A COMPANION TO THE BIBLE

A COMPANION

TO THE

BIBLE

GENERAL EDITOR

J.-J. VON ALLMEN

Professor in the Theological Faculty
of the University of Neuchâtel,
formerly Pastor of the Reformed Church
of France, Lucerne

INTRODUCTION

by

H. H. ROWLEY

Professor of Hebrew Language and Literature,
University of Manchester

NEW YORK
OXFORD UNIVERSITY PRESS
1958

This book originally appeared as Vocabulaire Biblique, *published by Delachaux & Niestlé, Neuchâtel and Paris, 1954. Translated into English from the 2nd French edition, 1956, by* P. J. Allcock, J. Austin Baker, W. R. F. Browning, W. Fletcher Fleet, A. W. Heathcote, Philip E. Hughes, Harold Knight.

English translation © 1958 *Lutterworth Press*

PRINTED IN GREAT BRITAIN

INTRODUCTION

IN INNUMERABLE ways the reviving interest in biblical theology
which has marked the last thirty years makes itself felt. Volumes
on the theology of the Old or New Testament or on both have
appeared, and countless articles and monographs on aspects of the
subject. In addition the great German *Theologisches Wörterbuch
zum Neuen Testament*, which is not yet complete and which
contains not a little on the Old Testament background of the New
Testament as well as on the New Testament itself, has both brought
its own important contribution to the subject and inspired lesser
works in various languages. Amongst these is the Swiss work
which is here translated. Its authors include a number of well-
known French and Swiss scholars, and it was prepared to serve
French-speaking students, ministers, and laymen. Its authors are
all Protestant, and it was published by the well-known firm of
theological publishers, Delachaux and Niestlé. At the same time,
its authors are aware of the growing co-operation in biblical study
between Protestant and Catholic scholars, which is one of the
significant trends of our time. That this work has been translated
into English means that its value has been recognized beyond the
circle of those for whom it was first intended.

A valuable feature of the volume is its concentration on a limited
number of longer articles with abundant cross references, rather
than on a large number of very brief articles. While this may mean
that the reader will not immediately find what he seeks, it will
mean that he will find something more rewarding when he finds
it in a larger context. He must not expect to find a Bible Dictionary
here. What he will have in his hand is a dictionary of the major
theological terms and ideas found in the Bible, and by the careful
and diligent use of this work he will acquire a considerable understanding of biblical theology. The layman will profit greatly from
its use, since all is written simply and with no unnecessary use of
technical jargon, and the minister will find rich suggestions for
expository preaching in many of the entries.

It is much to be hoped that this and similar works will bring
about the revival of theological preaching—not to weary but to
instruct. In the great periods of the history of the Church men
knew what they believed, and a deeper theological interest to-day

would lead to greater vitality in the Church. For theology is not something dull and remote, but something exciting and relevant. The Bible brings Good News to men, the stirring message of the wonder of God's love and the redemption whereby we can be lifted to share His life and power, and enter into His purpose for the world. No generation has been more thrilled than ours to deepen its knowledge of the mysteries of nature and the universe. To understand the spirit and will of the Creator of the universe, the mysteries of the purpose and destiny for which man was created, is yet more thrilling. In so far as this volume excites interest in these things and helps to satisfy that interest it will fulfil its purpose.

The good cook knows how to stimulate appetite as well as to satisfy it: this volume will be found both satisfying and stimulating, and if the reader, like the present writer, is inclined to ask for more, it will be the tribute to the quality of what he has found here.

H. H. ROWLEY

PREFACE
TO THE ORIGINAL EDITION

THERE IS NO NEED for us to emphasize the well-known fact that our generation is seeking anew and rediscovering, in Holy Scripture, the Word of the living God, and that it looks eagerly to its preachers, teachers and editors for their help and guidance in an ever-increasing understanding of it. To borrow the title of a famous manual, the contemporary Churches are living in the time of a "Biblical Renascence" the full consequences of which cannot yet be estimated, to such an extent is its influence penetrating and illuminating every aspect of Church life.

If one of the constant duties of the Church is to encourage orientalists, philologists, exegetes, historians of Israel, of Judaism, and of the early Church to intensify their researches, it is also her duty to place within the reach of those who are not specialists the result of all this scholarly work—and it is the aim of this *Companion* to contribute to such an end.

This implies in the first place that it has been prepared in order to be of use to the greatest possible number of readers. In the world of to-day the Church is in so great a need of members who are capable of witnessing, not only by their behaviour but in their speech, to the salvation which has laid hold upon them, that she cannot but wish to see them fully at home in the world of revelation, and hence increasingly in possession of a better understanding of the biblical message. So the first task which we have set ourselves is to present to the wider public an exact realization of the full and rich significance which our words assume when they are chosen to be the vehicles of the Word of God—and in doing so not to disappoint the theologians. We have also felt obliged to avoid a narrow parochial spirit and hence to interest and help not Protestants only, but those outside the Church who are puzzled or revolted by the Bible, and further—without any ulterior proselytizing motive—those Roman Catholics who are taking part in the work of biblical renewal which is going on within their own Church. In short, we realize that the coincidence of this biblical renascence with the quickened hope of Church unity is not a matter of chance.

In order to realize as closely as possible the aim we have set ourselves to achieve, it was necessary to choose a suitable method.

7

Now every choice implies limitation. Let us enumerate one or two of the possibilities we have had to give up. First of all it was necessary not to make the book too burdensome and hence too unwieldy: as a result there are many terms which we have not been able to include. This does not mean that such terms are without theological significance, but that they are not an essential part of the key-words of the Bible or that their meaning is expressed also by other words which are found in the *Companion* (hence the frequency of the asterisk, which refers the reader to the article devoted to the term immediately following it). It was also necessary to avoid a whole mass of technical erudition: Hebrew or Greek terms, annotations, discussions or refutations of exegetical hypotheses, etc.

Despite this limitation in the carrying out of their task, the collaborators have tried to provide a work of profound and far-reaching theology and exegesis. We hope they have succeeded in doing this and that this restriction has not resulted in any lowering of the general standard of the *Companion*. With one or two exceptions, it has also been necessary to exclude bibliographical notices: clergy who are at all well-read will know where to find such information: as for the laity, it hardly seemed necessary to refer them to publications which for the most part would bewilder them by their scientific character. Broadly speaking, however, it may be noted that the collaborators in the *Companion*, while consulting their own special sources, have had recourse above all to the articles in the *Theologisches Wörterbuch zum Neuen Testament*, edited since 1933 by G. Kittel and later by G. Friedrich, and published by Kohlhammer of Stuttgart, and to the best *Theologies* of the Old and New Testaments. This amounts to saying that the *Companion* may be considered—and in that case one of our aims would be realized—as a popular manual of biblical theology the principal ideas of which are classified alphabetically.

In fact, after having read and compared all the contributions, my impression was much more that of the unity of a manual than of the diffuseness of a dictionary, and the idea did occur to me (though I was asked to give it up as it sounded too pretentious) to entitle the work *La Parole et les mots* ("Words and the Word of God"). I merely allude to my proposed title in the preface in order to emphasize what seems to me to be the result of our labours, and I hardly dare add (for I hope so much that I may not be contradicted by the reader) the sign of our success. In effect such a title would have suggested that, by whatever word we enter the world of the Bible, so rich, so varied, so subtle and so strange, we are inevitably led to what forms the heart of it: the Word of God incarnated in Jesus Christ. Whether we speak of the Church, of Jerusalem, of the law, of sacrifices, of the ministry, of edification, of the Temple, of man or of the covenant, each of these words only yields its secret when referred to the Word, Jesus Christ. That is why the unity of the *Companion* does not seem to have been affected by the number of collaborators: in spite of their differences of approach and method, of the varying degrees in which their competence was already proved, and of their inevitable prejudices, and although each of them was marked by the joys and the anxieties of the *hic et nunc* of his ecclesiastical vocation, the collaborators have worked for eighteen months at a common task.

It remains for me to express my gratitude to all those who have made possible the realization of a plan which I have had at heart for many years. First of all to our contributors: they have spared neither time nor pains to make this work as useful as the public has a right to expect. I am thinking in particular of those among them who are accustomed to write for specialists, and who have here tried to express the conclusions of their scholarly work in a language which will reach a much wider circle of readers. My gratitude also goes out to the pastors whose wholehearted and fraternal co-operation I have enjoyed: their collaboration proves that it is well worth while, after the completion of a university course, to set apart some time for further study. It is very wrong of us to bear them at times a grudge because they so jealously insulate from the claims of their parochial duties the few hours of meditation and research which they need if they are not to become buried in routine work: after all it is in the service of the Church that one is a theologian!

And what would become of the Church and its theological thinking were it not for the publishers who consider their fine job to be a vocation and a real spiritual ministry? It is desired that, if only to thank them, those who use this *Companion* will help to make it widely known, will offer it as a gift to friends, confirmation candidates, students, will speak of it to those who they know are lovers of the Bible and to those who they know are troubled or irritated by it.

Before submitting the detailed plan of our *Companion* to the approval of the editorial committee, four previous drafts had been drawn up and then abandoned since 1945. Hence I know well enough that in such a work it is difficult to attain perfection: the

1*

choice of the articles, their length, and the authors to whom they should be given, are points likely to arouse much discussion. One thing nevertheless is more important than such discussions, however important they may be: namely to encounter, in the human witness of Holy Scripture, Jesus Christ the Word of God. Our aim has been no other than to facilitate this "one thing needful".

J.-J. VON ALLMEN

Lucerne, Autumn 1953.

P.S.—It has been impossible to avoid the use of certain technical theological terms if the articles were not to be made heavy and cumbrous by constant explanations. It is a question of the following terms in particular:

Aeon: a Greek term normally translated "century", not in the sense of a time period of a hundred years but in the sense of a certain manner of life defined with reference to God and eternity. *The present aeon* is the world as we know it characterized by rebellion against God and destined to come to an end on the return of Christ: *the aeon to come* is the age which will be fully manifested after the return of Christ, but which at the same time is already present since the Nativity (see article *time).

Eschatology, eschatological: terms derived from the Greek *eschaton*— meaning "the ultimate". Hence eschatology is the complex of biblical doctrines concerning the end of the world and the life of the world to come. Since the event of the coming of Jesus Christ, which means the breaking into this world of the Kingdom of God, the sphere in which eschatology is operative is already mysteriously present in our world, signifying for it both a challenge and a promise (see article *time).

Yahwist, Elohist: these terms denote the oldest literary sources of the early books of the O.T. It is known of course that these books as we read them to-day constitute a sort of puzzle, the several parts of which have been provided by at least four main sources (to the two sources mentioned must be added the so-called deuteronomic and priestly sources). The designation of the two sources in question by the terms Yahwist or Elohist is derived from the name by which they refer to God, i.e. Yahweh or Elohim.

The *Septuagint* (*LXX*) is the Greek translation of the Hebrew O.T. It owes its name to the legend according to which seventy translators arrived at their version independently only to discover later the perfect identity of their translations. The aim of this legend was to give credit to the idea that the Bible of the Jews of the Dispersion who spoke Greek was just as much inspired as the Hebrew Bible of the Jews of Palestine.

The Pentateuch is the collection of the five books attributed by Jewish tradition to Moses, namely Genesis, Exodus, Leviticus, Numbers, and Deuteronomy.

The Synoptic Gospels or more briefly the "*synoptics*" are the Gospels according to Matthew, Mark and Luke. They are so called because, broadly speaking, they follow the same general lines and so—in accordance with the etymology of the term—can be compared or viewed as a whole or in the same perspective.

An asterisk (*) preceding a word indicates that there is an article on that word elsewhere in the *Companion*.

ABIDE, *see* ENDURE

ABRAHAM, *see* NAMES (PERSONAL)

ADOPTION

1. The language of the O.T. does not possess a substantive equivalent to that of "adoption" in the N.T. This is worth noting because it proves for us the total absence of a legal form of adoption among the Jews.

However, the idea of adoption is not entirely absent: the term for son (*ben*) has as verbal root "to build" (*banah*). By extension: to build a family means to assure oneself of descendants, to live again in one's own children (*Marriage, *Death). Then what happens when the wife is barren? A woman can become mother of a child "by means of" another. Gen. 16:2, "The Lord has prevented me from bearing children; go in to my maid; it may be that I shall found my house by her." Compare Gen. 30:3, ". . . that I may build a house through her (= through her I shall be a mother)." The text of Exod. 2:10 which we translate "Pharaoh's daughter adopted Moses" reads literally: "Moses became a son to her" (cf. 1 Kings 11:20; Est. 2:7).

There is then an incipient idea of adoption in the O.T. but it is not codified juridically as in Roman law, where adoption has the result of placing the adopted person within the legal power of his father by adoption.

2. In the N.T. the texts where the term adoption appears are not numerous: five in all, and all in the Pauline epistles (Rom. 8:15,23; 9:4; Gal. 4:5; Eph. 1:5). The idea of adoption, without disowning its judicial sense, is heavy with religious content. We are at the very centre of the Christian message. The Christian cries, "Abba", that is, "Father" (literally "dadda!", cf. Gal. 4:6). A new filial relationship is established between God and the believer, on the basis of the work accomplished by Christ on the cross. *Sin had shattered every normal relationship between God and the creature. Doubtless, the law indicated to man what the will of God was, but since that law crushed man under superhuman demands man trembled to appear before an inexorable judge and remains a slave, chained by the power of sin. It was necessary for Christ to intervene to break the power of the curse of the law. By the death of Christ on the *cross (he was made sin for us, 2 Cor. 5:21), the believer, freed from all fear, is re-established in a new relationship with God, he is a "child of God" by adoption, and no more a timorous slave. He is a son, not by nature or essence as in the case of "*the Son*", but by adoption. Through the Son we are sons and children adopted by God. We now find ourselves in the same relationship with regard to God as Jesus with regard to His Father.

However, the status of "son of God"— even though it is already acquired by faith —will only be fully realized in the glory of the Father, when our body will be glorified. The adoption of our entire being remains an object of hope. That is why we still await the adoption of our body (Rom. 8:23).

What about the case of *Israel? God had declared in the O.T.: Israel is my son (Exod. 4:22). Adoption appertains also to Israel. The restoration of Israel will reinstate the nation in its true position of "son of God" (Rom. 9:4).

We are therefore "children by adoption through Jesus Christ" (Eph. 1:5; cf. Jn. 1:12f.) and this act of God adopting us as His children reveals the mercy of Him who saves us by Jesus Christ so as to re-establish us in a new and normal relationship, that of children of God who live by the grace of their Father.

M. BERNOULLI

ADVENT

Our versions render by this term different words which, with various shades of meaning, denote the coming, the arrival, the appearance or the glorious presence of the Messiah, of Christ, of the Son of Man or of the Lord taking possession of His Kingdom, exercising sovereign power and the last judgment. It concerns an act or transcendent event towards which the hope of the faith is directed and which will mark the end of time or of the "present age" by inaugurating the "new age", that of the manifestation on earth of the "Kingdom of heaven" (*Time and *Kingdom).

1. The O.T. already announces this event along two lines of thought which, in the end, come together:

(a) The Lord Himself through pity, zeal (or jealousy), faithfulness to His covenant, will reveal His kingdom to His people. This kingdom belongs to Him at all times (Num. 23:21; Deut. 33:5; Isa. 44:6). But it has been opposed or rejected. That is why, through all history, God prepares one event without precedent, whose announcement is one of the principal themes of prophecy: the coming, the arrival, the return of the Lord Himself to His people, Himself becoming the shepherd of Israel (Ezek. 34:11ff.), revealing His judgment and His mercy to Jerusalem and to the nations at the same time (Isa. 46:9-13; 52:7-8; Zech. 1:3,16; 2:9-13; 8:2-3, etc.).

(b) Moreover, it also concerns the coming of a King of the latter times, the heir of the promises made to Judah (Gen. 49:10) and to David (2 Sam. 7:16; Jer. 23:1-6), it is the "*servant", the Lord's "anointed" of Second Isaiah. He is announced sometimes as a temporal and political king, sometimes as an apocalyptic character; sometimes he is "raised up", sometimes he comes "on the clouds of heaven". His coming is accompanied by warning signs of *judgment and of the vengeance which he comes to exact (Isa. 40:10), or of paradisal *peace which he brings with him (Isa. 9:6 and 11:6f.), or else of universal *reconciliation among the peoples (Isa. 2:2-4).

He is surrounded with *glory and clothed with sacerdotal power (Ezek. 43:5; Ps. 110:4; Mal. 3:1-3). Finally, the Messianic hope is linked with the coming of a heavenly personage "like a son of man", "coming on the clouds of heaven" and to whom God Himself grants the eternal kingship and dominion which belong to him (cf. Dan. 2:44; 7:13-14 and Ps. 24). His coming is identified with or is a substitute for the "day of the Lord" (Amos 8:9-10; Zeph. 1:14-16 and 3:14-16).

2. The preaching of John the Baptist links directly with the prophetic message of a justiciary Messiah whose coming is imminent (Matt. 3:11-12). This same expectation is situated in the perspective of a temporal event which is at the basis of the eschatological hope around the person of Jesus. The eschatological statements in the first three Gospels (Matt. 24-25 and parallels) are a reply to the question asked by the disciples: "What will be the sign of thy coming?" Jesus replies with the description of "the coming of the Son of Man". Similarly, in John 7:25-52 and 10:22-30, the Jews on several occasions ask Jesus whether He is, or is not, the Christ. His answers, often ambiguous, His refusal to "reveal himself" at the instigation of His brothers (Jn. 7:2-9) as well as His word before Pilate (Jn. 18:36), show clearly that His glorious manifestation is subordinate to the accomplishment and completion of His earthly ministry by His death and resurrection. This glorious manifestation, illustrated by the parables of Matthew 25 in particular, is always announced as a temporal event which will take place in a manner which will be sudden, impossible to foresee and yet accompanied by signs that are discernible to faith. Jesus frequently insists on the impossibility of knowing the moment of His "arrival" (Mk. 13:32; Matt. 24:42; Lk. 12:39f.; Acts 1:6-7) and on the necessity of waiting for it with confidence, in watchfulness and prayer. Even in John, who tends to confuse resurrection, the coming of the Holy Spirit, and a glorious coming at the end of time, Jesus expressly speaks of His "return" (Jn. 14:3).

There has been much discussion of the question of knowing whether Jesus Himself believed, as did the first generation of

Christians, in the imminence of His Coming. Three texts appear to indicate this (Mk. 9:1; Matt. 10:23; Mk. 13:30). Without entering into detailed exegesis of these texts, which clearly designate the generation living at the time of Jesus as the witnesses of His advent, one must recognize with Cullmann that "the announcement of the proximity of the Kingdom has for Jesus and for early Christianity, a far greater significance" than the fixing of its ultimate date. What is decisive, is that the cross and resurrection mark the accomplishment of redemption which the final coming of Christ in glory will only make manifest, whatever period of time will elapse between the accomplishment and the final manifestation.

One text in the Epistle to the Hebrews is, in this respect, essential for a precise statement of the eschatological hope of early Christianity: "Christ, having been offered *once* to bear sins . . . will appear a *second time* . . . to save those who are eagerly waiting for him" (Heb. 9:28). This link between the expiatory work for salvation and the last coming is characteristic of the early Christian hope: "*this Jesus*, who was taken up from you into heaven, will come in the same way . . ." (Acts 1:11). He who shall come is the same as the one who came. The importance of the coming or return of Jesus Christ lies then in the fact that He will manifest in its fullness His eternal actuality and His universality, which was already completely secured, accomplished and consummated at the time of Christ's first coming. That is why also in the Apocalypse the conquering Christ appears in the likeness of the sacrificed Lamb (Rev. 5:12, etc.). Ultimately, that is why the point of all the apostolic preaching concerning the advent is in the frame of mind which its expectation requires, far more than in the manner in which it will take place. The Epistles speak of the "day of judgment" (Rom. 2:5–16), of the "day of the Lord" (1 Cor. 1:8; 5:5; 2 Cor. 1:14) of the "day of Christ" (Phil. 1:6,10; 2:16), in terms which recall the admonitions and warnings of Jesus Himself, and which also link up with the tones of the prophets announcing the "day of the Lord"

(1 Thess. 5:2–3; 2 Pet. 3:10). It is a question of a sudden and catastrophic event which is at the same time secret ("like a thief") by which the whole of mankind will be confronted with the Holy and Just One. The expectation of Christ's coming is mingled with the hope of the *resurrection of the dead (1 Cor. 15:23) and of the last *judgment, for which it is a matter of being "preserved blameless" (1 Thess. 5:23). But the only assurance of the Christian is found in the fact that the one who will judge is the one who gives salvation by His death and resurrection (1 Thess. 5:9–10). In this assurance, the coming of Christ can and should be awaited with hope and joy (1 Thess. 4:15ff.; 2 Thess. 2:1–9) as also with love and patience (Jas. 5:8; 2 Pet. 3:4; 1 Jn. 2:28; 2 Tim. 4:1,8).

The moment of the glorious appearance (Epiphany) of the Lord (Tit. 2:13) must in any case be preceded by a time of struggle and trial, of which one text, 2 Thess. 2:1–12, summarizes in an allusive manner the main data (allusion to the "mystery of iniquity", to the manifestation of "the lawless one", *Antichrist, accompanied by signs and by lying marvels; cf. Matt. 24:15–27). The book of Revelation is partly devoted to the description of the last eschatological struggles, in a succession of images of which the one of the "reign of a thousand years" preceding the final defeat of Satan underlines the participation of the martyrs and saints in the final triumph and the glory. Without doubt we must see in Rev. 20:4–6 an echo of Jesus' prediction to His disciples at the time of the Last Supper (Lk. 22:28–30).

H. ROUX

AFFLICTION, *see* PERSECUTION

AGES, *see* TIME

AMEN

Amen is a Hebrew word which, frequently used in synagogue worship, has passed from there into the N.T. and has maintained itself in the liturgical language of all Christian

Churches. It comes from a root which implies the idea of firmness, of reality, from which have been derived terms as diverse and important as: to exist, to believe, truth, solidity, faithfulness, certainty, faith, and perhaps even Mammon.

Amen signifies then: true, truly, certain, certainly; it often corresponds simply to "yes" (cf. 2 Cor. 1:20). It has been translated into Greek by an expression which we render "so be it", which has lost the suggestion of firmness, of truth, which is characteristic of the Hebrew, and finally only expresses, for many, a sort of wish.

Now the use made of Amen in the O.T. allows us to say that it signifies much more: that it serves to confirm and support what has been said. By pronouncing it the listener associates himself with what has been uttered; he recognizes it as valid, he makes it his own, he is ready to conform to it. Thus, Benaiah replied "Amen" to the orders of David (cf. 1 Kings 1:36; Jer. 28:6). So Amen is tantamount to a signature, to the giving of a promise; whence its legal use. The people say "Amen" to the commandments which Moses gives them, and by that they agree to follow them and they accept in advance the consequences implied (cf. Deut. 27:15ff., 12 times; Neh. 5:13; Num. 5:22).

Amen has passed as well into religious language. It confirms a prayer. It underlines the solemn nature of a doxology (cf. 1 Chr. 16:36; Neh. 8:6; Ps. 41:13; 72:19, etc.). The congregation shows by its Amens the part which it takes in praising God; it unites itself with the adoration and invocation of its Lord.

Similarly in the N.T. Amen functions as a response; it has its place in worship, as the writings of the early Church show (cf. 1 Cor. 14:16; Rev. 5:14). It is found at the end of prayers and doxologies to underline their importance and truth (cf. Rom. 1:25; 9:5; 11:36; 16:27; Gal. 1:5; Phil. 4:20, etc.). It has a place in hymns addressed to God, where it is sometimes associated with Alleluia (Rev. 19:4), and it is uttered by the believer or by the entire congregation. It is

only later that the priests reserve for themselves the right to say the Amen.

In the N.T. Amen preserves its original force of true, veracious. It reveals the certainty of a Church which responds with confidence to the promises of its Lord. As one commentator has said, the "Yes" of the Church echoes the "Yes" of God and this "Yes" is none other than Jesus Christ whom the Apocalypse designates the Faithful Witness, the Amen, the true Amen, the final Amen—no doubt alluding to an O.T. affirmation (cf. Rev. 3:14; Isa. 65:16).

The expression: "Amen (truly) I tell you that . . ." which opens many of Christ's discourses must be understood in this way. It is a solemn formula—it appears 30 times in Matthew, 25 in John who also doubles the word—by which Jesus of Nazareth affirms there and then His Messianic authority. He presents Himself as the one who speaks in the name and in the place of God, and He has the right to do so, for His Word is true and effective as that of His Father, and equally implies and demands a response. "Amen, amen, I say unto you . . .": it is the Lord who is speaking, the Son of Man, the true and faithful interpreter of the mind of God.

R. MARTIN-ACHARD

ANGEL

O.T.

An angel is a "messenger"; his nature is of no consequence. Ambassadors (Isa. 37:9), prophets (Isa. 44:26; Hagg. 1:13), priests (Mal. 2:7; Eccl. 5:6) are called "angels"; similarly the forerunner of the Lord (Mal. 3:1), without our knowing whether he be a man or a celestial being. Besides, the difference of nature between celestial and terrestrial beings is not clear in the O.T.; the former do not always have wings (Gen. 28:12), they move about on the earth (32:1), enter into union with the daughters of men (6:2), eat and strongly resemble men (18:1ff., 16; 19:1; Ezek. 40:4). They are their superiors, however, in strength, knowledge and intelligence (1 Sam. 29:9; 2 Sam. 14:17,20; 19:27).

1. Before the Exile.

(a) Angels and the Promised Land. Before the Exile there is no elaborate angelology. Yahwistic monolatry has relegated the ancient Canaanite gods to the rank of servants of Yahweh who presided over their celestial Council (Job 1 and 2; 1 Kings 22:19ff.); their submission shows that now Yahweh possesses and controls the land of Canaan in their stead (Josh. 5:13ff.). The angels played their part in it (cf. Gen. 32:1, 2,28 and Hos. 12: 4,5; Gen. 28:12); they show that Yahweh has relationship with this land and with the men who live in it.

(b) Angels and the chosen people. As bearers of a divine Word (1 Kings 13:18), angel of pestilence (2 Sam. 24:16f.; 2 Kings 19:35) or destruction (Gen. 19:21f.), guardian angel of Elijah (1 Kings 19:3ff.; 2 Kings 1:3,15) or of a believer (Ps. 34:7; 91:11), the angels normally act as protectors of the people of Israel or an individual in so far as he is brought into the divine covenant (e.g. Gen. 24:7).

(c) The Angel of the Lord (J and E sources of the Pentateuch). Certain expositors see here the second person of the Trinity; others Yahweh Himself and His "double", or a simple theological gloss, or an angel primum inter pares. This last view, which philology does not invalidate, has in its favour the interpretation of the LXX. Originally, this angel appears to be determined only by his connection with the relations of God with His people, in the framework of the promise made to Abraham and in reference to its realization (posterity, inheritance, deliverance from Egypt). Differentiated after the Exile, he is to retain the same function: Zech. 3:1ff.). At times, mention of him is quite arbitrary (cf. Judg. 6:14 in its context). He is exceptionally well distinguished from God in Num. 22:22ff.: God acts in heaven; His angel appears and speaks directly on earth with a pagan (as in Gen. 16 and 21). But in general this angel speaks and acts absolutely as God Himself does in other passages: compare Gen. 22:15ff. with 12:1ff.; Exod. 14:19 with 20:2. God acts fully through him; His "*Name is in him" (Exod. 23:21).

This alternation of distinction and confusion between God and His angel, without being at all systematic, makes it clear that: (i) the holiness of God in His relation with man is safeguarded: the anthropomorphism of Yahweh's meal in Gen. 18 is doubly attenuated in Judg. 6 where a sacrifice is received by the angel (compare similarly Exod. 19ff. with Acts 7:53 and Gal. 3:19). God can hardly appear on earth and talk to men because of His holiness. His alter ego replaces Him. (ii) Israel is not harmed because the action of this angel is not inferior to that of God Himself. (iii) There is less danger in the presence of the substitute than in that of God (Exod. 33:2ff.,20). Unquestionably there is a hint of the mystery of the incarnation in this figure. On the other hand this angel is the "accidental" mode of the presence and action of God amongst His people (*Ark).

Notice that angels are not mentioned by the pre-exilic prophets, nor in the priestly writings, for the word of the seer, temple and cultus establish the communication between God and men attributed earlier to angels.

2. After the Exile.

Angelology is elaborated little by little after the Exile up to the point of becoming an autonomous speculation. Ezekiel receives his revelations in visions or by means of an angel (40:3). Zechariah needs an angel interpreter who explains to him the visions and transmits to him the replies of God (1:9,13, etc.). In apocalyptic writings all divine revelations are mediated by dreams or visions, explained most often by an angel (Dan. 7:16; 10:14).

Angelology will develop within the following two sets of limits:

(a) God is unique, infinitely holy and elevated to the highest heaven. The distance which separates Him from the angels grows. They are abased before Him to such a point that sin may be found in them (Job 4:18; 15:14-15). The ancient divine beings (Ps. 29:1; 78:25; 97:7; Gen. 6:1ff.) no more share in the unique divine nature; they form a class of creatures intermediate between God and men: they are the angels of the LXX. Very numerous (Dan. 7:10), they form different hierarchical classes: the archangels Gabriel, Michael, Raphael, etc. God thus will have a court of celestial adorers (Ps. 103:20; 148:2).

(b) In principle, God no longer acts directly on the earth: He is replaced by angels with specialized functions: angels of revelation, of healing, of intercession (Job 33:23), watchers (Dan. 4:13), judges (Dan. 7:10), guardians of individuals (Tobit), heads of nations (Dan. 10:13). That of Israel, the ancient "angel of the Lord", henceforward will bear the name of Michael (Dan. 12:1).

3. *Cherubim.* These are not angels. Mythological animals (Ezek. 1) borrowed from a Babylonian setting, they acted as a mount for Yahweh (Ps. 18:10), they are guardians which forbid to mortals access to the deity (Gen. 3:24; and on the lid of the Ark, Exod. 25:20), and they seem to have the rôle of intercessor in the holy place (Exod. 26:1,31).

Finally we may mention other mysterious beings, the *Seraphim* (burning ones) of Isa. 6, who praise the Lord in His palace; and the *'ophannim* (wheels) which allow the throne of God to be moved (Ezek. 1:15ff.).

A. LELIÈVRE

N.T.

In a general way it can be said that the N.T. in its turn repeats the conception of the O.T. and of late Judaism on the subject of the ministry of angels. Without speculating any further on their nature, it presents them to us as celestial beings, belonging to the world on high, yet creatures of God and never to be the object of worship or prayer (Col. 2:18; Rev. 22:8f.). The Lord uses them in His service to execute His purpose, in the heavens and on earth, and to come to the aid of His elect (Heb. 1:14). Their appearance is always the sign of a direct and decisive intervention of God, who at that point no longer allows events to take their course but cutting across the course of events takes things miraculously in hand. As under the old covenant they had been instruments of Yahweh to guide His people, to summon His servants, to reveal them-

selves to His prophets, they likewise play a part in the great events of the life of Jesus Christ. Their rôle is attested particularly in the narratives of His birth (Matt. 1:20ff.; 2:13; Lk. 1:11ff.,26ff.; 2:9ff.) and His resurrection (Matt. 28:2ff.; Mk. 16:5ff.; Lk. 24:4ff.,23; Jn. 20:12ff.), as well as in the scenes where we see Jesus Christ fighting the decisive battles of the Kingdom (temptation in the desert, Matt. 4:11; Mk. 1:13; agony of Gethsemane, Lk. 22:43). They are like signs of the double aspect, visible and invisible, of the drama of salvation and their presence witnesses that in Jesus of Nazareth God Himself engages in the final struggle which has its repercussions on the earth and in heaven. Likewise in the book of Acts their interventions are landmarks in the first stages of the Church; they take an active part in the progress of the Gospel and so show the essential continuity which unites the witness of the apostles and the earthly ministry of Jesus Christ (5:19; 8:26; 10:3; 12:7; 27:23, etc.).

Finally, the Revelation attributes to them a decisive rôle; on the one hand in the vision given at Patmos, and on the other in the struggle of the latter times as shock-troops of the Son of Man (cf. the expression "his angels" in Matt. 25:31; 26:53). They surround the throne; they are the executive agents of the final cosmic drama; they engage in the last heavenly battles which echo the combat pursued on earth by the Church.

But although the angels play an active part in the whole period of the history of salvation, that which is behind us and that which lies ahead of us, it seems that the N.T. points to something like an interruption of their earthly ministry during the time of the Church. A capital event has taken place in which they did not take part, viz. the incarnation. They have no carnal body; the humiliation, sufferings, death and resurrection of Jesus Christ remain foreign to them. And the N.T. not only clearly notes their inferiority in relation to Christ (Heb. 1:4ff.) but even in relation to the Christian himself; the believer has a fellowship possible with the Lord which escapes the angels (it might be called a bond of kinship) and this the sacraments attest, in which they have no part (cf. 1 Pet. 1:12; 1 Cor. 6:3). In Jesus Christ we become *children* of the Father; the angels remain His *servants* (cf. Jn. 15:15). To the incarnation of God in Jesus Christ there corresponds henceforward the personal and intimate coming of God in the Holy Spirit. Hereafter the Paraclete alone has the power to bear witness to Jesus Christ; it is He who is the craftsman of the new creation, who chooses our bodies to make His dwelling there; it is He whom the Father sends (Jn. 14:15ff.; Acts 2:17). If they were the mediators under the old covenant, in the new their ministry as intermediaries between God and man has ended (Gal. 3:19. Notice also that the first intervention of an angel had been after the Fall). This is very clear in the Gospel and the Epistles of John as well as in those of Paul. (It is interesting to observe that with Paul the intervention of angels to guide him is replaced little by little by the Holy Spirit: stopped, impelled, led, bound by the Spirit . . .)

Angels of Satan (Matt. 25:41; 2 Cor. 12:7; Rev. 9:11; 12:7): heavenly powers who have revolted and entered the service of the *Devil.

Angels, Powers, etc.: on the relation of angels to celestial powers see *Authorities.

Angels of the Church (Rev. 2–3): The interpretations are various: (*a*) messengers sent by the churches to John; (*b*) the bishops or ministers of these churches; (*c*) their protective guardian angels. By relating this passage to Matt. 18:10 (the angels of children) we prefer to see there an expression of the secret and invisible reality of our life hidden in God. The apostle is, as it were, translated to heaven and it is the other aspect of the life of these churches which is revealed to him and which he expresses by this term.

M. BOUTTIER

ANGER

The Bible speaks more frequently of the anger of God than it does of the anger of

man; nevertheless, the divine anger is described on the analogy of human anger, which serves then as our point of departure.

1. *The anger of man.* The early Hebrews had observed that, when a man is angry, his nose swells and his nostrils tremble. For them, therefore, the expression "his nose burned" means "he became angry" and the substantive "nose" or "nostril" is very often used to denote anger. It is useful to compare the two following examples in their literal rendering, one being applied to a man, the other to God:

"And the nose of Jacob burned against Rachel" (Gen. 30:2).

"And the nose of Yahweh burned against Moses" (Exod. 4:14).

The identity between the two is most striking. The fleeting nature of human anger is underlined in Gen. 27:45; however, man's restlessness, which is the source of his anger, will not cease until he is at rest in the abode of the dead (Job 14:1; 3:17).

The Christian, and most especially the bishop, is bidden to shun anger (Lev. 19:18; Eph. 4:26,31; Tit. 1:7).

Like men, the *Devil can be seized by a mighty wrath (Rev. 12:12). Babylon is described as having caused the nations to drink a draught which provokes the anger of God (Rev. 14:8). But, generally speaking, it is man who, by his sins, angers God and excites His wrath (1 Kings 16:13; Jer. 32:32).

2. *The anger of God.* The example supplied in the preceding paragraph has shown us that the terms used to describe the anger of God and the anger of man are identical. Yet, despite the very realistic descriptions such as are found in Ps. 18:7–15, the anger of God is something entirely different from the anger of men.

The wrath of God is a holy wrath; it is sinless because it is freely directed against sin; Jesus Christ has this anger in His eyes when He looks round upon His hard-hearted hearers (Mk. 3:5), for the divine wrath is motivated by the passionate love of God for His people (Deut. 6:15; Ps. 79:5).

(*a*) *The anger of God can be manifested at*

all times. Yahweh is a God who is slow to anger (Num. 14:18; Neh. 9:17; Ps. 103:8; Joel 2:13), but when He hears that which displeases Him or when He sees impiety revealing itself, His anger is aroused (Num. 11:1; Rom. 1:18; 1 Thess. 2:16) and none can stand against it (Ps. 76:7; Nahum 1:6; Rev. 6:17). The divine anger can be kindled against an individual (2 Chr. 25:15), against dishonest Israelites who afflict the widow and the orphan (Exod. 22:23f.), against a country and its inhabitants (Deut. 29:27f.). It is Yahweh in His wrath who gives the Israelites a king (Hos. 13:11). He pours out His wrath upon the nations (Ps. 79:6) or else He causes them to drink the cup which contains His wrath (Jer. 25:15; Rev. 14:10). The anger of Yahweh can be appeased when the guilty have been punished (Num. 25:4; Josh. 7:26); sometimes, however, it is slow to abate (Jer. 4:8; 23:20; 30:24). When it is directed against obdurate sinners, its effect is to bring about in their specific case what is announced in general terms in the declaration of the curses (Deut. 29:19f.); it overtakes the children of wrath (Rom. 9:22; Col. 3:6; Eph. 2:3; 5:6). According to the descriptions of Yahweh such as are to be found in the following passages: Isa. 5:25; 30:27; Amos 1:2; Nahum 1:2, we are led to understand that Yahweh, in His anger, induces men to commit acts of which He Himself disapproves (2 Sam. 24:1, 17), that He punishes the iniquity of the fathers upon succeeding generations (Exod. 20:5; 34:7), that He drives out the inhabitants of a whole country (Deut. 29:27), that He utterly destroys men (Exod. 22:24; Jer. 10:24).

(*b*) *Divine anger in the Last Day.* Although, from the biblical texts quoted in the preceding paragraph, it is clear that the divine anger can be manifested at all times, there will be a special day reserved for the manifestation of the wrath of God, the day of Yahweh, the day of *judgment, the day of wrath and anger (Ezek. 7:19; Zeph. 1:15, 18; Matt. 3:7; Lk. 21:23; Rom. 2:5; 1 Thess. 1:10; Rev. 6:17; 11:18).

3. *Relation between the anger of God and*

the anger of man. Although it is possible for human anger not to be sinful (Eph. 4:26), yet because this anger springs from human sources, even if the man who is angry is King David (2 Sam. 6:8, which should be rendered "David was angry . . .") it does not bring about the righteousness of God (Jas. 1:19f.). God's anger, however, is always a revelation of His righteousness (Rom. 1:17f.).

H. MICHAUD

ANOINTING

1. By the practice of anointing—for which oil expertly prepared was used, cf. Exod. 30:23ff.—Israel used to consecrate to God that which He had chosen with a view to His work among the elect people or in the world: whether places (Gen. 28:18) or objects connected with worship (Exod. 30:26ff.; 29:2), but above all men to whom a particular *ministry was entrusted: the king (1 Sam. 9:16; 16:3; 1 Kings 1:34, etc.), the prophet (1 Kings 19:16), and the high priest (Exod. 28:41; a later redactor extends this custom to all the priests in the place of simple sprinkling, cf. Lev. 8:30). This means that anointing always designates a person for a particular work in the service of God, who is moreover—even though it is performed by men—the true author of anointing (cf. 1 Sam. 16:13; 1 Chr. 11:3; 2 Chr. 22:7, etc.), whence the frequent expression "the anointed of Yahweh"=the Christ of God (1 Sam. 26:9,16; Lam. 4:20; cf. Jn. 6:69). By this deed the anointed one is set apart and made to participate in the divine sphere: he is able to appear before God on behalf of the people and to act as a representative of God. There is, however, nothing magical about this anointing, and God is able to reject His anointed (Saul) or to disqualify him who would have usurped the anointing (Absalom).

2. If oil (the fruit of the olive, that tree which, like the *vine, symbolizes election) was used for anointing, it is because, as was the case with all antiquity, Israel regarded oil as a substance with saving properties: not only is it a sign of joy, prosperity, and

liberty (Ps. 23:5; Joel 1:10; Mic. 6:15; cf. Matt. 6:17)—whence its importance also for a person's toilet—but it brings health (Isa. 1:6; Lk. 10:34; Jas. 5:14), that is to say, it makes a person strong. It is therefore well fitted to enable those who have been anointed to do extraordinary things (for health and holiness are not far apart in the biblical perspective, the latter signifying a stage further on in the possession of vital power): it might almost be said that it is the vehicle of the Spirit of God (cf. 1 Sam. 10:1–6; 16:13; 2 Sam. 23:1–2; Isa. 61:1), who invests him whom the Lord has chosen with the necessary power to fulfil the vocation to which he has been called.

3. The association of the *Spirit and anointing is especially appropriate to the N.T. where—a remarkable thing—oil is no longer mentioned as "a visible sign of this invisible grace".

(a) In the first place this is true of *Jesus whom, at the time of His baptism (Matt. 3:13ff. and parallels) "God anointed with the Holy Spirit and with power" (Acts 10:38). He is not one anointed among others, but He is the Anointed One *par excellence* (in Hebrew: *Messiah*; in Greek: *the Christ*): "*the* Christ, the Son of the living God" (Matt. 16:16 and parallels). This term "Christ", which from the first Christian generation seems to have been annexed to the name of Jesus, designates in the first place a state. Being *the* Christ, he is primarily and above all the king, the new David expected at the end of the *times (cf. Matt. 2:2; 21:5; 27:11 and parallels; Lk. 23:2; Jn. 12:13; Acts 17:7, etc.), the one who enhances and fulfils all that the kingship signified under the old covenant. But ecclesiastical tradition, taking its stand on the O.T. texts which speak of the consecration, by anointing, also of prophets and priests, has certainly been right in affirming that the title of Christ brings together and contains the fullness of the ancient ministries which Jesus enhances and fulfils, and thus also the ministry of the prophet (cf. Lk. 4:18ff. = Isa. 61:1ff.) and of the priest (in the N.T. anointing is not brought into direct relationship with the sacerdotal ministry of Jesus, unless it is in Acts 4:27 where it is linked to His ministry as the *servant who dies vicariously for the people, and, very frequently, when he is spoken of as *Christ* who dies on the *cross). It should also be mentioned that already in the O.T. the *king* could perform a *ministry that was prophetic (cf. 1 Sam. 10:6,10; 2 Sam. 23:1–2) or sacerdotal (cf. 1 Sam. 14:35; 2 Sam. 6:14; 1 Kings 8:55).

(b) The anointing of the Spirit, however, was not conferred only on Jesus: after His ascension the Spirit was poured out also upon the *Church which, until the second advent of Christ, represents Him on earth and serves Him by continuing His eschatological work of salvation (Acts 2:1ff.). This anointing of the Spirit is closely linked with *baptism, which it precedes or follows immediately (cf. Jn. 3:5; Acts 2:38; 9:17f.; 10:44–48; 19:5f.; 1 Cor. 12:13, etc.). Thus all who have been baptized are "christs" (2 Cor. 1:21; *Seal). It is probably of this same anointing of the Spirit at the time of baptism that St. John speaks in his first Epistle (2:20,27), rather than of *laying on of hands performed after baptism (cf. Acts 8:14ff., the intention of this text probably being to emphasize the integration of the Samaritan Church into the Apostolic Church).

(c) Anointing with oil is not, however, unknown in the N.T., where its value for the healing of illnesses is stressed (Mk. 6:13; Jas. 5:14). As for the action of the woman who poured over the head or the feet of Jesus a vase of perfumed ointment, and which is reported in different forms (cf. Matt. 26:6–13; Mk. 14:3–9; Lk. 7:36–50; Jn. 12:3–8), in this a confession of the Messiahship of Jesus should be seen.

D. LYS

ANTICHRIST, *see* DEVIL

APOSTLE

1. In the N.T. this term admits of two very different uses, issuing however from one fundamental meaning which originates

in Judaism: an agent possessing a delegated authority. Very rarely it signifies one who is sent in a general sense which the context sometimes makes precise (Jn. 13:16; 2 Cor. 8:23; Phil. 2:25; Heb. 3:1). Most often it is applied to a group of people, the *envoys of the risen Christ*. In fact, the two genuine prerequisites of the apostolate are: (*a*) to have seen the Risen One (Lk. 24:48; Jn. 20:21; 1 Cor. 9:1; 15:7); (*b*) to have received from Him the mandate to witness to His resurrection and, in the light of that resurrection, to the totality of His person and His work (Matt. 28:19; Jn. 20:21; Rom. 1:5; 1 Cor. 1:17). Certainly, all the witnesses of the resurrection are not apostles. The 500 brethren of 1 Cor. 15:6 are not. But all the apostles have been witnesses of the resurrection (cf. 1 Cor. 15:7). This means that the vocation to the apostolate is limited historically to the appearances of the Risen One, and that Paul is the last apostle (1 Cor. 15:8).

Though the distinction between apostle and simple envoy is evident, it is less easy on the other hand to fix with precision what men comprised "the apostles" in the narrow sense. Only the Twelve can be named here with certainty: Simon Peter, Andrew his brother, James and John sons of Zebedee, Philip, Bartholomew, Matthew (=Levi in certain passages of Mark and Luke), Thomas, James the son of Alphaeus, Simon the Cananean (the Zealot according to Luke), Jude the son of James (=Thaddaeus, or Lebbaeus according to Matthew and Mark) and Judas Iscariot (cf. Matt. 10:2–3 and parallels), *Matthias* (Acts 1:26) and *Paul* (Rom. 1:1, etc.).

The interpretation is doubly uncertain for all the other persons named who might come into the list (Barnabas and the "brothers" of the Lord, 1 Cor. 9:5–6; Andronicus and Junias, Rom. 16:7; James, the "brother" of the Lord, Gal. 1:19; Apollos, 1 Cor. 4:6,9; Silas and Timothy, 1 Thess. 2:7; cf. 1 Thess. 1:1). In fact in all the passages cited it is possible philologically to concede that the term apostle does not refer to these men. Besides, even supposing that Barnabas, Andronicus and Junias, etc.,

might have been regarded as "apostles" it is still not said that they were so in the strict sense. They might only have been "envoys" of one Church or another, or missionaries. The best way of accounting for the sometimes varying usage met with in New Testament texts (and in the Didache, a noncanonical yet very early writing) is to acknowledge that the term apostle, first of all restricted to the Twelve and Paul, was later enlarged in the course of the first missionary period, only to be limited anew and canonized as a result of the false teachers who abused this title.

However that may be, we can only get an idea of the Christian apostolate by basing it on the Twelve and Paul, since these alone are the ones we know for a certainty were apostles and whose activity also we know (and moreover for the majority of the Twelve this activity appears to have been only collective).

2. *The apostolate of the *Twelve*. From the beginning of His ministry in Galilee, Jesus chose the Twelve "to be with him, and to be *sent* out" (same root in Greek as apostle) "to preach and to have authority to cast out demons" (Mk. 3:14–15). The choice of the Twelve and their ultimate apostleship, confirmed by the Risen One, are thus intimately united. By choosing *twelve* men, and more precisely twelve *Jews*, Jesus confirmed the covenant of God with the twelve tribes of Israel (cf. Matt. 19: 27–30). There is continuity between the new work which He commences and the ancient work of God in Israel. However, by choosing unknown Galileans Jesus indicates clearly that His work would be new. Moreover, in associating the Twelve with Himself "that they might be with him" Jesus shows straight away that He did not wish to be alone. He wishes to have men who would be "his own" (Jn. 13:1). Where He is, there He wants His own to be also. Even before His cross and resurrection He associates His own with His person and work. Not only does He proclaim His Word and perform His miracles under their eyes, but He also sends them out to preach this Word and to

perform these miracles. With them He celebrates the Passover and by celebrating it He renews it. It is especially to them that He appears when risen; with them He "eats and drinks after his resurrection" (Acts 10:41), and to them He gives the Holy Spirit (Jn. 20:22). The Twelve are not thereby the only witnesses authorized by Christ, but they constitute the foundation of His work on earth. It is on them that He will build His Church (see *Peter). Precursory signs of the end of time (Rev. 21:12), they are henceforward the guarantee of God's faithfulness to His promises. Just as Christ will be with them always (Matt. 28:20), so during His earthly ministry He wanted them always with Him. Thus the Twelve will not only be preachers, they themselves will be a constitutive element of the evangelic message (cf. 1 Cor. 15:1–7). Signs of the faithfulness of God to His promises, the Twelve will proclaim the Gospel first to the Jews, then to the Samaritans—schismatic Jews—and finally to the Gentiles (cf. Acts 1:8; Gal. 2:9; Matt. 28:19).

3. *The apostolate of *Paul.* In distinction from the apostolate of the Twelve, the apostolate of Paul arises at a time when the Church already exists, gathered around the Twelve who are its basis. The extraordinary character of the appearance of the risen Christ to Paul (Acts 9:1–9)—well after the appearances to the Twelve and outside the Promised Land—shows that the Jewish framework is broken from without. Paul will be essentially the apostle to the Gentiles (Gal. 2:9), the one who will bear to non-Jews the salvation entrusted to that renewed Israelite community, to the New Israel which is the Judaeo-Christian Church of Jerusalem. He has to enter the Church, be baptized, and—in spite of the direct call addressed to him by the risen Christ—receive by tradition the primitive catechism (cf. 1 Cor. 11:23–26; 15:1–7). The specific bearing of his apostolate will be to make plain on Gentile soil the power of the Gospel. The process of evangelization undertaken by the Twelve was from the centre, Jerusalem, to the periphery, the Gentiles. Evangelization by Paul, although also concerning the Jews in the highest degree, will run foul of Jewish unbelief, and it is finally by the detour of the conversion of the Gentiles that Paul envisages the conversion of all the Jews (Rom. 11:25–32). In virtue of his particular apostolate, Paul will be essentially a missionary, who will found Churches and will set free the universalistic bearing of the Christian message.

4. *The unity and uniqueness of the apostolate.* The apostolates of the Twelve and of Paul, though distinct, are in perfect union. Each recognizes the other (Gal. 2:7–10), thus testifying to the unity of a Church composed of Jews and Gentiles. From that moment there was set up for the future the central reference of the entire life and preaching of the Church. The Church is built on the foundation of the apostles (and *prophets) (Eph. 2:20). Apostolicity will be the criterion which the later Church will use for the recognition of canonical writings, that is of those worthy of possessing for ever authority over her. Certainly that does not imply in any degree a servile, literal or mechanical authority. The apostles received the *Holy Spirit and their witness can only be understood and accepted through the Holy Spirit. But it is also *their* testimony by which the glorified Christ will manifest Himself to the world and which He will confirm by the power of His Spirit. In this sense the apostles are the "stewards of the divine mysteries" (1 Cor. 4:1) and apostolicity, that is, conformity (in a form which cannot be discussed here) to the apostles, to what they are and to what they say, will be one of the essential marks of the Church of Christ, of the Christ who is with them to the end of the world (Matt. 28:20).

J.-L. LEUBA

ARK

According to a late description given in Exod. 25 and 37, the ark is a rectangular chest 4 x 2½ x 2½ ft. It includes poles for transporting it, two cherubim with outstretched wings (*Angel O.T.), a lid called the mercy seat and a protective curtain; inside were the two tables of the Law (cf. Heb. 9:3ff.).

1. *The ark is the "appointed" place where the God of the covenant is present.* Where the ark is found, God is present in the midst of His people. By its means He is Immanuel. This presence is so real and so definite that in coming to the ark the faithful come in fact "before Yahweh" (cf. 1 Sam. 1:19,22; 2:18; 3:3; 7:6; 2 Sam. 7:18; Exod. 25:30), so that one says "O God!" on seeing the ark (1 Sam. 4:6,7; Num. 10:33f.; Ps. 68:34), and so that certain critics have been led to conjecture that there was inside or above the ark a visible representation of God (stone, statue, teraphim) perhaps called the "Face of God" (cf. Num. 12:8; Ps. 27:4; Exod. 33:14f.).

This presence of God at the ark was never questioned prior to the Exile; this is noticeable in the account of the taking of the ark by the Philistines: if the ark is no longer in Israel then God, emigrating with the ark, has abandoned—not the ark—but Israel; and that indeed is the tragedy of this defeat (1 Sam. 4:18,22; Ps. 78:60f.). Certainly, one of the literary sources of the Pentateuch presents that presence as intermittent: God descends towards the ark when someone comes to consult Him there (Exod. 33:9–11). However, much later than that source the priestly texts are to declare that God "dwells" in the midst of His own people thanks to the ark (Exod. 25:8ff.).

It will also be said that the ark is the throne of God (1 Sam. 4:4) or His footstool (1 Chr. 28:2). So all the texts testify that the ark is the one place chosen by God at Sinai to manifest His perpetual presence among His people (Exod. 29:42ff.).

2. *The ark is the instrument of God's power.* God displays His power by means of the ark. It is charged with power; and this force manifests itself for the purpose of the salvation of the people of the covenant. This divine action by means of the ark is not only psychological, reassuring or intimidating; it is exercised on the Jordan

(Josh. 3), on Dagon, on the bodies of the Philistines; it directs the cows (1 Sam. 5 and 6); it kills or loads with blessings (1 Sam. 6:19; 2 Sam. 6:6,7,12). Yet God will remain free to suspend the exercise of His power because of the sins of the people: thus it will not aid Israel against the Philistines, who will be able to take it away from them (1 Sam. 4:11; 5:1).

(*a*) *The royal function of the ark.* Making tangible the presence of the divine King of Israel, the ark guides Israel in the desert (Num. 10:33–36; Josh. 3:3,4). Regarded as the palladium of the *wars of Israel, the ark is called by the name of the "Lord of hosts" (2 Sam. 6:2). When the conquest of the Promised Land was completed, the ark was installed in the most holy place of the *Temple (1 Kings 8:6) during the reign of Solomon. It was certainly the focal point of the processions mentioned in the Psalms of the enthronement of Yahweh (Pss. 24; 47; 68). Even if many details of these liturgical processions escape us, at least they must be regarded as a reminder and an actualization of the royal function of the ark during the pre-monarchic period.

(*b*) *The prophetic function of the ark.* It is above the ark that God speaks to Moses and makes Himself known to him by communicating His will. The ark of the covenant, or the ark of testimony, is the ark which contains the two tables of the *law. The ark is then simply conceived as a receptacle designed to receive them (Deut. 10:1–8).

(*c*) *The sacerdotal function of the ark.* The ark is finally the place where God and His people meet (Exod. 25:22). There God is accessible to His people. But this encounter is not natural. The holy God cannot live in the midst of a sinful people, and they cannot approach or even see the sacrosanct ark without special precautions: the curtain, special rites for the wrapping up of the ark, its service exclusively confined to the high priest and only in certain conditions (Lev. 16) avert the death of the children of Israel before the holiness of Yahweh (cf. Lev. 10:1–2; Num. 16:35,46).

The lid of the ark played an essential part in the annual *feast of atonement. This lid is called the "mercy seat" in our translations (Rom. 3:25; Heb. 9:5). The Hebrew root of this word has the meaning "to cover". This lid is "covered" by seven sprinklings of blood. By this rite the high priest covers before God the sins of Israel by bringing to Him the *blood (= the life) of the victim (cf. Lev. 16).

3. *The disappearance of the ark.* We do not know when and why the ark disappeared. In spite of the late reference in 2 Chr. 35:3, it must have disappeared at the latest in the reign of Josiah. In fact Jeremiah speaks of its destruction as a very sad affair which is still remembered (Jer. 3:16). But in the period of general conversion which will usher in the Messianic era, another ark will not be made. The holy city will take its place and will become in its stead the throne of God in the midst of His people (v. 17; cf. Rev. 22:3–4).

4. *The ark in the later theological systems.*
(*a*) According to a tradition of the Apocrypha the ark was hidden by Jeremiah in a cavern on Mount Nebo at the time of the destruction of Jerusalem; it will reappear at the end of time (2 Macc. 2:1–8; Rev. 11:19).
(*b*) The spiritual current: the receptacle of the tables of the law will be the heart of believers (Jer. 31:33–34).
(*c*) The most holy place of the second Temple will remain empty. From that time onwards it is the Temple, the "House of God", which will be the place of the presence of God in the midst of His people. The realism of this phrase in the late Psalms or in the writings of the Chronicler must not be attenuated.

Two currents emerge: first, in Judaism after A.D. 70, when the Temple has been finally destroyed, the tabernacle of the synagogues where the rolls of the Law are kept will be called the "ark"; secondly, in the N.T., Jesus substitutes Himself for the Temple and the ark (Jn. 2:21). He is the one place on earth where God is present, the instrument for His omnipotence for the salvation of the world (Col. 1:19f.; 2:9). As

Christ, Jesus is King, Prophet and Priest. Rom. 3:25 will even compare Him with the cover of the ark. By Him there takes place the unique sprinkling which purifies the sins of the whole world.

The *Church, the body of Christ, is now in the midst of the world what the ark was in Israel (Eph. 2:20–22).

A. LELIÈVRE

ARMAGEDDON, *see* NAMES (GEOGRAPHICAL)

ASCEND, *see* DESCEND

ASCENSION

This term, though rather unfortunate in some respects, serves nowadays to designate the "going up" of the risen Christ into the heavens. The third Gospel and the Acts of the Apostles are alone in the N.T. in explicitly mentioning this event. In Lk. 24:50–53 we read that the risen Christ "parted" from His disciples while He was blessing them (a less well attested reading in v. 51 adds that He "was carried up into heaven"). The context here indicates that this parting took place the same day as the *resurrection of Jesus. In Acts 1:2 it is a matter of a "taking up" of Jesus into heaven and v. 3 states definitely that it took place 40 days after the resurrection of Jesus, a period during which Jesus "presented himself alive" to His disciples and spoke to them "of things concerning the kingdom of God". Then in Acts 1:9 we read that the Risen One "was lifted up" whilst His disciples were looking at Him and that "a cloud took him out of their sight".

On analysis these three texts call for a certain number of comments which can be summarized in the following way:

1. The Greek words used to describe the "ascension" of the Risen One present that event as a "taking up" (verbs in the passive, presupposing that God is the subject of the action) rather than an "ascension". Christ does not scale the various heavens which separate Him from the deity,

to arrive ultimately in supra-terrestrial light, as one finds in myth, familiar to many religions, concerning the ascent of souls (and in certain apocryphal gospels concerning Jesus). The one who is taken up *already possesses*, though in various modes according to the texts, the glory of life; it is the Risen One who is taken up in sight of His disciples. 2. Considered in its N.T. context, the theme of the ascension appears as quite secondary in relation to that of the resurrection-exaltation of Jesus. In fact, the most ancient texts of the N.T., though they return constantly to the idea of the Risen One "seated" at the right hand of God, do not attach this statement to the fact of the ascension (cf. for example 1 Thess. 1:10; 4:16; 2 Thess. 1:7; 1 Cor. 4:5; Rom. 8:34; 1 Cor. 15:4, where, however, the appearances of the Risen One are concerned: Eph. 1:3,10,20; Phil. 2:9ff.; 3:20f.; 2 Tim. 2:8; 4:18, etc.). In short, the fact of the ascension appears neither in the Pauline or deutero-Pauline Epistles, nor in the catholic Epistles (1 Pet. 3:22 apart), nor in Revelation, nor in the first Gospel. It is mentioned in Mark 16:19, which is a late text, added at a later date to the second Gospel and which, moreover, says nothing on our subject other than what is said in Luke and the Acts, and in John 20:17, where, as in Luke 24:50–53 the ascension takes place immediately after the resurrection. 3. It can be seen that the ascension theme itself, later than that of the resurrection-exaltation of Jesus, was not, at first, an integral part of the theme of the appearances for 40 days (compare Acts 1:3 and 9; Jn. 20:17 and Jn. 20:26; 21:1).

But if the fact of the ascension, as a fully authenticated event, is but poorly and tardily attested in the N.T., the reality of this ascension is much more widely supported. In this connection theological statements are concerned, without any narrative or documentary character; statements that may be classed in two main groups.

In the first, we place Eph. 4:10 ("He who descended is he who also ascended far above all the heavens, that he might fill all things"), then the liturgical hymn of 1 Tim. 3:16 on the "taking up to glory" of Jesus, then three texts in the Epistle to the Hebrews (4:14; 6:19f.; 9:24) where the ascension is compared with the entry of the high priest of the old covenant into the Holy of Holies; then finally 1 Pet. 3:22 on Jesus Christ "who has gone into heaven" and to whom the angels, authorities and powers have been subjected. Concerning these theological rather than narrative statements about the ascension, we notice particularly (a) the subordination of the ascension theme to that of the resurrection, (b) the link often underlined between the cross and the ascension; this draws its significance from the fact that it was the Crucified, that is to say, the man Jesus, who entered into celestial glory, (c) the fact that the ascension is never presented as the end of Christ's work, since He was raised to intercede before the Father, to reign over all creatures, to send the Spirit to His followers, to return at last to earth, in glory, on the last day.

In a second group of theological texts on the ascension it would be necessary to mention all references to the "sitting" of Christ at the right hand of God. As we have already shown, this last theme, most often treated with that of the ascension, belongs primarily to that of the resurrection of Jesus (*Right hand).

P. BONNARD

ASHTAROTH, *see* GOD O.T.

AUTHORITIES

1. In the Pauline Epistles many important passages contain the words "authorities", "powers", "thrones", "dominions", "principalities", in the very particular sense of beings related to *angels and to demonic powers (*Devil). Other expressions must be compared with them, expressions with which these passages are often connected, such as "rulers of this age", "elements", "height", "depth", "things in heaven", "things under the earth". How has the term "authorities", which at first signifies the power delegated to someone and exer-

cised by him, then the persons themselves who hold it, been able to take on this specific sense which it assumes with the apostle Paul and, before him, in Judaism contemporary with the birth of Christianity?

2. (a) In accordance with secular usage, the words "authority", "powers", correspond in other writings of the N.T. to the earthly *powers* of civil or military leaders (Matt. 8:9; Lk. 20:20; 23:7; Acts 9:14; 26:10–12), and the abstract word is extended to the *rulers themselves* (Lk. 12:11; cf. also Tit. 3:1).

(b) In Acts 1:7 it is a question of the authority with which God "fixes the times and seasons" with respect to the establishment of the Kingdom. Jude 8 and 2 Peter 2:10 announce the punishment of those who have opposed the (divine) "authority". The synoptic Gospels attribute divine authority in the absolute sense to Jesus; this is found behind His words (Mk. 1:22; Matt. 7:29) as it is behind His acts (Mk. 2:10; Matt. 21:23). It is fully granted to the risen Christ: "All authority in heaven and on earth has been given to me" (Matt. 28:18; cf. 11:27). In a less absolute sense, it can be transmitted to the apostles (2 Cor. 10:8; 13:10). In Revelation many beings are invested with it (2:26; 6:8; 11:6; 13:7; 14:18; 18:1).

(c) Just as on the earthly plane the words "authority", "power" are also applied to the people who are their instruments, so the immediate servants of God in the invisible world, the direct instruments of His "Authority", are themselves called "authorities", "powers". On this heavenly plane, this terminological use is pushed even further, and consistently all the expressions implying power are connected, at the same time, with invisible *beings*. Thus, it is not only the words "authorities" and "powers" that take on a personal sense, but also the words "principalities", "dominions", "thrones". We must consider here the personifications of the attributes and functions of God (hypostases) which we meet in Judaism. Perhaps the very difficult passage 1 Cor. 11:10 on "the authority the woman should have on her head because of the angels" can be explained by this very tendency to make concrete the divine authority which protects against all other authority; likewise for the "dominion" already mentioned in Jude 8.

(d) For the Devil himself exercises an authority. He claims to have at his disposal the kingdoms of the earth: "To you I will give all this authority . . ." (Lk. 4:6). In Luke 22:53 there is a question of the "power of darkness". Eph. 2:2 speaks of the Prince who exercises power over the air, and in Rev. 13:2 the dragon gives to the beast (= the Empire) "his power and his throne and great authority". It is characteristic that these terms are the very ones that in Paul's writings denote the invisible beings. This confirms that power and authority— either those of the Devil or those of God— can assume form in real beings just as empirical authority is sometimes attributed to the power that is exercised, sometimes to the persons who exercise it.

(e) The fact that the same expressions are used at the same time in reference to the power, authority and throne of God and to the power, authority and throne of the Devil explains why it is often difficult to say whether their personification is good or bad. The indefinite character which, in this connection, strikes us with reference to these powers has been explained in Judaism by the doctrine of the fall of the angels.

3. In any case, the belief relative to "authorities" and to "powers" presupposes the idea that, *behind all these visible phenomena*, invisible beings, good and bad, are at work. It is so for the "elements" mentioned in Gal. 4:3,9 and Col. 2:20, and which are known to the author of 2 Pet. 3:10,12: they are cosmic principles, probably personified, who direct the course of the universe. Moreover, every man has his "angel" (Acts 12:15); Jesus Himself seems to have shared this concept (Matt. 18:10). In Revelation, there is reference to the "angels of the Churches" (chap. 2–3). Jewish sources bear special testimony to the conviction that every *people* has its angel.

The book of Daniel (chap. 10) speaks of the angels of Persia and of Greece, Enoch 89:59ff. mentions the 70 shepherds of the peoples, and in Rabbinic sources we meet the same belief.

It is clear that these angels of the peoples are considered as the invisible prototypes of actual princes. Thus we understand that the same expressions can denote at the same time the invisible authorities and the authorities of earthly states. So it is in 1 Cor. 2:8: "None of the rulers of this age understood this; for if they had, they would not have crucified the Lord of glory." We know that the "princes of this world" are, according to the religious terminology of Judaism, the invisible "powers", hostile to God, who (with God's permission) superintend the present age, while in the future age nothing will oppose further the reign of God or of the Messiah. But it is clear that the apostle is thinking here, at the same time, of the terrestrial instruments of these invisible princes, of Herod and of Pilate (Lk. 23:12; Acts 4:27; 13:27). There is also the need to recall the part, already mentioned, that is played in the story of the Temptation by the Devil, who (still with God's permission) has the kingdoms of the world at his disposal; the images which Revelation uses to denote the Roman state rest on the same conception. While taking account of this Jewish and Pauline belief and terminology we must very probably interpret the "authorities" to which Paul invites the Romans to submit (Rom. 13:1) in the same sense, that is to say, by understanding there at the same time the invisible powers and their instruments, the chief men of the Roman Empire. This is all the more evident since the apostle never uses the Greek word for "authorities" in the plural without implying the powers of which we have spoken. This image conforms completely to the Jewish terminology, where the same Hebrew word (*sar*) denotes, at the same time, the king, the prince and the invisible rulers (Dan. 10:13,20; cf. Josh. 5:14).

It is certain that beside the ancient conception of the "celestial army", foreign elements, especially Babylonian, influenced all this Jewish angelology. But whatever its origin it was widely current in Judaism at the time of the N.T., and the first Christians, Paul especially, gave it an important place in their theology.

4. If we knew in greater detail the Jewish speculations concerning this invisible world, we should know what distinction the apostle made between "authorities", "powers", "principalities", "dominions", "thrones", "elements", "rulers of this age". For it is certain that they were not synonyms for him and that he did not heap them together to attain a rhetorical effect. We know, moreover, that the Jews clearly distinguished different "orders" of angels (Apoc. Baruch Syr. 59:11). In one of the lists found in Enoch 61:10 there appear the "powers", "dominions", "authorities", and in Slavonic Enoch 20, "principalities" and "thrones" as well. It probably depended on a more or less secret teaching. In the sect of the Essenes, the doctrine of angels appears to have been particularly developed (Josephus, *Jewish War* II:142). This is confirmed by the writing which is called the *Testament of the Twelve Patriarchs* which, according to the recent discoveries at the Dead Sea, comes from the same sect: the Testament of Levi (chap. 3) gives teaching about angels. Other Jewish books of the same type speak of them Jub. 2:2,18; 15:27; 31:14). However, none of these texts allows us to assign a particular rôle to each of these powers, nor is it possible, for example, as it has been thought, to place for instance the "thrones" and "dominions" nearer to God than the others.

5. In any case, it is undeniable that for Paul it is no question of a belief of secondary importance. On the contrary, not only does he share with Judaism and the whole of early Christianity the firm conviction that these powers really exist (1 Cor. 8:5), but he is persuaded that, *behind all that happens before our eyes*, there are events in which the celestial powers are involved: "For we are not contending against flesh and blood, but against the principalities, against the

powers, against the world rulers of this present darkness, against the spiritual hosts of wickedness in the heavenly places" (Eph. 6:12). The angels see all the dramas which are enacted on earth: "(the apostles) have become a spectacle to the world, to angels, and to men" (1 Cor. 4:9). The failings of the Churches have connections with the attacks made by these "powers".

God created them from the beginning in Christ: "In him all things were created, in heaven and on earth, visible and invisible, whether thrones or dominions or principalities or authorities" (Col. 1:16). In Romans 8:38f., the apostle designates them all equally as divine "creatures".

To say that they were created *in Christ* is to say that the whole history of salvation concerns them equally. Because the first Christians take seriously their impact on earthly events, they also take seriously the victory that Christ won over them. Henceforward all these invisible "powers", whatever their name and rôle, are subject to Christ. There is only one mediator who counts: He who is "the image of the invisible God, the first-born of all creation" (Col. 1:15). It is true that the "powers" still exist, but practically speaking their existence has no further significance, since they are bound to Christ, and since every attempt on their part at emancipation and attack is doomed in advance to failure by virtue of the decisive defeat that they have already suffered. The N.T. texts which speak of the victory that Christ has won by His death over the invisible "powers" seem to consider them always as powers which previously had been hostile to God. Do they presuppose that they have *all* more or less departed from the divine will, or do they envisage only one section of these powers, those that opposed God, because Christ's death concerns them only? The texts afford us no answer. Whatever may be the answer, it is clear that in the story of salvation, at the end of which everything will be *subject* to God so that He may be "all in all" (1 Cor. 15:28), the decisive stage is already reached by the subjection of *all* the invisible powers which took place at the moment of Christ's death:

"to reconcile to himself all things, whether on earth or in heaven, making peace by the blood of his cross" (Col. 1:20).

6. This conviction is bound up with the Christian interpretation of the royal Psalm 110 which the Jews had already explained in a Messianic sense: "Sit at my right hand, till I make your enemies your footstool." There is no O.T. text that the first Christians quoted more frequently. The avowal contained in all the symbols, "He has sat down at the right hand of the Father," comes from this psalm. But all the ancient formulas regularly add, as a fact already accomplished in principle, the next part of the quotation: victory over the enemies, *and those enemies are always identified with the invisible powers.* So it is in the old text used in 1 Pet. 3:22, which after the mention of the death of Christ for our sins and of His preaching to the spirits, continues: "who has gone into heaven and is at the right hand of God, with angels, authorities, and powers subject to him."

For a long time it has been thought that in the famous passage Phil. 2:6ff. the apostle has used a Christological confession of the early Church. It culminates in the affirmation of Christ's elevation and dominion "confessed by every tongue": the Lord ("the name which is above every name") is Jesus Christ, and there again appear the beings which are "in heaven and on earth and under the earth"; their "knee bows at the name of Jesus" (vv. 10-11).

It can be shown (cf. O. Cullmann, *The Earliest Christian Confessions of Faith,* Lutterworth Press, 1950) that until the second century the creeds of the early Church never omit a mention of the submission of these powers (Ignatius of Antioch *ad Trall.* 9:1; Polycarp 2:1; Irenaeus *adv. haer.* I,10:1). The fact that it figures in these short summaries of the Christian faith proves its importance to the early Church. Eph. 1:21 joins as well the elevation of Christ with His reign over these powers: "He made him sit at his right hand in the heavenly places, far above all rule and authority and power and dominion and above every name that is named, not only in this age but also in that which is to come", and by quoting Ps. 8:7, the next verse adds "and has put all things under his feet". The invisible powers are not annihilated but subjected. The introduction of the famous baptismal directive given by the risen Christ at the time of His appearance to the disciples also certainly alludes to this subjection: "All authority in heaven and on earth has been given to me" (Matt. 28:18). With bright colours, Col. 2:15 describes the subjection of the powers: by the *cross of Christ God has "disarmed the principalities and powers and made a public example of them, and through Christ has led them in triumph".

Psalm 110 considers the victory over the enemies as *subsequent* to the elevation of the royal Lord to the right hand of God. We have just seen that, according to the Christian interpretation, it has already taken place at the moment of Christ's death. But there are other passages in the N.T. in which it will take place only at the end of time. Thus it is in a Pauline passage which speaks of the final consummation, of the total submission of all things to God: "Then comes the end, when he delivers the kingdom to God the Father after destroying every rule and every authority and power. For he must reign until he has put all his enemies under his feet" (1 Cor. 15:24ff.). The following verses develop this theme of submission by combining, as in Eph. 1:22, Ps. 110 with Ps. 8:7. So long as there remains the least element of revolt in the powers, their final submission at the end of time will mean their destruction. On the point of Christ's elevation to God's right hand, Heb. 10:13 also quotes Psalm 110 in making mention of the victory over the "enemies", but the author specifies that this is still to come while the elevation has already taken place: "he sat down at the right hand of God, then to *wait* until his enemies should be made a stool for his feet."

7. How are we to explain that victory over the powers is sometimes presented as an accomplished event and sometimes as a future event? At this point we must indicate in connection with this particular problem of the "powers" a phenomenon which we can call the chronological tension (*Time): the decisive battle has already taken place at the moment of Christ's death; victory is assured and yet the war still continues; the proclamation of victory, the final consummation, is still to come. The new era is inaugurated, and yet the former aeon ("the present age") still exists. The fact that the same author, the apostle Paul, considers victory over the powers sometimes as a fact of the past, sometimes as a thing of the future, confirms that this tension is indeed a constituent element of the thought of early Christianity. Indeed, the one Greek verb which is used to express the defeat of God's invisible enemies should be translated sometimes by "disarm", when the victory already gained is in question (2 Tim. 1:10), sometimes by "annihilate", when the victory to come is in question (1 Cor. 15:26).

The N.T. contains traces of an idea that offers a suitable explanation of this tension: the invisible powers, by the death of Christ, have been "bound", and obliged in this way to perform the divine will already. It is true that the picture of "Satan bound" is found explicitly only in Rev. 20:2f. and is applied there to Satan only and the reign of a thousand years. But it is probable that the first Christians held an analogous conception of the situation in which the powers find themselves between Christ's death and His return. It is only thus that certain contradictions in their evaluation disappear. Being finally conquered, but only bound, these powers can still attempt an apparent and *temporary* emancipation so long as the present age lasts. To use the image of the bond, it could be said that God can still allow the leash to be longer or shorter, but that the bond can nevermore be broken. Thus, these powers, though conquered by Christ and set to serve Him, can still become demonic again but for a limited time; for instance the beast (=the Empire) in Revelation (chap. 13:1ff.).

8. The expression "rulers of this age", which is certainly a collective appellation

for the whole or part of these powers, throws into relief the same correspondence between their present and their future lot. At the basis of this appellation there is a conception according to which each "aeon", each cosmic period, is ruled by one or several invisible powers whose authority ends with their "age". For Christians, the future "age" had already begun with the death and resurrection of Christ, and yet the present "age" endures until the final consummation at the time of Christ's return. That is to say that the "rulers of this age" still exist although they have no independent part to play, and though their function is, so to speak, absorbed by that of Christ the only mediator, to whom all is subject, while waiting until He Himself submits to God after the final act (1 Cor. 15:28).

But what is important in the whole N.T., what is the foundation of the "*joy" of the first Christians, is the conviction that there is now but one "ruler" of the time in which we live between the resurrection and the return of Christ. He is seated at the right hand of God, and all powers are already subject to Him. They are all already made like the "ministering spirits" (Heb. 1:14) who carry out the divine plan in the present phase of the story of salvation; "that through the church the manifold wisdom of God might now be made known to the principalities and powers in the heavenly places" (Eph. 3:10). Worship must no more be offered to the powers (Heb. 1:2ff.; Rev. 19:10; 22:8f.; Col. 2:18); no further fear, no slavery in connection with them (Gal. 4:3,9) is possible for the man who knows that there is no other than one true Lord even if the others still exist (1 Cor. 8:5ff.). "For I am sure," says the apostle, "that neither death, nor life, nor angels, nor principalities, nor things present, nor things to come, nor powers, nor height, nor depth, nor anything else in all creation, will be able to separate us from the love of God in Christ Jesus our Lord" (Rom. 8:38f.).

O. CULLMANN

BAAL, *see* GOD O.T.

BABYLON, *see* NAMES (GEOGRAPHICAL)

BAPTISM

1. The ministry of John the Baptist opens a new chapter in the story of salvation; it prepares the Lord's coming announced by the prophets (cf. Mk. 1:2ff. and parallels; Lk. 1:14ff.; Jn. 1:31). His ministry is like a boundary which indicates a radical change in history (cf. Acts 1:22; 10:37; 13:24), and so we must not be surprised that the governing groups in Jerusalem sent to ask him if he was the Christ (Jn. 1:19ff.). Indeed, it needed a special mission of God Himself to dare to apply to the children of Abraham (Lk. 3:8) the baptism that for generations the Jews had been applying to those who were converted to the faith of Israel (cf. Matt. 21:25ff. and parallels), and to dare to declare that in submitting to such baptism one enters into God's design (Lk. 7:29ff.). Recent research has indeed proved that John's baptism did not take its origin from the ritual lustrations which were known to nearly all the religions of the Near East and which were practised by certain Jewish sects; it is, on the contrary, an application to the Jews themselves of the baptism of proselytes. Different reasons have been sought to explain what John meant by the baptism that he administered: a unique baptism, by immersion and involving moral undertakings (cf. Lk. 3:1–18). The most credible reason is found in the idea, known to the Rabbis and mentioned by St. Paul, that to receive the law of God and to reach the Promised Land, the people had to be baptized into Moses by passing through the sea (1 Cor. 10:1–2). If proselytes were baptized, it was then in all likelihood with the idea of applying to them, too, *a posteriori*, the crossing of the Red Sea. Now, according to a considerable part of the Jewish tradition, the events of the Exodus are prefigurative of the last events: they suggest what will happen at the coming of eternal salvation. So it is to "make ready for the Lord"—whose coming is imminent—"a people prepared" (Lk. 1:17) that John baptizes. In the *desert (Matt. 3:7) he

gathers the Messianic people together, by a baptism of repentance (Matt. 3:6 and parallels, 11; Acts 19:4) and forgiveness (Mk. 1:4) which accomplishes the crossing of the Red Sea. It is a baptism by *water only (Matt. 3:11 and parallels), that is to say that it purifies (cf. Ezek. 36:25), that it passes sentence (cf. Gen. 7ff.) and that it gives hope (cf. Isa. 35:7): it makes preparation for salvation without granting it yet; it only puts an end to the state of things which God condemns without replacing it by the *Kingdom of God; it signifies the end of the present age without giving birth to the age to come. That is why John the Baptist is not yet under the new *covenant (Matt. 11:9–15).

2. Jesus Himself underwent the baptism of John (Matt. 3:13ff. esp.; cf. Jn. 1:32ff.), not because He needed it for Himself, but to fulfil all righteousness (Matt. 3:14f.), that is to say, in order to assume the ministry of the Son or the *servant of God (Mk. 1:10f.=Isa. 42:1), whose task it was to accept solidarity with the people and to take their sins as His burden (cf. Isa. 53). In this sense, the baptism of Jesus is a preparation for His death on the *cross, which, moreover, He qualifies expressly as a baptism (Mk. 10:38; Lk.12:50): His baptism singles Him out as the Lamb of God (Jn. 1:29–34). This is why the first three Gospels —there is some hesitation in John's Gospel (cf. Jn. 3:22ff.; 4:1ff.), though it reaches the same theological conclusion (Jn. 3:30)—say no more about the Baptist's activity from the time of Jesus' baptism, and even stop all mention of baptism until the moment when, as John the Baptist had predicted, Jesus will baptize with the Holy Spirit (Matt. 3:11 and parallels; Jn. 1:33). Now this moment could come only after Jesus had borne and borne away God's judgment against the sin of the world (cf. Jn. 7:39), therefore after His resurrection (cf. Acts 1:5; 11:16); and so it is only after Easter that the Lord gives His disciples the order to baptize (Matt. 28:19f.). From the days of John to Easter morning, all the significance of baptism was to some degree concentrated in Jesus, whose whole life—as the creed says—was nothing but a suffering.

3. After Pentecost, the Church obeys the order to baptize (cf. Acts 2:38–41), and the N.T. does not consider that anyone could be a member of the Church without undergoing baptism (cf. Acts 8:12,36; 9:18; 10:44ff.; 16:15,33; 19:5; Rom. 6:3, etc.). Is this baptism John's, or is it a new one? It is certainly a new baptism (cf. Acts 19:1ff.), and yet, like John's, it is still a unique baptism (cf. Eph. 4:5), a *baptism by water* (cf. Acts 8:36; 16:13ff.) and a baptism of repentance with a view to pardon (Acts 2:38). It is then, like John's, a baptism that means, for the baptized, that the present age has gone bankrupt, that it is condemned and under sentence. But, different in this respect from John's, Christian baptism is also a *baptism of the Spirit*; that is to say, not only does it put an end, for the baptized, to the present age, but it also places the baptized henceforward in the age to come, of which the Spirit is the guarantee (2 Cor. 1:22; 5:5). Being a baptism by water and by Spirit, Christian baptism bears forceful witness to the paradoxical situation of the Church in which the temporal world and the world to come join together; a situation which makes of the Church, in the world of the first Adam, a sign of the real presence of the world of the second Adam (*Jesus, *Time). Even if sometimes the moments of baptism by water and by the Spirit do not coincide (cf. Acts 10:44ff.), the two moments concern a single baptismal act (cf. Jn. 3:5). (The account of the conversion of the Samaritans, who, in spite of their baptism by Philip, had not yet received the Holy Spirit, which was communicated to them by Peter and John who had made a special journey from Jerusalem (Acts 8:4–17), is clearly intended to underline the integration of the new Samaritan Church with the apostolic Church in Jerusalem, rather than to mark a difference between the baptism by water alone and baptism by the Holy Spirit. If this obscure account has any theological significance, it is not in an opposition between the two baptisms, but

in the idea that the *apostles alone can give Christian baptism in its fullness.)

4. An event so all-important as baptism had straightway to give birth to a baptismal theology (cf. Heb. 6:2 where "baptisms" probably refer to Christian baptism contrasted to John's baptism or to those analogous rites celebrated in paganism). Within the limits of the canonical writings this theology contains the following main elements, listed here without any logical order:

(a) *Baptism is essentially a work of God*, the Father (cf. Acts 2:41), the Son (cf. Eph. 5:26) and the Holy Spirit (cf. 1 Cor. 12:13) in whose name it is administered (Matt. 28:19). It means that the one who is active in baptism and gives it its power is, in the first place, neither the baptizer nor the baptized, but the Lord. That is why—if the baptism were Christian (cf. Acts 19:1ff.) —it could not be repeated without blasphemy (cf. Eph. 4:5).

(b) *Baptism makes the death and resurrection of Christ effective.* This is the central doctrine of the N.T. on baptism. In and through baptism, it becomes true that Jesus dies for the trespasses and is raised for the justification of the baptized (Rom. 4:25). Now, in the passion of Christ the last judgment was anticipated: the anger and curse of God against the rebellious world fell on Christ alone on the cross for Him to bear them and bear them away (2 Cor. 5:21; Gal. 3:13); and on Easter morning Jesus became the first of those who have been raised (1 Cor. 5:20). The final fate of the world was played out in anticipation on Calvary and in the garden of Joseph of Arimathea. Baptism has as its power the validation of the ending of our world and the recommencement of the new world of God; it is, for each person baptized, a sacramental anticipation of his final destiny. But this individual anticipation is only possible because it is attributed to the universal anticipation of the last judgment which took place in the death and resurrection of Jesus Christ. That is why baptism is administered in the *name of Jesus (Acts 2:38; 8:16;

10:48; 19:5; cf. 1 Cor. 1:13ff.), which means (the term "in the name of" being a technical term for the transfer of bank accounts, for example) that it is administered on the basis of the substitutionary death and resurrection of Christ and with reference to them. It can thus be understood why St. Paul can declare that baptism drenches and drowns (=etymological meaning of the word baptism) in the death of Christ, buries with Christ, in anticipation of resurrection with Christ (Rom. 6:3ff.; Col. 2:12); why he says that by his baptism and through his baptism, the baptized becomes one plant with Christ (Rom. 6:5), and why—like Christ—the baptized is henceforward dead to sin and alive towards God (Rom. 6:11). Recent research has shown that this amazing manner of thinking is not an image nor a symbol but that it describes a reality: in his baptism and by his baptism, the baptized dies with Christ and is raised with Him; his carnal life there finds its end and his spiritual life its beginning. Baptism then overturns completely man's religious and moral position: it applies in fact to an individual what is true in law for the whole world, namely that in Jesus Christ, who dies and is raised up, the fallen creation comes to an end and the new creation begins. But —and this must be underlined—if baptism kills and restores to life, the person who emerges from the baptismal water is the same as the one who was plunged into it (*new): just as the Risen One is the same as the Crucified (cf. Lk. 24:38f.). Baptism does not interrupt the identity of the baptized, and it is still possible to speak to him of *his* "once" in contrast to *his* "now" (cf. Eph. 5:8, etc.).

(c) *Thus baptism inserts the baptized into the crucified and glorified Christ*, who becomes the life of the baptized (Rom. 14:7f.; Gal. 2:20; Phil. 1:20). Now it is in the *Church that the Crucified and Risen One manifests and reveals Himself since the ascension. That is why baptism adds to the Church (Acts 2:41), or leads to the Church (1 Cor. 12:13; Gal. 3:27–28). Just as one cannot conceive of members of the Church who are not baptized, so one cannot conceive of baptized people who are not, by a conscious and faithful undertaking, members of the Church. By admitting a new member to the Church, which is the place where the discomfiture of the Devil is known, confessed and lived out, every baptism thus means a victory over the power of the Evil One.

(d) Baptism is a new birth (Jn. 3:5), a washing of regeneration (Tit. 3:5) which makes, from a child of the flesh, a child of God (Jn. 1:12f.). That is why the baptized must prove the validity of his baptism by a new life (Rom. 6:8ff.; Col. 3:1–15; Heb. 10:19–25; cf. 1 Cor. 10:1–14). The first Epistle of John lays much stress on this fact by declaring that he who is born of God practises righteousness (2:29), knows how to love (4:7), sins no more (3:9, 5:18), is victorious over the *world (5:4; cf. 5:1–13). St. Paul says the same thing by declaring that the baptized has put on Christ (*garment) (Gal. 3:26ff.).

(e) Baptism is a condition of entry into the Kingdom of God (Jn. 3:5), and it can even be said that it saves him who undergoes it (1 Pet. 3:21). Such New Testament statements may lack dogmatic wisdom: this does not alter the fact that a great deal of exegetical acrobatics is needed to deny the close and very realistic link by which Scripture binds salvation and baptism together (cf. also Mk. 16:16; Acts 22:16; 1 Cor. 6:11; Tit. 3:5). It was for this reason (see below) that the apostles were doubly cautious in the practice of baptism. It may be asked whether indiscretion in the practice of baptism does not of necessity arise at that point where, through prudence in the doctrine of baptism, one wishes to contest or reduce the realism of the connections between baptism and salvation.

(f) In spite of Matt. 28:19, St. Paul states that he was not sent to baptize (1 Cor. 1:17). What is known of the activities of the apostle to the Gentiles however (cf. Acts 16:15,33; 18:8; 19:1ff.; 1 Cor. 1:14ff., etc.) prevents our pressing too far a text which is probably a reminder that St. Paul, after baptizing the first Christians in a town, made them responsible for baptizing those who were added to the Church later: indeed, of those that the apostle claims to have baptized in Corinth, Crispus was the first Jew to be converted (cf. Acts 18:8) and the family of Stephanas is called the "first-fruits of Achaia" (1 Cor. 16:16), a term which clearly means the first pagans to be converted. This term, which is taken from the language of sacrifice, permits the supposition that St. Paul is alluding to the baptisms that he is celebrating when he says that he is "a minister of Christ Jesus to the Gentiles in the priestly service of the gospel of God, so that the offering of the Gentiles may be acceptable, sanctified by the Holy Spirit" (Rom. 15:16). In this light, baptism becomes, for the baptizer, a method of sacrificing to God, that is to say, to consecrate to Him, to dedicate to Him, those who henceforth do not wish to live for themselves but for His glory.

5. But baptism has not only provoked some intense theological thought; it has demanded also some standards of discipline, of which the following may be noted:

(a) In order that nothing may stand in the way of baptism (cf. Acts 8:36; 10:47; 11:17; cf. Mk. 10:14 and parallels), a divine indication is required, which allows the Church to know that it can administer the rite with authority. This sign is either the confession of Christian faith by the one who requests baptism (cf. Acts 8:13,36f.; 16:14f.,33f.; 18:8; Mk. 16:16, etc.), or the gift of the Holy Spirit (Acts 10:44ff.). This faith or this gift of the Spirit show that God is willing to put these candidates for baptism within the effective benefit of Christ's death: they also allow the hope that these candidates will not compromise, by a life of sin, the baptism which they request.

(b) However the indication may be, the candidate's faith can also be valid for all those who, according to biblical law, depend on his authority: namely his *family or household. The head of the family's faith is then a kind of guarantee allowing the hope that he will be able to keep his dependants in the nurture and admonition of the Lord (Eph. 6:4). In this way on several occasions we find a whole family admitted to baptism (cf. Acts 10:24 and 48; 16:15,33ff.; 1 Cor. 1:16). Not to see in these texts—granted, of course, that the head of the house has a living faith—an authorization to baptize children, must imply the rejection of the biblical doctrine of family unity (this family unity being what authorized, under the old covenant, the *circumcision of Jewish boys: indeed, St. Paul makes baptism the parallel of circumcision under the new covenant, Col. 2:11f.).

(c) At Corinth, certain Christians had themselves baptized substitutionally for some of the dead who had not had the opportunity of hearing the Gospel, in the desire to place them too within the benefit of Christ's death (1 Cor. 15:29f.). This baptism had the aim of giving these dead a chance of rising again for salvation. The curious thing is that St. Paul does not condemn this practice; something which allows us to measure the realism of his doctrine of baptism. If this practice did not spread in the Church, and has even disappeared completely, it is because of the certitude that, since Christ's descent into hell, the Gospel is also proclaimed to those who, during their life, heard no Christian preaching (cf. 1 Pet. 4:6; *death).

(d) One cannot baptize oneself: the rite is always performed by another. Who then has the right to perform valid baptism? This question seems to have preoccupied the Church at Corinth to such an extent that it caused a division (cf. 1 Cor. 1:12ff.). We should notice first of all, on this point, that the N.T. never shows us a woman administering baptism. Next we should also recall that the account of the baptism of the Samaritans (Acts 8:4–17) seems to have the purpose of showing that only those directly authorized by Jesus can give baptism in its fullness. Perhaps there were added to these the ministers of Churches united to the one in Jerusalem, for example, Ananias who baptized St. Paul (cf. Acts 9:13f.,18,21). Yet nothing allows us to suppose that the baptism administered by Philip to the Ethiopian eunuch was not fully valid (Acts 8:36f.), and it will be noted too that it was not St. Peter who baptized Cornelius and his house, but that he gave instructions for their baptism (Acts 10:48. Did he give this order to one of the brethren of the Joppa Church who had gone along with him, Acts 10:23? See what is said above about the Pauline practice of having subsequent baptisms administered by the first converts in a town). These few remarks on the right of baptizing allow us to say no more than this: the infant Church was not unaware that there might be a problem here both theological and disciplinary.

J.-J. VON ALLMEN

BEATITUDES, *see* BLESSED

BEGINNING, *see* TIME

BISHOP, *see* MINISTRY N.T.

BLASPHEMY

N.B. Our versions often say revile or speak evil of, sometimes curse or slander in places where they should say blaspheme (e.g. 1 Kings 21:10,13; Matt. 27:39; 2 Pet. 2:2).

1. Blasphemy is an *attack against God's majesty and honour*. The blasphemer lays blame on the absolute Master of his life, and thus commits an irreparable act; the Law of Moses condemns him to death (Lev. 24:11ff.). It is also possible to blaspheme God in His representatives: Moses (Acts 6:11), Jesus Christ (Matt. 27:39; Lk. 23:39); before his conversion, Paul is a blasphemer, because he denies that God is revealed in Jesus, and he wishes to make Christians blaspheme (Acts 26:11), to lead them to deny that Jesus is the Christ.

2. *Jesus is accused of blasphemy* (Matt. 9:3 and parallels), because He forgives the paralytic's sins, which God alone can do: the Jews do not recognize this simple man as the Son, that is, God's representative and plenipotentiary (Jn. 10:33,36). The charge of blasphemy is also the one that brings the condemnation of Jesus (Matt. 26:63–65).

Obviously the statement of Jesus is not judged as blasphemous in itself, but the fact that it is this Jesus, a prisoner and powerless, this man clearly lacking all signs of God's power (Phil. 2:7), who declares Himself to be the Son of God: in the eyes of His enemies, the humiliated and suffering Son can only be an impostor.

3. Believers must *be careful not to cause others to blaspheme*. By his adultery David caused the enemies of the Lord to blaspheme (2 Sam. 12:14)—the pagan nations who surround Israel and who should see God's holiness shine forth in Israel. The respectful attitude of Christian slaves to their masters, the humility and spirit of service of the Christian wife, will prevent blasphemy of God's name and word by their masters or husbands who are still heathen (1 Tim. 6:1; Tit. 2:5).

4. Any *sin, even blasphemy against the Son of Man, may be forgiven, *but not blasphemy against the *Holy Spirit* (Matt. 12:32; Mk. 3:28–29). This saying, which has caused heartache among many timorous believers, means that only conscious and deliberate rejection of present grace, recognized and tasted (Heb. 6:4–6) brings death; the Holy Spirit is in effect the presence of God openly revealed in the heart that He has enlightened. The Son of Man is God present under the veil of His humanity; it is certainly a sin to blaspheme Him, not to recognize Him, to doubt, but it is a sin that each must combat unceasingly by prayer for the Holy Spirit (Lk. 11:13), repentance and obedience.

CHR. SENFT

BLESSED (HAPPY)

O.T.

1. Yahweh is never Himself called happy, after the fashion of the Greek gods, the blissful ones, and this indicates at once the gulf which separates the faith of Israel from the religions of antiquity. For the latter, the deity is a privileged being, to be envied; he enjoys a good fortune which it is a standing temptation to emulate. Yahweh by contrast is a God who comes to His people. He does not consider good fortune to be His prerogative (see Phil. 2:5ff.); He bestows it. As Creator, He is its source, being the source of life. Blessed therefore is he to whom He has been pleased to reveal Himself and with whom He has made His covenant. Conscious of an ineffable privilege, Israel's faith extols the blessedness of him who fears the Lord; for he sees that he is the object of an extraordinary grace, that of knowing only the living God. Yahweh is unique; and the blessedness of those who belong to Him is unique, delivered as they are in faith from the oppression of foreign gods, and the prestige of the surrounding cults, and the perpetual temptation to self-glorification. "Happy are you, O Israel! Who is like you, a people saved by the Lord, the shield of your help?" (Deut. 33:29). The more the faith of Israel is put to the test, the more resounding are the declarations to attest her blessedness. The Psalms above all sing of it, with all the variations which could issue from this theme ("Blessed are all who take refuge in him", 2:12; "Blessed is he whose transgression is forgiven", 32:1; "Blessed is he whom thou dost choose and bring near, to dwell in thy courts!" 65:4; "Blessed are those who dwell in thy house", 84:4; "Blessed are they who observe justice", 106:3; "Blessed is the nation whose God is the Lord", 33:12; 144:15, etc.).

2. By a process of derivation, especially in the Wisdom literature, e.g. in the Apocrypha, blessedness, the fruit of God's blessing, seems to take the form above all of fullness of life. Riches, success, prosperity, wife, children, beauty, wisdom here figure as manifest signs of *blessing and the direct cause of the blessedness which Yahweh showers upon His own. But gradually the certainty emerges that even in adversity and quite specially in martyrdom the faithful experience blessedness (cf. the Maccabees). Finally, through the vicissitudes of late Judaism, blessedness assumes increasingly an eschatological and Messianic accent.

3. It is chiefly in prophecy (cf. Isa.) that there is developed, by contrast, the cry of Woe! Woe is proclaimed against those who invite the wrath or the judgment of Yahweh by their disobedience, whether it be of the moral, social, political or spiritual order. It is striking to notice, however, that this terrifying possibility is reserved not so much for the heathen as for those who have been called by Yahweh and have then turned aside from Him (Hos. 7:13; Jer. 13:27) and have appropriated for their own gain, in arrogance, the mission they were charged to fulfil (cf. Isa. 10:1ff., Assyria, the rod of my anger; Ezek. 13:3, the foolish prophets). Finally, in Isa. 6:5, the cry attains its most religious expression: the mortal cry of the sinner who meets face to face the thrice holy.

N.T.

1. Here the eschatological drama opens: in Jesus Christ the advent of the Kingdom is fulfilled. Henceforth blessedness is tied exclusively to this decisive event, which inaugurates the coming of the Messiah. The destiny of the world takes on a dramatic turn; an unexpected and astonishing process of separation is at work among men: blessed are those to whom it is given to recognize the supreme intervention of God and take part in it; woe to those who pass by the good news! The earthly ministry of Jesus occasions the first sifting: Lk. 7:23, "Blessed is he who takes no offence at me"; Lk. 10:23, "Blessed are the eyes which see what you see"; Lk. 11:28, "Blessed are those who hear the word of God and keep it!"; and above all, Matt. 16:17, "Blessed are you, Simon." On the other hand are Matt. 11:21, "Woe to you, Chorazin!"; Matt. 26:24, Matt. 23:13,16, "Woe to you, scribes and Pharisees, hypocrites!" An encounter with the person of Jesus therefore leaves behind in its wake both blessedness and woe, which are continued by means of the preaching of the Gospel by the disciples (Jn. 20:29; 1 Cor. 9:16) and which are to reach their term at the last day with the parousia (cf. Matt. 24:19,46; Rev. 16:15;

19:9, etc.). Notice in Revelation: (a) The more general sense of the word woe where it is used of the great tribulation at the end: (b) "Keep the words of the book" is a kind of pledge of the blessedness which the last judgment brings for those found faithful.

2. All this is as it were recapitulated in the royal proclamation of the *Beatitudes* (Matt. 5:3–12; cf. Lk. 6:20–23, and their antitheses in Matt. 23:13–33; Lk. 6:24–26). Their solemn character is due to the catastrophic reversal of established values. Paradoxes: yes, for they take hold of the present after the manner of the future—and in Jesus Christ the future is here! The promised blessedness is not a hypothetical consolation prize; it is the word of Him who can see and judge the present from the last day. When the rich and the powerful and the Pharisees find themselves with empty hands (cf. the prophecy of the *Magnificat*, Lk. 1:51ff.), the poor, the humble, the hungry will find themselves suddenly to be the blessed: nothing but the coming of the Kingdom can make them full. Their human and social condition (Lk.) or their interior disposition (Matt.) shows that they are waiting for and expecting someone or other. These are then those for whom the Gospel is destined. It is for these that the King comes, crucified and risen again. Their cause is revealed as one with that of God.

M. BOUTTIER

BLESSING

1. The blessing is *a word charged with power*, through which God Himself, or a man who represents Him, causes the effective descent upon people, living beings or things, of salvation, prosperity, the joy of life. God blesses man, woman, and the animals (Gen. 1:22,28); bread and water, so that they bring no sickness (Exod. 23:25); the seed of the earth so that it may be fertile (Ps. 65:10); the work of man (Deut. 2:7). Life is not a natural phenomenon, but a gift, miraculously safeguarded by God Himself. When man gives a blessing, he does not draw from within himself, but

from the wealth of God: he prays (Gen. 24:60; 49:25; Num. 6:22–27; 1 Sam. 2:20).

2. The blessing is in a general way the manifestation of God's generosity: but it is particularly the *hallmark of the history of salvation*, and it intervenes in a clear-cut manner at each stage of salvation. (*a*) At the creation, God blesses living things, granting them the grace of life and being Himself its guarantor; it is the most general form of God's *covenant with creation. (*b*) After the flood, He blesses Noah and his sons and concludes with fallen humanity a new covenant, under the sign of patience (Gen. 9:1,11). He does not bow before sin, but confirms His grace which is alone capable of repairing it. God's plan will be revealed at the third stage. (*c*) God blesses Abraham whom He has chosen not for himself, but with a view to the salvation of all nations (Gen. 12:1–3). Abraham and the people descended from him will be the sign of the promise which will be fulfilled in Jesus Christ (Gal. 3:14; Jn. 8:56). It is this blessing, not a simple paternal blessing, which is at stake between Jacob and Esau (Gen. 27).

3. The man or the people that God blesses responds by blessing God, that is to say, in *thanksgiving*. The believer blesses God whose creature and child he is. Blessing is given to God who is faithful to His creatures (Ps. 104:1,35; 145:10,21), who hearkens or will hearken to prayer (Ps. 28:6, 63:4ff.). Eliezer gives thanks to God for His faithfulness to Abraham (Gen. 24:27); David prostrates himself on his bed, blessing God who has assured His succession and thus confirmed His promise of a kingdom for ever (1 Kings 1:47–48; 2 Sam. 7:11–16); the people gathered for worship bless God who has chosen them and revealed Himself to them (Ps. 115:18); Zacharias and Simeon bless God who fulfils His promise of a Saviour (Lk. 1:68; 2:28–32).

N.B. "The cup of blessing which we bless" (1 Cor. 10:16): this word should not evoke a gesture of blessing that confers on the cup a more or less magic power; here to bless means to give thanks: the cup, the sign of the communion in Christ's blood, is the gift of God who saves the Church, and as such is an object of praise.

CHR. SENFT

BLOOD

1. (*a*) The blood is *the *life*. In the Bible blood is never simply one element in the constitution of the human body: it is the principal one. "It is the blood which gives life to the flesh"; this is the meaning of the fundamental definitions of Gen. 9:4; Lev. 17:11ff.; Deut. 12:23; the "soul" of the flesh resides in the blood; the soul of all flesh lies in its blood. In these contexts the word soul has no connection with Greek ontological dualism which sees in the soul an alien principle opposed to the body. In biblical anthropology the soul on the contrary is an integral part of the body: "the soul" (the blood) animates the flesh of animals. In such texts the Hebrew word soul would be well translated by our word vitality.

(*b*) The blood implies *limited life*. The vitality of the blood is not conceived as a potentiality or reserve of life which is at the disposal of the flesh. It can be perpetuated only in so far as it is transmitted by paternity and maternity (Jn. 1:13); only in this sense is blood a generator of life. As a characteristic of the human species (Acts 17:26) the blood emphasizes the precariousness of life. This also is the implication of the expression "flesh and blood": in dissociation from sin since Christ shared in it (Heb. 2:14) it contrasts the frailty and limitations of human life with the eternity of divine life (1 Cor. 15:44–50; cf. also Matt. 16:17; Eph. 6:12; Gal. 1:16). From this point of view we might draw a further contrast between biblical anthropology according to which *man has not life in himself (Gen. 2:7; 3:22) and the Babylonian creation story of Berossus where the animals created by the mixture of earth with the blood of the god Marduk naturally participate in divine life.

(*c*) The blood implies the fact that *life is limited by *death*. When blood is seen to have been shed it signifies the loss of life and that we are face to face with death, generally a violent death (Gen. 37:31f. and Matt. 23:30,35). That is why the issue of blood sullies in the case of the menstrual flux (Lev. 15:19ff.; Ezek. 22:10) and of murder (Num. 35:33).

Water changed into blood (Exod. 7:14ff.; Rev. 8:8ff.) makes life impossible. In the field of eschatology blood is always a sign of death and irremediable misfortune (the moon changed into blood, Joel 2:30ff.; feasts of blood at the day of judgment, Ezek. 39:17ff., etc.; cf. on another plane 1 Cor. 11:27 and 30).

Thus since life resides in the blood, God the Lord of life is the sole Disposer of the blood which is devoted exclusively to Him. There flow from this three prohibitions and an exclusive use of blood in sacrifices (cf. 2 and 3).

2. (a) It is absolutely forbidden to eat blood or bloody meats in the O.T. and to do so is punishable by death. This interdiction is not a hygienic rule; to claim to increase one's vitality by eating the blood of an animal is a violation of the right of God who is alone the sovereign Lord of life (Lev. 3:17). The prohibition applies also to the Gentiles (Gen. 9:4; Lev.17:12ff.). The law obliges one to bleed every animal intended for human consumption and to cover its blood with dust (Lev. 17:13).

In the N.T. this rule figures among those imposed on the Gentile Christians of Antioch, but its enforcement is prompted solely by the motive of charity towards the Jews (Acts 15:19–21) since Christ has become Lord of the living and dead (Rom. 14).

(b) The prohibition against shedding the blood of another man. O.T.: Murder is not an ethical transgression nor an injury done to the victim or society. It is a violation of the right of God (cf. Gen. 9:5–6). Thus God demands a reckoning for blood that has been shed and avenges it: the homicidal ox is stoned as a murderer but no damages can be claimed (Exod. 21:28); in the case of deliberate human homicide the blood that has been shed necessarily falls on the head

of the murderer (Exod. 21:12). God bids the avenger of blood to cover innocent blood by that of the murderer (Num. 35:31ff.); (he covers the cry of this blood, i.e. its soul: Gen. 4:10; Job 16:18; 27:8,9). The avenger thus fulfils a religious duty which later will be entrusted to the magistrate (Rom. 13:4). This is the greatest principle of Exod. 21:23. In the case of involuntary homicide, the murderer although in principle punishable by death may take refuge in a city of refuge where he will be eventually acquitted by the death of the high priest, who will thus cover his murder (Josh. 20:6).

N.T.: The interdiction remains and doubtless also the punishment (Matt. 5:21f.; Rev. 16:6). But as far as the Christian martyrs are concerned the interest is centred in Jesus; the cry of their blood is covered by His blood (Heb. 12:24; Rev. 6:9–11, to be compared with 7:14); and henceforth the terrible formula "His blood be on our head and on our children" must be understood in the light of the prayer: "Father, forgive them, for they know not what they do."

(c) It is forbidden to offer blood to demons. This is why blood can be shed only on the altar of God in the sanctuary (Lev. 17:3ff.; Ps. 16:4; 106:38).

3. (a) Blood as sealing the covenant between God and the people. O.T.: Exod. 24 describes the ritual by which the covenant of Sinai was sealed. The blood of the sacrificed beasts is shed partly on the altar and partly on the people. Vows having been made, this blood establishes between God and Israel the bond of a common life. In such circumstances to break the covenant would be equivalent to disowning the life which one shares with the other partner. The O.T. alludes to this bond of blood when it presents God as the father of the children of Israel (cf. Zech. 9:11; Exod. 4:24–26).

N.T.: The new covenant promised in Jer. 31:31–34 is sealed by the blood of Jesus shed on the cross. Here we see an eternal covenant (Heb. 8:6) which will not be violated and one whose efficacy is superior to the first (Heb. 8:6). By the blood of His own Son God effects a supernatural community of life between Himself and men, whom He thus makes sharers of His own nature (2 Pet. 1:4) and of His own plenitude of life: with a play on the word covenant, meaning in secular Greek testament, Heb. 9:15ff. emphasizes the validity of this transmission of the divine heritage to men, which is consequent on the death of the Son, the legitimate heir.

Connected with this notion of the divine covenant as a secondary idea is the *reconciliation and peace between God and men wrought by the bloodshedding of Christ (Rom. 5:9–10; Col. 1:20) and also the new brotherhood between Jews and Gentiles which flows from their participation in the same covenantal blood (Eph. 2:13).

Further the doctrine of redemption by blood is relevant here (Acts 20:28; Heb. 9:14; 1 Pet. 1:18–19). The "redeemer" in the O.T. denotes the nearest kinsman who has the right of buying back an object or a person; similarly Christ unties the bond which linked men in their corruption with their earthly fathers and becoming our elder brother introduces us into the family of His Father in heaven.

(b) *The use of blood in *sacrifices.* O.T.: In the framework of the covenant of Sinai, blood is the sacrificial element intended to repair the covenant which the sins of Israel have ceaselessly profaned (Lev. 16:15).

Sprinkled while still warm (i.e. living) wholly or partly on the horns of the altar it represents the offering to God of the life of the victim already identified with the offerer by the imposition of hands. Its function and use are defined in Lev. 17:11: "I have given you the blood to make atonement for your souls." Although of uncertain etymology, we shall connect the expression "make atonement" with the Hebrew root meaning "to cover". As in the case of murder (cf. 2, b) the sins of Israel are covered by the blood of the victim. They are thus purified (see *Clean). This is the meaning of the *feast of atonement (Lev. 16) where the sins of the whole year are covered in the sight of God by the blood of the goat. In the same way the leper, the

unclean house (Lev. 14) the altar or the high priest (Lev. 8) were cleansed. As regards the latter, the ritual of purification is clearly intended to prepare him for his consecration for the service of God.

N.T.: Heb. 9:22 reminds us of this essential function of blood which according to the Law purifies almost everything. We are not here faced by any intrinsic changeless principle but by a rule which has been decreed by God because of that blood which will truly effect the purification of sins; namely, the blood of Christ. While awaiting the time when it would be shed the Israelites had the duty of celebrating in all seriousness the bloody rites of the law. As far as men were concerned these rites had a pedagogic function, and from the point of view of God they effected expiation because they foreshadowed the bloodshedding of Christ (Heb. 9:8f.). The thought of the purifying effect of the blood of Christ (remission of sins) occurs frequently in the N.T. (Rom. 3:25; Eph. 1:7; Heb. 9:12; 1 Jn. 1:7; 2:2; Rev. 1:6). A unique work of salvation, accomplished once for all and for all mankind, this forgiveness of sins sanctifies believers for the service of God (Rev. 5:9; Heb. 13:12; 10:29) the priestly service of the Church (Rev. 1:5,6) and for entrance into the holy place in the very presence of God (Heb. 9:24; 10:19).

4. *Blood and the *Lord's Supper.* (a) *In the synoptic Gospels and* 1 *Cor.* 11. Believers are maintained in membership of the new covenant in the blood of the cross by their sharing in the cup of *blessing. This eucharistic blood conveys to them the necessary atoning efficacy of the covenant, and keeps and strengthens them in the forgiveness of their sins. Let us note that the formulas of Matthew and Mark are an imitation of the formula of Exod. 24:8.

(b) *In Cor.* 10:16. To share in the sacramental cup is to communicate in the blood of Christ shed on the altar of the *cross for the expiation of sins.

(c) *In Jn.* 6:53–57. An evident eucharistic allusion. The expression "drink blood", absolutely shocking to the mind of a Jew, should be set side by side with its use in 1 Chr. 11:19, where it suggests the idea of death: to be drunk, blood must first of all have been shed. But in this context the blood that has been shed no longer suggests simply that Christ loses His life but that He gives life. This blood is therefore life-giving to all who drink it; it is "drink indeed", i.e. a drink which satisfies eternally. In fact the blood of Christ, the vehicle of His eternal life as the Son of God, effects the generation of children of God, which the blood of men could never do (Jn. 1:13; cf. 1, *b*).

It is also possible that this double mention of the flesh and blood is an allusion to the sacrifice of the paschal lamb (Exod. 12:7,8) whose flesh nourishes and whose blood protects from death (cf. 1:29,36; Rev. 5:12).

(*d*) *In Jn.* 19:34 *and* 1 *Jn.* 5:6. The blood in itself serves to denote the Lord's Supper. All the sacramental realism of St. John is subordinated to the work of the cross. The Lord's Supper should not be neglected any more than baptism. In the parallelism of water, representing baptism, and blood (not wine) representing the Lord's Supper, is to be found the source of a later sacramental hierarchy.

To speak of the blood of Christ is not a formula interchangeable with others; in the N.T. it suggests: the humanity of Christ; the reality of His death, as real as the death of other men; the violence of His death; the fact that this death is above all a sacrificial act by means of which God founds His new covenant, forgives sins, sanctifies, brings about the redemption of the world and gives His life.

A. LELIÈVRE

BODY, *see* MAN

BODY OF CHRIST, *see* CHURCH

BREAD

O.T.

The etymology is uncertain. The term may perhaps come from a root which means to "enclose" or "grind". A kinship is noticeable with very different words, such as war, destruction, and, if the text of Zeph. 1:13 has not been corrupted, with the word flesh (a kinship which is confirmed by the language of the nomadic Arabs). But at all events bread was regarded as suffering (bruised by the teeth, cf. Num. 14:9, where, in order to make clear that a people will be destroyed, it is said that they will be bread for the Israelites) or being the result of suffering endured by grain; in the Ugaritic ritual the god Mot, a divine son, is cut, tormented, imprisoned, and crushed.

In the O.T. bread has the following significances:

1. It is regarded, above all, as the *symbol of the gifts* which God provides so that man may live, often in association with water (as we shall see, the perspective varies, but completes that in which *wine is taken as the symbol of these gifts) (Exod. 23:25; Num. 21:5; Isa. 33:16; Ezek. 4:17). To be without bread is therefore a terrible plight (Ps. 37:25; 2 Sam. 3:29, etc.). It is true that man shall not live by bread alone (Deut. 8:3), but without bread he cannot live at all. Likewise the first obligation of charity will be to share one's bread with him who is hungry (Isa. 58:7).

2. In the same class of ideas it reminds us that *this life is dependent on God*. Because it is essential to man, it reminds him that he is only a creature (Deut. 8:10–18).

3. Because of the *toil* which its provision involves, it will become the symbol of man's curse. God continues to grant man bread, but by the sweat of his brow (Gen. 3:19). That is why in the Messianic age he will have his bread without toil (which does not imply without work) and without money (like wine and milk) (Ps. 132:15). Isa. 55 does not mention bread, but the idea is the same: no more will either toil or money be necessary in order to eat. This is also why the manna acquired without toil and without money is called bread (coming) from heaven (Exod. 16:4; Neh. 9:15). This is the bread which Yahweh gives (Exod. 16:15).

2*

4. The *unleavened bread* of the Passover recalls the flight from Egypt; it is also called the bread of affliction (Deut. 16:3). It is meant to be a reminder that the Israelites were slaves, that they were delivered by Yahweh, and, as the whole ceremony of the Passover proclaims, that the Israelites are strangers and pilgrims on this earth (Ps. 39:13; 1 Chr. 29:15). Like wine, leavened bread is a sign of establishment. But it should not be forgotten that sometimes leaven is regarded as corrupting.

5. *To share one's bread* is not only to perform a charitable act, but also to make peace with the person to whom it is offered (Gen. 14:18; Judg. 8:5–6 and 15). At the time of Aaron's consecration bread was placed in his hands (Exod. 29:23–24), without any explanation of this action being given.

6. Bread is a very important *sacrificial element*: the table of shewbread is a sacrificial table (Ezek. 41:22). It is associated with many *sacrifices. Is this done by substitution, that is to say, the bread replacing the victims as the wine replaced their blood? This would be supported by the kinship between bread and flesh.

Is this an agrarian rite? This would be supported by the Mesopotamian myths in which bread (and also grain) is a materialized divinity on which the gods feast.

Is this in order to nourish the divinity who, like men, has need of bread? Chapter 21 of Leviticus calls sacrifices the bread of God. This implies that God eats, but not that He eats bread (vv. 6, 8, 22). Moreover, if, in this chapter, God eats, it is when the sacrifice is consumed (v. 6) or by the "vicarious consumption" of the priests (v. 22). Is this again because bread is closely associated with life and because the sustenance which it provides is the result of the dying of the grain? This idea of life which arises from a necessary death (which Jesus made use of in another connection: He speaks of the death of the grain *in the ground* in order that it may bring forth fruit,

Jn. 12:24) is common to the peoples of the Orient. Accordingly bread would be sacrificed because of this special life which it contains, life which it would communicate temporarily by consumption, and much more fully by sacrifice.

Beyond doubt all these notions come into play, and it is very difficult to say which of them is primitive and which preponderates.

N.T.

Bread is one of the first things which man should ask from God (cf. Matt. 6:11). And is it not significant that in two parables on prayer (Lk. 11:11 and Lk. 11:5–10) Jesus takes bread as a symbol of asking? We are tempted not only to see in bread a symbol, but to accord it a more profound significance. The main passage, however, is that of John 6 where Jesus claims to be the bread of God. By this He means:

(*a*) that He is the food of all men: it is He, and He alone, who gives life to men;

(*b*) that the manna (of which it is not said in the O.T. that it was the bread *of* heaven, but the bread [coming] *from* heaven—only Ps.78:24 calls it the grain of heaven) was only temporary, giving life temporarily, and prefigured the true bread which Jesus Christ now gives;

(*c*) that His coming and His sacrifice are the actual gift of the true bread to the world; that is to say, of true life;

(*d*) that whoever wishes to live must eat this bread. By this bread Christ transmits the life which He has Himself received from His Father (v. 57). How is this bread to be eaten to-day? By faith (vv. 29, 35, 40) and by the sacrament of the *Lord's Supper (vv. 53–56).

It is thus above all as a sign of life that Jesus took bread as a sacramental element, but we must also remember that it is a necessity for us. Properly understood, it is also taken as a "sign" of suffering flesh, of compassion: to share one's bread is, as we have said, a sign of reconciliation and a sign that one accepts as table-companions those to whom this sign is accorded.

A. MAILLOT

BROTHER, *see* FAMILY, NEIGHBOUR

BUILD

1. In the O.T. the verb to build (in Greek derived from *oikos*, a house=build a house) appears first in the literal sense, e.g., to build an altar, etc. (Exod. 20:25; cf. 1 Chr. 21:18; 1 Kings 16:24; Amos 9:14, etc.). Then the sense expands and is applied to Israel as a building of Yahweh's making: "I will establish your descendants for ever, and build your throne for all generations" (Ps. 89:4). In the same psalm God's favour is an eternal building (v. 2 renders literally: "Thy mercy shall be built up for ever"). In Jer. 12:16 Yahweh proposes to build up not only His own people but also the Gentile *nations: "they shall be built up in the midst of my people." The conception here is of a real incorporation of the heathen into the religious community of Israel, an incorporation which presupposes their being won to the faith of Israel's God: ". . . if they will diligently learn . . . to swear by my name, 'As the LORD lives' . . . then they shall be built up in the midst of my people." Yahweh will *build* the walls of Jerusalem (Jer. 31:4,12): these expressions must be taken in the most realistic sense; Jeremiah is promising to those carried away to Babylon a return to Palestine and the reconstruction of Jerusalem and the national community. By using this verb to build to describe the action of Yahweh in the world, the O.T. stresses four aspects of this action in particular:

(*a*) It is action conceived as action *in history*. God makes a real entry into history to build up a people (a royal house, families, a town, etc.) which, for all that, is yet to be exposed continually to all the ups and downs which mark the history of peoples: victories and disasters, internal revolutions, fidelity and infidelity to the faith of its fathers, popular pride and despair, etc. It cannot be too carefully noted that the God of Israel does not "build" an *élite* of a number of religious souls, but a *people in its entirety, which is called as a people to bear witness to the nations. Moreover, Yahweh does

not speak to humanity as a whole; He builds up in the midst of it a social and religious "group", which is to speak to it from within of the God of the whole earth.

(*b*) The social building that is Israel, therefore, when seen as such, affords throughout its history an illustration of the *judgment and *grace of God. Set in contrast to the verb to build we often find its opposite, to destroy; but if Yahweh frequently "destroys" His people, it is only to rebuild them closer to the ideal. "I will set my eyes upon them for good, and I will bring them back to this land. I will build them up and not tear them down; I will plant them and not uproot them" (Jer. 24:6). These promises and hopes of reconstruction originally had reference to the return from Exile, but they were soon taken in the sense of an eschatological rebuilding that would be perfect and final.

(*c*) In the O.T. the two metaphors of the building constructed by Yahweh and the field cultivated by Him are frequently found side by side; and they are complementary. The metaphor of planting completes that of building by adding to it the idea of continuity: in building terms, it would mean that the builder is always on the scaffolding, working on a building continually under construction. In turn, the building imagery completes that of the planting by adding to it the idea of community: it is not sufficient to think of Yahweh growing individual plants; again in building terms, His work is more like a house, of which the different sections contribute to His glory because they form a single whole (Jer. 12:14; 31:27; 1:9ff.; 18:7–10).

(*d*) Finally, the O.T. often combines the ideas of building and *creation. In Gen. 2:22 Yahweh "builds" the woman (in the sense of creating; cf. also Amos 9:6). The building of the people of God is always a creation in the sense that it is brought about only by the authority and free election of Yahweh.

2. It is obvious that in this connection the N.T. depends on the O.T. (Matt. 21:33 and parallels recall Isa. 5:1ff.; Ps. 118:22

appears in Matt. 21:42; Mk. 12:10; Lk. 20:17; Acts 4:11; 1 Pet. 2:7; cf. also Rom. 9.33 recalling Isa. 8:14). When the N.T. quotes the O.T. on this subject of building, it is always with a polemical note. This is not, however, in any way for the purpose of denying that the old Israel was really God's building, but simply to assert that this building came to completion and found its true meaning in the person of Jesus Christ and the new people of God (Mk. 12:10f.). The *stone* rejected by the heads of the nation, Jesus Christ, is probably not to be understood as the corner-stone, which bears the weight of the building, but that at the apex, which crowns the whole and gives it its meaning: cf. 1 Pet. 2:4,7 where the stone is no longer the Christ of the parousia (Mk. 12:10f.), nor the Christ dead and resurrected (Acts 4:11), but the glorious and spiritual Christ, a "living stone" of the building formed of other living stones— for this the members of the Church also are.

Further, we find in the Gospels numerous echoes of thought on the subject of the *Jerusalem *Temple, its building and, especially, its approaching destruction (Mk. 13:1; 14:58; 15:29; Matt. 26:61; 27:40; Jn. 2:19; Acts 6:14). In all these passages the Jerusalem Temple is the Israelite building *par excellence*. Even though it is true that in the time of Jesus the local synagogues were playing a large part in the religious life of the people, the Temple continued to be the supreme witness to the tradition and to the presence of Yahweh, and the guarantee of both (Ps. 46; 48; 76; 84; 122; 125; 132; 133; cf. Mic. 3:12; Jer. 7:14,26ff.). To prophesy the destruction of the Temple was to predict the utter ruin of the people of God. In Jn. 2:19 (cf. Mk. 14:58; 15:29; Matt. 26:61; 27:40) a significant relation is established between the destruction of the Temple and the resurrection of Jesus, the new Temple, i.e., the new meeting-place of the faithful.

The saying of Jesus to Peter: "You are Peter, and on this rock (Greek *petra*) I will build my church . . ." (Matt. 16:18) opens up new lines of thought.

(*a*) It is Jesus, and no longer God, who builds up the chosen people; in this lies His work as Messiah, already begun in His lifetime by the call of the apostles.

(*b*) Just as, in Rabbinic thought, God created the world on the rock of Abraham (or the foundation of Israel), so Peter takes the place of the supreme patriarch of the people of God. It is to be noted that, in several places, the building up of the people of God is based on a particular individual, a believer chosen for this purpose; but in a building up of this kind the historic rôle of Peter would be unique and never to be repeated.

(*c*) Peter is to be the foundation of the building; but the builder will always be Christ: "I will build", not "thou shalt build" or "direct".

(*d*) That which is to be built is the *Church. This Greek word appears only here and in Matt. 18:17 in the Gospels. Whatever the Aramaic term that Jesus used, it would, without doubt, have referred to the Messianic community of the last times, charged with proclaiming the Kingdom and with even now giving to the world the signs that herald it.

Turning now to the Epistles, there is evidence, first of all, of very careful reflection on the basis and establishment of the building that is the Church (1 Cor. 3:9–15). In this chapter, the apostle begins by declaring (vv. 1–8) that in the Church all ministries are equal before God, to whom alone belongs the power and the glory of causing the Church to "grow". Nevertheless, he goes on (vv. 9–15) to distinguish his own ministry (which was, at Corinth, to lay the foundation of the Church by preaching Christ) very sharply from the ministry of his successors (Apollos, etc.), who are building the Church on this foundation, laid by him alone (v. 10). The trend of the argument is to free the apostle from further responsibility: he has done his work—let his successors take care how they "build" on that basis! (cf. the same term in other contexts: Rom. 15:20; Eph. 2:20; 1 Tim. 6:19; 2 Tim. 2:19). Theologically, the most remarkable feature here is that the foundation of the Church is neither a man, nor an institution, nor any grouping of men, but *Jesus Christ, "laid" at Corinth by the apostolic *preaching.

The other Pauline texts on the apostolic "building" may be arranged in two classes. In the first (2 Cor. 10:8; 13:10; 12:19) the apostle defines his ministry as one of building up: in the second (1 Cor. 3:5–17; Rom. 15:20; Gal. 2:18; Eph. 2:19–22; 4:11–16), he is rather describing the conditions in which this ministry can be accomplished. In the Epistle to the Ephesians, this process of building up is considered from the angle of the *unity of the Church: the unity of former Gentiles and former Jews in the single "building" of the Church (Eph. 2:19–22); the unity of the whole Church, "growing" under the authority of a common "head", Christ (Eph. 4:11–16). Here, as often in the O.T., the two images of building and growth are mingled and complementary, so that, although the combined image is inconsistent from the point of view of logic, yet in the matter of theological insight its consistency is perfect. In it Jesus Christ appears at one and the same time as the foundation of the Church (through the apostles and prophets), its authority or "head" that causes its growth, i.e. builds it up, and also the end of this growth, towards which the whole life of the Church is moving.

It is to be noted that the faithful also have the task of building up the Church; and among the faithful not only the apostle, as we have already seen, but also the prophet (1 Cor. 14:3), he who speaks with tongues (v. 4), the interpreter of tongues (v. 5) and all the faithful, in so far as they are charismatically endowed (v. 12)—in short, "all things" serve to edify (i.e., all the gifts of the Spirit, v. 27). In other passages it is *love that edifies (1 Cor. 8:1); or we are warned that "not all things" are for edification (1 Cor. 10:23, where "all things" refers not this time to gifts of the Spirit, but to every kind of moral conduct); or again, peaceable behaviour "builds up" (Rom. 14:19), or each of us as an individual (Rom. 15:2; 1 Thess. 5:11; 1 Pet. 2:5;

Jude 20), or teaching that is only indirectly apostolic (Col. 2:6f.). Even if it is always Christ, then, who builds His Church, this only involves the members of that Church the more in the undertaking. Moreover, the object that is builded is not always the Church as such. The N.T. knows nothing of a Church apart from the extremely concrete reality of the men and women who constitute it, and who have themselves to be built up, "constructed" into the complete building. On the other hand, the N.T. never gives the word "edification" the sense of a purely interior and individual religious feeling, such as Pietism understood by it. As for the ultimate purpose of the building process, the Epistles conceive it sometimes as the judgment to come, in which the erected building will be tested (1 Cor. 3:13f.), sometimes as God's dwelling in the Church (Eph. 2:22; 4:12–16), sometimes as the proclamation of the Gospel to the world (1 Pet. 2:4–10). These differing passages have this in common, namely that they all emphasize that the building up of the Church is not an end in itself but is for the service of a divine presence and a universal mission which transcend it.

Finally, it should be observed that the building up of the Church is constantly endangered—endangered from without, certainly, but most of all from within. Hence arise the numerous exhortations in the Epistles, which seek to provide for the building up of a community and to prevent its being imperilled, whether by individualism in religion (1 Cor. 14), in morals (1 Cor. 8:1,10; 10:23; Rom. 14:19; 15:2; 1 Thess. 5:11; Col. 2:6), or last of all in doctrine (Jude 20; 1 Pet. 2:4f.; Eph. 4:11–16; Col. 2:6). Analysis of these three groups of passages shows with what precision of thought and what authority in the cure of souls the apostles of Christ provided for the building up of the first Christian communities.

P. BONNARD

BURNT OFFERING, *see* SACRIFICES O.T.

CALL

The profane usage of this verb and its derivatives is found in the Bible, in the sense of summoning, inviting or naming. But the term belongs to the special language of the Bible and receives a radically new significance when God is its subject; then the verb, its participle *called*, and the condition of the one called, which is to have a *vocation*, are a unique expression of Revelation.

The Greek LXX version uses a single word to express the power of that divine act which is expressed in Hebrew by three different verbs. When God calls He makes His voice heard, of course, but besides He calls into being, He creates the universe by naming its constituent parts (Gen. 1); He lays hold for His own sake in order to accomplish His designs. In a general sense, the call is God's way of encountering man.

1. *The encounter of God and man.* God is in fact by definition "he who calls" (Rom. 9:12; Gal. 5:8). He does it "according to his own purpose" (2 Tim. 1:9); by this He took the initiative from the start, refusing to abandon His fallen creature: "The Lord God called Adam, and said to him: Adam, where art thou?" Thus God opened the dialogue which He unceasingly pursues with Adam. It is on the earth that the voice of God echoes (Ps. 19). In this summons God reveals Himself, gives Himself, humbles Himself: He enters into relationship with humanity, the history of individuals and of nations; while guarding His secret and sovereign liberty of action, He penetrates even into this history. All that is contained in the O.T. as a promise of which the N.T. shows the fulfilment in Jesus Christ: Christ, the "Word of God" (Rev. 19:13), incarnates the call of God to men.

Before analysing the diverse forms which the call of God can take, it is necessary to notice its essential character: it is a function of the redemptive work of God, it proceeds from God's mercy, and it aims at the salvation of men. The history of these men is none other than that of the *covenant of God and it shows "the grace which he gave us in Christ Jesus ages ago" (2 Tim. 1:9).

Under the old as under the new covenant God called men whose witness and rôle have been unique in that history. Yahweh called Moses (Exod. 3:4; 19:20; 24:16), Samuel who was already pledged to the service of the Temple (1 Sam. 3:4), Isaiah (49:1); but it goes without saying that the forms and the effects of these calls do not change: they are typical, because the parties are always God and man. Matthew interprets a word of Hosea (11:1) as a call of God to His Son, fulfilling the prophecy of the return from Egypt; but an interesting though later variant says: "I have called him my Son." Jesus calls His disciples, and they leave all to follow Him (Matt. 4:21). Paul speaks of himself as "called to be an apostle" (Rom. 1:1; 1 Cor. 1:1); in saying this he defines his particular function and recalls at the same time the coincidence of this with the birth of his faith in Christ; he will be enabled to give validity to this title which he has received and which he bears like his own new name Paul (1 Cor. 9:1; 15:9).

We are led to remark here that God often names those whom He calls. The work in which He enlists them is so novel that the one who is called must carry the sign of that novelty, and the upheaval produced in his existence or by means of it is equivalent to a (re)creation by God. The verb "to call", so far as its most compulsive implication is concerned, can then be a synonym for "to nominate". The *name is significant at the same time of the destiny of the one who bears it and in the prophetic, even eschatological, sense which it can have. Thus, amongst other instances, Isaac (Gen. 17:19), the laughter of God, announces the resurrection and the conversion of the Gentiles; at the threshold of the Gospel, John, given this name by God, interrupts the tradition of the family of Zacharias (Lk. 1:13,59–63). Moreover, the name of the Messiah could only come from God: "You shall call his name Jesus. He will be great, and will be called the Son of the Most High" (Lk.

1:31–32). And the name which Jesus gave to Simon, when He met him for the first time, prefigures the commission of the apostle in the primitive Church:

"So you are Simon the son of John? You shall be called Cephas (which means *Peter)" (Jn. 1:42).

However personal it shows the encounter of God with man to be, this call goes beyond the destiny of the man it comes to: the call addressed to Abraham established the people which God chose from among the nations; the new name given to Jacob is generic and will serve for their name. We therefore see why the prophets, and especially second Isaiah, re-echo the call of God to His people, as laden with meaning, and full of hope and reproach, as that which God might address to an individual: "I, Yahweh, have called you to make righteousness triumph" (Isa. 42:6); "why did no one answer when I called?" (Isa. 50:2). It is still more urgent when God lays stress on the name which He has given him: "Hearken to me, O Jacob, and Israel, whom I called . . ." (Isa. 48:12, cf. also 43:1; 45:3); "But you, Israel, my servant, Jacob, whom I have chosen . . . and called from the furthest regions, saying to you: You are my servant" (Isa. 41: 8–9). Ever afresh God comes to encounter His people to save them and take them into His service. In effect, this call is a saving invitation for the one who is its object, and it must show its effects far and wide in space and time. The N.T. discloses to us the secret of it, the means and the end.

2. *A saving invitation.* (*a*) *The secret of the call.* It springs from the mysterious and sovereign grace of God manifested in Jesus Christ, in the Gospel. He who, during His earthly ministry, called men with an authority He could only hold from His Father, continues to call men by His Holy Spirit. Reminding the Romans of their pagan origin, Paul writes to them: ". . . you who have been called by Jesus Christ . . ." (Rom. 1:6). And in the triumphal act of thanksgiving which opens the Epistle to the Ephesians, one well-attested variant of 1:11

reads: "It is in him (Christ) that you have been called." That God, in Christ, is its sole author, allows the apostle to take up as well as to develop the striking expression of Isaiah (49:1; cf. also Jer. 1:5): "When he who had set me apart before I was born, and had called me through his grace, was pleased to reveal his Son to me . . ." (Gal. 1:15). The call precedes the response and decision of man, because it depends upon the sole freedom of God, so that Paul can further expound this mystery by saying: "And those whom he predestined he also called; and those whom he called he also justified" (Rom. 8:30). It is this which leads Paul to affirm that his ability and his ministry come from God alone: ". . . to me who am not worthy to be called an apostle. . . . But by the grace of God I am what I am" (1 Cor. 15:9–10).

This calling of the grace of God is ordinarily translated by vocation. But in the N.T. this word does not have the confused meaning currently attributed to it; it expresses the initial overture of God in *revelation: the sovereignty of Him who calls is never confused with the blossoming forth of the gifts, tastes or talents of man. God alone (or Jesus Christ) is the subject of the verb, and the substantive participle ("called") like the substantive ("vocation") always refer back to Him. Since He who calls is holy (1 Pet. 1:15), this vocation is qualified as "holy" (2 Tim. 1:9); it is "heavenly" (Heb. 3:1); it comes "from above" (Phil. 3:14); so many attributes which refer to one subject! (One particularly difficult text, 1 Cor. 7:17–24, is discussed below, 3*c*.) The aim of the calling is, besides, perfectly clear and lets no doubt exist about its significance.

(*b*) *The aim.* When God calls man it is to Himself and to His Son that He calls. He invites them to participate in all the blessings of salvation, and He incorporates them in His redemptive work so that they may benefit by it and be witnesses of it. The multiple expressions that are found in the N.T. are so many diverse testimonies to the unique work of "him who called you in the grace of Jesus Christ" (Gal. 1:6). That work, whose glorious plenitude will be manifested at the end, is already unfolding in the present time its beneficent effects.

In the Gospels, Jesus calls men into the coming *Kingdom, of which He is secretly the king. The most characteristic text is the parable of the wedding feast (Matt. 22:1–14 and parallels): it announces the refusal of Israel to answer to its vocation (vv. 3–4,8) and the entrance of Gentiles into the glorious promise (vv. 9–10). This call into the Kingdom is found only in one passage in the Epistles (1 Thess. 2:12) and Revelation: "Blessed are those who are invited to the marriage supper of the Lamb" (19:9). Pauline and deutero-Pauline language habitually uses other terms to express the glorious fulfilment of the divine work into which men are invited to enter; it is eternal *life: "Take hold of the eternal life to which you were called" (1 Tim. 6:12); *glory: "To this he called you through our gospel, so that you may obtain the glory of our Lord Jesus Christ" (2 Thess. 2:14; cf. also 1 Pet. 5:10; 2 Pet. 1:3). The N.T. also takes up the O.T. figure of *inheritance: "those who are called receive the eternal inheritance promised to them" (Heb. 9:15; cf. also variants of Eph. 1:11 and Col. 1:12). And Paul makes use of the comparison familiar to him of the race in the stadium ". . . to obtain the prize of the upward call of God in Christ Jesus" (Phil. 3:14).

But although God manifests His work "so that you may know what is the hope which his call brings to birth in you" (Eph. 1:18; cf. also 4:4), the present aspect of the work has no less importance. Its present virtue conditions its ultimate fulfilment. God calls into the fellowship of His Son Jesus Christ (1 Cor. 1:9), and its effects apply to the diverse circumstances of the life of the Church and of Christians. To the Colossians, seduced by heresies which threaten the Church, Paul teaches that it is to the peace of Christ that they have been called (Col. 3:15); he says the same to divided couples (1 Cor. 7:15); to the Galatians, tempted to put themselves under the yoke of Jewish prescriptions, Paul speaks vigorously: "You were called to

*freedom, brethren" (Gal. 5:13); and the Church of Thessalonica ought to understand better the moral bearing of the divine call: "God has not called us for uncleanness, but in *holiness" (1 Thess. 4:7). But to whom is this imperious call addressed, with the promises which it contains and the demands it involves?

(c) *Those who are called.* Who can they be, if not all men (Rom. 11:32)? God's redemptive work is on a world-wide scale. This revelation turned upside down the thinking of the Jew Saul of Tarsus, only to become the main perspective within which the doctrine of salvation is inscribed. "(I speak) even of us whom he has called, not from the Jews only but also from the Gentiles. As indeed he says in Hosea: Those who were not my people I will call 'my people', and her who was not beloved I will call 'my beloved'. And in the very place where it was said to them, 'You are not my people', they will be called 'sons of the living God' " (Rom. 9:24–26). In effect: "to all those who are called, both Jews and Greeks, Christ is the power of God and the wisdom of God" (1 Cor. 1:24).

But God remains master of His plan of salvation, and that is why the verbs to choose and to *elect often accompany the verb to call and its derivatives. They lay the stress on the freedom of the call of God, "who has mercy on whom he will" (Rom. 9:18; cf. also 1 Cor. 1:26–27; Rev. 17:14). In this fact lies all the believer's assurance. K.-L. Schmidt (*Theol. Wörterbuch zum N.T.*, III, 488) throws light on the declaration of Matt. 22:14: "For many are called, but few chosen", by showing that these terms are synonyms and are comprehensible in a dialectical sense. This text evokes the central paradox of the Gospel: salvation is a gift, and nevertheless it must be grasped; the context (vv. 11–13) would suffice to make it clear; the man who has neglected to go to the dressing-room to put on the wedding garment prepared for that purpose for each guest by the master of the house is cast into the outer darkness. Thus the calling of the believer must always be related to the merciful and just purpose of

God (Rom. 11:20), and Christians must apply themselves to making their calling and election sure (2 Pet. 1:10).

Furthermore, this call of God is a word so efficacious that it even defines the condition of the Christian. All Christians have received a calling: the called man is the believer of the new covenant (1 Cor. 1:24; Rom. 8:28; Jude 1; Rev. 17:14). The expression "called (to be) saints" (Rom. 1:7; 1 Cor. 1:2) denotes both the goal of the calling and the name of those who have received it. This calling gives them also the new name of "children (or sons) of God" (Matt. 5:9; 1 Jn. 3:1), of "brethren" (Heb. 2:11). Those to whom the call comes are particularly such as are sick, the sinners (Matt. 9:12-13 and parallels), those who are in the highways and along the hedges: the poor, the maimed, the blind and the lame (Lk. 14:22ff.). Indeed, the apostle remarks that amongst those who were called at Corinth "not many were wise according to worldly standards, not many were powerful, not many were of noble birth" (1 Cor. 1:26).

It remains to underline a characteristic aspect of the call of God: it is *communal* as well as personal. This is particularly clear in the Epistles: the Christian receives his call by means of the *Church, for the Church, and in the Church for the world. The call to salvation is only made real by the integration of the one called into the posterity of Abraham (Rom. 9:7), into the body of Christ (Col. 3:15); he participates in the building up of that body and in its ministry (Eph. 4:11-12); in this respect Paul's vocation is typical (Gal. 1:15; Rom. 1:5). That leads us to examine how the response of one who is called is expressed.

3. *The response of the believer.* (*a*) *Faith.* The call of God can be heard only in *faith, and at the same time it gives birth to the obedience of faith. "It is by faith that Abraham obeyed the call of God and set out for the country which he was to receive as an inheritance" (Heb. 11:8). In the Gospel, the preaching of Christ is a call to repentance, which shows clearly the response of

those who believe in Him (Lk. 5:32). Paul, explaining his call to the Galatians, adds: I obeyed immediately "without consulting flesh and blood" (Gal. 1:16).

(*b*) *Ministries.* The man who responds to the call finds himself thereby engaged in the work of God, which is that of the body of Christ on earth. It is with a view to His redemptive work that God calls. No one can arrogate to himself any title or assume for himself any function: "but he is called by God, just as Aaron was" (Heb. 5:4). But every call is always a call to service, either in the mutual relations between Christians (Gal. 5:13), or in the *ministry of the Church under the forms which it has instituted (1 Pet. 4:10-11).

(*c*) *The condition of the Christian in the world.* In a still more general manner, a call determines the condition of a Christian in the world, which is that of total dependence on God in Jesus Christ: thereby he belongs to a people who are "strangers and pilgrims on the earth" (Heb. 11:13). But at the same time this people shows its vocation in the personal life of its members, as well as in their social life (1 Pet. 2:9-10).

This is so true that a good number of exegetes and the majority of our versions interpret the calling of which Paul speaks in 1 Cor. 7:17-24 in the sense of condition, state. That interpretation implies that the social or professional situation becomes the vocation of the Christian, that he should regard it as such since it is this that "the Lord has assigned to him". In this passage (says J. Héring) Paul "would extend the discussion by exposing the relativity of human situations in relation to the coming of the Kingdom. The apostle's point of view could be summarized in a word: make the least possible change in human conditions of existence, so long as they do not oppose the realization of the Christian call. . . . Even human slavery is of so little importance in relation to the liberation from another slavery from which Christ has freed us, that it is best to make no change." But exposition in detail contradicts this; starting from the parallelism of the phrases in verse 17, Héring concludes that "it is therefore a matter of accepting the social situation (celibacy or marriage, freedom or slavery) in which we may find ourselves at our conversion, as a way of realizing our individual Christian call. . . . As a result, 'call' does not denote here the 'vocation' which calls us to be a Christian, but the one which we must make real by accepting our situation." He remarks afterwards that "the use of this term in our text has flourished extensively in Christian ethics and notably in Protestant ethics, which readily uses 'vocation' for the rôle devolving upon Christians" (Héring, *Commentary on the New Testament*).

This exegesis is seductive, but K.-L. Schmidt, following H. Cremer, has treated it justly (*op. cit.*, III, 492). He shows that it has the unanimous testimony of the N.T. against it, for which calling always denotes the call of God to salvation. We read that passage in the ethical perspective of the Reformers rather than in that of early Christianity.

In fact, the Reformers revalued the situation and the profession of the Christian in the world. For Luther, faith raised the humble toil of the peasant in his field or the housewife in her home to the level of a sacred service. Calvin, whose doctrine is inspired by the thought of God's sovereignty over everything and His glory which the Christian must seek in all his acts, says that "we have also to observe diligently that God commands each of us to give heed to our calling in all the actions of our life . . . And in order that none should lightly overstep his limits He called such manners of life vocations." After this "He" one must at all events put a question mark! Calvin extends the sense and the strictly biblical usage of this term. But the ethics of the Reformers drew the practical consequences of the doctrine of the Gospel by showing that God's call must be expressed in the obedience of the believer and that it unifies all his acts.

The internal testimony of the N.T. thus invites us rather to understand the thought of the apostle in the following way: he who has received a call has been redeemed

by a ransom (v. 23); he therefore remains attached to the calling of God (v. 20), and he lives in a way which conforms to this (v. 17). Grace and the promise of salvation are of so much more importance than the external and temporary situation of the believer!

It goes without saying that in faith the Christian is able to regard that situation as one that "the Lord has assigned to him". It is always in some precise circumstances, in such a place and at such a moment that the Christian has to obey. Paul can pray to God that He will make the Thessalonians worthy of the call which God Himself has addressed to them (2 Thess. 1:11). As a "prisoner for the Lord" he writes in the same way to the Ephesians (4:1). That means that they must comport themselves in a way which conforms to the requirements of the Gospel (Phil. 1:27), to the will of the Lord (Col. 1:10), behaving in a manner "worthy of God, who calls you into his own kingdom and glory" (1 Thess. 2:12).

In the end, God may be served in no matter what situation, and most particularly by the *sufferings of Christians and even their *death in order to demonstrate the power of the Gospel. It is thus that Paul considers himself a "prisoner for Christ" (Phil. 1:13; 2:17); and Christians must know like the recipients of 1 Peter (2:19,21) that "one is approved if he endures pain while suffering unjustly . . . for to this you have been called."

ED. DISERENS

CANAAN, *see* NAMES (GEOGRAPHICAL)

CAPTIVITY, *see* FREEDOM

CHIEF, *see* AUTHORITIES, MINISTRY O.T.

CHILDREN, *see* FAMILY, MARRIAGE

CHRIST, *see* ANOINTING, JESUS

CHURCH

1. *The word Church and its synonyms.* The Church is designated in Scripture sometimes by the Greek term *ecclesia* (hence

French *église*), sometimes by figures of speech. *Ecclesia* was current in the Hellenistic world for the regular assemblages of a particular social group or even of the whole population (cf. Acts 19:39f.). But *ecclesia* was never used by the Greeks in a religious context. For religious meetings they employed other terms, not one of which is retained in the N.T. to signify the Church. The word Church has therefore its origins elsewhere, namely in Jewish tradition. There the word has the same general sense of being called together as in Greek usage, but it acquires a religious connotation in view of the fact that the person who convokes is God. In the O.T. the "Convocation (Church) of God" is the chosen people, constituted by the calling of God by whom they are summoned. Similarly in the N.T. the Church is the assembly of believers, constituted by the calling of God in Jesus Christ; she is the Church of God or the Church of Christ. The word *ecclesia* has always a positive implication: it refers to an assemblage of those who obey God rather than a negative conception of those called out of the world.

For the mission of the Church is not that of withdrawing from the world but of being present within the world to convey to it the summons of God. The Church is by definition the opposite of a sect of the Pharisaic kind.

In the N.T. then the Church must be understood first and foremost in the light of the redemptive work accomplished by God in Christ; she is the concrete expression of what this work has done to those who believe: i.e., of their unity in a single organism directed to God and Christ. This explains the following fact: the term *ecclesia* is relatively rare in the N.T.: it occurs only in one Gospel out of four, and is not found in eight of the Epistles. But the reality of the Church is expressed by the images which illustrate the contents of the term *ecclesia* as just defined. Hence a study of the Church must inquire not only into the simple term *ecclesia* but also into such expressions as the *people of God, the *building of God, the ploughed field, or

the *vine of which Christ is the trunk, the flock of which God or Christ is the *shepherd, the bride of Christ, the body of Christ. We shall meet these various titles again as we study the fact and the theology of the Church in the witness of Scripture.

2. *The fact of the Church.* (*a*) *O.T.* In the O.T. the expressions "the Church of God", "the Church of Israel", denote the chosen people inasmuch as they are party to God's covenant and the human instrument of the history of salvation. God has made a *covenant with Israel at Sinai. This people whom God chose from amongst all the peoples of the earth in order to make His name known (Exod. 19) is "all the assembly (church) of Israel, and the women, and the little ones, and the sojourners who lived among them" (Josh. 8:35). Thus in its origin the civil and religious communities coincide: they are constituted by the same covenant and governed by the same law. But over the centuries this unity was shattered by the disobedience of a great number to the law and the covenant of God. The prophets warned their countrymen who were seduced by idolatry and pagan customs of the punishments which awaited them. Isaiah specifies that the truly faithful alone remain within the sphere of the promises of God; it is this "*remnant" of the people who will be called "holy", that is, recognized as His people by God, Himself "the Holy One of Israel" (Isa. 10:20; cf. 4:3). Jeremiah for his part announces the coming of the days when God will make a "new covenant" with His people (Jer. 31:31–34).

The two ideas of the remnant and the new covenant are asserted in the centuries which followed the Exile, and they nourished the Messianic hope. The redeemer to come at the end of the age was to fulfil his mission by grouping round him the community of the true faithful, distinct from the nation. Three facts are relevant here. First, according to the vision of Dan. 7:13–27, the Son of Man represents "the people of the saints of the Most High", with whom he appears actually to be identified. From the second century B.C. there appear within Judaism such societies as the "Community of the New Covenant", which was born in Palestine and later exiled to Damascus. The documents discovered in the neighbourhood of the Dead Sea are evidence of the importance of such communities. Finally on the very threshold of the Gospel stands the preaching of the Baptist, who summons the sons of Abraham to repentance, and, by offering his *baptism even to those who were already marked with the seal of circumcision, proclaims that neither membership of the chosen people nor the sign of the first covenant would suffice for the coming Messiah to see in every Israelite the good wheat which he will gather into his barns.

The two ideas of remnant and new covenant disclose their prophetic origin inasmuch as they are definitely not sectarian. They do not imply that salvation is reserved for a small number of the elect. They affirm on the contrary that the people of God is created anew, starting with the remnant, by means of the new covenant sealed by the expected redeemer. Thus by means both of the Saviour and the community which He has first to gather round Himself, Salvation spreads to a great number. Both the Jewish idea of the remnant and the Church in Christian usage always possess an inclusive rather than an exclusive meaning.

(b) *Jesus*. The two ideas of the community and the new covenant are predominant in the teaching of Jesus. He comes forward as the Son of Man in search of the people of God whom He would gather round His own person and reconstitute in view of the approaching Kingdom of God. In fact, Jesus does not confine His activity to teaching the multitude; He gathers round Him a more restricted circle of disciples and of those the Twelve are the core who form His "family" (Mk. 3:33f.; cf. Eph. 3:15). It is to this "little flock" (Lk. 12:32; cf. Matt. 26:31; Jn. 10:1–18) that the Father will give the *Kingdom. To designate His own and to indicate their relation with Him and with God, Jesus makes use of another image which, like that of the flock, comes

from the O.T., namely that of the building of the Temple. The new *Temple which Jesus will build (Mk. 13:2; 14:58) is nothing but the community of those who believe in Him who is the agent by whom God manifested His presence among men. It is by His death that Jesus achieves His "work": this He states clearly by saying that He must die and rise again and afterwards return in glory. The institution of the Lord's Supper fully explains this declaration; His blood poured out makes a new covenant which supersedes that of Sinai; His disciples must renew this act of communion just as they must preach the Gospel in the whole world before their Master will return in power and great glory (Mk. 13:10). In other words, the earthly mission of Jesus, and still more His death and resurrection, have as their aim the formation of a community of the faithful which shall endure and expand during the interval between His first coming and His appearing at the end of the age. Everything in the teaching of Jesus—the term Son of Man which He uses of Himself, and which in the tradition and in His own thought cannot be separated from the community of the last days; the essential actions of His ministry, such as the gathering of the disciples, the institution of the Lord's Supper and the mission entrusted to the apostles—show that the idea of the Church is at the very heart of Jesus' thought and governs all His actions, even though the Church is especially designated by the traditional images of the flock and the building and the Temple.

Seen in this perspective, the two texts where Jesus does employ the word *ecclesia* do not seem to stand isolated. In Matt. 16:16–18, in reply to Peter's confession, Jesus declares that the apostle is the Rock on which He will build His Church. Here is nothing which contradicts the general attitude of Jesus. To every man, whether he is a Peter or a Paul, He offers a particular and specific vocation. He must rule over a people whom the Church will begin to mould; and the Church is His Church, for she will be born and take her place in the world at the conclusion of His redemptive act, with the gift of the Spirit to the apostles. (On this text cf. O. Cullmann, *Peter; Disciple, Apostle, Martyr*, S.C.M. Press, pp. 155–212). In Matt. 18:15–17 ("If your brother sins against you, go and tell him his fault. . . . But if he does not listen, take one or two others . . . that every word may be confirmed. . . . If he refuses to listen to them, tell it to the Church") the word *Church* bears the sense of a local fraternal gathering and might be equally applied to a Jewish Synagogue of the time of Jesus or a Palestinian Church of the apostolic era. The word has not the specific sense of the text just discussed. But the passage is an interesting confirmation of the contention that the word *Church* is not a Christian creation, but was, as we said above, inherited from Judaism.

(c) *The Church of Jerusalem.* What was promised and indeed prefigured in the time of Jesus was actually realized in history after the resurrection and the gift of the Spirit. The preaching of the apostles had the result of disclosing a reality that was new alike from the theological point of view and as a mere social phenomenon. Summed up in the single word "Church" are "brothers" (Acts 1:15, etc.), "believers" (Acts 2:44, etc.), "disciples" (Acts 6:1, etc.), those who "call on the name of Jesus" (Acts 2:21; 9:14, etc.). So, Acts 5:11; 8:3, etc.

The Church appears as the *people of God, in continuity with the people of the old covenant, for the promises of the O.T. are realized in Christ (Acts 2:25, etc.) and through the gift of the *Spirit (Acts 2:16f.), and in discontinuity, for with unbelieving Judaism there is a rupture. More exactly, the Jews cease to be the people of God in virtue of their persistent unbelief. The Church indeed marks itself off from Judaism by confessing as "Lord and Christ" that Jesus whom the Jews had crucified (Acts 2:36) and whom God raised up (Acts 2:24, etc.). This confession is the authentic sign of the new people of God.

Entry into the Church is through belief in Jesus Christ, by being baptized in His name, by receiving the Spirit (Acts 2:38). All are called, both those at Jerusalem and those who are afar off (Acts 2:39). The Church lives in expectation of the return of Christ at the end of the age (Acts 3:20–21). During the interval the apostles—and before long they are joined by others—labour to consolidate the Church by their teaching and extend it by their missions (Acts 6–11), the faithful meanwhile leading a renewed life (Acts 2:42, etc.), in which communion, in the specific sense of the *Lord's Supper, occupies the central place (Acts 2:46, etc.).

By all these characteristics the Church is seen as a force powerful and unique in history and in eschatology—in short, as the people of God which is reconstituted in Jesus Christ, and not simply as one synagogue amongst many others. This people is present in various places, at Jerusalem (Acts 8:1; 9:31; 11:22), in Galilee and Samaria (Acts 9:31), Antioch (Acts 11:26; 13:1, etc.), in Syria and Cilicia (Acts 15:41), and elsewhere too, as a result of the missions of Paul (Acts 16:5, etc.). Everywhere this people *is* the Church in the fullest sense. The dispersal of the Church, so far from distorting her character, actually assists her function to be the people of God which must expand, like the preaching of the Gospel, from Jerusalem to the ends of the earth (cf. Acts 1:8).

(d) *Paul.* Paul had the same conception of the Church as the apostles of Jerusalem. For him too she was the people whom God is calling together in Jesus Christ. Jerusalem was the seat of the historical origin of the Church; here Christ had been first preached and believed in (Rom. 15:19), and everywhere the apostle preached, there too the Church arose. Paul preached the same Gospel as those who had been apostles before him (1 Cor. 15:11; Gal. 1:17). The message of salvation was addressed to all, Jew and pagan alike (Rom. 1:16, etc.). All who believe in the same Lord form a single Church comprising both Jews and pagans (Eph. 2:11–22).

Like the book of Acts, the Pauline Epistles use *Church* both for the whole people of God and also for the concrete manifestation of this people in a particular place. The believers of Corinth are "the Church of God which is at Corinth" (1 Cor. 1:2, etc.); that is to say, they constitute on pagan soil the same unique reality which was present in Judea amongst the Jews and which before his conversion Paul had persecuted (Gal. 1:13; 1 Cor. 15:9). Paul uses the plural "the Churches" or "the Churches of God" (1 Thess. 2:14; Gal. 1:22; 1 Cor. 16:1; 2 Cor. 8:1), which does not appear in the Acts. He speaks of the Churches in particular places or provinces (Rom. 16:1; 1 Thess. 1:1; Col. 4:16, etc.) and even of "house-Churches" (1 Cor. 16:19; Col. 4:15; Philem. 2). But "all the Churches" (Rom. 16:16; 1 Cor. 7:17, etc.) are so many living realizations of "the Church". The plural indicates only the plurality of places where *the Church* exists, in virtue of the geographical dispersion of believers, isolated from each other in the provinces of the empire or in the districts of the large towns.

In spite of this dispersion, the Church is one. Paul emphasizes the unity by making use of an expression which is peculiar to him. He declares that the Church forms a body (1 Cor. 12:12f.; Rom. 12:5f., etc.), whose head is Christ and whose members are the faithful (Col. 1:22,24; Eph. 1:22–23, etc.). This is for the apostle an ontological reality and no mere image. The Church is the organ by which Christ is present and active in the world during the interval which separates His resurrection from His parousia. The body of Christ takes a visible shape when it meets for worship in the presence of its head and the Lord's Supper is celebrated (1 Cor. 10: 16–17).

The two expressions, "the Church of God" and "the Body of Christ", together express everything that the Church is in the eyes of the apostle Paul. She is the Israel whom God gathers together on the foundation of the confession that Jesus is the Christ; and it is Christ who brings to fruition the promises of the old covenant and, through His people, henceforward manifests Himself as the Lord to whom all dominion has been given.

(*e*) *John.* The word *Church* does not come in John, but the fact of the Church is there. The disciples whom the Johannine Christ gathers during the ministry are only the first members of the "little flock" of whom Jesus is the "true *shepherd": He unites the sheep of Israel and those not of "this flock" (Jn. 10). Jesus prays not only for the disciples whom the Father has given Him (Jn. 17:6) but also for those who will be led to the faith (Jn. 17:20) by the apostles; for, after His glorification, Jesus wills to draw all men to Himself (Jn. 12:32). In His prayer Jesus asks that all who believe may be *one, as the Father and the Son are one (Jn. 17:20–23). This unity is illustrated by the image of the *vine: as the branches only live through their union with the main stem, so communion with Christ makes the faithful a single organism whose unity makes it possible to grow and to bear fruit (Jn. 15). Here we have the equivalent of the Pauline conception of the Church as the body of Christ, just as the image of the one flock expresses the same thought as the Pauline elaboration of the Church comprising both Jews and pagans.

The certain facts that the Church owes her existence to Christ and that she is one and universal are moreover expressed in the N.T. by the other images which have been mentioned in connection with the synonyms of the name of the Church, and notably in the texts where the Church is called the Bride of Christ (Jn. 3:29; 2 Cor. 11:2; Eph. 5:32–33; Rev. 21:2,9; 22:17) or the building of which Christ is the chief corner-stone (1 Pet. 2:6–7; cf. 1 Cor. 3:9; Eph. 2:20).

3. *The Theology of the Church.* The preceding historical inquiry could be summarized in the following assertions which express the thought common to the authors of the N.T.

(*a*) *Definition of the Church:* The Church is God's people, of the new covenant, comprising men of all races and languages, who respond to the preaching of the Gospel by faith in Jesus Christ. As a people whom God calls together in Christ, the Church shares in the unity of her Lord: there is one God, one Lord, one Church (Eph. 4:1–6), which is the Church of God or the Church of Christ. The Church is not the property of the believers: the expressions "my Church", "our Church" have no place in the N.T. scheme of thought.

(b) *Composition of the Church:* God Himself gathers together His Church through His word in the apostolic witness, made powerful by the life-giving Spirit. Hence names are applied to the faithful which remind them that it is by divine action that they are grafted on to the Church. They "are called" (Rom. 1:6); they are "the saints" (Acts 9:13; Rom. 8:27), "those sanctified in Christ Jesus" (1 Cor. 1:2), "all who believed" (Acts 2:44). They are within the Church from the moment when they believed and were *baptized in the name of Jesus—it is not possible for a believer to remain unbaptized (Acts 2:41; 10:48; Gal. 3:27). In baptism the believer is united to the dead and risen Christ; he is placed within the benefits of Christ's work of redemption; he is made a member of His body or flock; he shares in the gifts of the Spirit; he is born again; he leads a new life (Rom. 6:3–11; Jn. 3:3–16).

The Church is the place where the believers continue in the faith (Acts 2:42); it is in the Church that the new creature can grow under the influence of the Spirit (1 Cor. 3:1, etc.). The baptism which unites us to Christ also unites all those baptized in the name of the same Lord to one another; they live together in the Church the same spiritual life, being "of one heart and soul" (Acts 4:32), "bearing one another's burdens" (Gal. 6:2). In short, the faithful enjoy a corporate existence which is lived within the Church.

. (c) *Mission of the Church:* The Church is not of the world (Jn. 17:14), but she lives in the world (Jn. 17:15). She confesses her faith in her Lord who came, who reigns, and who will come again (Phil. 2:6–11; 3:20–21, etc.). She proclaims to the world the *Gospel of the salvation which God offers in Jesus Christ (Acts 1:8; Rom. 10:14; Jn. 17:18). By her unity and her love (1 Cor. 1:13; Jn. 17:21–23; 2 Cor. 5:14; Jn. 13:34–35), she provides the proof of the Gospel's power. To sum up, she is the means by which God draws the work of

redemption to its appointed end, a redemption which had been declared in the old covenant and is realized in Christ. She is Christ's presence among men until the end of the world.

PH.-H. MENOUD

CIRCUMCISION

Circumcision is a surgical operation which consists in cutting away the foreskin of male children. It has long been practised among the Jews, in carrying out what the law prescribes (Gen. 17:12–13; Lev. 12:3). Every male child must be circumcised on the eighth day after birth (Lk. 2:21), and this ceremony, religious in character, is solemnly performed in the synagogue in the presence of the congregation which recites prayers and liturgical songs, while the child's father and the *mohel* (the one who performs the circumcision) carry out the rite according to rules and with well-defined instruments. This custom is not, however, limited to the Israelites, for many peoples, even to-day, practise it the world over. About 200 million men are estimated to observe the custom still (the Arabs for instance). The study and observation of these different peoples permits, moreover, a clearer insight into the meaning of the rite which must in all probability have had an analogous meaning in Hebrew antiquity. The few passages in the O.T. which mention it explicitly give a glimpse of the ancient and also of the more recent conceptions which have been held about it in the course of the centuries.

What was the original meaning of circumcision in ancient Israel? The explanation given by ancient historians like Herodotus, who saw in the custom a measure for hygiene and health, is no longer held to-day. It is much more probable that it was a magical or religious initiation rite, going back to very early times. The fact that the operation was performed with sharpened stones or stone knives (Exod. 4:25; Josh. 5:3) is proof of a time earlier than the Bronze Age.

Originally, it seems fairly certain that we

are in the presence of a puberty or marriage rite: just before marriage the young man must undergo a certain number of initiation tests, of which one was circumcision, so that he might fully accomplish his function as a man. Now these initiation rites were not carried out without blood sacrifices which were offered to the deity as a request that he should make the marriage fertile. The O.T. has retained some traces of this original meaning: in Gen. 34:14–17 the condition necessary for a marriage to be possible between the descendants of Jacob and foreigners is that the latter should be circumcised. The very terms that denote in Hebrew the fiancé and his father-in-law (the father of the wife)—*Ḥatan* and *Ḥoten* —come from a root which means to cut and which is used in Arabic to express: to circumcise. The father-in-law circumcised his future son-in-law at the moment of marriage. The curious incident of the circumcision of Moses' son by Zipporah (Exod. 4:24–26) at the moment when the Lord is attacking Moses to kill him, cannot be explained otherwise. It is likely that the original story told how Moses, uncircumcised, and having taken a Midianite wife (the Midianites practised this rite), almost suffered mortal attack by the deity, because he had not undergone this test. Zipporah would then have circumcised him and said to him, according to the ritual formula: "You are a bridegroom of blood to me!" (vv. 25–26). But subsequent tradition, not understanding clearly the meaning of the episode, has transferred to Moses' son the act of circumcision; the child replaces the father. In this way the practice of the circumcision of children would be explained and justified, at a time when this rite was no longer a marriage rite.

In a more general way, it must have been a rite of initiation to a function or an important responsibility of man: in this way the story of Josh. 5:2–9 would be explained. Joshua gives orders to circumcise all the men at the moment of the conquest of Canaan, at the place which was called Gilgal. The name of the hill (v. 3) means in Hebrew foreskins (*Areloth*).

Similarly, at the celebration of the Passover which marked the exodus from Egypt, all those not already circumcised had to be operated on (Exod. 12:44).

But the all-important significance of circumcision, in the O.T., appears in the narrative of its institution ordered by God to Abraham (Gen. 17:9–14 and 23–27): it is a *covenant rite which is the sign of belonging to a family, a race or a people. In this passage, which is a less ancient tradition than that contained in chapters 12 or 15, the covenant between God and Abraham is marked, on man's side, by circumcision performed on every male, whether son of the house or foreigner bought with money; the uncircumcised male will be "cut off", that is cut off from the people, for violation of the covenant (v. 14). On God's side, the covenant will consist in the granting of a numerous and blessed posterity, whilst the names of Abram and Sarai are to be changed to Abraham and Sarah (vv. 5, 15–16). Henceforward, circumcision will be the mark of the true Israelites, sons of Abraham, and will distinguish them from foreigners and heathen. However, the religious importance attached to circumcision was only to appear gradually in the history of God's people, and even though the custom had existed for a long time, its theological import was made precise only at a relatively late period. Indeed, before the Exile, the Israelites lived in a world of Semitic peoples who practised this rite. Only the Philistines did not observe it; that is why the term of uncircumcised, with the sense of heathen, is specially attributed to them (1 Sam. 14:6; 17:26; 31:4). It should also be noted that in the most ancient legislation of the Hebrews (Exod. 20–23; 34) and particularly in the Decalogue, circumcision is not mentioned as a law to be observed. Only after the Exile, when the Jews had lived among uncircumcised people (Babylonians, Persians) was circumcision to become a religious obligation for Israel, and one of the essential duties (taking precedence indeed over sabbath observance, Jn. 7:22–23) imposed on Jewish proselytes. A distinction was even made, about the time of the Christian era, between proselytes of the door who might be admitted to the synagogue without accepting all the prescriptions of the law, and proselytes of righteousness, who were to accept all, particularly circumcision.

Circumcision, a sign of the ritual and racial purity of true Jews, was envisaged, however, from ancient times, as an act of more symbolical than real value. A fruit tree could be spoken of as uncircumcised; its fruit was considered as unclean (Lev. 19:23). Above all, in order to speak of purity of heart, of obedience and of faithfulness to God, images such as circumcision of the heart (Deut. 10:16; 30:6; Jer. 4:4), of the ears (Jer. 6:10), or of the lips (Exod. 6:12) were used. This type of circumcision is more important than the circumcision of the flesh (Jer. 9:25). It is the sign of the true faithfulness of the believer who is a member of the chosen people. The heathen are uncircumcised in heart and flesh (Ezek. 44:7). It is in this symbolical sense that the word is used in the N.T., particularly by the apostle Paul, who explains that the true sons of Abraham are circumcised in heart (Rom. 2:25–29; 1 Cor. 7:19; Gal. 5:2–6) and that true circumcision exists in Jesus Christ alone (Phil. 3:2–3; Col. 2:11–15).

F. MICHAELI

CITY

1. If the word city has acquired a theological significance the reason, to a large extent at least, is to be found in what *Jerusalem, the greatest of all cities, meant to Israel. It goes without saying that the word is used in a completely different sense from the one that it has in the civic tradition which has its roots in classical Greece. In this tradition it denotes the excellent and typical creation of human genius which is dominant through its reason and which organizes life and human relations in a rational way; man fashions his world, formulates laws to which he will freely submit: as a member of the city he is a complete man, free and responsible, a man in possession of himself and realizing his

ideal of humanity. Jerusalem is a city in a very different sense. Jesus called it the city of the great King (Matt. 5:35): it is *the* city, because there God dwells and is present among His people. In it stands the *Temple, the place where, by the will of God, heaven meets earth, and the worship is offered which makes real for Israel the covenant of which God is the author and surety; in Jerusalem, the Messianic promise took form in the line of kings which issued from David. It is the tangible sign of the salvation promised to Israel, and through Israel to all peoples (cf. e.g. Isa. 56:6–8; 60:1–9; Zech. 9:9–10). As a city not through the will of man but through the work and election of God, it foreshadows the city that God is preparing, and towards which His plan of salvation guides the world.

2. In the N.T., which bears witness to the fulfilment of the promises and the end of "appearances", the city is the *Kingdom of God*. The Kingdom is the new Jerusalem, the Jerusalem from above (Heb. 12:22; Rev. 3:12; Gal. 4:26), the city which is to come (Heb. 13:14), which has solid foundations, because God is its architect and builder (Heb. 11:10), the city of the living God (Heb. 12:22). It will be in reality what Jerusalem merely foreshadowed in figures drawn from earthly reality, chosen by God to reflect divine reality: the place of the omnipotent presence of God and of consummated salvation, the sure and permanent city, because nothing will have gone to its construction which is not the work of God alone.

3. *The people of God are waiting for this city and are on the march to it.* The people wait and can march, not through their own initiative but because God has granted them freedom of the city by creating for them, in Jesus Christ, the past to which they can appeal and the future to which they may look forward. We have our city in heaven, whence we await also the Lord Jesus Christ as Saviour (Phil. 3:20; cf. Gal. 4:26, Jerusalem our mother): our present life is shaped and determined by our belonging

to the future world, whose first-fruits are already to hand and have been given to us in Jesus Christ. It may also be said that believers have approached (that they have returned to) the city of the living God (Heb. 12:22), not that the Kingdom has already come, but because, as members of the Church founded on Jesus Christ, they have already received the earnest of the Kingdom and can already see the first signs of the triumphant revelation of salvation. The Church is on the march between the past and the future given by God, as is shown by the two sacraments: *baptism plunges the believer into the death of Christ and establishes him on the past given by God (in Jesus Christ you have been brought near, that is, made beneficiaries of the grace bestowed on Israel, Eph. 2:11-13); established on this past, the Church assembled for the Holy Supper (see *Lord's Supper) keeps vigil and rejoices in the expectation of the city that is to come ("you proclaim the Lord's death until he comes," 1 Cor. 11:26).

4. Originating in the city which is to come, the *Church must not settle down in the world* and set itself to live in human security. Here we have no permanent city— this is not a resigned complaint on the brevity of life, but the declaration of faith which has its future in God alone—we are on a quest for the city that is to come (Heb. 13:14). We live in this world as alien exiles (1 Pet. 1:17; 2:11); in the world, not of the world (Jn. 17:14ff.). Abraham, who left his city to live as a stranger in Canaan, is with the other patriarchs the symbol of the Church, and the pattern for believers (Heb. 11:9ff.): certainly he dwells in the land of promise, but in the movable shelter of a tent, because the land is not yet given to him; if he were settled he would live no longer by the promise and by faith, his life would no longer be the quest for the heavenly city which God has prepared for him and his (Heb. 11:16).

God does not require the believer to flee from the world, but to live a life in accordance with the laws of the city of which God

has made him a citizen, and which offers clear witness of the reality of the Kingdom, of God's rights over men, of redemption and judgment. "Conduct yourselves with fear throughout the time of your exile" (as strangers on the earth, 1 Pet. 1:17); Believers are not spoilt children who can allow themselves to flout the Father's will (Schlatter), and live with impunity as unbelievers: all their life must show that they are redeemed not by perishable goods, such as the world gives, but by the blood of Christ, by God who judges the unbeliever and grants him by His grace his only future. As sojourning strangers, they must abstain from fleshly covetousness which makes war on the soul (1 Pet. 2:11ff.; cf. Col. 3:5ff.), must keep away from all those undertakings by which man believes he ensures himself a full life and salvation and which ruin him; all this must be observed not only so that they themselves do not fall from grace, but so that they may, without equivocation, be regarded by the heathen as strangers, unassimilable, who bear witness to the kingdom which is to come.

5. *The relations between the Church and the world are then not only negative.* If the presence of the Church, its life determined by its belonging to the future city, are a judgment on the world, the denial given to its attempts to find in itself a reason for existence, the faithfulness of the Church to the better country (Heb. 11:16) is also its only faithfulness to earthly countries. Joseph is a stranger in Egypt not only for the salvation of himself and his family, but for the salvation of Egypt, as Abraham is a stranger in Canaan for the salvation of all nations. The Church is an exile, not an isolationist, because her existence is closely bound up with the world's and because she is responsible for all. She does not withdraw from public life. Thus Christians should pray for the powers that be, for the Church cannot fully perform her mission towards all men in a country given to corruption and to disorder or if she is hounded by *persecution (1 Tim. 2:1-8; cf. 1 Pet. 2:13-17; Jer. 29:7). However,

the Church's loyalty is not unconditional; if she renders to Caesar that which is Caesar's, she must render to God that which is God's (Matt. 22:21), and thus remind the authorities of the earthly city that they are subject to the King of the city that is to come.

CHR. SENFT

CLEAN

O.T.

1. *The laws of cleanness* (cf. especially Lev. 11–15). The distinction between clean and unclean is not exclusively biblical: it is found in countries surrounding Israel; it may even be said that it is one of the fundamental elements of "religion". But in the Bible these notions assume a new significance. To understand it, the simplest thing is to consider the effects of uncleanness.

If the priest infringes the laws of cleanness, he is unfit for priestly duties (Lev. 21:1–15; 22:1–8). The layman in a state of uncleanness cannot eat hallowed things (1 Sam. 21:4), nor sacrificial victims (Lev. 7:20–21), nor enter the Temple (Lev. 12:4), nor take part in the cultic feasts (2 Chr. 30:17–20), nor fight in the holy war (Deut. 23:9–14; Num. 31:19–20). In the case of a leper who has been healed, his uncleanness drives him from the camp, and he can regain access to the Temple only by stages: entry into the camp but outside his tent, access to his tent, then presentation before the tent of meeting (Lev. 14:1–11). All that concerns the cult must be pure (Exod. 25:31; 30:35; Lev. 4:12; and also Neh. 12:30; 13:30). Thus uncleanness involves exclusion from the sacred precincts. And if anyone in a state of uncleanness performs an action that requires cleanness, he or she must be cut off from the people of God (Lev. 7:21).

Lev. 10:10 draws a parallel between holy–common, and clean–unclean. Let us make it clear that there is no question of equivalence. What belongs to God is holy; what belongs to the creation is common.

But this distinction is not a rigid division: there is no frontier between the transcendent and the material. To understand this we must appeal to the fundamental notion of Israelite psychology: the soul, or (better) the potentiality. There is potentiality in a being or object when that being or object manifests efficacy or purposiveness: thus in the profane the presence of the sacred, the divine, is revealed. God is absolute potentiality. And Yahweh is jealous of every other potentiality.

As a result the common may be clean or unclean. Its greater or lesser potentiality involves its greater or lesser participation in holiness. But if the potentiality is foreign to Yahweh, there is opposition between the two: thus unclean may be defined as what must be kept away from the holy, while the clean–common may on the contrary become holy. It would be mistaken to come to the over-hasty conclusion that unclean and holy are equivalent: on the contrary they are mutually exclusive; what is holy in one religion is unclean in the eyes of another (especially Israel); the unclean must always be shunned; if it so happens that anyone must be kept away from what is sacred, it is because he is not ready to meet what is of itself a source of blessing.

What is unclean is unclean of itself; but it may communicate its uncleanness. As a result he who has undergone this sort of defilement must cleanse himself, that is, he must sanctify himself in order to be in relationship again with Yahweh, who is the Holy, either in the cult or even simply among the people. Thus, apart from God Himself, that is holy which God chooses and reserves for Himself by causing it to share in His own potentiality, or in other words in His Spirit (Ps. 51:12–13).

What is common and has been hallowed may be desecrated=made common, and return to everyday common life. This profanation is good if it is done according to the rules (rites of going out, offering and hallowed eating of the tithe and the first-fruits: cf. Deut. 14:22–23); it is evil if it consists in an insensitive juxtaposition of the common–clean that is holy with what risks being common–unclean or at the least common–defiled (cf. 1 Sam. 5–6; 2 Sam. 6:6).

2. *Unclean things*. Everything is more or less defiled by corrupting influences: the land because of the heathen, the heathen because of idols. But to Israel all this is unclean of itself since it participates in a spiritual world that is opposed to Yahweh. Let us draw up a list of what causes defilement for Israel, on the understanding that division into two paragraphs is merely for clarity of classification within one whole. The following are unclean:

(a) *All that has links with paganism:* (i) *certain animals:* it is not forbidden to touch them but to eat them; to eat is to appropriate a part of the soul of what is eaten; the hallowed people must eat only what its soul may assimilate, and makes a special point of forbidding things that are sacred for foreigners. Perhaps the discrimination between animals sometimes comes from this (in cases where discrimination derives from evidence of a strange potentiality, the animals would have to be listed in the following paragraph). As a result, the heathen will be unable to eat at an Israelite table and Israel will remain holy (Lev. 11; 20:25–26; Deut. 14:1–21; Gen. 43:32). (ii) *Meat offered to idols:* this appears quite late, when Israel is no longer "separate" from the nations and when, scattered through the world, it finds that in the market meat coming from heathen sacrifices is being offered to its people (cf. 1 Macc. 1:62–63; Acts 15:29). (iii) *The fruits of Canaan* during the first three years of cultivation, deriving from the fact that they have connections with previous worship of Baal, the god of the soil (Lev. 19:23–25). (iv) *The land occupied by the heathen* (Lev. 18:25; Num. 33:51–56; Ezra 9:11), the homes of the heathen and finally the persons of the heathen: cf. the "forbidden" set upon the Canaanite towns at the time of the settlement (Josh. 6:24–7: 26). Forbidden is the opposite of *holy. Its cause is the *idol—the source and at the same time the symbol of a spiritual world

different from that of Yahweh's people (Gen. 35:2; 2 Chr. 34:3; Ezek. 23:7).

(b) *Anything that manifests a potentiality independent of God.* Let us make separate mention of *blood, the pre-eminent vehicle of the soul, unclean or holy as the case may be, and therefore a source of defilement (Num. 35:33) or of purification (Lev. 14:52), but a thing that must not be eaten (Gen. 9:4; Lev. 7:27). In connection with the unclean things which follow there was perhaps awareness of a danger: the mysterious character was primarily the source of a taboo, and not of a rule of hygiene. (i) *The dead bodies* of men (Num. 19:11; 2 Kings 23:13–14; Ezek. 39:12), of unclean animals (Lev. 11:27–28), and of clean animals not killed by men for food or sacrifice (Lev. 17:15). Tombs are whitened before the Passover so that pilgrims may see and avoid them. The dead participate in a sphere of holiness incompatible with God. (ii) *Sacrificial victims* not eaten within the first two days (Lev. 7:16–18). (iii) *Leprosy* in persons, on cloth or in houses (Lev. 13–14). (iv) *Everything connected with the mystery of procreation:* childbirth (Lev. 12); menstrual flow or any other flow, normal or unhealthy (Lev. 15); normal sexual relations (1 Sam. 21:5; 2 Sam. 11:4). This uncleanness increases in culpability if unlawful or unnatural acts are involved (Lev. 18). (v) *The red heifer* and her ashes (Num. 19) although holy, perhaps in anticipation of the fact that they are used for expiation.

Objects in contact with these unclean things are unclean and must be avoided for the same reason (Lev. 15:4), except spring-water and seed for sowing (Lev. 11:36), without doubt because of the cleansing potentiality of water and the mystery of germination. Uncleanness is more contagious than holiness (Hagg. 2:11–13).

3. *Moral cleanness.* In the prophetic message, uncleanness takes on an ethical sense connected with the holy will of God (Isa. 6:5; Jer. 13:27; Hab. 1:13; cf. Ps. 19:9f.; Prov. 15:26). Moral purity is not a mere surpassing of legal cleanness, and

legal cleanness is not simply an object-lesson and a symbol of moral purity. The fact that later on the Pharisees exaggerated the first to the point of neglecting the second, and that the second was separated from the first which had become hypocritical, should not lead us into error. One passes from legal cleanness to moral purity not by reaching out from the body towards the soul, while keeping only the idea of obedience required by the law of cleanness—but by careful study, through reflection on the idea of the fear of Yahweh. The unclean is of itself contrary to Yahweh's potentiality. Not to purify oneself when one is unclean (legally) is a sin (morally): not through simple disobedience to the order of purification, but through opposition to God in His very essence; for God is the Holy One *par excellence* (Lev. 11:44-45). Thus, if the very ancient laws of cleanness are codified at the time of the Exile, it is most assuredly so that they shall not be forgotten despite the absence of the Temple, but it is also an echo to the message of the prophets: physical purification is a sign or sacrament of moral purification.

The moral code derives from the definition of "clean". An action performed by the hands ("clean hands"="to be faultless", 2 Sam. 22:21; Job 17:9) comes from the soul as a whole; it is right if this whole is involved. Uncleanness destroys the soul's integrity and causes the ruin of the whole being (Mic. 2:10). A clean heart (Gen. 20:5) is the opposite of a divided heart, a soul broken by an alien will. What is set apart by God does not receive His will as an external order, but is placed within the sphere of His holiness and participates in His Spirit; then one can approach God: pray to Him (Job 16:17), go into the Temple (Ps. 24:4). *Sin is rebellion, that is, ontological opposition to God by submitting also to another will and therefore to another potentiality (that is why Israel's sin is greater than the sin of the Gentiles: Amos 1:1–3:2).

Uncleanness comes from without: but to condone uncleanness is a sin (from within); and inversely sin is an uncleanness. Un-faithfulness to God is a defilement like adultery or prostitution (Hos. 2). An unclean soul cannot develop and becomes stunted: the covenant relationship with God is upset. In the beginning there were automatic consequences. But the personal relationship between God and man appears: hence the jealousy of the holy God under whose wrath man cannot live.

4. *Purification*.   God is holy: man is defiled (Lev. 11:44; Job 4:17; Hab. 1:13): by corrupting influences, by behaviour, and even by nature (Job 14:4; Ps. 51:7). Purification is necessary, after which one will strive like Job (33:9) to remain clean.

(*a*) First of all the dual rôle of *fire* is to be noted: it purifies certain objects like metals (Num. 31:22–23; Mal. 3:3), and perhaps it is for that reason that enemy treasure can enter God's treasury when the country is "purified" by fire (Josh. 6:24); and it consumes the offering, purifying it and releasing from it the life principle which rises to God. But it is obvious that its action normally destroys whatever it acts upon; hence, for Israel and its welfare, the rôle of *water*.

*Washing must always take place, sometimes with the removal of hair which is a seat of the life-principle and therefore easily contaminated (Num. 8:7). The basis is bathing and the cleansing action of water: partial or total washing, at birth (Ezek. 16:4), at marriage (Ruth 3:3; Est. 2:3), in order to seek and express health and joy (*Anointing) by cleaning and perfuming (one's body, feet, hands, face).

Often there must be the *sacrifice of a victim whose *blood washes away the unclean potentiality (expiation) and of another whose blood restores the link with the divine potentiality (holocaust): after giving birth (Lev. 12:6), after contact with a dead body (Num. 19; 2 Sam. 12:15f.), after leprosy (Lev. 14), after an issue (Lev. 15). The duration of uncleanness is variable: until evening after the contact (Lev. 11:24), seven days after being healed (Lev. 14:8–9) or contact with a human corpse (Num. 19:11), forty days after giving birth (Lev. 12:2–5) and double that time if the child is a daughter.

The priest, the sanctified person, conducts this ceremony not only in cases of accidental defilement but for the people, the country and especially for the *Temple (centre of the country and closely connected with the people): all that goes to the Temple must be purified, and the holiness of the Temple (where impure man meets the holy God) must be maintained by the yearly removal of sin (Lev. 16). For all this, priests and Levites must themselves be purified (Num. 8:6–22; 2 Chr. 29:15–19; Ezra 6:20).

(b) But neither the washing (Jer. 2:22; Job 9:30), nor the sacrifice (Ps. 51:17) has any magical power; they are signs. It is not a question of purifying oneself, but of being purified, by God's *forgiveness (Ps. 32:1–2) and not by a human rite. In a mysterious way God leads the sinner towards the need for pardon (2 Sam. 12; Isa. 38:17; Dan. 11:35), which will be asked for in prayer, any rite being replaced by the confession of sin (Ps. 51).

The action of purification is not, however, done away with; but it comes from an act of God the creator (Ps. 51:9–12; Isa. 1:18; Ezek. 36:25–26; Dan. 12:10). The sacrifice itself is not debarred but will be offered by God Himself in the person of the Messiah (cf. Isa. 53:12). The greatest crime is to refuse to be purified (Ezek. 24:13).

D. LYS

N.T.

In the *synoptic Gospels*, Jesus appears as the one who transforms certain people who are said to be unclean into clean beings. Thanks to certain of His cures, lepers are healed. The Gospel writers say: "the lepers are cleansed." This cleansing is not merely a miraculous act which changes physically sick men into ritually clean beings, irreproachable before the Jewish law. Its meaning goes deeper: it manifests the intervention of God who transforms what is corrupt: the body or the whole being. The episode of the ten lepers is significant in this respect (Lk. 17:11–19). Jesus not only insists on cure, but on conversion.

Ritual cleanness, even of men in good health, is clearly not enough: Jesus says so in strong terms to the Pharisees (Matt. 23:25–26; Lk. 11:39). The only true cleanness comes from a purification of the heart, from real communion with God (Matt. 5:8). Cleanness is then not the privilege of certain men upright of themselves. It results from the intervention of God who makes clean the unclean heart of man (Mk. 7:18–23). It is translated into conduct in harmony with the will of God. This cannot be obtained by the mere application of rigid principles. A man is not clean because he may have done his duty or because his conscience is clear. He is clean, when the Lord acts in his life. No one is clean of himself. But each one becomes clean through faith in the Lord. The writer of the fourth Gospel makes Jesus say: "You are already made clean by the word which I have spoken to you" (Jn. 15:3).

This purity in living, resulting from an ever renewed and strengthened communion with Christ, is infinitely wider and stronger than the principles to which mankind would like to reduce it: the apostle Peter himself (according to Acts 10:15; 11:9) is obliged to acknowledge that the Gentiles are not more unclean than the Jews, and that faith alone creates a distinction, not race.

The apostle Paul takes up this idea of purity and, in order to describe the various human situations before God and Christ, uses several words which can be thus rendered into English: guileless, without blemish (Rom. 16:19; Phil. 2:15), blameless (literally) (Phil. 2:15), innocent (Phil. 2:15), pure (Phil. 1:10), without offence (Phil. 1:10). The variety of the expressions, with certain almost imperceptible shades of meaning, does not matter so much as the spiritual reality expressed by the apostle.

Jesus told Christians to be "innocent as doves" (Matt. 10:16). The apostle desires that believers should be wise in what concerns good, and "guileless as to what is evil" (Rom. 16:19). It is the result of obedience of faith (Phil. 2:12–15): "Do all things without grumbling or questioning, that you may be blameless and innocent, children of God without blemish in the midst of a crooked (lit. warped) and perverse (lit. which squints) generation." Uprightness and simplicity of heart allow the believer to "discern" what is important in daily conduct and will guide him until the day of Christ, until His return, when he will have to be pure and not be the object of scandal (Phil. 1:10). The present purity of Christian conduct (Phil. 4:8) only has value because it will allow the final meeting with Christ. It is henceforth the result of the hope and the joy of the life to come in the visible presence of the Lord who will purify us thoroughly and for ever.

It is in the same sense that the Pastoral Epistles speak of a pure *heart* (1 Tim. 1:5; 2 Tim. 2:22) or of a pure *conscience* and that the first letter of Peter cites the pure conduct of Christian women (1 Pet. 3:2). For the purification of the being (or of the soul, 1 Pet. 1:22) results from obedience to the truth.

In the Epistle to the Hebrews, purification, a human work, the result of rites doomed to extinction, is contrasted with the purifying work carried out by Christ's sacrifice, the result of which is to lead us to serve the living God (Heb. 9:13–14; cf. 10:2).

In short, it can be seen that through the various words which are used to translate the idea of purity in all N.T. writings there is a remarkable unity of view: man, having become impure through his estrangement from God, becomes pure through constant communion with Christ. His purity is never acquired, but always received until the day when Christ returns and makes visible that purity which until then is only the fruit of faith.

M. CARREZ

CLOTHES, *see* GARMENT

COMFORTER, *see* HOLY SPIRIT

COMMANDMENT, *see* LAW

CONFESS

To confess means: to declare oneself in a categorical and personal way to be in definite relationship with God. Confession is the public expression of faith, which by this expression is pledged. While *witness is addressed to men, confession is addressed, in the presence of men, to God in a voluntary impulse of gratitude and praise. By confession the congregation of believers— and each individual believer—pledge themselves to their Lord and openly commit themselves before the world. To confess is not merely to express a personal opinion: confession has in view the absolute, it brings the demands of the living God into the very midst of human discussions. Nor is confession the statement of an eternal and impersonal doctrine: whoever confesses pledges himself, at his own risk and peril, in a very definite situation.

1. In the O.T., "to confess" has the three following meanings: (*a*) to praise, to celebrate; (*b*) to declare (the Lord and the deliverance He has wrought); (*c*) to recognize one's faults. The O.T. recognizes an inward connection between these three acts: one can praise God only by proclaiming His acts of deliverance, and one can only sing of deliverance by recalling the wretchedness and sin from which God has delivered His own. These three acts are found in association in certain prayers (Gen. 32:9–12; Neh. 9) and in many of the Psalms (Ps. 22; 32; 40; 51; 116; Isa. 38:9–20), psalms of mourning or hymns of gratitude in which the believer relates the deliverance of which he has been the object, describes his wretchedness, avows his sin, celebrates the mercy of God; making the appropriate sacrifice, he pledges himself to make God's mercy known to his brethren. The framework in which these O.T. confessions are made, individual or collective, public, liturgical or spontaneous, is the Temple at Jerusalem; their customary pattern is described in Job 33:26–28.

2. In the N.T. the word rendered "to confess" means primarily "to assent to, to agree on a common basis": confession implies in effect that he who makes confession acquiesces fully in the will of God.

Now this same word inherits from the O.T. tradition the supplementary meaning "to praise, to celebrate" (it is the term used in Matt. 11:25; Rom. 15:9). Confession in the N.T., as in the O.T., is an act of praise: not the simple sharing of views by two equal partners, nor the declaration of a human consensus of opinion, but the acceptance, enlightened and convinced, grateful and submissive, of an adored will. When one confesses, one prays, as it is fitting to do in the presence of an almighty and merciful Lord.

3. Confession has two objects: on one hand *the person of Jesus Christ*, on the other *the sins of the believers*. These are the two aspects of one and the same revolution: Jesus Christ came, indeed, to bring the forgiveness of sins. To confess Jesus Christ involves at the same time the recognition of one's own sin; on the other hand one cannot confess one's sins and effectively repent except "according to God" (2 Cor. 7:9–11): all other "grief" is barren. The old man, as he dies, confesses his sin; the new creature confesses Jesus Christ who assumes possession of him.

(*a*) *To confess Jesus Christ* means to confess a name, a person, and not a religious system. The N.T. thought of confession takes up that of the O.T. in its very words (Deut. 6:4, "Hear, O Israel, the Lord our God is one Lord") but it makes quite clear what is the name of this Lord. One confesses ' Jesus Christ", "the Lord Jesus", "that Jesus Christ is Lord" (Phil. 2:11), "the Son of God", "the Gospel of Christ" (2 Cor. 9:13), "the name of God" (Heb. 13:15), "our hope" (Heb. 10:23). The recognition of the lordship of Jesus Christ, the knowledge of His name, constitutes all the teaching that must be held. Thus the confession, once formulated, serves as a summary of the *teaching which is to be faithfully guarded (1 Tim. 6:12; Heb. 3:1) especially in the face of heresy (1 Jn. 4:2; 2 Jn. 7–9), and that not on account of pride but in true humility.

(*b*) With regard to the *confession of sins*, already practised in the O.T., we find this revived by John the Baptist (Mk. 1:5), it is an accompaniment of the ministry of Jesus (Lk. 5:8;19:8; in the Parables, Lk. 15:21; 18:13), of that of the apostle (Jn. 20:23; Acts 19:18) and becomes the object of apostolic injunctions (1 Jn. 1:9; Jas. 5:16). Such confession has no intrinsic meaning as a religious practice. Its true meaning is that it is the consequence of the renewal which Jesus Christ brings: its secret is that pardon has come and that Christ is Lord even of the wasted years of the past.

4. *Perspectives of Confession*. (*a*) Confession is addressed to God: it is a response to His call, it is also prayer and praise (Matt. 16:16; Phil. 2:11; Heb. 13:15). Men (Matt. 10:32; Lk. 12:8; Jas. 5:16) can be witnesses of a declaration which is addressed to God, or they can be His special ambassadors.

(*b*) Confession is a *revealing act*, not designed in the first instance to persuade others: it may persuade them, but it may equally offend them (Matt. 10:32–39; Jn. 9:22). It demonstrates to the world the fundamental harmony between the Creator and the redeemed creature, an agreement which is not only possible but which has been actually rediscovered by the witness. Confession is a spontaneous act which can be very costly (Jn. 12:42).

(*c*) To confess—or not to confess, to hold one's peace, to deny—has an *eschatological significance*, that is to say one which has a connection with the last judgment and the salvation of believers. This connection is seen in John the Baptist and is made fully apparent in the words of Jesus: Matt. 10:32; Lk. 12:8; cf. Rev. 3:5 and 2 Tim. 2:11–13 (where the reader is reminded that it is the Saviour who is Judge). We shall be accused by *Satan before the judgment-seat of God, where we shall need the defence of Christ, advocate and redeemer who is not ashamed to call us "brethren": shall we then in this day refuse to defend His name before men? Paul underlines this eschatological perspective by stating explicitly that confession with the mouth leads to future salvation (Rom. 10:10,13), and to resurrection (2 Cor. 4:13f.). Confession is not something added on to faith: it is at one and the same time a manifestation of faith in view of the last day and a testing of it (Jn. 12:42). The confessing community foreshadows the community of the last days (Rom. 14:11f.; Phil. 2:11), whose solemn confessions we hear in Revelation (5:9f.; 11:15, etc.)

(d) Confession takes place *before men*, either to a limited circle or in public. This public may be the assembly of the faithful (1 Cor. 12:3) or the universal Church (2 Cor. 9:13), the ignorant or hostile crowd (the "confessor" is often to become a martyr).

(e) Confession is *the work of the Holy Spirit* (Matt. 10:20; 1 Cor. 12:3; 1 Jn. 4:2ff.). It is the confession of an unbroken community, not of isolated individuals, for it transmits the knowledge of historical facts the truth of which is guaranteed by the whole body of the Church. Confession has its place in *baptism (Acts 8:37; 10:44–46; cf. Matt. 3:16–17) or in ordination to a *ministry (1 Tim. 6:12, in all probability).

CH. BIBER

CONSCIENCE, *see* MAN N.T.

CONSECRATE, *see* ANOINTING, HOLY, MINISTRY, SACRIFICES

CONSULT, *see* SEEK

CONVERSION, *see* REPENTANCE

CORNER STONE, *see* BUILD, JESUS

COVENANT

O.T.

In Israel life is only possible within the community, the isolated individual being an exception who arouses horror. Now, that life which blossoms within the community is incomprehensible without the concept of *covenant*, by which the bonds uniting the members of the community are expressed. Still further, the relations between the God of Israel and His people are thought of under the form of a covenant. This conception alone affords an understanding of the religious life of the people of God. Many conceptions depend on it, such as *righteousness or *sin. Thus, in the O.T. covenant has a significance the importance of which cannot be exaggerated.

1. We must be clear, however, respecting the extension which can be given to the concept of covenant as able to exist and be present without the observance of suitable rites at the moment of its conclusion. A covenant exists every time that there are beings united together and belonging to the same totality. The smallest unit at the heart of which is a covenant is also the most natural. It is the family, in which the members are united by the ties of blood. They have common blood, as the Arabs say, or common flesh, as the Hebrews say. To break the sacred ties of the covenant which unites the members of the same family or the same clan or the same tribe or the same people is to commit sin, to be wicked, unrighteous. To observe these ties is, on the contrary, to be righteous and good. The obligations cease outside the group united in the covenant. With regard to strangers, enemies for example, the Israelite can act as he pleases. He is righteous when he destroys them.

2. Nevertheless, life is not so simple. In reality, covenants overlap each other, which gives rise to terrible conflicts. It is the drama of Jonathan, who, in order to remain faithful to the covenant of the family, ought to follow his father and hate David, at a time when he has concluded with this same David a covenant whose depth may be conjectured from 1 Sam. 18. He is caught between his duty as a son and his duty as a friend, which are equally sacred. When a covenant is concluded between two men, that does not signify that the two parties are equal. On the contrary, the more powerful imposes his will. It is he who gives direction to the group formed by the covenanting parties. This is the case with Hezekiah and Sennacherib (2 Kings 18:13ff.). If the

covenant exists within the people it can be extended to other nations. Thus the Gibeonites manage by a trick to form a covenant with Israel (Josh. 9). From that instant they are sacred and Joshua can no longer treat them as enemies. The expression "the man of my covenant" can also mean my neighbour, him to whom I have obligations. Within the group formed by a covenant, peace and well-being reign. In it each one can develop and live freely. His duty will be to respect the rights of the others, in doing which he will be acting with justice, but at the same time his own legitimate rights must be respected. If this is not the case, he will be justified by having them restored, that is, by the repairing of a community which had been destroyed.

3. The Hebrew word for covenant can be translated by pact or contract. It is used with a verb meaning to cut, an allusion to the rite of which Jer. 34:18f. speaks. The conclusion of a covenant can be accompanied by a complicated ritual or, on the contrary, be reduced to its simplest expression: sacrifice, meal, oath, handshake. It is probably to a meal that the expression a "covenant of salt" refers (Num. 18:19; 2 Chr. 13:5; cf. also the covenant between Laban and Jacob in Gen. 31:44). It is to be seen that life is not possible without the covenant which underlies the entire life of the group or community. As God is the sustainer of life, He also sustains the covenant. To act contrary to the covenant is to commit a sin (Jer. 11).

4. What gives the concept of covenant in the O.T. an incomparable theological significance is that the relations between God and His people are expressed thereby. It can be said that *the entire religion of Israel presupposes for its basis a covenant between God and the nation He has chosen.* Abraham makes a covenant with God in Genesis 15. It is an imposing scene, in which God passes between the animals which have been divided asunder, in the form of a flame of fire, while Abraham is plunged in a profound sleep. The Deity

could be called the God of the covenant in passages which reflect the period when the Israelites were not yet in Canaan (Judg. 8:33; 9:4,46). At Sinai the God of their fathers made a covenant with Israel, as at the exodus from Egypt (Exod. 19 and 24). If the people are faithful to their obligations, if they observe all the ordinances imposed by their God, He will show the feelings which are implied in the covenant: love, goodness and grace. God will be faithful. At the great Jewish feasts, above all at the Passover which celebrated the deliverance from Egypt, and at the autumn festival the people solemnly renewed their covenant with God. The promises which He had made had a concrete character. They comprised what the Bible calls the *blessing, that is to say security, prosperity, fertility of the soil and the maintenance of the world which God had created and which depended entirely upon Him.

Quite early in the history of Israel, the idea that God could be the partner of His people appeared unworthy of the majesty of God. That is why the biblical writers, instead of using the expression "conclude" a covenant, wrote "give" or "establish" a covenant. When Israel was exiled in Babylon, the covenant with God still remained. It formed part of Israel's nature. By restoring His people, by reinstating them in a rebuilt Jerusalem, God remains faithful to His covenant. He performs an act of righteousness. This is the beautiful message of Isa. 40–55 which sings of the re-establishment of Zion as the manifestation of the eternal righteousness of God. Righteousness and love, grace and salvation have here the same meaning.

There was a covenant with Adam, a covenant with Noah, a covenant with Moses at Sinai. Repeatedly in the course of history the covenant is renewed by impressive ceremonies: by Joshua on Ebal and Gerizim (Josh. 8:30), by Josiah (2 Kings 23), by Ezra and Nehemiah (Neh. 8). If God has remained faithful, Israel has disobeyed her God. Like the contemporaries of Jesus, she has remembered her privileges as the chosen people and forgotten her obligations. So God has intervened to punish, but His chastisement had as its aim the purifying of the people in view of the conclusion of the new covenant, written no more on tables of stone but in the heart of a transformed people (Jer. 31:31ff.). Only the idea of covenant makes it possible to understand that of the love of God, His righteousness, His grace and His salvation; it alone also makes comprehensible the character of sin. This explains the central place which it occupies in the theology of the O.T.

G. PIDOUX

N.T.

Translations generally render the Greek word *diatheke* by two terms: covenant and testament. For example, in Heb. 9 the R.V. gives testament in vv. 16 and 17 and covenant in v. 18. The current expressions Old and New "Testament" (cf. 2 Cor. 3:14) come from this same Greek word which is most often translated by covenant. These diverse translations of one Greek term strive to give the sense of the biblical context, but they can lead to misunderstanding. It is all the more necessary to analyse the original term with the help of its historical context.

It appears 33 times in the N.T. (7 times in quotations from the O.T.): 9 times by Paul; 17 times in the Epistle to the Hebrews; 4 times in the synoptic Gospels; twice in the Acts and once in Revelation. The verb from which the substantive is derived only rarely appears in the N.T. (Lk. 22:29; Acts 3:25; Heb. 8:10; 9:16; 10:16).

1. We can start by isolating the expression in the canticle of Zacharias (Lk. 1:72) which moves entirely within O.T. and traditional Jewish perspectives. Here the appeal to the "holy covenant" underlines especially the continuity of the pattern of the history of salvation, a continuity based upon the faithfulness of God to the "oath" made to Abraham. This covenant is invested with the three principal Old Testament aspects:

(a) It is a sovereign and merciful initiative by God (for the canticle of Zacharias does not sing of the benefits of a religious institution or of a bipartite agreement, but of the faithfulness of God);

(b) It creates a definite history, the history of a people sustained and upheld by that covenant in which God binds His name to that of a group of human beings (for this is the significance of His "oath", v. 73); this history has a beginning and an end; the covenant is not an intermittent association, it is directed to a goal, namely, the salvation of Israel by the "remission of sins" (v. 77ff.; Rev. 11:19 describes this temporal end to the covenant).

(c) If God binds Himself to His people by an oath, the covenant especially binds the people which is held to "serve Him in holiness and righteousness" (v. 74ff.); and this may be called the moral aspect of the covenant (cf. Rom. 9:4, where the gift of the covenant and of the law are joined together). This same fundamental meaning is also found in the Acts: in Acts 3:25 the expression "sons of the covenant" underlines the creative power of the covenant which has brought into being in history a people which owes its existence entirely to it; while on the other hand this text clearly recalls the fact that the covenant made with Abraham after all concerned "all the families of the earth" (Gen. 22:18). The meaning of the text is that the time has come through Jesus Christ when the blessings of the covenant will burst forth upon all nations (for this is the significance of the Pentecost narrative). In Acts 7 Stephen takes up the great prophetic theme of the unfaithfulness of the Israelites to the covenant of God. In v. 8 the expression "covenant of circumcision" (Gen. 17:10; 21:4), current in contemporary Jewish circles, reminds us that in the various O.T. narratives of the covenant of God with Israel "memorials" or witnesses of that event are always set up before the people (rainbow, altars, ceremonies of worship, popular festivals, circumcision, etc.). This aspect of these texts is too often neglected. It underlines first of all that the covenant always risks being forgotten or neglected by the people and that it must therefore be regularly and solemnly recalled to them; but chiefly it shows that the covenant, although founded upon an initial unique event, is renewed—from year to year and from generation to generation; hence the decisive importance of the ceremonies of the covenant in the O.T. which alone can make comprehensible the words of Jesus at His last meal with His disciples. But the great temptation of the people of God (denounced by the prophets and by Stephen in Acts 7) was of attaching themselves so much to the title-deeds and ceremonies of the covenant (festivals, cult, circumcision) that they neglected the covenant itself and its demands for faithfulness and justice.

2. In the Pauline Epistles, Gal. 3:15ff. gives us our term in its Greek legal sense of will and *testament* (as Heb. 9:16,17). The verbs which the apostle uses here (annul, append) show clearly that he is using a comparison borrowed from the Greek law of his time and not from the vocabulary of the Septuagint. The point of the text bears upon the idea of the definitive validity of a testament drawn up in the proper manner: the comparison must not here be pressed so that considerations about the death of the testator or the age of the beneficiaries enter in (cf. Gal. 4:1–7). In other words, the covenant of God concluded with Abraham is here compared (and not identified) with a will which nothing afterwards can annul or modify. The most important theological note in this passage is that the covenant, in its essence and its historical origin, was a promise of God to Abraham (and through him to all humanity). If therefore God has made a covenant with man it is not in the first instance in order to impose upon him His law (added long after, and provisionally, in the history of salvation), nor is it to make him immediately (=without mediator) a recipient of salvation, but to "promise" him the salvation now accomplished in Jesus Christ. In the other Pauline or deutero-Pauline texts (we reserve for the moment 1 Cor. 11:25) the thought flows directly from the O.T.:

(a) It is interesting to notice in Rom. 9:4 that "the covenants" (an allusion to the various covenants mentioned in the O.T.; some important manuscripts give the singular: the covenant) belong to a group of "privileges", or rather of favours, given by God to Israel. These privileges are most diverse: adoption, glory, covenants, law, worship, promises. According to Paul the Jews are still the recipients of these things, and his distress (vv. 2–3) is that they now risk being dispossessed by their rejection of Jesus Christ. This text takes its full significance by its opposition to the situation of pagans, "strangers to the covenants", described in Eph. 2:12.

(b) In Rom. 11:27 the apostle quotes Isa. 59:20–21 (Jer. 31:33–34), not to apply it to the redemptive work of Christ but to the last day, when, the pagans having been converted, God will in the end "obliterate" the sins of the Jews. In conformity with the most profound intuition of the O.T. the definitive covenant of God with man is here conceived as a remission of sins: the idea of a bipartite contract gives place to that of a free and sovereign gift of God to sinful man. The thought of the apostle is doubtless that this ultimate covenant of grace has become an historic possibility since the sacrifice of Jesus Christ.

(c) It appears from 2 Cor. 3:14 and Gal. 4:24 that the Jews have not understood the free gift of the covenant described in the O.T.: they have made from a covenant of grace (depicted by Sarah) a covenant of bondage (depicted by Hagar, Gal. 4:21–31); they have been perniciously drawn towards bondage and legalistic presumptions. A "veil" (2 Cor. 3:14) has ever since hung for them over their entire spiritual destiny and has distorted even their understanding of the *Scriptures, the document of the freely bestowed covenant. To deliver them from this, according to the apostle Paul, nothing less than their conversion to Jesus Christ is needed, in whom alone the saving import of the O.T. is revealed (vv. 16–18).

3. We may now consider the declaration of Jesus during His last supper with the disciples (*Lord's Supper: Mk. 14:24; Matt.

26:28; Lk. 22:20; 1 Cor. 11:25). Without entering into a detailed analysis of the text we can notice:

(a) The text preserved by Paul (1 Cor. 11:25) seems to be the most ancient, both in form and content. Mark, followed by Matthew, gives the words "poured out for many", probably an allusion to Isa. 53:12 (the same expression Mk. 10:45). Only Luke and Paul speak of a "new" covenant (certainly an echo of Jer. 31:31-34; cf. also Exod. 24:8; Zech. 9:11).

(b) According to Lk. 22:29,37 the one who speaks here is the suffering servant of Isaiah (42:6; 49:8). It is because of his obedience "unto death" (Phil. 2:5-11) that he has received the power to bring men into the Kingdom of God and to seal a new covenant between God and men.

(c) The act of Jesus in breaking the bread and handing the cup must therefore be understood as an interpretation of His sacrifice upon the cross: His blood poured out (i.e. His death) is the blood of the new covenant (Exod. 24:3-8) instituted by God for the salvation of men. As in the Old Testament, it is a covenant completed in a single act (the *cross) and given form in a "ceremony" intended for its continuous recall among God's people.

(d) In the Gospel texts Jesus appears to arrange to meet His disciples in the imminent Kingdom of God (Mk. 14:25; Matt. 26:29 adds "with you"). In the Pauline text it is rather a ceremony which is repeated and which "proclaims" the return of Jesus Christ, gathering the Christians together with this expectation. In both cases the new covenant meal has this two-fold implication of being founded upon the unique sacrifice of Jesus Christ and of being the temporary act of a people who await another *meal: the Messianic banquet in the finally established Kingdom.

(e) In the expression "new covenant" (1 Cor. 11:25; 2 Cor. 3:6; Heb. 8:13; 9:15; cf. Jer. 31:31), the adjective new means that Jesus fulfils the Old Testament covenants which, by that very fact, receive their precise meaning although limited in time. It also signifies that the covenant sealed by Jesus

Christ already participates in the Kingdom of God where all things will be made new.

4. In Heb. 9:16f., as in Gal. 3:15, it is a matter of will and testament in the legal Greek sense. Here the point of the comparison is no longer the ultimate validity of the will but the death of the testator. It is clearly seen in the text that the blood sprinkled in the rites of the old covenant (Exod. 24:3-8; Num. 19:4ff.; Lev. 14:5) must be understood in the sense of death because "without the shedding of blood there is no forgiveness of sins" (v. 22=without a substitutionary death). For the rest, the thought of this Epistle is completely summarized in 7:22, "Jesus is . . . the surety of a better covenant" (superior in the sense of having a greater efficacy and being more fundamental for reconciling man to God). It is this superiority which the Epistle establishes throughout its argument. The "new" covenant (8:13; 9:15) is not superior in itself but because of the decisive superiority and the ultimate sufficiency of the work of its "surety", Jesus Christ. But Hebrews also uses the converse argument: it establishes the superiority of Jesus Christ by the superiority of the "promises" of which He is "mediator" (8:6). Here, more clearly than anywhere else in the New Testament, we are in the presence of a functional Christology: the person of Christ is defined by the work which He came to accomplish. Finally, basing itself like Paul and like the Gospels on the prophecy of Jer. 31:31ff., Hebrews insists on the obsolete character of the first covenant (8:13, "what is becoming obsolete is ready to vanish away"), obsolete, not because of intrinsic imperfection but because of the new work of Christ: the first covenant is simply "old", superseded by new happenings. The cultic offering for sins is therefore now cancelled by the remission accomplished in Jesus Christ (10:18; 9:15,16; 10:29), so the covenant of which Jesus Christ is the mediator can be called "eternal" (13:20).

P. BONNARD

COVET

1. The Bible does not look at man from a naturalistic point of view in which all desires and passions are considered lawful, but rather views man from the standpoint of the revealed will of God. Indeed, in the O.T. the purport of the tenth commandment is to show that sin is not to be found in actions only, but in the heart and will of man.

2. The tenth commandment (Exod. 20:17; Deut. 5:21) lists the objects of covetousness: wife, servants and cattle belonging to the neighbour. Sexual covetousness plays an important part (Gen. 39:7; 2 Sam. 11:2; Job 31:1,7; Prov. 6:25; Matt. 5:28; Rom. 1:24); alongside this, the coveting of property (Mic. 2:2), of silver and of gold (Acts 20:33). The seat of covetousness is the heart (Rom. 1:24), the body (Rom. 6:12), the flesh (Rom. 13:14; Eph. 2:3; 1 Pet. 2:11; 2 Pet. 2:18; 1 Jn. 2:16), the eyes (Gen. 3:6; Job 31:1; 1 Jn. 2:16) and the soul (Rev. 18:14). It must be added that it is not the eye only but the whole man that is guilty (Mk. 9:47).

3. The fault lies not in the objects which are coveted; it lies in the man who covets. "What comes out of a man is what defiles a man" (Mk. 7:20-23). Covetousness shows that *man is "flesh", that he does not love God with all his heart and with all his strength (Deut. 6:5; Matt. 22:37), but pursues his own will in opposition to God. The law, having for its aim to make this nature of man apparent, can be summed up in its prohibition of covetousness (Rom. 7:7); to yield to covetousness implies living as do the pagans (1 Pet. 4:2; Eph. 4:17), after the manner of the world (Tit. 2:12; 1 Jn. 2:16). References to covetousness colour the opposition body-spirit (Eph. 2:3; Rom. 8; Gal. 5–6) and the enmity between earthly and spiritual things (Phil. 3:18-20; Col. 3:1-8).

4. Covetousness does not come from God (Jas. 1:13-15), but it dwells in everyone as a corrupting and enslaving power (Eph. 4:22; Tit. 3:3); it comes from the "world"

and drags those who harbour it into destruction with the world (1 Jn. 2:15-17). The man who yields to it is engulfed in death (Jas. 1:15).

5. Covetousness is a sign of discontent and rebellion (Jas. 4:1-4). Believers are called to be content with what God gives them (Phil. 4:11-13; Heb. 13:5f.), making their wants and necessities known to God in trust (Heb. 13:5; Matt. 6:25-34; Phil. 4:6f.; 1 Pet. 5:7). Reinstated in the love of God and of their neighbours (Rom. 13:9f.), they are set free from covetousness as from all other sins, by the Holy Spirit whom Christ causes to dwell in them. But this deliverance remains linked to faith and to the effort required to keep faith intact. Hence the exhortations of the apostles to their readers not to live as they lived formerly (Eph. 2:3; 4–5; Gal. 5:16,24f.; 1 Pet. 1:14f.; 4:1-4), but to live as the redeemed (1 Cor. 6:20) and as children of the light (Eph. 5:8).

F. BAUDRAZ

CREATION

All the peoples of the lands around Israel —Sumer, Babylon and Egypt—possessed traditions concerning the creation of the world. These accounts of the beginnings of existence had a religious character. In Babylon, the great epic *Enuma Elish* was solemnly recited at the New Year Festival. One of the outstanding features of these cosmogonies is their mythological aspect. The various parts of the world, sea, sky and earth are represented as so many divinities engaged in a life and death struggle, out of which emerges the created world. Although living in an environment where the creation myths played an important part, Israel did not take them over wholesale. If the O.T. has retained certain vestiges of the old myths, they are sporadic and stereotyped. In combat Yahweh overthrew the dragon who in the creation stories represents the great ocean, the abyss, and is called Rahab, Leviathan or the dragon (Ps. 74:12-17; 89:9-12; Job 26:12-14; Isa. 27:1; 51:9), before He created the world. Elsewhere it is the ocean itself which was brought under the dominion of Yahweh (Job 38:8; Prov. 8:29; Jer. 5:22; Hab. 3:9; Ps. 18:15; 33:7; 65:7; 104:5-9).

The Bible contains two accounts of the creation of different origin and of different date: (A) Gen. 1:2-2:3 and (B) Gen. 2:4-17. The differences between them are important, relating not only to the order of the events of creation but to more fundamental matters. At the time of the creation, the world was depicted in (A) as an ocean without shore, wrapped in darkness, a chaos in which earth, water and night were commingled, whereas in (B) it is described as a dry, arid wilderness. Both accounts presuppose, as indeed does the whole of the Bible, a view of the world entirely different from the modern view, but which was very widespread in antiquity. The most striking factor in account (A) is the complete absence of mythological features. The elements have lost the personality which they possessed in the old myths. They are no longer gods but things. This account with its carefully weighed phrases reads like a confession of faith. There is no attempt to answer the question whether God made the world out of nothing (ex nihilo), for such an idea would have been foreign to the Semitic mind. The word used to describe the process of creation, the Hebrew bara', leads us to no definite conclusion on this matter. At the moment when God intervened, the world was a mass of water and land in which no life was possible. When God exerted His creative ability, He made life in the world possible.

Considered from this point of view, the different phases of creation as well as the purpose which lay behind them fall into a clear pattern: to make life possible in a place where previously it did not exist. Verse 2 describes the state of chaos which existed on the first day: a vast ocean covered an earth plunged into total darkness. There exists some doubt about the identity of the Spirit of God which, according to the same verse, hovered above the surface of the waters, for the original text could support the translation: "a mighty wind was blowing over the surface of the waters". Vv. 3-5:

creation of light, the prelude of life. Vv. 6-8: as the world was conceived as a vast accumulation of water, the author represents God as fashioning the firmament or sky in the form of a solid vault which holds up the upper or celestial ocean. Vv. 11-13: the appearance of vegetable life. Vv. 14-19: creation of the great luminaries, sun, moon and stars. Attention has been drawn to the fact that light itself was created before the heavenly bodies, and that the most important of these, the sun and the moon, were not indicated by their names, but merely called "lights". In this deliberate "degradation" of the heavenly bodies, which at Babylon were deified, the writer reveals his very clear intention. Vv. 20-23: the earth produces the birds and fish, as though they belonged to the same species. God blesses them; that is, He gives them power to reproduce themselves and to multiply. Vv. 24-25: the earth brings forth the animals. Vv. 26-28: God Himself intervenes in person to make man, the crown of creation, the creature for whose benefit all that has gone before was created.

It is impressive that, at this point, the author discards the third person which he has been using: "Let there be light . . .", in favour of the first person plural: "Let us make man." The question arises whether the God of Gen. 1 was, as in Isa. 6:8, surrounded by a court of divine, celestial beings. "Let us make man in our image" could, it is claimed, mean: let us make him in the image of one of the divine beings who surround the throne of God. This conclusion seems to me forced. When the author used the first person plural, he did so in order to insist that, in the case of man, the lord of creation, God resolved to make a personal intervention. This *image, this likeness (in Hebrew selem and demût) has for centuries been a topic for debate among theologians. This is understandable, for beneath these words is hidden the mystery of the emergence of *man and of his relationship to his creator. The meaning is, however, clear, for the words used here always mean in the Bible an external, physical appearance. Man is created in the image of God. His external guise is that of his creator. God blesses him and gives him the power of procreation. Vv. 29–30: plants and fruits are allotted to man for food, while the animals have the grass for their use. V. 31: on the evening of the sixth day God surveys His handiwork and finds it perfect, "and behold it was very good."

It is the theocentric character of this passage which must be stressed: nothing comes to pass except through God. It is on Him, or rather on His creative word, that this life rests. He alone made the earth habitable and life possible. If He were to withdraw His word, there would ensue the return of darkness, of the destroying waters and of death. The sight of the waves of the sea lashing the shore but seemingly held in check by an invisible force, the sight of the sky supporting the celestial waters, serve to remind man of what might happen if God withdrew His word, just as the oncoming of night reminds him of the primeval darkness. At the very peak of this divine work, a visible reflection of the creator, lord of the world of grace, of light and of life, stands created man.

The second account (B) takes us into an arid desert, from which all life is banished, an expanse of scorched clay. Suddenly a stream of water issues from the earth to irrigate the surface of the ground. From the moist clay Yahweh, like a potter, fashions a figure. He breathes into its nostrils and it becomes a living being. Then follows the story of the garden of God, planted with trees, the formation of the animals, the creation of woman made from one of man's ribs. This account, older than the one which precedes it, reveals a less systematic character and presupposes a totally different world-view.

Although these accounts were, at a relatively recent date, placed at the beginning of the Bible, we find very little echo of them in the rest of the O.T. Ezekiel is familiar with the Eden myth, but in quite a different context (Ezek. 28:13). Their significance is to be seen not so much in the view of the *world which lies behind them and which is peculiar to their own age—with the earth thought of as being rather like a disc resting on pillars with the sky like a solid vault held up by the mountains and in turn supporting the upper ocean—as in the religious attitude to which they bear witness and which still holds teaching and example for modern man.

According to the Bible, the world and man did not succeed in keeping the perfection which they possessed at the time of their creation. This perfection was impaired by a mysterious happening which is vividly described in Genesis 3. It is difficult to assess the place occupied by the event of creation in the Israelite cult. If it seems improbable that it played as important a part as it did for instance in Babylon, the numerous allusions to the creation which we find in the Psalms do indicate that in the cult God was also extolled as creator. When we speak of creation, we always think of an event in the past, of an act accomplished and effected once and for all. In the O.T., on the contrary, the created world, which is the world of life, is constantly threatened by the powers of death. God has constantly to intervene to repel them. He sees to it that the floods of chaos do not overflow the bounds which He has appointed for them (Jer. 5:22; Prov. 8:29). After the vengeance exacted by the powers which are hostile to life at the time of the Flood, God ensured the stability of the world and of life and the regular sequence of the seasons (Gen. 8:22; Ps. 74:16f.; Jer. 31:35). God sustains the world in justice, that is to say that He maintains its character as a world where life is possible (Joel 2:23; Ps. 148:6).

The God of the Bible is continually worshipped as Creator God. These declarations are intended not so much to remind worshippers of the origin of things as to magnify the power and the wisdom of God (Ps. 93:1; 96:5,10; 102:25; Isa. 40:21), His power and wisdom constantly operative. It is to Him that the universe belongs. He has power over nature and can use this power to carry out His plans (Ps. 24:1; 65:10; 78:26; Isa. 40:26; 44:24; 45:12,18; Job 9:4). He looks after the world which He has created (Ps. 104). As creator, He is the one who is mighty to help (Ps. 146:5; Isa. 45:9). The purpose of the biblical allusions to creation is not to recall what happened in the very beginning. The biblical idea of creation is not a theoretical question, but something which vitally affects man's very existence. If the biblical writers refer again and again to the activity of the creator, it is in order to emphasize His power and the corollary of this power, the littleness of man and his dependence on God (Ps. 33:8; 103:14; Job 10:9; 33:6; Ps. 139:13–16). When speaking of the creative ability of God, the Bible deliberately uses a present participle, which gives to this work a permanent quality: Isa. 44:24: "I am Yahweh who *make* all things, who alone stretch out the heavens, who spread out the earth—who is with me?" This implies that creation is a permanent act of God, as is also His redemption of Israel. It might be interpreted by saying: in the past, in the present and in the future, I am and I remain the creator. It is upon me that the stability and the solidity of the world are based. The God who made the world can also destroy it. In numerous passages the end of the world is described (Jer. 4:23–26), an event which is equally a manifestation of the Creator's power. In the book of Proverbs, He is assisted in His work by *Wisdom (Prov. 8:22–31).

The teaching of the O.T. on the subject of creation is extremely rich. If it has its roots in ideas which to-day are outdated, it affirms this truth of vital importance to us all—that the world exists only through God, that without Him there would be no life— that His relations with the world and with created beings are those of a creator with his creatures, relations of absolute dependence. His power over the world and over life remains unimpaired, that is to say that the life of men derives solely from the grace of Him who has created the world and who maintains its life simply because that is His will.

G. PIDOUX

CROSS

The Romans probably took over from the Carthaginians the practice of crucifixion, which was a penalty of oriental origin. At first confined to slaves, its use was later applied to condemned criminals from the provinces. The cross, which was most often T-shaped, was of a height just sufficient to enable the condemned man's feet to clear the ground, his hands being fixed to the transverse beam (*patibulum*) by means of ropes or nails. The interest which the N.T. writers take in the cross is neither archaeological nor historical, but Christological. When they speak of the cross, it is always of the cross of Jesus, the Christ, the Son of God.

1. *The cross of Jesus Christ.* In the synoptic Gospels, the announcement of the Passion (Mk. 8:31; 9:31; 10:32 and parallel passages) connects the death of Christ with the divine purpose which willed that the Messiah, delivered by the leaders of Israel to the Gentiles, should die, not by the Jewish penalty of stoning, but by the Roman penalty of the cross (Matt. 20:19). As the accusation seemed to him to be groundless, Pilate would have been willing to release Jesus, but the populace, stirred up by the chief priests, demanded the death of Jesus with their shouts of "Crucify him" (Mk. 5:13f. and parallels). Pilate, having tried in vain to secure acceptance for his own will, sent Jesus to the cross, after first having Him flogged in his presence (Mk. 15:15). We are informed that Jesus, worn out by this torture, was incapable of carrying His own cross (the *patibulum*) as was customary, and that a passer-by, Simon of Cyrene, had to be requisitioned to carry it for him (Mk. 15:21 and parallel passages). On this point John corrects the synoptic tradition by asserting that Jesus Himself carried His cross (19:17), perhaps because he could not harmonize the very human weakness which the synoptic tradition acknowledged, with the sovereign majesty with which Christ is invested in his Gospel. The full horror of the nailing of Jesus to the cross and its erection on Golgotha (Mk. 15:22 and parallels) is expressed in these simple words: "and they crucified him" (Mk. 15:24 and parallels). On either side of Him were

3*

crucified two thieves, who were probably not so much common offenders against the civil law as terrorists of whom the occupying power was striving to purge the land (Mk. 15:27 and parallels). He whom the inscription affixed to the cross (*titulus*) described as "the king of the Jews" (Mk. 15:26; Matt. 27:37; Jn. 19:19), died thus between two zealots, advocates of the direct action which He had always repudiated. Those who stood by watching mockingly urged the king of Israel to come down from the cross so that they might believe in him (Mk. 15:29ff.; Matt. 27:39ff.) and poured derision on the crucified Messiah, the Saviour who could not save Himself, adding the last touch to His shame. According to John (19:25), Mary, the mother of Jesus, was near to the cross with the disciple whom Jesus loved, and Jesus, before His death, committed them to each other's care. Also according to the fourth evangelist, the death of Jesus synchronized with the day and hour when the paschal lambs were slain; the Jews asked Pilate that the bodies of the men crucified on Calvary should not remain hanging on their crosses lest the land should be defiled by their presence on a sabbath day which was a high feast day (Jn. 19:31; Deut. 21:23).

If the Gospel accounts of the Passion raise for the historian a great number of delicate problems, the fact of the death of Jesus on the cross may be regarded as having been historically established. By the words: "He suffered under Pontius Pilate", the Creed adduces the historical character of the revelation of God in Jesus Christ to confound every attempt to transform the Gospel into a timeless gnosis.

2. *Human reactions to the cross of Jesus Christ.* Apart from the Gospels, the words cross and crucify are found only in the Pauline letters and in Acts 2:36; 4:10; Heb. 6:6; 12:2 and Rev. 11:8, the book of Acts and the Epistle to the Hebrews having some links with the apostle Paul. Why does the cross occupy such a predominant place in the thought of the apostle? Driven to give a summary answer, we should say:

because Paul came violently up against the cross of Jesus before he recognized it as the cross of Christ, the act by which God had reconciled the world to Himself (2 Cor. 5:19). How could he have come to believe that Jesus of Nazareth, delivered by the Sanhedrin to Pilate, a crucified felon smitten by the curse of God (Gal. 3:13), was the Christ, the Messiah of Israel? To convince him that Jesus was the Christ it needed the cataclysmic revelation on the Damascus road, a vision of the crucified and risen Christ (Gal. 1:16). From that moment he was quite certain that Jesus was the Christ, a certainty which came to him not despite the cross but because of it. This complete reversal of Paul's judgment concerning Jesus Christ crucified dominates all his thought.

The crucified Christ is at the very heart of the Gospel and by this Word of the cross (1 Cor. 1:18; 23; 2:2) God passes judgment on every claim made by man to be the master of his destiny and to gain his salvation by his own efforts. To believe, the Jews demand miracles (1 Cor. 1:22); they ask that God Himself should make clearly known the identity of His Anointed. And the Gospels proclaim Jesus, the crucified Messiah! The Jews see in Him only weakness, defeat, condemnation and curse, the *stumbling-block (1 Cor. 1:23) which flings them back into unbelief. What could be more opposed to all that the Jews believed than having to admit that the people of God had delivered their Messiah to the heathen to be crucified, that the observance of the law had led them to this sin of sins, and that all they had to do was to believe in the crucified Christ and to trust in God's grace alone! So the cross of Christ stands between Church and Synagogue, and the error of the Judaizers was that they failed to understand this. They wanted to enforce *circumcision and the observance of the Mosaic law upon believers who had come over from paganism "in order that they may not be persecuted for the cross of Christ", said St. Paul with vehemence (Gal. 6:12). For to have preached the necessity of circumcision would have been completely to disarm the hostility of the Jews, but it would have meant making light of the judgment which the cross passes on all self-righteousness, blunting the sharp edge of the Gospel, and reducing to a mere shadow the scandal of the cross (Gal. 5:11). Paul would never for a moment consent to that. Of themselves, the Greeks are no more enthusiastic than the Jews in their reception of the preaching of the crucified Christ. "They seek wisdom" (1 Cor. 1:22). Before they can believe they must understand.

The only teaching they can accept as true is that which harmonizes with their conception of the world and which satisfies their reason and their sense of proportion. So they turn in scorn and mockery from the idea of a crucified Christ, which they term "folly"! (1 Cor. 1:24). The cross confuses them and they cannot regard it seriously without abandoning all the values which add worth to their existence.

So only those on whom God bestows faith, "those who are called" (1 Cor. 1:24) have real insight into the paradoxical meaning of the cross, of this folly which is the very wisdom of God and of this weakness which is the very power of God (1 Cor. 1:24f.). For in Christ the weakness of man and the power of God have met: "For he was crucified in weakness but lives by the power of God" (2 Cor. 13:4). He was crucified when God delivered Him helpless unto death, but He lives by the power of God who raised Him up and made Him to be alive for evermore. Since the cross is the method by which it pleased God to reveal His power for the salvation of the world, any recourse which the preacher of the crucified Christ might have to the arguments of human wisdom or to the prestige of eloquence would strip the cross of its divine efficacy (1 Cor. 1:17).

3. *The meaning of the cross of Jesus Christ.* (*a*) To speak of the meaning of the cross of Christ is really to speak of the meaning of His *death. We must content ourselves here with marshalling the evidence of the texts which mention the cross. The N.T. focuses attention not on the physical sufferings which Jesus underwent on the cross, but on the shame and degradation which accompanied His agony. For the Greeks and Romans it was the ignominious death of a criminal slave and not to be spoken of by decent people; for the Jews the death endured "outside the gate" (Heb. 13:12) proclaimed the curse of God upon a criminal condemned and cut off from His people (Gal. 3:13). When He endured the cross, it was this shame that Christ despised (Heb. 12:2), revealing thus the full measure of His obedience (Phil. 2:6–8).

(*b*) In 1 Cor. 2:8 St. Paul sets the cross in a cosmic significance. The wisdom of God, of which he speaks here, is revealed in the plan of redemption in which the death of Christ is the decisive event and the fulfilment of which will bring believers to *glory (1 Cor. 2:7; Rom. 8:17ff.,20,30), the divine life in all its fullness. The rulers of this age are the angelic powers (Eph. 1:21; Col. 1:16; etc. *Authorities) to whom God has entrusted the government of this sinful world and who guarantee to the world a certain social and moral law based on religious beliefs, laws and authorities. That is why behind the Sanhedrin and Pilate, guardians of this world order, Paul discerns the action of the rulers of this world and declares that "if they had understood the wisdom of God, they would not have crucified the Lord of Glory" (1 Cor. 2:8). They would have taken great care not to have a hand in the redemptive death of the Lord Jesus which was to put an end to their rule by bringing men under the immediate authority of God in Jesus Christ through the Holy Spirit.

(*c*) The effect of the cross of Christ is described in a similar way in Col. 2:14f., where we are told that God has pardoned our sins "having cancelled the bond which stood against us . . . this he set aside, nailing it to the cross." We now no longer confront God as bankrupt debtors, since He has of His own free will annulled the bond which He held against us and through the cross has proclaimed the cancellation of our debt. This pardon has had a cosmic repercussion, for in allowing us to draw near to Him openly and directly, God has, by the same act, repudiated the angelic powers who were guardians of the order of the sinful world, He has made a public spectacle of them, triumphing over them through the cross (2:15). Men in quest of salvation no longer have anything to expect from them. According to Col. 1:20, all creatures on earth and in heaven—men and the angelic powers— have been reconciled to the Son, and through Him to God, because He has made peace by the blood of the cross. Universal reconciliation is attributed here to the blood of the cross, by which must be understood the life given by Christ on the cross, without reference to any particular theory of redemption. In Eph. 2:16 we see a particular application of this idea. By abolishing the law (v. 15a), the cause of the hostility which divided Jew and Gentile (v. 14), by bringing to each the same grace, Christ has reconciled both to God and has united them in one body by the cross. Christ is thus the peace of Gentiles and of Jews reconciled to God and united in the Church which is His body.

4. *The cross in the life of the believer.* (*a*) Jesus declared that he who would be His disciple must deny himself and take up his cross (Mk. 8:34 and parallel passages); he must take (Matt. 10:38) or bear (Lk. 14:27) his cross, as the Master had done during the whole of His ministry and as He did when He ascended Calvary. No one denies himself unless, out of loyalty to Jesus, he accepts death in advance, even the most ignominious death. The measures taken by the Romans to repress continual plots had made the cross familiar enough to the inhabitants of Palestine for Jesus to speak about it before having Himself experienced it.

(*b*) The Judaizers who, according to St. Paul, were seeking to persuade the Galatians to be circumcised in order to avoid persecution for the sake of the cross of Christ (Gal. 6:12) had shown themselves unwilling to bear their cross. But as for the apostle, he would glory in nothing "except in the cross of our Lord Jesus Christ, by whom the

world has been crucified to me and I to the world" (6:14). Far from being ashamed of it, it is in the cross alone that he glories, for it is by its power that he has become a new creature (6:15). Judged by the cross of Christ, the world with its wisdom and its righteousness has ceased to count for Paul, just as he ceased to count for the world from the day when he accepted the judgment of the cross in order to receive the righteousness of God and to know His wisdom.

(*c*) The case of the Judaizers is a warning: consciously or unconsciously Christians may reject the cross of Christ and thus deprive the Gospel of its true character and its efficacy. Paul speaks with tears of alleged Christians who are the enemies of the cross of Christ, whose end is destruction, whose god is their belly, who glory in their shame, who set their minds on earthly things (Phil. 3:18f.). Most commentators see here a further description of the Judaizers as in Phil. 3:2, but the features in their conduct which Paul stigmatizes are obviously more applicable to people who imagine that they can reconcile the sensual habits of the old life with their Christian faith. Heb. 6:6 affirms that it is impossible to bring back to repentance those who, after having known the grace of Christ, have fallen again into sin and by their apostasy "crucify the Son of God on their own account and hold him up to contempt". If you crucify Him who was crucified for you, you commit the sin for which there is no hope of pardon, the sin which transforms the very work of grace into condemnation.

(*d*) The vision of the dead Christ on the cross ceaselessly reminds Christians of the source from which their new life springs and of the standards of conduct which are the sign of that new life. That the Galatians before whose very eyes "Jesus Christ was publicly portrayed as crucified" (Gal. 3:1) should so far disregard these standards as to be willing to accept circumcision was proof to Paul that they had been bewitched by some malign influence. Faith in Christ crucified involves for believers a radical break with the law, with sin, with the flesh. Those who belong to Christ "have crucified the flesh with its passions and desires" (Gal. 5:24), for *baptism was for them the sign of their participation in the death of Christ (Rom. 6:3). Our old man—that which we are by birth in distinction to the new man which we are in Christ—has been crucified with Christ (Rom. 6:6); we ought then to live—and we can live—a new life in obedience to the Spirit (Gal. 5:25). All the ethical exhortations of Paul are based on this fact, and he sets before the Church the paradox of this life which has death as its prerequisite: "I have been crucified with Christ; it is no longer I who live, but Christ who lives in me" (Gal. 2:20).

CH. MASSON

CUP

The O.T. employs a number of substantives to denote, according to its shape or size, this utensil of Egyptian or Phoenician origin, from which rich and poor alike drink. Cups were used also in the Temple for the offerings and libations (1 Chr. 28:17). The most precious were of silver (Gen. 44:2) or of gold (1 Kings 10:21); the brim was ornamented with lilies (1 Kings 7:26). The cups mentioned in the N.T. were in the form of the Graeco-Roman patera, widemouthed and shallow.

In the course of secular feasts (Gen. 40:13; Mk. 7:4) each one had his own private cup from which he drank and sometimes got drunk. As a sign of welcome, the host offered a cup of wine to each guest. To drink from anyone's cup is a sign of great intimacy (2 Sam. 12:3).

These customs lie behind the symbolic meanings which the word assumes in Scripture:

1. *The cup of thanksgiving*, literally the "cup of deliverances" (Ps. 116:13): this symbolic expression refers to the festal meal at which a cup of wine was offered to God as a token of gratitude for past deliverances (Ps. 116:17). The Passover ritual, in particular, included four successive cups which were elevated as a thank-offering (cf. Lk. 22:17,20). The elevation of the cup retains, in the celebration of the Lord's Supper, this eucharistic value: it is the *cup of blessing*, that is to say, the cup by means of which we give thanks to God (Matt. 26:27; 1 Cor. 10:16) (*Lord's Supper).

2. *The cup of consolation* (Jer. 16:7) is an allusion to the cup of wine which was offered during a funeral feast to the bereaved relatives. In this connection the idea refers principally to *wine which is a symbol of joy.

3. *The cup of destiny:* As in the literature of other oriental peoples, the cup symbolizes in the Bible, and especially in the Psalms, the earthly destiny of man. This usage arises from the idea that man receives his lot from the hand of God just as a guest receives the cup from his host. The cup of wine is a symbol of the happy destiny of the man on whom God showers His blessings (Ps. 16:5 23:5). The reverse is that the punishment and death reserved for evil-doers are represented as a cup of fire and brimstone (Ps. 11:6), of desolation and ruin (Ezek. 23:33): a bitter cup which must be drained to the very dregs (Ps. 75:8).

The prophets made frequent use of this symbolism to proclaim the wrath and judgments of God; they built up from it a rhetorical figure: God Himself fills a cup with His anger; this cup God hands, or charges the prophet to hand, to all who revolt against Him, Israel and Judah (Isa. 51:17; Ezek. 23:31ff.) as well as to the heathen (Jer. 25:15ff.); of this cup they must drink until they stagger and fall. With the cup here is linked the idea of intoxication and falling. The people whom God uses to execute His wrath are themselves compared to a cup (Jer. 51:7; Zech. 12:2). Through the prophets this image entered into the general biblical language (Hab. 2:16; Ps. 75:8) and it is this image which the author of "Revelation" uses to describe the *anger of God (14:10; 16:19; 18:6).

It is in a similar vein that Jesus, in alluding to His death, speaks of a cup which He must drink (Matt. 20:22f.; Jn. 18:11) and that in Gethsemane He prays to the Father to spare Him by removing this cup from Him (Matt. 26:39,42). This word is not simply a synonym for death: it suggests that God Himself has decided upon the death of His Son and is handing to Him the cup as His true destiny, asking Him to drink it of His own free will.

4. *The cup of communion:* when it circulates among the guests, as happened in certain religious festivals, the cup becomes a token which binds together those who share a common meal (1 Cor. 10:21). It is not certain that this common cup, a sign of a sharing in gratitude and expectation, was a familiar feature in the Jewish Passover ritual. But when He institutes the Lord's Supper, Jesus distributes to His apostles the cup of His sacrifice (*Blood) to bring home to them the fact that, from that moment, they are sharing in the destiny of the Messiah, at present humiliated but soon to be glorified. The cup of the Lord's Supper is, then, the seal given to believers of the share they have in the sacrifice of Christ (1 Cor. 10:16) and in His glory in the Kingdom (Lk. 22:28–30) .

S. AMSLER

CURSE

1. The curse is *a word by which God caused misery and death to fall upon man or upon things, because of sin.* The serpent is cursed (Gen. 3:14), or the ground (Gen. 3:17; 5:29), or Cain (Gen. 4:11). On the lips of a man it calls the judgment of God upon an enemy (Num. 22:6; 23:8; 2 Kings 2:24; Lam. 3:65). When directed against God Himself (Lev. 24:11,15; Job. 2:9), it is the greatest sin of all and results in death: he who curses God is excluded from the covenant and from life. The same is the case with him who curses his parents, because it is through them that God has given him life (Exod. 21:17; Prov. 20:20; 30:11), or of him who curses the king, the earthly representative of the divine King (1 Kings 21:13; 2 Sam. 19:21).

2. It should be noted that the divine curse *is not on the same level with God's *blessing;*

it is its corollary, but it is not in the original intention of God. The curse is possible because there is blessing: it is the lot of those who reject blessing. Those who, on meeting Abraham, recognize in him one who carries grace will be blessed, but those who curse him, those who hate in him (or in his people) the divine act of election, will be cursed (Gen. 12:3; cf. 27:29). When God places His people before blessing and cursing (Deut. 11:26–28), He does not place them before two abstractly equal possibilities, between which they will make their choice—for Israel is blessed—but He causes them to know on what condition they will continue to be blessed: if they love God, keep His commandments, and turn from idols (Deut. 11:28; 30:15–18). The nation of Israel will be cursed if it is unfaithful to God who has elected it, precisely because He has elected it: its sin and its condemnation are proportionate to the grace which has been granted it. Likewise those cursed in the parable of the judgment (Matt. 25:41ff.) are not people eternally predestined to cursing, but those who, having encountered Christ in His brothers, the least ones, have refused to love Him in them.

3. *Christ became a curse for us* (Gal. 3:13). Throughout this chapter Paul shows the Galatians the folly of a return to the *law as a means of salvation. Not only is it impossible for us to become righteous through it, because in fact we are constantly breaking it, but above all because the very fact of entertaining this wish rests upon a total misconception of what is *righteousness before God: instead of receiving it (v. 11) one wishes to glorify oneself (cf. Lk. 18:11–12). By using the law as a means of salvation we place ourselves in opposition to God and fall into the curse. Christ has redeemed us by becoming a curse for us, by taking the place of the man who wished to save himself by the law and whom God has cursed. Thus he shows that this means of salvation is impracticable, and at the same time offers another, the true means: the suffering of the Son for sinners, the gift of grace received by faith.

4. Delivered from the curse by grace, *the believer has not the right to curse* (Lk. 6:28; Rom. 12:14; Matt. 5:44). To pronounce a curse, which excludes one's neighbour from grace, is a sort of last judgment pronounced against him. This is impossible for him who knows his own true situation before God and who himself lives by the grace which saves the one who is cursed.

CHR. SENFT

DARKNESS, see LIGHT

DAVID, see NAMES (PERSONAL), JESUS

DAY, see JUDGMENT, TIME

DEACON, see MINISTRY N.T.

DEATH

O.T.

1. The *covenant which God made with Abraham and his seed (cf. Gen. 12:1ff.) and which He renewed at Sinai (cf. Exod. 19ff.) demands the faith of Israel. This faith is national and communal before being individual and personal. Since the elect people can rely for ever on this covenant the death of members of their nation is not a particularly pressing problem: because of the covenant the permanence of the people is assured despite the ephemeral quality of its members (Ps. 103:15–18). Abraham is disturbed at the prospect of death so long as he has no posterity (Gen. 15:2f.; 17:17ff.; cf. Isa. 66:22); but once he is certain of continuing in his posterity (cf. also Deut. 25:6, and what is said, so frequently, of David and his posterity, e.g., Ps. 89:20–38), he dies "in a good old age, an old man and full of years" (Gen. 25:8). The father of the faithful by his quite simple and, one might say, quite natural death participates simply in the normal lot of men: he goes "the way of all the earth" (Josh. 23:14; 1 Kings 2:2). "We must all die, we are like water spilt on the ground, which cannot be gathered up again" (2 Sam. 14:14). The length of our life is no more than a hand-breadth (Ps. 39:5) and those who exceed seventy years are uncommonly strong!

(Ps. 90:10). The O.T. abounds with passages which speak of death with this calm moderation (cf. Job 7:7ff.; Gen. 25:17; 35:29; 49:33; 2 Sam. 7:12; 1 Kings 2:10; 11:21,43; 14:20, etc.).

2. The first territory which Abraham acquired in the land that God had promised him was a burial ground (Gen. 23:1–20; 25:9; 50:13): to bury one's dead is in fact an essential duty of piety and it could give rise to moving scenes (cf. 2 Sam. 21:7–14; 1 Kings 13:11–32). Not to be buried is the worst misfortune that can happen to a dead person (cf. 1 Kings 14:11; 16:4; 21:19ff.; 2 Kings 9:10,30–37; Ps. 79:1ff.): even a man condemned to death had the right of burial (Deut. 21:23). Israel, however, vigorously opposed the funeral rites of paganism (Lev. 19:28; Deut. 14:1ff.) together with attempts to communicate with those who have died (Lev. 19:31; 20:6,27; Deut. 18:11; 1 Sam. 28:1–25), but piously lamented her dead (cf., e.g., 2 Sam. 18:33ff., but also Ezek. 24:16ff.) during a more or less long period of mourning (Gen. 23:2; 50:10, etc.) which in exceptional cases was national in scope (Deut. 34:8; 1 Sam. 28:3). The beautiful lament composed by David after the death of Saul and Jonathan will be recalled (2 Sam. 1:17ff.). But—and this is a significant fact—there is no instance of these funeral ceremonies being accompanied by prayers or sacrifices for the repose of the dead. Though pyres might on occasion be erected, it was for putting living persons to death in the flames (Gen. 38:24; Lev. 21:9; Josh. 7:15). The only corpses which are said to have been burnt are those of men whom God had rejected from His covenant (Josh. 7:25; 1 Sam. 31:12; 1 Kings 13:2; 2 Kings 23:16,20; 2 Chr. 34:5; cf. 1 Kings 16:18): their burning seems to be an anticipation of eternal fire. To burn a corpse is not, in the Bible, a pious manner of rendering it the last respects: it is an abomination (cf. Amos 2:1), a way of getting rid of it (cf. Judg. 15:6).

3. Where do the dead go once they have been buried? They are gathered to their

fathers—whence the use of family tombs (Gen. 15:15; 47:30; Deut. 31:16, etc.)—they descend to the abode of the dead (Gen. 37:35), the meeting place of all the living (Job 30:23; cf. Ps. 89:48f.; Isa. 14:9ff.; Ezek. 32:21ff., etc.). The Israelite faith did not indulge in much speculation on this infernal and insatiable place (Prov. 30:16) which was situated in a dark cavern (Job 10:21) under the ocean (Job 26:5), and which was pictured with closed gates (Job 38:17; Isa. 38:10). In primitive times it was believed that those held there were there for ever (Job 7:9f.; 16:22), and that they were separated from God, incapable of serving or praising Him any further (Isa. 38:10ff.; Ps. 6:6; 30:10; 88:11–13; 115:17), denied His protection (Ps. 88:6): "Sheol cannot thank thee, death cannot praise thee; *those who go down to the pit cannot hope for thy faithfulness*" (Isa. 38:18). Seen in this perspective of exclusion from the grace and from the presence of God, death is no longer the serene fulfilment of a life full of years: it becomes something to be dreaded and a punishment (cf. Gen. 3:3,19), as though there were a general application to the entire populace of the penalty of death which cut off the transgressors of the law from the elect people, and thus from life (cf. Exod. 31:14; Lev. 20:2ff.,16,27; 24:16; Deut. 13:5ff.; 17:5; Josh. 7:25, etc.). Without doubt it is for this reason that death and the dead are unclean (cf. Num. 9:6; 19:16).

4. The question arises as to whether death should really be the final word for man. Without reaching a clear and univocal answer, or even a generally agreed answer, the O.T. declares what only the event of Easter will be able to complete and confirm. Within its limits, the O.T. revelation arouses inquiries, hopes, and certainties, in the following ways:

(a) We have already observed that in a general manner man could, at least partially, ward off death by perpetuating himself in his posterity, by transmitting his life to his children (*marriage): a son is a guarantee of endurance (cf. Gen. 29:32; 30:1; 19:30–37; Deut. 25:6, etc.).

(b) Over a long period eschatological hopes did not affirm an eternal life, but rather a protracted postponement of the onset of death (Isa. 65:20; cf. Zech. 8:4), and thus an ample duration of life as in the earliest times (cf. Gen. 5:5,25; 9:28, etc.).

(c) It is known also that God kept certain of His notable servants from death by taking them direct to Himself at the end of their life (cf. Gen. 5:21ff.; 2 Kings 2:5–13; cf. Deut. 34:5ff.).

(d) God is the defender of those who are His (Job 19:25ff.; Gen. 48:15f.; Ps. 119:154; Jer. 50:34, etc.) and their security (Ps. 16:9ff.): therefore He will not permit the tomb to devour them (Ps. 49:16) and His grace is strong enough to rescue them from all affliction, even that of death (cf. Ps. 73:23ff.). One can therefore enter into the experience of death knowing that God is able to manifest His presence there also (Ps. 139:8; Amos 9:2) and that He is powerful enough to rob death of its prey (cf. Isa. 53:8).

(e) This was to affirm that, by God's command, the abode of the dead would at last render up its prisoners (Isa. 26:9), who will be raised up like the bones of Ezekiel's vision (chap. 37), that it would spew them out as Jonah was spewed out by the great fish (Jon. 2:11). God, in fact, is the God who "kills and brings to life, who brings down to Sheol and raises up" (1 Sam. 2:6; cf. Hos. 6:2): He is stronger than death (Hos. 13:14). This faith, hesitant at first, is affirmed ever more confidently, and ends by proclaiming—in the most recent book of the O.T.—the resurrection of the dead for the last judgment (Dan. 12:2). It should be noted, however, that faith in the resurrection was never an article of Israelite orthodoxy and that it was possible to be a member of the people of God without holding it (*Jews): it was professed by the party of the Pharisees, but rejected by that of the Sadducees (cf. Acts 23:6ff.; Matt. 22:23ff.).

N.T.

1. What the O.T. was able only to set forth by certain sayings (cf. above) or

certain prophetic deeds (cf. 2 Kings 4:17–37; 13:21) the ministry, the death, and the resurrection of Jesus fulfilled and confirmed: death is vanquished! is the great message of the *Gospel (2 Tim. 1:10). That is why, for the N.T., faith in the *resurrection is no longer either optional or debatable as was the case under the old covenant: it is absolutely essential (cf. 1 Cor. 15:2, 12–19, 32, etc.). In other words, since the coming of Jesus Christ it is possible to speak of death only as conquered and impotent (1 Cor. 15:55): it is no longer master of itself, for Jesus has the key of death (Rev. 1:18). In the joy of this victory it is possible even to say that we no longer belong to death, but that it is ours (1 Cor. 3:22).

(a) This victory is manifested in the first place by the fact that at the coming of Jesus death was repelled by resurrection and *life: its threat has ceased to be oppressive (Lk. 1:78; Matt. 4:16), and in certain cases it has had to yield up its prize (cf. Lk. 7:11ff.; Matt. 9:18ff. and parallels; 11:5 and parallels; Jn. 11:1–46; cf. also Matt. 8:28ff. and parallels; 27:52f.). Likewise it is driven back before the servants of Jesus (Matt. 10:8; Acts 9:36–43; 20:7ff.; cf. 1 Cor. 11:30; Mk. 16:18).

(b) Such exploits are only the prelude or the echo of the victory which Jesus gained over death by dying Himself. This death is in fact our death, which He Himself bore: He died for us, that is to say, in our place (Mk. 14:24 and parallels; Rom. 5:6,8; 2 Cor. 5:14; 1 Thess. 5:10; 1 Pet. 3:18, etc.). This death of Jesus on the *cross for the sake of our *ransom and our *reconciliation with God should have come upon men in order to punish them for their sins (cf. 2 Cor. 5:21; Gal. 3:13f.): it is therefore efficacious for them, on condition that they in turn participate in it (by *baptism), that is to say, that they die with Christ (Rom. 6:3–11; Col. 2:11ff.,20; cf. Gal. 2:19). By taking our death on Himself Jesus thus entered into death, but in order that He might remove its claims and nullify its power: by assuming responsibility for the *sin of the whole world He took upon Himself the death of the whole world—

since death is the wages of sin (Rom. 6:21,23; 7:5; 8:6,13; Gal. 6:7f.; Jas. 1:15, etc.)—in such a way that those who believe in Jesus Christ have henceforth advanced beyond death, they died on the first Good Friday. Thus they have passed from death to life (Jn. 5:24f.; Col. 2:12), like Christ, whom death could not hold (Acts 2:24).

(c) The assurance of this victory was so strong in the first days of the Church that some went so far as to assert that the last resurrection had already taken place (2 Tim. 2:18), while others seem to have thought that certain leaders of the Church would experience, at their death, an assumption into heaven (cf. Rev. 11:11ff.), and for the majority the fact that it caused sorrow in the Church was an unexpected stumbling-block (1 Thess. 4:13; cf. 1 Cor. 11:30). The apostles, however, said again and again that it was by their behaviour and obedience that Christians should display the risen life in which they already shared (Rom. 6:4–14; Col. 3:1–17; 1 Jn. 3:14, etc.).

2. If death has been conquered by Jesus Christ, it may well be asked why those who have been "united with him" (Rom. 6:5) should yet die, and especially why death is not treated by the N.T. writers as a trifling matter but as the last enemy still to be vanquished (1 Cor. 15:26; cf. Rev. 20:14).

(a) The reason for this is that for the N.T. the victory of Christ has already been won without being yet manifested in all its fullness; that is to say that the coming, in the person of Jesus Christ, of the *Kingdom of God when there will be no more death (cf. Rev. 21:4; Matt. 11:3–6 and parallels) is a coming that is as yet hidden and unperceived. During the *time between the first and second *advents of Christ there is a commingling of the present age with the age to come, between the world which passes away and the one which will not pass away. While they already are citizens of the heavenly *city Christians still walk in the flesh (*Man), that is to say, in an atmosphere that is the result of man's rebellion against God: like all the descendants of the first Adam (1 Cor. 15:22; Rom. 5:12–19), which also and originally they are, they are mortal (Rom. 6:12; 8:11; 2 Cor. 5:4).

(*b*) But this common and general death (cf. however Jn. 21:20–22; 1 Cor. 15:51; 1 Thess. 4:15–17), which continues to be the greatest fear of unbelievers (cf. Heb. 2:15; Rom. 8:15), is no longer feared by Christians (Rom. 14:7f.). What Christians fear is the "second death" which will shut out not only from temporal life, but from eternal life (Rev. 2:11; 20:6,14f.; 21:8). For faith, in fact, the concepts of *life and death are no longer governed by one's temporal decease: when a man's life is lived outside of the Gospel even when "living" he is "dead" (Matt. 8:22 and parallels; Col. 2:13; 1 Tim. 5:6), whereas in Christ even one who is "dead" is "living" (Jn. 11:25f.; 6:50). That is why it is a matter of *eternal* life or death to die as quickly as possible to one's first life, to this body of death (Rom. 7:24), in other words, to renounce one's self in order to confess Jesus Christ as our true life (Phil. 1:21; Col. 3:3). When one is placed on this level of "life" and "death" then physical death can no longer take possession of us, but can only deliver us to Christ.

(*c*) It is, however, important that this physical death should be encountered with the courage of faith. In the N.T., indeed, we frequently find that it is mysteriously linked to that of Jesus. By dying a physical death (*Persecution) one dies "to the Lord" (Rom. 14:8), that is to say that in our death His is repeated and fulfilled (cf. Jn. 16:2; Rom. 8:36ff.; 1 Cor. 15:31; 2 Cor. 4:7ff.; Col. 1:24; 1 Pet. 2:18ff.; 3:13ff., etc.). The suffering of Christ, with its terror and its peace (cf. Mk. 14:34ff. and parallels; Matt. 27:32–50; Mk. 15:21–37; Lk. 23:26–49; Jn. 19:17–30), is thus an example for the suffering of Christians, and it is understandable that many have wished to glorify God by a death similar to that of Christ (cf. Jn. 21:19; Acts 21:13; Phil. 1:20; 3:10).

3. The N.T. is not clear concerning the manner in which burial was understood. Judaism, in order to ensure "an everlasting renown" for the noble dead (1 Macc. 13:29), had introduced the veneration of tombs to which reference is made not without a certain irony (cf. Matt. 23:27–29; Acts 2:29). But to deduce from this that the N.T. writers scorn funeral ceremonial is an unjustifiable step, especially when one considers the details of the burial of Jesus in a virgin tomb (Mk. 15:42ff. and parallels). Refusal of burial is treated as a particular insult (Rev. 11:8ff.), and it is accorded even to the corpses of those whom Satan has snatched from the Lord (Acts 5:6,10). To discover the first traces of Christian funeral ceremonial Acts 9:37ff. should be read again.

4. The N.T. affirms with unanimity the resurrection of all the dead at the return of Christ, but unanimity is less apparent when it comes to saying where the dead are to be found until that moment arrives.

(*a*) In a general manner its authors believe —together with Judaism—in the abode of the dead (Hades, which is not the same as *Gehenna), situated at the centre of the earth (Matt. 12:40), and regarded as a prison (1 Pet. 3:19; cf. Rev. 20:2,7) with locked gates (cf. Matt. 16:18; Rev. 1:18). Without offering any criticism of it, Jesus made use of a Jewish opinion according to which this abode of the dead was divided into two sections, of which one, for the wicked, is a place of torment, while the other—"Abraham's bosom"—is a place of repose (Lk. 16:22ff.). What is distinctive about this view of the current doctrine of purgatory is that no passage is possible from one place to the other (16:26). It is often thought that the paradise of which Lk. 23:43 speaks is the same as "Abraham's bosom" or, what comes to the same thing, the "eternal habitations" (Lk. 16:9). But one may ask whether it is not preferable to translate as follows: "Truly, I say to you, to-day—that is to say, on this cross where I seem to have been deprived of all power— you will be with me in paradise"—that means, I still have power over eternal life and eternal death, and I promise you life— paradise having here its eschatological connotation as in Rev. 2:7.

(b) Between His death and His resurrection Jesus Himself also descended into Hades: He did not descend there, however, in order to wait for the end of the world, but partly in order to proclaim there also the deliverance of captives (1 Pet. 3:19; 4:6) and partly that He might snatch from death (=from the Devil? Heb. 2:14) the keys of this abode (Rev. 1:18). To picture the sovereignty of Christ when dead, which is emphasized in Jn. 10:18 and Acts 2:24, one may imagine this descent into Hades as a New Testament counterpart of the episode of the seizing of the ark by the Philistines (cf. 1 Sam. 5–6). Having thus descended into the lower parts of the earth (Eph. 4:9), there is no longer, in the world, any place where the lordship of Christ is excluded (Phil. 2:10f.).

(c) For this reason those who henceforth die "in the Lord" (1 Cor. 15:18; 1 Thess. 4:16) can no longer be separated from Him (Rom. 8:38f.): hence it is possible (without being self-centred, however!—Phil. 1:24ff.) to wish "to depart and be with Christ" (Phil. 1:23; 2 Cor. 5:6–8). But where is one with Him? In Hades (cf. Rom. 10:7)? In Jerusalem (Heb. 12:22f.) or under the altar (Rev. 6:9) or before the heavenly throne (Rev. 7:9)? The essential thing is not to locate the place, but to know that until the time when Hades has rendered up the dead (Rev. 20:11ff.) those who have died in Christ are not abandoned by Him, nor are they far from Him, even though they have not yet attained to the fullness of felicity (cf. Rev. 6:9ff.), since they have not yet been clothed with their body of glory, that body which is fitted for eternal life.

(d) Sometimes (but perhaps it is a euphemism?) death is compared to a sleep (Mk. 5:39 and parallels; Jn. 11:11f.; 1 Cor. 15:18; 1 Thess. 4:13f.; 5:10; cf. Matt. 25:5). The idea involved is the same in the sense, firstly, that this sleep is only temporary and will be followed by an awakening; and, secondly, in the sense that sleep does not destroy the identity of the sleeper: while he is unconscious, he remains himself. The absence of the idea of the immortality of the soul in the N.T. does not therefore point to the view that in death there is a suppression of human existence, for he who is to be raised is the same as he who has died (cf. Lk. 24:39f.; Jn. 20:26ff.). Despite the Judaism of the diaspora, which taught this, the N.T. does not allow the infiltration in any way of the Greek idea of the immortality of the soul. Why? In the first place because man has not the guarantee of his existence in himself (God alone is immortal, 1 Tim. 6:16); and also because, believing that salvation does not suppress but transforms the creation of God, the N.T. does not envisage an eternal existence other than on a new *earth* (2 Pet. 3:13) and in a new *body* (1 Cor. 15:35ff.). Biblical teaching does not countenance the idea of a dualism of incompatibility between that which is "material" and that which is "spiritual": on the contrary, it affirms the incarnation (Jn. 1:14). To reject the realism of the resurrection in favour of the spiritualism of the immortality of the soul implies either that God is not the Creator or that He can save only a portion of His work; in particular it amounts to an affirmation that Jesus Christ has not risen from the dead (1 Cor. 15:13ff.), and thus that death has not been vanquished, and thus that men remain for ever in fear and servitude (Heb. 2:14ff.).

J.-J. VON ALLMEN

DECREE, *see* ELECT

DELIVER, *see* FREEDOM

DEMONS

O.T.

Demons in the Bible are of a fourfold origin:

(a) Nature spirits, relics of the so-called animistic view of the world, only spoken of in the Bible as being evil. These spirits inhabit for choice regions or places of ill-fame, such as deserts, ruins, cemeteries, rather like certain Djinns among the Arabs.

(b) Pagan deities degraded to the rank of demons, such as Beelzebub (*Devil) or the gods of Hellenism, which the apostle Paul and the Church Fathers put on the same footing as the demons.

(c) Evil spirits sent by Satan or by God Himself from highest heaven to test, to tempt or to punish men.

(d) Fallen angels (Gen. 6:1f.; Jude 6; cf. the books of Enoch) or angels who are liable to fall (1 Cor. 11:10?)—"Ghosts", however, do not seem to have been confused with demons. At least in the only case where the spirit of a dead man appears (at Endor, 1 Sam. 28:11f.), the spectre plays a very honourable part.

On (a): In Isa. 34:11–15 hairy satyrs ("goats") are listed along with Lilith (the night hag), owls, dragons, vultures, cormorants and ravens (cf. Isa. 13:20–22), to describe the desolation into which Yahweh will cast Babylon (chap. 13) or "the nations" (chap. 34). The prohibition of sacrifices to the demons is expressly given in Lev. 17:7. One still finds, however, embedded in the Mosaic religion a curious survival of the cult of the spirits of the wild, in the form of a rite which might be described as negative worship offered to one of them. It is the rite which consists in transferring the sins of the people to a he-goat who is then dedicated to the demon Azazel, to whom he is driven into the desert. In order to remove every pagan feature from this ceremony care is taken to dedicate another he-goat to God (Lev. 16:8–22).

On (b): All the Canaanite gods to whom, in their syncretism or in their apostasy, the Israelites used to sacrifice on the high places are at times called "demons" (Deut. 32:17; Ps. 96:5; 106:37). These pagan deities were doubtless the gods of vegetation and fertility. The modern translation *"idols" is not an exact rendering, because it does not convey the demoniac climate of their worship which the Hebrew authors wished to emphasize. It is again possible that the demon Asmodeus, who plays so sinister a part in the story of Tobit (6:10ff.; 8:1ff.), was originally a Babylonian god.

On (c): With regard to evil spirits who come from heaven, we have information in the book of Judges (9:23) where God sends an evil spirit to bring division between Abimelech and the men of Shechem; in 1 Sam. 16:14; 18:10; 19:9, where God vexes the house of Saul in the same manner; in the vision of the prophet Micaiah, related in 1 Kings 22:19–23, who sees before the throne of God a spirit who volunteers to seduce King Ahab by inciting 400 false prophets to promise victory to the king.

On (d): Fallen or falling angels are clearly referred to in Gen. 6:1–4. Their sin consisted in falling in love with the daughters of men, and of entering with them into a union from which sprang a race of giants. The books of Enoch provide ample details on this story and on the punishment of the angels. When the Epistle of Jude, who quotes Enoch 1 (v. 14) speaks of angels bound in chains in the nether gloom until the day of judgment (v. 6), the writer certainly has in mind, along with others, these beings.

N.T.

In the N.T. period, however, there is scarcely a trace of the differences between the various categories of demons, of whom Satan (called also Beelzebub) is regarded as chief. Attention is drawn particularly to cases of persons possessed by "demons" or by "unclean spirits", and whom Jesus healed. We may observe that the demons can drive their victims to madness, as did the "legion" of demons at Gadara; these were regarded by the Jews as being an especially unclean brood, because they dwelt in the tombs and agreed to enter into a herd of swine (Mk. 5:1–20 and parallels). Another case of possession by more than one demon is cited by Luke, where Mary of Magdala is described as one "from whom seven demons had gone out" (Lk. 8:2). A case of epilepsy aggravated by dumbness (noted in Mk. 9:17–29; cf. Lk. 9:38–42) is attributed to the influence of a demon, who on this account is called a "dumb and deaf spirit" (Mk. 9:25; cf. 7:32). In Matt. 12:22 we have a description of a demoniac whose evil spirit had caused its victims to lose not only speech but sight.

On the other hand, there is no justification for regarding the demoniac in Mk. 1:23–28 as an epileptic; for it appears that it is only as a result of the art of exorcism that the demon casts the sufferer to the ground before leaving him (cf. Lk. 4:35). In this case, the *sickness is not clearly described; but the most interesting aspect is that the spirit speaks through the mouth of the possessed man whom the demon uses as a kind of medium.

It must be pointed out, however, that only those diseases which are called nervous or mental are attributed to the demons. Jesus cured many other diseases in which there was no question of demon-possession; e.g. the fever of Peter's mother-in-law (Mk. 1:29–31 and parallels), the congenital blindness of the beggar (Jn. 9:1–7), forms of paralysis (Mk. 2:1–12 and parallels). Nor is there any hint of the use of exorcism in the cases where Jesus raised people from the dead. There is one single exception in the case of the woman who was "bent over and could not fully straighten herself out" (Lk. 13:10–13), who is described as "bound by Satan" (which could have a more general meaning) and as having a "spirit of infirmity".

It must be borne in mind that, even when He is exorcising demons, Jesus uses no magic formulas. He gives a peremptory order to the spirit, threatening it if need be. In only one single case, we are told, did Jesus agree to enter into discussion with the demons and to lighten the sentence (the Gadarene demoniac possessed by a "legion" of demons). In certain cases, the demons distinctly recognized the superior nature of Jesus. Thus the unclean spirit in Mk. 1:23 calls Him "Nazarene", which here is the equivalent of "Nazirite" (="the Holy One of God").

Nor is there any doubt that Jesus considered these expulsions of demons as signs which foretold the coming of the *Kingdom. In the account of the stilling of the storm on the Lake of Gennesareth (Mk. 4:39 and parallel passages), this event takes place in a manner strangely reminiscent of an incantation, which suggests that, in the writer's mind, the storm had been caused by elements "animated" by malevolent spirits.

It is well known that the disciples of Jesus, during His lifetime and acting expressly on His command, practised the expulsion of demons. He reminds them in this connection of the difficulty of such cures (Mk. 9:28–29 and parallels) and of the dangers of a relapse (Matt. 12:43–45 and parallels). After His resurrection, however, He gives them a new assurance that all power is given to them in heaven and on earth, that is, power over the visible and invisible forces (Matt. 28:18; Mk. 16:17).

It was in the name of Jesus that they drove out demons (cf. Acts 3:6); but this name was only effective when the healer possessed the Holy Spirit (Acts 19:13–16). Among the recorded healings of demoniacs details are given of the case of a girl at Philippi who was demon-possessed (Acts 16:16ff.): she had a "python spirit", i.e. a spirit which gave oracles, as did Apollo through the intermediary of the "pythoness" of Delphi; perhaps this was a case merely of intermittent mediumism.

That leads us to speak too of the intervention of unclean spirits in Christian worship, of which the apostle Paul was so afraid. There again it appears to be a case of otherwise sane persons who, when they fell into an ecstatic trance or into some other supranormal state, could be used as the mouthpieces not only of the Spirit of God, but also of evil entities. Those who prophesied and those who spoke with tongues were particularly exposed to the danger of such unfortunate happenings.

The distinction between good and evil spirits took on then so great an importance that the "ability to distinguish between spirits" is listed as being very useful and necessary (1 Cor. 12:10; 14:29).

For the "powers" who crucified Jesus: see *Angels and *Authorities.

In conclusion, it is obvious that the reassurances given to believers against the wiles of the Devil are valid also against the demons, provided that the faithful keep the faith and develop their power to "test the spirits to see whether they are of God" (1 Jn. 4:1).

J. HÉRING

DESCEND

Apart from their obvious sense, the expression to descend and its antonym to ascend have in the Bible several technical meanings: a *geographical* meaning (to go up to Jerusalem, to go down to Egypt) and a *cultic* meaning (to go up to the Temple, to the Mountain); but these two technical meanings themselves depend on a prior *theological* sense. The verbs to go up and to go down point, indeed, to the relationship between God and man (a relationship expressed, for example, by the vision of Jacob's ladder and the angels ascending and descending on it, Gen. 28:12; Jn. 1:51). This usage can only be understood from the viewpoint of the biblical conception of the *world: heaven where stands God's throne, the earth where men live, and the underworld where dwell the dead, form three superimposed storeys. To descend, then, indicates any movement which proceeds from heaven to earth, from God to man (e.g. "every perfect gift is from above, coming down from the Father of lights", Jas. 1:17), or from the earth to the abode of the dead (e.g. Gen. 37:35 where the expression is equivalent to "die", *death). To ascend indicates, on the other hand, any movement which proceeds from the underworld to the earth (e.g. Ps. 71:20 "from the depths of the earth thou wilt bring me up again"), or from earth to heaven, from man to God (e.g. Acts 10:4: "Your prayers and your alms have ascended as a memorial before God").

It is *above* that man, creature of God, finds life and salvation; *below* he finds death and perdition. But for man, because of his disobedience, there is no natural way of access. To seek to rise is the very heart of sin (cf. the Tower of Babel and the text of Isa. 14:13f., where "to ascend to heaven" is synonymous with "I will be like the Most High"), and the way back from the abode of the dead and the way to heaven are barred to man unless God descends miraculously to his help.

In the O.T. we see God intervene over and over again in this way, to judge or to save, sometimes by sending down from heaven fire, a voice, an angel and sometimes coming in person to deliver Israel (Exod. 3:8; cf. Acts 7:34), to speak to Moses (cf. Exod. 19:11), etc. But the people long for a final advent of their Saviour (cf. Isa. 64:2). It is with the news of this event that the Gospel thrills; the Holy Spirit which "came down" like a dove designates Jesus Christ as the one who Himself came down from heaven to fulfil the Father's will and to give to men the life from above, eternal life (cf. Matt. 11:23; by His presence Capernaum was exalted to heaven). He is the true bread which *descended* from heaven (Jn. 6:30ff.). He sends to His disciples His Spirit which *descends* at Pentecost on the assembled apostles (cf. also Acts 8:16; 10:44; 11:15). But to the abasement and humiliation of the Son of Man (which will involve His descent into the realm of the dead), God replies by *raising* Him into glory. When considered along with Jn.3:13, Eph. 4:8–10 gives a full insight into this descent and into this exaltation of the Son of Man: He is henceforward the fullness of all things. There is once more intercourse between earth and heaven; He who descended is He who ascended. Christ is our life; wherever I go, "above" or "below", He is my companion. He has summed up everything. Such is the meaning of the striking passage in Rom. 10:5–13: "No one need any longer ascend up into heaven to seek for a Saviour and for salvation, for He has become Man; no one need again seek Him among the dead, for He is risen!" It is the fulfilment of Psalm 139 which describes the omnipresence of God: "If I ascend to heaven, thou art there; if I make my bed in Sheol, thou art there! If I take the wings of the morning and dwell in the uttermost parts of the sea, even there thy hand shall lead me." Finally the expression "to descend" has an *eschatological* sense: it refers to the final appearance of the Lord at the time of the parousia (1 Thess. 4:16). With Him will appear also the New Jerusalem which descends to this world (Rev. 3:12; 21:2–10). This final descent from heaven marks the complete end of all separation between God and His creation.

In conclusion we ought to call attention to: (*a*) the use of the word "descend" in the rite of baptism (Acts 8:38) which bears witness to the meaning it has of dying with Christ in order to rise with Him, (*b*) that according to Rev. 12:12 (cf. Lk. 10:18) the Devil had his dwelling in the celestial regions until he was dislodged thence by the victory of Christ.

Geographical sense: to go up means "to go to Palestine", whereas one "goes down" to Egypt. But these expressions have nothing to do with altitude and latitude; they originate in the analogy which is evident in the Bible between the Holy Land and the Kingdom of God, and between Egypt (or the pagan lands) and the Kingdom of bondage and death (to go up out of Egypt=to be delivered).

Cultic sense: To ascend is the characteristic expression in the Bible to denote the action of going to Jerusalem, the Holy City, and to the Temple, to carry out the worship which God demands (cf. "go up to the feast", "go up to the Temple", etc.). To ascend means then in this context "to go to adore", not merely because primitive worship was offered on the high places, nor because the Temple of Jerusalem was actually on the highest point of the city, but because every cultic action, prayer, sacrifice, festival, is a movement towards heaven, the only "ascent" towards God which sinful man is allowed to make, and because the *Temple is a kind of symbol on earth of the heavenly sanctuary. The whole cultic life of Israel finds its fulfilment in the ascent into heaven and in the entry into God's presence, the Holy of Holies, of Jesus Christ, the great High Priest (cf. Heb.).

M. BOUTTIER

DESERT, *see* NAMES (GEOGRAPHICAL)

DEVIL

The Hebrew word *Satan* means "adversary". Thus King Hadad of Damascus is called the "satan of Solomon" (1 Kings 11:14). In a more precise way this expression designates the adversary before a tribunal, i.e. the accuser (cf. Rev. 12:10, where the Devil is called "the accuser"). Quite naturally the word "satan" comes to mean "denouncer" or "calumniator". The translation of "satan" by "Devil" is therefore quite justifiable, for the meaning of the Greek "diabolos" is exactly that of "denouncer" or "calumniator" (cf. Jn. 6:70-71, where Judas is called "devil").

In the earlier sections of the O.T. Satan is not yet an independent personage, nor even a maleficent being. According to Zech. 3:1, the oldest text in which Satan is mentioned, he takes his place at one side of God's throne with the "angel of the Lord" at the other side. In the book of Job he assumes a will of his own; at least he makes a wager with God, with Job as the stake, just as he does with the soul of Faust in the later legend. Nevertheless he acts solely with the express permission of God and keeps within the limits which God has fixed for him (Job 1:12; 2:6). According to 1 Chr. 21:1, it was Satan who suggested to David the evil idea of numbering the people, whereas in the older version of 2 Sam. 24:1 it was God Himself who drove him to this folly, because His anger was kindled against the king.

However, the pessimistic strain in the teaching of certain prophets, the terrible political experiences of the Jews, as well as the influence of Persian religion favoured the development of a dualistic conception of the world. Satan came to play a more dramatic and more independent part in history, although he never became an antagonist of God as he did among the Zoroastrians and the Manichaeans, for he was always conscious of being a creature inferior to God. He becomes the commander of an evil army which strives to hinder the purposes of divine Providence, the "angels of Satan" (Matt. 25:41; Rev. 12:7,9). The book of Revelation even speaks of a "throne of Satan" (2:13). The Jews, however, did not develop very precise notions concerning the hierarchy of the satanic world. Sometimes Satan is identified with Beelzeboul=Lord of the dunghill (a corruption of Beelzebub, the name of a Philistine god, cf. 2 Kings 1:1–3, who was considered by the Jews to be very evil). Cf. Mk. 3:22f. and parallel passages.

Belial, a name which originally could be applied to any wicked person, is used in the N.T. as a synonym of Satan (2 Cor. 6:15).

While it cannot be proved that the author of Gen. 3 intended to identify the serpent with Satan, this creature acts in a manner which corresponds so closely to his intentions (tempting, lying, hurling humanity into death) that it is easy to understand why the book of Wisdom (2:24) and later the Revelation of John (12:9; 20:2) identify the Devil with the "old serpent" who played so nefarious a rôle in the beginnings of human history. The same holds true for the "dragon" which is not clearly differentiated from the serpent and which is to be defeated by the archangel Michael. In any case the (occasional) identification of the Devil with the serpent must not lead us to think that he exerts his power only on the earth. This power is manifested in heaven as well as in the intermediary worlds.

Whatever name is applied to the Devil, his manner of acting is always the same. Not content with denouncing before God the faults of men, he seeks to lead them into sin, because he himself is a sinner (1 Jn. 3:8). That is why he is called the "Tempter" (Matt. 4:3; 1 Thess. 3:5). He tempts men by promising them, as a reward for disobeying God, delights (1 Cor. 7:5), or earthly power (Matt. 4:8–11 and parallels), or a knowledge like that of God (Gen. 3:5). To accomplish this he makes great use of lies, a practice which earns him the title of "liar" and "father of lies" (Jn. 8:44).

Another of the methods of working for which he shows a marked predilection is murder: he is the "Lord of Death" (Heb. 2:14; cf. Jn. 8:44 and Rev. 9:11; Matt. 10:28; cf. 1 Jn. 3:11–12). It is he who is responsible for every attempt to overthrow a morally superior power by destroying the physical basis of its action. It was in this fashion that the "rulers of this age" (1 Cor. 2:6–9), without being actually of satanic origin, became the servants of the Devil by

crucifying Jesus and by persecuting the saints.

The constant use of violence and deceit by Satan and his henchmen requires that believers shall manifest courage and extreme vigilance (Eph. 6:11f.; Jas. 4:7; 1 Pet. 5:8f.; 2 Cor. 2:11), all the more so because the Devil can disguise himself as an "angel of light" (2 Cor. 11:14). A healthy suspicion, and the wisdom of "the serpent" (Matt. 10:16) towards "wolves" in sheep's clothing and "dogs" (Matt. 7:15; Acts 20:29–30; Phil. 3:2; cf. Matt. 7:6) are the cardinal virtues taught by the N.T.: and no man who is deceived can plead as excuse his naïve credulity or his generous confidence.

It must be emphasized, moreover, that it is not only individuals, but also—one could almost say: particularly—communities that Satan tries to deceive and to bring into his service. Thus the political powers are "servants of God" only in so far as they make every effort to maintain right and justice (Rom. 13:1–7). A government which substitutes despotism and terror for justice and which persecutes the innocent, becomes, as the book of Revelation reminds us in vivid pictures, a servant of one of the infamous "beasts", who are nothing but creatures of the Devil.

The total effect of all the biblical references is to present the picture of a Satan who is the supreme evil-doer. Because of this, he is known as "the Evil One" (2 Thess. 3:3; Matt. 6:13; 1 Jn. 2:13, R.V.). He is the arch-enemy of the human race (Matt. 13:39). His might in the present world is such that sometimes the title is accorded him of "ruler of this world" (Jn. 12:31; 14:30; 16:11) and once even "god of this world" (2 Cor. 4:4). His power, in our aeon, is operative not only on the earth, but in the upper regions: he is also the "prince of the power of the air" (Eph. 2:2).

What is to be the destiny of Satan? He has already suffered a smarting defeat as a result of an event which, if his plans had carried, ought to have brought him certain victory: the death of Jesus on the cross. Through it the writ of accusation, which was destined to destroy humanity, was cancelled

(Col. 2:14–15); that is one of the most curious aspects of the great paradox of the *cross. The struggle, however, goes on, especially in the invisible world. The insight of Jesus, who sees Satan "fall from heaven" (Lk. 10:18), appears to be a prophetic vision rather than the revelation of something happening at the time.

The Christian feels in his life, and even in his flesh (2 Cor. 12:7), the repercussions of this strife between Christ and the hostile powers. That is why the believer must be ready to face martyrdom, if need be, and never to look upon the precepts of the Sermon on the Mount as a way of living which guarantees his own peace and security. On the other hand, those who sow the good seed of the Word of God cannot be held responsible for the weeds which spring up in their field: it is the work of "the enemy" (Matt. 13:39).

But the believer has no doubt that in the end Satan and "his angels" will be utterly destroyed, for this is clearly taught in the N.T., especially in the Epistles of Paul and in the Revelation of John (Rom. 16:20; 1 Cor. 15:25–28; Rev. 14:10; 19:20; 20:10; 21:8; cf. Matt. 25:41).

Origen's thesis of the probable conversion and final redemption of the Devil appears to have no biblical foundation.

In all the distresses brought upon him by the Devil, the believer is assured of the love and faithfulness of God, who promises that he will not be tempted beyond his powers of resistance (1 Cor. 10:13). Since it is clearly stated that it is not God Himself who tempts men (Jas. 1:13), the well-known sixth petition in the Lord's Prayer ought to be translated: lead us not into trial. God may indeed test man by tribulations, whereas Satan seeks to bring about his fall—a fact which does not exclude the possibility that the same happening may be in God's sight a testing and in Satan's intention a *temptation.

It must be pointed out that the expression "Son of the Devil" does not necessarily bear a mythological meaning. His servants may be described in this way (the unbelieving Jews in Jn. 8:44, sorcerers in Acts 13:10).

On the other hand, a more literal interpretation must be put on the texts where Satan is described as "entering" into certain persons, e.g. Judas Iscariot (Lk. 22:3; Jn. 13:27) and taking possession of them, e.g. Peter (Mk. 8:33 and parallel passages).

The rite by means of which a sinner, whose presence in the Church involves a risk of contamination, is vowed to Satan (1 Cor. 5:5) must be explained in the light of the excommunication practised by the synagogue: the guilty man was expelled from the community and by that same act delivered to the forces of evil; in the eyes of the apostle, however, this calamity may be the means of bringing to the sinner the opportunity of repentance and salvation.

What has the Bible to say about the *Antichrist*? An Antichrist (in the singular) is merely mentioned by name in 1 Jn. 2:18, "you have heard that antichrist is coming"; according to 1 Jn. 4:3, he is even now in the world. The first text, however, adds "many antichrists have come". The reference here is to those who deny the reality of the incarnation of Christ (2 Jn. 7) and the identification of the heavenly Christ with the historical Jesus. The supreme Antichrist (in the singular) is not definitely identified with the Devil, but rather with one of his myrmidons such as the "man of lawlessness" who, according to Paul, will come before the end of the ages (2 Thess. 2:3–4), whom he calls also "the son of perdition", the "adversary", "who exalts himself . . . proclaiming himself to be God" (*ibid.*). He will bring about a great apostasy, as will also the beasts of Revelation, creatures like him of the Devil.

J. HÉRING

DISEASE, *see* SICKNESS

DISCIPLE

1. In later Judaism (see *Jews), the law became the object of systematic teaching on the part of the rabbis around whom gathered their pupils (cf. the importance of the Scribes or of the teachers of the law in our Gospels). The master teaches, the

pupils listen and put questions. The incident of Jesus in the Temple at the age of 12 (Lk. 2:46) is characteristic. But it is the teaching rather than the personality of the "doctor" or "master" which is important. He is the interpreter of the will of God as expressed in the law, and the scholarship of an Hillel or of a Shammai, however remarkable this may be, has one aim—the exact interpretation of Holy Scripture. A great importance attaches to the tradition formed by a school. The apostle Paul sat at the feet of a great teacher, Gamaliel, but it never occurred to him to make his master an object of especial veneration! These "doctors", at the same time jurists and theologians, all appeal to the unquestioned authority of Moses, the supreme revealer of the counsels of God. In this respect, the Jewish masters are similar to the Greek teachers whose wisdom is an object of teaching and veneration. Both form schools, and their thought, along with their interpretations, is handed on from one generation to another.

2. In the N.T., the word "disciple" appears about 250 times, but strangely enough only in the Gospels and in Acts. Even in our language, the shade of meaning which distinguishes a pupil from a disciple is evident. Doubtless the disciple, like the pupil, receives instruction, but the former embraces the teaching of the master. In the Gospels "disciple" has a deeper significance: the disciple adheres closely to the very person of Jesus. That is where the disciples of Christ differ completely from the disciples of a philosopher or of a rabbi; these latter are attached primarily to the master's teaching, to his thought or to the tradition which he hands on, whereas the disciples of Jesus are linked body and soul *to the person of the Lord.* Apparently Jesus can give the impression of a rabbi surrounded by his pupils, but in actual fact the case is quite different: the Jews, even through the medium of the Scribes, are "disciples of Moses" (Jn. 9:28) whose instruction they receive. The disciples of Jesus share even the fate of the person of their Lord, and the

teaching of the Master, vital as it is, is not nearly so important as their faith in His personal mission; the summons: "Follow me!" (Mk. 2:14; 1:17; Matt. 4:19; 8:22, etc.) is the true call to discipleship. The people whom Jesus calls to follow Him are not those who are particularly endowed with intellectual gifts, but the humble, sinners, and even Levi a toll-collector. Jesus Himself selects His disciples, a fact which confers a unique value upon the relations of Jesus with His disciples: they are wholeheartedly in the service of their Lord, and they are called not merely to be pupils capable in their turn of instructing others, but to become *witnesses* of historic events linked to the person of Christ, to His death and His resurrection. Jesus is Lord and the disciples are servant-witnesses. After the exaltation of Christ into glory, they are to live in expectation of His royal coming (Matt. 24:45ff.; 25:14ff.; Lk. 12:35ff.,42ff.). The disciple who shares his Lord's destiny will also be called upon to suffer too; Jesus felt the need to warn His followers about this (Matt. 10:24–25; Mk. 8:34–35; Lk. 14:26–27; Jn. 12:25–26), which does not imply necessarily that the disciples had understood the meaning of the mission of Jesus. How many times Jesus had to teach them the fuller significance of certain sayings or parables and even more of His approaching death! (Mk. 4:10; Matt. 16:22ff.). But the disciple is a disciple of the Lord just as truly in that which relates to His teaching as in that which relates to His person. All the apostles are to be disciples of Jesus, even if all the disciples do not become apostles.

The conclusion of the matter is that, for His followers, Jesus is not a "teacher" (He does not speak as the Scribes, Matt. 7:29), but because He speaks with authority, He is their Lord and they depend upon Him absolutely. The disciples are to be witnesses of what Jesus was in His life and in His death and resurrection.

In Acts the term disciple is extended generally to include all Christians (Acts 6:1; 9:1,25; 11:29; 21:16); it is the equivalent of brother or believer. This use of the word is symptomatic, for it proves afresh that the word disciple implies a faith without reserve in Him who is the Lord.

M. BERNOULLI

DOCTRINE, see TEACHING

DOMINATIONS, see AUTHORITIES

DOOR (GATE)

In addition to their literal meanings, the words door and gate are used in a number of figurative expressions to denote:

(a) a house, a town or a place of habitation, the part being taken to indicate the whole (Exod. 20:10; Zech. 8:16);

(b) a vulnerable spot: "to possess the gate of the enemy"=to conquer them (Gen. 24:60);

(c) the imminence of an event, of a threatening danger (Gen. 4:7, "sin is couching at the door"; Mk. 13:29, "you know that he, the Son of Man, is near, at the very gates"; Jas. 5:9, "the Judge is standing at the doors").

(d) the place where good and evil reputations are fashioned, the gates of the town being the place where business is transacted, where news is passed on, and where justice is carried out in the assembly of the elders (Prov. 31:23; Job 31:21; Ps. 69:12; 127:5; Ruth 3:11; Amos 5:10–15);

(e) the place where a king's servant (Dan. 2:49) or God's servant (Ps. 84:11) stands to address to him his petitions or his praises.

In the theological sense the gate or the gates suggest the idea of a dangerous and formidable power, either the "gates of Sheol" (Isa. 38:10), "the gates of death" (Ps. 107:16,18) which God alone can break, or the "gate of heaven" which Jacob discovers at Bethel as an "awesome" place (Gen. 28:17) for through it at any moment the holy God may appear. Generally the opening of the gates of heaven, or "of God", or of "the holy place" symbolizes the free flow of the gifts which God bestows on His creatures or on His people (Ps. 78:23; Mal. 3:10), and also the entry of the King of Glory into His Kingdom (Ps. 24:7–10). In the same way the opening of the gates of

Jerusalem, the holy city, like those of the Temple in the vision of Ezekiel, stands for the free access to the grace of God enjoyed by the sacred nation (Isa. 60:11; 62:10; Ezek. 43:6–11), and it is from under the threshold of this temple that there flows the river of the water of life (Ezek. 47:1). Again, the vision of the opening heavens is given to Stephen (Acts 7:55f.) and to John on Patmos (Rev. 4:1). It is doubtless by analogy with this general sense of the outpouring of measureless grace that the expression "an open door" is frequently used in the N.T. to indicate the possibilities open to the apostolic preaching (Acts 14:27; 1 Cor. 16:9; 2 Cor. 2:12; Col. 4:3). Conversely the "closed door" points to the execution of divine justice beyond which there is no appeal, whether it refers to the door of the ark which God Himself shuts when Noah has gone in just before the Flood (Gen. 7:16) or to the door of the room where the marriage feast was held which was shut immediately after the arrival of the bridegroom (Matt. 25:10).

The use which Jesus makes of the figure of the door or gate may be understood as:

(a) in Matt. 7:13, the "narrow gate" refers to the only gate which leads, through the justice and grace of God, into life;

(b) in Jn. 10:1–10, Jesus Himself is pictured as the door of the sheepfold (see *Shepherd), the Kingdom of Heaven, for He alone gives access to grace through the fulfilment of righteousness. He is "the true one, who has the key of David, who opens and no one shall shut, who shuts and no one opens" (Rev. 3:7). And yet, by a kind of paradox which runs through all the Gospel preaching, He is also the one "who stands at the door and knocks", like a beggar or a petitioner, in the expectation that the one within will open the door to Him (Rev. 3:20).

H. ROUX

DOVE

The dove (or the turtle-dove) is frequently mentioned in the story of Israel. Its gentle gait (Hos. 7:11), its soft eyes (Song of Sol.

1:15), and its whiteness (Ps. 68:13) have made it a symbol of tenderness (Song of Sol. 2:14; 5:2; 6:8) and later of innocence and simplicity (Matt. 10:16).

Of all the birds, the dove alone seems to have been widely used as a sacrificial victim. The Yahwistic narratives, committed to writing in the 8th century B.C., speak of the sacrifice by Abraham (Gen. 15:9) of a turtle-dove and a young pigeon. This custom certainly dates back to a very early age: Noah had already sacrificed clean birds to mark the end of the Flood. But the first to prescribe the use of the dove in the sacrifice, especially in certain purification ceremonies (Lev. 4:4f.; 14:30f.; 15:14) are those jurists who compiled the sacrificial legislation during the exilic and post-exilic periods. It would seem that this legislation is one of the results of the general impoverishment of the country and is designed to make it easier for the poor to offer a burnt offering (Lev. 5:7; 12:8; 14:21f.).

But none of the characteristics of this bird nor yet any of its uses in the sacrificial system can explain the enigmatic text which refers to the baptism of Jesus (Mk. 1:9–11 and parallels), where it is related that Jesus "saw . . . the Spirit descending upon Him like a dove". Without going so far as to identify the Spirit and the dove, there is here more than a mere comparison. An appearance of such revealing nature designates the Spirit as the power of God at work in the person of the one baptized: a new age is beginning; the heavens have opened above the head of Jesus. Just as in the book of Revelation Jesus appears as the Lion of Judah or as the Lamb slain, so here the Holy Spirit appears as a dove. Are we justified in seeing in this appearance a sign of the age of the new covenant? We should remember that, at the time of the making of God's covenant with Noah, and later with Abraham, doves had been sacrificed. In any case, already in Judaism the dove suggested the active presence of the Spirit, especially to express the creative or reconciling work of God. The interpretation of Gen. 1:2, "the Spirit of God was moving over the face of the waters" as a dove spreads her wings over her young brood, could also be compared with the account of the baptism of Jesus.

M. CARREZ

DREAM

1. *The circumstances of the dream.* An examination of the relevant biblical passages suggests as a definition of the dream a vision which takes place during sleep (Job 33:15; Isa. 29:7), and is dispelled on awaking (1 Kings 3:15; Ps. 73:20), vanishing for ever (Job 20:8). The fleeting nature of the dream has sometimes caused it to be considered as the opposite of reality (Ps. 126:1; Eccl. 5:6; Isa. 29:8; Jer. 23:32) or of truth (Jude 8: the latter passage seems to apply to gnostic heretics). For Ecclesiastes dreams are the result of the agitation of the day-time (5:3); however, the old idea, generally accepted, is that God uses dreams in order to communicate with men (Gen. 20:3,6; 31:10–11,24; Num. 12:6; 1 Kings 3:5), or to terrify them by the sense of His majesty (Job 7:14; 33:15ff.).

As regards Hebrew and Aramaic at least, an attempt has been made to connect the word for dream with an Arabic root which means both to dream and to reach the stage of puberty; even if this connection is valid from a philological point of view we should not too rapidly conclude that dreams were characteristic only of young men in the process of developing their manhood; as a matter of fact, with the exception of Joseph, son of Jacob, all the other characters to whom dreams are attributed were nubile; in any event we should admit that dreams were granted rather to people of mature years, and hence it is understandable that on the Day of the Lord when everything will be different from normal reality the dreams of old men will be for them the certainty that the divine spirit has come upon them (Joel 2:28, a prophecy taken up in Acts 2:17 and applied to the events of Pentecost).

2. *The forms of the dream.* (a) The dream may assume the form of a succession of images (Gen. 37:40,41; Judg. 7:13,15; Dan.

2:4,7; in Aramaic the expression "to see a dream" is frequent), and in this form it comes near to vision pure and simple (thus Acts 11:5-11).

(*b*) The dream may also contain a direct message from God and take on at times the manner of a dialogue (Gen. 20:3-7; 31:10-13,24; 1 Kings 3:5-15; Matt. 1:20-23; 2:12,13,19-20,22; Acts 18:9-10), as also happens in certain visions (Acts 9:10-16; 10:3-6).

(*c*) Finally these two types of dream, images and words, are combined in the nocturnal vision reported in the Book of Acts, 16:9.

3. *The meaning and explanation of dreams.* (*a*) The dream reveals the future to persons who stand outside the elect people of God: Abimelech (Gen. 20:3,7), Laban (Gen. 31:24), the officers of Pharaoh (Gen. 40:5ff.), Pharaoh (Gen. 41:7), the Midianites (Judg. 7:13-15), Nebuchadnezzar (Dan. 2:1ff.), the Magi (Matt. 2:12), the wife of Pilate (Matt. 27:19). Apart from the cases where the necessary rapidity of the action involves immediate understanding of the dream, it may be said that the Gentiles need to receive the interpretation from a member of the elect people: thus it is difficult to imagine the Midianites not immediately understanding the meaning of the cakes of barley bread causing the tents to crumple up, but on the other hand the officers of Pharaoh and Pharaoh himself have recourse to Joseph just as Nebuchadnezzar has to seek counsel of Daniel. The fact that God speaks by dreams to Gentiles is a mark of His favour; that is why, unless He Himself grants the interpretation, the privilege of interpreting always devolves on one of His children.

(*b*) When God grants a dream to one of His children He gives at the same time the necessary explanation, i.e. if He has not spoken in direct and clear language: thus Joseph (Gen. 37), Daniel (Dan. 2:4,7) and St. Paul (Acts 16:9).

4. *Was prophecy obtained by dreams?* According to Deut. 13:1-5, it would seem that this question should be answered in the affirmative, for there the prophet is mentioned alongside the dreamer, and the same inference may be drawn from Jer. 23:25,32. In 1 Sam. 28:6, revelation by dreams is cited as the chief means of divination. In another passage (Num. 12:6-8) the dream, probably in the form of images, is considered as an inferior means of prophetic revelation, the higher level of prophecy being mediated by direct verbal communication (see *Word) as the case of Moses pre-eminently shows. Later *revelation as mediated through dreams was violently criticized by the authentic representative of Yahweh, who lived in intimate communion with God (Jer. 23:25-28,32; cf. also Zech. 10:2).

Opposing to the dreams of the false prophets the word of God heard in the immediacy of religious communion, Jeremiah said: "What has straw in common with wheat?" (Jer. 23:28). Without disparaging the variety of means which God uses to speak to men, let us in conclusion remember this precious thought of Jeremiah.

H. MICHAUD

EARNEST (GUARANTEE)

Twice the apostle Paul speaks of the earnest of the Spirit. He thereby utilizes a commercial and judicial term of Semitic origin to express a spiritual reality: the earnest or the guarantee in fact consists of the part actually received of the total, which itself will be given later (cf. for example Gen. 38:17,18,20).

Writing to the Corinthians (2 Cor. 1:18-22) the apostle recalls the faithfulness of God, the realization of all the promises in the person of Jesus Christ, then he adds: "But it is God who establishes us with you in Christ, and has commissioned us; he has put his seal upon us and given us his Spirit in our hearts as a guarantee." Later, addressing the Ephesians (1:14) the apostle insists on the fact that they have believed in Christ and as a result "were sealed with the seal of the promised Holy Spirit, which is the guarantee of our inheritance". Believers are thus in a particular situation:

by His death and resurrection Christ has freed them from sin. They now have the possibility of sinning no more. The Spirit has become active within them, indicating the arrival of the last days (as in Acts 2). But the totality of the believer's nature is not yet transformed. The Spirit constitutes in fact the guarantee or the earnest of the total transformation which will be completed at the day of resurrection of believers, when sin and death have been finally eliminated and when Christ, until then the unseen Lord, will reign in a visible manner. Such is the object of Christian hope.

Notice also that in place of guarantee or earnest, we also find mention of the *first-fruits* of the Spirit (Rom. 8:23). Chapter 8 of the letter to the Romans shows us how the victory of the Spirit will be made real: following the liberation wrought by Christ a new humanity exists in the power of the Spirit, of those who must live in a world where sin, though vanquished, is yet active. To possess full enjoyment of the liberty of the children of God it is necessary to await the day when corruption will be annihilated. They do indeed suffer; but this suffering is nothing in comparison with the glory to come: creation itself longs for that day, and mankind also. "We ourselves, who have the first-fruits of the Spirit, groan inwardly as we wait for adoption as sons, the redemption of our bodies. For in this hope we were saved." The first-fruits are the first of the harvest which is near. The earnest or the first-fruit of the Spirit in our heart gives us the assurance that our entire being will become a spiritual being (1 Cor. 15:44).

M. CARREZ

EASTER, *see* FEASTS, RESURRECTION

EATING AND DRINKING (MEAL)

1. The Bible is too near to human life not to speak often of matters connected with eating and drinking. Many of the passages in question have not an immediate theological bearing. With regard to food and drink in general the following points in particular should be noted:

(*a*) since the fall of man (Gen. 3:17ff.) the right to eat is dependent on *work (cf. 2 Thess. 3:6–10) but this right wherever work has been done must be respected (cf. 1 Cor. 9:4–14);

(*b*) if food communicates and sustains life, it is by a sort of exchange, i.e. by the destruction of other life (cf. Gen. 9:3; Exod. 12:1–12; cf. again Jn. 6:48–58);

(*c*) food is a gift of God for which we must thank Him (cf. 1 Tim. 4:3ff.): this is especially clear from the notable fact that God gives food and drink to His people (cf. Exod. 15:22ff.; 16:1–36; 17:1–7; cf. again Jn. 2:1–10; Matt. 14:13–21, etc.) or His servants (cf. 1 Kings 17:4,9; and again Matt. 4:11) and also from the fact that we must pray to God for our daily *bread (Matt. 6:11, etc.).

2. But in biblical thought meals have also a far more profound meaning: they are both sources and signs of communion, that is to say that by means of eating and drinking, a metaphysical bond is created between those who share in them. "The cup of blessing which we bless, is it not a participation in the blood of Christ? The bread which we break, is it not a participation in the body of Christ? because there is one loaf, we who are many are one body: for we all partake of the same loaf" (1 Cor. 10:16ff.). This statement of Paul summarizes very accurately the fellowship realized among the guests of any meal: the fact that they all participate in the same source of life creates among the participants an identity of life.

(*a*) First of all, this communion is established on the purely human level: to eat together unites or seals a unity, such as a covenant (cf. Gen. 26:26–31; 31:45–55; Josh. 9:3–19). That is why it is particularly reprehensible for the partaker of a feast to betray the community which such feasting involves (Ps. 41:10; cf. Jn. 13:18,26ff.; Matt. 26:23ff.) and why it requires all the diplomacy of Joseph to make his brethren eat with Egyptians under the same roof (Gen. 43:32). For a meal shared commits one to a bond of loyalty. Hence it is very understandable that Paul should have struggled passionately at Antioch to prevent Jewish Christians and Gentile Christians from splitting up for their eucharistic meals, for such a divorce implied a total rupture of the unity of the Church (Gal. 2:11ff.); and this explains also why with equal vigour he objected to a continuation of eucharistic fellowship with such as by their sins were compromising the holiness of the Church (1 Cor. 5:11).

(b) This communion is also established on a religious level, between men and God. That is why God is so angry with those of His people who, seduced by the daughters of Moab, have taken part in feasts celebrated in the honour and presence of Baal-Peor (Num. 25:1–5) or with those who, in violation of the old covenant, dishonestly shared in pagan festivals (cf. Judg. 9:27; Ezek. 18:6,11,15; 22:9). For through sacramental communion with pagan gods, a unity was created comparable with the sexual bond: to share in heathen feasts is therefore for Israel a sort of prostitution. It is against such a background of ideas that we should understand what Paul says about meats sacrificed to idols (cf. 1 Cor. 8–10).

(c) But if the biblical authors are so opposed to the presence of Israelites or Christians at these sacrificial pagan feasts, it is in the light of the realization that God too, or His Christ, wishes to be united with Israel or the Church by means of fellowship meals. The O.T. knows a type of *sacrifice usually called sacrifice of thanksgiving, but which it would be preferable with the LXX to call sacrifice of peace or sacrifice of communion (Lev. 3:1ff.; 19:5ff.); after having drained the victim of its blood and reserved for God certain portions of fat (the food of God, Lev. 3:11; Num. 28:2) which the priest causes to smoke on the altar (the table of God, Mal. 1:7,12), the flesh of the victim is consumed by the priest and his guests (cf. 1 Sam. 1:3ff., 9:13ff., etc.). Thus a fellowship is set up not only between the human participants but also between the latter and God, the author of the *covenant (cf. Exod. 24:3–11; Deut. 27:7; Ps. 50:5,

etc.). In the perspective of the N.T. it is through the feast of the *Lord's Supper that communion is established and sealed between Jesus Christ and His own, and perhaps Paul came near to understanding the Christian communion in the light of the communion sacrifices of the old covenant. At least this might be inferred from 1 Cor. 8–10 where the polemic against heathen sacrifices springs from concern for the Lord's Supper and its momentous significance for Christian unity and fellowship.

(d) The meal of fellowship also plays a part in the hopes of the people of God: it is the Messianic banquet foretold by the prophets (cf. Isa. 25:6; 34:6ff.; Zeph. 1:7, etc.) and expected also by the Church (cf. Matt. 8:11; 26:29; Lk. 22:29ff.). But this eschatological feast, a feast of the marriage of the Lamb (cf. Matt. 22:2f.; Rev. 19:9) is anticipated already in the meals which Jesus takes with His disciples (cf. Matt. 11:16–19; Jn. 2:1–10), in the miracle of feeding (Matt. 14:13–21, etc.), in the meals which mark His resurrection appearances (cf. Lk. 24:30f., 41ff.; Jn. 21:9f.; Acts 10:41), and—what sums up all these meals—in the Lord's Supper (cf. 1 Cor. 11:26; 3:20). This is why the ancient Church celebrated this meal in the *joy of salvation (Acts 2:46; 16:34).

(e) When we see the apostolic Church refuse to hold fellowship with sinners (1 Cor. 5:11) we may wonder if it was not contradicting its Lord, who, as it happened, insisted on sharing His meals with sinners (cf. Mark 2:15ff., etc., Lk. 15:2; cf. however Acts 11:3). On this the following observations may be made: firstly in agreeing to eat with sinners Jesus (rather like at the time of His *baptism) was showing His solidarity with them and declaring that it was for their sakes that He had come; secondly that the apostolic Church did not forbid eating with sinners if the latter were not of the Church (cf. 1 Cor. 5:10; 8:7ff.; 10:25–31): but that since it was, since Pentecost, the Body of Christ or the temple of the Holy Spirit it could not tolerate within its bosom anything that would have violated its sanctity.

A. LELIÈVRE

EDIFY, *see* BUILD

EGYPT, *see* NAMES (GEOGRAPHICAL)

ELDERS, *see* MINISTRY N.T.

ELECT

O.T.

1. The fundamental word for the doctrine of election in the O.T. is the verb *bahar*, whose primary sense is that of casting a rapid glance, as an animal run to earth glances at the huntsman. From this first meaning the idea of inspecting is derived, then that of choosing. Like a large number of other verbs, it can be used in all instances where it would be possible to employ it in our own language.

In the sphere of daily life, one might choose an *object* (stones, 1 Sam. 17:40; one's way, Ps. 25:12; a refuge, Deut. 23:16) or a *person* (a wife, Gen. 6:2; heads over the people, Exod. 18:25) or a *moral reality* (good or evil, Isa. 7: 15–16; life or death, Deut. 30:19). There is a word derived from this root which is used of young people, the gallant, the men of choice, the *élite* (*bahur*, Judg. 20:16). So far as one can judge, a choice, whatever it may be, presupposes an investigation, a process of reflection which is more intellectual than emotional in character. The considerations for and against having been carefully weighed, a decision or choice is made. Nevertheless this choice cannot be entirely divorced from feelings of preference: a man chooses what he himself loves best, and so the verb choose comes to mean also love (Isa. 1:29; Job 36:21).

2. More commonly, the verb choose is used in connection with the religious life of a man or people, God being either subject or object. Thus, when man meets God with His claim upon him, he chooses; and the object of choice is what comes from God: His law, His will, His way (Ps. 119:30, 173; Prov. 1:29). Only rarely is God Himself the object of choice: it is not the people who choose God but God who chooses His people: though the idea is not entirely absent, as can be seen from Josh. 24:15,22, one of the few texts where it is actually explicit: "Choose this day whom you will serve. . . . You have chosen the Lord, to serve him." The people were confronted with a choice between God and the idols; they chose God, even after Joshua's stern warnings against making a superficial and too rapid choice. But even here the people's choosing seems to be secondary to God's choosing, for if they choose the Lord it is because God has delivered them, guided them and jealously loved them (vv. 16–20).

3. This brings us to the essence of the election idea in the O.T.: *God has chosen the nation of Israel* from among other peoples, to make of her His own people. This choice on the part of God was especially exhibited in two events to which Israelite tradition constantly referred: the election of the people even before its historical existence in the person of Abraham and his descendants (Gen. 12:1–2; 22:15–18; 26:4; Isa. 41:8; Neh. 9:7); and the election of the people at the moment of the exodus from Egypt under the leadership of Moses, who had been called by God for this redemptive mission (Exod. 3:7–10; Deut. 6:21–23; Ps. 105:26). Though this choosing by God is a fundamental certainty of Israel's faith, it remains nevertheless outside the realm of rational explanation. On what grounds did God choose Israel? No positive reply is given to that question, for God alone is master of His decision. Deuteronomy does attempt some sort of negative reply: if God has chosen Israel, it is not because they were a numerous people—on the contrary, they were the fewest of all peoples (Deut. 7:7); it is not because they were more righteous than others and so deserve this privilege—on the contrary they were a stiff-necked people (Deut. 9:4–6). If God has chosen them, it is because God *loves* them and desires to be faithful to His covenant and His promise made to their ancestors (Deut. 4:37; 7:8; 10:15). The people is elect because it is loved by God (Deut. 23:5).

Election then corresponds to the *love of *God for His people. But this explanation does not satisfy the reason; for why did God love this people and not some other people?

The only explanation, and that goes beyond human reason, is that election simply has its ground in God Himself, in His sovereign freedom of action, as He determines. He is bound by nothing and by nobody, and if He chose Abel rather than Cain, Isaac and not Ishmael, Jacob and not Esau, it is because He is sovereign and has the right to act as He pleases (Mal. 1:2). The most striking picture of this sovereignty is that of the potter who makes some vessel that he has in mind and then smashes it, if he likes, in order to start another—what he does with the clay in his hand is entirely his own affair (Jer. 18:2–6). And yet God's election is not like the arbitrary caprice of a despot; it is always directed towards a precise end, namely, the fulfilment of a plan for the salvation of the world. There is no election for its own sake; there *is* election for a predetermined mission, for service. The people has been chosen to execute a mission among the nations, and while its election does carry with it certain privileges (divine blessing, promise, protection and deliverance), it also imposes an obligation which cannot be shed without being unfaithful or breaking the covenant. The notion of election is therefore allied to that of *covenant.

At the same time there is obviously a limitation to the election in that infidelity involves the breaking of the covenant. The people's infidelity can take two possible forms: on the one hand through forgetting the mission with which she is entrusted, since God chose her; on the other hand through a feeling of superiority and pride before other nations, and the idea that God owes her His protection and His preference in all circumstances (e.g., the idea that Jerusalem will never be conquered and destroyed, because it is the city which the Eternal One inhabits). Against the erroneous conception of election the prophets struggled; they showed the people

that contrary to the popular idea which tended to see in the heathen those whom God had rejected and in Israel the people elect for ever, God's choice did involve a completely responsible act of obedience and fidelity: otherwise it would be *Israel who would be rejected, and not the idolaters. "You only have I known of all the families of the earth; therefore I will punish you for all your iniquities" (Amos 3:2; Jer. 7:16–34; 37:17–20; Ezek. 6–7; Ps. 78:59–67, etc.). The Babylonian Exile is held out by the prophets as God's great punishment of His faithless people, at the very time when the nation's leaders were proclaiming: God is with us, no evil shall come upon us! (Mic. 3:11; Jer. 5:12; Ezek. 13). The righteousness of God demands that His people be not blinded by this election to the extent of forgetting their mission (Amos 4; 9:7–8).

4. However, apart from certain rare exceptions, the prophets do not declare that the people will be totally rejected by God. Though the Lord punishes and tries them, He Himself remains faithful to His promise and to His covenant, and the people's mission continues. Israel will be punished, but a *remnant will survive in order to accomplish the will of God. The remnant conception is an important aspect of election, for it is the remnant which is to inherit at once the privileges and the responsibility of mission which the Lord had laid on His people (Isa. 4:3; 10:22–23; 37:31–32; Zeph. 2:3; Mic. 5:7–9). After the Exile, the little Jewish community which returned to Jerusalem regarded itself as the remnant of whom the prophets had spoken, but there again two divergent ideas begin to appear at the heart of Judaism: the idea of the remnant who had been saved by God—the community of those who were pure and faithful—an idea which culminated in Pharisaic pride, narrow particularism and intolerant nationalism; and also the idea of the remnant who had indeed been saved by God, though to fulfil a mission amongst the nations and bring them the message of the Salvation of the Everlasting One, an idea which implied the missionary universalism

4

which finds expression in some of the most beautiful passages of the O.T. (especially in Isa. 40–55; cf. too Zech. 8:20–23).

The result of this ambivalent notion of remnant can be noticed in the attitude of Judaism towards the Gentiles; either the Gentile nations will be finally rejected by God at the end of the age; or else they will all come to the knowledge of the true God, thanks to Israel who will have been the light of all peoples.

5. The O.T. speaks also of an election which concerns not the people, but certain individuals. Men of God are chosen by him: Abraham (Neh. 9:7), Moses (Ps. 105:26), David (Ps. 78:70). The priests too are the object of God's choice (Deut. 18:5; 2 Chr. 29:11). Equally, the prophets are chosen, though the actual term is not often used in their case: they are called by God or set apart from their birth (Jer. 1:5). Kings are very specially regarded as chosen by God (1 Sam. 10:24; 16:6–13, etc.). In this choosing on the part of God we again find the idea previously pointed out, namely, that the action of God is not arbitrary, though it is completely free and, on the purely human level, non-rational. It has in view a mission or a service which is entrusted to the man thus selected. To such a degree is this essential that in very many texts God's election appears under a peculiar form, possibly even outside the nation of Israel. God chooses nations or men to serve as the instruments of the fulfilment of His purpose, and those nations or men may well be even Gentiles.

By way of punishment, God sends the army of the Babylonians against His people and Jeremiah advises submission since such is the will of God (Jer. 27; 32). Nebuchadnezzar is sent by God to carry out His orders as "his servant" (Jer. 25:9); so too Pharaoh had shown his hardness of heart towards the Hebrews so that the glory and the power of the Lord could be released (Exod. 14:17–18); so too Cyrus shall be called the anointed of God, appointed to give back their liberty to the captive people (Isa. 45:1; Ezra 1:1–3). All these men are not made part of the chosen people; they are in some cases its mortal enemies. But in spite of that, and for the sake of some particular service, they have been chosen by God.

We reach then a conception, in some sort, of a divine decree for the direction of the world and the control of history. Once again it is in the chapters of the second Isaiah (Isa. 40–55) that the idea of God directing events according to His sovereign will is clearly expressed. He has foreseen from afar what would happen and He has overruled men so that His will should be fulfilled (Isa. 41:21–29; 42:8–9; 44:6–8, etc.). Here is a theological understanding of history which expresses explicitly what is latent in the whole biblical revelation.

Contrariwise, the idea of individual predestination is rarely met in the O.T. The sole text which could really be adduced is Ps. 139:15–16.

F. MICHAELI

N.T.

The idea of election is expressed in the N.T. by the verb choose (19 times), the adjective chosen (23 times) and the noun election (7 times). A glance over these passages and their context shows that we are concerned with a characteristic theme of primitive Christian reflection.

1. In the four Gospels the verb describes in the first place the *choice* that Jesus made of His apostles (Lk. 14:7 and 10: 42 are exceptions; these are instances of a more general and more Greek use of the term, the sense being of choosing or reserving for oneself—a seat at a banquet, or the "good portion" in the story of Martha and Mary). On the choice of the apostles the following points may be noted:

(a) Only Luke (6:13) uses the verb choose in his narrative (cf. Mk. 3:13–19; Matt. 10:1–4); (b) the Gospels without exception present this choice on the part of Jesus as a sovereign and perfectly free action; the election is in no way a recognition of the merits or the qualities of the apostles; the apostles are made to stand out from the anonymous multitude of "disciples" but no reason can be given for this choice except the authority of Jesus; (c) election is never merely for its own sake but has always a definite "instrumental" character: the disciples are chosen with a view to a mission which is at the same moment entrusted to them, that of announcing the Kingdom, casting out demons, healing the sick (Matt. 10:1–4; Mk. 3:13–19; but in Lk. 6:12–16 only, the account of the choosing of the Twelve does not coincide with their authorization for the apostolic ministry); (d) in the narratives of the choosing of the Twelve the name of Judas appears with the explicit qualification "he who betrayed him" (or another formula to the same effect). While the synoptists merely emphasize thus Jesus' choice of the traitor, the fourth Gospel unfolds a mature and developed thought. John brings out far more clearly than the synoptists do that through the call of Jesus God's own work is being accomplished, but there are in addition these two suggestions: divine election is accomplished only through the Son and is always therefore historical in character; John does not know of any non-temporal decree (Jn. 6:65; 13:18). Secondly, this election is a call to faith and obedience. It does not eliminate man's obligations; on the contrary, it makes them both practicable and pressing (Jn. 6:70; 15:16, "chosen that you should go and bear fruit").

On the subject of Judas, the fourth evangelist declares on the one hand that he has been chosen by Jesus in full knowledge of the situation (his being chosen was neither a mistake, nor an accident, nor an ill-considered act of generosity "to see if that would be successful"), but also, on the other hand, he declares that Judas "did not believe" (6:64); the traitor was preeminently one who doubted, and, because a doubter, "a devil" (6:70). Moreover his revolt against Jesus did not apparently exempt him from doing just that for which he had been chosen "in order that the scripture might be fulfilled" (13:18). As Jesus unmasks him, he is told: "What you

are going to do, do quickly" (13:27). The texts therefore do not bring into relief the personal responsibility of Judas so much as the fact—and a very terrible fact for anyone who cares to meditate on it—that it "was necessary", doubtless on account of the gravity of sin, that the demon of the betrayal should play havoc even with the inmost group of apostles themselves.

In the Gospels the adjective *chosen* is applied to Jesus (twice by Lk., 9:35 and 23:35). In the Greek version of the O.T. (LXX) this word, with its Christological implications, was never applied to the Messiah as such, but only to the servant of the Lord in Isaiah (42:1). But it was very often used of the Messiah in Jewish apocalyptic literature: which is a reminder that Jewish thought simply could not conceive of an authority or a mission, whether human or divine, whose fundamental explanation did not lie in a sovereign act of divine choice.

In the other texts, the adjective *chosen* is used substantively in the plural to denote the members of the Messianic community, always in a very eschatological context: the fundamental conception is that the elect (Matt. 24:22,24; Mk. 13:20,22,27; Lk. 18:7) will, in the last days, endure terrible trials, but that they will overcome them entirely by the grace of God. The spirit of self-righteousness and proud security which often marks the later Jewish apocalypses here finds an echo, but a purified echo. The same expressions may be recognized, but man now trembles again before the tribulation and the judgment to come; he trembles and trusts, come what may, in the "last" assistance of God. Mk. 13 and Matt. 24, while being a solemn warning to the elect against those who would lead them astray, also contain a promise and message of help: the Lord "has shortened" (Mk. 13:20 and parallels) those days because of, and for the sake of, the elect. As for the famous conclusion (Matt. 22:14) of the parable of the wedding feast, "For many are called, but few are chosen", it must probably be understood in the sense of a warning of Jesus against the illusory security of the

Jews (or His own disciples); it is not enough to rely on the Messianic invitation: it is still necessary to recognize it and embrace it at the moment when it is resounding (in this case, v. 14 would be the conclusion of the parable itself, vv.1–10); or, it is not enough to accept this invitation but it is necessary also to come to the feast, stripped of all self-righteousness and clad only in the mercy of God, represented by the wedding-garment (in this case, v. 14 would be related only to vv. 10–13, as Lk. 14:16–24 seems to indicate). It might also be that here, as frequently in the N.T., the adjectives *called and chosen* have the same meaning and that the verse is a warning, in paradoxical form, against religious illusions: there are fewer truly chosen than you think!

2. As in the third Gospel, so also in the Acts of the Apostles the idea of election is prominent, is indeed one of the points where the kinship of the two narratives is manifest. Only the verb to choose is found, never the adjective derived from it. In Acts the verb is applied, first, to the choice, within the Church, of an apostle (1:24), and deacons (6:5—though the actual word deacon is not used here), and delegates (15:22,25). On this, it is to be observed that (*a*) these "elections" were not regarded as anything more than a recording of the sovereign choice of God. "Show [by the lot] which one of these two *thou* hast chosen" (1:24). The Church's rôle, though it is certainly very real, is limited to "putting forward" two men (1:23) between whom the lot should decide (26); and (*b*) this election by the Church was followed by the "putting forward" of the elected to the apostles who, after prayer, laid their hands on them (Acts 6:6). (*c*) This election was carried out by the apostles and elders, with the concurrence of the whole Church, and apparently within the restricted group of apostles and elders only (15:22,25).

What is more striking in the several texts is the variety of methods of election: two principal ingredients were required for reaching any decision—the mind of the

entire Church, and the authority of particular ministers (apostles or elders); and it was felt that the will of God was indeed made known, whatever may have been the exact procedure in each case (15:28). According to Acts 13:17 "the God of this people Israel chose our fathers", and this divine act of election is followed by an imposing list of God's interventions in the course of history for the purpose of preserving the nation, for the primary reason for the election was to make ready the way for the coming of a "Saviour" in the midst of and for the benefit of the chosen people. It is evident from this verse that Israel's election only had any meaning for the first Christians because it made possible the salvation through Jesus. In 15:7, as in the Gospels, election has a decidedly instrumental character: Peter was chosen by God in order to make the Gospel heard among the heathen; the words "from the early days" no doubt refer to the beginnings of the Church of Jerusalem.

3. In the Epistles, while any notion of election by members of the Church is quite unheard of, the conception of God's activity of choosing is more widely and more profoundly expounded, and rings with clear theological echoes from the Gospels.

It is the divine election alone which gives the Church at once an exalted destiny and a missionary vocation, both of which conceptions are fundamental to 1 Cor. 1:27–31. In this amazing passage, four points are specially noteworthy: (*a*) The triumphal note which makes God alone the creator of the Church; (*b*) the fact that election means a real creation by God and certainly not the adoption of human values (v. 28); (*c*) the fact that God's election of "low and despised" things had one single aim in view, namely, that no human being might boast in the presence of God (vv. 29, 31); (*d*) all this reflection by the apostle on the weakness of those chosen by God does not rest on general philosophical conceptions, nor on a peculiar taste for paradox, but derives from meditation on the *cross of Jesus Christ (vv. 17f.). This Pauline passage might be compared with the idea of the "chosen vessel" of Acts 9:15 and, more especially, with the panegyric in Jas. 2:5 on the poor, chosen and made rich by faith.

In Eph. 1:4ff. the author is dealing with a very different matter. This is the only passage in the N.T. where election is explicitly stated to have its roots in eternity (cf. 1 Pet. 1:2): "before the foundation of the world"; and yet this does not deprive it of the historical character of being founded on Jesus Christ: ". . . he chose us *in him*" (v. 4). Moreover the end of election is no longer here the evangelization of the world, but the sanctification of the faithful and the "praise of his glorious grace".

As for the adjective *chosen* or *elect*, Paul hardly ever uses it. When he does it denotes the members of the Church and would appear to be synonymous with the saints (see *Holy) (Rom. 8:33; Col. 3:12; note Rom. 16:13 where the adjective is applied to a single member of the Church, Rufus; cf. also 2 Jn. 13). Plainly the apostle is much more impressed by the historical event of divine election "in Christ" than he is concerned with the simultaneous existence of people chosen and people not chosen.

It is indeed significant that the very idea of rejection (as the opposite of election) is entirely absent from the N.T.: even in Rom. 9:13 ("Jacob I loved, but Esau I hated," cited from Mal. 1:2–3) the context shows that this phrase is again intended to emphasize the merciful grace of God rather than His decree of death; the verb hate, moreover, does not here contain any implication of eternal reprobation. In the Pastoral Epistles election leads also to faith (Tit. 1:1) and leaves open the question of the final salvation of the "elect", for which the author will "endure everything" (2 Tim. 2:10). In 1 Tim. 5:21 it is said of the angels that they are the elect of God. This election by grace, acting concretely in history, accompanying, as it were, the people that it has created, preserving a "remnant" of the same people and leading it at last to Jesus Christ—this lies at the bottom of all Paul's reflection on the destiny of Israel (Rom. 9:11; 11:5,7,28).

4. Less explicit but no less characteristic are the expressions found in the Epistles of Peter and John. The elect are the members of the Church (1 Pet. 1:1); and the expression in this sense would seem to have become quite common (cf. also Rev. 17:14). On the "elect" stone, Jesus Christ (1 Pet. 2:4,6; cf. Isa. 28:16) is raised the new building of the Church, also called "a chosen race" (v. 9), as in the O.T. Here again then election preserves its absolutely Christocentric nature: the Church is only elect in virtue of its dependence on The Elect, Jesus Christ. In the first verse of the Epistle the idea of election is actually expressed within a trinitarian formula: the Christians are "chosen" by the foreknowledge of God the Father, sanctified by the Spirit, for obedience to Jesus Christ. Election is inconceivable without both the sanctification and the obedience which are its fruit: 2 Pet. 1:10 goes so far as to exhort believers to "confirm" their call and election, a paradoxical expression to be sure, but it is not, as has been asserted, in sheer contradiction to the teaching elsewhere in the N.T.

5. These observations can be summed up by listing the chief characteristics which the writers of the N.T. attribute to the idea of election:

(a) it is sovereign and it is free;

(b) it is worked out on the plane of history, *in* Jesus Christ;

(c) it confronts man with the demand to believe and obey;

(d) it means that God's final verdict on the believer is always held in suspense;

(e) it has a decidedly communal character —election does not isolate a man, but unites him to the others who are chosen;

(f) it is plainly instrumental: God chooses Jesus, apostles, Church, in order to entrust to their care a missionary task in the world.

6. The election terminology and conception are reinforced and made explicit by a collection of verbs and nouns which all centre round the idea of *predestination*, and each of them would have to be the subject of a separate investigation. In the abstract,

however, these terms add nothing fundamental to the wider concept of election; rather they are dependent on it and acquire the same theological nuances. These are primarily: God foreknowing (Rom. 8:29; 11:2; 1 Pet. 1:20; 2 Pet. 3:17) and the corresponding noun, foreknowledge (Acts 2:23; 1 Pet. 1:2): He "has prepared beforehand" (Rom. 9:23; Eph. 2:10); He "predestined" (Acts 4:28; Rom. 8:29,30; 1 Cor. 2:7; Eph. 1:5,11); He "set forth" (Eph. 1:9; cf. Rom. 1:13; 3:25) and the corresponding noun, "purpose", "aim", "setting forth" (Matt. 12:4; Mk. 2:26; Lk. 6:4; Heb. 9:2; Acts 11:23; 27:13; Rom. 8:28; 9:11; Eph. 1:11; 3:11; 2 Tim. 1:9; 3:10). All these terms have in common that they are formed with the assistance of the Greek prefix *pro-*, which means *before*, *in front of*, and is to be understood in a strictly temporal sense (with the possible exception of the shewbread expression in Mk. 2:26 and parallels). They all lay emphasis on the fact that the salvation wrought by Jesus Christ which is made known to the world by the preaching of the apostles, and will shortly be openly declared before the eyes of all, has been prepared by God since the beginning of the ages.

P. BONNARD

ELIJAH, *see* NAMES (PERSONAL)

ENDURE (ABIDE)

1. Both in the O.T. and the N.T., "to endure" refers to God and indicates the permanent duration of the divine person and action. The terms "kingdom" and "eternity" intensify this thought, but the verb "to endure" underlines the contrast between God and the divine world, which endure, and creatures and creation which are transient, without permanence and stability (Ps. 102:25-27 = Heb. 1:10-12). God is "the living God, enduring for ever; his kingdom shall never be destroyed, and his dominion shall be to the end" (Dan. 6:26), whereas earthly empires pass away (Dan. 7:1-12) and the wealth of man does not last (Job 15:29).

Just as God Himself endures, so the word of God endures, whilst every creature withers like the grass (Isa. 40:6-8 = 1 Pet. 1:24-25). The purpose of God remains firm, unlike the plans of the human heart (Prov. 19:21). From this standpoint the eschatological hope consists of the certainty that God and His kingdom will still remain, when the first creation will have disappeared (Isa. 66:22 = 2 Pet. 3:13; Heb. 12:27).

Already in the O.T. the idea emerges that the righteous man, through his very righteousness which draws him into close relationship to God, will not be subject to the ephemeral nature of this world, but will endure for ever (Ps. 112:4,9 = 2 Cor. 9:9). It is the N.T., however, which gives full play to this thought.

2. The coming of Jesus into history does not change the nature of this world. So long as the kingdom of God has not arrived in power and glory, "the form of this world is passing away" (1 Cor. 7:31). But in conferring the divine life upon believers, Christ has made them sharers henceforward in that which endures. Eternal life was for the Psalmist no more than a hope; by the coming of Jesus and by the gift of the *Spirit, it is for the believer a certainty already realized.

The four evangelists record that the Spirit descended upon Jesus at the time of His baptism, and John states explicitly that the Spirit remained on Him (1:32). Before ascending to His Father, Jesus imparts the Spirit to the disciples (Jn. 20:22; cf. 7:39). According to the N.T. as a whole, the age of the *Church is the age when the Spirit is poured out upon the believers and manifests in them His presence and His power (Acts 2:17f.; 10:44f.; Rom. 8:23; Gal. 3:2; Heb. 6:4; etc.). The Spirit creates in the believer a new life which nothing can destroy (Jn. 11:25-26; Rom. 8:36-39, etc.). This means not that the Spirit acts on rare occasions in the form of ecstasy and inspiration but that He abides in the Church and on the faithful.

Indeed, according to Paul, the Spirit "dwells" in the believer and the believers "are in the Spirit" (Rom. 8:9-11), just as Christ lives in the believers and the believers live in Christ (Gal. 2:20, etc.). According to John, just as, during the incarnation, Jesus is in God (14:20; 15:10) and God abides in Jesus (14:10), so the believers abide in Jesus and Jesus abides in the believers (6:56; 15:4–7; 1 Jn. 3:24); in the same way the believers abide in God and God in the believers (1 Jn. 4:12–16). The believer, who does the will of God, abides for ever (1 Jn. 2:17), but the unbeliever remains in sin (Jn. 9:41) and in death (1 Jn. 3:14).

In short, although believers live in a world which is passing away and in which "they have no lasting city" (Heb. 13:14), they themselves "endure" in the absolute sense, that is to say that, from the moment when they first believed, they are living that divine, spiritual life which has no end.

3. This theological setting helps us to understand the true nature of the Christian life. Through *faith the believer is lifted from the level of the ephemeral, which is the level of the world, up to the level of the permanent, which is the level of God, of Christ and of the Spirit. The believer must make a supreme effort not to fall back. That is why the verb "to abide" expresses the fundamental imperative of the life of the faithful. This life began for them at the moment when, through faith, they recognized Jesus as Christ and Lord. They must now persist in the decision which they have taken and in the behaviour which they adopted when they believed and when they entered into the spiritual life.

Thus the N.T., which is addressed chiefly to believers, contains more exhortations to abide in the faith than appeals to believe. Using a variety of expressions and figures, it reminds readers on every page that the Christian life is a state which ought to last and in which the faithful must remain at the cost of constant vigilance and perseverance. In His parables Jesus compares eager disciples to patient and unflinching servants who watch till dawn as they await their master (Mk. 13:34ff.). The Johannine Christ declares to the Jews who believe in Him: "If you continue in my word, you are truly my disciples" (Jn. 8:31). In other words: the act of faith by which a man recognizes Jesus as the revealer come from God, must be followed up by an "abiding in the word of Jesus", a fixed settlement in His teaching, the food which sustains his life. To keep His commands is to abide in love (Jn. 15:9–10) and in light (1 Jn. 2:10). That is the condition which must be fulfilled by one who would remain in communion with Christ and with God, as the apostle emphasizes it: "Let what you heard from the beginning abide in you. If what you heard from the beginning abides in you, then you will abide in the Son and in the Father" (1 Jn. 2:24). St. Paul expresses the same idea when he presents the Christian life now as the growth of the new creature born by the action of the Spirit (1 Cor. 3:1; 2:6; Eph. 4:13; Col. 1:28), now as a race in which the act of faith is the start (1 Cor. 9:24f.; Phil. 3:12f.). The Acts of the Apostles describes this abiding in faith as perseverance: "And they continued steadfastly in the apostles' teaching and fellowship, in the breaking of bread and the prayers" (Acts 2:42 R.V.). The Christian life in its fullness can be summed up in these four distinctive features which the Church must guard if she is to be the true Church and remain faithful to her Lord.

PH.-H. MENOUD

ENEMY, *see* DEVIL, WAR

ETERNITY, *see* TIME

EVIL, *see* GOOD, SIN

EXALTATION, *see* ASCENSION, GLORY

EXORCISM, *see* DEMONS, MIRACLE, SICKNESS

FACE

This word can be used in a most general way simply to express the visible aspect of some object, as, for example, the "face" of the earth (Gen. 2:6; Lk. 21:35), of the fields (Ezek. 32:4), of the waters (Eccl. 11:1), or of the heavens (Lk. 12:56). But strictly it applies to man and to God.

1. *The face of man.* Scripture often speaks of man's countenance, for it is in the countenance that his innermost feelings find expression. "A glad heart makes a cheerful countenance" (Prov. 15:13); on the other hand, anxiety is betrayed in a darkened countenance (Gen. 40:7). In the same way, Cain's countenance is downcast (Gen. 4:5) and Laban's is altered when his feelings alter (Gen. 31:2). The face of a frightened man goes pale (Jer. 30:6). In the case of a resolute man it is hardened (Isa. 50:7; Ezek. 3:8; Lk. 9:51, which may be literally rendered: "He hardened his face to go to Jerusalem"). "Confusion of face" is the sense of shame which causes a blush to rise (Ps. 34:6; Dan. 9:7) and which a man may seek to hide by covering his face (Mic. 3:7). Similarly, the face may be covered to hide tears (2 Kings 20:2) or as a sign of contempt (Isa. 53:3). The man who prays in humility prostrates himself before God with his face to the ground (Gen. 17:3; Matt. 26:39). The human face is, therefore, the reflection of man's hidden feelings.

But it is also the most individual feature of a human being, so that to speak of a man's face is really to speak of him as a person (Isa. 3:15). Especially is this so in the case of Jesus: His transfigured countenance is the sign of the glory that belongs to Him as a person (Matt. 17:2), and when He is struck across the face, it is a humiliation inflicted on His whole person (Matt. 26:67; cf. Matt. 5:39). The language of the Bible goes so far, indeed, as to use the face as a synonym for the individual person: thus the prophecy "I send my messenger before thy face" (Matt. 11:10=Mal. 3:1) simply means "before thee", and the Pauline expression concerning "the glory of God in the face of Christ" (2 Cor. 4:6) refers to His person and work regarded as one complete whole.

2. *The face of God.* The O.T., because it presents God in the image of man, talks of Him as having a face. Sometimes this is pure metaphor, for the purpose of conveying, by the picture of a wrathful (Lam. 4:16; Ps. 80:17) or a lightened countenance (Ps. 4:7), the feelings of anger or of goodwill inspiring God's attitude toward men. But even more frequently the term is used to denote the very being of God in His dealings with men; for God to turn His face toward man (Num. 6:26) is to show man His favour; conversely, to declare that "the face of the Lord is against those that do evil" (1 Pet. 3:12) is to say that He is demonstrating His wrath toward them. The face of God, therefore, denotes just so much of His invisible being as God for the present vouchsafes to reveal to men. Supremely, it is His goodness, His favour. Blessing, for the believer, is that Yahweh should cause His face to shine upon him (Num. 6:25); while to punish the sinner God turns away His face or hides it from him (Deut. 31:18) and so abandons him to death (Ps. 30:8; 104:29).

As has happened with His *angel or His *glory or His *name, so the face of God is sometimes personified in the O.T. It then plays a mediatory rôle between God and men. By this means the Jews avoid involving God too closely in human history. Thus: "He brought you out of Egypt with his own presence" (Deut. 4:37), or again: "The angel of his presence saved them" (Isa. 63:9). But the face of Yahweh is intimately bound up with His being to a greater degree than is the case with any of the other mediatory personifications. It is no more in fact than a respectful way of speaking of Yahweh Himself.

3. *God and man face to face.* Because God reveals Himself to man by showing him His face, man can and must *seek the face of God. This very common expression denotes the attitude of the pilgrim, who goes to the sanctuary to learn God's will (2 Sam. 21:1), and, in a more general sense, that of the believer who desires to live in the presence of God, or, as it is said, "in his sight" (1 Chr. 16:11). On the other hand, the unbeliever with a bad conscience tries to escape from the presence of God: he hides himself far from God's face, like Cain (Gen. 4:14,16), or flees from it like Jonah (Jon. 1:3,10). God Himself drives the wicked far from His face (Jer. 15:1). But

the Psalmist (Ps. 139:7) is well aware that in fact no one can escape the omnipresence of the Lord. Every man is, therefore, in the presence of God, and it is the essence of his human situation—towards which he is free to adopt an attitude of acceptance or rejection—that he exists face to face with God.

In addition to the normal mode by which every man lives in His presence, God grants special revelations to His servants, in which they are allowed to "*see" or to "behold" His face; thus Jacob at Peniel claims to have "seen God face to face" (Gen. 32:30; 33:10), as does Moses at Sinai (Exod. 33:11; Deut. 34:10; cf. Deut. 5:4). This does not mean that they have seen God with their bodily sight, for in this present world man cannot see the face of God and live (Exod. 33:20,23). The use of these two verbs in Scripture serves to convey the truth that God's faithful servants enter into an un-mediated relation with the very being of the invisible God who reveals Himself (Job 33:26; Ps. 11:7; 17:15).

But at the last day the partial vision of faith is to be replaced by the vision of God face to face, a full and complete knowledge of God in eternal love (1 Cor. 13:12), a knowledge which the angels in heaven already enjoy (Matt. 18:10). Meanwhile, the presence of the glorified Christ before the face of God (Heb. 9:24) gives the believer a pledge of this fulfilment.

S. AMSLER

FAITH

O.T.

Israel's religion was founded on the covenant concluded by God with His people at Sinai. This covenant was the foundation of the Israelites' faith. To believe is to hold as truth the existence of the God who spoke to Moses and who has revealed Himself as creator of the world and head of the people; it is to recognize the sovereign authority of the *law which He has given; it is to await with confidence the realization of the *promises connected

with the covenant. In short, to believe is, in Israel, to confess that God exists and that He acts in the past, the present and the future, and it is to live with trust in this God who governs history and directs His people. Without this faith in God, the people of Israel would not endure (cf. Isa. 7:9; 30:15). It is in faith that the people lives out its destiny.

Parallel to this collective expression in Israel is an individual expression. It is the attitude of assurance and trust in God of the righteous, who find in communion with Him strength and courage in the midst of trials (the Psalms, e.g. 73; or Job). Personal faith has its foundation in the certainty that God is sovereign. Through that it is written into the form of the people's collective faith in God.

Faith, a certainty that the God of the covenant governs the universe and will realize His promises, and faith, a personal trust of the righteous man in a God who Himself cares personally for him, are found united in the portrait which the O.T. gives of Abraham, the believer *par excellence* (Gen. 15:6, etc.). Faith was the attitude of Abraham throughout the trials to which he was submitted: the call to go out of his country, the promise of an heir when he was already advanced in age, the sacrifice of Isaac. By faith Abraham knew that God would carry out His promises; he handed over to God his destiny, which was also that of God's people.

N.T.

1. *Definition of faith*. The first term which the Christians used to describe themselves was "the believers" (Acts 2:44, etc.). The word faith or the verb to believe occur on almost every page of the N.T. But there is only one formal definition to be found in the N.T., which is in Heb. 11:1: "Faith is the assurance of things hoped for, the con-viction of things not seen." That is to say, the believer in virtue of his faith holds to be true those realities which now are invisible, either because they are still to come—in this case faith is equivalent to *hope—or be-

4*

cause they cannot be empirically known simply in view of what they are. What are these realities? Chapters 11 and 12 of the Epistle to the Hebrews state that faith is first faith in God ("Whoever would draw near to God, must believe that he exists, and that he rewards those who seek him", Heb. 11:6) who created the world through His word (11:3), and who prepared within the old covenant a salvation now realized in Christ. Jesus is "the pioneer and perfecter of our faith" (12:2). Or in other words, Christ, the mid-point of the two Testaments, is the head of all believers past and future, of Israel and of the Church; "He takes control of the faithful at the beginning and conducts them to the end" (C. Spicq). Believers can only reach salvation by means of this faith-union with Him who is the "head of salvation" (Heb. 2:10).

2. *The object of faith: *Jesus Christ.* On Jewish territory, faith in God is always taken for granted. So it is, for example, in Jn. 14:1, where Jesus says to His disciples: "You believe [R.S.V., marg.] in God"— which is obvious, since they are Israelites— "believe also in me." The heathen are moved to believe first in God the living and the true (1 Thess. 1:9) and then in "his son from heaven, whom he raised from the dead, Jesus, who delivers us from the wrath to come" (1 Thess. 1:10). The proper object of faith, according to the N.T., is Jesus Christ, who is the revealer of God, who brings salvation to its fruition in His name, and who, uniting believers to Himself, unites them to God and saves them.

Even in the first three Gospels believing means to maintain the truth of the Gospel which Jesus preaches: it means too that this Jesus is saluted as the Messianic saviour who works with all the power of God towards the salvation of mankind. Faith is trust in the person of Jesus and in the truth of His message, and, as a result, a total submission to His person and message, which are accepted as from God. Believing is to admit that by His preaching and miracles Jesus is established as the long-awaited deliverer (Matt. 11:4–6): it is to

confess Him, in one way or another, to be the Christ (Mk. 8:29; Matt. 8:10). To believe in Jesus is to believe in the *gospel (Mk. 1:15).

John wrote his Gospel "that you may believe that Jesus is the Christ, the Son of God, and that believing you may have life in his name" (20:31). Believing is to confess that Jesus is not just "the son of Joseph, from Nazareth" (1:45; 6:42), but also and at the same time the Son who has come from beside the Father in order to give life to the world. The thought is, essentially, the same as that of the other Gospels, but John emphasizes still more, if that is possible, that Jesus has come from beside the Father (8:23) in order to reveal Him and make Him known among men (1:18); He alone is the Way which leads to the Father (14:6); He is the Resurrection and the Life (11:25); He gives eternal life and the promise of resurrection at the last day (6:40, etc.) to those who believe in Him, i.e. who come to Him as the only Saviour (6:68) and who perseveringly abide in His communion (8:30–31).

After Pentecost, *Peter* and the apostles preach faith in Jesus as being the Christ sent by God, who has died and been raised up (Acts 2:36; 10:40–42); and, having believed, the first essential step was to be baptized into His name and to receive the Holy Spirit (Acts 2:38). This Jesus, Christ and Lord, whom the apostles proclaim, is the only name given among men by whom they may be saved (Acts 4:12).

Paul's teaching is no different; cf. the summary of this point given in Rom. 10:9–10: "If you confess with your lips that Jesus is Lord and believe in your heart that God raised him from the dead, you will be saved. For man believes with his heart and so is justified, and he confesses with his lips and so is saved." To believe is to assent that Jesus is the Lord who, acting in the name of God, has reconciled sinners with Himself (2 Cor. 5:19) and so created a new medium of salvation. This new order has brought the reign of Law to its end; it is based on faith and becomes concrete in the obedience of the faithful to

Christ, with whom they live in personal communion.

In short, the N.T. conception of belief is a confession that Jesus' declarations on His person are true, together with the apostolic witness which, after the death and resurrection of Jesus, affirmed that He is very Lord and Christ. This faith moreover implies that by it the believer is totally committed; he is bound to Him who is henceforward his Lord and who makes him live in newness of life. At all times and in all places faith is at once a confession and a life renewed in obedience to Christ, who is the object of faith and confession.

3. *The effects of faith.* In his act of belief, the Christian says "Yes, and Amen" to the message of Jesus and, after Him, to that preached by the apostles. He realizes that Jesus came to inaugurate the new covenant and to accomplish the redemption which the old covenant had foreshadowed. He knows that with the life, death and resurrection of Jesus, and the apostolic witness which published these facts, the history of salvation has entered into the last epoch and is to reach its term "at the last day" with the return of Christ. He knows that meanwhile Christ is present in the midst of His own through the Spirit and He gathers together in this Church those who belong to Him. Faith is thus a new vision of history and of the world.

At the same time the believer himself participates personally in this last stage of the history of salvation. By faith he is included within this history, which becomes his own destiny. The apostle Paul expresses in incomparable language the solidarity which exists between Christ and the believer when he says that he who believes in Christ is "dead with him" (Col. 3:3), "buried with him" (Rom. 6:4), "raised with him" (Col. 2:12), "lives with him" (Rom. 6:8), is to be "glorified with him" (Rom. 8:17) and "reign with him" (1 Cor. 4:8). By his faith, the man of faith understands that the work of Christ for the salvation of sinners has been accomplished, including of course himself, and that he has been saved provided

that he believes in Christ and remains in His allegiance, living henceforward "in the obedience of faith" (Rom. 1:5, etc.). Faith gives life and salvation.

4. Unbelief appears everywhere in the N.T. as the supreme evil. Not to believe is in fact practically to annul the work of Christ: it means that the individual remains in his sin, far removed from all possible salvation. That is the reason why the faithful are exhorted without ceasing to "*abide" in the faith. It is also why spreading the faith appears as the duty *par excellence* of the Church confronted with the world (Mk. 13:10; Jn. 20:31; Acts 1:8; 1 Cor. 9:16, etc.).

PH.-H. MENOUD

FALL, *see* SIN

FALSEHOOD

O.T.

There are more than a dozen terms which are more or less closely connected with falsehood. This term is firmly associated with the notion of *word in the O.T. For the latter, the word is powerful, effective, not by an immanence which is proper to itself, for in itself it is empty, but by a privilege which Yahweh has accorded to the human word. The word can thus be an instrument that is magnificent or dangerous. Falsehood will be an *autonomous* word, that is to say, a word whose power it is desired to use outside of the will of God. The liar will say, "By my words I am strong" (Ps. 12). But this will also be an *evil* word, for man, imagining himself to be master of this power, will wish to make use of it against Yahweh, against his neighbour, and for his own advantage; this last pretension will in the end be only illusion. This deception of falsehood is of primary importance for the O.T.; and perhaps it is also that which most distinguishes it from *truth, which is *stable*. Against Yahweh, falsehood will correspond to magic—the utilization of forces other than His—or idolatry; against one's neighbour, it will again correspond to magic: wicked, hurtful words, or that which we are accustomed to call falsehood or calumny, and the words are also wicked because they deceive those who hear them and hurt him who is their victim. All would act as though the word spoken were true.

By falsehood man wishes to produce an effect upon men, upon things, upon the past and also upon the future, not only to rewrite history, but also to "remake" it; that is why, for St. John, the fundamental falsehood will be to deny either the divinity or the humanity of Christ, who Himself is the centre of history (1 Jn. 4:1 and 1 Jn. 2:22). (It is interesting to see that in Genesis 3 the serpent recreates the past in order to produce an effect upon the future.)

1. *Magic and falsehood* (cf. Ps. 59:13 and Isa. 28:15, where falsehood is a power of the infernal world). As is the case with idolatry, falsehood applies not only to the words, but to the attitude and to the existence of the "liar", as well as to the power of which it makes use and which it serves (the nature of everything is perverted by falsehood). It may be asked whether, fundamentally, falsehood was not for the Israelite a power (one of those which Christ "despoiled"), illusory indeed, but on which men confer a potency.

2. *Idolatry and falsehood*. Similarly idols will be called "Falsehood", and are closely related to it (Amos 2:4; Jer. 10:14; Zech. 10:2): one term, in fact, signifies falsehood or folly as well as a little idol; and another term can, dependent on its pointing, signify nonentity, falsehood, and perhaps charms or force. And, turn and turn about, we find expressed in the same terms the redoubtable force as well as the nonentity and the folly of these idols. Falsehood is at the very heart of the mystery of sin, which at one and the same time is a nonentity and illusory, but also harmful because this nonentity and this illusion are disintegrating and destructive. We should note that the sincerity of those who worship idols is not taken into account. Paul follows the lead of the O.T. when he says that the creatures have *changed* the truth of God into false-

hood (Rom. 1:25). It is remarkable, moreover, that he does not say that they "have abandoned the truth of God for falsehood". Falsehood has not a personal, autonomous existence. For the O.T., as for Paul, the deified creature is a falsehood, a pseudo-deity, which arrogates to itself that which belongs to the true God. It promises man that which it is unable to give him. It will give him the very opposite, but man obstinately believes that this creature will grant him this deification. This is the grand mockery of the prophets (Isa. 44:6–10, especially v. 20; Jer. 10:6–16; 51:15–18, especially v. 17).

3. *Genesis* 3. The tempter, moreover, will begin his work of death with a falsehood (indeed, several), and it is noteworthy that (in v. 2) the Samaritan Code reads "liar" instead of serpent, an interesting dogmatic correction (cf. Jn. 8:44). Besides, it may be asked why the serpent has been taken as a type of the liar: to begin with, because of its divided tongue (Ps. 52:4?), for one of the terms used for false signifies either slippery or divided (one can think of the ambiguous language of Genesis 3), and all the more so as duplicity, "duality", is one of the characteristics of the liar (cf. Ps. 12 where the liar, in particular because of his words, has a double heart—literally, a heart and a heart; cf. also Jas. 1:8, the "doubleminded" man). To have two lives, for example, one for Sunday and one for the rest of the week, is what the O.T. would call falsehood. If the serpent has been chosen as a type of the liar, it is perhaps again because of its fascination, by which it persuades its prey of impotence. This strange power, which resides more in the victim than in the serpent, could not have failed to make an impression on the Israelites. The corrector of the Samaritan Code understood fully that it was falsehood: at the origin of sin it is a deception which causes man to follow an imaginary goal, and which for that very reason is hurtful, fatal, since by trusting in it man loses himself.

4. *The law and falsehood*. In the Deca-

logue there is no commandment "Thou shalt not lie" (cf. however Lev. 19:11), but: (*a*) it is implicit in the first three commandments. (The third commandment should in fact be translated "You shall not take the name of Yahweh for the purpose of sinning", and not "in vain", that is to say, you shall not make use of the power of God's name for the purpose of doing wrong to your neighbour.) (*b*) "You shall not bear false witness against your neighbour" is a particular case of falsehood, the most obvious case. There are, however, two reasons for the omission from the Decalogue of the commandment "You shall not lie": it would mean ultimately "You shall not sin" and would run the risk of lapsing into a general prohibition; secondly, the thinking of the Israelites is realistic: for them, falsehood is not something relative to an abstract or inner truth. Truth is what Yahweh has done or will do in history and what He wishes to be done. Thus to boast was not, at first, necessarily to lie, and Yahweh blesses the midwives of Exodus 1. Truth is also the integrity of one's neighbour, and falsehood attempts not only to harm him, but also to corrupt him. The proof of this is that, if in a case of false witness the judgment confirmed that it was such, the accused, regarding himself as forsaken by God, came to acknowledge himself a sinner.

5. *Prophecy and falsehood.* One lies if one speaks when Yahweh has said nothing or when one distorts what He has said (prophet of falsehood, Jer. 29:9; Ezek. 13). By telling or foretelling a false story the prophets of falsehood ensnare the people and lead them to their perdition.

Without being radically separated from its primitive sense, the term falsehood later took on a more modern sense, but the main criterion seems clearly enough not to have been primarily subjective: to lie is to take away from or to add to that which is true (Prov. 30:6). The final verdict of the O.T. concerning falsehood is that it is an illusion and a folly, for sooner or later the word returns to him who is its author. Falsehood is false to him who is false.

N.T.

1. It is John who has accorded most space to falsehood. Jn. 8:44, perhaps under the influence of the Samaritan Code (cf. above), calls the Devil "a liar and the father of falsehood" and also, in parallel, "a murderer". The Jews are his children because they do not acknowledge the divinity of Christ (cf. 1 Jn. 2:22 where falsehood is also the denial of the divinity of Christ). With John falsehood stands in relation to Christ—more exactly, the historic Christ is the *Truth (14:6), and whoever does not acknowledge this is in falsehood. Thus everything seen apart from Christ will be seen in a falsified manner. In 1 Jn. 1:6 falsehood, for the Christian, occurs when there is contradiction between what he *is* and how he *lives*; contrariwise, in 2:4, it is to affirm the existence of that which is not. There is a strange and instructive link between "being a Christian, saying that one is a Christian, and living as a Christian". If one of these three parts is in contradiction with the others, it is a falsehood. This is again the case when there is inconsistency between one's relationships with God and one's relationships with one's neighbour (1 Jn. 4:21). The reality of an affirmation which runs the risk of being subjective should be verified by an objective conformity: the N.T. also leads to the conclusion that sincerity does not remove from falsehood its character of falsity. Hypocrisy is in no wise the opposite of sincerity. Hypocrisy is incompatibility between what one is and what one pretends or believes oneself to be. And even though his true nature constantly keeps on obtruding itself, the hypocrite is unable to reach a clear understanding of it. It is for this reason that Jesus "belabours" the Pharisees so strongly. Hypocrisy is the normal outcome of sin by which man believes in that which is not and believes himself to be what he is not.

2. In falsehood Paul sees the characteristic work of the "old man" (Col. 3:9). We have already encountered above the text Rom. 1:25. It is partially explained by Rom. 5:12ff. which shows: (*a*) that sin,

despite its power, has created nothing: it only destroys and leads to death; (*b*) that even while doing this sin does not create for man a history that is independent of the purpose of God, and thus (*c*) that it is God alone who, through His grace, saves man. Sin has been false all along the line.

3. The following passages should also be noted: Matt. 26:59, which shows that it is with the help of falsehood that the Sanhedrin proceeds to condemn Jesus; according to Acts 5:1ff. falsehood is the sign of death (cf. also Rev. 21:8); let us also remember the important text which shows that God cannot lie (Heb. 6:18).

Apostles of falsehood, or false apostles, false prophets, etc. It is in 2 Cor. 11:1–15 that we have some information on the subject of such men, but the question is far from being solved. They are, however, (*a*) men who set themselves up above the apostles. They call themselves super-apostles (v. 5). Is this meant with respect to doctrine or ethics because of a particular asceticism? Both, without doubt. (*b*) They introduce another "Christ" whom they support in a different spirit (v. 4); that is to say that another doctrine, without doubt gnostic, has been revealed to them by another Pentecost (their own).

In every respect falsehood is present because there is an attack on the historic person of Christ, failure to recognize those whom He has chosen (the Incarnation and Pentecost are unique), and seduction of the Corinthians who are moving, like Eve, towards their destruction (v. 3).

False Christ (Mk. 13:22; Matt. 24:24). The false Christ does not deny the existence of a Christ; on the contrary, his position is based on the expectation of the world concerning such a person, only he appropriates to himself this expectation.

A. MAILLOT

FAMILY

O.T., *see* *MARRIAGE

N.T.

1. "Call no man your father on earth, for you have one Father, who is in heaven" (Matt. 23:9). The meaning is that with the coming of Jesus the family set-up of the O.T. dispensation is abolished, at the same time as everything else in God's first creation: it is the end of our world. In this sense, He has come "to set a man against his father, and a daughter against her mother, and a daughter-in-law against her mother-in-law; and a man's foes will be those of his own household" (Matt. 10:35f.), and Jesus will not allow that domestic reasons should interfere with God's call to a man to embrace the *Kingdom (Matt. 8:21). The time has now come when the structure of the family must cease to be decisive: for the Kingdom is present: and to enter into salvation a man must be able not only to renounce family ties, but even to repudiate them with hatred (Lk. 14:26; cf. Mk. 10:29f. and parallels). Jesus Himself experienced this wrench for the sake of the Kingdom (cf. Matt. 13:57; Mk. 3:21,31ff. and parallels; 6:4, *Mary).

Nevertheless, the abolition of the natural order of the family does not imply the fragmentation of society into individualism; on the contrary, out of the death of the natural family arises a supernatural family, namely the *Church, the family or household of God (1 Tim. 3:15; cf. Heb. 3:6). In this new family, given back by miracle to those who have renounced their first family (Mk. 10:30 and parallels), the pattern of relationships is restored. St. Paul "begets" Churches like the father of a family (1 Cor. 4:15; 2 Cor. 6:13; cf. 1 Thess. 2:11), or brings them into the world like a woman who is delivered of a child (Gal. 4:19; cf. 1 Thess. 2:7); in Timothy, Titus or Philemon he has indeed his "children" (cf. 1 Cor. 4:17; Phil. 2:22; 1 Tim. 1:2,18; 2 Tim. 1:2; 2:1; Titus 1:4; Philem. 10); he tells pagans who are baptized that henceforth they form part of the family of God (Eph. 2:19; cf. Gal. 6:10); he requests Timothy to think of the members of the Church as people of his own kin (1 Tim. 5:1f.); he compares bishops to fathers of a family (1 Tim. 3:5) and he knows of women who are mothers for the Church (Rom. 16:13). Furthermore the

Church is herself understood, in the phrase of Calvin, as the mother of those whose father is God (cf. Gal. 4:26ff.; 2 Jn. 1,4,13). In ancient Christianity this family-conception of the Church was so strong that one of the charges most frequently levelled against believers by pagans was that the Church encouraged incest. They could not understand how those who called each other fathers or mothers, brothers or sisters, could be their husbands or wives.

2. A family divided against itself because of the coming of the Kingdom cannot stand (Matt. 12:25 and parallels). But the breaking in of the age to come does not necessarily imply that natural families are to be entirely discontinued. Jesus gave back their little girl to Jairus and his wife (Mk. 5:40 and parallels), her son to the widow of Nain (Lk. 7:11ff.), their brother to Martha and Mary (Jn. 11). In order to restore them to their parents, He healed a lunatic child (Mk. 9:21ff. and parallels), a Roman official's son (Jn. 4:46ff.), a Canaanite child (Matt. 15:21ff.), and on others He laid His hands (Matt. 19:13ff. and parallels); He even included amongst His followers certain of the disciples' mothers (Matt. 27:56); He healed Peter's mother-in-law (Mk. 1:29ff.; cf. Acts 28:7f.). Within the family of God there is therefore room for human families—one might think also of Jesus' instructions about marriage and divorce!

In accordance with the custom of the time, which the N.T. nowhere disputes, the family (called also by the beautiful name *house*) comprises parents, children and also servants (often designated in Greek by terms which show they belong to a particular "house": Matt. 10:25,36; 24:45; Lk. 16:13; Acts 10:7; Rom. 14:4; Phil. 4:22; 1 Pet. 2:18). When the father is alive, or when he is a Christian, the house takes his name, and this social unity is so closely bound up with him that he is able to take decisions on behalf of the whole household which have eternal effects. This is seen for example in the narratives of conversion or of baptism (Acts 10:2; 11:14; 16:31; 18:8; 1 Cor. 1:16; cf. again Acts 16:15; Jn. 4:53

and Matt. 18:25). Moreover within God's family—often perhaps because they acted as headquarters—there are Christian families, honoured and blessed, who nobody would suggest ought to separate and split up in order to demonstrate their authentic membership of the Church (cf. Acts 21:5; 1 Cor. 16:15; 2 Tim. 1:16; 4:19. There is, however, also the danger of these families slipping as a whole into heresy: Tit. 1:11). It is even probable that in the life of the Church they form the centres for worship (cf. Acts 2:46; 5:42; 20:20), and precisely as families they have a ministry of public witness to bear as to what every human family ought to be: hence the importance of their being well conducted (cf. 1 Tim. 3:4,12; 5:14; Titus 1:6).

There is in consequence the clear outline of a moral code for the family which probably first of all demands that, at the family's origin, marriage should be contracted "in the Lord" (1 Cor. 7:39; by contrast, see 1 Cor. 5:1ff.) which means that it is contracted between Christians and is regarded as indissoluble. Children born of such marriages are "holy" (1 Cor. 7:14, even if only one of the parties, having been married when pagan, has been converted) which means that the whole of married and family life belongs henceforth not only to the realm of the first creation, but also to that of salvation. A father, who reflects the fatherhood of God (Eph. 3:15), must show for his household both firmness and consideration which will maintain its unity: it is his duty to assure its means of subsistence and clothing (cf. Eph. 5:29), to love his wife as Christ loves the Church (Eph. 5:25ff.), to bring up his children so that they will willingly learn to love and to serve the Lord (Eph. 6:4; Col. 3:21), to remember that his servants have the same Lord as he has (Eph. 6:9; Col. 4:1, etc.). A mother is to recognize the authority of her husband (Eph. 5:22f.; Col. 3:18; 1 Pet. 3:1-6), and with him to make plans for the future—temporal again—of their children (2 Cor. 12:14), to make her house honourable (cf. 1 Tim. 5:14) and welcoming (cf. 1 Tim. 5:10; Rom. 16:3,13; Acts 18:26), and, lastly, to remember that what constitutes her womanhood is not so much the capacity to have children as to have a husband (cf. 1 Cor. 11:8f.): in the structure of the family according to the N.T. the marriage union itself has precedence over the production of children, and it is in respect of this unity which their parents form that children have to learn their obligations and their rights (cf. Eph. 6:1f.; Matt. 15:4ff. and parallels; 19:19 and parallels). As to the obligations, they should know that it is pleasing to the Lord that they should see in their parents the delegated authority of God Himself and therefore see them as somehow the representatives of God (which does not overlook the fifth commandment's still forming part of the first table of the law; cf. also Heb. 12:9); and it is through seeing this that they will also support their aged parents (1 Tim. 5:4). As to the rights, by means of a Christian education they will discover how it will be possible for their ambitions to coincide with their calling and so to find the meaning of their life (Eph. 6:4). As for the slaves who form part of the establishment, their duty is to see in their master, with all that the term implies of goodwill, a vicegerent of the Lord (Eph. 6:5ff.; Col. 3:22ff.; cf. 1 Pet. 2:18–25); their right (over and above just wages, see *Money) is to be able, with their owners, to rejoice in their salvation (cf. Acts 10:2ff.; Matt. 25:21,23).

To find the structure of the family morality of the N.T. the numerous parables should be re-read where Jesus describes a father of a family (cf. Matt. 21:28ff.; Lk. 11:11; 15:12ff., etc.) or a householder (cf. Matt. 13:27,52; 20:1; 24:43 and parallels; Lk. 13:25; 14:21, etc.). It is hardly likely that this biblical picture of the Christian family depends essentially on the social conditions of the ancient world, for it is too deeply rooted in the doctrine of the Fatherhood of God or the indissoluble unity that is between Christ and His Church. If social conditions change, then it will be the Church's task to discover in the new setting a form of family life where the core of the biblical teaching on the family can continue to flourish without alteration.

J.-J. VON ALLMEN

FASTING

Most of the religions of antiquity recognized the practice of fasting. Abstinence from food was most often considered to be the means of escaping from the power of demons who enter into man by food, so that one might prepare oneself to meet the deity and to receive his ecstatic potencies.

O.T.

Before becoming an officially instituted cultic practice, fasting is, in the O.T., at first an act of individual or collective piety performed on the occasion of a particular personal or national event. The Israelite fasts after a bereavement (1 Sam. 31:13; 2 Sam. 1:12; 3:35), or when he is in the grip of serious difficulties and is awaiting the help from God which he needs (2 Sam. 12:16; 1 Kings 21:27; Ps. 35:13). Fasting is undertaken also as a way of preparing to receive the revelation of God (Exod. 34:28; Dan. 10:2f.) or before a difficult venture (Ezek. 8:21; Est. 4:16). At critical moments in their history the entire people show by fasting that they are looking for divine aid (Judg. 20:26; 1 Sam. 7:6; 2 Chr. 20:3; Joel 1:4; 2:12; Jer. 36:6,9). There were, besides, official days of fasting, and woe betide him who failed to observe them! Before the Exile, fasting took place only during the great feast of atonement (Lev. 16:29ff.; 23:27ff.; Num. 29:7); after the Exile, there were four days of public fasting annually.

Fasting is never an ascetic exercise designed to liberate the soul from the slavery of the flesh. On the contrary, its purpose is to express to God that one is humbly waiting upon Him. It is a remarkable fact that the technical term which designates to fast is frequently replaced by the expression "to humble one's soul" (Lev. 16:29,31; 23:27,32; Num. 29:7; 30:14) which is its equivalent, as Ps. 35:13 and Isa. 58:3,5 show. Also, he who fasts behaves as an afflicted person (1 Kings 21:27; Joel 2:13; Est. 4:3; Neh. 9:1; Jonah 3:5), he puts on sackcloth and ashes, he prays (Jer. 14:12; Ps. 69:11; Neh. 1:4), he intercedes (Ps. 35:13). Fasting is thus the expression of a profound repentance (1 Kings 21:27; 1 Sam. 7:6; Jonah 3:5), as also of the fearful expectation of the day of Yahweh (Joel 1:14; 2:12). From this attitude fasting could easily pass—especially in later Judaism with its mercenary piety—for a means of making an impression on God, a sort of obsequious begging. That is why the prophets protested (though without much success) against this manner of fasting. True fasting, that is to say, the true manner of abasing oneself before God and of preparing to meet Him, is to break the chains of injustice, to set at liberty those who are oppressed, to share one's bread with the hungry, and to gather in the lonely (Isa. 58:1–16; cf. Jer. 14:12; Zech. 7:5ff.).

N.T.

In the time of Jesus Judaism encouraged the practice of fasting: the Pharisees used to fast (Lk. 18:12, on Mondays and Thursdays), and so also did the disciples of John the Baptist (Mk. 2:18 and parallels).

Jesus Himself fasted during His temptation (Matt. 4:2). This fasting, however, which recalls that of Moses on Sinai (Exod. 34:28), is an expression neither of repentance nor of the expectation of the divine revelation: it is the manner in which Jesus displays His absolute dependence on His Father (see *Wilderness). In the Sermon on the Mount He makes it quite plain that those who belong to Him faithfully observe the practice of fasting, but He enjoins them to do it in secret (Matt. 6:16–18), so that this practice may be a true humbling before God alone. Fasting should also be linked with prayer for the performance of certain particularly difficult acts of healing (Matt. 17:21).

In no place do the Gospels state explicitly that Jesus fasted during His public ministry; neither did He require that fasting should be a regularly observed practice. Fasting, in fact, is the expression of the expectation of salvation (Lk. 2:37); so when Jesus is present the moment for fasting has passed (Mk. 2:18 and parallels); it is then the time for *joy, except perhaps during the passion and before the resurrection (Jn. 16:20; cf. Mk. 2:20).

This joy of salvation which has been manifested dominates the whole life of the primitive Church which lives in the certitude of the resurrection. It is for this reason that no fasting was instituted by the apostles. When facing certain important decisions, however, the primitive Church recognized fasting—rather like "emptying oneself" in order then to be "filled with the Holy Spirit" to the maximum—for example, before deciding to set out on a mission (Acts 13:2f.) or before choosing ministers for the churches (Acts 14:23). Thus fasting was linked with prayer and signified openness to the orders of the Lord. We recall also that "for the sake of the Gospel" (1 Cor. 9:23) St. Paul practised a certain discipline for himself and recommended it to the Churches. Like the contestant in the stadium, he knew how "to bring his body into subjection" and "to impose upon himself all sorts of abstinences" in order to obtain the prize: he knew that the denial of self for the confession of Christ could lead very far and be very exacting (1 Cor. 9:15–27; cf. also 2 Cor. 6:5 and 11:27, where beyond doubt the "fastings" are not spiritual exercises, but due to external necessity: he had come to the point of having nothing to eat!).

The fact that St. Paul so frequently speaks against ascetic tendencies—when, whether it be fasting or other abstinences, they have their root in a dualistic conception of *man and the *world—proves that Christian fasting was not an exercise designed to release the soul from the prison of the body (as will often be the case in the later tradition of the Church), but an exercise which makes it possible, on the one hand, to regulate one's self-control and, on the other, and above all, to devote oneself freely to the "one thing needful" (cf. Col. 2:16–23; 1 Tim. 4:1–5, etc.).

J. D. ROBERT

FATHER, *see* FAMILY, GOD

FEAR

O.T.

The O.T. has no expression which translates our word "religion" (and even in the N.T. such an expression is found only twice: Acts 26:5 and Jas. 1:26f.). The Bible speaks rather of the "fear of God" to characterize the attitude of man towards the God of love who desires to enter into a *covenant with him. The O.T. does, however, make reference to other fears. The origin and development of the idea of fear show what is the response of man to the grace of the Lord.

1. *Original fear.* In order to understand this in the historical and geographical context in which Israel found herself (not forgetting that in the O.T. this familiar theme eventually transcends its context and takes on a new meaning), it must be related to the fundamental idea of primitive psychology, that of "potentiality".

(*a*) Anything may be a seat of potentiality which is empirically established when an astonishing event or chance encounter reveals to man a power or an "intentionality". The being or the object in which potentiality is located is then *holy*, for it is the vehicle of "mana".

But potentiality is not confined to certain places or moments. It is everywhere and always present, but passes unnoticed and is localized occasionally when some sign which reveals its presence unexpectedly appears.

Moreover, this global potentiality is organized into psychic totalities around centres, such as holy places (*Temple) or holy persons (commander, king, priest, *Ministry O.T.): thus a Moabite is not just an individual member of that nation, he represents Moab as a whole, the psychic totality to which he belongs over against the psychic totality of Israel (Deut. 23:3f.).

(*b*) Face to face with the extraordinary nature of every manifestation of power, man experiences a feeling which ranges from astonishment to dread and which may be called "fear". When man asserts that the person or object charged with mana is "tabu" (from the Polynesian verb *tapui*=to sanctify), it is as though he were crying out "Beware! Hands off!"

The idea of morality does not yet emerge: the violation of a tabu involves not so much a punishment as an automatic reaction (rather like an electric shock, 2 Sam. 6:6f.). But, inversely, when someone suffers an injury, it is inferred that he has violated some tabu: every misfortune is an indication of a hidden sin, whether or not there has been any sinful intention. Thus man, always in danger in a hostile world, lives in a state of distress: fear and a guilty conscience become associated.

To be divested of this power to produce distress, fear must be "organized" by being brought into contact with sacred centres. The life which emanates from the centre (person or place behind which is the god) constitutes around it a psychic totality: so there emerges the fear of the chief (with rites and festivals to bring about a transition from the secular to the sacred). In consequence there arises an antagonism against every other psychic totality, an antagonism which explains the fear of everything which is charged with an unfamiliar power (foreigner, corpse, etc., with the consequent distinction between *clean and unclean and the dietary and sexual tabus).

(*c*) Thus the conception of fear is ambiguous. Man is searching for security. He must of necessity flee from anything of which he is afraid. But anything may make him afraid: of what use then is flight? On the other hand potentiality is not the appearance here and there of the supernatural *within* nature, but the unusual which reveals the life *of* nature. That is why fear is not simply flight, but also a quest for this life-principle.

Whether he likes it or not, everyone must participate in this life-principle in order to live: the people are identified with the king, who "gives breath" to the people (Lam. 4:20); the small man fears the great: that is, he is at his mercy primarily because all his prosperity comes from the great man's hand. Inversely a man can never feel unconcerned about the foreigner; greetings, hospitality and war are holy activities. It is possible to go so far as to say that "*war is a psychic struggle"; if a warrior fears the enemy, it is the psychic totality of the enemy that he fears: as his fear jeopardizes the psychic totality to which he belongs, he cannot take part in the combat, not merely because his fear is psychologically contagious, but because it breaks the ontological unity of the army (cf. Deut. 20:8 and Judg. 7:3 of which this is the original sense).

2. *Objects of fear in the O.T.* The O.T. makes it clear that man is inclined by nature to fear many things. It is impossible to separate them into categories of different values, and the following classification is given only for the sake of clarity: the common element in all manifestations of fear is that this emotion arises when man comes face to face with some revelation of the force of life.

(*a*) Fear is the *basic relationship beween creatures:* even if the horse is intrepid (Job 39:25), it is nevertheless a fact that the beasts are afraid of man, their lord and the master of their life (Gen. 9:2). Man, in his turn, lives in a state of anxiety, heedful of every cosmic sign (Ps. 46:3; Jer. 10:2). As soon as misfortune strikes him he feels that he has been plunged into doom, even if he is just (Job 3:25); this feeling is all the more strong if he is a sinner (Ps. 38:18).

(*b*) Fear is the attitude adopted towards the *other personality*: it is occasioned by respect for his authority, which derives from God (old men: Job 32:6; parents: Lev. 19:3; chieftain: cf. below), generally because of the danger which his power represents (Gen. 4: 8–14; 26:7; 1 Sam. 15:24; Jer. 1:8): fear is supremely the fear of death (Ps. 91:5f.).

(*c*) But it is contact with another psychic totality which produces by far the greatest feeling of dread: *the foreign land and its inhabitants* (Gen. 46:3; Num. 14:9); *enemies* (Deut. 20:1; Judg. 7:3; Isa. 10:24; Ps. 27:3); especially the *enemy captain or king* (1 Sam. 17:24; Isa. 7:16; Jer. 42:11); and the *heathen gods* (2 Kings 17:35–38; Jer. 10:5). By contrast, the Canaanites (Exod. 15:16; Josh. 2:11), the Edomites (Deut. 2:4) fear Israel, that is to say, they fear the powerful God around whom the Israelite psychic totality exists.

(*d*) Then again to the Hebrews *the holy* is an object of fear: they avoid coming into contact with it, looking on it or being in its vicinity. The places where God is to be found are tabu, for they are charged with danger: Bethel (Gen. 28:17), Horeb (Exod. 3:5), the ark (1 Sam. 5–6; 2 Sam. 6), the Temple (Ps. 5:7; 68:35; Isa. 6). Contact with the dead is to be feared, among other sources of contamination. Moses is afraid to look at God (Exod. 3:6); the people are afraid to approach Moses whose face shines (Exod. 34:30), and later fear his successor Joshua (Josh. 4:14); to speak against Moses has fatal consequences (Num. 12:8). The people fear the prophet *and* God (1 Sam. 12:18); and Saul, after his rejection, fears David because of the presence of God which is with him (1 Sam. 18:12). When Samuel is afraid to relate his vision to Eli, it may not be simply out of respect or affection (1 Sam. 3:15). Here the positive character of fear is apparent: it is no longer a question of flight and struggle, but rather a determination to know and to observe the technique which enables a man to draw upon the source of life's power.

(*e*) Furthermore man fears *God* (Gen. 31:42,53; Exod. 24:17; 33:20; Deut. 5:26), *His *name* (Ps. 99:3; 111:9), *His *angel* (Judg. 6:22; 13:6; cf. Lk. 2:9). This is so evident that, when God draws near to man, He prefaces His revelation with the formula "Fear not", a formula which has reference to God Himself independently of any other danger in which man would need His help (Gen. 26:24; Judg. 6:23; perhaps Hagg. 2:5; cf. Lk. 2:10). This fear links up with (*a*): the same Hebrew word denotes "strength" and "God". It is only the love of God which can prevent this meeting from being fatal (Judg. 13:22f.); Gen. 32:30: "I have seen God face to face, and yet my life is preserved", which is a miracle, not the normal consequence.

3. *The Fear of God.* But in the texts: (*a*) the oftener God commands men not to fear such objects, including Himself; (*b*) the

more certainly does a new "fear of God" emerge. An attempt to distinguish between a bad-servile and a good-filial kind of fear is inadequate. The truth is that the potentiality of Yahweh cannot tolerate being one among others, but desires jealously to abolish not only respect for other potentialities but the very existence of these. What is *new* in the O.T. conception of fear is the conviction that it is not man's concern to walk warily amid all the various powers which surround him but rather that the power of Yahweh is the only one to be feared and completely destroys every other fear (on the understanding that fear of king or prophet remains fear of God: 2 Sam. 23:3; 1 Sam. 12:18; Deut. 1:17; Jer. 17:8; and especially Isa. 8:12–13; Ps. 23:4).

God, *the creator* of the incomprehensible forces of nature, is by that very act of creation also *the saviour*.

The fear of Yahweh alone is man's response to the covenant God offers to him. That is why sin, which is a break with God, brings afresh in its train the fear of enemies (Lev. 26:14–17; Ps. 38:19f.), fear of everyone else (Gen. 4:12–14) and the fear of God (Gen. 3:10). On the other hand, the fear of anyone other than God is a snare: it is futile (Prov. 29:25) and moreover it induces men to be unfaithful to God (Isa. 57:11). To fear Yahweh is to recognize His omnipotence and in the last resort His oneness.

Thus the fear of God is the basis of morality (Exod. 18:21; 20:20; Job 2:3; 28:28; Prov. 8:13), for it consists of the quest for purity before Him who is the Holy One. It must be noted that "fear of Yahweh" is much more common than "fear of God": Yahweh is the personal name of the Lord; it is a case of being afraid not so much of what God *might do* as of what He *is*. Far from saying that God is feared through dread of punishment (Jer. 3:8), the O.T. claims that punishment, the discipline of the God of love (Prov. 3:12), leads man to a healthy fear of God (Deut. 13:11).

This wisdom, of which fear is the beginning (Ps. 111:10) is radically different from human self-sufficiency. This fear, grounded in a painful sense of impotence which is the basis of the sinful conscience, is a sharing in the sole potentiality of God (Ps. 51:10–12; 68:35); it consists of submission to His revelation and obedience to His word (Exod. 9:20; Isa. 66:2,5; Ps. 2:11). This fear is the supreme attribute of the Messiah (Isa. 11:2), who will come supremely as the "slave of Yahweh" (Isa. 53). It blossoms into *love, the essential bond of beings who live in fellowship (Deut. 10:12; cf. 1 Jn. 4:18). That is why to fear God finally comes to mean to honour Him, to revere Him, to adore Him: it is the worship due to Him alone (2 Kings 17:24–41). Thus paradoxically fear is the source of confidence, and weakness the source of strength (Job 4:6): that is the work of grace.

D. LYS

N.T.

The verb "to fear" may be followed by an infinitive: "to fear to do . . .", or by a conjunction "to fear lest . . .". In this usage, there is no specifically religious connotation (e.g. Matt. 1:20; 2:22; Acts 23:10; 2 Cor. 11:3, etc.). Used in the absolute sense, it denotes, as does the substantive "fear", an attitude of man brought about by his surroundings or more particularly by the motive which drives him. The sense of the transitive verb differs according to the nature of the direct object, which may be God, or men and their actions, or various happenings. The idea of fear plays a less important part in the N.T. than it does in the O.T.; its meaning in the N.T. is not always precisely defined.

1. *Fear as a human emotion.* (*a*) *Fear reveals men's unbelief.* The Gospel shows that those who oppose God's purpose as it is made known in Jesus Christ are under the dominion of fear. Pilate, when he heard the charge which the Jews brought against Jesus ("he has made himself the Son of God") "was the more afraid" (Jn. 19:8); without doubt he had a presentiment of the unique character of the accused. At the foot of the cross, the conclusion of the drama and its cosmic repercussions filled the soldiers

with a religious dread (Matt. 27:54). The angel of the resurrection exposed the weakness of the soldiers who guarded the tomb: "and for fear of him the guards trembled and became like dead men" (Matt. 28:4). It is apparent time and time again that people in positions of authority, whose first concern was the security of their own person and the maintenance of their own position, spoke and acted in a certain way because of their fear of the people (Mk. 11:18; Matt. 21:26 and parallels; cf. also Matt. 14:5). After having listened to the Parable of the Vineyard, in which they recognized themselves all too plainly, the chief priests and Pharisees had to curb their anger. "They feared the multitudes, because they held him to be a prophet" (Matt. 21:46 and parallels). On the other hand, the hostility of the authorities towards Jesus prevented the ordinary people from declaring openly for Him (Jn. 7:13).

(b) *Fear reveals also the doubt of the disciples.* In fact, the Gospel makes it clear that those who had answered the call of Jesus were far from appreciating the full range of His teaching about His Kingdom. In the boat, they were frightened when they saw their master coming towards them, walking on the waters (Matt. 14:26f.); and after Peter had thrown himself overboard to go to meet his lord "when he saw the wind, he was afraid" (Matt. 14:30 and parallels). Despite the promises that the Lord had made to them, the prospects of the sufferings and death of Jesus, and doubtless the risks which they themselves would have to run, filled them with fear (Mk. 10:32). Who then could have grasped the announcement of the resurrection and believed this miracle which surpassed all human thought? Equally the Gospels show us that the women who discovered the empty tomb were far from interpreting it as a sign of the triumph of Christ. "They . . . fled from the tomb; for trembling and astonishment had come upon them" (Mk. 16:8); Matthew adds, however, that their fear was mingled "with great *joy" (Matt. 28:8).

Moreover it was not the ungodly only who were subject to the fear of other people.

Joseph of Arimathea, who took charge of the body of Jesus, was His disciple, but "secretly for fear of the Jews" (Jn. 19:38); and even the testimony of the women had not been enough to give to the disciples a complete assurance, for they too shut themselves in from the same motive (Jn. 20:19). The attitude even of the apostle Peter was not without weakness: Paul took him secretly to task because, after having eaten with the Gentiles, "he drew back and separated himself, fearing the circumcision party" (Gal. 2:12).

(c) *Fear is a human reaction to the Revelation of God.* When God manifests in Jesus Christ His Kingdom, men are surprised: they discover, in a vague, emotional way, the immeasurable distance which separates them from the living God; and fear joins hands with astonishment. A great many miracles, reported in the Gospels, arouse this reaction in the crowd and even in the group of disciples. The stilling of the storm (Mk. 4:41 and parallels), the healings which Jesus performed, expressions of the divine compassion, signs of His coming Kingdom (Matt. 9:8; Mk. 5:15 and parallels), the "many wonders and signs . . . done through the apostles" (Acts 2:43): all these are manifestations of divine power which fill the observer with fear. The woman who had been healed through touching the *garments of Jesus, "came in fear and trembling" (Mk. 5:33). The Gospel adds, after the raising of the young man at Nain, that "fear seized them all; and they glorified God saying, 'a great prophet has arisen among us!' and 'God has visited His people!' " (Lk. 7:16); similarly, after the healing of the paralytic: "and amazement seized them all, and they glorified God and were filled with awe, saying 'We have seen strange things to-day' " (Lk. 5:26). To the fear which the natural man feels when God displays His merciful power there may be added, then, a sign of faith, even if this is only an evanescent crowd-emotion. Even more are men overcome with fear when God displays His justice; "Acts" tells us that after the death of Ananias and Sapphira "great fear came upon the whole church, and upon all who heard of these things" (Acts 5:11; cf. also 5:5). The Gospel proclaims that, at the coming of Christ, the effect of God's judgment will be "men fainting with fear and with foreboding of what is coming on the world" (Lk. 21:26; cf. also Rev. 18:10,15).

(d) *When He makes Himself known, God liberates believers from every fear.* The opening of the Gospel of Luke is significant. God prepares for the birth of His Son, the crucial act in His *revelation, by sending His angel: in the case of Zacharias (Lk. 1:12f.), of Mary (1:30) or of the shepherds, the angel calms and strengthens those whom he meets, in order to bring them within the scope of God's purpose, with the words "Fear not!" It can easily be understood how the magnitude and the mystery of this purpose dismayed those who discovered it! (Lk. 1:65). When Jesus called Peter to follow Him, He reassured him (Lk. 5:10); and in the storm, He drew near to them and calmed them (Matt. 14:27 and parallels). When God spoke on the Mount of Transfiguration to bear witness to the divinity of His Son, "when the disciples heard this, they fell on their faces and were filled with awe, But Jesus came and touched them saying, 'Rise and have no fear' " (Matt. 17:6f. and parallels). The prophecy (Zech. 9:9) which Jesus quoted at His entry into Jerusalem demonstrated His Messianic reign: "Fear not, daughter of Zion; behold thy king is coming, riding on an ass's colt" (Jn. 12:15). In Revelation, the seer fell as one dead at the feet of the Lord (Rev. 1:17). The angel messenger of the resurrection spoke as did he who announced the nativity: "Do not be afraid . . ." (Matt. 28:5); and Jesus appeared to the women confirming the angel's words (Matt. 28:10). The Lord's imperative: "Fear not!" far surpasses the special circumstances in which it was spoken. The mission of the Twelve has so clear an eschatological reference that the whole Church knows that she need fear no adversaries (Matt. 10:3,26ff. and parallel passages). The disciples are given the assurance that they shall possess the *Kingdom (Lk. 12:32); and in "Acts" we see the Lord

or His angel strengthening the apostle to meet the conflicts which he has to face (Acts 18:9; 27:23f.). Abundant testimonies in the Epistles confirm those which have been quoted: the believing wife must be submissive to her husband and not let any fear upset her (1 Pet. 3:6); even in suffering, Christians must not let themselves be disturbed, but must glorify Christ (1 Pet. 3:14; cf. Rev. 2:10). The Epistle to the Hebrews applies to Christians the declaration in Ps. 118:6; "With the Lord on my side I do not fear . . ." and sees in the story of Moses two examples of this attitude (Heb. 11:23,27); the incarnation and the death of Christ lead to deliverance from the fear of death, which formerly held mankind in bondage (Heb. 2:15).

Paul, in a striking epitome, supplies the secret of this deliverance: "For you did not receive the spirit of slavery to fall back into fear, but you have received the spirit of sonship" (Rom. 8:15). The redeeming work of God, made effective by the Holy Spirit, sets the believer free from fear. John, in his own language, says just the same thing when he declares that the love of God, which creates in man love for God, "casts out fear. For fear has to do with punishment, and he who fears is not perfected in love" (1 Jn. 4:18).

2. *Fear as an expression of faith.* However much it may seem to contradict what has been said, fear is one of the expressions of *faith; but its connotation is obviously defined by the complement which accompanies it. This is so true that several times in the N.T. believers are called "those who fear God". This very general expression embraces alike those who belong to the old covenant (Lk.1:50), the "devout proselytes" (Acts 13:43) such as Cornelius (Acts 10:22), and the Gentile sympathizers (Acts 10:35; 13:16). The Revelation counts them as being among the servants of God; the twenty-four elders greet in these terms the advent of the Kingdom of God: "the time for the dead to be judged, for rewarding thy servants, the prophets and saints, and those who fear thy name, both great and

small" (Rev. 11:18; cf. also 19:5). The lack of fear is a sign of unbelief or rebellion: the attitude of the judge in the parable (Lk. 18:2,4), or of the "unrepentant" thief on the cross (Lk. 23:40). It is the chief sign of the state of sin in which humanity lies (Rom. 3:18).

(a) *Fear glorifies God or Christ.* It is striking that Revelation associates fear with the praise and adoration of the elect in heaven. The victors sing the song of the Lamb: "who shall not fear and glorify thy name, O Lord?" (Rev. 15:4). The angel who carries the eternal Gospel announces God's judgment: "Fear God and give him glory, for the hour of his judgment has come: and worship him who made heaven and earth, the sea and the fountains of water" (Rev. 14:6f.). From this one can easily understand how fear is one of the manifestations of faith on the earth as well.

(b) *Fear in the life of the believer.* God, whom the believer calls Father and whom he loves with a child's freedom, still remains the One who will judge every man according to his deeds. From this view-point, Jesus could say to His disciples: "fear him who can destroy both body and soul in hell" (Matt. 10:28 and parallel passages). It is because "we must all appear before the judgment seat of Christ" that the apostle can write "Therefore, knowing the fear of the Lord . . ." (2 Cor. 5:10f.). The Pauline doctrine of *salvation is profoundly paradoxical: precisely because salvation is a gift of God, the believer's security is in God, in faith: "but you stand fast only through faith. So do not become proud, but stand in awe" (Rom. 11:20) and Peter confirms Paul (1 Pet. 1:17).

In the life of the Church, the fear of the Lord is shown in obedience to His commandments; it is the condition of the sanctification of Christians. Along with gratitude and hope, it is the deeply-rooted motive of sanctification: "Since we have these promises, beloved, let us cleanse ourselves from every defilement of body and spirit, and make holiness perfect in the fear of God" (2 Cor. 7:1); it is one of the fruits of "godly grief" (2 Cor. 7:11). It is in the

fear of the Lord that the Church "is built up and walks" (Acts 9:31).

In concrete terms the fear of God means that all Christians must be subject to one another (Eph. 5:21). It is significant that the apostles invite Christians to a life of obedience to the Lord when they are dealing with the respect which they owe to civil *authorities; indeed this respect is the ethical expression of the fear of God. The same attitude must characterize the conduct of Christians towards magistrates (Rom. 13:3–7), towards God's servants (2 Cor. 7:15), that of the wife towards her husband (Eph. 5:33; cf. 1 Pet. 3:1f.) or of servants towards their masters (Eph. 6:5; cf. 1 Pet. 2:18). Fear is still one of the elements in ecclesiastical discipline. When used by the members of the Church, it proves the efficacy of the public rebuke of offenders (1 Tim. 5:20; cf. 2 Cor. 7:11). To those who are outside the Church the bishop must make reply "with gentleness and reverence" (1 Pet. 3:15), but towards some the Church must sometimes feel "mercy with fear, hating even the garment spotted by the flesh" (Jude 23).

ED. DISERENS

FEASTS

O.T.

In this subject less than in any other is it possible to derive a general pattern from history; for it is only in following the development of the various feasts that we are enabled to understand what they meant to the Israelites at different periods, and what they had come to mean by the beginning of the Christian era. We can see that they underwent very considerable evolution; but it is not always possible to follow closely the details of each stage, even if, as a whole, these correspond to the variations in the development of Israel's religion. Frequently it is in the latest documents that we find the traditions of the earliest phases preserved. Any exposition of this process, however, has to be punctuated with numerous question marks; for in many cases it must follow the line that seems logical to us, rather than anything the texts explicitly state.

1. To understand certain features, it is obviously necessary to go back to the nomadic period of Israel, even before the time of Moses; for by then the feasts already marked the great occasions of pastoral life. Later, the settlement in Canaan brought about considerable changes. The principal events of the agricultural year are different from those of the nomadic, and new feasts are incorporated. Later still, the deutero-nomic and priestly reforms introduced important modifications into the concept of even the oldest festivals.

Two of the great annual festivals probably date from the period of nomadic life; the feast of the *Passover* in the spring, and the *Atonement* festival in the autumn. We find the archaic features of these festivals pre-served especially in the priestly narratives. Passover is marked by the sacrifice of a lamb in the setting of the family and by the distinctive rôle of the *blood, which during the departure from Egypt serves to protect the Israelites from the destroying angel. Much of the ritual is to be understood in the context of nomadic life, where it forms a kind of reconsecration of the flocks to the deity, who, in turn, re-establishes his covenant with his people. At a later stage, the slaying of the first-born is quite naturally understood as a rendering back to the deity of that which belongs to him by right, in return for his continued maintenance of the fertility of the flocks. The origins of the Atonement festival may go equally far back; at any rate, the rite of the goat for Azazel (Lev. 16:20-28), laden quasi-physically with all the sins of the people, is far from belong-ing to the much more spiritual context of the priestly piety; but we do not know exactly what were the primitive rites of this festival.

The lunar, and therefore monthly, festi-vals, with their two critical moments of full moon and new moon, may possibly go back to somewhat the same period; but they also play a large part in agricultural life.

Many of the festivals indicate their origin by their close connection with the agri-cultural life of the Palestinian peasant. The *Feast of Unleavened Bread*, celebrated in the spring at the same season as Passover, marked the beginning of the harvest. The first of the new flour is eaten, and naturally nothing made from the reaping of the previous year must be mixed with it; whence the necessity of using no leaven in the baking of the loaves. Other ceremonies become attached to this one: offering of the first-fruits of the reaping; offerings of the first-born of the flocks, for the purpose of assuring the fertility of the fields and herds. Fifty days later, the *Feast of Weeks* (Pentecost) marks the end of harvest.

The great harvest festival, however, which always remained the supreme festival in the calendar, took place in the autumn. It was called the *Feast of Tabernacles* (i.e. tents), because at this season of the year everyone camped in the midst of his vines under little booths of branches. This feature—in the towns the huts were frequently replaced by cloth tents—has led some to see in the festival a relic of the nomadic period. Indeed, this was the interpretation given to it later; but it does not seem at all likely that it was the primitive one. In any case, we find the festival already being celebrated by the Canaanites of Shechem (Judg. 9:27).

The *lunar festivals* also played a large part. The prophets frequently mention the new moon in conjunction with the *sabbath*, which latter term cannot yet refer to the weekly festival but must denote the feast of the full moon (Isa. 1:13; Hos. 2:13). These events are family or clan festivals (1 Sam. 20:18,29). Consequently, they had a closer link with the small local sanctuaries; they were occasions for rejoicing, sometimes even for licence, which explains the severe condemnation of them by the prophets and the bad reputation given them by the writers of Deuteronomy. The Feast of Unleavened Bread was naturally linked to that of the Passover, and the Atonement Festival to that of Tabernacles, because they were celebrated at the same seasons, in the spring and autumn respectively. The ancient legislation, of which only fragments survive, gives us but an imperfect picture of these annual festivals. Thus, in the case of the spring festivals, the Yahwist (Exod. 34:18–

26) and the Elohist (Exod. 23:14–16) sources tell us very little about the Passover and give all the prominence to the Feast of Unleavened Bread. In the case of the monthly festivals, new moon and sabbath, the prophets, when they do mention them, never provide any details. To the list of annual festivals must be added in the autumn, together with the New Year festival, the Festival of the *Coronation of Yahweh*, of which we know very little for certain, almost all the references being late. It must go back to the beginnings of the monarchy and, without being identical, correspond to those which were celebrated elsewhere, e.g., in Babylonia (enthronement of Marduk).

2. *The Reform of Josiah* was not intended to be an innovating movement, but a reforming and purifying one, introducing into the religious life something of the high moral teaching of the prophets. However, as in all reforms, the new elements were nevertheless important. In the case of the festivals, the centralization of the cult at Jerusalem led to considerable changes. They completely lost the orgiastic character which, in the smaller sanctuaries, they too often possessed. The rejoicings went on, of course, but they became completely secularized. The feasts thus became separated from everyday life; for it was a practical impossibility for everyone to gather in Jerusalem. The agricultural character of many of the festivals tended to fade away. It was Deuteronomy that reintroduced into the great springtime festival the features characteristic of the Feast of the Passover (Deut. 16:1–8).

The principal feasts kept at Jerusalem quite naturally took on more importance and solemnity. Their agricultural origin was forgotten and they were gradually regarded more and more as commemorations of the great events of Israel's religious history. It was probably at this stage, in the course of general systematization, that the festivals began to be fixed by the calendar and no longer by Nature. Up to the time of Deuteronomy, several of these festivals were genuine national festivals, but Deuteronomy began the process of giving them that very definite character of commemorations of Israel's past religious history, which was so in keeping with the movement. The joyful atmosphere of the ancient festivals was replaced by the gravity of an anniversary celebration.

Probably also about this time—though we cannot follow the development exactly—the sabbath became no longer a monthly but a weekly festival, a beneficial time of rest after labour (Exod. 23:12; Deut. 16:9ff.), with that marked humanitarian quality so entirely in the spirit of Deuteronomy.

The priestly reform followed the course set by the Deuteronomic and drew out all the implications of the latter; but, being composed for the most part in exile, it is sometimes rather detached from real life. The festivals themselves are not modified, but they are fixed by the day and month (Lev. 23:5ff.; Num. 28:16). There are, however, some new elements. The feast of the new moon, which had been abandoned by Deuteronomy, is restored in full authority (Num. 28:11–15), which suggests that in fact there were probably extensive circles where its celebration had never been given up. The weekly sabbath is no longer merely the cessation of work; it is inactivity pure and simple. It becomes an ascetic practice even (Exod. 16:27–30; 31:12–17) and, with *circumcision, is to be the distinguishing mark of those Jews dispersed among the heathen. The relative importance of the festivals is indicated by the length of celebration. Seven days are assigned to the Passover (with which the Feast of Unleavened Bread is closely united) and to the Feast of Tabernacles, while the Feast of Weeks (Pentecost) lasts for but a single day. The Feast of Tabernacles becomes the memorial of the old nomadic life, the blessed "golden age" of Israel's history. It is not in fact the commemoration of a particular event, but a time when, for a few days each year, the old style of life once more becomes a reality; and the hope is that the old faithfulness will accompany it. The

Feast of the Passover retains, or rediscovers, a good many ancient features which the Yahwist, Elohist and Deuteronomic texts had not preserved, but which in all probability had never ceased to form part of the festival (Lev. 23:1–14, and the account of the festival at the time of the departure from Egypt, Exod. 12:1–20). In the case of the other festivals, we find a standardization of ritual, marked by holocausts, *sacrifices for sin, the sabbath rest and the gathering together at the Jerusalem sanctuary of worshippers from all the townships of Judah. The offerings at these festivals are no longer happy freewill offerings. They are fixed by the law; they are an obligation on the community; and their presentation obtains the divine favour for all the people, present and absent.

3. *Later development within Judaism* continues along the lines marked out by the Priestly Code. In the case of the sabbath, for example, the rules laid down and their interpretation become increasingly strict. The historical character at first ascribed only to the great festivals is now extended to the others. Thus, after the destruction of the Temple, the Feast of Pentecost becomes a commemoration of the giving of the law on Sinai. The festivals, like the calendar as a whole, were regulated by the moon and rested on observations made at Jerusalem. The indications thus arrived at took time to reach the diaspora; and in some years it could happen that a feast would be celebrated twice, to ensure that the date fixed by Jerusalem was observed. The practice also obtained to some extent in all parts, when there was an intercalary month (which was a repetition of the month preceding), of celebrating the feast of *Purim*, which fell in the preceding month, for a second time.

The practice of marking the destruction of the Temple by two days' fasting continued. The historical character acquired by each of the festivals is well demonstrated in the attitude taken at the time of the Maccabean struggle first for the religious and then the political independence of the

people of Judah. The great deliverances of that period were commemorated by special feasts, which recalled both a particular event and also more especially the deliverance granted by God in that event. Thus we have the *day of Nicanor* (1 Macc. 4:48), commemorating a victory of Judas Maccabeus over that Syrian general; and the *Dedication of the Temple* (1 Macc. 5:59), the day when, after the Temple had been reconquered and purified by Judas, celebration of the normal cultus according to the traditional rites began once more. There was also a feast to celebrate the taking of the Akra, the Syrian citadel in Jerusalem, which, for more than twenty years after the early victories, continued to resist the attempts of the faithful Jews to restore the worship and political independence of the country. This feast, however, had already lapsed by the time of the historian Josephus in the first century of our era. In the case of the feast of *Purim* we have no evidence of its origins; it seems, like the book of Esther which tells of it, to have been of an extremely profane character.

In all the religions of Israel's neighbours the festivals ended by losing a large part of their naturalistic and agricultural character, and instead the great myths of these religions were represented in their celebration. In Israel, on the other hand, the myths properly so-called were restricted within the limits of what was possible, and these were the past events recalled year by year in the festivals. Nevertheless, these events were not celebrated merely as events, but rather as a memorial of a particular mighty work of God on behalf of His people—one might almost say, as a memorial of the ever present and ever possible action of God, who had of old miraculously delivered His people from bondage in Egypt, had led them into the land of Canaan, and still to-day both could and would deliver them from all oppression, actual and potential. This historical or, to be more exact, historico-religious character is pronounced even in the case of the festivals of the Maccabean period, which were instituted soon after the actual events. It is not the noble deeds of Judas Maccabeus which were thus celebrated (in the way that, for example, in France the festivities of July 14th commemorate the taking of the Bastille) but it is the direct work of God by the hand of Judas, which each year is recalled to the mind of the Jews. This idea is to be found, already clearly and powerfully expressed, in the work of Deutero-Isaiah, but without its yet being linked with the keeping of the festivals. In his writings the deliverance from Egypt continues to be the great pledge of the even more wonderful deliverance, which God will not be slow to grant His exiled people. We might even say, in more general terms, the pledge of all the deliverances that God can ever grant to His own. Christians later took over many of the festivals of Judaism. Beside the traditions of their Jewish past they set the quite recent traditions of the life of Jesus, and in time these latter come more and more to the forefront; but fundamentally they continue to be celebrated in the same spirit.

G. NAGEL

N.T.

St. Paul said to the Christians: "Let no one pass judgment on you . . . with regard to a festival or a new moon or a sabbath: these are only a shadow of what is to come: but the substance belongs to Christ" (Col. 2:16; cf. Gal. 4:10f.). In other words, because of the coming, the death and the resurrection of Jesus, the feasts of the O.T. are now fulfilled, and to maintain them "signifies a falling back into the old covenant, as if Christ had never come" (O. Cullmann).

1. Until His resurrection, Jesus and His disciples faithfully observe the Jewish festivals and days of worship (cf. Matt. 26:18ff. and parallels; Lk. 2:41f.; 4:16; 23:54f.; etc.). The fourth Gospel even insists strongly on the fact that Jesus is eager to be present at the Jewish feasts: He goes up to Jerusalem for the Passover (2:13ff.; cf. 12:12ff.; 11:56); for another feast (Purim? 5:1); for the feast of Tabernacles (7:2ff.); and for that of the Dedication (10:22). This determination of

Jesus to be present is, as it were, a declaration that He Himself is the "substance" of these festivals and that He is come to fulfil them, as He also comes to fulfil the whole law (cf. Matt. 5:17). These passages may therefore be set side by side with those telling of Jesus' attitude toward the *Temple at Jerusalem.

(a) This is shown particularly in the matter of the sabbath. The seventh day of the week is the one favoured by Jesus for His work: not only does He choose it for preaching in the synagogue (Mk. 6:2ff. and parallels; cf. Matt. 4:23 and parallels; 9:35; Lk. 4:15; Jn. 6:59ff.; 18:20), but He seems to prefer it to the others for working His *miracles (Matt. 12:9–14; Mk. 1:21ff. and parallels; Lk. 13:10ff.; 14:1ff.; Jn. 5:1ff.; cf. 7:23; 9:14). It is the day above all others when, after the manner of His Father, He "works" (Jn. 5:17), that is to say, when He makes manifest the breaking into this transitory world of the world to come. Thus He fulfils the expectation of *rest and of God's presence, foreshadowed by the sabbath: He makes it "His" day, the day which is His to use for His work, the day of which He is "lord" (Matt. 12:1–8 and parallels). It is, in fact, quite wrong to interpret the liberty which Jesus takes in the matter of the sabbath as a demonstration of a general principle of anti-formalism: it is the sign of His Messiahship. It is for man's salvation (Lk. 13:15ff.; 14:5, etc.) that Jesus is lord especially of this day, the raison d'être of which is not to be found in itself (Mk. 2:27), but in Jesus the Messiah. Therefore anyone who violates the sabbath for a reason other than the coming of the Christ is "accursed and a transgressor of the law" (according to one textual tradition of Lk. 6:5), whereas those who know that Jesus is the Messiah, and therefore the inaugurator of the reign of God, are dispensed from observing the law of the sabbath (Matt. 12:1ff. and parallels); it no longer concerns them. They will be free, nay, they will be obliged to find another day for their worship; just as they will be both free and obliged to abandon the Temple and *circumcision; they are the new *Israel.

(b) But Jesus does not fulfil the sabbath only; He does the same for the Jewish *Passover*, which was but the shadow of the Passion of Christ, "our paschal lamb" (1 Cor. 5:7). This is why the evangelists so strongly emphasize the connection between this Jewish festival and the death of Jesus (cf. Matt. 26:2 and parallels; Jn. 11:55ff.; 12:1–8; 13:1). It is also the reason why the fourth Gospel—with a view to stressing the connection even more—does not place the death of Jesus at the same moment as that indicated by Matthew, Mark and Luke. Finally, it is the meaning of the very definite link established between the Jewish Passover and the institution of the *Lord's Supper (Matt. 26:17ff. and parallels; cf. Jn. 6:4).

2. Some time was needed after its first formation for the Christian Church to understand all the implications of the fulfilment of the Jewish feasts and ceremonies in the person and work of Jesus. We know that some Judaizing Christians wanted to see the Church remain faithful to Jewish customs (Col. 2:16; Gal. 4:10), whereas many Gentile Christians, and most of all St. Paul, were only concerned to make the fullest use of the doctrine of the new Israel, which was acknowledged by the whole Church and found unanimous expression in the replacing of the sabbath by Sunday.

Since the sabbath was the day on which the Jews gathered in their synagogues (Acts 15:21), it is true that this day remained, at Jerusalem (Acts 6:9) as well as everywhere else, the most suitable day for missionary work among Jews (Acts 9:20; 13:5,14,42,44; 14:1; 16:13; 17:1,10,17; 18:4,19,26; 19:8). In this sense it may be said that the first Christian missionaries continued to observe the sabbath, just as they continued to frequent the Temple (Acts 3:1; 5:20,25). Nevertheless, they were aware of their being something different from Jewry (see *Church).

For this reason—even though at the start the Jerusalem Christians came together every day (Acts 2:46)—Christian worship was transferred from the seventh to the first day of the week (Acts 20:7; 1 Cor. 16:2), soon called the "Lord's day" (Rev. 1:10). This day was established, because it was that on which Jesus rose from the dead (Matt. 28:1 and parallels; Jn. 20:1) and on which He appeared to the disciples (Mk. 16:14; Lk. 24:13ff.,34,36ff.; Jn. 20:19; cf. Jn. 20:26). By making the first day of each week a festival of Christ's resurrection, the first Christians laid down one of the essential principles of a theology of Sunday and of worship: it is the day and the hour when the Risen Christ is present among His own; the day and the hour when the crucial moment of the history of salvation is re-presented, actualized; the day and the hour when the Lord, in answer to the prayer of His Church (Marana-tha, 1 Cor. 16:22="Come, Lord!" Rev. 22:20), comes to rejoin them. The climax of this encounter and reunion takes place in the *Lord's Supper, when Jesus, as on the eve of the Passover (Mk. 16:14; Lk. 24:30ff.,41ff.), presides at the common meal of His people (Acts 10:41).

The first day of the week, however, is not only that of the memorial of the resurrection (though in biblical thought a memorial is much more than an act of remembrance). It is in addition—and here we have the second essential principle of a theology of Sunday and of worship—the day on which, by anticipation, is realized the Christian hope of Christ's coming in glory, the "day of the Lord" (Rev. 1:10); that is to say, that "last day" of which the prophets spoke (Isa. 2:12; 13:9; Joel 2:31, etc.). It is the day of hope and of fear, the day of the marriage of the Lamb and of the condemnation of the wicked, the day when Jesus drinks the new wine (Matt. 26:29) and when the man who has no festal *garment is cast out of the banquet (Matt. 22:11ff.). When we remember how vital the idea of the Messianic banquet is to the biblical concept of the Lord's Supper, and combine with this what has just been said about the idea of memorial, we can understand the extent to which this sacrament was central not only to the theology but also to the reality of worship for the first Christians (Acts 20:7, etc.), and how it made of the first day of the week a true *dies dominicus* (Fr. *dimanche*).

The Lord's Day—memorial of the resurrection, anticipation of Christ's return—is therefore the day, between these two events, on which supremely the work of salvation is accomplished; so that to experience a Christian Sunday is to expose oneself to the grace of the redemptive mystery of God. We could have arrived at the same conclusion by considering, instead of the Lord's Supper, the preaching that went with it (Acts 20:7ff.); for *preaching, quite as much as the Lord's Supper, is embedded in the eschatological work of God: it, too, recalls the resurrection of Jesus (Acts 2:24ff., etc.); it, too, by gathering the elect (cf. Lk. 5:10; Matt. 9:37ff.), anticipates the return of the Lord (cf. Matt. 24:31). It may be said, therefore, that the Lord's Day constitutes the Church. It may also be said, that those who think it their duty to abandon Sunday to keep the sabbath instead are in effect denying the passage from the Old *covenant to the New, and therefore the Messiahship of *Jesus.

It is a matter for some surprise that the N.T. never transfers to the Lord's Day the laws relating to the sabbath rest. If it was in the evening—and so after a day's work and, in the case of the young man who fell asleep, a hard day's work—that the church of Troas came together (Acts 20:7), it is therefore not necessarily by inactivity that the Lord's Day is to be hallowed. Moreover, the Church waited three hundred years before making Sunday a holiday. What sanctifies the first day of the week is much more, then, the act of worship with all its normal features.

3. Since every Sunday is, in some sense, a Passover festival, it would seem that the Jewish paschal ceremonies had not already been transformed in the Apostolic Age into that which they were later to become—the primary and essential festal cycle of the ecclesiastical year. It should, however, be noted that at the time of the controversies over the date of Easter appeal was made to traditions said to go back to the apostles

themselves. Passages like Col. 2:16; Gal. 4:10f.; Rom. 14:5 suggest that some Christians wished to transfer to the life of the Church other Jewish festivals. By contrast, there seems to have been complete unanimity in the matter of the Feast of *Pentecost*. Among the Jews at that period, its celebration recalled the gift of the Law on Sinai, the creation of the people of God. The Christians, for their part, must have celebrated it as the day of the re-creation of the people of God by the outpouring of the Holy Spirit (Acts 2). Why is it, then, that St. Paul writes to the Christians at Corinth, of whom the majority were converts from paganism, that he expects to remain with the church at Ephesus—equally a church with a Gentile majority—until Pentecost (1 Cor. 16:8), if that festival was known only to the Jews? It is much more reasonable to suppose that the *Christian* Pentecost was celebrated at Jerusalem, since the apostle is so eager to reach Jerusalem by that date (Acts 20:16). The latter passage suggests that this festival, which for Christians brought to mind the day on which "devout men from every nation under heaven" (Acts 2:5) had heard tell of the "mighty works of God", was, in St. Paul's view, celebrated not only as a memorial of the outpouring of the Holy Spirit but also as a means of emphasizing the unity and universality of the Church. Thus it is precisely to demonstrate this unity of the world-wide Church that the apostle goes up to Jerusalem; for he is taking with him the collection which he has made among his own churches (cf. 1 Cor. 16:1–4; 2 Cor. 8–9; Rom. 15:25–28).

4. Though the remembrance of the death and resurrection of Jesus and of the outpouring of the Spirit was regularly celebrated by the apostolic Church, yet the anniversary of the *Birth of Jesus* was not the subject of any celebration whatsoever. The Bible, moreover, as Origen was to recall later, has a certain mistrust of birthdays— it mentions only those of Pharaoh (Gen. 40:20) and Herod (Matt. 14:6). Further, in sharp contrast to Easter and Pentecost, the

date of Jesus' birth is only very vaguely indicated—it was "during the time that Quirinius was governor of Syria" (Lk. 2:2). We have to wait several centuries for the Church to arrive at any nearly unanimous agreement on the 25th December as the memorial-date of the birth of Jesus.

5. In connection with the text of Col. 2:16 quoted at the head of this article, it may be wondered whether to reintroduce festivals into the life of the Church is not to go against the teaching of the N.T. But we must remember that it is against the continuance of the *Jewish* festivals that St. Paul protests, not the celebration of *Christian* ones. We might derive from this the following rule: it is permissible to celebrate festivals in the Church, provided that they emphasize that with Jesus the Messiah has come, and therefore that the Kingdom of God is here; these festivals cease to be permissible just as soon as they cease either to recall clearly the saving work of Jesus (Pentecost being the work of Jesus, who sends His Spirit: Jn. 15:26), or to proclaim decisively His return in glory. In other words, Christian festivals must be first and foremost Christological. They become parasitical from the moment that they separate the person and work of Christ from the focus of the Church's faith and joy. This rule is all the more important in so far as it may be necessary to define the limits and intentions of any celebrations based, directly or indirectly, on such passages as Heb. 11 or Matt. 26:13.

Above all, it should be noted that the usefulness of Christian festivals resides in the fact that they emphasize the essential truth of Christianity—the knowledge that salvation is not an idea but a historical fact, which finds its centre and its meaning in the person and work of Jesus Christ.

J.-J. VON ALLMEN

FIRST-FRUITS, see EARNEST, SACRIFICES O.T.

FLESH, see MAN

FOLLOW

1. In the O.T. the Hebrew expression denoting the idea of following is used normally in reference to the idolatry of Israel, i.e. the suggestion is that of following false gods and abandoning the Lord (cf. Judg. 2:12; Deut. 4:3; 6:14; 1 Kings 21:26; Jer. 7:6,9; 9:13; 11:10; Hos. 1:2, etc.).

It is used more rarely to express devotion to the cult of Yahweh (Deut. 1:36; 1 Kings 14:8; 18:21; 2 Kings 23:3; Jer. 2:2) and this reserve is no doubt—with justice—to be explained by the fact that the phrase, very concrete and materialistic as it is, was the technical term in use for the practice of pagan cults with their processions of the faithful following the images of idols. It was of great importance to preserve the idea of a transcendent God who would tolerate no material representation of Himself.

2. In the N.T. this expression takes on a new meaning, richer and more specialized. Whereas the closely related verb "imitate" has as its object God Himself (Eph. 5:1), this does not apply to the verb "follow", the object of which is always Christ. Moreover, the latter appears solely in the four Gospels and once in the Book of Revelation (14:4, an allusion to Matt. 10:38). In the Epistles on the other hand we find expressions implying the idea of imitation and usually suggesting submission to the glorified Lord and His Spirit.

From these observations it becomes fairly clear that primitive Christianity wished to express by the verb "follow" the special tie which united the disciples to the historical Christ. The exclusive application of the term in the N.T. to the disciples of Jesus shows beyond doubt that the early Christians had in mind the unique character of this relationship.

This unique character is evident from the very first meeting of the disciple with his Master: "Follow me"; it is this imperative which is at the point of departure of the new relation about to be established. For the disciple it means the irruption in his life of an unusual authority, of a truly Messianic demand, to which the only fitting reply is that total and immediate obedience which the four evangelists delight to emphasize (Mk. 2:14; Matt. 4:19,20; Lk. 9:59; Jn. 1:43).

We may state more precisely those implications of discipleship contained in the term "to follow":

(*a*) Following Jesus involves in the first instance a sharp break with the past. The disciple must give up everything, must cut all those ties which had been formed prior to his encounter with Jesus, so as totally to belong to his new Master (Lk. 9:61; Mk. 10:28; Matt. 19:21).

(*b*) Following Jesus also involves sharing in His earthly destiny. It involves the obligation to share His wandering and homeless life (Matt. 8:19) and in a certain measure to participate in His passion (cf. Matt. 26:40). Yet we should notice that it is never a question of a total imitation of Christ. Some were disciples of Jesus who did not completely follow Him as regards His wandering life. The lot of the disciple cannot be quite the same as that of the Master. Jesus tries to make the disciples understand the necessity of His suffering and death. But the disciples cannot follow Jesus to the point where He hangs in desolation on the cross (Jn. 13:36–37; Mk. 10:38). Yet if the disciple's following of the Master stops on the threshold of that unique event—the death and resurrection of the Master—it remains none the less true that a destiny of suffering, similar to that of his Lord, is reserved for the disciple who remains faithful. Jesus alludes to the possibility of following Him even after His death (Jn. 13:36; 21:22); it is in this future as much as in the present that the disciple will have to bear *his* cross, which is not identical with that of Christ (Mk. 8:34 and parallel passages).

(*c*) Lastly, to him who follows Jesus the promise is given that he will enjoy the salvation which the Lord offers. While not conferring any special privilege on the disciple (cf. Mk. 10:40) his following of Jesus makes him fit to enter into the Kingdom of God (Lk. 9:61ff.) and to share in eternal life (Mk. 10:28; Jn. 8:12). The destiny of the disciple is henceforth linked with that of Jesus (Jn. 12:25,26; Jn. 10:27,28).

But in conclusion it should be noted that to live as a disciple it is less a question of attaining a sort of *imitatio* such as was later advocated in certain ecclesiastical interpretations than of entering into, *abiding in and progressing in the new life of belonging to Jesus Christ, marked by faith in and obedience to Him. To follow, in the thought of the N.T., suggests an event; not an idea or a state. The term is closely connected with the appearance of the historical Christ proposing to men a radical redirection of their lives (expressed in the N.T. by the idea of *repentance) and in discipleship to Himself, orientating them towards a new aeon, which is that of eternal life and the Kingdom of God.

H. MEHL-KOEHNLEIN

FORGIVENESS

1. *Definitions of forgiveness.* A whole series of expressions in O.T. and N.T. designate the act of forgiveness and make it possible to define its nature. To begin with, there is the most common expression "to remit", "to cancel" (a transgression), in comparison with the remission of a debt (Ps. 32:1; Matt. 9:2; Lk. 7:48). There are the expressions "not to impute" (Num. 12:11; Ps. 32:2; Rom. 4:8), "to cover" something which one no longer wishes to see (Ps. 85:3; Rom. 4:7), "to forget" something the memory of which one does not wish to retain (Ezek. 33:16), "to blot out", "to cleanse", as one does with a stain (Isa. 6:7; 43:25; Ps. 51:4). The following may also be cited: "to cast behind oneself" (Isa. 38:17), "to tread under foot", "to cast into the depths of the sea" (Mic. 7:19). Sometimes the verb "to forgive" is employed in the absolute sense (Mk. 4:12; Matt. 6:15; 12:32). When it is followed by a complement it is essentially connected with sin and sins (Ps. 32:1; 51:4; Mk. 2:5; Lk. 17:4), with transgression, iniquity (Ps. 32:1–2; Rom. 4:7), offences (Matt. 6:14), blasphemies (Mk. 3:28).

Thus forgiveness is seen as the act of God which puts an end to the unhappy situation created by the *sin of man, a situation offensive to God and grievous for man. It is the act which re-establishes man in his true relationship to God by removing the element which destroys that relationship, namely, sin, man's transgression.

It must, however, be observed that, according to all these definitions, this act of forgiveness does not consist in denying purely and simply the fault of man, as though it did not exist. But it puts an end to a situation of fact which is perfectly recognized. God, the author of forgiveness, acts with full knowledge of the matter and in full sovereignty. In His mercy and long-suffering He refuses to execute a judgment which is deserved and grants man a reprieve.

2. *The conditions of forgiveness*. The O.T. describes a number of human attitudes which make the forgiveness of sins possible. The prophets affirm vigorously that sacrifices and external rites of purification are vain (Mic. 6:6-7; Jer. 6:20). What is of importance is the recognition of one's fault and the acknowledgment of guilt (Jer. 14:20), the act of suffering for this state of affairs, of realizing the gravity of sin and the grief of having offended God, contrition of heart (Ps. 51:19; Isa. 57:15; Ps. 6). It is, finally, conversion that is important, the act of changing one's way and returning to the Lord (Jer. 3:14; Ezek. 18:30-32; 33:11, 14-16, etc.). This is the essential condition for the exercise of forgiveness.

John the Baptist takes up this theme in his preaching of *repentance as a necessity for the remission of sins (Mk. 1:4 and parallels). It is, finally, the necessity for repentance which the Messianic preaching of Jesus stresses, placing it in close relationship with the coming of the *Kingdom of God (Mk. 1:15 and parallels).

3. *Forgiveness in Jesus Christ*. In the N.T. forgiveness is presented in a double perspective.

On the one hand, emphasis is placed on the *unmerited* character of forgiveness. In reality the indispensable conditions for forgiveness of which the O.T. already speaks are requirements impossible of realization by man left to himself. Man is an insolvent debtor (Matt. 18:23-35). The sinner is incapable of rehabilitating himself before God and of keeping His law. He cannot save himself (Mk. 10:26-27 and parallels). From man's point of view, forgiveness is seen to be impossible.

On the other hand, despite this human powerlessness to obtain forgiveness, this forgiveness is announced and proclaimed (Mk. 2:5 and parallels; Lk. 7:47-49; Lk. 1:77). It is the good news of the free gift of God to sinful man. This is the significance of the parable of the prodigal son (Lk. 15:11-32). Thanks to the pure compassion of the father, the unworthy son becomes a child of his father once again, his access to the paternal home and to life is restored.

But the Gospels not only proclaim this forgiveness: they connect it closely with Him who brings it, namely, *Jesus Christ who confers forgiveness. Jesus is seen as the one who has the power to forgive sins, power similar to that of God (Mk. 2:5,7,10). Moreover, His death is presented as a redemptive act which makes possible the remission of sins (Mk. 10:45; Matt. 26:28 and parallels; see *Cross).

In this way everything connected with forgiveness converges in Jesus Christ. It is through Jesus Christ that forgiveness becomes a living experience for man, essential for the establishment of the new *covenant (cf. Heb. 9:15,22). Thanks to Him, the assurance is given that every sin will be forgiven to men. Only the sin against the Holy Spirit cannot be forgiven, neither in this world nor in the world to come. He who *blasphemes against the Holy Spirit will not experience salvation (Matt. 12:31).

4. *Forgiveness in the Christian community*. For the Church, therefore, forgiveness is inseparable from Jesus Christ. She preaches forgiveness because of Jesus Christ, she grants forgiveness in His name (Acts 13:38; 10:43; Lk. 24:47; Col. 1:14; Eph. 1:7;

Jn. 20:23; 1 Jn. 2:12; Jas. 5:15). This grace of forgiveness is especially signified in *baptism and the *Lord's Supper (Acts 2:38; Mk. 1:4; Matt. 26:28). Moreover, in conformity with the teaching of Christ the Church considers the practice of forgiveness towards the brethren as a requirement and a consequence of the forgiveness of God (Matt. 6:12–14; 18:21,35; Mk. 11:25; Lk. 6:37; 7:47,49; Eph. 4:32; Col. 3:13). To live by the forgiveness of God without forgiving one's neighbour is inconceivable.

Thus, contrary to Judaism, for the Church of Christ forgiveness does not concern only the things of the past. It is the living action of God which man knows in forgiveness and which unceasingly opens the future to him. Forgiveness is an eschatological gift, bound to the coming of the Spirit, in the expectation of the Kingdom of God (Acts 2:38).

H. MEHL-KOEHNLEIN

FREEDOM

1. Freedom is the condition of those who belong directly to God. According to the dictionary, freedom is the "condition of a person who does not belong to a master", a purely negative definition which humanistic or political idealism could embellish. According to the Bible, he is free who, as a creature of God, enters into His *covenant and there defies all the totalitarian pretensions of men and their world. He is enslaved who has not yet been liberated from an absolute human control, or, which is less serious, who is temporarily deprived of the material realization of the freedom of God (exile, persecution, foreign domination). Since, by definition, God is the only possible liberator, it is from Him alone that all deliverance can be awaited with watchfulness, and it is to Him that it will continue to be owed.

In the Bible freedom is not, in the first place, a conquest or an emancipation, individual or social, of man in the midst of his fellows. Far from placing man in isolation by making him the hero and the end of all freedom, Scripture sees him face to face with God, at one and the same time

the object of His love and the possible toy of the forces of the world, and regards his freedom as a reintegration into the hierarchy of Creation and accordingly under the authority of God, in the *peace of the first and the last day. What profane history calls freedom, deliverance, is not biblical, except for a change of master, since it is not the freely awaited and accepted prerogative of the power of God over His children.

Before the Fall, Adam was free because of the generous disposition of the Creator. Jesus Christ is free because of His total submission to the Father, with whom He is one. The people of the old covenant are free in proportion as they recognize and confess God's miraculous liberation of their fathers, and in the new covenant the Church participates in advance in the "glorious liberty of the children of God" (Rom. 8:21) in proportion to its faith in Jesus Christ and its resistance to every rival authority.

2. The liberating work to which the O.T. bears testimony is the *election of Israel as the direct property of God (Exod. 19:5)—in historical terms, the departure of the Hebrews from Egypt under the leadership of Moses. The liberation of this nation coincides with its foundation. In fact, when God sets free and takes possession of men He makes of them a new reality which is historically perceptible. The free nation of Israel is the work of God alone, as Exodus persistently shows by emphasizing that it owes its existence neither to the initiative of Moses (Exod. 3), nor to the goodwill of Pharaoh (Exod. 5–14), nor to the revolutionary enthusiasm of the Hebrews! (Exod. 2:14; 5:21; 14:11–12). It is in God that Israel finds its independence with respect to all the great powers of the world. All the other acts of deliverance of the O.T. are the confirmation of this liberation and expressly refer to it (the "promises to Abraham", the "land which God swore that he would give to your fathers", etc.).

In the time of the judges, as also of the first kings, the wars of independence are the proof that the liberating God remains faithful to His promise and to the work which

He has begun: He protects the national territory against the enemies from without and their arrogant gods. Later on, Israel will have an ever-diminishing consciousness of its direct dependence on God; the kingdom (1 Sam. 8) will interpose itself between the nation and its Liberator, the people will see and follow only their human king, and thus will allow themselves to fall from the freedom of God into the tyranny of men. A new liberation will then become necessary, less and less territorial, and more and more spiritual. The heralds of freedom will no longer be military leaders, but prophets. The enemy will be not so much Egypt or Babylon as contempt of being the Lord's possession (Isa. 1:2ff.), national pride with a veneer of religion (Jer. 7:3–15), the exploitation of the weak (Jer. 34:17), and recourse to strange gods. Catastrophe will put an end to this false freedom and to this imaginary independence without Lord and without covenant. At last, during the Exile, the proclamation of liberation will ring forth anew (Isa. 40; 49:8ff.; Zech. 9:9ff.)—not merely territorial liberation—the proclamation of the new covenant within which there will be provision for a final deliverance (Isa. 61:1–3; Mic. 4:1ff.; Mal. 3:1ff.).

The conditions of freedom had been displayed beforehand in Gen. 1–2, where man is in the direct service of the Creator, and in Gen. 12–50, where the nomadic patriarchs already enjoyed, thanks to their strict dependence on the Lord, a foretaste of the freedom of God's elect.

3. The N.T. proclaims Jesus Christ as the liberator for all men: for Israel in the first place, and then for the Gentiles. Jesus Christ brings liberation (Lk. 4:19,21) because He re-establishes the direct relationship of possession and belonging between God and men, at least believers. His advent replaces God in the life of men, driving out false masters (the *forgiveness of sins, the liberation of the *demon-possessed) and at the same time restoring to man his solemn responsibility before God and his unhoped-for dignity amongst his fellows. Jesus Christ is "God with us" (Immanuel);

henceforth He is the end of all dictatorships. For him who acknowledges His sovereignty, freedom has commenced, freedom which is not just a defensive reaction against circumstances (individualism, assertiveness compensating for subconscious inferiority) nor contempt of the world, but the law of a new creature whom his Creator has taken in hand again. In a world that is separated from God, freedom returns by Jesus Christ (Jn. 8:31–36). Where the Spirit of the Lord is active, there is freedom (Rom. 8:2; 2 Cor. 3:17; Gal. 5:1).

In the N.T., then, it is not a question of freedom in the merely social, relative sense of the word (to have the same rights as others): these social distinctions are known, noticed (Jas. 5:4–6), called in question (Philem. 21; Eph. 6:9), but they are not regarded as decisive (1 Cor. 7:20–21, where the translation should be: "Even when you could become free remain a slave rather"). The source of freedom is not in institutional reforms; it is in the Lord, for him who submits to Him and serves Him (1 Cor. 7:22; 12:13; Gal. 3:28). By Him, however, all the forces of slavery are threatened and shaken.

4. The tyrants from which Jesus Christ delivers men are *sin and *death, the latter being the regular consequence of sin. No longer is it a question of national liberation, as in the days of the old covenant: the liberating activity of God is extended to all men, universally and individually; it is radical in form because history has now entered upon its final stage. God deals with the roots of tyranny, thus with internal corruption (2 Pet. 2:19), with sin (Rom. 6:18–23) which engenders death. The Messiah comes and works accordingly: He is not the liberator of ancient times, modelled on past hopes. He comes now to attack the roots of evil, which man neither would nor could eliminate, nor even recognize in himself. He comes to liberate man from himself, to reveal to him that his pretended ("internal") freedom is slavery, to give His life in order to purchase forgiveness, and to rise again in order that the way

of freedom might be opened up. Man resists his own liberation; but he who follows Jesus to the end passes into the world of freedom and into *life eternal, even though death may still intervene. And the time of the "glory of the children of God" approaches. For faith and for hope the time of freedom has commenced, and sin and death are already vanquished.

5. To live free is to place oneself under the active sovereignty of the living God, it is to be "possessed" by the Holy Spirit. Freedom, which has nothing in common with chaos (Gal. 5:13; Eph. 4:14; 1 Pet. 2:16), has a structure, and this structure can even take the name of law (the "law of the Spirit of life", Rom. 8:2; the "law of freedom", Jas. 1:25; 2:12; the "pattern of teaching", Rom. 6:17). The apostles, indeed, do not leave to chance the task of instructing Christians how to live free. Together with them, they examine the concrete will of the liberating God, seeking its distinctive marks, which they set down in writing as practical signposts (cf. Paul's exhortations at the end of his Epistles). Where the Spirit of the Lord is, there is freedom: now, the Lord is not a God of disorder, but of peace (1 Cor. 14:33). To live free is therefore to follow His "law" in faith and "obedience from the heart" (Rom. 6:17).

(a) To wish to define a priori, by means of a *law, the concrete effects of the sovereignty of God would, however, result in a complete absurdity. The living Lord would then be supplanted by a dead letter. And it would be not only an error but an ungrateful retrogression to regard the law of the old covenant, as it was observed in the synagogue, as the law of freedom in the kingdom of Christ. This would render vain the coming of Christ and, although using His name, would be to take refuge in conservatism in the era, which is now over, of the old covenant. The law of the O.T. (which is not, however, a natural morality, but rather the code of the covenant of God) has in fact never had a liberator. It is God, its inspirer, who has delivered; and it is He who, in Jesus Christ, now brings

radical deliverance (Rom. 8:3–4). In no way does this deliverance permit a return to a list of moral and religious requirements. Man would be powerless to deliver himself in this way by his own works. Hence the earnest, anxious, unremitting struggle of Paul against the Judaizers, against all those who in practice assign more importance to the observance of a law than to believing submission to the work of Jesus Christ. Christians with a legalistic outlook have failed to understand that Christ is the beginning of a new era, of a new creation, and that by their moralism they at once overthrow the significance of Jesus Christ (Gal. 5:11; 6:12) and of the law which they extol (6:13; cf. Rom. 3:19–28; Phil. 3:2–3; Col. 2:10–23).

(b) While there is room for withstanding legalists, yet there is absolutely no place for a display of strength, that is to say, for openly demonstrating a freedom which runs the risk of being nothing more than the boasting and desire of the flesh. The true freedom given by Christ has effects which are less ostentatious, but more radical (Gal. 5:24–25). If everything is permissible, not everything is expedient (1 Cor. 8–10); what is of importance is to be integrated with love into the *building up of the body of Christ and to facilitate the integration into it of others (Rom. 14–15). This attitude of entire renunciation of matters of personal advantage, and of sacrifice in order to avoid all cause of offence to the Gospel, is already the attitude of Jesus (Matt. 17:24–27); it is also that of Paul (1 Cor. 9; 1 Thess. 2:5–9). This is perfect freedom, without internal shackles.

(c) Finally, to live free does not imply social anarchy. The Christian, initiated by his own salvation into the mercy of the Lord of lords, will submit to human *authorities in so far as the established order does not seek to impose itself as absolute and eternal. The task of the state is to maintain the best possible provisional order, and the freedom of the Christian consists in living in this state while at the same tine giving the first place to the Lord. His attitude is thus compounded of loyalty and respect (Rom. 13:1–7; 1 Pet. 2:13–17), and also of resistance (for the greater good of the state when it is no longer fulfilling the function assigned to it by the Lord: Acts 4:19–20; 5:29), of resolution in making use of all his rights (Acts 16:35–39; 22:25–30), and at times also of suffering and martyrdom. The trial of Jesus and that of Paul are models of the attitude of freedom, which, although misunderstood and condemned, is loyal and constructive, and which is the result of God's liberating work. It is here that the freedom which the Bible proclaims reveals its political and social aspect.

CH. BIBER

FULFIL

1. When the term "to fulfil" has theological significance it serves essentially to express the great event in the history of salvation, the coming of Jesus Christ, in relation to that which precedes. The O.T. was the time of promise; in Jesus Christ the fulfilment is attained.

But that which is fulfilled would not be known if it had not been announced. Promise and fulfilment imply each other; hence the importance for the N.T. of the witness of the O.T.

Jesus refers expressly to the O.T. in that which concerns His word and works (Matt. 11:4–6), His passion and His death, which is an offence for the Jews as well as for the disciples (Mk. 14:21; Lk. 24:26–27). He is the one who was to come and Scripture has traced the way He must follow. Matthew puts the events of the life of Jesus into almost minute relationship with the Scriptures (1:22; 2:5,15,17,23; 3:3,17; 4:14; 12:17; 13:14,35, etc.); the other evangelists emphasize chiefly the accord with the Scriptures of the facts of the Passion (Mk. 15:28; Jn. 18:9; 19:24,36–37; Acts 4:25–28; 8:32–35; 13:27), of the resurrection (Jn. 20:9; Acts 2:31; 13:32–37), and of the ascension of Jesus (Acts 2:34–35). In other words, the Scriptures show that Jesus is the Christ (Lk. 24:27,32,45; Acts 17:2f.; 28:23; 1 Cor. 15:3–4).

2. Fulfilment of the Scriptures signifies more than the correspondence of a particular word in the O.T. with a particular event in the life of Jesus. It is the Scriptures in their totality which witness to Him (Jn. 5:39–47). The O.T. was written with Jesus (Jn. 5:46–47; 8:56) and the Church (Rom. 15:4; 16:26; 4:23–24) in view. Therefore the profound meaning of the Scriptures is only recognized in the Church (Rom. 9:10ff.; 10:11; 2 Cor. 3:14–16), which reads the Scriptures in the light of their fulfilment.

Jesus fulfils the Scriptures by what He is as well as by what He does, in His person as well as by His work. He not only brings the word of God: He is it in Himself (Jn. 1:1,14); through Him the Kingdom of God has drawn near and is present (Mk. 1:15; Lk. 7:18–23; 11:20); His works are the signs of the Kingdom, the testimony to what He is (Jn. 5:36). It is no longer merely the promise of salvation but its reality (Lk. 4:21) which is manifested in Him.

In his perfect obedience to the will of God, even to the cross, Jesus fulfils the *Law and the *Prophets (Matt. 5:17; Mk. 10:45; Rom. 5:18–19; Phil. 2:8). Henceforward the Law and the Prophets surrender their authority to Jesus Christ (Matt. 5:18; Lk. 16:16; Rom. 10:4); it is then no longer the law which governs the relations of men with God, but Jesus Christ.

3. Just as for things past (Heb. 8:4ff.; 10:1), the things to come, the end of the world, must also be regarded in the light of Jesus Christ. Jesus Christ will return in the glory of the Father for the judgment, the resurrection and the completion of salvation (Matt. 25:31; Mk. 8:38; Rom. 8:18,23; 1 Thess. 4:13–14; 1 Jn. 2:28–3:3). But that which remains to be accomplished is less than that which Jesus Christ has already done (Rom. 5:1–10); the *resurrection will only make manifest the eternal life already present (Jn. 5:24; 6:39–40). For that which determines the destiny of men is their faith or disbelief with regard to Jesus Christ (Jn. 12:47–48).

4. The new righteousness which surpasses

that of the Scribes and Pharisees (Matt. 5:20), is *love, which summarizes both the old law (Mk. 12:28–31; cf. Deut. 6:4–5; Lev. 19:18) and the new commandment (Jn. 13:34; 1 Jn. 2:8).

In this sense love fulfils the whole law (Gal. 5:13–14; Rom. 13:8–10): all the work of God leads to this, that believers devote their lives to the service of their neighbours (Eph. 2:10; Matt. 25:31–46), following the example of Christ (Jn. 15:12–13; Eph. 5:2). Love is the only reality which will remain in the world to come (1 Cor. 13:8); it is the "royal law", the law of the Kingdom of Heaven (Jas. 2:8), the sign that one belongs to the Kingdom and that one belongs to Christ (Jn. 13:35).

F. BAUDRAZ

GARMENT

1. (a) If it is not a sign of innocence (Gen. 2:25) or an expression of the ecstasy of self-surrender in love (Song of Solomon) the nakedness of the human body is a thing of shame which should not be exposed (cf. Lev. 18) but carefully concealed (cf. Gen. 9:22ff.). That is why it is the duty of the Christian to be generous in providing for the need of one's brother to cover his nakedness (cf. Matt. 5:40; 25:35ff.; Lk. 3:11; 6:29; Jas. 2:15), as God concealed the nudity of the first man and woman (Gen. 3:21; cf. Ezek. 16:8). To be naked in effect is to be forsaken (cf. Lk. 8:27) or even punished by God (Isa. 3:22ff.; Ezek. 16:39; Acts 19:16). Certainly the body is more than the raiment (Matt. 6:25) and even nakedness cannot separate from Jesus Christ those who are His own (Rom. 8:35); but raiment is part of the vital needs of man like food and shelter (Gen. 28:20; Exod. 21:10; 22:26ff.; Deut. 10:18; 24:17; 1 Tim. 6:8).

(b) But the aim of clothing is not merely to protect and cover man in his nakedness: it also discovers and exposes his inmost nature. In the first place this fact enables us to recognize the wearer by his clothing. For this reason the O.T. forbids a man to wear a woman's garments and a woman to wear those of a man (Deut. 22:5; cf. 1 Cor.

11:14ff.), and for the same reason all disguise is considered tantamount to a lie (Gen. 27; cf. 2 Cor. 11:14ff., Matt. 7:15): clothes must be so infallible an index to the identity of the wearer that it becomes a species of deception to choose clothing which is contrary to one's rank or state in life. Furthermore, this kind of trick is regularly exposed (cf. 1 Sam. 28:8ff.; 1 Kings 14:1–6) or fails of its effect (1 Kings 22:30–35; 2 Chr. 35:22f.). Among revealing garments may be noted those of the angels (Lk. 24:4; Acts 10:30, etc.), of the prophet (Zech. 13:4; Matt. 3:4; 2 Kings 1:8), of kings (Acts 12:21; cf. Matt. 11:8), of the rich (Jas. 2:2), of the widow (Gen. 38:14,19), of the still virgin princess (2 Sam. 13:18), of the leper (Lev. 13:45), of the prostitute (Gen. 38:14,19), etc. On the basis of such a conception of clothing it goes without saying that priests also wore a distinctive garment, all the details of which are minutely described (cf. Exod. 28; Lev. 16:32; Ezek. 44:17). And if the Christian woman should be clad decently and simply (1 Tim. 2:9–10; 1 Pet. 3:3) it is to show thereby that she considers her honour and glory to consist in the adornment of good works rather than in that of precious jewels. The revealing character of the garment is also suggested by the fact that changes of garment are significant like changes of *name: he who receives a new garb becomes a new man (Zech. 3:3ff.; Gen. 41:42; cf. Lk. 8:35). The importance that the promise of new white garments (cf. Rev. 6:11; 7:9,13ff.; 3:5,18, etc.; cf. Eccl. 9:8) assumed in the baptismal practice of the early Church is well known. The garments of Jesus are also revelatory of His person and mission: thus their dazzling radiance at the moment of His transfiguration (Matt. 17:2), the whiteness of the robe with which Herod arrays Him (Lk. 23:11), His seamless dress (Jn. 19:23) or the golden girdle with which He is girt when He appears to the seer of the Apocalypse (Rev. 1:13; cf. Exod. 28:8) all reflect His office of supreme high priest, just as the scarlet robe placed on Him by the soldiers (Matt. 27:28) symbolizes His royal state.

But the garment is not merely revealing

of what one is; it also indicates what one does or the state of mind in which one finds oneself: thus it is said that men wear wedding garments (Isa. 49:18; Rev. 19:8; 21:2ff.) or garments of mourning (2 Sam. 14:2; Jon. 3:8; Matt. 11:21) and the wearing of such garments may be considered obligatory (Matt. 22:11; cf. Isa. 52:1). To show sadness (Gen. 37:34, etc.), fright (2 Kings 22:11), extreme amazement or anger (Matt. 26:65; Acts 14:14) or repentance (Joel 2:13), in other words to mark that he feels, in one way or another, affected to the depths of the soul, a man will rend his garments; as a mark of readiness for action a man girds his robe (Exod. 12:11).

(c) Thus we have seen that to change the garments may be the sign of a far deeper change taking place in the very soul of him who is unclothed and reclad, and that for a man to rend his garments has a similar significance. This means that for the Bible as for primitive man in general the clothes are an integral part of the very personality of the wearer: the garment partakes of the wearer's inmost being. Thus when Jonathan gives David his cloak, it indicates that he vows himself to the service of David (1 Sam. 18:4), and if the latter is so shaken with fear at the thought of having cut off the skirt of Saul's robe (1 Sam. 24:5ff.) it is because he fears to have assaulted the Lord's anointed. It is in this light also that we must understand why, on the death of Aaron, no new garments are made for his son Eleazar but he receives the priestly robes of his father (Exod. 29:29; Num. 20:26ff.) or why it is that Elisha inherits the powers of Elijah by inheriting his mantle (2 Kings 2:13ff.; cf. v. :7ff.). Likewise it is in this perspective that we must understand the miraculous power of the garments of Jesus (Matt. 9:21; 14:26) or of the apostle Paul (Acts 19:12). This unity of person and dress is also shown by the fact so often attested that to cleanse oneself completely one must also wash one's garments (cf. Exod. 19:10; Lev. 11:25,40; 14:8,47; 15:8; 16:26,28; Rev. 7:14; 22:14) or by the fact that to sully the garment is to sully the person (Rev. 3:4; cf. 16:15; see also the parallel between the

laws about leprosy of the body and that of the dress, Lev. 13ff.).

2. If the garment assumes such importance in biblical thought, if it is to this extent bound up with the person of the wearer and the index of his character, we need not be surprised that verbs meaning to strip and reclothe have been susceptible of coming into such close connection with ideas of election, baptism, vocation, salvation and the Christian life as a whole. To be found naked before God, i.e. to be found before Him in the state of guilty exposure in which Adam was found in the Garden of Eden, is what is most to be feared, for in that case man again runs the risk of being driven from the kingdom and presence of God; whereas if He finds us clothed, the celestial habitations will be open to us (2 Cor. 5:3ff.). But this new garment which will enable man to bear the divine judgment —like the first couple's aprons of skins (Gen. 3:21)—it is God alone who can give it, and man knows well that the girdles of leaves which he may fabricate for himself (cf. Gen. 3:7), his attempts to hide himself from the sight of God, are incapable of assuring him salvation: in order to be able to abide in the presence of God man must receive from his heavenly Father a garment of salvation (Isa. 61:10), just as the prodigal son on his return received the best robe (Lk. 15:22). The point is that man must have the white robe of the elect (see above); i.e., that he must be renewed in the whole of his being, and in some sort re-created wholly. This garment of salvation, which does not merely clothe man but which becomes an integral part of his entire being, is Jesus Christ (Rom. 13:14) the new Adam (Eph. 4:24; Col. 3:10); it is put on in baptism (Gal. 3:27) which is a stripping naked of man in revolt, of man without a future, of the man we were before the coming of Jesus Christ, and a putting on of the new man, the resurrected man who we are in Jesus Christ (cf. Rom. 13:12ff.; Eph. 4:22ff.; Col. 3:9). The Fathers saw in this putting on of the Christ not merely the acquirement of divine righteousness and an

anticipation of future glory, but also a restoration of paradisal innocence, of the state in which they thought the nakedness of the first couple—since they were not conscious of it—was already clothed with a "stole of holiness" (Irenaeus) or with a "garment of innocence" (Ambrose).

Thus clothed with the garment of salvation, believers must deliberately adopt it and identify themselves with it, especially in the form of an armour (Rom. 13:12; Eph. 6:11ff.; 1 Thess. 5:8ff.) which will enable them to confront the world and the Evil One without losing the innocence which they have gained through the forgiveness of God; but also they will wear it as a garb of humility (1 Pet. 5:5) and compassion (Col. 3:12) which will make of them a peaceable and loving people. As for those whom Jesus Christ entrusts with a special *ministry, He will clothe them with power from on high (Lk. 24:49) to enable them perfectly to fulfil it.

J.-J. VON ALLMEN

GATE, see DOOR

GEHENNA

1. This name is a transcription of the Hebrew *gehinnom*, "valley of the son of Hinnom" (Josh. 15:8; 2 Kings 23:10), a deep depression situated to the south of Jerusalem. It was the site of the worship of Moloch, to whom the kings Ahaz and Manasseh sacrificed their sons (2 Chr. 28:3; 33:6). Josiah, the reforming king, declared it an unclean place (2 Kings 23:10) for the burning of refuse and the disposal of corpses (Jer. 31:40; Isa. 66:24). The prophets proclaimed oracles of doom on the valley, which in their preaching became the scene of the coming chastisement (Jer. 7:31f.; 19:6; Isa. 31:9). In the Jewish Apocalypse of Enoch it is the place where God will punish the wicked in the sight of the righteous on the mount of Jerusalem (cf. Lk. 16:23,26).

In the N.T. Gehenna designates eternal punishment, no longer localized in the valley of Hinnom.

2. Gehenna has numerous synonyms or equivalent phrases: the eternal fire (Matt. 18:8–9; 25:41); unquenchable fire (Matt. 3:12; Mk. 9:44–48); the fire and the worm (Mk. 9:48; cf. Isa. 66:24); the furnace of fire (Matt. 13:42); the lake of fire (Rev. 20:14), or of fire and brimstone (Rev. 14:10; 19:20; 20:10; according to Gen. 19:24; Ps. 11:6; Ezek. 38:22 this was the punishment of Sodom and Gomorrah); the torment (Rev. 14:10–11; Lk. 16:23,28); the pit (Rev. 20:3; cf. Matt. 25:41); eternal punishment (Matt. 25:46); the outer darkness (Matt. 8:12; 22:13; 25:30).

How can Gehenna be at once "fire" and "darkness"? Fire was, for Israel, a sign of the presence of God (Exod. 19:18; 40:38; Deut. 4:12; 5:4) but also of His holiness, which cannot endure evil: God destroys by fire all that displeases Him (Deut. 32:22; 2 Sam. 22:9; Jer. 5:14; 15:14; Heb. 12:29). Gehenna has no power of itself; it is God who there imposes punishment by fire. On the other hand "outer darkness" is the opposite of *light, symbol of salvation and eternal life (Jn. 8:12; Rev. 21:23): outside the banquet of the Kingdom of Heaven there is only darkness (Matt. 22:13).

St. John speaks not of Gehenna but of perdition (3:16); of the enduring *anger of God (3:36); of *death (6:50; 8:21; 11:25; 1 Jn. 3:14f.); of judgment, in the sense of final condemnation (5:24,29); of darkness (12:46); of being cut away (15:2); cast out (15:6); of being driven far from Christ at his coming (1 Jn. 2:28).

Nor is the term Gehenna found in St. Paul; it is replaced by wrath (Rom. 2:5; 5:9); wrath and fury, tribulation and distress (Rom. 2:8f.); perdition (Rom. 9:22; Phil. 3:19); corruption (Gal. 6:8); rejection (1 Cor. 9:27).

The antonyms of Gehenna are *salvation, eternal *life, the heavenly *city.

3. We must distinguish between "Gehenna" and "the abode of the dead", also called "hell" (cf. *World, N.T.): to the latter go all souls after death to await the resurrection, whereas Gehenna is the place to which the wicked are delivered after the

last judgment to undergo their punishment; it is "the second death" (Rev. 20:6,14).

4. In contrast to Jewish apocalyptic the N.T. takes no pleasure in describing the torments of Gehenna. Jesus Christ came not for an immediate final judgment, which would restrict Him to pronouncing a decisive sentence, but to give His life as a ransom to snatch men back from perdition (Mk. 10:45; Jn. 3:16; Rom. 6:23); those who believe in Him have passed from death to life, from perdition to the Kingdom of God (Jn. 5:24; Col. 1:12–14).

But the coming of Jesus Christ can also have the opposite effect: those who do not believe in Him, who reject His words, condemn themselves (Jn. 12:47f.). Jesus Christ confronts every man with a life or death decision; each must decide for himself what his eternal portion is to be. Left to themselves men go straight to Gehenna; only the intervention, the work of Jesus Christ, accepted in faith, can give them a different destiny.

Gehenna is the doom hanging over those who from the start turn away from Christ (Matt. 23; Jn. 8:44–47), but it also threatens those disciples who do not persevere in the witness they ought to bear to Christ in word and deed (Matt. 10:28; Mk. 8:38; Lk. 12:4f.,8f.). The believer must break with all forms of sin (1 Cor. 5:9f.; Gal. 5:19ff.; Phil. 3:18f.; 1 Jn. 3:14f.; Rev. 21:8; 22:15); to this end no sacrifice is too great (Mk. 9:43–49), having regard to the severity of God's judgment on sin (Matt. 5:22). The "children of Gehenna" are the hypocritical Scribes and Pharisees and those who model themselves on their example (Matt. 23:15); they are the sons of the Devil, who is a liar and a murderer (Jn. 8:44), because of the attitude they have taken toward the Christ.

James (3:6) warns of the hellish power of the tongue.

To sum up: when the N.T. speaks of Gehenna and perdition, it is not to predestine some to an inevitable doom, but to warn and exhort all to seek salvation and eternal life in faith in Jesus Christ.

F. BAUDRAZ

GENEALOGY, see FAMILY, GENERATION

GENERATION

1. Begetting, birth: see *Family.

2. In the sense of the length of a human life, "generation" is used to reckon time: past time (Acts 14:16; 15:21); the time of God's punishment, which continues to the fourth generation (Exod. 20:5; Deut. 5:9); the time of His mercy, infinitely greater than His anger (Exod. 20:6=Deut. 5:10; 1 Chr. 16:15; Ps. 105:8). The phrase "from generation to generation", which may also be translated "from age to age", signifies "for ever", "in perpetuity" and is connected with God's faithfulness, His rule and His love (Exod. 3:15; Ps. 33:11; 90:1; Isa. 60:15; Dan. 4:3; Lk. 1:50).

3. Elsewhere "generation" denotes the men of a particular period (Exod. 1:6; Num. 32:13; Eccl. 1:4; Deut. 2:14); the men of the past (Job 8:8), of the future (Deut. 29:22; Job 18:20; Ps. 22:31; 48:14; 78:4,6; Lk. 1:48), of the present (Isa. 53:8; Lk. 16:8).

In this sense the "generation" is the object of the severe judgments that the prophets pass on the men of their time and on the whole people of Israel: a crooked and perverse generation (Deut. 32:5,20); an evil generation (Isa. 1:4), a generation of adulterers and harlots, who love other gods than the Lord (Isa. 57:3; Jer. 2:20; 3:1–5); a lying generation (Isa. 57:4).

Jesus takes up these judgments of the prophets and applies them to His own contemporaries: an evil and adulterous generation (Matt. 12:39; cf. Isa. 57:3; Jas. 4:4); adulterous and sinful (Mk. 8:38); a faithless generation (Mk. 9:19); faithless and perverse (Matt. 17:17; Lk. 9:41); the Scribes and Pharisees are classed by John the Baptist and Jesus as "broods of vipers" (Matt. 3:7; 12:34; 23:33), but they are not the only ones so condemned; Jesus makes no exception for individuals but considers the people as a whole. The men of other generations were no better (Matt. 23:29–37) but by putting the Christ to death the generation of Jesus' contemporaries draws particular attention to itself, carries sin to the limit and therefore will receive a more terrible punishment (Matt. 23:36).

The believer is separated from his perverse and corrupt generation, which continues to live in religious hardness of heart and moral corruption (Acts 2:40; Phil. 2:15), to form a new *people (1 Pet. 2:9; Tit. 2:14). This is at once the gift of Jesus Christ and His requirement.

4. A special problem concerns the difference in the number of generations in the genealogies of Jesus (Matt. 1:1–17 and Lk. 3:23–38). The two passages have differing purposes and the names they list coincide only in seventeen instances, but they have a certain schematization in common. Matthew has six sets of seven generations, Luke eleven such sets. It is probable that these figures correspond to various calculations on the coming of the Messiah: according to Enoch, for example, the Messiah is to come after nine weeks of generations; according to 4 Esdras after eleven weeks. Thus, each in its own way, the genealogies testify that *Jesus is the Messiah.

The genealogies referred to in 1 Tim. 1:4; Tit. 3:9, are not those of Jesus but of the O.T. patriarchs, which the rabbis used and interpreted; a practice which gave rise to interminable disputations, against which the apostle seeks to put his readers on their guard.

F. BAUDRAZ

GENTILES, see NATIONS

GIFTS, see MINISTRY N.T., HOLY SPIRIT

GLADNESS, see JOY

GLORY

O.T.

The Hebrew word which corresponds to glory implied originally the idea of weight or mass—whence the Pauline expression "an

eternal weight of glory" (2 Cor. 4:17). In Greek, glory, according to classical usage, denotes simply opinion and thence reputation. For the Semite, what has weight has importance and value. In secular usage, glory is a synonym for riches and property (Gen. 31:1; Isa. 10:3), for success and power (Gen. 45:13; 1 Kings 3:13) and so finally denotes the subject's honour, splendour or greatness.

1. The idea of glory plays an important part in the theology of the O.T.; in particular, the phrase "the glory of Yahweh" is frequently employed as a technical term. The whole content of revelation is, indeed, nothing else but the glory of Yahweh. The whole biblical history conspires to manifest this glory. Yahweh acts for His own glory, and when He creates, punishes or saves, the basic motive of His action is the glorification or, as it may also be described, the sanctification (cf. *Holy) of Himself or of His holy name. Ezekiel and Deutero-Isaiah pay particular attention to this theocentric aspect of God's intervention (Ezek. 20:9,14; 36:21–23, etc.; Isa. 42:8; 48:9ff.; Ps. 79:9, etc.). According to the most ancient ideas, the glory of Yahweh is associated with natural phenomena such as storms and tempests, and perhaps even volcanic eruptions. Yahweh, a kind of storm-god, spreads panic among animals and men by His lightnings and His terrible voice, the thunder. He shoots out flames of fire, His lightnings lighten the world, the earth trembles at His approach. In the same way, Sinai, where Moses talks with God, is encompassed with the glory of Yahweh as with a consuming fire (Ps. 29:3,7; 97:3f.; Exod. 24:15–18; 19:16, etc.).

On first inspection, therefore, the glory of Yahweh is presented to us—and it will never lose this character—as something at once radiant and terrible, too deeply mysterious ever to be comprehended, revealing itself in swiftness and might, intervening here below after the manner of the lightning which strikes suddenly down to earth.

2. Consequently, the glory of Yahweh

5*

connotes for Israel, first and foremost, the majesty of a God who infinitely surpasses man. Yahweh is the "wholly other", not lightly to be approached: His power, His energy, His essence evade all comprehension. His brilliancy is such that He cannot be regarded face to face; the magnificence of Yahweh is so dazzling that even Moses can only have sight of the rearward or reflection of it (Exod. 33:17-23). The divine splendour and the frailty of humanity, which, in accordance with the ethical categories introduced by Isaiah, is the same as to say the holiness of Yahweh and the impurity of creatures, are separated by an immeasurable distance, of which every being suddenly confronted with the presence of the Most High must be aware (Isa. 6:1-7).

3. But the O.T. offers us yet another conception, dear to the priests, according to which the glory of God, far from confining its flight to the heights of heaven, comes to dwell among men. Yahweh of His goodness allows His glory to rest in the midst of Israel. At first, the Tent of Meeting is the privileged place of this abiding. In accordance with the divine promise "the cloud covered the tent of meeting and the glory of the Lord filled the tabernacle" (Exod. 40:34; cf. Exod. 16:10; 29:43; Lev. 9:6,23f.; Num. 14:10, etc.).

God bestows His glory on Israel, but it should be noted that at the same time He veils it with a cloud. Thus it escapes the gaze of the sacrilegious, it is protected from any kind of profanation and it remains independent of those in whose midst it has come to dwell. The glory of Yahweh belongs to Him alone at all times, even when it is present among men.

After the ark (1 Sam. 4:21f.; Ps. 24:7-10), the *Temple at Jerusalem, built by Solomon, is the place chosen by Yahweh to be the especial dwelling-place of His glory (1 Kings 8:10f.). "I love the habitation of thy house, and the place where thy glory dwells" sings the Psalmist. It is true that the reflection of the glory of God appears to Ezekiel in the land of exile, amid overwhelming noise, a blaze of light and a confusion of extraordinary figures (Ezek. 1). The prophet is not forgetful, however, that Jerusalem remains the normal seat of the divine glory (Ezek. 8:4; 9:3). Yet what a drama is here unfolded! the glory of the God of Israel, the only source of the glory of the Holy City, forsakes that city where crime and sacrilege are multiplied! Ezekiel, astonied, is present at the departure of the cherubim, who bear the glory of Yahweh on their outspread wings (Ezek. 10). Nevertheless, he foresees the solemn moment that will succeed this time of desolation, he foretells the return of the glory of the God of Israel to a purified Jerusalem, he already hears the approach of the tremendous procession (Ezek. 43:1-7; 44:1-4). The whole drama of the chosen people is suggested in this departure and return of the glory of Yahweh.

4. If the priestly theology prefers to connect the glory of Yahweh with particular places, hymn and prophecy associate it with particular times. The liturgy sings of Israel's past, witnessing to the marvels accomplished by God on behalf of His people. The glory of Yahweh is revealed in the Creation; but it manifests itself especially during the days of the Exodus, when the Egyptian tyrant is struck down. The prophets predict the universal triumph of the divine glory; from east to west the name of Yahweh will be feared and His glory reverenced (Isa. 59:19). Even now the heavens declare the glory of God, but it is still needful that the nations should join in these praises (Ps. 8:2ff.; 19:2ff.; 24:7ff.; 104:1ff., etc.). The whole earth is full of the glory of Yahweh—so sing the seraphim in the highest. Nevertheless, what is already true in heaven is still awaited by men; but the day is coming when all flesh will see the glory of God (Isa. 6:3; 40:5; cf. also Isa. 60:1-5).

While the O.T. closes with the mysterious vision of one "like a son of man" to whom the Ancient of Days gives "dominion and glory and kingdom" (Dan. 7:13f.); while the chosen people, following in the steps of Ezekiel, go on to meditate on the disturbing fortunes of the glory of God, which, transformed into a kind of hypostatized figure (*Shekinah*), goes into exile to join the Jews driven from the Holy Land; the Gospel proclaims to all the fulfilment of that which under the old covenant was but vaguely discerned and hoped for:

"And the Word became flesh and dwelt among us, full of grace and truth; we have beheld his glory, glory as of the only Son from the Father" (Jn. 1:14).

R. MARTIN-ACHARD

N.T.

1. We may distinguish three senses of this word in normal usage:

(*a*) Its content may be dynamic, a legacy from certain strands in the O.T. (the Yahwist tradition and the prophets, especially Isaiah, etc.). In this sense "glory" expresses the active and radiant presence of God the Lord. There are three ways in particular in which the glory of God acts, which have influenced the thought of the evangelists and apostles: (i) By means of His glory God helps and succours the believer or the chosen people; conversely, by the same means He punishes, whether it be the enemies of His people or the people themselves in rebellion. (ii) It is the guide that leads the way to the Promised Land. (iii) It is the means of God's self-revelation.

This dynamic sense is found occasionally in the *synoptic Gospels*, but most especially in the *apostle Paul*, where it expresses the resurrection life. In the *fourth Gospel* "glory" is extended to denote the drama of redemption in its entirety, though with the emphasis on the result of that drama.

(*b*) Its content may be visual, with light playing a prominent part. Ezekiel was the first to present the glory in the form of extraordinary brilliance and light. This sense is found to some extent in all parts of the N.T., sometimes combined with sense (*a*), sometimes, though more rarely, by itself.

(*c*) In hymnody (psalms, canticles and liturgical formulas), "glory" has lost much of its force. Judaism affords examples of

composite formulas with two or three or four terms, among which the term glory is included.   Here and there in the N.T. examples of this usage may be found. We may quote: Phil. 1:11; 1 Pet. 1:7; Rev. 4:9,11; 5:12,13; 7:12, etc.

2. We must now examine the part played by "glory" in particular N.T. writings. It is in the thought of *Paul* that it occupies the most important place. The complete pattern may be described thus: (i) In the beginning man was subject to God and could see His glory (Rom. 1:21,23). (ii) As soon as he was subject to sin, this glory became foreign to him and an object of terror (Rom. 3:23; 2 Thess. 1:9). (iii) After the death and resurrection of Jesus Christ, man is rescued from the complete domination of sin, although he still has to die. He sees the glory in the face of Christ (2 Cor. 3:18; 4:6). (iv) After the work of redemption is fully accomplished with the return of Christ, man will neither sin nor die any more; not only will he see the glory, but he himself will become a glorious body, a being in glory (1 Cor. 15:43; 2 Cor. 3:18; Phil. 3:21), subject to the active, radiant power of the Lord.

Three important aspects of this thought must be emphasized:

(*a*) The believer finds himself in a world where sin is still active. The presence of Christ in such a man is, therefore, at once a source of hope and a cause of suffering (Rom. 8:17–30): the glory of the Risen Christ is already giving him his freedom, but, on the other hand, it makes him more aware of the activity of sin in the world. His sufferings thus have a very definite meaning: they assure him of his belonging to Christ and strengthen his hope of glory (2 Cor. 4:17; Col. 1:27f.).

(*b*) The rôle of glory in the matter of Christian conduct is of primary importance. For the believer, as for the Church, there are difficulties of every kind (doctrinal divisions, 1 Cor. 3:1–9; litigation, 1 Cor. 6:1–9; sexual misconduct, 1 Cor. 6:12–20; the spirit of condemnation, Rom. 14–15; 1 Cor. 8:1–13; 10:23–33, etc.).   In face of these difficulties their duty is to glorify God. When a Christian acts in such a way as to endanger the spiritual life of his neighbour (whether that neighbour is a believer or not), he may no longer rest content simply with an appraisal of the motives of his conduct from his own standpoint—even though these motives may seem to be good ones— because he is required to glorify God. For, by obliging him to do everything for the glory of God (1 Cor. 10:31; Rom. 15:6f.), this process of glorification has two effects: (i) It teaches him no longer to consider his own reasons for acting, even if they are good in principle, but to look to the effects of his actions and conduct on the relationship between the Lord and other men. (ii) By this means, glory becomes the goal of Christian action, because the glorified Lord is its fountain head.

It may be said, therefore, that just as the glorification of Christ has created a new union between God and men, so also the glory of God is still uniting men in a mutual relationship (Rom. 15:6; e.g., "such harmony", "together", "with one voice"). It triumphs over all that may oppose it. It does not merely *assert* the existence of difficulties or the disastrous consequences of sin; it rises above them, is victorious over them and finally eliminates them.

(c) Glory manifests God's covenant (2 Cor. 3; 4:1–6). Under the old covenant, received by Moses, man only reflects the glory for a time. Under the new covenant he may contemplate it for ever in the face of Christ. Glory is not satisfied with transforming a possible bond between God and men: it creates one and guarantees it.

We may conclude, therefore, that glory is at the heart of Pauline thought just as much as is the resurrection of Christ. God is the Father of glory and to that glory He destines the believer. *Resurrection and glory are almost completely identified. It is impossible to think of the resurrection, whether of Christ or of the believer, without thinking of the glory that follows it, or to think of glory without thinking of the resurrection that precedes it. Were it not for the resurrection of Christ, no one would ever again have enjoyed the presence of the divine glory, nor understood its meaning. Were it not for that resurrection, the life of Christ would not have been "in glory", the Lord would not have had a "glorious body", nor a "being in glory". By his actual communion with Jesus Christ the believer is introduced to the contemplation of Him. On the day when he is "with Christ", he will be a "glorious being" completely after His likeness.

3. In the *fourth Gospel* glory appears as the outstanding attribute of the Son.

(a) He possesses it from before the creation of the world (17:5).

(b) When He comes to earth, He "reveals" it and it "reveals" Him (1:14). It manifests Him as one sent by the Father (11:4) and is itself manifested when Jesus performs certain signs (11:4; 2:11; 11:40)—for example, at Cana, when Jesus changes water into wine, and at Bethany, when He restores Lazarus to life. The evangelist can therefore say that, by His earthly ministry, Jesus has been glorified and that the Father has been glorified in Him, for it is in the course of this ministry that the revelation of Jesus as the one sent by the Father emerges (13:31f.). The ambivalent character of the signs, recognized for what they are by the believer alone, is echoed in the process of manifesting the glory, which the believer alone can behold (11:40). This double aspect of the manifestation of the glory in the earthly ministry of Jesus recalls a similar feature in certain O.T. traditions, according to which one and the same divine glory simultaneously succours the believer and blinds and punishes the unbelieving. The Semitic character of certain phrases in the fourth Gospel is here plainly recognizable.

(c) Frequently, the phrase "Jesus has been glorified" is used to mean "Jesus has died and risen again". Glorification thus denotes the totality of the drama of redemption and emphasizes its final outcome—entry into glory. It expresses at once God's victory over the enemy, death, and the triumph of Christ; and signifies that in this fact the saving plan of God is revealed in its entirety (7:39; 12:16,23,28; 17:5).

(d) Similarly, the disciples are to be recognized by the fruits they bring forth, fruits which, in their own way, will also glorify the Father (15:8; 14:12ff.). Even their deaths will thus acquire significance (21:19).

(e) Neither is the Spirit excluded from this work of glorification. In a manner reminiscent of the action of the divine glory He guides toward the truth, declares things to come and reveals the Son; and by these means He glorifies Him (16:13–15).

4. Outside the Pauline literature and the fourth Gospel, where we have found "glory" set in a framework of original thought, there are numerous other passages, which may be tentatively classified as follows:

(i) The appearance of radiant light, signifying the nearness of God and His intervention (either directly or by an angelic intermediary): Lk. 2:9; 9:31; Rev. 18:1.

(ii) The glory of the places where God reigns: the Temple (Rev. 15:8); the New Jerusalem (Rev. 21:10).

(iii) As a characteristic of the Messianic Age or of the heavenly sphere: Mk. 8:38; 13:26; 10:37; Matt. 25:31–46.

By way of summary, we may say that, except in certain liturgical formulas, "glory" expresses the active and radiant presence of God manifesting itself in the most diverse forms. In the present world we may already be aware of it; in the world to come we shall behold it and our whole being will thereby be transformed.

M. CARREZ

GOD

O.T.

1. "Yahweh is the true God: he is the living God and the everlasting King." This affirmation made by the prophet Jeremiah (10:10) is a fairly complete summary of what God was for Israel.

The Living God. The fact of God was so obvious that there is in the O.T. not a single trace of speculation on the origin or the provenance of God, whereas theogony occupies a considerable place in the beliefs of the peoples around Israel. Without doubt, Yahweh was not always the god of the Israelites, but His connection with the gods of their fathers who had preceded Him was merely one of succession, not a genealogical relationship; as soon as He appears, He is recognized as a greater, a sovereign god, because He is a living god. Just as *life is a mysterious reality which can only be accepted and which no one dreams of disputing, so God is an undeniable datum. The theological character of the expression "Living God" is not so generally accepted as that of other expressions such as "King" or "Holy One", but these other affirmations are conditioned by that which declares that He is a living God; His life is the condition of His eternal nature, of His power and of the existence of men who live by His breath of life (Ps. 104:29). Faith in the Living God reached its highest expression in anthropomorphic language. The thought of the Living God gives to biblical anthropomorphism a meaning quite different from that which is conveyed by the application of similar terms to the pagan idols; "it is because God is living that one can speak of Him as of a living man, but it is by speaking of Him as of a human being that one constantly calls to mind that He is living" (F. Michaeli).

Anthropomorphism is found throughout the O.T.; it is in no sense a primitive way of speaking of God and is not incompatible, e.g. in Deutero-Isaiah, with a highly spiritual theology (cf. Gen. 6:12; Exod. 16:12; 1 Sam. 26:19; Ps. 2:4; Isa. 7:18; 63:6; 66:1, etc.). Along with anthropomorphisms are found expressions implying anthropopathism. God experiences all the feelings which are known to men: joy (Zeph. 3:17), loathing (Lev. 20:23), regret (Gen. 6:6), jealousy (Exod. 20:5). The Israelite faith, however, imposed certain limits on a thorough-going anthropomorphism; while speaking of God in human terms, the Israelites always remembered the essential dissimilarity between God and man. "I am God and not man" (Hos. 11:9) and the prophet Isaiah expresses the irreducible difference between God and man in terms of flesh and spirit (Isa. 31:3), where the antithesis is not between the spiritual and the carnal, but between the strong and the weak. Then again in the O.T., a man has no real existence apart from his membership in a community; now God is self-sufficient and has no need of a female partner. The Hebrew language does not even possess a special term to denote the goddess and makes use for this purpose of the general term *Elohim* (1 Kings 11:5). God has no sons; the beings described as sons of God (Gen. 6:2; Job 1) are divine beings, but not sons begotten by God. Another limit set to the anthropomorphizing tendency was the prohibition forbidding the making of a carved representation of God (Exod. 20:4). Israel understood clearly that it was impossible to reduce God to the human level or to define a reality as mysterious and yet as manifest as life itself.

The One God. Although the affirmation that the God of Israel is the one and only true God is one of the dominant ideas of the O.T., it expresses a truth which is less evident than the truth that He is a living God. Monotheism is affirmed theoretically only at a comparatively late date, but it may be stated that, from the very beginning, or in any event from the Mosaic period, the faith of Israel is practically monotheist. Moses was not a religious reformer like Amenophis IV who introduced a new religion by persecuting the one already in existence. Israelite monotheism, too, is different from the movement which in Babylon had assured the supremacy of Marduk by the reduction of the other gods to mere personifications of his various functions. The problem of the existence or non-existence of other gods was not the immediate concern of Moses; rather he received the revelation of a god who by his power and vitality and by his demands for the complete obedience of his worshippers leaves no room for other gods beside him (Exod. 20:3). W. F. Albright believes

that it is possible to speak of "monotheism" from the age of Moses, and finds confirmation of this in the affirmation "of only one god, creator of everything, the source of justice, who is powerful in Egypt, in the desert and in Palestine, who has no sexuality and no mythology, who is human in form but cannot be seen by human eye and cannot be represented in any form" (*From the Stone Age to Christianity*, Johns Hopkins Press, p. 207).

The god of Moses is a jealous god, and the figure of the conjugal bond which the prophets use to illustrate the reality of the *covenant demonstrates clearly that the God of Israel looks upon the presence of other gods alongside Him as an act of infidelity. However, at this period the existence of other gods is not denied; if Yahweh is god in Israel, Chemosh is god in the neighbouring land of Moab (cf. Judg. 11:24); in the eyes of the majority of the Israelites, who had not remained on the high level of the faith of Moses, the power of Yahweh did not extend beyond the limits of their nation and their territory; to go into a foreign country meant being exiled from the face of Yahweh (1 Sam. 26:19) and coming under the sovereignty of another god who for the time being might be more powerful than the God of Israel (2 Kings 3:27). But these limitations were to be shattered by the jealousy of the God of Israel, a jealousy which was manifested not only by the exclusive worship which He required of His people but which extended to the other gods; Yahweh could not remain indifferent to the gods of the peoples with whom His own people were constantly in contact; the struggle of Israel with these nations goes hand in hand with a conflict between Yahweh and the gods of these nations.

Nevertheless, the two struggles follow an inverse order: whereas the political history of Israel is marked by the progressive loss of national independence, her religious evolution is characterized by an increasingly emphatic affirmation of the unique sovereignty of God. That was essentially a victory for the faith of the prophets, who set Yahweh free from all the ties He might have with the race and the land to proclaim Him as the Lord of universal history (cf. Amos 3:2; 9:7); from that time the gods of the nations are no more than instruments in His hand; according to passages such as Deut. 4:19 and Ps. 82 the authority of the heathen gods was conferred upon them by the God of Israel.

God's mastery over universal history has its corollary in His lordship over creation (Amos 4:13; 5:8). The difference between Yahweh and the other gods is not a simple matter of hierarchy; the God of Israel is in a radically different and superior sphere. The monotheistic affirmation implicitly contained in the message of an Isaiah or a Jeremiah (Isa. 31:7; Jer. 2:5,11) is developed systematically in Deutero-Isaiah, who declares that Yahweh is the only God, that there was no god before Him and that there will be none after Him; He is the first and the last (cf. more especially Isa. 41:4; 43:10ff.; 45:3,6; 48:11, etc.). The other gods, and first and foremost the gods of Babylon who had, nevertheless, shown their power by subjugating Israel, are only idols, blocks of wood or of metal having no life (Isa. 41:24,29). Yahweh, on the other hand, is not only the Living God, but He dominates history and creation to such a degree that He was able to predict all that would take place (Isa. 43:12; 45:21; 46:9; 48:3,16). It is because he lays such stress upon the unique character of the God of Israel that this prophet feels that he has the right and the duty to bring all the nations to the knowledge of this one true God. From this time onwards the religion of Israel is clearly monotheistic and many passages reflect the influence of the great Prophet of the Exile (Ps. 96:5; 1 Kings 8:60; 2 Kings 19:15,19). Henceforth can be observed the frequent substitution of the name Elohim for that of Yahweh, and the use of the name Yahweh to convey the idea of God in general, especially in the prophet Ezekiel.

We may sum up by saying that Israelite monotheism did not emerge as the result of reflection on the unity of the divine nature or on the order of the world, but as a result of the struggle of a jealous god whose power was so strong that in the end it imposed itself on the whole world.

2. *Names of the God of Israel.* (*a*) *El, Elohim.* In all the Semitic languages the idea of divinity is expressed by the root *el* (in Accadian *ilu*, in Arabic *ilah* and, with the definite article *allah*), the root meaning of which is probably that of power. To the Semites, God is always the strong Being who inspires a feeling of fear and reverence and before whom man must prostrate himself, whether this power is manifested in the form of hate or whether, as in the O.T., in the form of a lord who chooses and commands. The name of *el* is, in the O.T., applied indiscriminately to all the gods, but we also find it used as a proper name for a particular god. The Ugarit texts have shown clearly that the god *El* occupied the preeminent place in the Canaanite pantheon; it is this great god *El* who is encountered in the stories of the patriarchs, e.g. in Gen. 33:20: *El*, God of Israel; more often the name *El* is followed by another word in apposition to indicate the place (El Bethel, El Olam, etc.) or the character of the theophany. The O.T. writers prefer to use as a proper name the word *Elohim*, originally a common noun used to denote all the gods and goddesses, which became a proper noun often replacing Yahweh, from the motive either of avoiding the use of the ineffable name or of showing that Yahweh was God in the highest sense of the word.

(*b*) *Yahweh.* This name occurs nearly 6,000 times. In the actual text, as it was established in the 6th century A.D. by the Massoretes, the association of consonants and vowels produces the name *Jehovah*. This name, which has enjoyed a certain favour especially through the liturgical use which has been made of it, is in fact a barbarism, since it is a hybrid form in which the vowels of the word *'Adonai* = my lord, which was destined to replace the ineffable name, were combined with the four letters of the sacred tetragrammaton. There is a fairly considerable weight of evidence to suggest that the true name of the god of Israel was Yahweh; certain of the early Fathers, speaking of the name of the god of Israel and of its pronunciation, give its transcription as *Yabe, Yaoue* or *Yao*; in the Assyrian documents the theophorous element *yah* in proper names is transliterated *Yau*; these various transcriptions would seem to bear witness to the idea that from a very early date the name of the deity existed in two forms, a short form *Yah, Yahu*, and a longer form *Yahweh*. The shorter form occurs in the O.T. in Exod. 15:2, "Yah is my strength and song", and in the doxological formula "Hallelu-Yah"= praise Yah. The form Yahweh is found as far back as the 9th century B.C. in the inscription of King Mesha of Moab and in the ostraka of Tell ed Duweir (Lakish); in the Elephantiné papyri, on the other hand, the divine name is always written *Yahu*; the two forms then must have been in use simultaneously. It is, however, more likely that the shorter form is a contraction of Yahweh than that the longer form is an expansion of Yah(u).

On the subject of the origin of the worship and of the meaning of the name of Yahweh we have in Exod. 3 a fairly detailed account according to which the name Yahweh was unknown before the time of Moses; Gen. 4:26 and 9:26 suggest, however, that the name Yahweh was in use long before Moses' time. The proposition that this name was borrowed from the Canaanites or the Kenites does not go beyond the stage of probability; it seems more exact to admit that the name Yahweh was already familiar to some of the ancient Israelite tribes during their nomadic period but that it was Moses who, in the revelation which was given to him at Sinai, added to this name a power and a prestige unknown before.

The meaning of the name Yahweh must be sought in the direction indicated by the narrative of the burning bush, where it is connected with the verb *hayah*=to be: *Yahweh* would then be the one who speaking of himself says: "I am" (*'ehyeh*) and of whom men say: "he is" (*yahweh*). This explanation is at the same time philologically more probable and more in harmony

with the narrative than the explanation that Yahweh is a causative form of *hayah* meaning "he who causes to be", "he who calls into being". It is still an open question whether God's reply to Moses is a revelation or a demurrer; in the former event it should be translated "I am he who is", in the latter "I am what I am", that is to say, "that is no concern of yours". There is probably some element of truth in both these interpretations, for the analogous verbal constructions in the O.T., e.g. Exod. 3:14; 2 Kings 8:1; 1 Sam. 23:13; Exod. 33:19; Ezek. 12:25, express sometimes an indetermination and sometimes, especially in the last two passages, an additional intensity: "I am indeed he who is". That is, in our view, the meaning of the word God to Moses, but the deliberately ambiguous pronouncement does safeguard the element of mystery which even God's self-disclosure does not entirely disperse. In every instance, in the verb *hayah* the emphasis must be put not upon the obvious idea of existence but upon the presence of God with Moses and with the people: the revelation Moses is charged to bring to the people is that of a God really present to guide, to judge and to save them.

(*c*) *Yahweh Sabaoth*=Lord of Hosts. This expression is found 279 times in the O.T., its commonest occurrences being in the prophetic books. This phrase is interpreted in three different ways: it may mean the terrestrial armies of the children of Israel, or the hosts of the stars, or again, the legions of spirits and angels. It must be borne in mind that the expression is often in juxtaposition with the ark of the covenant which was, at least at the beginning, a war-symbol (cf. Num. 10:35); again, when David goes out to meet the Philistine, he says to him: "I come to you in the name of the Lord of Hosts, the God of the armies of Israel" (1 Sam. 17:45). It seems then that the "hosts" means originally the warlike hosts; in the prophets this expression denotes the aggregate of the forces over which Yahweh claims the command, and is used with the motive of highlighting the dynamic function of Yahweh and His work of conquest. There is still room for the possibility that, alongside this basic aspect, the prophets used this expression to affirm that the host of heaven was also controlled by Yahweh, and consequently that this host of heaven had no claim upon the worship of the faithful.

(d) *Titles bestowed on the God of Israel.* The root *ba'al* expresses the idea of ownership and lordship; when this word is used as the title of any god, it signifies that the god is the owner of a place where he claims to dwell and the lord of a man or of a people over whom he claims to rule. Yahweh, then, was the *ba'al* of His people (Isa. 54:5), and in many proper names the theophorous element *ba'al* clearly means Yahweh: Yerubbaal, Eshbaal, Baalyada and especially Baalyah. But as a reaction against the Canaanite religion in which Baal was not only a title but the proper name of one of the chief deities, the name of *ba'al* was increasingly dissociated from that of Yahweh (cf. Hos. 2:16f.).

Yahweh is often called *'Adon*=lord, an expression more especially used in the vocative. It was this word *'Adonai*=my lord which a subordinate used when he wrote to his master and when he addressed him to his face.

The title of king, *melek*, is frequently applied to Yahweh, especially in the Psalms where great stress is laid on the kingship of Yahweh; but as this expression designated also the earthly king, its use as a divine title was subject to the fluctuations which the royal person and the ideology of kingship underwent in Israel.

3. *Some foreign gods.* When the O.T. writers speak of the strange gods who often proved to be a temptation to the Israelites, they call them the *Baals* and the *Ashtaroth* (Judg. 10:6; 1 Sam. 7:4). The O.T. uses the generic term *ba'al* to denote different deities. The Ba'al who in the days of the prophet Elijah appears as an actual rival of Yahweh was probably *Melkart*, the local god of Tyre—the birthplace of Queen Jezebel. Among the local baalim the O.T. mentions the god of Shechem, *Baal Berith* (Judg. 8:33; called *El Berith*, Judg. 9:46) and

the god of Ekron *Baal Zebub*, god of flies, who became the *Beelzebub* of the N.T., and who had the power of curing certain diseases (2 Kings 1:1–16; Matt. 10:25; 12:24; Mk. 3:22; Lk. 11:15–19).

Chemosh, national god of Moab (Num. 21:29; Jer. 48:7ff.; Judg. 11:24, erroneously described in the last passage as the god of the Ammonites) had been granted admission into Jerusalem under the great syncretistic movement which took place during the reign of Solomon (1 Kings 11:7–23) and was not eliminated until the time of Josiah (2 Kings 23:13).

Milkom, a common noun which developed into a proper name=the king, was the national god of the Ammonites. It cannot be established with any certitude whether the infant sacrifices offered in the valley of Hinnom near to Jerusalem were offered to this god or to a Canaanite god *Melek*, better known in the altered form *Molek* or *Moloch* according to the Greek transcription.

Tammuz is the type of the dying and rising god, the personification of the forces of nature which dies with the summer heat and is born again with the spring. This god, who originated in Sumer where he is found as far back as 3000 B.C., passed into Syria and Palestine, where his cult had secured a footing in the very heart of the Jerusalem Temple (Ezek. 8:14). In Phoenicia he was better known under the name *Adonis*.

Dagon, whom the O.T. mentions as a god of Philistia (Judg. 16:23; 1 Sam. 5:2–7), passed from the West into Mesopotamia where he is encountered occupying a well-established place in the Mari pantheon. He was not, as a tradition which goes back to St. Jerome suggests, a fish-god (*dag* in Hebrew=fish), but a vegetation-god (*dagan* =corn), whose attributes must have closely resembled those of Tammuz.

Among the goddesses, pride of place in the Canaanite pantheon is occupied by *Asherah*, who is known in the Ugarit texts as the consort of *El* and of *Baal*. She is mentioned in the O.T.: 2 Kings 21:7; 1 Kings 15:13; 2 Kings 23:7; 1 Kings 18:19; like Baal, she was associated with the nature cults of fertility and fecundity; in other O.T. passages, *asherah* denotes a wooden pillar, the object of cultic veneration; it is probable that the name of the goddess was applied at a later stage to the sacred pillar without the two being completely identified since according to Jer. 2:27 the tree was a male deity.

The goddess *Anat*, who was the great patroness of war among the Canaanites, does not figure as a deity in the O.T.; but from the papyri which come from the Jewish colony at Elephantiné in Upper Egypt (5th century B.C.) we learn that under the name *Anat-Yahu* she was assigned as partner to Yahweh Himself, which leads us to suppose that the cult of this goddess was practised among the Israelites of the kingdom of Samaria from which the Elephantiné colonists had come. *Anat* is found too as the proper name of an Israelite leader of the time of the Judges (Judg. 3:31; 5:6) and survives in place-names such as *Beth Anat* and *Anathoth*, the native place of the prophet Jeremiah.

Astarte, usually pointed *Ashtoreth* with the vowels of the word *bosheth*=shame, is the Babylonian *Ishtar*, the goddess of the morning star: Venus, the goddess of war and of love. In this latter character she was the patroness of sensual pleasure and fecundity. This goddess was of so rich a personality that many other goddesses came to be merged with her; that is why the Bible speaks of *Astartes*, meaning by that expression all the local female deities; but for her also the goddess-type was the queen of heaven who, as emerges so clearly from such passages as Jer. 7:16-20 and 44:15-30, has ever exerted a great power to seduce the feminine temperament.

ED. JACOB

N.T.

In the N.T. there is not—nor in the nature of things can there be—any original doctrine of God, for the God of whom Jesus and the apostles speak is none other than the God known by all the people, the God of the old covenant, the one, living, jealous and merciful God, the holy God to whom men owe obedience and loyalty. Contrary to what the intellectuals of Athens might imagine (Acts 17:19), there is no question of any new teaching about God in the N.T. message; the God who is active in the story of Jesus is one whom pious Jews cannot fail to recognize, for He acts as He has always acted and in harmony with His promise. It is through the exposition of the *Scriptures (as Jesus expounded them at Emmaus, Lk. 24:25-27, and as did the preachers of the early Church) that men can understand the new action which God has performed in Christ. The important thing to grasp is that it is the God of the covenants and of the law, the God of the prophets, who continues to act towards men as He has always acted. It is because of this that all the theological affirmations of the O.T. are implicitly accepted by the N.T.

1. First and foremost the affirmation of *the absolute oneness of God* is taken for granted. Throughout the N.T. the monotheism of the O.T. is looked upon as a tradition which is beyond dispute (cf. the conversation of Jesus with the Scribes who sought to test thoroughly the agreement of His teaching with the biblical tradition, Mk. 12:28-42 and especially vv. 29 and 32). Thus, every time that they refer to the unity of God the N.T. writers can fall back upon such formulas as: we *know* (1 Cor. 8:4), or we believe, in the strong and absolute sense of this word (Heb. 11:6; Jas. 2:19). Of course this affirmation is not to be understood in the intellectual sense, as if it were made in order to take sides in the argument as to whether the world is governed by a unity or by a multiplicity of principles. It has a polemical and exclusive meaning; to affirm the oneness of God is to affirm the worthlessness of the gods, their fundamental futility (1 Cor. 8:4; 10:19), much more than merely their non-existence; for the N.T., like the O.T., admits that man can hold communication with powers which are demoniac even if celestial, and that, consequently, the worship of idols must be thought of not as a matter of complete

indifference, but as a deadly participation in a kind of blasphemy (1 Cor. 10:7; Acts 7:40–43; 1 Jn. 5:21). The N.T., like the O.T., confronts us with this paradox: although the *idols are vanity, the Eternal God takes umbrage at them. The jealousy of God is one of the most original features of biblical monotheism.

This one God desires that men should recognize Him in His exclusive oneness. He is not satisfied with a purely intellectual knowledge (see *Know), for such knowledge does not bring a man into right relationship with God; the demons also possess this knowledge of the one God, but that does not prevent them from trembling (Jas. 2:19). What God does expect from man is that he should recognize in a concrete way His will, His demands, His holiness and also His kindness and His mercy; in other words, man's knowledge of God must be *faith, that is to say trust (Rom. 4:3; Gal. 3:6), faith in His justice, and hope (Rom. 4:18; 2 Cor. 3:4; Acts 24:15; 1 Pet. 1:21; 3:5).

This practical knowledge of God bears witness to the fact that the oneness of God cannot be stated in isolation; it can only be understood when one recognizes that it is linked with the holiness of God. He is the one God because He alone is holy. When God turns towards man, He shows him His holiness with the formidable demand which this involves: "be holy, for I am holy" (Lev. 11:44, a demand echoed in the N.T. in the injunction of Jesus "You must be perfect as your heavenly Father is perfect", Matt. 5:48). Faith in the holy God will inevitably mean obedience. It is by this obedience that men bear concrete witness to the truth that He is the only God. By serving God man pledges himself to refuse all service to Mammon (Matt. 6:24), to carnal appetites (Lk. 12:19), to idols (2 Cor. 6:16; 1 Cor. 10:21), to the cosmic powers (Gal. 4:8), to the *authorities of this world when they claim to set themselves above God (Mk. 12:17; Acts 4:19; 5:29). Thus, knowledge of God in the N.T., as in the O.T., is inseparable from an ethic which certifies that God is turned in man's direction, that God cares for man, and that

fundamentally and essentially He is on the side of man.

2. This conviction was translated in the O.T. by the concepts of *covenant and *election. The "definition" of the God of the O.T. is that He is the God of Abraham, of Isaac and of Jacob, the God of Israel, *the God who chose for Himself a people* to walk with them and to realize through them His purposes in history. This conviction is carried over unaltered into the N.T. There are numerous passages which refer to this special relationship between the one God and a particular people (Matt. 22:32 and 33, a decisive passage because it emphasizes that it is through the covenant with a people that God reveals His true nature: He is the God of the living: Matt. 15:31; Mk. 12:26,29; Lk. 1:68,78; 20:38; Acts 3:13; 5:30; 2 Cor. 6-16; Heb. 11:16; 2 Pet. 2:1; Rev. 14:11, etc.). In the same way that God was the God of the people of Israel will He be the God of the Church, the heir of *Israel (Acts 20:28; 15:14; Heb. 4:9; 11:25; 1 Pet. 2:10). This living relation of God with a historic community, this personal link uniting God and man shows us the inadequacy of the ideas which men generally use to define God: eternity, transcendence, etc. None of these concepts can be applied to the God of the Bible without particularizing or reservation. As King of heaven, creator of all, He is indeed transcendent, eternal, absolute, but He associates Himself with the history of the men whom He has created. He wills to be acknowledged by them, He chooses some among them to be His witnesses.

3. All these paradoxes culminate in the relationship which unites the Eternal God and the man *Jesus. It is in *the connection between the doctrine of the One God and the Christological teaching* that the originality of biblical religion emerges most clearly. This originality is so marked that the Jews could believe that monotheism was threatened by the teaching of Jesus Christ.

Jesus Himself clearly emphasizes the

absolute "transcendence" of the One God. By rejecting all those trifling calculations by means of which the Pharisees sought to regulate their relations with God, Jesus recalls men to the sense of the dignity of God. He makes it quite clear that the unity which binds Him to God is one of dependence. He seeks only to obey God and conceives of all His work as an act of obedience to Him (Matt. 26:39; cf. Phil. 2:8). He refuses to allow Himself to be called good, since this designation belongs only to the One God (Mk. 10:18). He puts Himself on the same ground with relation to God as His questioners: "My Father and your Father, my God and your God" (Jn. 20:17). He never claims to be in possession of God's secrets (Matt. 24:36) and draws His wisdom solely from the Scriptural revelation of God.

Despite this, He is the Son of God (Matt. 16:16f.), endowed with divine power or at least with some of its characteristic features: if He refuses to avail Himself of Divine omnipotence, He exercises the right to forgive sins, a power which in the view of Israel belonged solely to the One God; He gives to His disciples the keys of the Kingdom of Heaven (Matt. 16:19); He is the one who will pronounce judgment in the last days (Matt. 25:31f.). The earliest Christian theology accords to Him the title of Mediator equally in the process of creation and in the work of salvation (Heb. 1:2; Col. 1:16; 1 Cor. 10:4). He presents Himself as God's ambassador, which means, according to the idea of the times, that He is equal in dignity with Him who sends Him: "he who receives me receives Him who sent me" (Matt. 10:40). The prince of this world, the enemy of God, is also the enemy of Jesus: "The reason the Son of God appeared was to destroy the works of the devil" (1 Jn. 3:8). That God is on the side of Christ in an absolute and complete sense in this struggle, that the fight waged by Christ is also God's battle, is attested by the resurrection of Christ (Acts 2:32): the resurrection is the ratification by God Himself of the work of Christ and the kingly rule of the One God in heaven and on earth will be assured by the victory of Christ (1 Cor. 15:28).

Thus the unique teaching about God which the N.T. claims to give is the existence of an intricate relationship between God and Jesus Christ. That a Messianic envoy of God, "like a son of man" (Dan. 7:13f.) should one day appear and engage in the final struggle is in harmony with the hopes of Israel. That does not in itself constitute an innovation. In general, however, the O.T. writers envisaged that this Messiah would belong to the category of the prophets or would even be one of these prophets who had already appeared (cf. Matt. 16:14). What was hidden from the faith of these writers was that this emissary would be the only son of the One God and that God would in this way reveal the true meaning of His Fatherhood. The N.T. writers were fully aware of what was new and unparalleled in this revelation. Consequently they multiplied expressions with the intention of making clear at the same time the uniqueness of the position of Jesus and the fact of the complete revelation of the invisible God in Jesus Christ. God designated Him as High Priest (Heb. 5:10), sent Him (Jn. 3:34), raised Him up (Acts 7:35; 13:23), made him to be Lord and Christ (Acts 2:36), ordained Him to judge the living and the dead (Acts 10:42), bore witness to Him (Acts 2:22), set His seal upon Him (Jn. 6:27), anointed Him (Heb. 1:9), exalted Him (Acts 5:31; Phil. 2:9). John finds in a language which is not entirely borrowed from Jewish tradition expressions which indicate even more emphatically the divinity of Christ. Jesus comes from God (Jn. 3:2; 8:42; 9:16,33; 13:3; 16:27f.). But it is Paul who discovers the most decisive formulas in which to express the truth that the Eternal God, the Creator, became in Christ a creature of history (in John's Prologue the use of the idea of the Logos might possibly lead the reader to interpret the incarnation on the metaphysical rather than on the historical level): "God was in Christ reconciling the world to Himself" (2 Cor. 5:19); "in Him—in Christ—the whole fulness of deity dwells bodily" (Col.

2:9). What the N.T. affirms, then, is that we can have no authentic knowledge of God except in Christ, since it has pleased God to realize through Him His work of redemption. At no moment, however, is the transcendence or the eternity of God jeopardized by the miracle of the incarnation: heaven is not left void in consequence of the incarnation. God the Father never left His throne: Jesus never ceases to pray to the Father who is in heaven. Jesus presents Himself as one who is in harmonious contact with the will of the Father. This unity between the two wills is so profound ("I and the Father are one", Jn. 10:30; cf. Jn. 17:11 and 21), that belief in the Father and belief in the Son are one and the same faith (Jn. 14:1,9). The duality of the persons is nevertheless unimpaired: what Christ possesses, He receives from the Father (cf. Jn. 17:22: "the glory which thou hast given me") and it is to the Father that He returns when He has finished His work (Jn. 13:3; 17:11). This duality of the persons, with identity of will, does not result simply from the fact of the incarnation. The incarnation does not imply that God has in some way provisionally duplicated Himself and that the duality derives solely from an encounter between a principle and a substance which brings about a division. The N.T. writers could doubtless have found in the Hellenistic tradition the elements of such an interpretation. Although they were Jews and clung firmly to the belief in monotheism, they did not do so; they preferred to formulate the idea of the eternal pre-existence of the Son even if this meant running the risk of being accused of polytheism (Phil. 2:6; Col. 1:17; Eph. 1:4; and, of course, the Prologue of John).

It is certainly the exception for the N.T. writers to call Jesus "God" (Rom. 9:5, a contested passage; Jn. 1:1; 20:28; 1 Jn. 5:20), but He is regularly called *the Lord*, a title which in the O.T. belongs to God alone, and the Epistles ascribe to Him all the functions which belong properly to God. Scripture, then, bears unequivocal testimony to the divinity of Christ. But the Christology is not added later as an appendix to the theology: it is an integral part of it. Christology has for its aim to bring us to the knowledge of the One God, who is a living community, a fellowship of persons. The O.T. taught that God is the Living God and a Father. The N.T. teaches us what meaning to attach to these statements. No doubt this unity of God, in the duality of the persons, is difficult to grasp and to explain, and the N.T. formulas do not always possess the exactness we would wish. Especially do they leave in doubt the subordination of the Son to the Father: does this subordination spring from the abasement of the Son, from the fact that He was clothed with an authentic humanity which became part of His very nature (since it was still in existence until after the ascension) or was it already operative in Christ's pre-existent life? In the same way, even though the N.T. emphasizes the personal character of the work of the Son, it leaves no room for any distinction between the work of the Father and that of the Son (cf. the formula adopted by Paul: "yet for us there is one God, the Father, from whom are all things and for whom we exist", 1 Cor. 8:6). The attempts made by many of the early Fathers and theologians to share between the Father and the Son the various attributes or functions are purely speculative and have no foundation in Scripture.

4. The non-speculative character of the N.T. appears equally clearly in the way in which, in the revelation of the One God, the person of the *Holy Spirit* is introduced. No N.T. writing explicitly affirms the trinitarian nature of God. But the person and the work of the Holy Spirit stand out from the account of the work of salvation. While the N.T. rejects the notion of all intermediary powers between God and man and finds no place for angelology, while Wisdom and the Logos are integrated into the person of Christ, the Spirit, sometimes described in the O.T. as a kind of divine hypostasis, becomes, like Christ, but in close relation to Him, a divine person. He

too is called Lord (2 Cor. 3:17) and the well-known text of John 4:24, "God is spirit", seems indeed to identify Him with God. As the work of God cannot be subdivided, it is impossible to distinguish in any clear fashion what refers to Christ and what refers to the Spirit: in the course of the same chapter, Romans 8, Paul attributes intercession on behalf of the saints first to the Spirit (v. 27) and then to Christ (v. 34). All union of man with God or with Christ is effected by the Spirit (cf. 1 Cor. 6:17). The Holy Spirit is called sometimes the Spirit of God, sometimes the Spirit of Christ. But one thing is certain: the place filled by the Holy Spirit can only be understood in the light of the redemptive work accomplished by Christ.

The Spirit is the gift bestowed upon men who believe in Christ: that is why He is described as a promise of Christ. From the very strange passage in Jn. 7:39: "Now this he said about the Spirit, which those who believed in him were to receive; for as yet the Spirit had not been given, because Jesus was not yet glorified", the conclusion must not be drawn that the Spirit is a creation of God coming into existence only at a certain date in history, but rather that the Spirit mediates the divine presence for men only at the end of Christ's ministry. The N.T. is concerned, not with speculations about the nature of the Spirit and His relations with the other persons of the Trinity, but with calling attention to the various stages in the history of salvation, the conditions requisite for the presence of God for us. It is thus that the Holy Spirit, clothed with the very power of God, intervenes after the departure of Christ, at the same time as Comforter, Teacher and the one who makes us share in the divine life even in this present aeon (Jn. 14:26; 15:26; 20:22). Linked as He is to Christ, it is of Christ alone that the Spirit can speak (Jn. 16:13f.). This means that the Holy Spirit does not represent for us the discovery of a new attribute of God, previously unknown. The same qualities that are attributed to Christ may be ascribed to Him. If Christ is called, like the Spirit, "Paraclete"

(at the same time Comforter and Advocate, 1 Jn. 2:1), this is not the outcome of chance nor lack of clarity. The work of God for man is one, although the ways by which His personal presence with man are manifested are mysteriously varied.

5. Although the N.T. does not formulate any *trinitarian doctrine* of God, its constant testimony authorizes and even demands such a theological affirmation: the God who reveals Himself to man for his salvation is one in three persons. This triune nature of God can never be understood apart from His redemptive work, it cannot be separated from the history of salvation, as Gal. 4:4–6 strongly emphasizes: "But when the time had fully come, God sent forth His Son . . . so that we might receive adoption as sons. And because you are sons, God has sent the spirit of his Son into our hearts." All the formulas in which the three persons of the Trinity are mentioned are always formulas which refer to the history of salvation (1 Cor. 12:4–6; 2 Cor. 13:14; Matt. 28:19). This fact considerably limits theological speculations on the dogma of the Trinity. It is advisable, also, to point out that the term "person" used to designate the Father, the Son and the Holy Spirit is not a biblical term and that a critical examination of this philosophical term is a prior necessity. It signifies in any case that God always acts upon man in the manner of a personal presence and not in any magical way.

6. The N.T. applies to God a great number of descriptive adjectives. It is impossible, however, to reduce these to a system or to grade them in order of importance, as though one were describing a substance and were able to differentiate between primary and secondary attributes. For each of the epithets which the N.T. uses to characterize God refers to some manifestation of God's dealings with men on the plane of human history and relates to some action of God rather than to some attribute of the nature of God. It is only as this is kept in mind that the great scriptural affirmations can be understood: God is

faithful (1 Cor. 1:9; 10:13; 2 Cor. 1:18), God is *wise* (Rom. 16:27), God is *true* (Jn. 2:33; Tit. 1:2), God is *merciful* (Rom. 2:4), God is *just*, even in His anger (Rom. 11:22); He is the God of *peace* (Rom. 15:33; 16:20; 1 Thess. 5:23; Phil. 4:9; 1 Cor. 14:33; Heb. 13:20), the God of *hope* (Rom. 15:13), the God of *comfort* (2 Cor. 1:3), the God of *love* (2 Cor. 13:11). When John uses the formula: "God is *love", he does so to show us that love is not one separate attribute among others, such as might be used in the description of a substance, but that love is the full and final expression of all that God is towards us. As has often been emphasized, this statement does not mean that love has been deified, that man raises love to the absolute degree and then makes a god of it, but that we recognize the true nature of love in the work which God does for us in Christ and through the Holy Spirit. The only norm we possess for measuring true love is the gift which God bestowed when He gave His Son to the world (Jn. 3:16).

It should be noted that:

(*a*) Without ever calling into question the awful nature of God's holiness, so strongly highlighted in the O.T. (especially in Isa. 6), the N.T. rarely stresses it (except in Rom. 1 and 2).

(*b*) The N.T. writers generally avoid, when speaking of God, the traditional attributes used in pagan religions and in Hellenistic philosophy. Mention may be made by way of exception of 1 Jn. 1:5: "God is light", which has an Iranian ring. Paul makes use, too, of the expression "the eternal God", but the Greek text makes it quite clear that God is the ruler of eternity and that eternity is not a reality which would have any existence apart from Him (Rom. 16:26).

7. The N.T. teaching about God cannot be expressed in the concepts usually reserved for God. In particular, the notion of *transcendence*, although inevitable, is inadequate: God is no stranger to the world which He created (when He sends His Son, He sends Him "to his own people", Jn.

1:11). He is the Lord of the world. The only expression which befits God is the expression which denotes interpersonal relations. The incarnation results in the breaking of the schema which is implied in the idea of transcendence. The opposition between heaven and earth does not involve an opposition of the pattern sacred-profane, transcendent-immanent, for the will of God is destined to be accomplished as perfectly on earth as in heaven (Matt. 6:10). Nothing on earth can in the final issue stand against the omnipotence of God (Lk. 3:8; Mk. 10:27; Acts 5:39; 2 Tim. 2:9) and Christians have the right to await the day when God will be all in all (1 Cor. 15:28).

But it would be just as false to suppose that the coming of the Son of God leads us towards a conception of the *immanence* of God: the normal relation between man and God is one of faith and *prayer, which implies a personal relation with God, and consequently a certain distance between man and God. This does not imply that man and God stand apart from each other as strangers, rather that they belong to each other (1 Cor. 3:23; 6:19). It is in this sense that we must interpret certain statements which, taken by themselves and isolated from the scriptural testimony as a whole, might suggest an immanence of God in man and open the door to a mysticism radically at variance with the religion of the Bible (cf. e.g. Eph. 4:6, where the words "in all" must not be allowed to obscure the words "above all", or 1 Jn. 4:16: "he who abides in love abides in God, and God abides in him"—a statement which is only properly understood when it is remembered that to abide in love really means to abide in Christ, *made man*).

R. MEHL

GOLD, *see* MONEY

GOOD

1. Holy Scripture does not seek to define an essence of Good, for Good is not in the Scriptures an autonomous reality and, as such, absolute, which once defined in its

essence could then be put into relation with other notions and other realities. Nor is Good an idea of God, nor an attribute of God. It is on the contrary the very essence of God who is Good and Goodness (the two terms overlap completely in Greek). We must say of The Good what St. Augustine declares concerning Eternity. There is no analytical relation between the essence of God and The Good. But, God Himself is The Good and this term has no assignable sense except in God. Good has no existence outside God, and God does not consider Good as an external and objective reality. For God there is no norm of The Good. And so man has no chance of knowing The Good except by reference to the will of God: what God wills, that is the Good.

On this point there is a fundamental agreement between the O.T. and the N.T. The man who knows God can only praise Him, for God is good (Ps. 118:1; Ps. 117; 1 Chr. 16:36; 2 Chron. 5:13). And the N.T. recalls that this goodness, that is, the quality of willing and doing The Good, is God's privilege (Matt. 19:17). (The parallels Mk. 10:18 and Lk. 18:19 state it in still more exclusive terms: no one is good but God alone.) The revelation of God in history can therefore only be the revelation of His goodness: He alone proclaims what is Good. What He performs for His people —the exodus, the entry into the Promised Land, the protection which He grants to His people—that is The Good (Exod. 18:9; Num. 10:29f.). To a supreme degree the *Law which God gives to His people is Good (Rom. 7:12). Finally, the eschatological promise which God continually renews to His people and to His Church by means of *covenants is good: "I will make with them an everlasting covenant, that I will not turn away from doing good to them" (Jer. 32:40). Isaiah (52:7) prophesies the coming of the good messenger, the messenger of the good news who announces the salvation of the latter days.

Because God is goodness, all that comes from God is good, and that good is the salvation of men. That is why, far from being a static concept and defining a sort of political or ontological equilibrium, The Good always has an eschatological colouring: the Good which comes from God sends us back to the fulfilment of history. The Epistle to the Hebrews salutes Christ as the one who "appeared as a high priest of the good things to come" (9:11). It does not forget that the good which was the law already had that eschatological meaning and importance (recognized also by Paul when he calls the law a schoolmaster who leads us to Christ, Gal. 3:24), but the law gave us hitherto only "a shadow of the good things to come" (Heb. 10:1). Since Christ is the reality of our salvation, the benefit, the blessing of God to men is concentrated in Him. In Him we have been showered "with every spiritual blessing" (Eph. 1:3). Admittedly it is not always immediately apparent that Christ is their Good, and Nathanael begins by asking the question: "Can anything good come out of Nazareth?" (Jn. 1:46. It is, moreover, very remarkable that he says these words "anything good" when thinking about the salvation to come: cf. v. 45). But the true act of faith always consists in recognizing that Jesus Christ is our Good, because He is our salvation, that apart from Him we can do nothing (Jn. 15:5), that He has the words of eternal life (Jn. 6:68).

2. The identity of the Good and *salvation is thus the common thesis of the O.T. and the N.T. For the one as for the other, this good, which we receive from Him who alone is good, is not an object of contemplation: since it is given to us as part of the will of God, it contains a requirement for us. Good is only promised and given to us so that we may fulfil it, so that we may act in accordance with it. On this point the unanimous position of the O.T. is essentially simple: the law being the clear and unimpeachable expression of the perfect will of God, obedience to the law, its meticulous and faithful fulfilment, constitutes the Good of man, means life for man (Deut. 30:15–16). As the good is conceived in the perspective of salvation, the antithesis of good is not

abstract evil but rather *death. This very close relationship between the fulfilling of the commandment, good, and eternal life, is found again in the N.T., as is witnessed by the rich young man's question to Jesus: "Teacher, what good deed must I do, to have eternal life?" (Matt. 19:16). Jesus does not call this issue into question: "If you would enter life, keep the commandments" (v. 17b). Jesus simply adds a new and decisive condition: not only the complete renunciation of worldly goods for the benefit of the poor, but a renunciation that has no other purpose than to allow the man to follow Him, the Christ (v. 21). This attitude of Jesus, which accepts the basic issue of the O.T. and goes beyond it, confirms us in this twofold idea:

(a) There is a connection between the law and the Son of Man: both are given us as good things.

(b) The Son of Man is the summing-up and the fulfilment of all good things. It is in this sense that the law can be considered as obsolete and that the Son of Man has it at His disposal, in the sense that He subordinates it to the good of man and introduces into it, as a function of that good, orders of precedence and urgency (cf. Matt. 12:12, Jesus' declaration "So it is lawful to do good on the sabbath").

3. Yet the fact of following Jesus, to be united to Him by the bond of faith and therefore to live in Him, this "good" in short, will not turn us from the good that the law symbolized. Just the opposite. So long as man lives far from Jesus, so long as he has not become a new creature in Christ, that good of the law remains unattainable to him: "For I know that nothing good dwells within me, that is, in my flesh. I can will what is right, but I cannot do it. For I do not do the good I want, but the evil I do not want is what I do" (Rom. 7:18–19). In a word, so long as I live in the *flesh, the good things of God are turned aside by the power of sin from their destination. They are changed into their opposite. But as soon as the new creature is implanted in me by faith in Christ, original good

becomes good again: much as man must beware of good *works, he makes the following discovery: "We are his workmanship, created in Christ Jesus for good works, which God prepared beforehand, that we should walk in them" (Eph. 2:10). From the time of the new birth we are in some degree sent back to the law, to the good of the law, and this practice of the law does not carry in itself the mortal risks that it carried previously. The "perfect knowledge in all wisdom and spiritual understanding" which we henceforward possess will allow us to do good, that is to "lead a life worthy of the Lord, fully pleasing to him, bearing fruit in every good work" (Col. 1:9,10).

Lost through sin, the good of the law is found again in Him who delivers us from sin.

4. It remains to describe in concrete terms that good which is offered to man and to which he is so urgently invited by the apostolic writings (Rom. 12:9, "hate what is evil, hold fast to what is good"; Rom. 12:21, "Do not be overcome by evil, but overcome evil with good"; 2 Thess. 3:13, "do not be weary in well-doing", etc.). Obviously this term is no longer defined in precise juridical terms, as it was in the old covenant. In Christ we know that this good is inexhaustible and Jesus continually makes clear the indefinite requirement of the law. Now it is necessary to discern the good, and man can only achieve this with the help of the Holy Spirit. The precept of 1 Thess. 5:21, "test everything; hold fast what is good" has certainly not a purely theological sense; it has also an ethical one. Paul formulates the wish, "I would have you wise as to what is good" (Rom. 16:19), which shows clearly that good should be the object of spiritual discrimination. The N.T. ethic is not a "ready-made" one. We are not given prior indication of what is good. However, Paul especially is at pains to indicate the characters by which good may be recognized. Chapters 12 and 13 of the Epistle to the Romans, which form a whole, contain invaluable hints on the proper practice of good. The meaning of good is the

edification of the community, as is shown by 1 Thess. 5:15, "Always seek to do good to one another and to all."

Between two exhortations to good, Romans 12 seeks to show what constitutes good in the community of the Church and outside that community. It springs from that text that the heart of good is the love that does not puff itself up with pride (respect in the community for the diversity of gifts), which seeks peace, which exercises gentleness and patience, which avoids raising insurmountable barriers between men, but which, on the contrary, strives to join with others in sadness as well as in joy (cf. 1 Cor. 13). Rom. 15:2 gives the most complete characteristic of the good deed: "Let each of us please his neighbour for what is good" (or for his good) "with a view to edification". This term means, of course, the community of brethren *built up (edified) as a house is built. The idea of edification, of *unity, is always joined with that of good, even when a very humble good is concerned; thus in that precept: "Let the thief no longer steal, but rather let him labour, doing honest work with his hands, so that he may be able to give to those in need" (Eph. 4:28). *Work is a good thing in proportion as it allows the strengthening of the unity of the community by the bond of charity.

Finally, good is recognized in that it produces or permits a peaceful, hard-working, honest life (2 Thess. 3:6–15; 1 Pet. 3:11). But it is fitting to underline again that, if good is *love, in so far as the latter is the contents of the law, the appearances of good are as numerous as the faces of our neighbours. There can then be no question of asking the Scriptures for a complete description of good.

5. *Man can certainly never boast of accomplishing good. For man, even when saved, is not good and only "the good man out of his good treasure brings forth good" (Matt. 12:35). At least he who lives in faith in Christ has no reason to despair, for if he knows the power of the resurrection, he can with certainty consider baptism

as the "answer of a good conscience toward God" (1 Pet. 3:21 A.V.). On several occasions the N.T. can take account of the *Good* conscience of those who do *good* (Acts 23:1; 1 Tim. 1:5,19; 1 Pet. 3:16). The good conscience is not the proud satisfaction of him who believes he has mastered all the requirements of good, but the answer of the Christian who, because of the resurrection, knows that God will complete in him the good work which He has begun (Phil. 1:6) and that "in everything God works for good with those who love him" (Rom. 8:28).

R. MEHL

GOODS, see MONEY

GOSPEL

1. Gospel means *good news*. Modern versions (e.g. French and German) have usually kept the Greek word *evangelion*, which they are content to transcribe. [English versions use the word Gospel, derived from Old English, while the corresponding Greek verb is translated "preach the gospel", except at Lk. 2:10 ("I bring you good news") and 1 Thess. 3:6 ("Timothy has brought us the good news of your faith").]

2. The word is found only in the N.T. It signifies a reality which is not yet extant in the O.T. era. The newness of the news does not lie, as some have maintained, in certain of its contents—God as Father, God as love, forgiveness, universality of salvation, etc., for none of these is absent from the O.T. Nor does it lie in the enhanced emphasis on these truths (it is said, for example, that the O.T. lays stress on the holiness of God, the N.T. on His love); much more certainly it is to be found in the fact of *fulfilment*. What was promised in the O.T., the end towards which the whole process of history, which is the design of God, was being directed, has now been fulfilled and attained. The N.T. does not say anything of *God that is as yet unknown to the O.T.; it shows that God has fulfilled His promises (Matt. 1:22f.; 3:3; 8:17; Mk.

15:28; Acts 2:16ff.; Rom. 1:1ff.; Gal. 4:4; 1 Pet. 1:10ff., etc.).

3. The word Gospel is accompanied by various attributes to make its sense more precise. The most important are: The Gospel *of (Jesus) Christ* (Mk. 1:1; Rom. 15:19; 2 Cor. 2:12); *of the Kingdom* (Matt. 4:23; 24:14); *of God* (Mk. 1:14; Rom. 1:1; 1 Thess. 2:8). Paul speaks often of the Gospel, without qualifications: the Gospel is the News *par excellence*.

4. The Gospel is that of (Jesus) Christ: it is the announcement that Jesus is the Messiah, the Christ of Israel: in Him the promises which God made to His people are fulfilled. To show this is the purpose of the two tables of genealogy, of which one leads downwards from Abraham who received the promises, through David the King after God's heart (1 Sam. 13:14), to Jesus who is called Christ; while the other (Lk. 3:23-38) traces the generations backwards to Adam, son of God, proving that in Jesus, the Christ of Israel, all men are inheritors of the promise and are brought back to God (cf. Rom. 1:1-6). The frequent quotations in the Passion narratives are likewise intended to show this, as also the speeches in the book of Acts and the whole of the Epistle to the Hebrews. On this it is worth noting that: (*a*) it is fundamental, for understanding the Gospel, to understand the history which contains its promise and provides its form, i.e. one must know the O.T.; (*b*) that history is in fact part of the Gospel itself, and not, as is often said, an inferior and rudimentary counterpart of it. Moses wrote of Jesus (Jn. 5:46), Abraham saw His day and rejoiced (Jn. 8:56), the prophets contemplated the salvation and were its messengers (1 Pet. 1:10,12; Rom. 1:2). The fact that Jesus is the Christ is the foundation of the unity of the two Testaments.

5. In Matthew, Mark and Luke the Gospel is the proclamation of the imminent coming of the Kingdom of God. God will establish His rule and put an end to the present order; He will annihilate all that is in opposition, the power of Satan, sin, disease, and death, and will bring salvation to the people of God, who await the fulfilment of the prophecies. This message has as corollary the demand for repentance (Matt. 4:17; Mk. 1:15): man must abandon his religious safeguards, submit to the judgment of God, and obey His will. Advance signs of the Kingdom are given in the miracles, the "signs" of Jesus, healings, especially of demoniacs, and in the *forgiveness which He grants. In Jesus the Kingdom is already secretly present and is combating the power of the Evil One and restoring the order of God (Matt. 12:28; 11:2-6).

The meaning of the message and of the miracles of Jesus appears clearly only in His death and resurrection, towards which everything else leads up. He who pardons and heals is no master of psychological technique, the spurious benefactor who will save man as he wants to be saved, without being confronted with God, without humiliation and without death; He is, on the contrary, hated and rejected by man, but in being put to death He exposes man's sin and man's final and irreparable perdition. Moreover, He it is who undertakes to be the sign of sin and to be wounded for those who have wounded God (Matt. 26:26-28; Acts 8:32ff.; 2 Cor. 5:21; Gal. 3:13), and who through this very means is revealed by God, in the resurrection, as Lord and Saviour (Matt. 28:18; Acts 2:32ff.; 3:13ff.; Rom. 1:4). The Gospel is centred on the *cross, as is particularly clear in the case of Paul's Epistles, where he says he refuses to know or to proclaim anything else (1 Cor. 2:2); and in the cross he sees not only the saving *fact*—his predecessors did as much— but also the *form* (made necessary by the nature of sin) of the revelation and of the knowledge of God, as well as of preaching and of salvation (1 Cor. 1:17-25). It is also unquestionably the case with the four Gospels, which have very appropriately been called "narratives of the Passion with detailed introduction" (Kähler), and with the other N.T. writings. In the cross, God and man meet, not without violence, for judgment and salvation; together with the resurrection, in which its meaning is revealed, it marks the beginning of the end of this age, the event which inaugurates the *time of fulfilment and which is the foundation of the whole life of the Church and the believer.

6. The Gospel announces that *Jesus is the Lord* (1 Cor. 12:3; Acts 2:36; Phil. 2:11); the Risen One Himself says: "All authority in heaven and on earth has been given to me." Raised to the right hand of God (Acts 2:33), He is King with the authority of God Himself and with universal dominion. His dominion is founded on the work of redemption accomplished in an obedience even to the death of the cross (Phil. 2:8f.) and therefore on God Himself, who willed this work and in the sight of all men stamped it with His approval by raising up the Crucified (Acts 3:15; Rom. 1:4; 6:4). The Gospel is not therefore an empty word, but a powerful act of God, which really does save; the apostle is not ashamed of it (Rom. 1:16) and continues to proclaim it in spite of insults and conflicts (1 Thess. 2:2). It is the word of truth (Col. 1:5), i.e. the authentic revelation of God and of His intentions towards man; the Gospel of the glory of the blessed God (1 Tim. 1:11— another translation is possible, the glorious Gospel of the blessed God, R.S.V.), i.e. the manifestation of His victorious power (or His powerful manifestation). More explicitly, Paul can call it the Gospel of the glory of Christ, who is the image of God (2 Cor. 4:4), the word in which Christ is present with His power and truth, which are indeed God's; a word reliable and efficacious. Naturally, therefore, it is also called the Gospel of God; it is the good news whose author is God and by which God Himself reaches out to man and intervenes in his existence.

Having its foundation in the death and resurrection of Jesus Christ, the Gospel is the word of *reconciliation (2 Cor. 5:19), by which God takes away the obstacle which keeps man far from God, under judgment and in fear; the revelation of the *righteousness of God, who saves man

(Rom. 1:16) by making him die with Christ; the Gospel of *grace (Acts 20:24), of *peace (Eph. 6:15), and of *salvation (Eph. 1:13; 1 Cor. 15:1f.). Pardon makes a new creature of man, re-establishes normal relations between him and God and allows him to contemplate judgment without fear. Message of judgment and of grace, the Gospel is valid for everyone (Rom. 3:23f.,29f.). It is the announcement that the Christ of Israel is the Lord who calls the heathen also (Rom. 1:1–7), the Lord of all (Acts 10:36). By His death, which makes manifest the sin of Israel as well as of the heathen but also is a revelation of free salvation, undeserved and offering no ground for boasting, Christ has broken down the wall of separation between Israel and the Gentiles (Eph. 2:11ff.; 3:6); the Gospel is in the whole world (Col. 1:6), and alike from Israel and the heathen there is one single condition necessary for salvation, namely *faith (Rom. 1:16f.; 3:30).

7. Because the Gospel is God's revelation, and not a creation of the mind, or of emotion, or of man's religious instinct (1 Cor. 2:9), it is not an obvious truth: for those whom the god of this age has blinded (2 Cor. 4:3f.), it continues to be veiled. The apostle certainly does not think that the Gospel is itself absurd or obscure— he calls it wisdom (1 Cor. 2:6); it is a *stumbling-block to the Jews who demand miracles, that is to say, who will not understand how God humbles Himself, and foolishness to the Gentiles, who seek truth by means of ratiocination and are not aware that only God's mind, by which their own is shattered, gives the truth which really lights up the understanding. But it is the power and wisdom of God for those who are called and who submit to condemnation and to grace (1 Cor. 1:22ff.).

The Gospel must not be mistaken by those who hear it for one of those doctrines which philosophers are perpetually evolving as rational solutions to the problem of existence; it must remain, and be seen to remain, the word which maintains an impassable barrier between the wisdom of man and that of God. For these reasons Paul deliberately abandons the wisdom of words which would persuade by flattery (1 Cor. 1:17; 2:13; 2 Cor. 10:5). He does not spare the Athenians his appeal for repentance or the message of the resurrection (Acts 17:18,30f.). It should however be noted that believing does not mean blindly subscribing to incomprehensible assertions: "Repent, and believe in the gospel" (Mk. 1:15): faith is inseparable from *repentance; it comes to birth in the light which God relentlessly casts on all existence which tries to evade His will and in the clear acceptance of His verdict, and springs forth from the offered grace. It is the active response of man whom God has enlightened and which declares that he is in the right. It takes shape and is strengthened in a life which is clearly and consciously conducted: "Let your manner of life (or perhaps: Let your government of the Church) be worthy of the gospel of Christ" (Phil. 1:27f.); the life of the Church, its unity, the clear witness and the fearless obedience of the believers must demonstrate the truth of the Gospel, and leave no doubt about the perdition of those who resist it.

8. The *law and the Gospel are set in opposition chiefly in Romans and Galatians (cf. also the echo of Paul's preaching in Jn. 1:17). This opposition does not by any means imply that in the O.T. and the N.T. there are two different revelations, two ways of salvation—the O.T. placing man before God's demand, so that he may be justified by obedience to the commandments, and the N.T. realizing that this attempt on God's part resulted in failure, and therefore inaugurating as it were a régime of benevolence. The Gospel does not signify a new attitude of God to man, as if in the old times He had demanded justification by the works of the law and was now proposing justification by the Gospel of grace. The law is not against the promise of grace (Gal. 3:21) any more than the Gospel annihilates law—which, on the contrary, it upholds (Rom. 3:31). Paul shows that grace precedes law (Gal. 3:17), and that the introduction of

law was integral to the original and the only plan of salvation. The aim of the law is to provoke transgression (Rom. 7:7f.), to prove that man does not wish to receive grace, but to boast before God of his own righteousness (Rom. 10:2f.; Lk. 18:11f.); thus it preserves man in his real situation before God, in which alone he can be confronted by Christ and take hold of grace (Gal. 3:23f.).

9. In the Johannine writings (fourth Gospel, Epistles of John, Revelation) the word Gospel is never used in its specific meaning of good news; it comes only once and there it bears a different sense (Rev. 14:6f.). The Eternal Gospel which the angel announces is not the Gospel of Christ, but a kind of final warning addressed by God to mankind before the judgment. It is called eternal possibly because it is the appeal to which the works of God resound (Rom. 1:20) since the beginning of the creation.

10. The writings of the N.T. never employ the word Gospel to denote the first four books of the N.T. canon: for all preaching that bears witness to Jesus as Christ and Lord is the Gospel, the message of Paul or the Epistle to the Hebrews as much as the narratives of the evangelists. The use of the word current to-day was not found until the second century, when the intention was not to establish a difference between the words of the incarnate Jesus and the doctrines of the apostolic Church, or to oppose the "religion" of Jesus to the "dogmatism" of the apostles (the Gospels are, as it happens, as much permeated with theological reflection as the Epistles), but to separate off the history and the basic facts of the new covenant, as those of the old are put apart in the Pentateuch, and so to assert their definitive and normative character.

CHR. SENFT

GRACE

O.T.

1. Grace is not a thing, but its essential significance is simply God Himself in His

goodwill towards men. The grace of God is not something separable from God, but is a personal relationship which God establishes between Himself and men. He regards them with favour and with kindness (Ps. 31:21; 33:22; 42:8; 90:17; Num. 6:24–26; 2 Sam. 7:15). In this relation God has the initiative. He loves the people of Israel for no reason whatever, without any merit on their part (Deut. 4:37; 10:15; Hos. 3:1; 11:1). The *election of Israel is thus grounded on the grace of God (Deut. 7:7–8; 9:5–6).

2. The grace of God towards sinful men consists in the *forgiveness of sins (Exod. 34:6–7; Ps. 32:1–5; 51; 103:8; 130:4). God can indeed, when He so wishes, decline to inflict a just punishment, and to reconcile sinners with Himself by a free decision of His grace (Hos. 11:9–10; Isa. 43:25; 44:22; 48:8–11; Mic. 7:14,20). To bestow grace is therefore to forgive (Exod. 33:19; Prov. 3:34; Isa. 30:18). God will establish by His grace a new *covenant, whose foundation will be the forgiveness of sins (Jer. 31:31–34; Ezek. 34:25; 36:26–27).

3. The benefits which God accords are "graces", because they are undeserved gifts of His love (Gen. 32:10; Isa. 63:7). A grace is a favour, a particular act of deliverance (Ezra 9:8). To ask for grace=to beseech (Gen. 42:21; Est. 4:8). Grace can also signify charm or passing beauty (Prov. 31:30); being pleasing to God and men, which is won by obedience and trust in God (Prov. 3:4).

N.T.

1. Grace, which in the O.T. denotes God who comes towards men to do them good, is properly the expression of that essential event which the N.T. is witness to, namely, the coming of God in *Jesus Christ. By Him God comes personally to the earth; and henceforth grace is linked to the person of Jesus Christ and there is no distinction between saying that Jesus Christ is the grace of God, or that it is in Him, or that He gives it.

The consequences of the incarnation are grace and truth (Jn. 1:14,16–17): all God's love which gives and forgives, the whole of the revelation and the knowledge of God are within Christ, available for communication to men in order to draw them out of darkness. The capacity of giving in Jesus is inexhaustible, for it is up to the measure of the fullness of God. Grace and truth were known from the O.T. revelation, but in Jesus Christ they are fully manifested and given: the O.T. and Judaism must yield place to Him. They are succeeded, not by a religion which might again be surpassed, but by the gift of the perfect and final communication of God in His only Son. This is "the true grace" (1 Pet. 5:12).

2. Grace means the whole *Gospel, which is "the good news of the grace of God" (Acts 20:24), "the word of his grace" (Acts 13:43; 14:3; 2 Cor. 6:1; Col. 1:6). But the Gospel has not become something in the hands of men; grace is the power of the living Lord who spreads abroad the Gospel and enables it to bear fruit (1 Cor. 15:10; 2 Tim. 2:1); thus, for example, the missionaries are commended by the Church to the grace of the Lord (Acts 14:26; 15:40; 20:32).

The greetings and blessings of the Epistles must be understood in this sense. The greeting "Mercy and peace" used to exist in Judaism. "Grace" has a wider meaning and denotes the totality of the saving and protecting activity of God upon His Church; *peace is the effect of this activity, salvation in its present and future reality. The action of God, the gifts of God, are mediated through Jesus Christ; it is the great new thing as compared with Judaism (see *Jews). So also with the greetings at the end of the Epistles: the blessing of Aaron (Num. 6:24–26) has given way to various formulas which all attribute grace to Jesus Christ and expect it from Him (Col. 4:18; 1 Tim. 6:21; 2 Tim. 4:22, say simply "grace", but it is self-evident that it is the grace of Jesus Christ).

3. The grace of God in Jesus Christ

which meets sinful men signifies *forgiveness of sins, justification (see *Righteous), redemption (see *Ransom): Col. 2:13; Rom. 6:1. It was to this end that Jesus Christ gave His life (2 Cor. 8:9; 1 Tim. 1:14). Grace, in this sense, is very often mentioned in opposition to another means of salvation, circumcision and the observance of the law (Acts 15:11); the works of the law (Rom. 6:14; Gal. 2:21; Eph. 2:5,8; Titus 3:7). Paul insists on the "free", undeserved, character of justification (Rom. 3:24; Eph. 2:5,8): the condition of justification, i.e. faith, does not contradict or modify this character, but confirms it. The grace which God gives is justification by faith (Rom. 5:2); it belongs to *faith to receive (Rom. 4:16); faith is not something meritorious, for it is itself a gift of God, a grace (Phil. 1:29). Justification by grace, by means of faith, is the uncovenanted gift of God to which no one could make any claim.

This character of grace deprives man of every excuse for boasting (Rom. 3:27; 5:11; 1 Cor. 1:31; Eph. 2:9); he can only give glory to God for the free gift of His salvation. If man cannot be saved by *works, in other words by his own efforts, then only Jesus Christ has conquered sin and death which were reigning over all men (Rom. 5:12–21). Thus He inaugurates a new era and those who believe in Him share in a new world where death has given place to eternal life and sin to righteousness. There exists now a "rule of grace" which has succeeded the rule of sin (Rom. 5:21), which was the rule of the *law (Rom. 6:14). The believers are therefore exhorted not to revert to the works of the law (Gal. 2:21), or fastings (Heb. 13:9), or their former sins (Heb. 12:15), for they would be separate then from Christ and would fall back from the dominion of grace to that of sin (Rom. 6:12–14; Gal. 5:4). To be under grace is thus to live in the obedience of faith, with a view to holiness (Rom. 6:15–22).

The "time of grace" is that of salvation (2 Cor. 6:2, quoting Isa. 49:8), but the present time is still not that of salvation entirely realized; it is Jesus Christ who will accomplish that at the last day, because all grace is in Him (1 Pet. 1:13).

4. Grace signifies also ministry, an activity in the service of God. Especially the apostolic ministry ("the grace which has been given to me", Rom. 12:3; 1 Cor. 3:10; Gal. 2:9; Eph. 3:2,7–8); but also the various ministries entrusted to believers (Rom. 12:6; Phil. 1:7). Every service is a gift of the Lord, who calls to it those who are not worthy (Lk. 5:8–10).

Not only the actual calling, the starting point (1 Cor. 15:9), but also the whole range of activities as they develop, are works of grace; man does not work alongside grace, but grace works in him and by him (1 Cor. 15:10; 2 Tim. 2:1; Acts 18:27). God uses His servants (1 Cor. 3:7; 2 Cor. 4:7) and every work which God accomplishes is grace (Acts 11:23).

5. The gifts of the *Spirit are "gifts of grace" (charismata); the grace of God, the Lord Himself acting in the Church, gives to His body all its functions and services necessary to its life (Rom. 12:6–8; 1 Cor. 12:1–7; 1 Tim. 4:14; 2 Tim. 1:6; 1 Pet. 4:10; Eph. 4:7–13). These gifts are not however of equal importance (1 Cor. 12:28; Eph. 4:11) and the supreme gift, intended for all, is love (1 Cor. 12:31; 13). The term charisma emphasizes the free nature of the gift received; the ability to accept comes from God (2 Cor. 3:5–6).

6. Grace has sundry further meanings, but they all partake of its primary meaning of God's gift, His undeserved favour. (a) The favour of God, which men perceive (Acts 4:33; 6:8; it is also the sense of Lk. 2:52, according to verse 40; cf. Prov. 3:4; Acts 2:47, the favour of God enables believers to "find grace" with men). (b) To find grace with God (Lk. 1:30; Heb. 4:16) reflects a divine decision favourable to man. (c) The help of God—in man's suffering and weakness (2 Cor. 12:9); in the ministry (2 Cor. 1:12); (d) Deliverance, special favour—to Elizabeth (Lk. 1:25); to Mary

(Lk. 1:28); eternal life (1 Pet. 3:7); suffering for right (1 Pet. 2:20); suffering for Christ (Phil. 1:29; cf. Matt. 5:11–12). (e) All kinds of benefit, material and spiritual (2 Cor. 9:8; Eph. 4:29), for God is the God of all grace (Jas. 1:17; 1 Pet. 5:10). (f) The resurrection of Christ (Acts 13:34). (g) The collection on behalf of the Church of Jerusalem (see *One) bears the name of "grace" (1 Cor. 16:3; 2 Cor. 8:6–7,19); it is a work of God's grace, for He prompts believers to give freely.

F. BAUDRAZ

GROWTH

Just as the seed cast into the earth leads naturally to the full blossoming of the plant, so the work of God in the world holds within itself the promise of its fulfilment. Growth is characteristic of the work of God; it develops progressively from the less to the greater, from the imperfect to the perfect, from the inception to the completion.

Now, even if the Bible frequently employs the figure of growth, it never uses it in the sense of progress from a natural state to a supernatural state, as if the attainment of salvation were something which is conferred as a reward for continuous effort or for an ever-increasing virtue. When it announces the coming and extension on earth of the Kingdom of heaven, the Word of God knows nothing of the "progressist" meaning of progress, for it holds no brief for the idea of a natural evolution towards some hypothetical golden age. We find there an emphatic denial that man and the world are capable of achieving their own salvation.

The growth of the Kingdom of Heaven, of the Church and of the individual Christian is always an *inward* growth of the order of grace (2 Pet. 3:18). If there is progress here, it is not from nature towards grace, but from grace towards the full flowering of salvation.

1. *The author of all growth.* It follows from what has been said that it is not man who promotes growth (1 Cor. 3:6), but God to whom it belongs to know the mystery of life. But even if God is the originator of all growth, He is not its sole agent. Indeed His work is carried out by the Lord (1 Thess. 3:12), by the Word of God which enables men to grow into salvation (1 Pet. 2:2), by those who are the messengers of that Word and who work for the building up of the Church (Eph. 4:11–16) and through the obedience of those who have received the Word (2 Cor. 9:10).

Man, it must be repeated, is not the author of growth: whether he sleeps or keeps watch, night and day, the seed germinates and grows without his knowing how (Mk. 4:27). But he is a fellow-worker with God in that he is bidden to sow (Matt. 13:4) to plant and to water (1 Cor. 3:6), in that he is called to exercise the ministries of the Church, the perfecting of the saints and the building up of the body of Christ (Eph. 4:12), to shed abroad Christian love (2 Thess. 1:3), and to help in the progress of the Gospel (Phil. 1:12).

2. *The growth of the *Kingdom of heaven.* The Kingdom of heaven has taken root in the world, where it was sown as a tiny seed; it has been placed like leaven in the meal or hidden as a treasure in a field (Matt. 13:31–33,44). The birth of this Kingdom is obscure, its development mysterious and impeded by the action of the enemy (Matt. 13:24–30), but its scope is measureless, embracing the whole of creation. The field in which the Kingdom of heaven is to grow is larger than the hearts of believers, wider even than the Church, it is no less than the world (Matt. 13:38); it is the *whole* of the meal (Matt. 13:33). It is highly significant that the laws which govern the development of the Kingdom are exactly paralleled in the laws of nature, for it is within the order of creation that the order of redemption has to be planted, to grow and to express itself.

3. *The growth of the Church.* The agent which God has chosen to bring about the growth of His Kingdom in the world is the *Church. The growth of the Kingdom on earth goes hand in hand with the growth of the Church. The latter is destined to expand

in two distinct but complementary ways—quantitatively and qualitatively.

The Church must first of all grow in quality: she must take care to remain pure and faithful in the midst of the wiles and enticements of the world. If she would attain to the measure of the perfect stature of Christ, she must seek unity of the faith and of the knowledge of the Son of God and speak the truth in love (Eph. 4:13–15). This growth *in Christ* implies that the Church must always pay strict attention to its own organized life, for only a body which is well knit together and solid is capable of being built up (Eph. 4:16).

The Church must also grow quantitatively: she must increase in extent and in numbers. She only disclaims connection with the world in order to be more effectively present in the world. If she refuses to allow the spirit of the present age to flourish in her, it is in order that the Spirit of the Lord should flourish in the present age. Wherever the Church is faithful, the Word of God makes great progress and spreads more and more (Acts 12:24), the number of the disciples increases (Acts 2:47; 4:4; 6:1,7; 9:31, etc.), and God multiplies the posterity of him whom He has blessed (Gen. 12:2; Heb. 6:14). A Church concerned about the quality of her inward growth will of necessity be an outward-looking Church, a missionary Church.

4. *The growth of the Christian.* Whilst the body of Christ, through its own growth, contributes to the growth of all its members, in its turn it increases in numbers and in strength by the growth of each member. The Christian who has received the knowledge of salvation is called to go from triumph to triumph (1 Thess. 4:1), seeking to possess in rich abundance those spiritual gifts which make for the building up of the Church (1 Cor. 14:12). Every believer must pass from spiritual childhood to the state of the mature man (Heb. 5:12ff.), by his growth in the knowledge of God (Col. 1:10), in faith (2 Thess. 1:3), in love (Phil. 1:9; 1 Thess. 3:12), in the fruits of righteousness (2 Cor. 9:10). Those who thus grow in grace feel henceforth that their strength increases as they advance (Ps. 84:7).

The Christian, then, is not one who has reached his goal (Phil. 3:12) but one who, in his forward march, in his journey towards perfection, strives ceaselessly to attain, through the strength supplied by the Holy Spirit, the perfect stature of Christ. And in so far as it is Christ who grows within him, his own self grows less and less. "He must increase, but I must decrease" (Jn. 3:30). So the progress of the believer, far from leading him into pride, turns his steps in the direction of humility, for it induces in him the growing recognition that he who plants and he who waters are of little account, since it is God who gives the growth (1 Cor. 3:7).

J.-PH. RAMSEYER

HAND, *see* LAYING ON OF HANDS, RIGHT HAND

HARVEST

This term is found with three different meanings: firstly, in its proper sense; secondly, in a figurative temporal sense (ethical-psychological); thirdly, in a figurative prophetic-eschatological sense.

1. *Proper sense* (Gen. 8:22; Jn. 4:35; Jas. 5:4, etc.). In the Bible the harvest is not a matter of a merely material and self-centred order. It is associated with requirements, on the one hand, with respect to God: the first-fruits of the harvest must be offered to Him (feast of Pentecost: Exod. 22:29; Lev. 23:10), and on the other hand, with respect to one's neighbour: the harvester is to leave a corner of his field without harvesting it and this he is to set aside for the poor man and the stranger (Lev. 19:9; 23:22=Deut. 24:19). At length harvest-time became the occasion for festivals and rejoicings on the part of all the people (Exod. 34:22; Isa. 9:2), inasmuch as the season of reaping was seen as a notable manifestation of grace, the grace of a promise kept, the joy of ripe fruit corresponding to the expectation of the sower.

6

Subsequently the simile of the harvest, of reaping, is frequently utilized to indicate a relationship of cause and effect between an act and its consequences: what a man sows he also reaps (Gal. 6:7). There is here a general law which finds its application not only in nature, but also, on the one hand, in the moral economy of this world and, on the other hand, in the event of the end of the world, which is likened to the world's harvest.

2. *Figurative temporal sense.* In this world, in fact, it is already possible to ascertain, even though imperfectly, the mechanism of the moral laws and to discern the effects of an immanent justice: he who sows iniquity reaps iniquity (Prov. 22:8); those who sow the wind will reap the whirl-wind (Hos. 8:7), whereas he who sows according to righteousness will reap according to mercy (Hos. 10:12), and he who has sown spiritual benefits for others has the right to reap their temporal benefits (1 Cor. 9:11).

The manifestations of this law of correspondence between sowing and reaping invest all the actions of man with what may be called a gravity of history. None of his actions is indifferent since all bear within themselves the germ of a life to come, temporal—and future. All are written into a history which will be the consequence, the happy or unhappy development, of the positive or negative potential of his action. This provides moral preaching with a powerful lever and constitutes a warning and an exhortation at one and the same time: a warning to those who do evil without concern for the crop it is producing; an exhortation to do good, "for in due season we shall reap" (Gal. 6:9).

The time of harvest, however, though at present, during this age, it may show itself sporadically (Matt. 9:37–38; Jn. 4:35–38), will be realized perfectly only at the time of the last judgment, with which it is identified. The harvests of this world manifest and announce the harvest of the world, that is to say, the hour when the earth itself will be harvested (Rev. 14:15–16).

3. *Figurative prophetic-eschatological sense.* "The harvest is the close of the age" (Matt. 13:39). Here the law of correspondence between sowing and reaping finds its perfect expression and at the same time its perfect mystery.

The fruits of our actions will, in fact, reach their full maturity only in the day when God Himself shall reap them or reject them according to His righteousness. Then he who has sown to his own flesh shall of the flesh reap corruption, but he who has sown to the Spirit shall of the Spirit reap life eternal (Gal. 6:8). Thus the actions of men are charged not only with history, but also with eternity.

Precisely because of this, since it does not belong to man to dispose of eternity nor to describe any act, good or bad, as eternal, the ultimate harvest remains a mystery. The task of separating the tares from the good grain is not entrusted to God's servants here below, for fear lest when pulling up the tares they should at the same time eradicate the wheat, but it is entrusted to divine harvesters (Matt. 13:28–30, 39–43). Our actions are delivered over to the justice of God whose sun will be able to cause even the most obscure and insignificant seeds to fructify, while the fruits of pride and presumption will be destroyed. In our faith it is possible for us only to know, with a calm assurance, that in Jesus Christ the justice of God is the justice of His love.

This faith enables us to await with serenity the time of the celestial harvest. Will it not be, like our earthly harvests, a time of festival and of joy in which the threatening shadows of judgment will throw into clearer relief the realities of the promise and of salvation, the joy of the glad ingathering promised to those who have sown for the kingdom, the royal reward offered to them who, after having sown with tears, will reap with songs of delight (Ps. 126:5)?

The time of the harvest, then, is in God's hands. But to man is committed the time of sowing. Yet, in one aspect, the harvest is determined by what is sown. What God will cause to appear at the last day is that which man has brought to birth long beforehand. What is to be manifested in heaven will proceed from the earth. Only the light will be new, revealing, indeed transforming, but the harvest which it illuminates will be that, and none other, which has been produced on earth during the period of man's labours and sowings. In the classic passage which we have already cited the apostle urges that we should not be weary in sowing good seed . . . while we have opportunity (Gal. 6:9–10).

J.-PH. RAMSEYER

HEALING, *see* SICKNESS

HEART, *see* MAN

HEATHEN, *see* NATIONS

HEAVEN

In English, as in most other modern languages, the word heaven has sometimes a purely meteorological or astronomical significance, and sometimes a religious meaning, while the distinction between the two senses is not always clearly felt. It is not surprising that it was similar among the ancients. It may even be added that the ambiguity of the word is justified up to a point. For between the positional superiority of things above and the essential superiority of the supernatural world there exists an "analogy of being" which predisposes the first to be a symbol of the second.

For greater clarity we will distinguish the two senses of the word heaven even in the O.T., always bearing in mind that they are not always clearly separated.

1. *Heaven from the natural point of view.* First of all the word heaven in the Bible can signify what we call in these days the atmosphere. In this way "birds of the heaven" are commonly mentioned, just as one speaks of "fish of the sea" (cf. Dan. 4:12; Matt. 6:26; 8:20; 13:32, etc.). In the same sense Dan. 7:13 speaks of the clouds of heaven (cf. Mk. 14:62), unless in these texts the word cloud has a symbolic meaning. We note, too, that birds and clouds are

not the only inhabitants of the air. It is also peopled by invisible beings, of which some are frankly disquieting: cf. Eph. 2:2 (see *Demons, *Angels). But "heaven" means normally the *firmament* or the celestial vault, for which the Hebrew language sometimes uses a distinct term. According to Gen. 1:6, the firmament divides the waters "above" from those "beneath". The waters above the firmament constitute the reservoirs of the rain which passes through openings in heaven (cf. Ps. 148:4; Job 38:37 and especially Gen. 7:11). It was through these "doors" or "windows" that the manna, the "bread of heaven", descended, according to Ps. 78:23–24 (cf. Ps. 105:40 and Wisdom 16:20). In this sense, heaven is sometimes compared to a vast tent or to a great curtain, in conformity with some fairly common oriental conceptions (Isa. 40:22; Ps. 104:2). Let us note a further point, that among the Hebrews there are also traces of an image that is equally widespread in the East and even in the West, which sees in the heaven the royal mantle of the deity; thus Ps. 102 (v. 27) compares the heaven to a cloak that God will one day roll up like someone changing clothes (compare certain representations of the Virgin in Roman Catholicism where she is dressed in a cloak decorated with stars). Further, the Revelation of John (6:14) announces that God will roll up the heavens like a "book" (i.e. a manuscript in the form of a scroll).

Sometimes heaven is pictured as being supported on pillars (Job 26:11); elsewhere there is a vaguer reference to the "foundation" of heaven (2 Sam. 22:8). In any event, the idea of a heaven formed of a fairly solid mass is found elsewhere than in Genesis; Job 37:18 insists on its hardness and compares it with a shining mirror. The "sea of glass" of the Revelation (4:6; 15:2) is perhaps reminiscent of this conception.

To the firmament are attached the stars, according to Gen. 1:14ff. But the statement must not be taken too literally. For in this case the vault would have to move with the fixed stars, an idea that is not found in the Bible; these stars are suspended, rather, a little below the heaven, at a great height

(Job 22:12). Their number is enormous; no one can count them (Gen. 15:5). More than any other creature they proclaim, by their shining splendour, the glory of God (Ps. 19:2; cf. Dan. 12:3). All, including the sun and the moon, move round the earth, which is stationary. Among the planets only Venus (called Helel, Isa. 14:12) and Saturn ("Chiun"=Kenan, of the Chaldeans, cf. Amos 5:26) are expressly named. It is not known exactly to what extent the Hebrews identified Venus with the morning star; but it is certain that this brilliant body announcing the arrival of day plays a great rôle in their imagination, to the extent of becoming for them one of the symbols of salvation; thus ben Sirach (Ecclus. 50:6) compares Simon the High Priest to it, and the second Epistle of Peter (1:19) calls Christ "the morning star which must arise in our hearts". According to John the Seer (Rev. 2:28), the Risen One even undertakes to give the morning star to those who persevere, which must signify a supernatural light granted by the Lord.

Among the so-called fixed stars several constellations are named in the book of Job, who perhaps borrows his astronomical knowledge from the science of the Arabs. In any event he knows the Pleiades and Orion (9:9; 38:31), as well as the "Dragon" or "Serpent" (26:13). Other constellations are mentioned in the same book in terms whose significance is doubtful (the Great Bear? the Hyades? Aldebaran?). The Pleiades and Orion appear also in Amos (5:8).

The signs of the zodiac, well-known in Rabbinic literature, are perhaps referred to by the O.T. under the term Mazzaroth (cf. especially 2 Kings 23:5).

Sometimes the stars are considered as living beings; cf. Job 38:7, where certain stars "sing". According to Judges 5:20, the stars fought with the Israelites against Sisera. This personification obviously involved the danger of star-worship, and we know that the Israelites of the time of the Kings sometimes yielded to the temptation (cf. 2 Kings 21:3–5; 23:4–5), and Deuteronomy decreed stoning for these idolatrous

acts (17:2–5). The Bible also insists on the fact that the stars are only the creatures of God (Gen. 1:14ff.; Amos 5:8; Ps. 74:16; 136:7; Job 9:7–9, etc.) and that God ever remains master of heaven and of earth. It is thus that He can shake the earth (Job 9:6) or halt the progress of the sun (Josh. 10:12–13).

In the N.T., however, there is no explicit prohibition of star-worship, but it is implied in the interdiction of angel worship (see *Angels, *Authorities).

Comets are apparently nowhere clearly mentioned, unless they are hidden behind the "wandering stars" of Jude 13. But when the author of Revelation (12:4) sees a great "red dragon" sweeping the sky with its "tail" and throwing to earth a third of the stars, it strangely recalls the appearance of a comet accompanied by a shower of shooting stars. Similarly the "sword of God" hanging in the sky (Isa. 34:5) might well be a comet.

It goes without saying that God is also master of all meteorological phenomena, notably thunder, lightning and hail (Exod. 19:16; 20:18; 1 Sam. 7:10; Ps. 77:18; 104:7; Ecclus. 43:13–22; 46:17). In general terms, he makes rain and fine weather. Let us note as well that Job no longer shares the naïve conception of reservoirs of rain above the heavens. He knows that the clouds are formed of vapour (37:11; cf. Ps. 33:7), and bring rain.

Finally, what does the Bible think of *astrology*? No prohibition is mentioned. But the book of Isaiah (47:13) mocks astrologers, and Jeremiah (10:2) puts the faithful on guard against their superstitions. However, if a distinction is made between belief in the influence of heavenly bodies and in their prophetic virtue, it must be recognized that, in the second sense, astrology has received a sort of consecration by the Bible. For unusual celestial phenomena are often considered as *signs* of adversity, which God uses to warn men (Joel 3:15; Amos 8:9; Isa. 13:10; 34:4; Ezek. 32:7–8). And we also find this point of view in the "little apocalypse" of the synoptic Gospels (cf. Matt. 24:29 and parallels) as well as in the Revelation of John (cf. 6:12ff. particularly). In one case, at least, an unusual star announces a happy event—the star of Bethlehem, and no censure is made of the astrologer Magi who managed to interpret this sign; they seem, rather, to be praised for their promptness in taking it seriously.

2. *Heaven from the religious point of view.* Here the supernatural world is concerned, or more exactly the ensemble of the invisible worlds. Indeed it is striking to discover how many times the N.T., especially the first Gospel and the Epistles of Paul, uses the word heaven in the plural—"heavens". It would be vain to attempt an explanation of this peculiarity in philological terms alone. It is true that the Hebrew word normally used for heaven exists in the plural only; but this evidence only pushes the problem further back. For it must be asked if the Hebrews did not know several heavens, and a positive answer must be given to this question. Thus Deut. 10:14; 1 Kings 8:27; Ps. 148:4; Neh. 9:6, speak of "heaven of heavens" to denote the supreme Heaven, the dwelling place of God. According to Eph. 4:10, Christ ascended above "all the heavens" (cf. Heb. 4:14). And is it necessary to recall that the apostle Paul knows "a man" (i.e. himself) who was taken up into the third heaven? (2 Cor. 12:1ff.). Yet the Bible is quite reticent in its speculations about the different heavens, in opposition to the books of Enoch which abound in curious details about the "seven heavens".

As for God's throne, it is sometimes simply set "in the heavens" (Isa. 66:1; 2 Chr. 30:27; Ps. 11:4). But often better phrases are sought to express its transcendence; it is in the "heaven of heavens" (see above), above the firmament (Ezek. 1:26–27), above "the waters" (i.e. probably the waters above the firmament, Ps. 29:3), and texts such as Isa. 40:12 presuppose that God is above the whole universe.

The heavens are also the dwelling place of the angels, who sometimes form a kind of court around the throne of the deity, 1 Kings 22:19. (For the hierarchy of angels,

known to apocalyptic literature and St. Paul, see *Angels and *Authorities.)

The throne of God is also the object of certain grandiose visions related in the Revelation of John. According to chapter 4 His throne is surrounded by twenty-four other thrones, occupied by the elders, seven lamps "which are the seven spirits of God", as well as by the four beasts already mentioned in the famous vision of Ezekiel (chapter 1): Man, Ox, Eagle, Lion. Further, according to the Epistle to the Hebrews, in the highest heaven (an expression also used by the angels according to Lk. 2:14) there is a supernatural tabernacle, where the true High Priest, that is Christ, offers spiritual sacrifices and intercedes for the faithful (7:25; cf. 1:3; 5:10; 8:1; 12:2 and 1 Jn. 2:1). And according to some undoubtedly authentic texts in the synoptic Gospels, Jesus Himself predicted that the "Son of Man" would be seen sitting at the right hand of the Father (Mk. 14:62 and parallels; cf. Mk. 16:19 and the vision of Stephen, Acts 7:55). The seer of Revelation also sees in heaven the souls of the martyrs: "those who had been beheaded for their testimony to Jesus and for the word of God, and who had not worshipped the beast or its image and had not received its mark on their foreheads or their hands" (20:4ff.). Their souls take precedence over all others in heaven. John's Gospel states that the disciples will have their dwelling places in heaven, prepared by Christ (14:1–3), and similarly the Epistle to the Hebrews knows a "place" prepared there for the faithful (8:1; 11:8–10) and foreshadowed by the Holy Land.

J. HÉRING

HELL, *see* DEATH, GEHENNA, WORLD

HOLY

The idea of holiness (which often overlaps that of the sacred or of purity) is common to all religions but shows fairly marked fluctuations according to time and place. There are to be found almost always at the heart of the idea the two notions of separation (i.e. that which is set aside from common use) and of spiritual power: the holy is what has been separated from the common and consecrated to the gods (sanctuaries, offerings, priests, magicians, liturgical formulas, cultic objects, etc.) whether in order to be offered to them in sacrifice or to be dedicated in their service; it suggests also and in virtue of the first notion, that which is clothed with a certain power of control, both over the gods and over the destiny of men. Associated with these two ideas of consecration and spiritual power is generally to be found the human reaction of fear or the veneration which is due to holiness.

Whereas ancient Greek had a whole series of terms to express the various aspects of holiness, Hebrew had only one main term (*Kadosh*) which was probably Canaanite in origin; this root expressed the idea of separation in contrast with the common. To render this Hebrew term the translators of the O.T. chose the Greek word *hagios*, which of all the Greek synonyms denoting the idea of holiness was the least common. This word passed from the O.T. to the N.T. and into the language of Christianity, where it became one of the key words. If then the idea of holiness is common to Christianity and its neighbouring religions, the term which expresses it in the Bible is not lacking in originality; the fact is that, as we shall see, the biblical consciousness of holiness is marked by certain specific characteristics.

1. *The holiness of God.* The entire O.T. is dominated by the idea of the holiness of Yahweh. All the more particular teachings about holiness are connected with this fundamental intuition. Yahweh is holy in two main senses, which, although at first sight seeming contradictory, express the two poles of the Hebrew religion. Firstly, Yahweh is holy in the sense that He stands utterly above the created world; He is the wholly other, the incomprehensible, the unanalysable, the unfathomable. This insight is already expressed in certain ancient narrative passages (Gen. 28:16ff.; 1 Sam. 6:19ff.; 2 Sam. 6:6ff.; Josh. 24:19) and cul-

minates in the declarations of the prophets (Isa. 6; 57:15; Hos. 11:9; 12:1; Ezek. 1; 28:25; 36:22; 38:23: "I will show my greatness and my holiness and make myself known in the eyes of many nations; then they will know that I am the Lord"). In this first sense the ideas of holiness and of the *glory of Yahweh are often equivalent. But on the other hand Yahweh is holy inasmuch as He imparts Himself, inasmuch as He wishes men to share in His own divine life as He brings them within the scope of His judgment and mercy. His holiness is dynamic, exacting; it confronts man to pour out upon him a new life.

The explanation and the criterion of this new life can lie only in the purpose of Yahweh (Deut. 7:6; Isa. 8:13; Lev. 11:44,45; 19:2; 20:7,26; Num. 15:40, "You shall be holy, for I am holy"). This latter formula does not primarily express a moral requirement, but rather a religious one; the people will belong to their God and will be differentiated from other peoples by their scrupulous obedience to cultic laws. The context also shows very clearly that this holiness of Israel is rooted in and explained only by the deliverance which God has granted it: "For I am the Lord your God who brought you up out of the land of Egypt to be your God" (Num. 15:41; cf. also: Isa. 40:25; 41:14; 43:3,14; 45:18; 57:15, where, as in Hosea, the holiness of Yahweh, i.e. the most intrinsic element in His being, is not His wrath against sin but His active love). The expression "the holy one of Israel" means nothing else (Isa. 1:4; 5:19,24; 10:17,20; 12:6; 17:7; 29:19,23; 30:11, etc.).

It is significant that in the N.T. the idea of the holiness of God is only very rarely expressed. The reason for this is simple; the N.T. is not a speculative writing about the divine perfections, it is interested in the holiness of God only in so far as that holiness has just been revealed in the person of Jesus (cf. below, §2). However, formulas such as Rev. 4:8; Jn. 17:11; 1 Pet. 1:15ff.; Matt. 6:9 show that the O.T. insight is by no means forgotten. When they asked in their prayer that the name of God should be hallowed, Jesus and the first Christians were thinking not so much of the veneration with which the name of God should be surrounded as of the final revelation which God would give of Himself to all mankind at the end of time.

2. *The holiness of Jesus and the Spirit.* The N.T. never says that Jesus was holy or the pre-eminently holy one (not even in Lk. 1:35, the holy child) for this would be equivalent to saying that He had acquired in His person all possible moral and religious perfections. Such expressions as "the holy one of God" (Mk. 1:24; Jn. 6:69; Lk. 4:34; Rev. 3:7) or "holy servant of God" (Acts 3:14; 4:27,30; cf. Matt. 12:16f.) mean that Jesus is He in whom and through whom God finally accomplishes His work of judgment and mercy. It is for that reason that He has been elected and has received the Spirit, like the *"servant" of Isaiah 53 (cf. Ps. 105:16, where the holy servant is Aaron). It is the same with such phrases as "holy spirit"; they do not attribute to the Spirit all sorts of extraordinary qualities but merely emphasize His divine origin and authority; holy spirit and Spirit of God are two strictly equivalent expressions (cf. Isa. 63:10ff. where the holiness of the spirit comes to mean His operation in history and Ps. 51:13 where in the sphere of personal life the Spirit of God, "thy Spirit", effects a similar regeneration and deliverance). Again, the adjective "holy" adds nothing new to the noun "spirit". In the synoptic Gospels and the Acts it would appear that this adjective was often added later to the original text, doubtless in order to distinguish the divine spirit from the demoniac spirits with which the Gentile Christians were in danger not of confusing it but of comparing it. Now the action of the Spirit of God is always incomparable, holy (Matt. 12:32 and parallels; 1 Cor. 6:19; Eph. 2:19; Rom. 15:16; 2 Tim. 1:14, etc.; cf. Isa. 40:25; 43:15); it cannot be included in any preconceived category.

3. *The holiness of the elect people.* We have seen that the holiness of God,

according to the O.T. idea, is not a static perfection but implies rather the nature of divine in so far as the latter imparts itself to men and operates within history. The first objective of this divine action within history is the election and assembling of a "holy people" (Lev. 21:6,8; Exod. 22:31; Deut. 26:19; Lev. 20:8; Ezek. 37:28, etc.), i.e. reserved to the service of Yahweh. It is then Yahweh who in the first place sanctifies His people (i.e. claims them exclusively for Himself) by means of His *election and *judgments and the mighty acts by which He delivers them. But the O.T. emphasizes no less the sanctification of God by His people (Num. 20:12,13; 27:14; Isa. 5:16; 8:13; 29:23; Ezek. 20:41). This sanctification of Yahweh has assumed various forms according to the time. Originally and throughout the history of Israel it is effected above all in *worship; it is by gathering together in the holy place and enjoying the benefits of the substitutionary sacrifice that Israel sanctifies itself and dedicates itself to its God; hence the importance throughout its history of the places, the means, the times, the persons reserved for worship: *sabbath (Gen. 2:3; Exod. 20:8; Neh. 13:22; Jer. 17:22,24; Exod. 20:20), altars (Exod. 29:37; 40:10; 1 Sam. 16:5), offerings (Lev. 6:11,20), Temple (Hab. 2:20; Jon. 2:5; 1 Kings 9:3), priests (Lev. 8:12; Exod. 19:22; 1 Chr. 15:14; 2 Chr. 29:34); then, especially in the post-exilic period, the *torah* (see *Scripture).

Thus by all sorts of normal and tangible media the faithful Israelite dedicated himself to the service of his God. Two dangers threatened this piety, which was at once so deep and so concretely embodied. Firstly, there was the danger of growing more attached to the forms, ritual and instruments of worship than to its professed object: the God of Israel. The prophets were constantly protesting against this materialization of Israelite piety: "It is the Lord whom you must reverence" (Isa. 1:4; 8:13; 31:1; Hos. 11:9; Isa. 55:5; 60:9). Institutions, rites, feasts and sacrifices are holy only in so far as they are used in the service of the uniquely Holy One of Israel.

The other danger was that of forgetting that the sanctification of Yahweh inevitably involves personal submission to His law. At this point the idea of holiness connects with the biblical idea of *righteousness, understood in its specifically moral sense: to be sanctified means not only to be purified, to be separated from other nations or to submit scrupulously to the ritual of worship, but above all "to observe all the commandments" (Deut. 26:16). In this Deuteronomic context the commandments concern not only conventional religious life (worship, first-fruits, the levirate law, etc.) but the moral obligations of everyday life (the widow and orphan, the stranger, the poor, the landmarks of property, false witnesses, etc.): "the Lord of hosts is exalted in justice" (Isa. 5:16, a sentence of which the translation is disputed but which obviously expresses a characteristic emphasis of the prophets).

It has been widely asserted that Jesus and the early Christians abolished the cultic and ritual aspects of the O.T. idea of holiness and retained only its moral and spiritual phase. This assertion is probably mistaken. What is true is that (a) the N.T. emphasizes above all the work of God on behalf of the sanctification of His new people, a work accomplished once for all in Jesus Christ, the foundation of the new sanctuary, the Church (Jn. 17:19; 1 Cor. 1:2; Rom. 15:16; 1 Cor. 6:11; the whole of the Epistle to the Hebrews); (b) the N.T. like the O.T. has a cultic conception of the moral life, since the faithful are called upon to offer their bodies (i.e. their concrete behaviour) to God as a living and holy sacrifice (cf. Rom. 12:1; 15:16; Phil. 2:17); (c) the idea of holiness remains basically communal and ecclesiastic: it is just because they are members of a people with mutual and brotherly responsibilities that the saints are assembled and organized by the Spirit into a differentiated community (Eph. 4:12; 1 Cor. 16:15; 2 Cor. 8:4; 1 Cor. 7:14; 9:1, etc.). In all these texts holiness is not the prerogative of a few specialists in the moral and religious life but belongs to the brethren as a whole, inasmuch as they are all partakers of the benefits of the saving work which God has wrought in Jesus Christ: the "saints of Jerusalem" for whom the collection is organized have no special dignity in this respect; (d) holiness is nevertheless in the Epistles the theme of urgent exhortations, exactly as in the O.T.: those sanctified by Jesus Christ are called to sanctify themselves or to sanctify the Lord Jesus Christ (Eph. 1:4; 5:27; 1 Pet. 1:15; 3:15; 1 Thess. 4:3ff.; Rom. 6:19,22; Rev. 22:11); (e) already in the N.T. it is noticeable that there is a very clear warning against spiritualist teachings which tend to make of sanctity a professional ascetic thing; now "everything created by God is good, and nothing is to be rejected if it is received with thanksgiving: for then it is consecrated by the word of God and prayer" (1 Tim. 4:5; cf. the same warning with regard to purity, Rom. 14:20; Tit. 1:15).

P. BONNARD

HOLY SPIRIT

Reading the texts of the N.T. which speak of the Spirit, one experiences a certain difficulty. "As yet the Spirit had not been given, because Jesus was not yet glorified", says Jn. 7:39. Earlier in the same Gospel, however, John the Baptist saw the Spirit descend on Jesus (Jn. 1:32), and, according to Acts 4:25, it was the Spirit who inspired David to write Psalm 2. These contradictions, more apparent than real, are due to the different periods of history in which the Spirit worked, for He did not operate all the time with equal power or with the same ends in view. It is therefore necessary to follow the unfolding of this history to understand the coherence and the unity of the Spirit's activity through the time of the old covenant, and the years of the incarnation, and during the era of the Church.

1. *The Spirit as power of inspiration in the old covenant.* According to the witness of Scripture, the Spirit is the power by means of which God acts. The divine Spirit is at work in the creation (Gen. 1:2) and in

the preservation of human life (Job 33:4; Isa. 42:5). It rests in particular on those who are called to be the heads of the people of God (Gen. 41:38; Judg. 3:10) and on the "*servant of the Lord" (Isa. 42:1). Wisdom and discernment are gifts of the Spirit (Isa. 11:2; Prov. 1:23). Finally, the Spirit appears as the energy and divine intelligence which possesses the prophets and which lifts them above the calculating prudence of their contemporaries (Mic. 3:8; Isa. 61:1, etc.). However, according to the O.T. the Spirit only rests on certain men and as a temporary favour, with a view to the specific mission they are charged to accomplish. The old covenant lives in the hope that God will pour out His Spirit on all men at the dawn of the new age (Joel 2:28; Ezek. 37:1–14). The last expression of this prophetic message came from John the Baptist, who announced that his baptism of water was to be followed by the baptism of the Holy Spirit given by the Messiah, who was himself invested with the Spirit of God (Mk. 1:8; Lk. 4:18).

In short, in the old covenant the Spirit intervenes sporadically by quickening the men upon whom devolved the responsibility of leading Israel towards her providential destiny. But the Spirit does not act yet as a power of regeneration and new life. It is significant here that the work of the Spirit is not connected with the giving of the law at Sinai. The old covenant is the covenant of the *law and the *promise, and in respect of both the action of the Spirit always maintains its occasional character. But the utterances of the prophets do come authentically from the Spirit, and on this the N.T. confirms the witness of the O.T. and draws the logical conclusion from it. Since the prophets spoke by the Spirit—David (Mk. 12:36; Acts 4:25), Isaiah (Acts 28:25), the prophets in general (2 Pet. 1:21)—their word, now established in *Scripture, has conferred upon it the character of an inspired writing. It is the Spirit who speaks in the Scripture (Heb. 3:7; 9:8; 10:15).

2. *The Spirit a divine power associated with Jesus.* Jesus is distinguished from the prophets and from His forerunner by being clothed with the fullness of the Spirit. The four Gospels portray the descent of the Spirit upon Him at His baptism (Mk. 1:8; Matt. 3:11; Lk. 3:16); John says more precisely that the Spirit descended and remained on Him (Jn. 1:32–33) and that "it is not by measure that God gives the Spirit" (3:34). From that time the Spirit is united to the person of Jesus; He has, as it were, no existence apart from Jesus. That is the meaning of Jn. 7:37ff.: as a power independent of Jesus the Spirit did not yet exist. This Johannine testimony is confirmed by what the first three Gospels say. They reveal the Spirit in the ministry of Jesus as victorious over hostile forces, to wit, the *demons, *sickness, and *death. Every time that Jesus intervenes against one or other of these forces, it is the Spirit of holiness, the Spirit of life, who is acting through His person. That is what enables Jesus to say: "If it is by the Spirit of God that I cast out demons, then the Kingdom of God has come upon you" (Matt. 12:28). The book of Acts (10:38) sums up the course of Jesus' ministry in one verse: "God anointed Jesus of Nazareth with the Holy Spirit and with power; he went about doing good and healing all that were oppressed by the devil, for God was with him." John emphasizes a related idea when he describes the words of Jesus as "Spirit and life" (Jn. 6:63), and a very close idea it certainly is, for the words of Jesus have the same power as His acts; both sanctify. Jesus said to His disciples: "You are already made clean by the word which I have spoken to you" (Jn. 15:3).

The birth narratives (Matt. 1 and Lk. 1) both mention the work of the Spirit in the conception of Jesus, and this is the same idea as that of the anointing by the Spirit at the baptism. These narratives are designed to show according to their own mode that Jesus was a direct creation of the divine Spirit; as with the first man, a new beginning of the human race. That is the thought behind the title Son of Man which *Jesus chose to use of Himself, as also by the title Second Adam, used by St. Paul. What is

6*

new and unique in Jesus is that the Spirit finds His nature utterly without anything which might obstruct His entry: and this is the last meaning of the assertion in the Gospels that, since the baptism, Jesus and the Spirit are a single person and a single power who live and act in one perfect unity of will.

3. *The Spirit as power of regeneration in the Church.* The resurrection of Jesus set in motion the realization of the promises which the prophets uttered about the gift of the Spirit to humanity. The risen Jesus sent down upon the apostles the Spirit as He had Himself promised them (Jn. 14–16). Thenceforward the Spirit was present in the world as that power of life which had once brought Jesus from the grave. He is at work in the Church and, through the Church, makes believers to be new creatures: rescued from this world which is passing, they are transferred to the Kingdom of God which is on its way. There are three aspects of the reign of the Spirit, as a specific mark of the new covenant, which must be set out.

(*a*) *The Spirit and the Lord.* Between the glorification of Christ and His advent at the end of the age, believers are not left alone. The Spirit has been given to them (Jn. 20:22; Acts 2:1f.). In several passages John calls the Spirit the *Paraclete* (14:16–26; 15:26; 16:7), i.e. the Protector or Supporter rather than the Comforter. For His function is not to save the apostles from being submerged by despair, but in a very real way to succour them and strengthen them in their work of bearing witness to Christ and the Gospel. The Spirit-Paraclete leads the disciples into all truth, and this signifies, since Jesus is Himself the truth, that the Spirit gives them a full understanding of the revelation of God in Jesus and an ability to proclaim it to the world. By means of them, the Spirit extends the work of redemption which had been begun by Jesus during the incarnation, both in time and space. The Spirit, having been formerly associated with the person of the Jesus of history, and so with Palestine and with a particular generation, acts from henceforth

through the apostolic witness in the whole world. But it is the same power who is at work under this new form and it is the same salvation which is offered. It is also the fulfilment of Jesus' promise reported in Acts 1:8 and realized at Pentecost: "You shall receive power when the Holy Spirit has come upon you, and you shall be my witnesses . . . to the end of the earth."

Equally the apostle Paul maintains the close relation between the Spirit and the glorified Christ. The divine Spirit is the Spirit of Christ (Rom. 8:4; 2 Cor. 3:18; Gal. 4:6, etc.) for Christ works by Him. The apostle even writes: "The Lord is the Spirit" (2 Cor. 3:17). In this verse it must not be supposed that there is an absolute identification between Christ and the Spirit, since for Paul Christ is a personal being who was manifested in Jesus of Nazareth and who now lives in the heavens, so that the believer is still "away from the Lord" (2 Cor. 5:6), even though the believer, by definition, possesses the Spirit of Christ, since he belongs to Him (Rom. 8:9). Elsewhere the Spirit is the divine power communicated to believers and residing in them so that they no longer live "in the flesh" but "in the Spirit" (Rom. 8:4, etc.). Paul maintains an identity of function between the Spirit and the Christ in the work of redemption. Both equally are the same divine energy which works in the believer, and which from the present time onward renews his interior self and makes him walk in the obedience of faith, or, in a word, re-creates him after a mystical manner (Rom. 6:11–14; 2 Cor. 4:16; Gal. 5:22–25, etc.). At the coming of the Kingdom of God this energy will remake the believer after a physical manner by giving him a new and spiritual corporeity and by introducing him, by means of resurrection, into glory and incorruptibility (Rom. 8:11; 1 Cor. 15:42–50). And this brings us to the activity of the Spirit in the Church and in the individual believer.

(*b*) *The Spirit and the Church.* The gift of the Spirit caused the emergence of the Church. The new era inaugurated by the glorification of Christ can be called indifferently either the age of the Spirit or the age of the Church. The Spirit apart from the Church would be energy without any instrument through which it could operate. The Church without the Spirit would be a body without a principle of life. Therefore in the N.T. the Spirit and the Church are always conjoined and are inseparable from each other. Both are predicted and promised by Jesus during the time of the ministry (Jn. 7:39; Matt. 16:18). After the resurrection they operated in concert in the history of salvation and so have initiated the last age (Acts 2). Finally, the Spirit and the Church are united in awaiting together the advent of Christ (Rev. 22:17).

The Spirit directs the Church and acts in her and through her. It has often been observed that the chief personage in the book of Acts is neither Peter nor Paul, but the Spirit, who makes the Church increase in number and in vigour (9:31), who inspires the decisions necessary to maintain her unity (15:28), who guides the apostles and preachers of the Gospel in their missionary journeys (4:8; 6:10; 8:29; 10:19; 13:2–4; 20:23), who establishes the essential ministries (6:6; 20:28), who sends warnings by the prophets (11:28; 21:4–11). On this the Epistles of Paul confirm the evidence of the Acts. Every time that the message of redemption—which caused the Church to be—is preached, the power of the Spirit is manifested (Gal. 3:3–5; 1 Thess. 1:5, etc.). An identical pattern of events is repeated everywhere, for there is only one Spirit and consequently only one body, i.e. one *Church (Eph. 4:4). The Church is the temple of the Spirit (1 Cor. 3:16) and the Spirit enriches the Church by His gifts (1 Cor. 12).

The Spirit of the glorified Christ is not a force which comes and goes by chance. He is a power who acts within the framework which this power has built. There alone can the spiritual life of the believer be nourished and developed.

(c) The Spirit and the Believer. The believer is baptized in the name of Jesus. Having been added to the Church, he receives the Holy Spirit (Acts 2:38, etc.).

It may also happen that the Spirit comes down upon believers in order to reveal that they ought to be added to the Church by *baptism (Acts 10:44–48). Every way it is in the Church that the believer shares in the life of the Spirit (Eph. 3:20–21). To describe this new life would involve giving a picture of the whole of the Christian life, so this article is limited to a summary of the most notable aspects of it. The believer is "a new creation" (2 Cor. 5:17, etc.), a being born anew (Jn. 3:3–8, etc.). The Spirit who is given him henceforward is the sign and the pledge of his eternal salvation through the resurrection from the dead (1 Cor. 15:20–23; Jn. 6:40; etc.). Being the power of regeneration, the Spirit enables the believer to live in the communion of the Father and the Son as a child of God (Rom. 8:14–17; 1 Jn. 3:1) and in communion with the rest of the faithful (Phil. 2:1–5; 1 Jn. 2:20). The Spirit manifests His presence and His action in the Church by the gifts distributed among believers by which He builds up their common life (1 Cor. 12:7; 1 Pet. 4:10, etc.). Finally, the Spirit confirms for the faithful the truth of the apostolic witness concerning Jesus (1 Jn. 5:6–12; cf. 1 Cor. 12:2–3) and convicts the unbelieving world of sin in the light of the revelation (Jn. 16:8–10; cf. 1 Cor. 14:22–25).

Although the believer is now saved by Christ, whose redemptive work is already finished, he must nevertheless remain in this world which goes on and will go on until the last day (*Time), and he is still exposed to all the miseries of flesh and blood (see *Man); still he must pass through *death. But the Spirit who has now been given to him draws him forward, so to speak, and never ceases to remind him that his Lord has vanquished death, so that he knows for a certainty that no power on earth can separate him from the love of God manifested in Jesus Christ (Rom. 8:31–38).

4. The Holy Spirit and other spirits. The Spirit who proceeds from the Father and the Son is a Spirit holy by nature and sanctifying by His action. He is the Holy Spirit. The adjective here is not merely qualitative;

it is also adversative. The divine Spirit must not be confused with one or other of the evil spirits, such as the spirit of the world (1 Cor. 2:12), the spirit of bondage (Rom. 8:15), the evil spirit which provokes heresy (1 Tim. 4:1). Hence the apostle's wish that the faithful be kept in the communion of the Holy Spirit (2 Cor. 13:14) and John's exhortation to "test" the spirits: "Beloved, do not believe every spirit, but test the spirits to see whether they are of God. . . . For . . . the spirit of antichrist . . . is in the world already" (1 Jn. 4:1–3). The Spirit who comes from God has reference always to the revelation of God in Jesus Christ, as expressed in the apostolic tradition. The divine spirit is the truth as God is the truth (Jn. 15:26; 16:13; 1 Jn. 4:6).

PH.-H. MENOUD

HOPE

In order to be able to live, it is essential to have a future, be it most uncertain and dark. But having a future means having hope, good or bad. Hope belongs to life. What does not yet exist largely conditions what is in process of becoming. Thus, the things that we wait for, and our manner of waiting for them, partly make us what we are. In Greek thought it was possible to nourish hopes that were both bad and good, but the Bible employs the word only to denote a waiting for something good and favourable. Hoping is seizing in faith a promise of life and salvation. To have hope is to have a future which, even if it contains tribulations, will be good.

1. *The believer's hope does not come from within himself.* Christian hope, a heritage from the hope of Israel, is not born of an inward psychological process. If the believer has hope, it is not solely or primarily because he needs to hope, because some immediate anguish impels him to take refuge in the hope of something better in the future. It is true that utterances of hope are quite often associated with cries of despair or appeals for help or with lamentations (Job 5:16). It is true that it is always to one under

condemnation that grace offers hope. But sometimes, and in fact most frequently, the man in question is quite unaware of his condemnation. For man does not always feel his desperate situation at all profoundly. Does this mean then that when all is going well he has less need of the hope that the Bible talks of? By no means: for hope as the Bible knows it does not depend on our state of feeling: it does not come from time to time, but is essential to the believer's life; it does not ask vaguely for assistance, but offers indispensable salvation. According to the word of God, man does not create, but receives, hope.

2. *Hope is God's gift.* The hope of the Bible is a confident waiting upon a future given by God. It is not therefore for us to specify or to conjecture the object of our waiting, for we do not have hope at *our* disposal. When this ceases to be the prerogative of God, the surprise which He has laid up for His children, it becomes an idolatry. Man then begins to wait and to hope for what is no more than a projection of his dreams and ambitions, idealized and projected into the future. And the word of God which, in another connection, issues a continuous summons to true hope, ruthlessly denounces those who trust in vanities, such as man (Jer. 17:5), or personal riches (Job 31:24) or righteousness (Ezek. 33:13) or death (Job 11:20) or the umbrellas of religion: "Do not trust in these deceptive words: 'This is the temple of the Lord!' " (Jer. 7:4).

It is a property of hope in God that it cannot be acquired by us: we do not have it to dispose of, for it does not belong to the realm of visible objects that form the world of flesh and blood. The hope which one sees is no longer hope: does one still hope for what is seen? (Rom. 8:24).

We touch here on what it is that makes biblical hope so essentially paradoxical, that is to say, its being at once complete insecurity and complete assurance. It relies on nothing which is available to ourselves; it is utterly remote from all our requirements and claims. It is hope against all hope

(Rom. 4:18). But because it comes only from God, its guarantor, it is more certain than any human hope; it never disappoints (Rom. 5:5), it is steadfast (1 Thess. 1:3), it is without envy or fear, save fear of the Lord (Prov. 23:17-18), it rests on the faithfulness of him who made the *promise (Heb. 10:23).

Consequently it can be seen how closely hope is connected with faith. One is not possible without the other (1 Pet. 1:21), for it is in faith that hope derives its assurance (Heb. 11:1), and it is in hope that faith finds its joy and its peace (Rom. 15:13); it is on hope of life eternal that faith rests (Tit. 1:2); and, lastly, it is by hope that faith perceives the glories of the last day (Tit. 2:13).

Joined to faith on the one hand, hope is also united with *love. Any sort of egoism is quite alien to biblical hope. Anything one hopes for, one hopes that others equally will share (2 Cor. 1:7). No one can be abandoned to his fate or left as a prisoner of doom. The Good Samaritan gave evidence of his hope just as much as his love for the man who had fallen amongst robbers. It is not possible to love one's neighbour without also having hope for him and with him: which implies that hope must be accompanied by acts of charity.

So faith, hope and love together constitute the Christian's being at its deepest level. One evokes the other; all rely upon each other; these three abide (1 Cor. 13:13), because all three depend on the mercy of God in Jesus Christ.

3. Hope in Christ. The Bible is throughout the book of hope, and moreover, of the same hope. In the O.T. it is a hope veiled, but in Jesus Christ it emerges quite unobscured under its true title. Henceforward, for those who turn to the Saviour, the veil is taken away (2 Cor. 3:1-18).

What distinguishes the two testaments will certainly not be found by an examination of the actual concept of hope, for this hope has the same context for both. The difference between them is due on the contrary to their respective relationship to a single hope. The O.T. hopes for Him who is still to come, the N.T. hopes for Him who has come—and will come again. Christian hope is therefore based on historical knowledge of its object, it is nourished on a certain past event, and from this it derives its assurance. The paradox mentioned above finds here its justification: in Jesus Christ the Christian has the assurance of the things which he hopes for, he has the *demonstration* (!) of those that he does not see (Heb. 11:1). A bolder or indeed a more adequate definition could hardly be conceived. So, too, in a surprisingly concise expression, St. Paul describes the same paradoxical truth: it is in hope that we are saved (*not*, shall be saved) (Rom. 8:24). Hope has here become synonymous with Jesus Christ; and that He is indeed and most certainly our hope is stated in 1 Tim. 1:1; cf. Col. 1:27: "the riches of the glory of this mystery, which is Christ in you, the hope of glory."

(*a*) In Jesus Christ, hope is confident. The Christian is sure of a future because he has a past. Yet this future does not remain for him as something unknown and unfriendly, for he knows it from his experience of the faithfulness of Him who is the same yesterday, to-day and for ever (Heb. 13:8). And the future has lost its power to terrify, and hope is always a good hope and a refuge (Heb. 6:18), not in virtue of some illusory optimism, but because of the knowledge of Him who by means of His death is a pledge of a blessed future. He who has given His life for us can only desire our good. It is He who delivered us—and on Him we have set our hope that He will deliver us again (2 Cor. 1:10).

(*b*) In Jesus Christ, hope is living. It is not woven out of death and nothingness nor vitiated by the fatal chain of mechanical laws. Hopes not founded on the living Christ are moribund and sterile. In fact they leave men without hope (1 Thess. 4:13), which means that they inevitably abandon all idea of survival. But, properly, Christian hope does not rest on an idea, but on the living person of Jesus Christ, risen from the dead. He alone can guarantee an inheritance which is imperishable (1 Pet. 1:3,4).

By His resurrection, Christ laid the foundation of hope in eternal life and delivers us from the calamity of hopes which are for this life alone (1 Cor. 15:19).

(c) In Jesus Christ, hope is eschatological, which means that its object is future and yet already present. The Christian's future is not determined by an end which is both stationary and also out of reach. The future comes to us. At the same time as we advance towards it, it advances towards us. For Christ is also the one who comes. In Him what is hoped for is on the way to meet us, and already impinging on the present moment.

By the power of the Holy Spirit hope becomes confident and lively and is given in the present time as a pledge of the age to come (Rom. 5:5). Thus, not only do the hopes of this world carry the promise of life eternal, but the hope of the Kingdom is born in the midst of the economy of this era; it governs the believer's mode of behaviour and provides the context for Christian morality.

4. *Christian morality is a morality of hope.* Having been freed from his sinful past, the Christian is one who lives in conformity with his hope. Because he belongs to the Saviour who is coming, he is no longer subject to the fashion of this world which passes away (1 Cor. 7:31). Hope renders impossible any absolute attachment to sojourning here below (Heb. 13:14); it cannot accept the securities offered by visible things. Not that hope signifies flight from this world: on the contrary, it implies that the realities of this world must be taken seriously and not reduced to nothingness. Just because the believer has put his hope in the living God, he is able to work and to engage in combat on the earth (1 Tim. 4:10).

A Christian awaits the realization of his hope, that is, the return of his Lord (*Advent). Because of this the time of hope is also the time of watching (Mk. 13:33–37). The believer's vigilant expectation is not an affair simply of each individual Christian, but of the people of God corporately. The individual shares in hope only in so far as he is a member of the community. For the whole Israel of God, the whole Church, even the entire creation, has been given the promise. The Christian life is the exercise of hope and vigilance, but both of them are shared with others.

J.-PH. RAMSEYER

HOUR, *see* TIME

HOUSE, *see* BUILD, FAMILY

HYMN

Though it is incorrect to think that the Israelites regarded music as an art, in the modern sense of the word, for its own sake, it is quite certain that they did regard it as of supernatural origin and consequently privileged in its relation to the other arts.

Music could be used without words (especially in the ancient period). It could excite or still ecstasy, 2 Kings 3:15 (there is a close parallel with intoxication). It could expel demons or stimulate them (1 Sam. 16:16 and 23; 18:10; 19:10). The "good" musician (it is difficult to know by what standards such judgments were made) was an inspired man, one moreover capable by his art of communicating this inspiration to those who listened. Note the ephemeral, accidental nature of this inspiration.

It attracted the attention of God, and was acceptable to Him (cf. the trumpets of Num. 10:9–10). There were, too, a great variety of musical instruments (Pss. 149 and 150); instruments which served not only to render praise to God, but which could also be the instruments for the power of God (Josh. 6:20) or again could proclaim the day of Yahweh (Joel 2:1ff.,15f.; Rev. 8:6–9:21).

But music was increasingly allied with poetry and both became servants of prayer, so making it more expressive, i.e. more likely to be heard by God or a better offering of praise to God. Music could thus become "accompaniment" and musical instruments increasingly "instruments of song" (Amos 6:5).

Great efforts were therefore made to pray well and also to make beautiful music (though to us it would appear sheer cacophony). It must be remembered lastly that the Psalms were sung and that professional musicians were attached to the Temple (choirs of Korah and of Asaph), that there is frequent mention of singing in the N.T. (Matt. 26:30; Acts 16:25; Jas. 5:13, etc.) and that Paul saw in it a powerful means of edification for the Church (Col. 3:16; Eph. 5:19).

A. MAILLOT

HYPOCRISY, see FALSEHOOD

IDOL

O.T.

1. Among the Semitic peoples, whether settled or nomadic, there would seem in the earliest periods to have been no representations of the Deity. The Semites of Mesopotamia appear to have thought along different lines. Worship was paid to mountains, springs, trees, blocks of stone. These did not actually represent the god, but the latter was in some sense incarnate in them. Fairly quickly, however, these quasi-images took on very slightly more civilized forms—such as a block of stone or the lopped trunk of a tree standing in the middle of the sacred enclosure, which was the real sanctuary. Even at the end of the Roman period, we still find on coins pictures of the temple at Byblos, with its sacred enclosure and conical sacred stone; true, the colonnades of a Graeco-Roman temple, designed to suit the contemporary taste, are also to be seen, but the sacred stone remained beyond all doubt the real heart of the holy place. In the stories of the patriarchs we can still see very clearly the part played by sacred trees and even springs. The stone on which Jacob slept at Bethel and which he set up as a memorial of the appearance of his God (Gen. 28:11–22), was a sacred stone of a type which we find in fair numbers in the land of Canaan. The best example which has survived is the holy place of the town of Gezer, in the south-west of Palestine, with a row of sacred stones that is still impressive to-day; but we do not know to what precise period of pre-history it ought to be assigned. The sacred pole, the idol of his clan, which Gideon broke down and burnt (Judg. 6:25–32) is a typical example of such wooden representations. Human and animal images of the deity do not seem to have figured largely in Canaan, to judge at least from the results of excavation, which has provided us with very little in the way of evidence. When we do find some, they are mostly foreign coins, Egyptian, for instance, which may well derive from conquerors of the country and be in no respect indigenous.

2. In the few O.T. stories that speak of idols in Yahweh-worship the note of disapproval is certainly present, but frequently does not appear to be original. Thus, the golden calves set up by Jeroboam at the two great sanctuaries in the north and south of his country (1 Kings 12:26–33) do not seem to have shocked the contemporary Israelite—in fact, quite the opposite. The golden calf in the wilderness (Exod. 32:1–6), which enjoyed the patronage of Aaron, did not become an object of rebuke until several centuries later. For a long time now scholars have been suggesting that these calf-images, actually bull-images, were derived from Egyptian influence: but the Syrian parallels in our possession would seem to suggest otherwise. Here the animal is in no sense a representation of the god, as is the case in Egypt, but rather a form of seat on which he may be enthroned. This may help us to understand why the people of the time were considerably less repelled by them; they were to be regarded rather as works of art, to embellish the sanctuary and to bring it more into line with the fashions of the day. None the less, for a good many simple folk it must really have been a matter of a representation of God Himself. In the story of Micah (Judg. 17–18) we are told of a sculptured and even of a molten image, but we are given no indication at all of the form they took. As the latter eventually became that of the sanctuary of Dan, in the extreme north of the country, it is probable that we are already dealing with a bull-image. These

instances show clearly that, though there were occasional images of Yahweh, they were frequently invested with a degree of disapproval and regarded as exceptional.

3. There were, however, other idols, which may be described perhaps as lesser gods, the tutelary deities of the home. If we know nothing of their precise form, at least we have in the O.T. some indication of their size. The *teraphim* which Rachel stole from her father Laban must have been of small dimensions for it to have been possible to hide them under a camel-saddle (Gen. 31:31-35). On the other hand, the *teraphim* which Michal, Saul's daughter, put in the bed to give the impression that David, her husband, was sick (2 Sam. 19:11-17), while she was persuading him to escape, must obviously have been of a more imposing size. The excavations in Palestine have produced a large number of statuettes of naked women and other subjects, which allow us to form some idea of what these little household gods, to which the Israelites clung for so long, must have been like.

4. Apart from such household deities, it may be said that Yahwism was always very sceptical of, not to say repelled by the idea of human or animal representations. They were probably introduced under Canaanite influence, which may help to explain the disapproval with which they were regarded by an ever-increasing circle of people, who based their ideas on those who sought to return to the simplicity of the primitive cultus in the time of the sojourn in the wilderness.

Later, the tendency of idols to penetrate into the religion of Israel revived, but this was a result of foreign influences and came in a more artistic and elaborate form. The struggle then became, in truth, a struggle against strange gods. They were recognized as having power, but it was a power hostile to that of the God of Israel. We have to wait till the end of the Exile for a clear understanding that the idols were nothing but pieces of wood, stone or metal and not real gods: but, in consequence, it is at this period

that we also find the full expression in Israel of a true and complete monotheism. The strange gods are no longer, as in former times, gods who reign over other realms than that of Yahweh (for instance, Chemosh was the god of Moab as Yahweh was the god of Israel, cf. Judg. 11:24). It is only now that all real existence is denied them. Yahweh alone is God and the gods of the mightiest empires are nothing but common blocks of wood. Nor do the prophets moderate their sarcastic remarks at the expense of these false gods of wood, incapable of action (cf. Isa. 40:19f.; 41:7; 44:12-20; 46:1-7). The Fathers of the Church were to draw largely on this repertoire for arguments in the battle against the idols of their own day.

We know that Hezekiah (2 Kings 18:4) smashed in pieces a serpent of brass, which he called Nehushtan and which must have been an object of worship in the Temple at Jerusalem. It was regarded as the brazen serpent that Moses had raised in the wilderness. Since the Canaanites possessed cult-images of the serpent, it is possible that this cult had penetrated into the Temple. But our only indication of the kind of worship offered to it is the fact that it is mentioned along with the idols.

5. Idols, the tangible images of the deity, were treated with the honours due to a god. In the cult of the golden calf, mention is made only of dancing and rejoicing (Exod. 32) before the new god. But in other passages we read of the tender care lavished on the idol. When, at Bethel, Jacob sets up the stone on which he has been sleeping, he pours oil over it (Gen. 28:18). Elsewhere, we learn that it was the custom to cover the idol with kisses (1 Kings 19:18; Hos. 13:2). A touching witness to this practice is to be found in the sanctuary at Gezer: one of the standing stones, the smallest and no doubt the holiest, is almost polished with the touches of the faithful. As to the cult rendered to the household gods, the texts give us no information.

In the struggle against the idols that the Israelites worshipped, it would seem that at first condemnation was reserved for molten images, i.e., those worked with the greatest care and in the most costly materials (Exod. 34:17). It was not until later that radical condemnation was extended to all representations that might properly be considered idols, i.e., censurable representations of the Deity (Exod. 20:4; Deut. 4:16,23; 5:8; 7:25; 27:15).

G. NAGEL

N.T.

1. In the N.T. the word idol denotes, as in the O.T., heathen deities and their images. Idols are vain things; they mask no underlying reality. In opposition to them stands the living God, who created the heaven, the earth, the sea and all that is (Acts 14:15; Gal. 4:8), the living and true God (1 Thess. 1:9; 1 Jn. 5:20f.). They are dumb: it is not they who stand over against man; those who serve them are left in loneliness. The heathen are drawn to them by the vague instinct which drives all men to some religion and to the accident of particular customs and traditions (1 Cor. 12:2).

Paul gives an explanation of idolatry deserving of the most careful attention (Rom. 1:18–25). It is not, as is often thought, a kind of first stage or infancy of religion, from which, by development or evolution, emerge the so-called "higher" forms, spiritual and monotheistic: on the contrary, it is the lowest point of a fall, a perversion of original genuine knowledge of God. God made a real revelation of His invisible perfection, of His eternal power and divinity in His works: but men, after knowing God and being placed as creatures in the presence of their Creator, refused through pride to glorify Him as God and to give Him thanks, that is to say, to recognize Him as their Lord and their life as His gift (cf. 1 Cor. 1:21a). By refusing to live as His creatures ("You will be like God!" Gen. 3:5) they broke and corrupted the relationship on the basis of which alone a true knowledge of God is possible, and fell into the culpable absurdities and confusions of idolatry.

2. Because idolatry is not originally and essentially a primitive form of religion, but religion spoiled by sin, it is not by rational criticism that men can put an end to it: Athens, the city of Reason and Philosophy, is full of idols (Acts 17:16). It is only overcome by the revelation of God in Jesus Christ. It is a thing past and done with for the Galatians, because now they know God; or rather—in order to make it quite clear that this is no question of any light thrown on the matter by reason—because they have been known by God, who has drawn near to them and has declared Himself to be their God in Jesus Christ (Gal. 4:8f.). Similarly for the Corinthians idolatry is a thing of the past, because they have been taught by the Spirit of God to say: Jesus is Lord! (1 Cor. 12:2f.; cf. 6:9–11). But for the same reason, idolatry is not for the believer, as one might think, a danger done away with for ever: it reappears every time the believer forgets the lordship and grace of Jesus Christ. It is listed among the sins against which Christians must always be on their guard (Gal. 5:20; 1 Pet. 4:3); it reappears in the form of covetousness, the insatiable lust for possessions (Eph. 5:5; Col. 3:5), for Mammon is the type of all idols—it is impossible to serve him and God at the same time (Matt. 6:24). Idolatry threatens again when the Corinthians, proud in their faith and their freedom from the old superstitions, think themselves strong enough to move, without being contaminated, in the atmosphere of pagan ceremonies (1 Cor. 10:6,14; cf. § 3 below).

One particularly dangerous threat from idolatry is noted in the Book of Revelation: this is the cult of the Beast and his image (Rev. 13:14f.; 14:9,11; 15:2, etc.), that is to say, of the Roman emperor in the guise of his cult-images, or, as we might choose to express it, the cult of the state and the head of the State who is its incarnation. On the pretext of loyalty and good citizenship the state, now become totalitarian and its head divinized and exalted to the rank of Providence and Lord, demands worship and an absolute obedience, which Christians, who have Jesus as their Lord, must refuse even at the cost of their lives (Rev. 20:4).

3. A special problem is raised by the question of *meats sacrificed to idols* (Acts 15:29; 1 Cor. 8:1–11:1; Rev. 2:14,20). It appears that frequently the meat sold in the market came from the sacrifices (1 Cor. 10:25). Christians might be the guests of non-believers, who had perhaps purchased this meat (1 Cor. 10:27); it could also happen that Christians partook of public meals, which were, according to custom, prefaced by a sacrificial act and therefore had a cultic character (1 Cor. 8:10). Some Christians, the "strong" ones, had no scruples about buying and eating this meat: idols, they said, are nothing (1 Cor. 8:4; 10:19), therefore they can pollute nothing. Others, the "weak", were shocked at this, and if they allowed themselves to be governed by the example of the "strong" and their air of superiority, they felt that they were *sinning (1 Cor. 8:7,9–11). Paul agrees entirely with the "strong": for us, there is only one God and Lord (1 Cor. 8:6), the others are powerless. "The earth is the Lord's, and everything in it"; therefore there is no need to inquire the source of the meat offered for sale or set before you (1 Cor. 10:25ff.)—simply eat it with thanksgiving (1 Cor. 10:30). However, he puts forward against the "strong" two very serious arguments: (*a*) Even if the idols are nothing, it is none the less true that they are a tangible expression of something very real hidden behind them, the demons, who make use of them to divert to themselves the worship owed to the Lord. It is not possible, without arousing the jealousy of the Lord, to partake unthinkingly at the table of demons (1 Cor. 10:14–22). But, even more important, (*b*) we must avoid shocking the weak and causing them to stumble. This is to cause the weak to perish, the brother for whom Christ died (1 Cor. 8:11f.), and this simply for the boastful pleasure of displaying one's own enlightened faith. Rather than do such a thing, Paul is prepared to forswear all meat for ever (1 Cor. 8:13).

Note: This argument of Paul has always been employed—and with good reason—in the fight against alcohol, the problem of which may in many respects be stated in analogous terms.

CHR. SENFT

IMAGE

O.T.

For images of the deity in public and private worship, see *Idol.

1. A superficial reading of the O.T. would almost seem to suggest that the Israelites felt the same revulsion from all kinds of representation of living creatures as we meet much later among the most orthodox parties in Islam. But on closer inspection, we find that any statement on this question needs considerable qualification and that wholesale condemnation, though it may mark the final stages of the development of Israel's religion, is by no means to be found in the earlier periods. The commandment, "You shall not make yourself a graven image, or any likeness of anything that is in heaven above, or that is in the earth beneath, or that is in the water under the earth; you shall not bow down to them or serve them" (Exod. 20:4,5), is not only of comparatively late date, but only applies to cultic images; it does not seem to refer at all to other representations of a secular kind. It is true, however, that according to the evidence of excavations in Palestine, the Israelites, and the Canaanites before them, do not seem to have been possessed by the demon Art. A large number of statuettes, apparently portraying the benevolent deities of everyday life, have been found, but other representations seem never to have been of any great importance. There are censers and bases decorated with figures of animals and gods (?); also fine pieces of ivory, belonging probably to the decorations of royal furnishings (at Samaria and Jericho), with series of human figures and composite creatures. But the style of these pieces strongly reflects foreign influence, especially that of Egypt.

Though we possess some steles from an earlier period, they owe nothing to a native art: they are the work of Egyptians stationed in the country, such as soldiers or government officials (cf. the steles of Beisan).

2. The O.T. writings do, however, speak occasionally of images. First of all there are the *kerubim* (in order to avoid tedious confusion, these should not be referred to as "cherubim"—Exod. 25:18–22; 37:7–9; 1 Kings 6:23–28). They were placed on the lid of the *ark of the covenant in the Holy of Holies of the sanctuary. They served as a kind of throne for the Deity, and there are occasional references to God as "seated on the *kerubim*" (2 Kings 19:15; Isa. 37:16; Ps. 18:11; 80:2; 99:1). We have no description of them, but they are normally represented as human creatures with wings (to which reference is made in the texts). Goddesses of this type are found in Egypt, placed at the four corners of royal sarcophagi to protect the deceased with their outspread wings. However, it is at least a probable conjecture that the *kerubim* were not of entirely human form but also possessed certain animal characteristics, such as we meet elsewhere.

The O.T. mentions other images also. Semi-human, semi-animal creatures appear among other elements, perhaps geometrical or floral, in the decoration of the interior walls of the Jerusalem Temple (1 Kings 6:29–35; Ezek. 41:18–20). The book of Kings gives us practically no details. But Ezekiel, in his vision, is more explicit and describes this decoration appreciatively. His version is probably not identical with that which actually existed but it need not be substantially different. We observe that in these figures the human element is combined with the animal. There are plenty of examples of these composite figures in Mesopotamian art; usually they are the guardian spirits of the gates of palaces and temples. They probably originated in Northern Syria, whence their influence spread to the valley of the Tigris and Euphrates as well as toward Southern Syria and Palestine. The ivories discovered at Megiddo and Samaria afford us further examples of these creatures, the representations in these cases being strongly influenced by Egypt. The walls of the sanctuary were thus alive with strange creatures, in which were mingled the forms of man, bird, lion and doubtless the serpent also. In theory they were not objects of worship and ought, as in Assyria, to be regarded as guardians. It is likely that the *seraphim* which Isaiah saw in the vision that inaugurated his prophetic ministry derived from these figures; they were standing about the Deity, of whom the prophet could perceive no more than the train of His robe (Isa. 6). He speaks of their wings, but gives no description of them. The brazen serpent, to be found in the Jerusalem Temple up to the time of Hezekiah (2 Kings 18:4), and mentioned in connection with the idols, must have been a cult-object; but—probably to explain and justify the reverence accorded it—it was identified with the brazen serpent raised in the wilderness by Moses (Num. 21:8f.).

3. *The image of God.* The O.T. speaks of this only in Gen. 1:26f. The two other relevant passages (Gen. 5:1; 9:6) are closely bound up with this one. The priestly account of Creation is alone in telling us that God created *man in His own image. The assertion is found nowhere else in the O.T., but later Jewish writers devoted much space to an attempt to define its meaning and Christian authors have outdone them in prolixity. In the sense given to it by Genesis, the phrase is an attempt to emphasize the physical analogy between God and man, but it stresses equally strongly the fundamental distinction that separates man from the animals. Thus there is here a plain contradiction of the idea that found expression in many other religions, such as those of Egypt, which ascribed to the Deity an animal or semi-animal form.

But if it stresses the analogy between man and his God, it draws attention also to the distance between them. Man is not *as* God, he is merely "in his image, after his likeness". Between the one and the other there is no descending scale of beings, each a little less divine than the last; there is simply God on one side and man on the other, the latter being neither identical with nor diametrically opposed to God, but "in his image". It is on this foundation, with its misleading appearance of strict definition, that Jewish and Christian theologians have constructed their systems, many of which are impressive. But they continually go much further than the Genesis story and often in a quite different direction, in their efforts to base on this text a philosophical definition of the relation between man and God. Such views often hold the essential feature of the resemblance to lie in the moral nature. In going so far, they completely forget the simplicity of the original statement, of which they retain nothing.

G. NAGEL

N.T.

In our versions of the N.T., "image" appears as the translation of three Greek words of different, not to say opposite meanings: (1) In the vast majority of cases, the word translated "image", far from emphasizing (as would be the case in English) the unreality or the derivative nature of the image compared with that of the original, signifies on the contrary that the image is an authentic and adequate expression of the original: in the image the thing itself is made present, manifest, visible. Thus, Christ is the image of God (2 Cor. 4:4). (2) In two instances, however, "image" renders a Greek word which does express a derivative, non-original character; the inadequate shadowy reflection of one thing by another. Thus, the cult of the old covenant was an "image" of heavenly things (Heb. 8:5). (3) In one case the word expresses a likeness, a close relationship, which is not, however, an identity of substance: man is made in the "image" of God (Jas. 3:9, quoting Gen. 1:26). On this subject see *Image (O.T.) and *Man (O.T.).

1. *Image as revelation.* (a) *Jesus Christ is the image of God* (2 Cor. 4:4; Col. 1:15; 3:10). By this is meant that Jesus Christ is the revelation of God, He in whom God is adequately represented, in whom is manifested the plan of God for the world. It is no contradiction in terms to say that He is the "image" of the "invisible" God, for by "invisible" is understood not some physical property of the divine, but the fact that God is not a this-worldly reality at all, but the Lord who is over and above it; hence the phrase must mean that in Christ there is a genuine revelation of the invisible God. The same sense is conveyed a little further on (Col. 1:19), when it is said that all the fullness of the Godhead resides in Christ ("fullness" being a regular term of ancient theology to designate the world of the divine), or when Christ is called the "very stamp" of the person of God (Heb. 1:3). Much more frequently Jesus is referred to as the Son of God or simply as the Son; but all these expressions are equivalents. When Paul says: "(You) have put on the new nature, which is being renewed in knowledge (sc. of God) after the image of its creator" (Col. 3:10), he means that this renewal comes about through communion with Christ, the revelation of God and of His creative and saving Will.

(b) The new life is *the transformation of man into the image of Christ* (Rom. 8:29; 1 Cor. 15:49; 2 Cor. 3:18; Col. 3:10), that is to say, the reality of God, manifested in Christ and working and being made visible in man. The goal of our election, of the plan of salvation, is that we should be conformed to the image of the Son of God; that by the effects of justification His saving power and divine life should be manifested in us; that through the Son we should become children in whom God can recognize His own likeness (Rom. 8:29f.). In so far as it is based on the work of salvation, which is complete, this transformation can be regarded as something already achieved: "Those . . . he also glorified" (Rom. 8:30). But since it has to manifest itself in this world of sin and death, it may also be regarded as still in the future: "Just as we have borne the image of the man of dust, we shall also (*sc.* in the Kingdom, resurrected) bear the image of the man of heaven" (1 Cor. 15:49; cf. 1 Jn. 3:2). Paul can also say that by contemplating the glory of the Lord, God manifested in Jesus Christ, we are transformed into the same image from glory to glory: the salvation we have received is in process of realization, it is continually being effected; in the life of faith we are becoming that which by grace we already are (2 Cor. 3:18). This is not brought about by a kind of magic, but is expressed in the most practical way by a life of obedience to the commandments of God (Col. 3:5–10).

(c) When Paul calls man *the image and the glory of God* (1 Cor. 11:7) his meaning is obviously not the same as when he uses these words of Christ. Some women at Corinth, taking their stand no doubt on the apostle's own saying that in Jesus Christ there is no longer either male or female (Gal. 3:28), are seeking by their attitude in worship to obliterate the distinction between men and women: in opposition to the apostle's instructions, they abandon the veil which they normally wore for praying or prophesying (1 Cor. 11:5). By doing this they are breaking an order willed by God; they are forsaking their proper rôle and refusing to be what they are: women. Paul recalls them to their proper place. It is in her relation to man that woman finds that which determines her place in the order of creation, just as man finds the same thing for himself in his relation to God (cf. *Marriage).

(d) *The Beast and his image* (Rev. 13:14f.; 14:9,11, etc.) is a kind of monstrous inversion of God and His image. It is the God-state and its ruler, in whom it is incarnated and who requires to be served with divine honours (cf. *Idol).

2. *Image as shadowy reflection.* The Epistle to the Hebrews calls the cult of the old covenant the "image and shadow of the heavenly things" and the Temple "the image of the heavenly sanctuary" (Heb. 9:23; 8:5; cf. 10:1), with reference to the command given by God to Moses to make

everything according to the pattern which he saw in the mount (Exod. 25:40). They are but the shadowy reflection on earth of the true sanctuary and worship, not the substance of them. This does not mean, certainly, that they are devoid of all substance, since they are derived from the heavenly reality; but their relation to it is that of the shadow to the thing itself, of the promise to the fulfilment. This shadowy character is plain to those who believe in Jesus Christ, the true High Priest, who has entered into the true sanctuary and in whom the reality has been revealed.

CHR. SENFT

INHERITANCE

The biblical idea of inheritance plays an important part in the history of salvation. It is closely bound up with the idea of *promise. To say this, is to regard its meaning in the theological context as the essential one and its juridical use as only secondary. In the Bible the word inheritance does not simply refer (as it does in our ordinary usage) to the transmission or acquisition of wealth by succession, to the property bequeathed by one's forebears, but first and foremost implies the idea of an allocation or distribution effected by God, and is based, in the N.T. especially, on a clearly defined concept of sonship.

As far as the O.T. is concerned, it is almost impossible to give an exact statistical analysis of the passages in which the term inheritance appears, since, in our versions, the rendering "inheritance" is not uniformly employed for any one Hebrew word, nor does it always represent the same word in the original. We shall confine ourselves, therefore, to noting those books which contain the most fruitful thought on this subject: namely, the Hexateuch (i.e. the first six books of the O.T.), certain of the prophets (Jeremiah and Ezekiel especially) and the Psalms.

In the N.T. the term inheritance occurs thirteen times; and in addition there are thirty-two instances of cognate words: heir (10), co-heir (4), to inherit (17) and to give as an inheritance (1). The principal texts for the study of this concept are to be found in the synoptic Gospels, the Pauline writings (especially Galatians) and the Epistle to the Hebrews.

O.T.

1. In several passages of the O.T. the term inheritance is used in its ordinary sense simply to denote inherited property (e.g. Naboth's vineyard, 1 Kings 21:3ff.) or property in general (Prov. 13:22; 19:14) which can be handed on to one's sons (Gen. 21:10; Deut. 21:16; Judg. 11:2) and, in certain cases, to one's daughters (Num. 27:1ff.; 36:2ff.—In Job 42:15, the fact that Job can allot part of the inheritance to his daughters is intended to demonstrate the multitude of his riches). It is also in this ordinary sense that slaves form part of an inheritance (Lev. 25:46).

2. The concept of inheritance, however, came quite generally to acquire a deeper significance, a very definite theological content. At first, in the majority of texts, it refers to possession of the soil, i.e. the whole or part of the Promised Land (according to whether the inheritance of the entire nation or the share reserved for a tribe, a family or a particular individual is meant). The Israelites occupy the land of *Canaan only by virtue of the grace of God. God fulfils for their benefit the promise He had made of old to the fathers to give them a country for themselves and their descendants—a promise made in the first instance to Abraham (Gen. 12:1ff.; 13:14-17, etc.), then confirmed to Isaac (Gen. 26:3-5) and to Jacob (Gen. 28:13; 35:12) and renewed to Moses (Exod. 3:8,17; 6:8). Hence this country is not a patrimony pure and simple, handed down from generation to generation, but it is the inheritance which God alone has granted to Israel—"thy land, which thou hast given to thy people as an inheritance" (1 Kings 8:36; cf. Num. 34:2; Deut. 4:21,38; 12:9f.; 15:4; Ps. 105:9-11; 47:5)—and of which He Himself has fixed the boundaries (Num. 34:1-12). Joshua's success

in taking possession of it was due entirely to the fact that God had entrusted him with that task (Deut. 1:38; 31:7; Josh. 1:6) and that He intervened in His people's favour, giving "all their enemies into their hands" (Josh. 21:43-45; cf. Deut. 9:4f.; 11:25; Ps. 44:2-4).

God, therefore, supervised the conquest of the land He had allotted to Israel. Similarly, it was He who directed the partitioning of it among the tribes. The division was effected by lot, which means that it was regarded as a divine decision: Josh. 18:4-10 (cf. also Num. 26:52ff.; 33:54; 34:13ff.; Josh. 13:6f.; 14:2). Each tribe in this way received its lot (Josh. 15:1), its portion in the inheritance (Josh. 23:4; cf. Gen. 48:6). Moreover, the divine partitioning did not stop at the tribal level, but was equally concerned with the clan, the family and even the individual (cf. the families of Judah, Josh. 15:1,20; Caleb, Josh. 15:13; Joshua, Josh. 19:49f.).

In the last analysis, God is the real landowner and He alone can freely dispose of it as a settling-place for His chosen people ("the land is mine; for you are strangers and sojourners with me", Lev. 25:23; cf. Josh. 22:19). It is to establish this fact, and not to introduce a new conception, that certain passages describe the land or the people as the inheritance of God Himself (not an inheritance which He has received, but which He has chosen for Himself and which belongs to Him by right: for the land, cf. 1 Sam. 26:19; 2 Sam. 21:3; Isa. 47:6; Ps. 79:1; for the people, Deut. 4:20; 9:26,29; 32:9; I Sam 10:1; 2 Sam. 14:16; 1 Kings 8:51,53; 2 Kings 21:14; Isa. 19:25; Josh. 2:17; Ps. 28:9; 33:12; 94:5,14).

From what has already been said, it follows that, if God has Himself fixed the boundaries of the inheritance, no one has the right to alter them. They are sacred, inalienable, definitive. The "for ever" of God's promise (Gen. 13:15, etc.) refers not only to the allocation of the land to Abraham's descendants but also to its partitioning. Consequently, a share in the total inheritance cannot pass from one tribe to another (Num. 36:1-12) and coveting the property of another is forbidden (Exod. 20:17; Mic. 2:2), just as it is also a crime to move the boundary-marks of a field (Deut. 19:14; Hos. 5:10). It is only in the light of this conception that we can properly understand the astounding legislation for the Year of Jubilee, concerning the return of property to its first owner (Lev. 25:8ff.)—whether in fact this law was enforced or not. Even though it is possible to sell the crops that a piece of land produces (Lev. 25:16), it is not possible to make an outright sale of the land itself, for this belongs to God (25:23).

Nevertheless, the full possession of the inheritance is not automatic but conditional. It depends on the fidelity of the people to the *covenant granted by God, on their obedience to the divine commands (1 Chr. 28:8; cf. Deut. 4:1; 11:8ff.; 19:8f.; Josh. 1:7; 2 Kings 21:8; Neh. 9:8; Jer. 7:5–7; 25:5; Ps. 37:18). The punishment that will befall the Israelites, if they transgress these commands, is the loss of their country (Deut. 4:25f.; 1 Kings 14:15; Jer. 12:7–10; 17:4; Mic. 2:4), which they will not then be able to recover except by repentance and a new and complete submission to God (Isa. 57:13; 58:13f.). The great national disasters that culminated in the Exile were to be a terrible proof of this. Conversely, the sign that the divine favour is renewed, that God will once more be gracious to His people, will be their entering once again into possession of their inheritance. We can find this stated categorically in the texts proclaiming the return from Exile or in the Messianic prophecies (Ezek. 36:8–15; 37:21–28; Isa. 49:8f.; Ps. 69:37).

The period of the Captivity marks an important stage in the development of the idea of inheritance; for it now becomes of eschatological importance. The projection into the future of various elements of the concept is clearly to be seen at the end of the book of Ezekiel. Here God is presented as giving back the inheritance to His people with precisely the same boundaries and divisions as of old, in accordance with the promise made to the fathers (Ezek. 47:13f.; 48:29). Each man's share is to be absolutely inviolable (46:16–18). This simple reinstatement of the conditions of the past is, however, in various passages enriched by a universalist conception: not only will the stranger dwelling in Israel have a right to his own share in the inheritance (Ezek. 47:21ff.) but the *Gentiles will form part of the inheritance of God and of His Anointed (Ps. 2:8; cf. Ps. 82:8; Isa. 19:25).

3. But the idea was to expand in yet other directions. Thus it is that certain passages present God Himself as the inheritance of His people (Jer. 10:16) or of the individual believer (Ps. 16:5f.; 73:26; 142:6). Ought we to see the origin of this line of thought, as some have suggested, in the passages about the Levites? where it is said that, though they have no share in the nation's land (Num. 18:20ff.; 26:62), yet the Eternal God is their inheritance (Deut. 18:2; Josh. 13:33; Ezek. 44:28). But these texts can be understood in a purely material sense, in the light of Josh. 18:7 and, especially, of Deut. 18:1 (cf. Josh. 13:14), where the Levites receive their share in their priestly office or in the offerings presented to Yahweh. The conception put forward in Pss. 16 and 73, on the other hand, is much more profound, referring as it does to the joy and fulfilment which the faithful will find in communion with God.

4. In conclusion, certain particular instances should be mentioned. In Deut. 33:4 the inheritance is the Law (cf. Ps. 119:57,111); in Job, it is the personal destiny of the individual (20:29; 27:13); and finally, in Ps. 127:3, it is children.

N.T.

Apart from those passages where the word inheritance is used in its ordinary sense (Lk. 12:13; "Teacher, bid my brother divide the inheritance with me") or has reference to the possession of the Promised Land (Acts 7:5 and Heb. 11:8; where the promise to Abraham is recalled), the N.T. adds to the O.T. content of the term in two principal ways: first, by establishing a connection between this idea and the person of Christ (on to which the theme of sonship is also grafted) and secondly, by relating it to the Kingdom which He inaugurates.

In the synoptic Gospels the Parable of the Vinedressers already exhibits both these elements clearly (Mk. 12:1–12; Matt. 21:33–46; Lk. 20:9–19). Here, side by side, are to be found both the connection with Jesus Christ (the heir, i.e., the son, Mk. 12:6f.), and with the Kingdom (the inheritance, according to Matt. 21:43, is the Kingdom). The remainder of the N.T. only serves to work out this double relationship.

1. *Inheritance and Sonship.* In the O.T. the connection between sonship and inheritance, from the theological viewpoint, does not play a major part (except by implication: the Israelites are heirs because of the promise made to the *fathers*: Exod. 13:5; Deut. 1:8, etc.). By contrast, in the N.T. it occupies a central position.

In the first place, it is Jesus Christ who is the heir by virtue of His being the Son (Mk. 12:7 and parallels; Heb. 1:2). Next, the believers themselves are also sons and therefore heirs (Rom. 8:17; Gal. 4:7), but only in a derivative way. They acquire their status through Jesus Christ alone: they are "fellow heirs with Christ" (Rom. 8:17), because His work has placed them in a new relationship with God. Slaves though they were, Christ has made them sons and heirs (Gal. 3:26–29; 4:1–7). His death has made available to them "the eternal inheritance" (Heb. 9:15). It is in Him that they have been "sealed with the . . . holy Spirit, which is the guarantee of our inheritance" (Eph. 1:14; cf. Acts 20:32; cf. also *Adoption).

Chapters 3 and 4 of the Epistle to the Galatians are particularly valuable in this connection—all the more because they relate the new situation of the believer in Jesus Christ to the promise made to Abraham. In opposition to the Judaizers, St. Paul asserts that our being numbered among Abraham's posterity, who are the heirs of the promise (Gen. 13:15), depends

not on the law (Gal. 3:10,18; cf. Rom. 4:13) but on faith (Gal. 3:7–9; cf. Rom. 4:13–16; Heb. 6:12) and on faith in Jesus Christ (Gal. 3:14,22f.). In fact, Jesus Christ, together with those who are in Him (3:29), is the true posterity of Abraham (3:16).

This true posterity, then, based on Jesus Christ, is no longer according to the flesh (cf. 1 Cor. 15:50, "flesh and blood cannot inherit the Kingdom of God") but according to faith. This fact is of prime importance, because it implies a universalism no longer in the future, like that of the O.T., but already present: in Jesus Christ the promise transcends the limits of the Chosen People to speak to every man who believes in Him. In Jesus Christ "the Gentiles are fellow-heirs . . . and partakers of the promise . . ." (Eph. 3:6; cf. Gal. 3:28 and Matt. 8:10ff.).

2. *Inheritance and the Kingdom.* In the N.T. the equation of the inheritance with the Kingdom replaces the O.T. equation of the inheritance with the land of Canaan. The inheritance, the vineyard in the Parable of the Vinedressers, is the *Kingdom (Matt. 21:43), that Kingdom which, from the outset of His ministry, Jesus has declared to be at hand. Jesus, being the Son, is the heir (Mk. 12:7 and parallels) and those who are His will share in it with Him ("inherit the kingdom prepared for you from the foundation of the world": Matt. 25:34; cf. 1 Cor. 6:9f.; Gal. 5:21; Eph. 5:5; Jas. 2:5).

The verb to inherit in 1 Cor. 6:9f. and Gal. 5:21 is in the future tense ("the unrighteous will not inherit the Kingdom of God", "those who do such things shall not inherit the Kingdom of God"). Indeed, though the Kingdom is already in action here below, its complete possession is still an object of hope. In the Parable of the Vinedressers, it is to be noted that the Son Himself is not yet master of the inheritance, and that is why the vinedressers entertain hopes of depriving Him of it (Mk. 12:7)— He will only be Lord of the Vineyard after His resurrection (Matt. 28:18; Phil. 2:9f.; Heb. 1:4); and on the other hand, the passage already quoted (Matt. 25:34) from the great scene of the last judgment makes it clear that the waiting of Christ's disciples for their inheritance has an eschatological significance (cf. also 1 Pet. 1:3f.). Moreover, the Epistle to the Hebrews, despite certain passages where the idea of inheritance seems to apply to something already obtained (in the case of Noah, Heb. 11:7, this is righteousness; or, 6:12, in the case of all past believers, the promises), moves in the same direction. According to chapter 11, although the believers of old time (Abraham and the "heirs with him", Isaac and Jacob, v. 9) are heirs of the promise, they have none the less not yet "received what was promised" (vv. 13ff.,39). Similarly, chapter 6 exhibits the conditional, eschatological nature of this process of obtaining what is promised: it assumes the "faith and patience" (v. 12) of the readers, their zeal in waiting for the object of their hope "until the end" (the eschatological phrase *par excellence*, v. 11, cf. vv. 19f.). But their hope is firmly grounded, since it rests on a promise guaranteed by the oath of God (vv. 13ff.).

This inheritance, however, this Kingdom, the object of the believer's hope—what is it? what does it involve? It is the new *city, which God has created and is keeping for the faithful (Heb. 11:10,16), the new heaven and the new earth, the Holy City of Rev. 21 (cf. 2 Pet. 3:13). The believer is called to reign there for ever with God (Rev. 22:5; cf. Rom. 5:17). And when it says in Matt. 5:5 that the meek "shall inherit the earth", it is precisely to this reigning with God (cf. Rom. 4:13; Rev. 5:10) that it refers. Then the redeemed will enjoy the various treasures of the Kingdom they are to inherit (cf. the words "this heritage" in Rev. 21:7): eternal *life (Tit. 3:7; cf. Mk. 10:17 and parallels; Lk. 10:25), the grace of life (1 Pet. 3:7), *glory (Rom. 8:17f.; Eph. 1:18;=literally "the riches of the glory of his inheritance"), *blessing (1 Pet. 3:9), incorruption (1 Cor. 15:50ff.; cf. 1 Pet. 1:4).

In conclusion, we must emphasize certain fundamental aspects of the idea of inheritance.

(a) In the N.T., as in the O.T., possession of the inheritance depends on the fulfilment of the divine promise. The inheritance is a gift of God's sovereign grace. One must beware, therefore, of taking the biblical term in the modern sense of something owed to us, our rights in which are guaranteed to us by law.

(b) God had reserved an inheritance for His elect from the creation of the world (Matt. 25:34). This eternal plan of God finds a first fulfilment in the occupation of the land of Canaan, but it will only finally be fulfilled with the coming of the Kingdom (hence the typological significance of the conquest of Canaan in Heb. 11). Thus the temporal aspect of the concept, giving it a place in the unfolding of the history of salvation, is absolutely essential.

(c) The universalist and eschatological significance of the concept, already emphasized by certain passages in the O.T., acquires especial point in the N.T. The times of the end are really approaching, now that the Gentiles are fellow-heirs (Eph. 3:6) and that the believer has a foretaste of the inheritance to come through the Holy Spirit, which is also its guarantee (Eph. 1:14).

(d) The eschatological projection of the concept must not be understood in any "spiritual" or idealist sense. It retains a concrete character, clearly indicated in such texts as Matt. 5:5 ("they shall inherit the earth") and Heb. 11:10 ("the city which has foundations").

J.-CL. MARGOT

INSPIRATION, *see* SCRIPTURE, HOLY SPIRIT

ISRAEL

O.T.

1. The first instance of the name Israel in the O.T. is to be found in the story of the patriarch Jacob. On the occasion of his mysterious struggle with the divine messenger he received from God a new name, for which an etymology is furnished in the text (Gen. 32:24–32). "Your name shall no more be called Jacob, but Israel, for

you have striven with God and with men, and have prevailed" (v. 28). On this view the word Israel is derived from the two elements *sarah*, to struggle, fight, and 'EL, God. This etymological interpretation of the book of Genesis is also adopted in Hos. 12:3–4; ". . . he strove with God, he strove with the angel and prevailed." But the biblical explanation raises problems of grammar. In names compounded of a verb and a proper or a divine name the latter is the subject, not the object or predicate; so then the natural meaning of the word Israel would be rather "God struggles" or "God fights". Another possibility is that the verb itself is not precisely the one given in the explanation. In the course of centuries Jewish and Christian exegetes have proposed a number of other etymologies, e.g.: "God is he who makes war"; or "the man who has seen God" ('*ish ra'ah 'el*); or "the righteous one of God" (*yashar 'el*); or "God gives light" (from a rare root meaning to be bright, to shine); or "husband of Rachel" ('*ish raḥel*); or "He who is the prince of God" (from *sar*, prince), etc. At any rate it is certain that in this word God takes the place of first importance, and that the etymological meaning nearest to the facts of Scripture is to be found in the sense of God's ruling or victory, on the lines of the suggestion "God reigns" (from the verb *sarah* or *sarar*, which can mean to be ruler, to reign). The usage of the word seems to fit reasonably well with this interpretation.

2. We can hardly expect to know when the word Israel was first applied to the people who thenceforward were to bear, as their characteristic designation, the name of "the people of Israel". One piece of evidence, important because it is both ancient and extra-biblical, is that provided by the inscription of the Pharaoh Merneptah, who in a triumphal hymn carved on a stele (hence the name "Israel stele") records the names of the groups of population conquered in the course of his military campaigns. In this list Israel appears as a people still at the nomadic or semi-nomadic stage and not as an organized nation. This stele dates from about 1230 B.C., doubtless but a short time after the exodus from Egypt, and indicates that the name Israel as a designation of the Hebrews was already known among the heathen in the 13th century B.C.

3. In the books of the O.T. we must try to distinguish the several quite different senses in which the name Israel is used by the biblical texts at different periods in the history of the people of God.

(*a*) In the most ancient period, that is to say at the time of the nomadic life in the desert and of the settlement in Canaan before the establishment of the monarchy, the name Israel is applied to the whole body of the people made up of the twelve tribes, and clearly indicates the religious character of the bond that united these tribes in a common worship of Yahweh. Not at any time is Israel the name of an individual tribe, nor of any man except Jacob, and that before the people had even come into existence: but it attaches solely to the group of tribes whose unity is based on a common cult, not on a common national feeling or on an actual political situation of any kind (cf. Judg. 5:2, 7–11; the ancient Song of Deborah, in which we see several tribes joining together because of their consciousness of belonging to the same sacral community). It is by their common faith in the God of the patriarchs, the God who had promised the land to the seed of Abraham and Jacob, who had delivered His people from their bondage in Egypt, who had led them in the wilderness and was now giving them the Promised Land, that the tribes descended from the patriarch Jacob-Israel are firmly bound together. The new name of the ancestor of the twelve tribes emphasizes the sacral character of the great family of the people who bear his name: Israel. In Josh. 24 we find what may be called a common confession of faith by the tribes of Israel in the presence of Joshua at Shechem. The people of Israel is therefore a collective unity constructed not, as in the case of other peoples, on a national or political, but on a cultic and religious foundation. Israel exists only because God so wills, and because He has given them a mission. The *covenant which binds the people to their God is also the mortar that binds the members of the nation to each other, the principle unifying the individual sections into a collective whole. This is the true sense of the terms "people of Israel", "house of Israel", "children of Israel", which are so frequently used in speaking of this community (Exod. 40:38; Deut. 6:4; Judg. 1:1).

(b) Once the people acquire a political organization under the control of a king, the religious character of the bond uniting the twelve tribes tends gradually to disappear and consequently the meaning of the term Israel undergoes modification. It acquires a political and even geographical content that it had not originally possessed. In addition there is the fact that the southern tribes, Judah and Simeon, had remained a separate bloc from the rest and that the seeds of a division were thus latent within the body politic. By the time of Deborah it had already proved impossible to rally all the tribes of Israel. Saul, the first king, did not succeed in creating national unity (1 Sam. 11:8). David was at first named king only of Judah at Hebron (2 Sam. 2:1–4), while Ishbosheth was proclaimed king of Israel (vv. 8–11): it was not until seven and a half years later that David became king of all Israel and Judah (2 Sam. 5:5). Thus a distinction between Israel and Judah on purely national and political grounds was already emerging. It was one of the great merits of David that he succeeded in unifying the country by giving it a capital, Jerusalem, and a firmly established governmental and military organization. But in the same process the primitive religious meaning of the term Israel was entirely lost and when, after the death of Solomon, the split between the northern and southern regions widened so far that a complete break resulted, Israel became the designation of the northern kingdom and Judah of the southern under the Davidic dynasty (N.B. the expression "all Israel" as opposed to the tribe of "Judah", 1 Kings 12:20). Geographically, Israel was the mountainous area of Ephraim (the mountain of Israel, Josh. 11:16–21). The kings of Israel, of whom the first was Jeroboam, continued to reign in the northern kingdom for about two hundred years, until the Assyrians invaded the land, destroyed the capital, Samaria, and put an end to the monarchy in Israel (722–721 B.C.).

(c) It might be supposed that these events would result in the dropping of the term Israel from the vocabulary, since the historical reality of the kingdom of Israel had disappeared. Nothing of the kind. On the contrary, the religious sense of the word to some extent revived and it was applied to the kingdom of Judah as the sole survivor and genuine remnant of the people of God, maintained by the Davidic house. Instead of the word Judah, which never had a religious connotation, the prophets used "Israel" to refer to the nation which kept Jerusalem as its capital, and which was to exist for more than another hundred years before the captivity in Babylon and the destruction of the Temple. The prophets had already spoken of the "two houses of Israel" (Isa. 8:14), as if they refused to acknowledge the existence of the separation; but now they frequently employed the term Israel for the *southern kingdom* (Isa. 5:7; Mic. 3:1; Jer. 2:4; 10:1; Isa. 41:14), seeking by this means to recall effectively to mind the sacred covenant of the people with God and their election and mission, of which the traditions of the wilderness and of Sinai remained the true and authentic expression (Isa. 41:8; 44:1f.).

(d) After the fall of Jerusalem in 586 B.C., the Babylonian Exile, the Return and the restoration in the period of Nehemiah and Ezra, the religious content of the word Israel with its reference to the twelve tribes was bound to be stressed, since it was no longer a matter of a political and national federation but rather of a religious community. The word Judean or Jew kept a racial and national connotation, but Israel acquired an *ideal* significance, being applied to the nation of the faithful and the believers, both in the present and the future.

The major interest in the cult, in ritual and priestly regulations, in statistics and genealogies, which is characteristic of all the writings of the priestly school (e.g., in the books of Chronicles), is also displayed in a return to the idea of the Israel of God with its twelve tribes, each with a meticulously established genealogy (1 Chr. 2–9). Israel becomes once more, and in truth, the cultic community reunited round the Temple, preserving the religious tradition of the fathers and chosen by God for a clearly defined mission. In later Judaism the word Israel is the one used from choice by the faithful themselves in their consciousness of belonging to the elect people of God, while the word *Jew is employed rather by foreigners to designate those who belong to the Jewish race or nation. The Graeco-Roman world seems to have been almost entirely ignorant of the term Israel and to have used that of Jew exclusively. The latter word, moreover, acquired in the course of time a pejorative sense, which is equally noticeable in Christian circles in the early centuries.

4. Beside this idea of the true Israel, which at times encouraged in the body of the nation a feeling of superiority and pride to which non-Jews did not fail to draw attention, we must also note a use of the term which is not less interesting for being less frequent. The religious connotation of the word is emphasized in a particular usage, whereby it is employed in speaking of the ordinary people in opposition to the great and those in authority, and even to the priests and Levites (Ezra 9:1; 10:5). Perhaps there is here some suggestion that the lowly and humble (the "poor of Israel") are closer to the covenant made by God with His own than are the great and the powerful, even when these are members of the priestly body; for the latter often abuse their power and superior position and are thus unworthy of their mission. Nevertheless this use of the word is not sufficiently common to enable us to draw any definite conclusions.

5. Far more common, however, is the use of the word Israel in the visions of the future by the prophets of the exilic and post-exilic periods. For them Israel denotes, on the one hand, the grand gathering together of all the dispersed members of the two kingdoms of the North and South to reconstitute the true kingdom of David in the completeness of its twelve tribes (Ezek. 37:21–25; 48:1–7). This is to be the re-establishment in history of the people of God after the grievous trial of the Exile, a punishment made necessary by the unfaithfulness of the people in the course of the preceding centuries. But, on the other hand, Israel is also to be the people of God, restored, purified and sanctified, which at the end of time will receive the fullness of God's blessing and will be the witness of the Lord to the nations of the whole earth, so that they may know the salvation of God. "This one will say, 'I am the Lord's', another will call himself by the name of Jacob, and another will write on his hand, 'The Lord's', and surname himself by the name of Israel" (Isa. 44:1–5). God is called the Holy One of Israel (Isa. 43:3,14, etc.). This missionary and eschatological character of Israel is indeed one of the peaks of O.T. theological insight and finds its fulfilment in Christian thought.

F. MICHAELI

N.T.

Israel in the N.T., as in the O.T., is the name of the people of God, and the presence of this name bears its own witness to the oneness of the revelation in the old and the new covenants. It denotes the Jewish people in their unique relation to God who has chosen them and always marks them off, explicitly or implicitly, from the nations of the world.

1. *In the Gospels.* It is significant that in the synoptic Gospels Jesus is confronting not the Jews but Israel. But it is Matthew and Luke, the faithful interpreters of the oldest tradition, who best bring out this side of the ministry of Jesus. Mark, who wrote his Gospel for the Greeks, was not interested in this aspect. Only five passages

in the fourth Gospel mention Israel or the Israelites, in contrast to a constant concern with the *Jews. The author knows that Israel remains unbelieving and hostile and the unbelief of the Jews, despite their privilege of the divine revelation in the old covenant, seems to him simply an expression of the general unbelief of the world.

The first chapters of the Gospels of Matthew and Luke recount the birth of Jesus, the Messiah of Israel (Matt. 2:6; Lk. 1:30ff.; 2:11,25,34). The miracles of Jesus are exalted as the renewal of the favours of God to Israel (Matt. 9:33; 15:31), favours, moreover, which Israel could no more claim as a right now than she could in the time of Elijah and Elisha (Lk. 4:25,27). And yet Jesus knows that He is sent to the "lost sheep of the house of Israel" alone (Matt. 15:24), and it is because they recognize that His mission has this character that the Canaanite woman and the centurion of Capernaum have their prayers granted (Matt. 15:26ff.; Lk. 7:5; Matt. 8:8). Because of its obvious reference to the twelve tribes of Israel the account of the choosing of the *Twelve comes in the record of Jesus' ministry to Israel (Mk. 3:13ff.; Matt. 10:2ff.; Lk. 6:12ff.); and for the same reason Jesus is careful to limit to Israel the temporary mission which He entrusts to them, to the exclusion of Samaritans and Gentiles (Matt. 10:5f.), and promises them the government of Israel in the world to come (Matt. 19:28; Lk. 22:30). The narrative of the Passion tells how Jesus, the Messiah of Israel, was rejected by Israel. The inscription that Pilate had fixed to the cross bore these words: "the King of the Jews" (Matt. 27:37 and parallels), for the Roman governor was not alive to any but the political aspect of Jesus' Messiahship; but the High Priests and the scribes in their mockery of Jesus, with no suspicion that they are condemning themselves, say: "He is the King of Israel; let him come down now from the cross and we will believe in him" (Matt. 27:42; Mk. 15:32). On the first day of the week the Emmaus disciples are still talking sadly of Him who they hoped would deliver Israel (Lk. 24:21).

2. *In the Acts of the Apostles.* On the first page of the book the Twelve show that they are still preoccupied with the restoration of the kingdom to Israel by the Messiah, Jesus (Acts 1:6), but God's plan is quite different. As from the day of Pentecost (Acts 2) the Twelve, with Peter at their head, preach Jesus as the crucified Messiah (2:36; 4:10), whom God has raised to His right hand "to give repentance to Israel and forgiveness of sins and the Holy Spirit" (cf. e.g., 2:38; 5:30f.), as John the Baptist had proclaimed (13:24). When the apostles call their hearers "Israelites" (2:22; 3:12; 5:35; 13:16), they are giving them to understand clearly from the start that this message concerns them as members of the people of God. Even when the Gospel is preached to the heathen, Israel must not be denied it. After the conversion of Saul the persecutor, the Lord reveals to Ananias in a vision that Saul is the instrument He has chosen to "carry" His "name before the Gentiles and kings and the sons of Israel" (9:15). Thus it is that the apostle Paul begins by addressing the Israelites in their synagogues (Acts 13:16, etc.) and proclaims to them that God, in accordance with His promise, has raised up a Saviour for Israel in the person of Jesus (13:23). Finally, when the apostle is a prisoner at Rome, he summons to him the elders of the synagogue and tells them that he is undergoing his captivity "because of the hope of Israel" (28:20) fulfilled in Jesus Christ. Despite his universalism (1:8), the author of Acts is nevertheless convinced that the Gospel is in the first place intended for Israel.

3. *In the Pauline Epistles.* Paradoxically enough, the terms Israel, Israelite are entirely absent from those Epistles that bear the names of members of the College of the Twelve, Peter, James and John; yet they play an important part in the Epistles of Paul, the apostle of the Gentiles (Rom. 11:13).

It is in the writings of the apostle Paul, who is to be the victim of Jewish hatred, that we find the most intense love for the Jews (Rom. 9:1ff.; 10:1), the most lively sense of Israel's spiritual privileges (Rom. 9:4f.) and of its primacy in the plan of salvation (Rom. 1:16; 2:9f.). None felt more than he the offence of Israel's unbelief. How is one to expect faith from the heathen, when the Jews remain unbelieving? How is one to preach Jesus, the crucified Christ, to the Gentiles, if Israel persists in a refusal to recognize Him as the Messiah? Has the word of God failed? (cf. Rom. 9:6). St. Paul sought an answer to this central problem in Scripture, pondered in the light of the revelation in Christ and of the Holy Spirit (Rom. 9–11). We can only recall here those passages in which Israel is mentioned.

Paul calls attention in the first place to the fact that it is already true under the old covenant that "not all who are descended from Israel belong to Israel" (Rom. 9:6). To belong to Israel by blood does not necessarily mean membership of the true Israel, enrolled by the free and sovereign election of God (9:6ff.). Why is it that Israel does not believe in its crucified Messiah? Because He is the stone of stumbling, set in Zion by God (9:33). Engrossed in the pursuit of its own righteousness, Israel has passed by the righteousness which God gives in Jesus Christ crucified (9:30-10:4). Does this mean that God has rejected His people? Never! says Paul, himself an Israelite, of the stock of Abraham, of the tribe of Benjamin (11:1). Prefigured in the seven thousand men who, in the time of Elijah, had not bowed the knee to Baal, now, too, a minority of elect have received the salvation which Israel as a whole has rejected (11:7). Moreover, the unbelief of the greater part of Israel itself forwards the divine plan, for, in consequence, salvation has passed to the heathen with the effect of inciting the Jews to jealousy (11:11). Hence Paul in conclusion conveys to his readers a *mystery, that is to say, an event coming under the redemptive plan of God and revealed to the apostle by the Spirit: there is to be a partial hardening of heart in Israel, until the fullness of the Gentiles shall have come in (sc. to the Church) and by this means, in the end, all Israel will be saved (11:25f.). The

apostle's certainty is based not on the virtues of Israel but on this fact: the gifts and calling of God are irrevocable (11:29). If Paul was thus convinced of Israel's final sharing in salvation, it is not at all likely, though it is often asserted, that he opposed to "Israel after the flesh" the Church in the rôle of "Israel after the spirit" (an expression, moreover, that he never employs). In the thought of Paul "Israel after the spirit" is rather the minority of believing Israelites, who occupy in the Church that place which belongs by right to the whole Israel. Similarly, in Gal. 6:16, the "Israel of God" is probably not the Church but that part of Israel faithful to its vocation by belief in Jesus Christ, Israel marked out not only by circumcision but also by the faith of Abraham, the type of that faith which is counted for righteousness (Rom. 4:12).

4. *In the Book of Revelation.* Apart from a reference to the temptations of the children of Israel in the generation of the Exodus (2:14), Revelation only mentions Israel twice. By using the picture of the 144,000 marked with the seal of the living God and drawn from every tribe of Israel (7:4), the seer is inviting his readers to recognize the bond which joins the people of God at the end of time, those who are to pass through the furnace of persecution, to those twelve tribes of Israel which constituted the people of God at the beginning of the history of salvation. And when the seer describes the twelve gates of the New Jerusalem, on which are inscribed names that are those of the twelve tribes of the children of Israel (21:12), he is witnessing to the unity of the divine work, the completion of which is bound up with its commencement in the election of Israel and which without that people is inconceivable.

Thus everything that the N.T. has to say concerning Israel witnesses to the faithfulness of God. "For I tell you," writes St. Paul, "that Christ became a servant to the circumcised to show God's truthfulness, in order to confirm the promises given to the patriarchs" (Rom. 15:8).

CH. MASSON

JACOB, *see* NAMES (PERSONAL), ISRAEL

JERUSALEM, *see* NAMES (GEOGRAPHICAL)

JESUS

This personal name is the transcription of a Greek name which itself comes from a Hebrew root (*Jehoshua*) which means to help or to save. It was borne by a great number of Jews up till the time of Jesus Christ, but much less so from the second century A.D. onwards. In the O.T., for example, the name Joshua comes from the same root (Num. 27:18; 1 Sam. 6:14; 2 Chr. 31:15; Ezra 2:2) and the historian Josephus mentions twenty individuals of that name. From 35 B.C. to A.D. 63 four high priests were called Jesus. In the N.T. we find it again in Acts 7:45 and Heb. 4:8, where Joshua is intended, in the genealogy of Luke (3:29) where it is the name of one of the ancestors of Jesus of Nazareth, in Matt. 27:16f. as the second name of Barabbas (according to a well attested reading) and in Col. 4:11 where one of Paul's companions bears this name together with that of Justus; and, finally, according to Acts 13:6 the magician Bar-Jesus had a father called Jesus.

According to the Gospels of Matthew (1:21) and Luke (2:21), this name was given to the son of Mary and Joseph at the command of an angel in order to indicate that "it is he that will save his people from their sins". In this last context the name of Jesus signifies: (*a*) that the child who is to be born is truly a child of the Jewish people, in whose midst he will bear a personal name familiar to his contemporaries; it is his father (in the legal sense) who gives him his name, according to the custom in Jewish families (cf. Lk. 1:63). Jesus is thus a Jewish child amongst other Jewish children; (*b*) that the child who is to be born will not be an infant prodigy, a complete exception, but the last link in the long history of "deliverances" granted by God to His people; (*c*) that this saviour will be *the* saviour foretold by the patriarchs and awaited by his people, for he will deliver

them not merely from hunger, or from oppression, or from the mockery of their adversaries, but "from their sins". By this the N.T. indicates that the salvation of which man stands in need concerns not only his earthly, political, social, or personal condition, but above all his relationship with God which, having been corrupted, will be restored by Jesus.

In the Acts of the Apostles and in the Epistles the name Jesus is a constant reminder that the Saviour Christ is not a mythical personage or a heavenly figure, but was a man of flesh and blood who lived not long ago. This historical humanity of Jesus is strongly emphasized in the early sermons of Acts. There Jesus is presented as "a man approved of God" (2:22), and it is "this Jesus" (and not some imaginary and unreal person) whom God has raised from the dead (2:32). If the term Jesus appears less frequently in the Epistles, it is not because in them the Christ becomes an "ideal" figure (as the mythological school asserts). St. Paul's preaching in particular is dominated by the assurance that the Christ was "born of a woman, born under the law" (Gal. 4:4). In the context of his thought Paul could not have found an expression which would have stressed more strongly the *historicity* of the Christ. This historicity should not be understood only in the restricted sense of the *authenticity* of an event that has really happened. According to the N.T., Jesus has not only appeared in our history: He has assumed, recapitulated, and revealed in His person and His destiny the tragic significance of this history, both before God and before men. In Him we can recognize the true components of human history, in its bondages as well as in the promises which are attached to it.

The most ancient Christian confessions of faith declare that "Jesus is Lord" (Phil. 2:11, etc.). This formula lays stress on the historicity and the humanity of the Christ as much as on His genuine lordship; He who now reigns is precisely He who lived, suffered, and died for the salvation of the world. Here, too, the Christian hope is also involved, for He who is coming again is not a great unknown, but this Jesus Himself. Even in the most "spiritual" visions of Revelation it is this same Jesus of Nazareth with whom we are confronted. "The testimony of Jesus is the spirit of prophecy" (Rev. 19:10). The principal objective of the N.T., culminating in the Johannine writings (Gospel, Epistles, Revelation), is to direct the attention and faith of the Church to the historic person and work of Jesus, the author and perfecter of the faith (Heb. 12:2).

1. *Jesus—Servant of God.* The expression *Servant of God* is applied to Jesus in only one text of the synoptic Gospels (Matt. 12:18), which is a quotation from Isa. 42:1-4, and in four texts in the Acts (3:13,26; 4:27,30). But these texts are so important and appear to be so ancient that it is of importance to analyse their content, and all the more so since they belong to a much more numerous group of allusions, in the N.T., to the mysterious figure of the *Servant of deutero-Isaiah.

The context of Matt. 12:18 plainly shows, in this text, in what respect Jesus approximates to the Servant of Isaiah 42; like him, He does not draw attention to Himself and He exercises His ministry in the strictest humility before God. After having healed many who were sick, Jesus "ordered them not to make him known" (v. 16). It is in order to explain this prohibition that the evangelist cites Isaiah 42. The texts in the Acts of the Apostles all occur in the addresses of Peter; this may possibly suggest that this apostle, who originally had been offended at the sufferings of Jesus (Matt. 16:22), was the first to understand and interpret them with the help of the Old Testament figure of the Servant of God. These texts in the Acts show, in fact, that Jesus is called servant (*a*) in the sense that He was and did precisely only that which God willed that He should be and do; His unique greatness consisted in being the Servant of God and in serving God only; (*b*) in the sense that the "service" of Jesus was to save, to "bless" (3:26) men; He was

in the service of God in order to serve men; (*c*) in the sense that He was glorified because of this service, but always by God; like His service, His glory is received only from God; (*d*) in the sense, finally, that this service met with the opposition of men, and particularly of the great ones of this world who were "in league" against Jesus (4:27). Thus this service was a painful service which led the Servant to the cross.

This last observation suggests that perhaps the figure of the Servant of deutero-Isaiah was for the first Christians and, before them, for Jesus Himself the key to their reflections on the significance of the Passion. In fact, the N.T. allusions, more or less veiled, to this Old Testament figure are very numerous (Mk. 8:31; 9:31; 10:33; 14:24; 26:28; Lk. 22:20; 1 Cor. 11:24, etc.). Now the fundamental note sounded by them is that the Servant suffers "for many": the Servant *represents* his people, he dies *for* them (in their place and for their sake). His service is thus a substitutionary service. This idea of substitutionary representation is not confined to the N.T. It is found throughout the O.T., where the king, the prophet, and the high priest "represent" the entire people before God: it is by their mediation and in their persons that God makes a *covenant with His people, and the idea of the covenant dominates the Gospel accounts of the eucharistic Last Supper of Jesus. On the other hand, what is new in the N.T. is the union, in the same historic figure of Jesus, of the supreme Messianic dignity (cf. Son of Man) and the absolute humility of the suffering Servant.

Subsequent Christian reflection has not made wide use of the figure of the Servant of God. If the idea of substitutionary suffering is familiar to the apostle Paul, he does not express it by the image of the Servant (Rom. 4:25 alone refers explicitly to Isa. 53). It even seems that, later on, speaking of Jesus as the Servant of God was avoided through fear of doing injury to His dignity as the Son of God; hence the most ancient versions of the N.T. translate the Greek word "servant" unsatisfactorily by the term "child" (Latin *puer*), which is inappropriate as much in the context of deutero-Isaiah as in that of the N.T.

2. Jesus—Son of David.

With the expression Son of David as applied to Jesus other expressions which bring Jesus into association with King David may be linked, such as "the root and offspring of David" (Rev. 5:5; 22:16). In the account of the Annunciation it is said of the expected child that "the Lord God will give to him the throne of his father David" (Lk. 1:32). Jn. 7:42 declares that the Christ was to come "of the seed of David" (cf. also Rom. 1:3; 2 Tim. 2:8). The title Son of David itself appears in the Gospels in the first line of Matthew (1:1), and then on the lips of those who implore His help (Matt. 9:27; 15:22; 20:30f.; Mk. 10:47f.; Lk. 18:38f.). It is the expression with which the *multitude acclaims Jesus (Matt. 12:23; 21:9,15). In these last two texts Mark and Luke replace "Son of David" with terms more comprehensible to pagan-Christian readers (kingdom of David, the King who comes in the name of the Lord). Finally, Matt. 22:41–46 (Mk. 12:35–37; Lk. 20:41–44) is a difficult text which beyond doubt alludes to a dispute between Jesus and the Scribes regarding the term Son of David.

The idea that the Messiah would be a descendant of David only appeared at a late period in Jewish thought (Psalms of Solomon 17:21). None the less it has very definite Old Testament roots (cf. 2 Sam. 7:13–16; Amos 9:11; 1 Chr. 17:11ff.; 28:5ff.; 29:24ff.; 2 Chr. 9:8; 13:8). In the N.T. it presents Jesus as the king par excellence. It is important therefore to recall here the main lines of the kingly theology of the O.T. The king, in the O.T., with appreciable variations in different epochs and particular implications, (a) holds his authority from God alone (whether he has been imposed by force or chosen by his people is of little consequence). Yahweh is the King of kings, He exercises over them an absolute authority, not merely in principle, and His liberty is limited only in His own promises to this or that "house" which He has "elected". (b) It is through

this king that Yahweh makes His covenant with the whole people (2 Sam. 7; 23:1–7, etc.): the king is not an isolated "personality", he is king only for and with the people which he represents. (c) That is why the king remains always a man, at one with and answerable for the sins of his people. There is in Israel no process of deification of the king, as in Babylon and Egypt (even in Ps. 45 the "divinity" of the king rests on his divine adoption). (d) Finally, the king is at the same time the judge and the liberator of his people; it is by a king that, in the last days, God will re-establish His authority, His justice, His peace over the whole earth (*Kingdom of God). The Psalms contain numerous echoes of the importance of the king in ancient Israel, an importance always related to the royalty of Yahweh (Ps. 2:20; 45; 72; 101; 110; 132); in worship and in the festivals, when this double royalty was celebrated, the people of Israel expressed, perhaps better than anywhere else, their faithfulness to their God and to their King and their eschatological hope (Ps. 47; 93; 96; 97; 99).

These O.T. conceptions have contributed beyond doubt to the primitive Christian idea of Jesus as King. This idea, it should be noticed, is almost always opposed to that of the kings of the earth (Acts 7:10; Matt. 2:1; 3:9; Lk. 1:5; Matt. 14:9; etc.; cf. Ps. 2:2 and Matt. 10:18; Mk. 13:9; Lk. 21:12: the opposition of the kings of earth to the people of God). According to the Epistle to the Hebrews, it was Melchizedek, the mysterious king of Salem (7:1f.; cf. Gen. 14:18ff.), who was the "type" of Jesus Christ.

In view of the importance of the royal ideology in Jewish thought, it is surprising that it does not play a larger part in the N.T. Some have even gone so far as to think, on the basis of Mk. 12:35–37 and Jn. 7:42, that Jesus repudiated the Davidic dignity. These texts, however, do not require such an interpretation, but it is none the less the case that Jesus and the first Christian generations seem not to have accorded a very great importance to the traditional figure of the Son of David.

3. *Jesus—Son of God.* The term Son of God as applied to Jesus appears 31 times in the synoptic Gospels (11 times in Matthew), 42 times in the Epistles, 23 times in the fourth Gospel, 3 times in the Acts, and once in Revelation, under two forms of the same significance: Jesus—Son of God, and Jesus—the Son (=of God), the latter formulation being, apart from a few exceptions, a peculiarity of the Johannine texts and of the Epistle to the Hebrews. This indicates the importance which this Christological title had in the first Christian communities.

It should be observed that the N.T. often uses the word *son* in its ordinary sense; Jesus is the son of Mary, or of Joseph (Matt. 1:21,23,25 and parallels; 13:55; Lk. 3:23). The word appears also in numerous "family" parables (cf. especially Matt. 21:37; Lk. 20:13; Mk. 12:6 and Lk. 15:11ff.). In Matt. 8:12 "the sons of the kingdom" are the Israelites to whom the kingdom had been promised, whereas in Matt. 13:38 the same term designates the children of the kingdom and "the sons of the evil one" are represented by the tares (cf. again Matt. 17:25; Mk. 3:17; Lk. 10:6; 16:8).

Antiquity made considerable use of the expression "son of God" (or of the gods) in three principal senses: (*a*) of heroic and exceptional personages surpassing the common average of humanity (such as the heroes, demigods, kings, priests, etc., of Greek mythology); (*b*) of princes surrounding the king in the ancient oriental courts (Babylon); (*c*) of the elect forming as a community the "people" of God, and then of faithful examples of this people after it had lapsed into unfaithfulness (in the O.T.: Exod. 4:22ff., "Israel is my first-born son"; Hos. 2:1; Jer. 31:19; Deut. 14:1; Ps. 73:15; Wisdom 2:16ff.), and, finally, of the king of Israel as elect and enthroned by God (in the O.T., 2 Sam. 7:14; Ps. 89:27, and especially Ps. 2:7: ". . . The Lord said to me: You are my son, to-day I have begotten you . . ."). Whatever may have been said about it, there is no doubt that the N.T. term is dependent on this O.T. sense; but

primitive Christian reflection introduced into it significances all the more remarkable because Judaism was not acquainted with a Messianic usage even of the term Son of God (on the other hand, the Messianic interpretation of Psalm 2 was known to the Jews: Psalms of Solomon 17:23ff.; cf. Acts 4:25f.; 13:33; Heb. 1:5).

In the synoptic Gospels Jesus is not only *a* son of God, but *the* Son of God (Mk. 12:6f.; Matt. 11:27f.; Mk. 13:32, etc.). It is He who, in accordance with the ancient prophecy, has received the Spirit (Isa. 11:2; Ps. Sol. 17:37; 18:7; Enoch 49:3; Matt. 12:28f.; Lk. 3:18). Such is the significance, in particular, of the account of the *baptism of Jesus. Jesus is thus the one who represents in His person all the sons of the elect people and, at the same time, the unique son (well-beloved, elect) who surpasses them absolutely. It is He who is the son-heir, commissioned to negotiate in the name of His Father, so that in rejecting the son men reject the Father Himself (parable of the vinedressers, Matt. 21:33ff. and parallels). It is He who is the Son to whom by the resurrection all authority over the world has been entrusted (Pauline perspective, Rom. 1:1ff.). It is He whose filial intimacy with God was both unique and also creative of a new filial relationship of men to God (Pauline perspective, Gal. 4:6, and Johannine).

The fourth Gospel insists on this particular and absolutely unique character of the divine sonship of Jesus, the "only Son" (Jn. 1:14,18; 3:16,18; cf. also 1 Jn. 4:9; Heb. 11:7). This uniqueness expresses itself in a perfect identity between the thought of God and the ministry of Jesus, so that it is possible to speak of a practical and historical equality, for men, between the Father and the Son (Jn. 10:30; 5:20; 1:51; 12:45; 14:9). Moreover, this communion of will and action has always existed between the Father and the Son (Jn. 17:4–8; 14:7) and it will continue for ever (17:9). This historical equality of the Son with the Father, with its decisive consequences for mankind, expresses itself in particular in the prayer of the Son (Jn. 17:1ff.; 11:41; 14:16) which is characterized by a sovereign confidence; it expresses itself also in the obedience of the Son (5:30; 6:38), for the Johannine idea of filial obedience, so far from contradicting that of the divine sonship of Jesus, is its foundation and explanation. This equality of Father and Son expresses itself, finally, in the *love which unites Father and Son, the Father giving to His Son all that He possesses for men, and the Son possessing nothing for men other than what He receives from the Father. It is not probable that the idea of the begetting of the Son by the Father, which was soon to occupy a large place in Christian reflection, was indicated by that of the "only Son", but rather, indirectly, by a text like 1 Jn. 5:18. Judaism was acquainted with the idea of a Messiah begotten by God (Prov. 8:25 asserts this of Wisdom). But it is not there that one will find the centre of the evangelical affirmation, which is little concerned with the relations between the Father and the Son for their own sakes; for it, what is important above all is to affirm that, in history, Jesus the Son, and He alone, has caused us to know the Father perfectly.

4. *Jesus—Son of Man.* This Christological designation is by far the most important in the Gospels. A glance at a Greek concordance immediately discloses three important facts: (*a*) This expression belongs peculiarly to the Gospels; it appears elsewhere only four times, of which three are quotations from the O.T. (Heb. 2:6 = Ps. 8:5; Rev. 1:13; 14:14 = Dan. 7:13; Acts 7:56; in the Gospels: 14 times in Mark, 30 in Matthew, 25 in Luke, 12 in John, which gives the impressive total of 81 Gospel texts on the Son of Man). (*b*) This expression always designates Jesus, except in Mk. 3:28, where in the plural it designates men in general. (*c*) Finally, a still more remarkable fact, these words are encountered only on the lips of Jesus, speaking of Himself. The Greek expression is probably a translation of two Aramaic words (*bar 'anasha'*) which designates man, the human individual as distinct from the human mass (just as "the son of that which grows" = a tree, Gen. 49:22, and the son of a nobleman = a nobleman, Eccl. 10:7).

This expression could, in theory, be derived, in the N.T., from three principal literary and religious sources. The words "Son of Man" could mean, as is frequently the case in the O.T., simply man, the human individual considered especially in his limitations as a transitory creature in distinction from the omnipotence and eternity of God (cf. especially, in this sense, numerous passages in the Psalms: 4:3; 8:5; 12:2,9; 21:11; 36:8; 58:2; 62:10; 66:5; 80:18; 144:3; but also: Num. 23:19; Job 25:6; Prov. 8:31; Isa. 51:12; 56:2; Dan. 8:17). In this sense Jesus used this expression in order to emphasize His humanity, His limited, threatened, frail humanity. In the second place the expression could have come from the religious language of the surrounding territories (Syria, Iran, Babylonia, Asia Minor, etc.) where Man frequently designated the Saviour sent to humanity (when and where is scarcely apparent) in order to lead him back to his original destiny. In this sense the Gospels applied to Jesus a soteriological designation which was widely prevalent but rather vague, in order to present Him, without more preciseness, as the unique Saviour of humanity. In the third place, the expression Son of Man could be derived, by way of the Jewish apocalypses, from the mysterious figure of Dan. 7:13. In Jewish apocalyptic this figure was delineated with the features of the *heavenly Judge*, pre-existent, universal, cosmic, of the last days. The Son of Man had become one of the most common Messianic figures.

An examination of the Gospel texts leads one to prefer, almost without hesitation, this last interpretation. In describing Himself as the Son of Man Jesus chose the Messianic title which was least compromised with Jewish nationalism and warlike hopes. It was also connected with the reflection of little-known Palestinian circles who were awaiting the *Man of the last times*, the new Man or the new Adam (Rom. 5:12–21; 1 Cor. 15:22; Phil. 2:5–11), the inaugurator of the new humanity, as opposed to the first Adam through whom death entered into the world. According to the N.T., Jesus was thus indeed the Man *par excellence*, but not just any man. He was above all the Man-Judge of the last days, invested with judicial authority over all humanity (Matt. 25:31–46). But with reference to the surrounding ideas, the new Man of the N.T. was distinguished in that (*a*) his earthly work is accomplished in suffering and ignorance (the figure of the Man-Judge joining here with that of the Servant of Isaiah); (*b*) this work was not accomplished in the evening of time or in a perpetual and cosmic process, but in the historic person, very close to us, of Jesus of Nazareth. He who will return to judge the living and the dead is the same as He who has saved them by dying for them; He is thus the creator of a new humanity, nay even of a new world; and, finally, (*c*) this new Man does not come to snatch the individual from the clutches of time and matter, but to reveal to him his responsibility toward *other men*, particularly the weak and the suffering, in declaring His oneness with them (Matt. 25:31–46).

5. *Jesus—Lord*. The Greek word most frequently translated "Lord" in English appears more than five hundred times in the N.T.; it must have been one of the most widely used Christological appellations in the first Christian communities. As it was also a term current in the surrounding world, both in religious parlance and in a variety of profane usages, it is important that it should be given the particular significances demanded by the biblical context.

In the synoptic Gospels it is found that Mark and the most ancient texts do not apply this term to Jesus (Mk. 11:3 excepted) whereas Luke, on the contrary, frequently uses it in the sense of *rabbi-master* (5:8,17; 7:13; 9:54; 10:1; 13:8; 14:21,22,23; 17:37, etc.). In this sense the word Lord serves to indicate the profound respect, and at the same time the complete submission, of the disciple to his master. The Palestinian rabbis were surrounded with *disciples who showed them a veneration which at times reached a servility that Jesus often stigmatized.

In this first sense, Lord= *Master*, those texts may be adduced where the same word corresponds rather to the *head* (of a family, Lk. 1:43; Eph. 6:5; 1 Pet. 3:6, etc.), the *director* (of a business, Lk. 16:3,5, etc.), the *owner* (of a vineyard, of slaves, Matt. 13:27; Lk. 13:8; Matt. 9:38, etc.), the *superior* (of a soldier or of an official, Acts 25:26= the Roman emperor), a *governor* (Matt. 27:63= Pilate), any mysterious and impressive person (Acts 16:30= Paul and Silas), etc. These varied connotations of the word Lord remind us that in structure ancient society was essentially hierarchic: such a condition was not characterized by its proper qualities and possibilities unless by its relationships of submission or of liberty. It is only more important to notice that it is for Jesus alone that primitive Christian faith reserved absolute lordship.

But it is probably not in these current and profane connotations of the word Lord that the literary and theological source of the primitive Christian formula "Jesus-Lord" is to be found. The synoptic Gospels set us on the right track by reminding us that the Greek version of the O.T. (i.e. the Septuagint) translates the Hebrew '*Adonai* by the word Lord, and also especially the untranslatable group of letters which designates the *God of Israel, Yahweh (cf. Mk. 1:3= Isa. 40:3; 12:11= Ps. 118:22f.; 12:36= Ps. 110:1, etc.). Psalm 110 in particular played an important part in Christian reflection of the first days. In applying it to the person of Jesus it was held (*a*) that it is God who (by the resurrection) raised Jesus to the supreme Lordship (Phil. 2:5–11); (*b*) that this lordship could therefore be only understood as an authority perfectly putting into effect that of God, in such a way that in practice the two constitute no more than one (1 Cor. 12:3; 8:5–6); (*c*) that this lordship of Jesus is characterized by a victory already won over the false *authorities which govern the world, already won but not yet entirely manifested (Col. 2:6,10; 1 Pet. 3:22); (*d*) that the "people" of this lord (the *Church) are now gathered from amongst all the *nations, and that they can and should count on the certain victory of their king; it is thus not a matter of making Jesus king, but of combating and conquering those who have not yet recognized His effective authority.

Jesus therefore exercises the same authority as God. The "day of the Lord" (=of Yahweh) awaited by the Jews will thus be *His* day (Matt. 24:42; Acts 2:20; 1 Thess. 5:2; 2 Thess. 2:2): like the Oriental sovereigns of old, He will have His "parousia" (Latin *adventus*), His triumphal entry into the world transformed by His mercy. The Church, in its prayer, longs for this coming: *Marana tha*: Come, Lord! (1 Cor. 16:22). In the O.T. this lordship of Yahweh has two principal characteristics. In the first place, it is the government of *history*: contrary to every appearance, it is Yahweh who leads Israel toward the fulfilment of the destiny which He has planned for them, and who, to this end, stretches out His powerful hand over all the nations of the earth. On the other hand, this lordship is that of the *king-judge* who alone has the power of the remission of sin. These two characteristics are encountered again in the primitive Christian conception of the lordship of Jesus.

This lordship of Jesus retains an extremely concrete character for two principal reasons. Firstly, the lord ever remains He who has suffered and died for the salvation of men. The right to rule comes to Him from His total humiliation on the cross; He is thus lord because He was first the saviour of the world (Phil. 2:5–11; Rom. 5:6,8; 6:4,9; 1 Cor. 1:23f.). On the other hand, this lordship extends not only over history in general or sin in principle, but also over the history and the sin of each particular man; it governs the personal life as well as the celestial and terrestrial principalities (1 Cor. 7:39; 11:27; Col. 3:22), and the internal life of the Church, in its minutest details, as well as the general and universal design of salvation (1 Cor. 15:58;

4:17; 16:10); it is this lordship, finally, which is invoked in the miraculous and pneumatic outpouring of prayer (2 Cor. 3:17; 12:8). It is therefore at the same time the most secret and the most universal reality both in the life of peoples and in that of the believer (Phil. 3:8; Rom. 15:30; 1 Cor. 1:2); it remains a constant object of faith (and not of sight or of sentiment) and because of this governs the believer as no other earthly authority can.

6. *Jesus—Saviour*. The word saviour is applied to Jesus only rarely in the N.T. (Lk. 2:11; Jn. 4:42; Acts 5:31; 13:23; Phil. 3:20; 11 times in the deutero-Pauline Eph. and Pastorals and 7 times in the other Epistles). It is characteristic especially of the latest writings of the N.T. This fact ought to be weighed in view of the extreme frequency of this term in the surrounding world of the first century, and of the primary importance which it acquired in subsequent Christian reflection.

In ancient paganism the divine saviours were, in accordance with the times and the places, numerous and very diverse. Very different conceptions of the *peril* in which man is supposed to be placed lie at the root of these mythological speculations or narratives. To a peril conceived as accidental (war, social upheavals, storm, sickness, etc.) "specialist" saviour gods will correspond (Asclepius, Poseidon, Artemis, etc.), who stretch out a helping hand to man, if such is their intention at the time— that is to say that the salvation of threatened man hangs upon the unpredictable decision of the saviour gods. In a very different sense Hellenistic thought will recognize mansaviours, chiefly among warriors, generals, founders and benefactors of cities. The idea of salvation then becomes more communal and historical (such a city was "saved" on such a date by such a person-saviour). The Roman Empire certainly answered a universal need of "salvation", that is to say, before all, of peace and economic prosperity (Virgil's fourth Eclogue). Then the idea of salvation was turned inward and individualized again. At the beginning of the Christian era there were numerous religious or philosophical techniques designed to ensure *salvation by moral discipline and initiation into immortality. In pagan gnosticism, salvation was conceived as a deliverance of the soul imprisoned in the material body, a deliverance brought by a divine messenger whose heavenly and luminous principle "saved" the divine spark shut up within *man by summoning him to life. Salvation and the saviour were thus conceived in terms which were cosmological and mythical rather than personal and historical.

Against this background of the surrounding thought the Saviour of the N.T. is characterized (a) by a historical conception of the Saviour, born at a particular time in a given place and, above all, at the end of a prolonged expectation aroused by a *promise of God to His people (Lk. 2:11); (b) by a universalistic conception of the activity of the Saviour-Jesus; He does not come to save one particular people from oppression (like the Jewish go'el), nor certain souls prepared to meet Him, but the *world, all humanity conceived as totally and globally lost (Jn. 4:42; 1 Jn. 4:14; 1 Tim. 2:4, etc.); (c) by a very radical conception of the "peril" from which man needs to be saved; this peril is *sin and the corresponding *anger of God (Matt. 1:21; 1 Tim. 1:1; 2:3; 4:10, etc.); (d) by the part which apostolic *preaching and teaching plays in this work of salvation (all the texts of the Pastorals); (e) by the eschatological character of the salvation envisaged; the Saviour has accomplished His sufficient work, He now gathers His people by apostolic preaching, and He will soon return to judge and save men in order to bring back to God all humanity, indeed the whole reconciled universe (Phil. 3:20; Col. 1 where, otherwise, the actual word Saviour does not appear).

7. *Jesus—New Adam.* The O.T. figure of the first man was, from before the Christian era, the object of speculations concerning which numerous evidences remain. The rabbis used the expression "first Adam", but they were unacquainted with the idea of a Saviour as second Adam. Hellenistic Judaism, however, was familiar with the idea that the expected Saviour would be another Adam, or Adam himself. Thus to the idea of the ideal man (familiar, e.g., to Philo) that of the Saviour as the original *and* new Man was added.

The apostle Paul, who undoubtedly knew these speculations, profoundly remodelled and defined them (Rom. 5:12–21; 1 Cor. 15:22,45–49). It is a remarkable fact that he is not interested in the figure of Adam for its own sake (as were the rabbis who exalted the perfections of the original man), nor even for the sake of depicting the person of Jesus considered in itself (he does not make a simple comparison between Adam and Jesus for the purpose of exalting the latter). Paul does not make use of the figure of Adam (undoubtedly historical for him) in order to bring about an understanding of the *historical* work of Jesus: Jesus is compared with Adam so that thereby He may be better distinguished. The work of God in Jesus Christ *recalls* His work in Adam; it is not identical with it. History does not repeat itself; it moves onwards to its final fulfilment, which is the salvation of all humanity. In other words, Adam is a "type" of Christ.

In Rom. 5:12–21 Paul contrasts Christ with the first Adam in order to throw into relief the victory of grace over condemnation and death. The principal phrase is the "much more" of verse 15 (if death entered into humanity by the trespass of the first Adam, how much more shall grace reign by the one man Jesus Christ!). At the basis of this reflection one recognizes the idea, fundamental in all the Bible, that God never "treats" with humanity in general, but with this or that man (or people) who represents humanity before Him and draws it into the destiny (of death or of life) which He has opened for it. In 1 Cor. 15 the figure of Adam enables Paul, by way of contrast, to establish the certainty of the bodily (that is to say, personal) *resurrection of believers. The creation of humanity by God was performed at two different times: first "earthly" or "animal" humanity, represented by the first Adam, then "heavenly" or "spiritual" humanity, represented by the second Adam, Jesus Christ. These two creative acts by the same God are not the object of any judgment of value on the part of Paul. For him they are *historical facts* with incalculable consequences, since, by faith in Christ (cf. "those who belong to Christ", 1 Cor. 15:23), man can pass from proto-adamic humanity, doomed to death (v. 50), to deutero-adamic humanity summoned to the last resurrection. This transfer from one humanity to the other is not understood, in Paul, as a cosmic, magical, or impersonal process, but as the personal act of faith in response to the gospel of grace.

In the Gospels we find some echoes of similar reflections. The account of the temptation of Jesus (cf. Mk. 1:13) probably presents Him as the faithful Man of the last times in contrast to the unfaithfulness of the first man. The genealogy in Luke (3:38) explicitly connects Jesus with the first Adam, "the son of God" (cf. also the Mediator-Man in 1 Tim. 2:5). And above all the designation of Jesus as the Son of Man presents Him as the inaugurator, the "first-fruits", of a new humanity, indeed of a new creation, in which those who trust in Him already participate through faith and the eschatological gift of the *Spirit.

8. *Jesus—Mediator.* The term mediator appears only five times in the N.T. (Gal. 3:19; 1 Tim. 2:5; Heb. 8:6; 9:15; and 12:24); the corresponding verb, only once (Heb. 6:17). This infrequency recalls that of the O.T. where this word is not found at all (in Job 9:33 the Greek of the Septuagint "mediator" is a bad rendering of the corresponding Hebrew word). It was Hellenistic and Rabbinical Judaism which reserved a term (*Sarsur*) for expressing the idea of mediation, without otherwise giving it much importance.

But this poverty of the biblical vocabulary must not lead one to think that the idea of mediation between God and men is foreign to the Bible. On the contrary, it plays a very important rôle in Scripture and in several respects is distinct from the corresponding ideas in the surrounding religious sphere. There the idea of mediation is most often linked with *cosmological* representations: what is at the centre (of the universe, of the earth, or of man) has a power of communication with the celestial and divine world. In Philo, for example, the Logos, divine reason immanent to the world, irradiates the universe from its centre to its extremities. Moreover, the idea of mediation is founded on a *pantheistic* conception of divinity: God is diffused within the universe, in souls, in the human "spirit"; accordingly communication with the divine is ensured by certain practices or certain persons (priests, prophets, heroes, etc.) whose function is only to reveal and interpret the religious treasure common to all men. Finally, doctrines of mediation are frequently clothed with a very pronounced *mythical* character: the exploits are recounted of a certain "envoy" commissioned to lead souls back to God by delivering them from matter and from their bodies, but these accounts describe rather a permanent becoming; they lose their way in the night of temporality or in the depths of a perpetual "present".

In the O.T. God governs the entire universe which He has created and which He sustains by His omnipotence alone. He is not at the centre of things, He is "on high". His authority does not come to Him from the place which He occupies: on the contrary, certain places acquire a mediatorial significance solely by the fact that God has *chosen* them in order to manifest Himself there (for example, the tabernacle, the altar, Jerusalem, etc.; see *Names, Geographical). These places are thus at the centre of the world in a completely new sense. Moreover, the mediator in the O.T. is always a *historical* figure: a man among men, he represents humanity equally well as divinity, he is never a demigod or a superman (hero); he is a man authorized by God's grace alone (thus principally Moses, the prophets, the king, and, in a sense at once more profound and more enigmatic, the

*Servant of Yahweh in Isaiah). Finally, the mediator is charged with a mission, a "work". He does not communicate God to men only by his religious or moral perfections. Whether prophet, king, or priest, he exercises a function, a *ministry: in particular, he *speaks* (or brings the word of God), he *suffers* "for" his people (cf. Moses in Deuteronomy, the Servant of Yahweh, Jeremiah, etc.) and he *prays* (that is to say, intercedes; it is in this prayer of intercession that the humanity of the mediator is best expressed, in it he is truly taking his place with men and "before God"). These three chief forms of his activity show clearly enough that the O.T. mediator is always such in the sense of a communication of the *will* or of the decree of God (and not of an impersonal divine essence); and, moreover, in the sense of a "representation" of the people before God and not in the sense of an operation (magical or ritualistic) of the people upon God (this is so even and especially in the case of intercession).

All these general characteristics are found in the primitive Christian idea of Christ-Mediator. It can be said, for the sake of schematization, that the synoptic Gospels present Jesus particularly as the mediator prophet (He announces the Kingdom, proclaims the new law of God, performs the signs which were to be precursors of the Kingdom, pardons sins with the very authority of God, and prosecutes His work "for" His people, Mk. 10:45, with the humility and obedience which lead Him to the cross); the Pauline Epistles and, from another point of view, the Epistle to the Hebrews, present Him as the mediator priest (Jesus, the last Man, suffers "for" sins and endures the divine curse "for" us); and the fourth Gospel presents Him as the mediator intercessor (He prays for those whom God "has given Him", He feeds them, guides them, gives Himself to them and for them, both in His historic ministry and in His permanent activity in the Church, these two perspectives being indissolubly linked in the fourth Gospel).

All this wealth of doctrine, more or less elaborated, is implicitly expressed in 1 Tim.

2:5. This text insists on the humanity of the Mediator ("the man, Christ Jesus") in order to establish the universal character of the grace offered to "men" by God (the mediator "a ransom for all"). Gal. 3:19 is an echo of Jewish speculations about Moses as the mediator of the law, with the object of depreciating this law. The texts in the Epistle to the Hebrews (see above) are especially significant because of the association of the two ideas of mediation and of *covenant. They confirm our two previous observations: it is God who takes and keeps the initiative in mediation (the mediator is *only* an "envoy"), but, also, the mediator truly has the historic and concrete authority to lead men back to God (he is the only mediator "authorized" by God alone).

9. *Jesus—Lamb of God.* The word lamb is applied to Jesus only four times in the N.T. (Jn. 1:29,36; Acts 8:32; 1 Pet. 1:19). In Jn. 21:15 and Lk. 10:3 the reference is to quite another matter, and besides, the Greek word is not the same. The same word as in Jn. 21:15 and Lk. 10:3 occurs again in numerous texts in Revelation (5:6,8,13; 6:1,16; 7:9,14,17, and in fifteen other texts). It is seen, then, that this term is especially associated with the Johannine writings.

The literary and theological source of this expression is found in the O.T. In this respect, two main references may be named. (*a*) Jesus can be the lamb of God in the sense of the paschal lamb of Exod. 12, sacrificed for the whole assembly of Israel. This paschal offering had three principal characteristics: firstly, it was in origin a rite instituted by God with the salvation of Israel in view; the blood of the lamb is a "token" (v. 13), and not the means, of this deliverance; the initiative of the Passover belongs to God alone. Secondly, this token was not only a memorial of the past (the exodus from Egypt), but a perpetual ordinance (vv. 14,17,24, etc.), a "feast", a "ceremony", in which and by which God renewed His covenant with Israel. Thirdly, this *feast, in which Israel always received anew the assurance that God was "sparing" His people once again (vv. 13,14,17, etc.)

was thus above all a *sacrifice of offering, of grace in action. It is in this sense that the apostle Paul (1 Cor. 5:7: "Christ our Passover has been sacrificed"), the Epistle to the Hebrews (11:28) and Revelation (texts as above) understand it.

(b) In Isa. 53:7 the Servant of God is compared to "a lamb that is led to the slaughter", and the text declares that God has "laid on him the iniquity of us all". As the figure of the Servant of God seems to have played an important part in the earliest Christian reflection, there is room for thinking that the doctrine of the substitutionary death of Jesus as the lamb of God was associated with it: a lamb "without blemish" (1 Pet. 1:19), as the paschal lamb had to be; a lamb silent and patient, as Jesus was during His Passion; a lamb smitten *for* mankind (Jn. 1:29,36; 1 Pet. 1:19f.), like the Servant of the book of Isaiah. It may also be suggested, although this has often been contested, that the idea of the lamb substituted by God for the people whom He wishes to save is not foreign to the Gospel accounts of the Last Supper of Jesus with His disciples.

10. *Jesus—High Priest.* Although the N.T. frequently connects with Jesus the idea of a sacrifice offered to God, the Epistle to the Hebrews alone sees in Him the "priest" or the "high priest" of the new covenant (Heb. 2:17; 3:1; 4:14ff.; 5:1,5; 6:20, etc.). In this there is a direct reference to the O.T. (cf. especially Lev. 16) with its general conception of the priesthood as a particular function of the high priest entering, once a year, on the great day of atonement, into the Holy of Holies of the *Temple. But it must not be thought that the Epistle to the Hebrews applies to Jesus only the characteristics and the function of the high priest of the old covenant. On the contrary, its aim is to show the *superiority* of the priesthood of Christ over the Levitical priesthood, this superiority residing not only in the fact that Jesus brought to perfection that which was only imperfect in the O.T., but also in the fact that it is a superiority that belongs to a new age of the history of

salvation and to a new purpose of God for the whole of mankind.

(a) As the priest of the old covenant "represented" the entire people of Israel before God, the Epistle to the Hebrews insists in the first place on the *humanity* of Jesus, a humanity in no way sinful (7:26), but obedient. The high priest Jesus was really able to save men because He was a man together with them, tempted with them (2:18; 4:15) in suffering and on the cross (5:7–10; 2:17). He is a priest as the submissive and obedient Son. The efficacy of His sacrifice is founded on His perfect humanity. (b) The priest of the old covenant began by sacrificing for himself (7:26–28). Jesus, "holy, blameless, unstained", offers sacrifice only for others. Thereby His sacrifice is clothed with a more certain efficacy. (c) Whereas the priest used to sacrifice every day, constantly repeating the purifying rite, Jesus has accomplished it *once for all* (7:27; 9:24–28; 10:10,12,14). His sacrifice thus has the character of that which is "eternal" ("of the order of Melchizedek"), ever sufficient before God for the consolation of believers. Therefore it cannot be repeated. He has opened a new age in the history of the relations between God and men, and He abides eternally (7:24). The present relevance of the sacrifice of Jesus is thus founded upon His eternity, and this eternity itself on the definitive character of the unique work of the cross. (d) Thereby Jesus has entered for ever into the presence of God; but, in contrast to the priest of the old covenant, He remains in this presence, clothed with the authority of the priest-king. His sacrifice therefore has had a double effect: He has been raised once for all to the priestly kingship and He keeps open an assured access for men into the presence of God (6:17–20; 9:23; 10:19).

The whole exposition of the Epistle to the Hebrews, which to-day can appear difficult, derives in reality from the power of its extreme *simplicity*. For the strengthening of faith its purpose is to emphasize just one thing: the perfect and eternal sufficiency of the unique sacrifice of Christ.

7*

11. *Jesus—Head of the Church*. In several places the Epistles to the Ephesians and to the Colossians apply the term *head* to Christ (Eph. 1:22f.; 4:15f.; 5:23f.; Col. 1:18; 2:10,19). It is not very probable that this figure of speech is a simple development of the image of the Church as the body of Christ which we encounter in the other Pauline Epistles (Rom. 12:4ff.; 1 Cor. 12:4ff.). It is equally erroneous to see in it a Christian borrowing of the Stoic idea of the world (or, for example, of the Roman Empire) as a collective personality: Christ being nothing without His body (the Church) and the Church being nothing without its head (Christ). The texts of Ephesians and Colossians carry a different connotation and lead one to think that their literary sources may rather be found in certain gnostic ideas concerning the rôle of the first man at the creation of the world, or, more simply, in the O.T., where the idea of *governing authority* is often conveyed by the term head (Judg. 10:18; 11:8,9,11; Ps. 18:44: "Thou didst deliver me from strife with the peoples; thou didst make me the head of the nations; people whom I had not known served me; . . . foreigners came cringing to me"; cf. also the curious text of Isa. 9:13ff. where the head exercises the governing authority over the people of God).

In Eph. 4:15f. and Col. 2:19 it is clearly the idea of the *head-authority* which is dominant (cf. the hierarchy of 1 Cor. 11:3). Christians are exhorted to grow in (literally, in the direction of) Christ. This *growth is not envisaged as an organic and impersonal process, but as a faithfulness to the evangelical "truth" and an "edification" in brotherly love. In Col. 2:19 the perspective is equally polemical: contrary to all sorts of spiritual "developments" taught by heretics, the text is a reminder that it is a matter of recognizing that a "master-head" has *already* been given to the Church, and that accordingly it is important and sufficient to remain faithful to Him by submission to apostolic truth, which is the only concrete and Christian manner of "holding fast to the Head".

In Col. 2:9,10; Eph. 1:22 and 4:15 this idea of Christ as head is applied no longer to the Church alone, but to the whole universe. Christ is there presented as the supreme head of every authority and of every power. These *authorities and powers are angels or demons regarded as presiding over the destiny of men, whose rôle was emphasized and worship enjoined by certain religious doctrines or practices (Col. 2:18f.). To them the apostle opposes the unique authority of Jesus Christ, an authority which extends not only over the Church, but over the whole universe. We should notice (*a*) that this cosmic rôle of Christ is the *result* of His rôle as Saviour and as Lord of the Church (Col. 1:20); the text does not explain the work of the cross by the cosmic authority of Christ, it does the contrary; (*b*) that the rôle of Christ at the *creation* of the world (a continuing creation since "in him all things hold together", Col. 1:17) is not introduced in order to stress the perfection of this universe nor to deny the existence of hostile celestial authorities, but, on the contrary, in order to stress the perfect sufficiency of the reconciling work of the cross; man cannot attain to Christ the creator except by way of the Christ of the cross (Col. 1:22); (*c*) that although Christ is head of the Church and of the universe, these two domains of His authority are never confused. The Church has not been called to identify itself with the *world in order to save it; it has been called to believe in it as saved and governed by Jesus Christ and to proclaim Him to it. In this present age of the history of salvation the unity of the Church and of the world under the authority of the same Lord can only be an object of faith; it is a reality, but it is not yet manifest. The universal "recapitulation" (Eph. 1:10) under the same authority, the ultimate goal of the purpose of God, can already be regarded as achieved by the cross and the resurrection of Christ, but it will only be fully manifested when "God shall be all in all" (1 Cor. 15:28).

P. BONNARD

N.B.   Jesus—Messiah—anointed—Christ, see *Anointing.

JEWS

1. *General remarks.* To imagine that in the time of Jesus Christ the majority of Jews lived in Judea would be to commit a serious error. A great number of them had their home in Galilee; these were judaized Israelites, more precisely, descendants of the tribes of Naphtali, Zebulun, and Asher which, in distinction from the Samaritans, were associated with the worship of Jerusalem. But the great majority of the Jewish people was to be found scattered outside of Palestine: these were the diaspora. It is difficult to estimate their number, but it is known to have been very considerable (some 6 to 7 millions in the Roman Empire, of which a million were in Egypt alone and 50,000 in Rome under Tiberius out of a population of 800,000 inhabitants). At all events, both pagan and Jewish authors agree with each other in affirming that the empire was "full of Jews". And, of course, to these must be added those who lived outside the Empire, notably in Babylon where rabbinical studies were particularly flourishing. In Palestine itself their number necessarily became less following upon the wars of A.D. 70 and 130; but this does not seem to have been the case elsewhere.

2. *The Jews of the Diaspora.* It goes without saying that the Jews of the diaspora were able to participate in the worship of the *Temple only to a small degree. Apart from a group of Egyptian Jews who had their own temple at Elephantiné, their religion revolved round the worship of the synagogue and certain rites which were independent of the worship properly speaking, such as circumcision, alimentary precepts, and the observance of the *sabbath. In the N.T. the Jews of the diaspora are habitually called "Hellenists" (Acts 6:1; 9:29; 11:20), because for the most part they used to speak Greek, either as their only language (like Philo) or together with Aramaic (like the apostle Paul). Similarly, when the fourth Gospel speaks of the "diaspora of the Greeks" or simply of the "Greeks" (7:35–36) the reference is to Jews who spoke Greek.

It goes without saying that the extent of the diaspora is only to a small degree explained by the deportations carried out by the Assyrians (722), the Babylonians (597 and 587), and the Persians (c. 350), whose number should not be exaggerated and which in any case were never responsible for carrying Jews off to any places other than Babylon, Media, and "Hyrcania". The second chapter of the book of Acts gives the following as the countries of the Jews who had come to Jerusalem: Parthia, Media, Elam, Mesopotamia, the different regions of Asia Minor, Egypt, Cyrenaica, Rome, Crete, and Arabia. But there were also large numbers of them in the land of the Philistines, in Phoenicia, in Syria, in Greece, in the island of Cyprus, and at Pompeii. In the second century of our era they are reported with equal definiteness to have been in Carthage and "Numidia" (that is to say, in Tunisia and Algeria), in Mauretania (Morocco), in Spain, and in Gaul. Evidently their social position varied a great deal. Most of them seem to have been merchants, and amongst them people in very comfortable circumstances were found, even in the lands to which they had been deported (see the story of Tobit).

From the theological and literary point of view, it was the Jews of Babylon and especially of Alexandria who distinguished themselves. It was in the latter city that the most important of the Greek translations of the Hebrew Bible were produced (not only for missionary usage among the Gentiles, but also for those Jews who could no longer speak Hebrew), and, again, it was in this cosmopolitan city that Philo published his celebrated works which together represent a remarkable synthesis of Greek philosophy, Oriental theosophy, and Jewish belief.

The situation of the Jews in the Roman Empire was privileged. They were excused from the imperial worship, except for a daily sacrifice on behalf of the emperor offered (to God, of course) in the Temple. As far as military service was concerned, in practice, if not in theory, they were exempt. They enjoyed, besides, the right (expressly confirmed by the emperor) of judging their affairs by their own tribunals, except of course in the case of offences and crimes committed against Gentiles. The Jewish war in Palestine (66 to 70) had repercussions in the form of persecutions in Egypt and in Damascus, and perhaps elsewhere, which were provoked by the populace rather than by the Roman authorities. But they were only short-lived. Likewise, the edict of the emperor Claudius expelling the Jews from Rome (Acts 18:2) was only of local and transitory significance. Everywhere the Jews used to make "proselytes", that is to say, converts (cf. Matt. 23:15; Acts 2:10; 6:5; 13:43). There were, as well, important groups of those who "feared God", that is to say, of sympathizers, excused from the observance of the law, like the Gentile Christians later on, who were in part recruited from their number (cf. Acts *passim*, especially chapters 10, 13, 16, 18).

3. Palestinian Judaism. (a) The Pharisees.

In Palestine, and at Jerusalem in particular, the Pharisees were distinguished for their religious zeal. Their name connotes "separatists", a designation which fitted them very well in view of the fact that they were at pains to separate themselves not only from the Gentiles, whom they regarded as altogether unclean, but also from those of their co-religionists whom they considered to be insufficiently zealous. They observed the laws of Moses with the greatest preciseness and in addition the regulations added by tradition, that is to say, by the rabbis, who were for the most part attached to their party (cf. Mk. 7:3 and parallels, and numerous passages where reference is made to the Pharisees in conjunction with the "doctors", *vulgo*: scribes). In the Mishnah (Sanhed. Babyl. 10:3) it is even presupposed that the injunctions of the doctors ought to be observed more literally than the law itself. Thus it was that the Pharisees became the creators of Jewish law in both sacred and profane spheres. Similarly, their influence on the worship of the synagogue, which, as is well known, was an entirely lay worship (without priests), was decisive. After the destruction of the Temple and of the priestly party, pharisaic rabbinism continued as the sole dictator of religion.

We know from elsewhere (e.g. from Acts 23:6f.) that they taught the *resurrection at the end of the world (one of the few points on which they were in agreement with the teaching of Jesus), as well as the existence of angels (*ibid.*), and that after the resurrection men would be *rewarded or punished in the hereafter, though not without the possibility of appealing to the treasury of merits accumulated by the patriarchs. Moreover, they encouraged Messianic hopes and showed an extremely nationalistic and anti-Roman front, but, in view of their expectation of liberation resulting above all from a divine intervention, they did not all associate themselves with the party of the "resisters" (zealots).

The conflicts between the Pharisees and Jesus were frequent. They could not pardon His violation of the laws governing *sabbath observance, nor His disregard of the ritual prescriptions (Mk. 2:16,23f.; 3:1f. and parallels; 7:15f. and parallels, etc.) nor His claim to forgive sins (Mk. 2:6f. and parallels), nor the fact that He was more powerful than they in the expulsion of demons (Mk. 3:22f. and parallels). Jesus, for His part, frequently reproached them because of their pettiness, hypocrisy, and vanity (cf. especially Matt. 5:20; 6:1–6,16–18; 23:1–36), as well as for their failure to arrange the commandments in a sane order, in which love of God and of one's neighbour should have represented the highest point.

None the less, the N.T. also provides examples of Pharisees who were sincere and sympathetic, such as Nicodemus (Jn. 3:1ff.; 7:50–51; 19:39), or Gamaliel, who (according to Acts 5:34–38) advised tolerance toward the apostles (cf. also the doctor of the law depicted in Mk. 12:32–34).

(b) The Sadducees. The conflicts of Jesus with the Sadducees were less numerous but more dramatic. The word Sadducees means descendants of the priest Zadok (1 Kings 2:35; 1 Chr. 29:22), who, according to

Ezekiel (40:46; 43:19; 44:15–16; 48:11), alone had the right of officiating in the Temple. They were the party of the priests, more exactly of the superior sacerdotal caste, as well as of the aristocrats who supported them. In politics their practice was that of collaboration with the ruling power, which in turn protected them. In the Sanhedrin they were in the majority. In ethics they refused to recognize the rabbinical prescriptions added to the law—this was their only point of contact with Christianity. Further, they denied the resurrection of the dead, not so much because of sympathy with Greek philosophy as because of their conservative spirit, seeing that this doctrine was of comparatively recent origin. Jesus does not seem to have argued much with them (cf. however Mk. 12:18f.; Matt. 21:23f. and parallels), without doubt because He considered them unimportant in religious matters. Yet He warned His disciples not only against "the leaven" of the Pharisees, but also against that of the Sadducees (Matt. 16:6). It is notable that in the parable of the Good Samaritan He draws attention to the attitude of the priest and the Levite as a very bad example (Lk. 10:31–32). The Sadducees, for their part, became His mortal enemies after the expulsion of the merchants from the Temple, an action by which He interfered directly in their sphere (Jn. 2:19; cf. 4:21; Matt. 26:61; 27:40).

As for the accusation brought by them against Jesus that He wished to be king of the Jews, it was, of course, in the political sense not only false but also most unscrupulous and designed to bring about His condemnation at the hands of the Roman authorities. It is not impossible, however, that certain of their number had really feared the breaking out of a new revolutionary movement of the order of those mentioned in Acts 5:36–37 (cf. Jn.11:47–50).

After the death of Jesus the Sadducees as a group continued in their hostile attitude to the preaching of the Gospel and attempted to stifle it (Acts 3–5).

(c) *Baptists, Essenes, Nazarenes.* Here we find ourselves in a region about which

sufficient is not yet known. It is, however, indispensable to point out that when the N.T. speaks of "John the Baptist" the purpose is to draw attention to the fact that he belonged to a sect of baptists (just as, e.g., the name "Simon the Zealot" indicated that that apostle was connected with the movement of the zealots). We know but little of these pre-Christian baptist sects (apart from the Essenes), except that they practised asceticism and ritual ablutions. We are somewhat better informed concerning the Essenes, who for the most part lived in the region of the Dead Sea in what were in fact monasteries.

If John, who actually preached in this region, was in sympathy with them, he must have separated himself from them by a considerable innovation: he made of *baptism a unique act, with a new moral and eschatological significance. The Gospel tradition, despite the sayings reported in the fourth Gospel (1:29 and 34), shows the Baptist as being rather hesitant toward Jesus: cf. particularly Lk. 7:18–35. In any case, his disciples felt themselves to be in open opposition to those of our Lord (Mk. 2:18; Matt. 9:14; Lk. 5:33), especially because of His rejection of asceticism. In fact, the movement claiming to follow the Baptist carried out a mission independently of Christianity: see the remarks on the Egyptian Apollos, Acts 18:25, and on the disciples of John in Asia Minor, Acts 19:1–7. In our days there are still descendants of these baptists to be found in Iraq who venerate John as the Saviour and who are violently hostile to Christianity, as also to Judaism: these are the Mandeans. Yet it is a curious fact that they call themselves Nazarenes, a term which at times was assigned to Jesus and His disciples (cf. the Greek text of Matt. 2:23; 26:71; Jn. 18:5,7; 19:19; Acts 2:22; 3:6; 4:10; 6:14; 22:8; 24:5; 26:9, and also, according to some ancient manuscripts, Mk. 10:47; Lk. 18:37; 24:19; Acts 9:5), a name which could hardly be derived from that of the town of Nazareth (despite Matt. 2:23). If this term used in primitive times to designate a baptist sect, and if, as the first chapter of the fourth Gospel suggests, Jesus was originally a disciple of John before commencing His ministry, this coincidence could be explained.

As for the *Essenes*, they are nowhere mentioned in the N.T. But it is proper to observe that in several respects their moral teaching anticipated that of Christianity, particularly in the emphasis which they placed on charity. As for their theology, we know that they were especially interested in the doctrine of angels and in eschatology. From the political point of view, they passed, after having been conscientious objectors, in large measure into the ranks of the "zealots" and even of the "assassins" (terrorists). As for the sacrificial cult, it is known that they took no part in it.

(d) The "poor in Israel". Here we are concerned not so much with a clearly defined sect as with groups of pious individuals who—somewhat like the pietists of modern times—endeavoured to live humbly and to practise a religion of the heart. We find echoes of their piety in numerous psalms, where they describe themselves as "the poor" who are persecuted by the "powerful", without ever losing their confidence in God (cf. in particular Ps. 10; 22; 69; 73; 94; 146), and also in the pseudepigraphic writing called the "Testament of the Twelve Patriarchs", especially in the "Testament of Issachar", and it is of interest to observe that this writing originated in Galilee where, at that period, the Pharisees were less influential than in Judea. On the other hand, we know how Jesus valued the sincere attitude of the "poor in spirit", of the "blessed" who endeavoured to be "peace-makers", "merciful", and "pure in heart" (cf. Matt. 5:3–10 and 11:5; the good news is preached to the "poor"). It is not impossible that the authors of the books of Enoch were associated with these "poor", as well as with the Essenes.

4. *The Samaritans*. To achieve a correct understanding as to who the Samaritans were it is necessary to set aside altogether the calumnies showered on them by the Jews, who detested them. Actually, they were for the most part Israelites descended from the tribes of the northern kingdom, in particular Manasseh and Ephraim. As for the Gentiles introduced into Samaria by the Assyrians at the end of the eighth century, they had long since been assimilated into the indigenous population, and, according to reliable information available to us, not the least trace of polytheism or syncretism was found among the Samaritans in the days of Jesus. Although they had been politically linked to Judea since the time of the Maccabees, what distinguished them from the Jews was that they had retained their altar on Mount Gerizim near Shechem (cf. Jn. 4); the Samaritan temple, however, properly so called, had been destroyed by John Hyrcanus in 127 B.C. and it seems never to have been rebuilt. Their priests claimed to have descended from Levi. The second mark that distinguished them from the Jews was that they acknowledged the Pentateuch alone as being canonical. Thus they rejected the second part of the Jewish Bible, the "Prophets", and much more the "hagiographers". The Pentateuch had been translated by them into their own dialect and written in special characters distinct from those of the Hebrew alphabet. All in all, therefore, they were more conservative than the Jews. Nevertheless, they also cherished Messianic hopes, and it is possible that the belief in a Messiah coming from the tribe of Ephraim, attested by the Talmud, was Samaritan in origin.

The records do not agree concerning their political attitude during the Jewish war against the Romans (66 to 70). It seems that they were allied in part to the Jews and in part to the Romans. Their worship was finally abolished by Hadrian, but they continued to observe all the other laws of Moses, including the feast of the Passover.

Jesus does not appear to have regarded them as Jews, for according to Matt. 10:5 He forbade His disciples to preach the Gospel in Samaria (a prohibition clearly annulled by the injunction of Matt. 28:19). It is all the more significant, then, that, in order to put the Jews to shame and to protest against their intolerance, He held up a Samaritan as an example, in the famous parable of Lk. 10:30–37. Nor should the fact be overlooked that, contrary to the usual custom of the Galileans who preferred the detour by Perea, Jesus did not hesitate to travel through Samaria on a number of occasions (cf. Lk. 9:52; 17:1ff. and especially Jn. 4: the meeting with the Samaritan woman). After Pentecost Philip the evangelist preached in Samaria with great success (Acts 8:5–8). Further, we are acquainted with the considerable part played by the Samaritans in the history of Christian gnosticism, particularly by Simon Magus (Acts 8:9f.). As for the non-Christian Samaritans, they decreased in number after A.D. 70. In our own day they number no more than about a thousand, resident in Nablus.

J. HÉRING

JOHN THE BAPTIST, *see* NAMES (PERSONAL), BAPTISM

JORDAN, *see* NAMES (GEOGRAPHICAL), BAPTISM

JOY

Like love, and in distinction from other gifts of the Spirit associated with our present condition, joy appears in the Bible as *the great mark of the world to come.* The Revelation is full of it when it celebrates the universal gathering together of creatures at the foot of the throne of the Lamb (cf. 19:7). Joy bursts forth from the immediate and supreme nearness of the Lord, from this communion of the reconciled creation, invited to take part in the marvellous works of God and to contemplate His glory (cf. Jude 24; 1 Pet. 4:13). To enter into the Kingdom is to enter into the joy of the Lord (Matt. 25:21,23). Moreover, as the cosmic and eschatological reality, joy is manifested even now: it is experienced in heaven whenever a sinner repents (Lk. 15:10), and on earth the Holy Spirit sows the preliminary signs of it. It is from now

onwards common to heaven and earth, to God and man: it is concerned with that inexpressible moment when the Lord and His unfaithful people are reunited (Isa. 62:5), when the Father and His wandering son are brought together again. Yet, in virtue even of our present condition, as long as salvation is still incomplete, it is joy unadorned, the pure and naked joy of expectation, of him who with empty hands anticipates the great encounter!

O.T.

The terms "to rejoice", "to leap for joy", seem to have a foreign origin. Gradually incorporated into the religious vocabulary of Israel, they designated transports of tumultuous and excited enthusiasm (long suspected by contemporary rigorists such as the Yahwist, the early prophets, and Ezekiel) which were in evidence during festivals, sacrifices, and enthronements—the feelings of exaltation of a people looking to their God or their king. Otherwise it is less a matter of the emotions or feelings than of a definite cultic rite: "The texts show the vocal, noisy, and enthusiastic character of this joy, a full-throated exaltation of Yahweh so noisy that it is sometimes heard outside the city (Neh. 12:43) and which constitutes the paroxysm of the hymns of praise: cf. 2 Chr. 29:30" (P. Humbert).

In its national and cultic character this joy is always taking on new accents. In Deuteronomy it will become a manifestation of family piety (Deut. 12:7 and 12); but especially in the Psalms this joy will find its truly religious and personal accents for expressing the overflowing adoration of joy of him who knows that he is in the presence of God (cf. Ps. 16:8,9), who has received His law (Ps. 119), His promises, His pardon (Ps. 51), His deliverances. Finally, Isaiah is bold enough to transpose this joy from the ritual plane to the eschatological plane (Isa. 9:1), and in the last chapters it expands into a cosmic rejoicing (49:13; 55:12, etc.). Thereafter, in later Judaism, joy is connected with the expectation of the last times.

N.T.

1. This accent predominates in *the Gospel*: the *Kingdom is at hand, the day has arrived (cf. Jn. 8:56): leap for joy!— Thus joy bursts forth each time that the nearness of the Kingdom is an immediate reality, at each of the culminating points of the life and ministry of Jesus: the account of His birth (and this assurance of an ultimate intervention of God in the Magnificat; cf. Lk. 1:46 and also Lk. 2:10 and 20); the witness of John the Baptist (the time of the Bridegroom, Jn. 3:29); the proclamation of the Gospel, at the heart of Luke's account, with the mission of the seventy, the rejoicing of Jesus (Lk. 10:17,20); the amazement of the crowds (Lk. 13:17); the salvation of those who were lost (Lk. 15); the conversion of sinners (Lk. 19:6); the account of Palm Sunday (the Messianic entry into the city; Matt. 21:1–11 and parallels); the last conversations of Jesus with His disciples, with the promise that they would see Him again after the resurrection; the gift of the Spirit and the parousia (Jn. 15:11; 16:20,24; 17:13, etc.); and, finally, the accounts of the Last Supper, and the reunion of the Risen One with the disciples heralding that of the Kingdom (Jn. 20:20; Lk. 24:41). All along a difference of accentuation will be noticed: in the fourth Gospel it is no longer the news of events, but it is Jesus Himself who communicates the fullness of joy. This joy has the depth of the communion which unites the Father to the Son, the Son to the disciples, and, through the Son, the disciples to each other.

2. An analogous joy is found in *Acts*, where the outpouring of the Spirit, the miracles performed in the name of Jesus Christ, preaching and the conversion of Gentiles, appear as preludes to the last day (cf. Acts 13:52; 8:8; 13:48; 15:3). It illuminates the hearts of the converted (the Ethiopian, 8:39; the Philippian gaoler, 16:34). In particular, this joy is evident in the eucharistic meal (see *Lord's Supper) inserted between the remembrance of Easter and the hope of the Messianic meal (Acts 2:46; cf. 16:34). (Cf. O. Cullmann, *Early Christian Worship*, S.C.M. Press.) It may be noted that here something of the primitive character of the cultic joy in Israel is found.

3. In *Paul's letters* one may attempt to group the principal aspects of apostolic joy:

(*a*) It is a gift of the Spirit (the second in the list of Gal. 5:22; cf. Rom. 14:17); it is the joy of the Lord because He is near (Phil. 4:4). In this double sense it becomes the object of *constant exhortation* on the part of the apostle: every believer partakes of it and is called upon to do so. As a gift of the Lord, it can be uninterrupted, and independent of circumstances (cf. 1 Thess. 5:16; 2 Cor. 13:11; Phil. 3:1, etc.).

(*b*) With the apostle it takes the form of an *exultation*, the exultation of him who knows that he is the object of God's marvellous grace. This outlook is opposed to the human glorying of him who seeks to gain merit before God (cf. Rom. 5:2,11; 1 Cor. 1:31; 2 Cor. 10–12; Gal. 6:14, etc.).

(*c*) It characterizes the *communion* of the members of the body of Christ: they are the sign to each other that God continues to work through His Church. All progress in the faith confirms this joy (cf. 1 Thess. 2:19 and 20; Phil. 2:2; 1:26; 4:1; 2 Cor. 1:14, etc.). Finally, the apostle rejoices even in his sufferings or in his martyrdom because in them others will find a source of God's grace (Col. 1:24; Phil. 2:17).

4. Here we touch the last characteristic of Christian joy, which is also the most paradoxical and is increasingly clearly affirmed in the N.T., namely, *joy in afflictions*, sufferings for Christ's sake, and martyrdom (cf. 2 Cor. 13:9; Jas. 1:2; 1 Pet. 1:8; 4:13; 2 Jn. 12; Heb. 10:34; 12:11; Acts 5:41; Matt. 5:12). Joy, yes, for to suffer for the sake of Jesus Christ is to share in His glory; joy, for every affliction hastens the pains of childbirth: the more pressing they become, the nearer approaches the hour of ultimate deliverance.

M. BOUTTIER

JUDGMENT

O.T.

1. In the O.T. the idea of judgment is understood from its association with the verb to judge, which for the Hebrews did not carry the juridical significance which we give it to-day. In the Bible to judge is inseparable from the concept of the *covenant. When two persons enter into a covenant they have rights and duties with respect to each other. They are *just* in so far as they observe the obligations imposed by the covenant. To judge is, above all, to act in such a way as to maintain the covenant. In the heroic epoch the Judges, such as Gideon, Samson, etc., were leaders who arose to deliver the people at critical hours in their history. Like all leaders, they administer justice, but they are judges because they deliver the people and restore them to a normal situation. The king also is a judge who, as such, administers justice and resolves the disputes which the people bring before him. Several times the kings of Judah are spoken of as administering justice (2 Sam. 15:4; 1 Kings 3), but their rôle is that of judging the people, that is to say, keeping each in his right place within the covenant, upholding the covenant by coming to the help of the weak and driving out the oppressor. The ideal and perfect king of Isa. 11 is described as administering this kind of justice (Isa. 11:3–5; cf. Isa. 61).

In view of the fact that the relationship between Yahweh and Israel is conceived under the form of a covenant, judgment for Israel means salvation, victory, deliverance, due to the intervention of Yahweh in virtue of His duties as the God of the covenant, together with their corollary, the punishment of those who are outside the covenant, Israel's non-Jewish enemies. This is the meaning of the acts of justice or judgments of Yahweh which the Bible interprets as victories in Judg. 5:11 and Mic. 6:15. They are victories for Israel, defeats for their enemies. On every occasion when God acts on behalf of His people He judges them, that is to say, He helps them, leads them, and saves them. The history of Israel consists of a succession of these judgments: the judgment of the world by the flood (Gen. 6:5), the judgment upon Sodom (Gen. 18:20) and on Egypt (Exod. 7:4). It will be noticed that here judgment signifies punishment because Egypt was not Israel. The judgments of Yahweh on His people are always conceived as acquittals, since judgment is deliverance and victory (Deut. 32:36; Isa. 30:18; Jer. 30:11; Ps. 135:4), with its corollary of the punishments of non-Israelites (Ps. 7:7; 9:4; 110:6).

In the Psalms the allusions to God as judge and to His judgments are numerous. He is celebrated as the judge of all the earth, He who judges its ends, that is to say, its limits, He who judges the world with justice (1 Sam. 2:10; Ps. 9:9; 96:13; 82:8; cf. Gen. 18:25). It may be inferred that the celebration of God and His judgments occupied an important place in worship, as also did the expectation of the judgment of Yahweh. It is certain that at the great festivals of the Temple in Jerusalem Yahweh was celebrated as the judge *par excellence*. On these solemn occasions, called the Day of Yahweh, the rôle of the divine judge was played by the king, who represented God in the worship. His justice and His judgments used to be celebrated in the year which the religious festivals inaugurated. The object of these ceremonies was to renew the covenant and to strengthen justice, which was the condition of life and happiness. In addition, all sorts of promises were associated with them: promises of victory, of happiness, of unprecedented fertility, for the justice of God consists also in the gift of an extraordinary fertility which it was the aim of the worship to ensure (Ps. 72:3; Isa. 45:8; Joel 2:23). It is not surprising that from these hopes, which were supported and nourished by the worship, there was born the idea of an ultimate victory of the divine judge, of the triumph of His judgments, of a final judgment or last judgment. This development was encouraged also by the notion which the Israelites had of *time, conceived as a line with a beginning and an ending.

2. This hope of the judgment of God existed in Israel from a time prior to the eighth century. Prophets like Amos, Hosea, and Isaiah found themselves confronted with a popular hope of the divine judgment or Day of Yahweh, but it had a static character. Israel was hoping for a day of Yahweh which would mean light and salvation for them, but defeat and ruin for their enemies, simply because of the fact that they were Israel. Amos 5:18: ". . . the day of Yahweh will be darkness and not light" (implying: as you imagine); 5:14: "Seek good, and not evil, that you may live; and so the Lord, the God of hosts, will be with you, *as you have said*." Here "to live" means, as in many other passages, to be spared in the day of judgment. It is certain that this epoch was permeated with the feeling that the judgment was imminent, that at any moment God was about to intervene in history.

The prophets reformed the popular hope of judgment by introducing a moral factor into it once more. In their message the Day of Yahweh becomes a day of punishment for all the unjust, even for those who boast of belonging to the people of the covenant (Amos 5:18; Hos. 5:8; Isa. 2:12). The covenant demanded of its participants an equal fidelity, whereas in the past the whole history of Israel presented a long succession of breaches of faith and forsakings of the true God. Judgment will be administered either by the intervention of God Himself, who will take in His hands the reins of history, which leads to descriptions of theophanies or manifestations of God in person (Mic. 1:2), or by means of cosmic phenomena or military catastrophes, the enemy invading the land and destroying all the cities and all living creatures (Amos 9; Hos. 5; 10). The judgment, however, does not mean the total destruction of the people, but its purification. A "*remnant*" will survive, will "live". This will be the nucleus of the new *Israel (Amos 5:15; Isa. 6:13; 10:23). The Kingdom of God and its king are described by means of characteristics borrowed from the golden age of Israelite history, the epoch of David (Amos

9:11). It is difficult to define the manner in which the biblical authors pictured the judgment because they readily made use of images (cf. Hos. 5:14: "I will be as a lion to Ephraim") and because it is difficult to discern the reality hidden beneath the image. One must emphasize the fact, finally, that prior to the Exile (587 B.C.) judgment intervenes in the field of history, like the restoration which must follow it.

3. Whereas with the prophets of the 8th century judgment was limited to Israel and her immediate neighbours, that is to say, to the political horizon of that epoch, with their successors this horizon was expanded. This development is linked with that of the notion of *God as it gains in depth. When the power of God came to be recognized as extending over the whole world, judgment took on a cosmic scope. Zephaniah 1:2: "I will utterly sweep away everything from the face of the earth" (cf. also Zeph. 2:4). The motives for the intervention of God also undergo a characteristic alteration. If God judges the world, it is no longer because of the merits of Israel, which are insignificant, but because of His name, that is to say, His honour (Obad. 15).

This is particularly evident in Ezekiel where the affirmation "and you shall know that I am Yahweh" recurs many times over like a refrain which is sufficient to justify the judgment. This prophet shows us Yahweh judging all the neighbouring peoples of Israel (chap. 25), the kingdom of the dead where all those whom Yahweh has judged are found (32:18), the supreme assault of the pagan world (Gog and Magog, 38–39), which is the prelude to its final annihilation. In a scene which approaches the apocalyptic Joel describes the judgment or Day of Yahweh in the valley of Jehoshaphat, a name which means "Yahweh judges" (Joel 3:1). Zechariah causes us to see the final conflict of Yahweh against the nations and the rising of the new Jerusalem, which is enthroned above the conquered nations (Zech. 14). Daniel, finally, the latest book of the O.T., brings us into heaven where God, in the guise of an ancient, surrounded by judges, opens the books and proceeds with the judgment, after which the Son of Man (= the Messiah) appears and establishes his kingdom to which those who are written in the book of life belong, even the resurrected dead, while the rest inherit eternal damnation (Dan. 7:12). Whereas before the Exile judgment intervened in the field of history, in these last books, belonging to the most recent epoch, it inaugurates a new age of the world; it establishes new heavens and a new earth, which implies the idea of a dualism.

4. We know that between the O.T. and the N.T. there is, from the literary viewpoint, a very fruitful period of which the apocryphal writings and a section of the rabbinic literature afford evidence. In this literature the Messianic times, that is to say, the advent of the Messiah or King of the end of the ages who is coming to establish His kingdom, are introduced and preceded by a judgment reserved for the Jewish nation alone, but this judgment is followed by a universal judgment when all souls are assigned either to Paradise or to Gehenna. Gentiles are condemned to eternal fire, while Israel is saved because of its merits (cf. the book of Enoch, 10). Alongside the idea of this discriminative judgment occurring at the end of the ages, and which can be called final judgment, late Judaism recognized in it another idea according to which judgment is exercised each year at the time of the great festivals, such as the Passover and the New Year, for this reason called the "day of judgment".

However rich, contradictory, and at times foreign the biblical representations of judgment may be, they should not hide the fundamental idea of the O.T., namely, that judgment is a living reality. The life of Israel unfolds itself entirely within this perspective, which gives it its true significance and which at the same time throws into relief the absolute dependence of the creature when face to face with God who has created him and who judges him.

G. PIDOUX

N.T.

If the verb to judge sometimes signifies in the N.T. the activity of a tribunal (Jn. 18:31; Acts 23:3), and if it is also used to express the estimate which one person forms of another (Matt. 7:1–2; Acts 16:15; Rom. 2:1–3), it most frequently has God or Christ as its subject. Judgment is, in fact, one of the aspects of the Kingdom of God.

1. Nowhere does the N.T. state why it is necessary to take the judgment of God into account. It confines itself to declaring it, and this declaration is given as a word of God (cf. Lk. 3:2 and 7; Acts 17:30–31). The expectation of judgment flows, on the one hand, from faith in the holiness of God, Lord of heaven and earth, and, on the other, from the recognition of the world's sin. It could indeed be imagined that God would not intervene and would leave the world to corrupt itself increasingly until it had brought about its own destruction. If the N.T. declares that a judgment is on its way, it is because God, in His mercy, has had pity on men who are perishing, and has wished to offer them, with His pardon, the possibility of being saved. The salvation of those who believe is possible, however, only by the elimination from the Kingdom of God of those who refuse to be reconciled with God (Matt. 13:24–30,36–43). Thus in the N.T., as in the O.T., judgment is an aspect of the deliverance of believers (cf. Lk. 18:1–8; Rom. 12:19; 2 Thess. 1:5–10; Rev. 6:10) and it proceeds, ultimately, from the mercy of God. It is for this reason also that judgment, which at first sight seems to be imminent to all who are on the alert for its coming—to John the Baptist (Matt. 3:10,12), to Jesus (Matt. 24:34), etc.—is delayed, for God is long-suffering in order that all men may be able to come to repentance (Lk. 13:6–9; Rom. 2:4; 2 Pet. 2:9). Moreover, God causes His judgment to be declared throughout all the earth before executing it (Matt. 24:14).

2. Thus the notion of judgment, common to the whole of Scripture, culminates

according to the writers of the N.T. in that of *the last judgment*. We continue, therefore, in line with the religious conceptions of Judaism; but the first Christians had a further and decisive reason for thinking that they were living in the world's last times: they knew that the Christ, the Messiah, had come, introducing the *time of the fulfilment of the divine promises and of the renewal of creation. It was not that the notion of present judgment in history had been lost: indeed, it continued very much alive (Lk. 13:1–5; Acts 5:1–10; 12:23; 13:11; Rom. 1:18–32; 1 Cor. 11:27–32; Rev. 2:5,16,22–23; 3:3, etc.). But attention was concentrated in particular on the conclusive judgment which would ensure the triumph of the divine will through the overthrow of every resistance which it encounters, both among the spiritual powers which dominate the world (1 Cor. 6:2–3; 15:26; Jn. 16:11; Lk. 10:18; Rom. 16:20; 2 Thess. 2:3–10; Rev. 12:7–9; 20:7–15) and also among men (Matt. 25:31–46; Rom. 2, etc.). This judgment will affect all men, because all are responsible before their Creator according to the grace which has been granted them (Matt. 11:20–24; Lk. 12:17ff.; Rom. 2:12–16). Christians will also pass through judgment (1 Cor. 5:10). This present world will itself be convulsed (Matt. 24:29) and destroyed (Matt. 24:35; 2 Pet. 3:7–12); this will be the "end of the world" (Matt. 13:29; 24:3). A new world will replace the present one (2 Pet. 3:13; Rev. 21:1).

The cosmic character of the judgment is connected with the fact that biblical thought, unlike modern thought, does not dissociate the moral plane from the physical and natural plane. The condemnation of man by God is realized not only in his conscience, but in the entirety of his existence: in his heart which is darkened (Rom. 1:21–22), in his body which succumbs to sickness and to death (1 Cor. 11:30; Rom. 6:23), and also in his setting (nature, the universe, see Rom. 8:19–23). This cosmic aspect of judgment remains secondary, however. It is, in fine, nothing more than an extension of the judgment of humanity, which is always of primary significance.

3. *Final judgment belongs naturally to God* (Matt. 18:35; Rom. 14:10; 1 Pet. 1:17, etc.). But God entrusts its administration to Christ at His appearance in glory (Matt. 3:11–12; 7:22–23; 13:41–43; 16:17; 25:31–46; Jn. 5:22; Rom. 2:16, etc.). The "day of judgment" (Matt. 10:15; 12:36; 2 Pet. 2:9; 1 Jn. 4:17, etc.) and the "day of the Lord" (1 Cor. 1:8; 1 Thess. 5:2; Heb. 10:25, etc.) are one and the same. The angels (Mk. 8:38; 2 Thess. 1:7), the disciples of Jesus themselves (Lk. 22:30), and indeed the whole Church (1 Cor. 6:2,3) will collaborate with Christ in judgment (cf. also Matt. 16:19; 18:18; Jn. 20:23). The unity of the Father and the Son, on the one hand, and the communion of believers with their Lord, on the other, explain these concepts which at first sight seem surprising.

4. If Jesus is indeed, in the midst of the men of His time, the divine judge who is to come, the judge of the last day, the attitude which they take up towards Him not only has immediate consequences in this world, but already decides the judgment which will be pronounced upon them on the threshold of eternity (Matt. 7:24–27; Lk. 9:26; Jn. 12:48). It is therefore not surprising to read in the Gospel of John that Christ has exercised, already in the course of His historic existence, a judgment on those who came into contact with Him, although He had not come to judge the world, but to save it. In His presence, in fact, the destinies of men are already being settled for the world to come: some hear His word and receive eternal life; others refuse to believe and are already judged, their unbelief being the sign of dispositions which will one day bring about their irremediable condemnation (Jn. 3:17–21; cf. also 5:22–27; 8:15; 9:39). Similarly, when Christ accepts death and hears the voice of God saying: "I have glorified it, and I will glorify it again", He is able to declare: "Now is the judgment of this world, now shall the ruler of this world be cast

out" (Jn. 12:31). God, in fact, has already brought His judgment upon the two parties in conflict: Jesus and the world subjected to Satan, when He promises glory to Him who is to die as the victim of the world's hatred. Yet the interest which the fourth Gospel displays in the present reality of judgment in no way detracts from its expectation of final judgment, when that which is now partially apparent will become fully manifested (cf. Jn. 5:28–29, etc.).

5. With the exception of several passages in the Johannine writings where to judge means to condemn, *judgment has a double objective*. The first is expressed by terms such as *joy in the presence of the Master, the *blessing of the Father, entrance into the Kingdom of God, *life eternal, *glory, honour, immortality, *peace, *rest, etc.; the second by concepts such as the outer darkness where there will be weeping and gnashing of teeth, everlasting fire, separation from God, wrath and indignation, distress and anguish, eternal perdition, affliction, etc. (cf. Matt. 25; Rom. 2; 2 Thess.). The adjective eternal which is used with some of these terms does not indicate, as in our language, an infinite duration, but denotes that we are dealing with matters resulting from the final intervention of God, when He will establish the new world. If life in the Kingdom is without end and participates in the perpetuity of God, it does not follow that the suffering of the reprobate must be prolonged indefinitely. Moreover, every attempt to determine exactly what awaits men beyond judgment comes up against the undefined nature of a concept which was elaborated not to satisfy our curiosity, but to cause us to fear the God who offers us His pardon and eternal life in the fellowship of His Son. Thus the manner in which the N.T. makes use of the notion of judgment encourages us to indulge neither in speculation nor in fantasies concerning heaven and hell; it leads us rather to live this present hour in the faith and obedience to God of Jesus Christ.

6. *In accordance with what standard shall we be judged?* In accordance with the *law, which Jesus has not abolished (Matt. 5:17–20; Mk. 10:19), but of which He has deepened our understanding (Matt. 5) and emphasized what is essential (Matt. 22:37–40; cf. also Rom. 13:8–10): the commandments enjoining love of God and of one's neighbour. For all who have heard the word of Christ the criterion will be, in a word, their attachment to His person (Matt. 10:32–33). It is obvious that this attachment will not be acceptable to God unless it is genuine: unless it is accompanied by zealous, intelligent, and faithful service (Matt. 24:45–51; 25:14–46), and unless its substance is something more than words (Matt. 7:21–23). It is this which makes it possible for the apostle Paul to replace the norm of the law by that of the Spirit of Christ (Rom. 8:1–17; Gal. 5:13–25; 6:7–9). But, like Jesus (Matt. 16:27), he says that each one will be judged according to his *works (Rom. 2:6), or according to what he will have done, whether it be good or bad (2 Cor. 5:10). It does not seem necessary for us to understand by this that we shall be treated according to our works taken in isolation, but rather according to the testimony which they give to the depths of our character (Matt. 12:33–37; Rom. 13:8–10).

In this perspective, the greatest problem with which every man is confronted is that of his *justification at the divine tribunal. Of this the Pharisees were especially aware, and this preoccupation was the basis of their piety. The apostle Paul shows (Rom. 7) the distress and the despair into which the man falls who has only his own powers to rely upon for the resolution of this problem. Because man is fundamentally a sinner, his only hope is that God should show mercy towards him.

This is exactly what Jesus proclaimed: God remits man's debt, however great it may be (Matt. 18:21–35; Mk. 2:1–12; Lk. 7:36–50). "The Son of Man," he said, "has authority on earth to forgive sins" (Mk. 2:10). But it must be noted that this *forgiveness can be received only through faith in the Messiahship of Jesus, faith which does not fail to be accompanied also by renewal of life. If faith does not produce this effect, then the pardon at which it has grasped remains illusory: the day of judgment will reveal it (Matt. 6:14–15; 18:23–35). One cannot receive pardon, therefore, without repenting and being converted (Matt. 3:2,8; 4:17; 11:20–24; Lk. 13:1–9; Acts 2:38; 3:19). The pardon granted will likewise be imperilled if one does not persevere to the end in faith and obedience to Christ. Hence the necessity for watching, lest one should be surprised in evil-doing by the judgment, of which neither the day nor the hour is known (Matt. 24:43 to 25:13; Rom. 13:11–14; 1 Thess. 5:1–11; Rev. 3:3).

Although it may be expressed in different language, the apostle Paul knows no other solution to the problem of justification than that which is supplied by the grace of God. Sinners are "justified by his grace as a gift, through the redemption which is in Christ Jesus, whom God put forward as an expiation by his blood, to be received by faith" (Rom. 3:24–25). And the apostle opposes justification by faith, as alone valid, to justification by the works of the law, which the Jews sought after. Thus he bases his security in face of the judgment to come exclusively on the work of reconciliation which God has accomplished in Jesus Christ (Rom. 5:9–10; 8:31–39). This holds good for all Christians: whatever transgression they may commit (1 Cor. 3:15), into whatever sin they may fall (1 Cor. 5:5), in the eyes of the apostle their salvation is assured, provided that they continue in the faith. The apostle, moreover, speaks to believers of the impending judgment according to works which they will have to undergo (2 Cor. 5:10; Col. 3:25; 1 Thess. 4:6; 1 Cor. 9:27). The reason for this is that there is justification only through faith in Christ. Now this faith normally produces a renewal of life in the fellowship of the Risen Christ (Rom. 6). If therefore we do not live according to the Spirit, it is because we are not really in Christ, and are deceiving ourselves in believing that we have received the benefits of His death for our sins. A life inspired by love ought to manifest the reality of our justification by Jesus Christ. Thus the idea of a justification according to works does not contradict the doctrine of justification by faith. On the contrary, the latter implies the former. St. James gives expression to this in his own way, which contradicts the great affirmations of St. Paul in appearance only: "Man is justified by works and not by faith alone" (Jas. 2:14–26).

7. A few words should be said about a problem engendered by the expectation of the last judgment—the problem posed by *death when it comes to put an end to man's life before the judgment has intervened. The Jews had already been concerned about it and had solved it by belief in the resurrection of the dead for judgment (Dan. 12:2). The primitive Church retained this solution (Jn. 5:27–29; 1 Thess. 4:13–18; Rev. 20:11–15), although St. Paul spoke only of the resurrection of believers, as though death, the wages of sin, had a final significance for all those who die in separation from Christ. What, then, is the state of the dead between the time of their death and the coming of Christ for judgment and salvation? Frequently it is said that they sleep (Matt. 9:24; Jn. 11:11; 1 Cor. 11:30; 1 Thess. 4:13; 5:10), but nothing positive can be deduced from this expression, for it is a common euphemism when speaking of death. On the other hand, the parable of the rich man and Lazarus (Lk. 16:19–31) and also the declaration of Jesus to the malefactor dying on the cross (Lk. 23:43) are based on the idea that after death the wicked man is in a place of torment and the believer in peace (cf. also Lk. 16:9; Rev. 6:9; 7:9–17; 14:3). Thus a provisional judgment awaits every man at the hour of his death. St. Paul, indeed, declares that for him death will be gain (Phil. 1:21) because it will make it possible for him to "be with Christ" (Phil. 1:23), to "be at home with the Lord" (2 Cor. 5:8), that is to say, to enjoy a less uncertain relationship with Him than at present; faith must be replaced by sight (2 Cor. 5:7). It should be observed that the expectation of a provisional judgment

intervening immediately after death has the effect neither of eliminating nor of weakening that of the last judgment at the coming of Jesus Christ.

In conclusion, it may be pointed out that the notion of judgment, which plays so important a part in the N.T., testifies less to precisely determined and logically articulated insights than to the presence in the world of the holy and merciful God who reveals Himself in Jesus Christ. It is for this reason that the fact of judgment is so strongly affirmed, whereas its modes (time, manner, place) remain uncertain.

J. BURNIER

JUSTICE

1. The collection of documents bearing on legislation is found in the Pentateuch which was known to the Israelites as the *law, since it serves as a rule of life and at the same time contains the *revelation of God. According to tradition, Moses is the author of Hebrew legislation; it is apparently due to him that Hebrew law was formed and was able to preserve its characteristic features throughout the course of the history of the chosen people. It is true that many of the O.T. texts were edited long after the Exodus, especially in the period of the 7th to the 5th centuries, but it is beyond question that Moses played a decisive part in the formation of the Israelite law which left so deep an impression on the spirit of Israel.

Among the mass of legalistic documents, specialists distinguish various collections, the most ancient being: (a) a ritual Decalogue (Exod. 34:10-26), which may well be earlier than Moses; (b) the Decalogue proper (Exod. 20:2-17; Deut. 5:2-21) which some scholars think dates, in its original form, from the Mosaic period; (c) the Book of the Covenant (Exod. 20:22-23:19), a compilation of cultic regulations and moral precepts. Later compositions include: (d) Deuteronomy (especially Deut. 1-26) discovered in Jerusalem in 622 B.C. under Josiah (2 Kings 22) which, in the form of an exhortation addressed by Moses to his people, recalls the unmerited grace which

prompted God to choose Israel and the gratitude which the Israelites must show towards Yahweh by obeying His commandments; (e) the Holiness Code (Lev. 17-26) edited during the Exile, which stresses the holiness of God and the precautions which must be taken to avoid the profanation of His name; finally (f) the Priestly Code (fragments of which are to be found distributed more or less in all the books of the Pentateuch) which is interested in the great institutions of Judaism (*Sabbath, *Circumcision, etc.) and in the organization of worship at Jerusalem.

2. Hebrew legislation has been compared with the laws of the Assyrians, the Sumerians, the Hittites and especially with the famous Code of Hammurabi from the 18th century B.C. There are undeniable similarities between these various codes, but their divergences are more striking even than their resemblances. The biblical laws were inspired by a very distinctive spirit, one which had a lasting impact on every phase of the life of the chosen people. The outstanding features of Hebrew legislation are:

(a) Hebrew law is based solely on God, it is not the expression of the will of the people nor of the ruler; it is in no sense secular, but entirely theological (cf. §3).

(b) Hebrew law equates the service of Yahweh with the service of one's fellows. The duties which the Israelites owe to their God are not confined to the religious realm, they are equally concerned with moral and social life. As the Decalogue had already made clear, as the prophets unceasingly reminded the people, the worship of Yahweh entails a respect for the rights of others (cf. Exod. 20:2ff.; Amos 5:14ff.; Isa. 1:10ff.; Mic. 6:6ff., etc.).

(c) Israel rejects the class legislation which was in force at Babylon. Justice is the same for all. Biblical legislation is designed to help especially those who are in danger of being the victims of injustice, widows, orphans and foreigners (cf. Exod. 22:21ff.; Lev. 19:15,33f.; Deut. 24:14ff., etc.).

(d) Since, for the Israelites, *life is the supreme good, the life even of a slave is the object of special protection. Israelite law insists on the respect due to parents, regulates sexual relations, forbids prostitution which the Code of Hammurabi accepts, eliminates over-brutal penalties by seeking to soften the rigours of the *lex talionis* (cf. Exod. 22:10ff.; 21:7ff.,20,26ff.; Lev. 18:6ff.; 20:10ff.; Deut. 27:16ff., etc.). Such are some of the features of biblical legislation. While it is obvious that a judicial system valid for our own time cannot be elicited direct from Scripture, it is possible to gain from Israelite legislation useful pointers, guiding principles which enable us to accept or to challenge the merits of laws in force to-day.

3. In Scripture, then, law is inseparably linked with God; it is quite independent of any rational or mystical principle. Israel possesses not a natural law, but a law which it is God's province to establish, to safeguard and to restore. The Hebrew root from which the word law is derived expresses the idea of judgment and that of sovereignty: law is the domain of the supreme head, it springs from a supernatural source. Judgments are reserved for Yahweh and for those who enjoy direct contact with Him such as judges, kings or priests (cf. Judg. 3:10; 6:34; 2 Sam. 8:15; 1 Kings 3:9ff.,28; Isa. 11:1ff.; Jer. 23:5ff.; Ps. 72:2ff.; Deut. 1:16ff.; 17:8ff., etc.).

Apart from God there exists neither law nor justice (see *Righteous), but the God of the Bible never acts as a capricious despot; His judgments are never arbitrary. The basis of biblical law is a *covenant which unites Yahweh to Israel. The decrees of God are always in harmony with this contract, in the making of which it was God who, in the time of Moses, took the initiative, and to which He remains loyal despite the attitude of His partner. The Israelite laws are, therefore, never vague nor theoretical; they are concerned with a people set in its own specific situations, they embrace the whole existence of Israel and at the same time each individual member of the chosen people, they confront the descendants of the patriarchs at every moment and in every circumstance with the absolute requirements of God, they make known the authority of a God to whom one must yield obedience or perish (Deut. 30:15ff.).

The covenant is not only the basis but also the objective of biblical law, which is never abstract and never degenerates into a futile casuistry. The sole aim of Hebrew legislation is to maintain or to restore the validity of a contract which is constantly being threatened or actually broken by Israel's sin.

In short, it is Yahweh who guarantees the law; His judgments confirm the covenant, they demonstrate His faithfulness, they are acts of mercy; law as a whole bears the stamp of *grace, it is a gift made to the people of Israel in order that they may truly be witnesses of God's Kingdom and of His righteousness.

4. Whoever reads the Scriptures cannot help being struck by the multitude of judicial terms which he encounters in the Bible and the importance which is attached to them; the ideas of judgment, of covenant-relation, of witness, of promise, etc., play a leading part in the revelation. It seems, then, that if biblical law is fundamentally theological, theology in its turn is influenced by the conception of law, since theology is thought out in the categories of law. The Bible shows us the cosmic dimensions of the gigantic contest between God and the demoniac powers, in which the principal actors, along with *God and *Satan, are Christ, the people of *Israel and the *Church. Salvation is wrought in the setting of a law court, where the Creator manifests His will to reinstate the entire creation in its primitive order and to restore to every creature his special place, the "law" which from all eternity has belonged peculiarly to Him.

The O.T. ideas of law are not to be thought of as mere mental images, as an outworn symbolism or as a dead legalism; Scripture sets before us quite simply, by means of the various thought-forms which it uses, the true understanding of the relationship between God and humanity. Any notion of a fundamental unity between God and man is entirely foreign to the biblical revelation; salvation is in no sense a kind of fusion of the human with the divine. God is not an anonymous natural force which man might succeed in taking hold of for the purpose of making himself one with it. The Bible establishes a categorical distinction between God and man. The judicial language which the Bible uses rules out any idea of an equivocal union inspired by a dubious sentimentality; it sets the Creator and His creature in their rightful places over against each other, like the judge and the accused in a court of law. *Man is not and never will be divine, but he has been made in the *image of God, that is to say, he is God's creation made to answer God as his vis-à-vis. The Scripture makes clear to him that there is One who stands before him, cross-examining him, challenging him with the words "I am . . . thou must"; he discovers that he must make reply to this partner who intervenes in his life, who unsettles his existence, addresses him in a manner which is always concrete, vital, personal. Man only truly knows God through the medium of His *Word who initiates the dialogue with him, who sets in motion the trial of the world and who, in order to give a verdict in favour of humanity, comes to live amongst us, full of grace and truth (cf. Jn. 1:14).

R. MARTIN-ACHARD

JUSTIFICATION, see RIGHTEOUS

KING, see JESUS, MINISTRY O.T.

KINGDOM

The very frequent use of this term in the N.T. and especially in the synoptic Gospels, without its being anywhere defined, shows sufficiently that its usage was familiar both to the hearers of Jesus and to the first generation of Christians. In fact, we are here faced by a conception common in the Jewish apocalyptic literature of the 1st century B.C. and derived from the O.T. itself. The "kingship of Yahweh" or the "kingdom of heaven" (cf. Num. 23:21; Deut. 33:5) is known not only to the prophets and the psalmists but also in the older writings of the old covenant. Such expressions denote not the place or extent of the Kingdom of God (i.e. the ordinary implications of the word kingdom) but rather the fact that God is king, i.e. the majesty and sovereignty of God. This sovereignty may be contested, disregarded, or rejected, but it is none the less real, since it is "of God" or "of the heavens". That means that it is not manifested in this world where a number of earthly kingdoms exercise their sway, but that "the day comes" when it will be fully manifested and when the Kingdom of God will be effectively realized in the whole terrestrial and celestial realms of creation. This "advent" of the kingship of the eternal God, disclosing His righteousness and mercy in power and glory, is in post-exilic literature bound up with the advent of the Messiah-King, the Son of David, the Son of Man, to whom will be committed the sovereignty of the eternal God Himself. Whatever be the form and content of this ultimate revelation of the sovereign majesty of God at the end of time, the expectation of the Kingdom of God was the essential element in the hope of Israel and also in the piety of the God-fearers who are sometimes mentioned in the N.T. as existing outside the strict circle of the Jewish communities. It is this hope which, although it is sometimes expressed without due discrimination, responds to the preaching of John the Baptist and of Jesus Himself (cf. Lk. 17:20; 19:11; Mk. 12:34; 15:43, and also the episode of the entry into Jerusalem, Mk. 11:10 and parallels).

Thus it is certain that in speaking of the Kingdom of God (or, in Matthew, of the Kingdom of heaven) or of the reign of the Son of Man, Jesus is only sounding anew a theme which is already familiar to His hearers. The theme itself is not new. What is new and what properly speaking constitutes the *Gospel, i.e. the good news which

Jesus proclaims and commissions His disciples to proclaim in their turn, is the declaration that the time is fulfilled and that "the kingdom has now drawn near". In the many statements which report the preaching of Jesus the verbs of which the Kingdom is the subject all express this coming, this nearness, this imminence of the movement wherein God draws nigh to man and particularly toward His people Israel with the effect of manifesting His sovereignty (Mk. 1:15; Matt. 3:2; 4:17; 10:7; Lk. 10:9,11; 21:31, etc.). Now, says Jesus, the *time (the moment) that was to come in the preaching of the prophets is about to be fulfilled, it is becoming present; and it is precisely through this announcement that the Kingdom constitutes the content of the Gospel.

1. *The Gospel of the Kingdom.* This expression precisely indicates an *event*; the proclamation of the coming of the Kingdom, the promulgation on earth and in human history of the sovereign decision of God now to manifest and exercise effectively His supreme kingship. Thus it is impossible to think of the Kingdom of God as the sovereign good or as an ideal to be sought or attained by man: still less is it a state or place of privilege. On the contrary, it is the Kingdom which comes to man and which by that very fact raises for him the question as to whether he belongs to it or not, whether he is ready to receive it and enter into it, to bear its coming and penetrate its mystery. Now the way in which the Kingdom comes to men and claims their attention is essentially and primarily the *word. It is the word of the Kingdom which Jesus preaches as the good news, and it is for that that He has come (Lk. 4:43; 8:1; 9:11; 16:16). This preaching normally takes place in the form of *parables, i.e. indirectly under the veil of analogy, for the coming of the Kingdom constitutes a *mystery the understanding of which is only granted to those who have eyes to see and ears to hear (Matt. 13:10–17).

Jesus adds to His preaching *actions*: He preaches the Gospel of the Kingdom and He heals, casts out demons, performs acts of power, *miracles, signs. Such signs form an integral part of the message itself, accompany it, underline it. The evangelists state specifically that these signs are the confirmation of what has been promised by the Word of God (Matt. 8:17) and Jesus emphasizes the point Himself in His reply to the disciples of John (Matt. 11:4–5). This text is a direct allusion to those passages of Isaiah which most clearly announce the advent of the reign of the Lord (Isa. 29:18ff.; 35:5ff.; 61:1ff.). Thus both the preaching and the signs of the Kingdom attest the present reality of the kingship of God which is now in process of being manifested; at the same time they confer on Jesus the authority which astonishes His hearers (Matt. 7:29; Mk. 1:27)—an authority of which He refuses to disclose the origin (Matt. 21:23–27) though He gives it to be understood that it comes from God (Matt. 12:25–28).

In particular, by the casting out of demons Jesus suggests that His presence and His ministry spell the irruption into the world of creation, "subject to vanity", of the liberating power of the Lord who now comes to take possession of His Kingdom. Thus the sovereignty of God appears among men, it dawns on the horizon, it springs up like seed cast in the ground, precisely in that earth which up to now has been handed over to the dominion of Satan, but of which the King of heaven is also Lord! It is not by chance that Jesus uses with regard to the Kingdom images such as those of seed growing secretly and the sowing of seed, light and lamps that are lit; for these are the images which in the prophets and psalms of the O.T. illustrate the advent of the Messianic King (1 Kings 11:36; 2 Chr. 21:7; Ps. 132:17; 119:105; Hos. 2:23–24; Jer. 31:27; Isa. 55:10, etc.).

Finally, the preaching of the Kingdom which is now coming and which must be apprehended by faith through the parables and miracles of Jesus, is focused on the very person of Him who is its preacher. In fact *Jesus is not merely the preacher of the

Kingdom, He is at the same time the bearer and fulfiller of it. The mystery of the Kingdom is identical with the Messianic secret of Jesus. Because He is there, the Kingdom is there in that mysterious presence which is authentically His (Matt. 12:28). This seems to be the meaning of the reply of Jesus to those who ask when the Kingdom of God will come: "The kingdom of God is not coming with signs to be observed; nor will they say, 'Lo, here it is!' or 'There!' for behold, the kingdom of God is in the midst of you" (Lk. 17:20–21).

It is this close correlation between the coming of the Kingdom and the presence of Jesus which illuminates the mysterious text of Matt. 11:12: "From the days of John the Baptist until now the kingdom of heaven has suffered violence and men of violence take it by force." Luke in the parallel text says simply that the Kingdom of God is proclaimed. The two versions are at one, for it is precisely the proclamation of the Kingdom and its embodiment in the person of Him who is its king which provokes the convulsion of faith and the victorious decision by which one enters it. Hence we can say that in preaching the Kingdom Jesus is preaching Himself. The Gospel is not only the message *of* Jesus but the message about the person of Jesus. That is why entrance into the Kingdom is entirely governed by faith in Jesus Christ.

2. *Entry into the Kingdom.* It is the question of knowing whether one enters or does not enter into the Kingdom of God which forms the crucial point of the *preaching of the Gospel. The latter is not merely a promise, a proclamation, the annunciation of good tidings; it is at the same time an appeal to repentance and faith: "The time is fulfilled and the kingdom of God is at hand: repent and believe the gospel" (Mk. 1:15). Now it is entirely consonant with the deep meaning of these expressions to understand them in closest connection with the imminence of the Kingdom: repentance implies decisive change, the reorientation of man and the reversal of his values, the surrender by him of his own royalty and his own righteousness; faith implies the acceptance and recognition of the royalty of God and of divine righteousness. Hence it becomes clear that all the conditions of entry into the Kingdom are inescapably contained in this twofold requirement: *repentance and *faith. The Kingdom is *given* to those who wait for it, seek it and long for it as for their sole treasure: it is given to "the poor", to those who become as little children (Matt. 18:3–4), to him who is born again (Jn. 3:3–5), who leaves everything for the sake of Christ (Matt. 19:28–30) and is willing to follow Him in the path of self-denial and sacrifice (Mk. 9:47; Matt. 19:12; Lk. 9:60–62). Poverty of spirit, unpretentiousness, humility are not virtues which render one worthy to enter the Kingdom of heaven, but they are the signs and the fruits of that sincere repentance and genuine faith which the promise of the Kingdom and the very words of Jesus evoke in the heart of man. At this point it should be observed that the Sermon on the Mount, which is often interpreted as the charter or the new law of the Kingdom, can only be understood thus if it is not only the Gospel preached by Jesus but also lived out and fulfilled by Him. In truth there is a new law only for him who in faith and repentance receives the promise and the grace of the Kingdom and enters it. This entry into the Kingdom is identical with the dynamic decision of faith in Him who is its king. Hence in the last resort the advent of the Kingdom must be understood in relation to the person and the ministry of Jesus Christ Himself. It is the fulfilment by Jesus Christ and in Him of the sovereign righteousness of God which makes possible that ultimate and total manifestation of divine majesty "from on High", which will put an end to all earthly time and all human expectation by uniting all things under the sceptre of the King of kings and Lord of lords.

3. *The Kingdom of God and the Kingship of Jesus Christ.* It is evident from the witness of history, as recorded in the Gospels, that the whole earthly ministry of

Jesus is controlled by and culminates in the central event of His death on the *cross and His *resurrection. The preaching of the Gospel of the Kingdom, the declaration of its imminent advent and manifestation, are not consummated in a glorious accession to power or enthronement but by the cross on which the Messiah, the King of Israel, dies. The whole drama of the ministry of Jesus unfolding itself at the heart of His people revolves around this stumbling-stone, this rock of offence, which causes the disciples themselves to be scandalized and fall: "The Son of Man must be crucified and the third day rise again." (Cf. 8:31 and parallels, 9:31 and parallels, etc.) What is more, it is just because Jesus describes Himself as Messiah, Son of God, and claims to be the king of the Kingdom of heaven that He is rejected and crucified as "the king of the Jews".

Hence the mystery of the Kingdom consists not only in the fact that it is invisibly contained in the person of Him who brings it both in word and promise; but also in the fact that it lies utterly beyond the term of the terrestrial history of Jesus, a history which culminates in the climax of the cross. In order that the Kingdom of God may come, the *righteousness of God must be fulfilled; His victory over the unrighteousness of this world must be achieved and that in a total, radical and manifest fashion. "My kingship is not of this world," says Jesus before Pilate (Jn. 18:36). Without going into the question of when this Kingdom will be disclosed in the future (*Advent) we will note simply that in His teaching to His disciples Jesus certainly subordinates the ultimate manifestation of the Kingdom of God to His own glorious manifestation and that the latter becomes effectual only through His death and resurrection, by which it is entirely conditioned. Thus the account of the last Paschal meal and of the institution of the *Lord's Supper is moulded not only by the imminent accomplishment of the sacrifice on the cross but also by the consummation of the Kingdom of God (Matt. 26:29; Mk. 14:25; Lk. 22:16-18). It is also in the course of this scene as recorded by Luke that Jesus declares His intention of appointing a Kingdom to His own, to those who, just because they have shared His trials and have eaten and drunk the body and blood offered for them, will likewise share in the heavenly banquet and with the king will execute judgment on Israel (Lk. 22:28-30).

We should also in this connection note the distinction which has been especially brought out by the work of Oscar Cullmann between the Kingdom of God and the kingship or reign of Christ. In fact, in the texts we find it is sometimes a question of the Kingdom of God and at other times of the Kingdom of the Son or the reign of the Son of Man (e.g. Matt. 26:29 and Matt. 16:28). This distinction is concerned not with the substance of these two ideas, which imply the same reality, but with the temporal difference between the reign of Christ and the Kingdom. As soon as the work of salvation is completed by the righteousness of the cross, Jesus Christ rises again and is then exalted to the right hand of God, He enters into His glory and takes possession of His omnipotence and sovereignty (Lk. 24:26; Matt. 28:18). Thus the Kingdom of Christ begins with the ascension, and it is at Pentecost that the Holy Spirit proclaims by the mouth of the apostles: "God has made both Lord and Christ this Jesus whom ye crucified" (Acts 2:36). Hence the kingship of Jesus Christ is now already being exercised both on earth and in heaven. This is the assurance which inspires the Church and lies at the basis of the apostolic preaching. But the Kingdom of God is entirely in the future, and its disclosure awaits that imminent end of earthly time which will be signalized by the return of Jesus Christ who has come and will come again (Acts 1:11). Thus the proclamation of the Kingdom of God, which formed the very substance of the message of Jesus, remains also the message of the Church which bears witness to the fact that He is Lord.

4. *The Kingdom of God and the *Church*.

For the apostles, the Kingdom is in fact the main theme of their preaching (Acts 19:8; 20:25; 28:23). To preach Jesus Christ crucified and risen or to preach the Kingdom of God are one and the same thing, for it is by His death and resurrection that Jesus Christ has become Lord and it is through faith in His name that the sinner receives pardon and entry into the Kingdom of God. The Kingdom is often described by Paul as the *inheritance promised to the believer (1 Cor. 6:9-10; 15-50; Gal. 5:21; Col. 1:13). And the whole moral teaching of the Epistles is governed by the perspective of the Kingdom which is yet to come through the appearance of Jesus Christ and His reign (Rom. 14:17; 1 Thess. 2:12; 2 Thess. 1:5; 2 Pet. 1:11; Jas. 2:5; 2 Tim. 4:1).

Subject to the kingship of Christ and His reign which it confesses and proclaims, the Church does not in itself constitute the Kingdom of God; up to the end of time it can but announce the latter as its ultimate hope and the hope of the world, and it is only because Jesus Christ acts within the Church and controls it by His Holy Spirit (1 Cor. 4:20) that the Church can here and now at the heart of this world raise the standard of the world which is to come. The present sovereignty of Jesus Christ can only be apprehended by faith, while men wait for the day when He will deliver up the Kingdom to God His Father after having destroyed the last enemy, *death (1 Cor. 15:24ff.). Until that day the Church possesses no other power than that of its prayer: "Come, Lord Jesus" (1 Cor. 16:22; Rev. 22:17,20). Such prayerful expectation must remain until the great voice of the book of Revelation trumpets forth: "Now the salvation and the power and the kingdom of our God and the authority of His Christ have come!" (Rev. 12:10; 11:15).

H. ROUX

KNOW

In order to understand the specific connotation of the verb to know in the Bible, it is essential to compare the Hebrew idea with the classical Greek idea. The precise details which such a comparison will furnish will enable us to understand the more complex data of the N.T.

1. *Hebrew knowledge and Greek knowledge.* To the Greeks, knowledge (and this characteristic may also be discerned in modern scientific knowledge which derives from it) is by its very nature intellectual. By that is understood that the known reality, whether this refers to a thing or a person, always remains an object which the subject who is aware of the reality may grasp through the medium of the senses and more especially through the sense of sight. The more adequate the idea is to the known object, the more complete this grasp will be. In order thus to appropriate the object to himself, the subject must, as far as lies in his power, keep the greatest possible distance between himself and the object. He will master it only in so far as he restricts himself to observing it objectively. Knowledge, to the Greeks, is essentially detached, impersonal learning, and the opposite of knowledge can only be ignorance and error.

Whilst, at the level of ordinary understanding, the Hebrew idea of knowledge does not exclude an analogous objectivity, from the very outset it goes far beyond it. In the O.T. "to know" implies observation and intellectual grasp, but it also has another and far more significant meaning: to encounter, to experience, to share in. The O.T. writers are less concerned with grasping an object by means of the "idea" of it than they are with allowing themselves to be encountered by a reality which invades the inner recesses of the personality of the "subject" himself and draws him into its control.

In this sense, man, according to the O.T., may "know" (in a sense which would have hardly any meaning at all in Greek thought) suffering and sickness (Isa. 53:3), the loss of children (Isa. 47:8), the power of God (Jer. 16:21) and His vengeance (Ezek. 25:14). In this sense, too, man may "know" woman (Gen. 4:1; Judg. 19:25) and woman may "know" man (Num. 31:17). Popular usage, which quite correctly speaks in this last instance of knowledge "in the biblical sense", has ignored, however, that this is only one particular example of a connotation which is much more general.

To the pure observation of things and persons which are assimilated by the mind through the medium of the idea, Hebrew thought adds, then, a new dimension, that of *time* in which there is unfolded a history which by its very nature implies a vital connection between the knowing "subject" and the known "object". From the O.T. point of view, "to know" means to be closely bound up with the history and to give one's consent to this personal commitment. It is not the intelligence alone which is involved; the will also comes into operation, whilst the opposite of knowledge, far from being reduced to mere ignorance and error, reaches its climax in disobedience, in rebellion, in independence—in *sin, in short.

This conception of knowledge colours the description of the relations between God and the people of Israel. From God's side, to know Israel means not just that God knows that Israel exists and is aware of what Israel has done; it means that God pledges Himself to Israel as a man pledges himself to his betrothed; it means that of His own free will God binds Himself to Israel by sharing her history (Hos. 13:5). Knowledge of that kind, which is specifically biblical and theological, implies of necessity *election, and may, in consequence, carry with it the possibility of rejection (Amos 3:2). From the side of Israel, to know God means not just that Israel is aware that "there is" a God; it means to accept His *covenant (Hos. 2:20), to keep constantly in mind His mighty acts (Deut. 11:2; Isa. 41:20; Hos. 11:3), to ascribe glory to Him and to obey Him (Isa. 11:2; Ps. 9:11; 36:10); it means to will what God has first willed.

2. *Knowledge in the N.T.* Basically the N.T. conception of knowledge rests solidly on the O.T. Knowledge is the obedient recognition of the work of God, with this one difference that from now onwards this work is fulfilled in Jesus Christ (Lk. 10:11; Acts 2:36; 1 Cor. 2:8; Phil. 3:10), and that this work, completed but still hidden, will be gloriously revealed at the end of the ages for the salvation of them that believe (Matt. 24:32f. and parallel passages). If man may know, it is solely because God has first known him and has already bound Himself to him (Gal. 4:9; 1 Cor. 13:12). We must, however, take note of two shades of meaning which are unknown in the O.T. but are required in the new situation.

In the first place, there are grounds for observing that certain passages (e.g. Rom. 1:18–23; 1 Cor. 21; Gal. 4:8f.; Rom. 2:20; 1 Tim. 2:4; 2 Tim. 2:25; 3:7; Titus 1:1, etc.) understand knowledge as something to be grasped by the mind. Being addressed essentially to Israelites, the O.T. could not stop short at the intellectual aspect. Very rightly it was assumed that the mighty acts of God were known in theory. The important concern was to bring out the moral consequences of these acts. As the apostolic message was addressed also to pagans, it became necessary to pass on to these the knowledge—intellectual at first—of the divine acts of which they were ignorant. It must be added that the texts make it quite clear that such knowledge could not remain at the theoretical level without becoming empty and meaningless (1 Cor. 13:2,8,9,12). An intellectual awareness of the mighty acts of God is a necessary condition, but in no sense an all-sufficient condition of true knowledge, which always remains a gift of God bestowed through the Holy Spirit (1 Cor. 12:8) and received through faith acting in love (Phil. 1:9–11; Philem. 6).

In the second place, it must be noted that the apostolic thought concerning knowledge, at times in Paul, but especially in John, has been worked out in opposition to gnosticism, often borrowing its very language. Gnosticism, a philosophic and religious movement which arose prior to Christianity and which very early constituted a grave threat to it, had an attitude to knowledge altogether different from that which we find in classical Greek thought: knowledge was not the product of objective observation but the result of an initiation which put the initiated in possession of spiritual capacities higher than reason. Gnosticism was combated alike by the exponents of Greek philosophy in the name of reason and by the Christians in the name of faith. In effect, gnosticism turned knowledge into a mysterious possession which illuminated the initiated and—according to its claims—rendered all faith superfluous. Paul (1 Cor. 8:1–3) and John (throughout the whole of his Gospel and his Epistles) remind their hearers that knowledge is not a faculty added on to man which he can use at will, but that it springs from faith in the historic revelation of God in Jesus Christ, who is the fulfilment of Israel's history. Faith and knowledge build each other up (Jn. 6:69; 8:31f.; 16:30; 17:7f., etc.); knowledge is never able to free itself from *faith; man can never be torn out of sacred history and surrendered to his own secular history. The knowledge of which the Gospel speaks is not the possession of an initiate, but the acknowledgment of the mighty acts of God on the part of a believer.

J.-L. LEUBA

LANGUAGE (TONGUES)

1. *Languages.* God speaks, and man created in His image is also endowed with speech. But if the gift of language is a result of God's creative work, the diversity of languages is a consequence of sin. The Yahwistic redactors inform us in Gen. 11 that there was once a time when the whole earth spoke the same language and used the same words. This oneness of language gave men a power of cohesion such that nothing could halt them in their enterprises: they resolved to mount up to heaven and for this purpose undertook the building of the tower of Babel. It was in order to put a stop to this attempt that God intervened and threw their language into such confusion that men no longer understood each other. Such is the explanation of the origin of the diversity of languages.

2. *The tongue.* To speak the same language is not a sufficient basis of unity. Looking at the varied characteristics of the tongue in the prophets and the psalmists it is apparent that its capabilities vary from what is worst to what is best. Is it not compared to poison (Ps. 140:4), to a razor (Ps. 52:4), to a scourge (Job 5:21), to a fire (Isa. 30:27), to a sword, to a bow, to an arrow (Ps. 57:5; Jer. 9:3,8)? "It is a little member," according to the Epistle of James, "but it boasts of great things" (3:5). Its smallness masks its tremendous influence. Since it is capable of all things, of blessing and of cursing, it is essential that it should be kept under control. On this point the psalmist, Job, the sages of Israel, and the apostles are unanimous. The author of the Pastoral Epistles even goes so far as to give wise and witty advice in this connection for the avoidance of the nuisance of scandal-mongering widows in church circles (1 Tim. 5:13) and the improprieties of empty and profane conversations and the ostentations of false science (1 Tim. 6:20). Did not Jesus attack with sarcasm those whose tongue is deceitful when he denounced the Pharisees as hypocrites because they "preach, but do not practise" (Matt. 23:3)? In several places Jesus stresses the fact that the tongue expresses what a person truly is: it is not from the mouth but from the heart that evil thoughts proceed (Matt. 7:21). Conversely, it is God Himself who inspires the confessions of martyrs, showing to all that these men belong entirely to Him. He will give them words to speak and a wisdom which none will be able to resist (Matt. 10:20).

To sum up: for all the biblical authors the tongue is only the means of expression given by God to men. Involved as it is with their whole being in sin, it requires an intervention of God and a conversion of man's being if the tongue is to be able to bless and to bring forth good things.

3. *The gift of tongues.* If the problem of the control of the tongue is part and parcel of the more general problem of Christian conduct, the strange phenomenon of "speaking in a tongue" constitutes a religious manifestation. The effect of a

spiritual gift, these sounds, which are inarticulate and unintelligible both to those who utter them and to those who listen, must be interpreted if the assembly is to be edified. The Church of Corinth (1 Cor. 12 and 14) is told by the apostle Paul that each believer ought to rejoice in the gifts which he has received from God. But these ought never to be regarded by him as a mark of superiority, and consequently it is deplorable that these various spiritual gifts should be viewed as competing with each other. The ultimate aim of every activity within the Christian community is the edification of the body of Christ (see *build). Those who speak in a tongue (*glossolaletes*) must remember this. In fact, they speak to God rather than to men. They are working, it may be, for their own edification and not for that of others. The apostle also tells them: "I would rather speak five intelligible words than ten thousand words in a tongue." It is fitting therefore to observe: firstly, that he neither despises nor forbids speaking in tongues; secondly, that he refuses to assign it a place of superiority over the other gifts. It is important therefore that the exercise of this gift should have its place like those of the other gifts within the Christian community, but in a manner conducive to order and edification.

The account of the miracle of Pentecost (Acts 2) does not admit of an easy interpretation. We do not know precisely what took place: either the apostles received that gift of speaking in foreign languages (*xenoglossia*) and were understood (which seems to us doubtful), or they spoke in a tongue (as v. 13 might seem to indicate) and those who surrounded them, placed in a state of receptivity, understood. This much is certain, according to the text (which does not attempt to explain a phenomenon that remained incomprehensible to him who reported it): men of every origin and every tongue hear the apostles speaking of the wonders of God and, thanks to the gift of the Spirit, the diversity of languages no longer constitutes an obstacle. The effect of this miracle is found in this mutual comprehension which ought to have been

hindered, firstly, by the diversity of origin of the hearers, and, secondly, by the multiplicity of their languages. Its profound significance is seen in this: that no distinction of class or language or nationality can prevent the formation of a community animated by the Spirit of God. This creation of a community amongst men is the reverse of the attempt to construct the tower of Babel.

In fine, the "gift of tongues" is a spiritual gift. Its disorderly manifestations (as at Corinth) as well as its absence are matters for Christians to deal with.

To conclude, the living God who gives us His Word would never allow the witness which must be borne to Him to be linked to a particular tongue, to a special form of speech, to a unique kind of spiritual manifestation. At all times, where and when He wills, He is able to bring together in Jesus Christ, through His Spirit, men of every language and of every origin.

M. CARREZ

LAST, *see* TIME

LAW

O.T.

The notion of law is one of the most important in the O.T. since the Jewish religion is frequently regarded as the religion of the law. But it is not a notion which is presented in a simple manner, for it contains elements which are very diverse both in their form and in their foundation. It is appropriate, in the first place, to define the terms, and then to study their content, in order to conclude with a rapid survey of the principal legislative codes of the O.T.

1. The vocabulary employed for speaking of the law or of the commandments of God is rich in expressions. The reading of Psalm 119, which is a eulogy of the law, affords us a glimpse of a good number of different words which our translations endeavour to respect: law, ordinances, commandments, statutes, word, judgments, precepts, ways, etc. Without pausing over any of these

terms, we wish to draw attention only to two categories of words the sense of which explains the twofold point of departure of Israelite law: words like *mishpat* (from the verb *shaphat*, to judge or administer) which denote the usages and customs that had acquired the force of law and correspond to common law, and words like *dabar* (word), *mitsvah* (precept), and above all *torah* (law) which are applied to a law coming from a superior authority, to a precept or decision of a commander, of a king, or of a god. Of these terms that of *torah* is the most characteristic and the one which gathers together the notions relating to the law.

The origin of this word, which occurs more than 220 times in the O.T., is no longer clear. Its verbal root (*yarah*) signifies to throw, to fling, and is used, for example, of the shooting of arrows (1 Sam. 20:36), the casting of lots (Josh. 18:6), or the foundation of a building (Job 38:6; Gen. 31:51). But the most usual sense is to instruct or to teach, although it is a matter of debate whether this significance comes from the gesture of him who teaches (he flings his hand forward in order to show the way) of him who casts lots (in order to obtain an answer from God). The noun *torah* is applied, therefore, to an instruction received from a superior authority and which serves as a rule of conduct in any particular case. It is almost invariably translated into Greek by the word *nomos*: law (from *nemo*, to apportion or distribute, whence comes the noun *onoma*: name, in other words, that which is attributed to each one). The etymology of the term, however, does not suffice to explain its content, which during the course of the centuries is enriched or modified.

Originally a *torah* was an oral instruction given by the priest or the prophet in the name of God in response to a particular question posed by the people or by an individual (Isa. 1:10; Mic. 3:11: his priests *teach* for a salary). Before long these divine oracles were regarded as the revelation of the will of God concerning a more general scheme and the mission of the prophets was to cause the people to know the *torah* of the Lord (Isa. 8:16,20; 30:9; Mic. 4:2). Just as the word of God had the validity of rule for the life of the people, it was in the form of prescriptions and laws that the divine will was proclaimed and committed to writing. This explains the important place in the O.T. of legislative texts relating to worship, to religious practices, and to the individual, social, and moral life of the Israelites, the most complete collections of which are found in the Pentateuch. Quite naturally, the term *torah* served to designate the books containing these laws, and, in the Hebrew Bible, the Pentateuch as a whole is always called the *torah* of Moses. In Judaism the law of Moses forms the fundamental part of the *Scriptures, a portion of which is read in the synagogue every Sabbath, so that during the year the whole of the Pentateuch is re-read. The other books of the O.T. have a secondary value; a passage in the Talmud expresses it in this way: "If Israel had not sinned, the five books of the *Torah* alone would have been given to him, together with that of Joshua" (Tr. Nedarim 22b). In the time of Jesus the sacred books were called "the law and the prophets" (Matt. 22:40). If, however, the word was used more and more in its restricted sense, its original sense did not entirely disappear; after the return from Exile it was used again in connection with a question put to the priests on a particular point (Hagg. 2:11). Again, it is in a very wide sense that the law plays a part in the eschatological prophecies: in the last days all nations shall know the law of the Lord (Isa. 51:4; 42:4).

Since the law represents the will of God it came to be regarded as the greatest blessing which exists and it was eulogized in the most enthusiastic terms. The Psalms (19; 119, etc.) express in poetical form the veneration and love of the faithful for the law. The *torah* becomes the centre of Jewish piety and worship; it is more and more envisaged as the sacred and eternal *wisdom of God. Not only will it never perish, but it has always existed, even from before the creation of the world. It possesses

8

an absolute quality and is not merely the means which God uses to enter into relationship with men: it exists in its own right. Its sanctity will become magical: profane hands will not be able to touch the scrolls of the law without peril. Having become almost an attribute of God, it will take His place little by little in Jewish piety. The idolatry of the law will, in many respects, characterize the religious life of the Jews in the time of Jesus, and as this immutable law is in need of being interpreted from generation to generation in order to be applicable to every circumstance of human existence, they will lapse into casuistry and its serious consequences: hypocritical legalism and narrow formalism. The abundant rabbinical literature which will constitute the Talmud will be nothing other than a vast commentary on the law, increasing with the development of tradition. Very frequently tradition will assume greater importance than the law, and religious life will be veritably crushed under the burden of the law through losing the joyful freedom which the grace of the Lord gives (Matt. 23:4). There is a great distance between this conception of the *torah* and that which in former times gave spontaneous expression, through the mouth of the prophets, to the grace of the Lord.

2. Whatever may have been the evolution in the meaning of the word *torah* in Judaism, the essential notions which are associated with the idea of law in the O.T. remain the same. We must now examine these.

In the first place, it is fitting to emphasize the notion of *authority*: a *torah* possesses authority because it comes from a superior person (father or mother, Prov. 1:8; a leader, Exod. 18:16,20) and above all because it comes from God (Exod. 21:1; 24:3, etc.). It is the *revelation of the will of the Lord to His people and the means whereby Israel may know that his God cares for him. The law is thus linked to the *covenant established between God and Israel, especially at the time of the revelation on Sinai. It is, in fact, to this moment in the history of the Hebrews that the most

important legislative passages of the O.T. are attributed, even those whose redaction may be considered as belonging to a later period (Leviticus). The law is the sign of the covenant: God has given it to His elect people who henceforth must show their faithfulness by obedience to this law. There is nothing rigorously judicial in this promulgation of the law for Israel; it is rather the manifestation of the Lord's merciful grace towards His people and the proof of His love and blessing (Deut. 7:6–15). The opposition between the law and grace never appears in the time of ancient Israel, because the law is a gift of grace.

Because it comes from God, the law contains a notion of *dogmatic truth*. Not only does it afford knowledge of the will of God, but it also instructs concerning what God is and does. "I am the Lord your God, who brought you out of the land of Egypt. . . . I the Lord your God am a jealous God, punishing iniquity and showing mercy" (Exod. 20:2–5). The Lord is a God merciful and compassionate, slow to anger, rich in goodness and faithfulness, who maintains His love unto a thousand generations (Exod. 34:6–7). He will gather together His people, will lead them back into the promised land, will overwhelm them with blessings and take pleasure in their happiness (Deut. 30:1–10).

Then we must also mention the notion of *completeness* in the idea of the law: the *torah* concerns the whole life of the people and of the individual. No sphere is foreign to it, for God reigns sovereignly over all and it is from Him that all the ordinances affecting the religious, moral, and social life of Israel come. The laws of Leviticus and Deuteronomy make no distinction between a religious sphere and a profane sphere. The prescriptions envisage the manner of the offering of sacrifices and of celebrating the annual festivals, as well as the method of punishing crimes, of treating one's cattle of behaviour before a stranger, or of observing the rules concerning the eating of pure or impure animals, concerning lepers or concerning sexual relationships.

Lastly, a notion of *finality* is apparent in

all the Israelite legislation. The laws have a practical aim and are designed to regulate and guide the life of the faithful in the concrete circumstances of daily existence. They are never abstract dogmas which may be known in a theoretical manner; they are practical rules of life and action. Very frequently, moreover, they are drawn up, not as impersonal judicial pronouncements, but as exhortations, appeals, promises, or threats, which reach the heart as well as the mind. In this respect Deuteronomy is a remarkable example of legislation in the style of preaching. Naturally, this does not exclude precise and absolute legal prescriptions: "Thou shalt . . .", "thou shalt not . . ." (the rabbis counted in the Pentateuch 365 prohibitions and 248 commands, or 613 laws in all). The negative character of many of them cannot be overlooked (8 of the 10 commandments of the Decalogue are negative). It is, further, impossible to separate the individual from the community when one seeks to know to whom these laws are addressed. The alternation of *Thou* and *Ye* shows that what is true for the nation is true also for each of its members, and *vice versa*.

3. In conclusion, we wish to draw attention to the principal legislative codes preserved in the O.T., in so far as it may be possible to place them in the order of their antiquity. The *ritual Decalogue* (Exod. 34:10–28) and the *book of the covenant* (Exod. 20:22—23:33) contain very ancient laws. The *moral Decalogue* (Exod. 20:1–17 and Deut. 5:1–21) in its two forms, which differ slightly where certain commandments are concerned, represents the fundamental element of the law of God whose value is eternal. The *deuteronomic code* (Deut. 12 to 26) is already much more developed than the preceding laws and seems to have been inspired by the spirit of the first great prophets. It insists on purity of worship, on the necessity of avoiding all compromise with paganism, and on the love of God and of one's neighbour. Leviticus is a collection of laws of which the principal part is sometimes called the *code*

of holiness (chapters 17 to 26), but whose other parts are also codified. Its redaction is without doubt less ancient than that of the other legislative texts of the O.T. and forms part of a great work of the priests, often described as the *priestly code*, other constitutive elements of which are also found throughout the Pentateuch, in particular in Exod. 25–31; 36–40; Num. 1–10. A comparison with the *torah of Ezekiel* (chapters 40–48) is of considerable interest for reconstructing the history of Israelite and Jewish law and understanding its development. Similarly, a comparative study of the legislative codes of the O.T. and of the Babylonian, Assyrian, and Hittite codes of antiquity (for example, the code of Hammurabi) makes it possible to postulate the existence of a common foundation of civil and penal laws throughout the ancient East, while at the same time causing the unique value of the religious inspiration of the Hebrew legislation to stand out. (See *Justice.)

F. MICHAELI

N.T.

Apart from very rare exceptions (Heb. 8:10 and 10:16, which are quotations from Jer. 31:33 in the Greek text of the Septuagint translation, which has replaced the singular of the original Hebrew by a plural), the term "law" is always found in the singular in the N.T.; not without reason, for, in the majority of cases, it expresses a precise notion which, while admitting of two correlative nuances—as is also the case in post-exilic Judaism whence at this point the N.T. has taken over the vocabulary—none the less possesses a profound internal unity.

The law, in fact, is a part of *the expression of the holy and imperative will of God* (Rom. 3:19; 4:15; 7:1, etc.). But, on the other hand, as this will is recorded in the O.T., the term "law" will be able to designate concretely *the Pentateuch*, the fundamental document of the revelation of God to Israel (Lk. 2:23–24,27,39; 10:26; Jn. 1:45; Acts 6:13–14; Rom. 7:7; 13:8; Gal. 4:21, etc.), and also sometimes, but more rarely

(1 Cor. 14:21; Rom. 3:19; cf. Rom. 3:10–18; Jn. 10:34; 15:25; 12:34; cf. Ps. 110:4), the *Old Testament as a whole*, which ordinarily is described by the more frequent expression "the law and the prophets" (Matt. 5:17; Rom. 3:21, etc.).

"The law" and "the law and the prophets" thus indicate formally the O.T., the document of the requirements of God with respect to man, and materially these requirements themselves, without its being possible or desirable to delineate a precise frontier between these two significances.

In exceptional instances identical or analogous expressions may be applied to the O.T. as the document of the promises of God (Matt. 11:13; Lk. 24:44. This latter passage gives the more complete expression: "the law, the prophets, and the psalms", an allusion to the threefold division of the Jewish canon). But, in this respect, the N.T. ordinarily makes use of a different term, namely, *Scripture.

It should be noted that by law the N.T. never means the Jewish oral tradition subsequent to the canon of the O.T. On the contrary, it draws a careful distinction between these two dimensions, of which the second alone is valid (Mk. 7:5–13; Col. 2:8).

We must indicate, finally, the more general sense which our term bears in passages such as Rom. 7:21,23,25; 8:2 ("law which I find within myself", "law of sin and death"), and Heb. 7:16, where, in a purely formal manner, it is describing a norm, a rule (of conduct), the sense of which is determined by the context (for example: "law of sin"=conduct determined by sin). This wider meaning has made it possible for Christian thought to express the new import of the requirements of God without abandoning the term law (cf. Rom. 3:27–28: "law of faith" opposed to the "law of works"; Rom. 8:2: "law of the spirit of life") the permanence of which testifies to the unity of the two covenants.

A study of the law in the N.T., however, must not be based solely upon those passages which contain the term itself. The subject, without the term, is also found very frequently elsewhere, especially in the Gospels.

1. *Jesus and the law.* At first sight the testimony of the first three Gospels concerning the attitude of Jesus to the law, in His behaviour as well as in His teaching, appears to be contradictory. In a seemingly incoherent manner, positive and negative evaluations follow each other. A more profound examination leads to the following conclusions which make it possible to grasp the real unity of both the practice and the teaching of Jesus.

(*a*) In line with the O.T., and in opposition to subsequent Judaism which culminated in pharisaism, *Jesus does not allow that the law, whatever its claims, can constitute a means of salvation.* For Him, as for the original Israelite thought, which was continued by the prophets, man can be saved only by the exclusive initiative of God. Just as the covenant of God with Israel was not based on the previous merit of the Israelites, but on the divine decree of election, so also the salvation of men does not depend on conformity of their conduct to the prescriptions of the law, but on their acceptance of the Kingdom of God now manifested in Jesus (Matt. 11:7–15; Lk. 16:16; Mk. 2:21). The salvation of men is founded, not on obedience to the law, but on faith in Jesus. Tax-collectors and harlots enter into the Kingdom of heaven before those who have not believed the word of the Forerunner (Matt. 21:31–32). The same is the case with the lost sheep, the lost coin, and the lost son (Lk. 15). In Jesus they are found again and come back to life. *Faith in Jesus decides the eternal *salvation of man (Matt. 10:32–33; Mk. 10:13–16).

(*b*) Yet the law is fundamentally good (Mk. 10:18–19; Lk. 10:25–28). It has not, it is true, the power to introduce man into the covenant of God but *it defines the conduct which he can and must exhibit* once he has accepted, by faith, that God is able to cause him to enter into it. It gives expression to the requirements to which he must conform if he is no longer to fall away from it (whence the, in general, negative formulation of the concrete commandments in the O.T.). It thus enables him to know whether he is within the covenant, without, however, giving him the means of re-entering it by himself if he has excluded himself from it. In this respect the law is like a thermometer, which indicates health or sickness, without in any way being a remedy.

When measuring his interlocutors by the standard of the law, Jesus leads them to discover that it is not so much the will as the ability to obey the divine commandments which they lack. It may be that they are endeavouring to observe them. But they are none the less outside the Kingdom, because they have not yet abandoned their persons to God and to their neighbour (Lk. 10:25–37; Mk. 10:20–22). It is this abandonment alone that makes possible an authentic obedience. It indicates, in fact, an abdication of man before God. Jesus "fulfils" the law (Matt. 5:17) by showing its absolute demands (Matt. 5:21–48), which are crushing for every man who thinks that he can satisfy them without first having turned away from himself and found his life in the Kingdom of God manifested in Jesus (Mk. 8:34–35). Thus the law reveals sin and invites to repentance.

(c) It is possible now to understand the violent opposition of Jesus, not, it is true, to the law, but to the fallacious use which man can make of it, to the false power which he attributes to it, and to the illusory rôle which he causes it to assume in the economy of salvation. By imagining that obedience to the law can be the basis of salvation *man deceives himself concerning his true situation before God*. He thinks that he is able of his own will to enter again into the covenant which he has left, whereas it is God Himself alone who can reinstate him in it, and who does so, provided that man renounces self-justification and implores His pardon.

Obedience to the commandments is dangerously illusory when man considers that thereby he is entitled to dispense with *repentance or to hold back the total gift of his person to God (present in Christ) and to his neighbour. Family responsibili-

ties are fallacious if they afford a pretext for not following Jesus (Matt. 8:21–22; Lk. 14:25–27). Sabbath observance is misleading if it sets aside the immediate love of one's neighbour (Mk. 3:1–6). The fulfilment of the commandments is deceptive if it obscures the necessity for repentance (Lk. 18:9–14).

Traced back in this way to its source, namely, life in the *Kingdom, in *love for God and one's neighbour, the law neither necessitates nor tolerates any kind of casuistry (cf. Matt. 23:14–33). Equally, sin does not consist merely in committing actions that are contrary to the law, but in the refusal of repentance and love, a refusal of which actions contrary to the law are only the symptom and which is more serious still when considered as an obedience independent of the Kingdom, external to it (and not only to the heart of man)—a double hypocrisy (Matt. 16:6; 23:13). So far as the Kingdom of God is concerned, the Pharisee commits an error identical with that of a man who imagines that he may acquire the nationality of a country by the sole fact that he has attempted to observe its laws. It is repentance and self-renunciation alone that procure that nationality.

2. *The theological elaboration of Paul.* Paul says, in substance, nothing other than what we have just noticed. But he has elaborated it theologically and given it a fullness which the Christian message as a whole and the questions posed by the evangelization of the heathen together demand.

(a) The Kingdom of God, as the first three Gospels understand it, and the new situation created by the coming of Jesus culminate for him in the death and resurrection of Christ. *It is in the light of these divine facts (and particularly of the *cross and death of Christ) that Paul handles the law.* Like the O.T., and like Jesus, he denies its power to save man. But he elucidates, to a greater extent than the Gospels, the internal bond between the law and the cross. If Christ has inaugurated the Kingdom of God amongst men, it is because He has been subjected to the "curse of the law" (Gal. 3:13) and has thus fulfilled, for the salvation of men, the righteousness which it prescribed (Rom. 8:4). What men could not do, He has done (Rom. 5:6), and it is in this sense that His death is the complete manifestation of the love of God.

(b) From then on, the rôle of the law consists in giving *the knowledge of sin together with the certitude that man cannot justify himself.* Sin, it is true, exists before the law (Rom. 5:13) and in places other than where the law is known (Rom. 2:12–16; 3:9). But the knowledge of the law brings it into prominence and makes it still more real (Rom. 5:20; 7:7–13; Gal. 3:19). Paul does not mean that the law prepares man to receive Christ. On the contrary, it reminds the believer that it is impossible for him to live otherwise than by faith. Furthermore, the promise of redemption was given before the law (Gal. 3:15–18). The powerlessness of the law to save only serves to emphasize the power of Christ. To be "in Christ" therefore is, necessarily, to be not "under the law" (Rom. 6:14) and to escape its just penalty (Rom. 4:15).

3. *Free obedience.* The obedience to God of the believer who is thus situated and the concrete dispositions of the law—here again the teaching of Paul is a precise continuation of that of Jesus—are found to be altogether "radicalized" and "relativized".

They are *radicalized*, for they are led back, by the sole perfect obedience of Christ, to the very source of all human life: the divine life. Having lost every autonomous significance, they are fulfilled in the love of one's neighbour (Gal. 5:14; Rom. 13:10; Gal. 6:2), founded on faith in God. Far from abolishing the law, faith therefore brings it to its perfection, and confirms it (Rom. 3:27–31).

For the same reason the concrete requirements of the law are found to be *relativized*. With regard to the literal prescriptions of the law the believer is free (Rom. 7:1–6; Gal. 5:1). The fullness of love will actualize for him—or, contrariwise, will suspend—the validity of the concrete demands of the law (cf. 1 Cor. 7:18–24; 9:19–23). This explains the liberty of Paul with respect to the ritual prescriptions which, in his eyes—and again in conformity with the teaching of Jesus—cannot serve as an excuse for breaking the unity of Christians in love (Gal. 2:11–14). On the other hand, whenever the concrete prescriptions are compatible with love they ought to be strictly observed. Man's salvation depends on this, since failure to observe them would show that the transgressor is no longer in Christ (1 Cor. 6:9–11; Gal. 5:19–21). Paul is thus as far from spiritual anarchy as he is from legalism.

4. Taking the question as a whole, the remaining writings of the N.T. have an analogous position. (Jesus fulfilling the law: Jn. 1:45; 8:17; 10:34; 12:34; 15:25.—The commandment of love: Jn. 13:34; 15:12–15.—The law of liberty: Jas. 1:25; 2:12.—The inability of the law to procure salvation: Heb. 7:11–22; 9:15; 10:1–3.)

To sum up: the law (moral and ritual) is the obverse of the salvation which God set forth in the old covenant, and which has been achieved through Christ. Henceforth it is found in Him in its entirety. While it is vain and fatal for man apart from faith in Christ, it bears testimony to Christ Himself, and, situated henceforth in Him, it calls the believer to live in repentance and obedience. This means that the O.T. can be understood only in the light of the N.T. It means also that it is in this light that there appears at last the salvation of which, by the will of God, Israel is always the guardian.

J.-L. LEUBA

LAYING ON OF HANDS

1. The laying on of hands in the O.T. is first a ritual gesture by which a man transmits his own characteristics, his personality, to an animal (cf. Lev. 1:3–4; Exod. 29:10, etc.) or to certain men (the Levites, Num. 8:10), so as to bring about a substitution of persons, i.e. to be validly represented in the cultus by such an animal sacrificed, or by

the Levites in the service of the Temple. To this first sense of the term a second may be added, which is closely linked with it: that of consecration, of setting apart for God. Lastly, when Moses lays his hands on Joshua (Num. 27:18 and Deut. 34:9), there is transmission, but it is transmission from the side of God; a responsibility and a spirit of wisdom are conferred by God.

2. As a visible sign and a human gesture through which and by which God wills to bestow His Spirit and certain gifts, the laying on of hands preserves the same sense in the N.T.; according to the realistic conception of the N.T. the gesture is efficacious (but not of course magical) inasmuch as it is the instrument of the action of God, of Christ.

In the N.T. use is made of the gesture in three ways:

(a) *In the healing of *sickness.* Without being tied to one gesture, Jesus does nevertheless seem to have often laid His hands on the sick for His healing miracles (cf. especially Mk. 6:5 and Lk. 13:13 where the laying on of the hands was both the sign and the agent of the full word of authority from the Master). This action was a clear demonstration that Jesus was no simple healer, but that, acting in the name of God, and filled with His Spirit, He gave the spirit of life to the sick; for healing is one of the Spirit's manifestations.

What Jesus did with the full authority of the Son of God in the course of His earthly ministry was continued by means of the disciples in the Church, according to the command and the promise of the Risen Christ: "They will lay their hands on the sick; and they will recover" (Mk. 16:18).

(b) *In connection with *baptism.* Drawing up his short list of the primary elements in the Christian message, the author of the Epistle to the Hebrews puts side by side baptism and the laying on of hands (6:2), and this is not by chance. In two incidents, the book of Acts (8:14–17 and 19:1–7) shows plainly that the act of laying on of hands is concomitant to baptism, in the course of which the forgiveness of sins is effected by the immersion, and by the laying on of hands the Holy Spirit is visibly transmitted. It has a further relationship to baptism in that when Jesus laid His hands on the little children (Mk. 10:13–16 and parallels), it must be understood as a prefiguration of Christian baptism.

(c) *In consecration to the ministry.* Two narratives in Acts, that of the institution of the seven ministers in 6:1–6 and the mission of Paul and Barnabas in 13:1–13, as also various passages in the Epistles (1 Tim. 4:14; 2 Tim. 1:6; cf. perhaps 1 Tim. 5:22) show that the laying on of hands is the action by which the Church, in the persons of her ministers, transmits to certain men the *ministry in the Church. In this ministry function and spiritual gifts are indissolubly united. Here again is one of the O.T. senses of the term: the consecration to God and the delegation of authority by the Church. These different texts are evidence that the Church is not to act on her own initiative, but in obedience to the Holy Spirit, recognizing those who are called. Thus her action is then a visible and effective instrument of God, namely, the giving of the Holy Spirit.

M. BERNOULLI

LEVITE, *see* PRIEST O.T.

LIFE

O.T.

When the O.T. speaks of the life of man, it remains on the material and concrete plane of existence without trying to find abstract solutions to theoretical problems concerning the destiny of man or the philosophy of his life. The study of the words it uses will enable us to understand fairly clearly the meaning which the O.T. attaches to the concept of life, which is somewhat different from what is connoted by our own normal vocabulary.

1. Life in the first place implies the idea of a deep unshakeable *unity* of the living being. Our own distinctions between physical, intellectual and spiritual life do not

exist at all. Man is a whole, completely unified. His body and his mind, his breathing and his soul are so closely linked together that one of the parts can without difficulty denote the totality. This is very true of one of the words most often used to speak of life: the Hebrew word *nephesh*, the original meaning of which comes from the verb "to breathe" and which means the vital breath manifested in every living being by its respiration. God gave life to man by breathing into his nostrils the breath of life (Gen. 2:7). The word therefore corresponds to our word soul in the original sense of the Latin *anima*, meaning "that which is alive", and not in the spiritual and mystical sense which we associate with the term. For example, this soul or life of man has its seat in the *blood (Lev. 17:11; Deut. 12:23) and in many texts of the O.T. where our translators have used soul the word ought rather to have been translated "life" (to have one's soul empty, or dried up, is to be hungry or thirsty; Num. 11:6; Isa. 29:8). The same word comes to denote *man in his totality and might in many cases be translated by the personal pronoun: I . . . etc. (Ps. 3:3, "many say of my soul" which means "many say of me"; Ps. 103:1, "bless the Lord, O my soul"). The same might be said of other terms (flesh, body) which represent the totality and unity of man. Life forms an indivisible unity. Each part of the body (flesh, heart, blood, etc.) has a total function which is both physical and psychological.

2. A second notion implied by the concept of life is that of movement and action. in Semitic languages the verb "live" (*hayah*) seems to have originally the sense of a muscular contraction, by contrast with the word for *death of which the verbal root signifies to be extended or relaxed. Life is then a tension of the whole being, animated by a power which reveals itself in movement. It consists not in the passive neutral fact of existence, but in the presence of an active energy which moves man and impels him to act. This is confirmed by the use of the adjective "living" as applied to inanimate things which are astir with movement: the

Bible speaks of a living plant by contrast with a withered one (Ps. 58:10), or better still of living water in opposition to stagnant water which is motionless (Gen. 26:19; Lev. 14:5). It is also with this implication that the noun *hayya* designates especially an untamed wild animal, as distinct from a domestic animal or the beasts of the flock whose existence is more peaceful than that of the animals of the fields and the woods (Gen. 7:14; 8:1; Lev. 11:2). The dead do not possess this active energy of life and become weak beings, powerless shadows, inhabitants of the underworld where life goes on at an extremely enfeebled slackened pace (Ps. 88:11; Isa. 14:9–10; 26:14).

3. A still more important idea connected with the Hebrew consciousness of life is that of plenitude and intensity of life. The word which corresponds to our word "life" is almost always used in the plural in the O.T.: *hayyim* or *hayyin*; this plural does not denote a real plurality, but a special intensity of life, a richness and fullness of life which it is easy to elucidate by the use of the verb "to live" in the texts. "To live" means not merely "to exist" in the ordinary sense of the word, but rather to be restored to life, to live again or to survive, in cases where weakness, illness and death were overcoming a living being. The man who is dying of hunger lives when he once more finds food (Gen. 43:8; 2 Kings 7:4); he who is threatened with death lives when he is rescued from peril (Gen. 20:7); he who is ill lives when he recovers his health (Josh. 5:8; Num. 21:8–9; 2 Kings 1:2; Isa. 38:9) so that the verb "to live" comes to mean to be cured and to regain one's hold on life after the menace of death by a full and entire restoration of vital forces. It is hardly possible to speak of life when one is ill, weak, tried, or wretched.

This intensity of life extends beyond the person, even, and is applied to all that concerns him and all that he possesses outside his body. Thus to live means not merely to enjoy good health but also to experience wealth and prosperity. To live in poverty and wretchedness is not true life for the men of the O.T. Whosoever enjoys life possesses abundance of material goods and obtains success in his undertakings. This is already true of the beasts which are well fed (people would say: "make one's cattle live"; i.e. give them plenty of fodder, 2 Sam. 12:3; Isa. 7:21–22); similarly with regard to a ruined nation or town which is rebuilt and becomes prosperous once again (Neh. 4:2); but it is especially true of man whose life and prosperity are identical (Deut. 8:1). Hence we arrive at the notion that life is synonymous with happiness and *peace (peace is not the absence of war but perfect felicity, well-being, and good fortune; this is the meaning of the formula of greeting "Peace be with you", Judg. 19:20; 1 Chr. 12:18). To possess life is then to possess the greatest good that there can be (Job 2:4) and what man desires most of all is to enjoy a long life because this means an overflowing of happiness (1 Kings 3:11; Prov. 3:16; Ps. 34:13; 91:16). The formula of acclamation "Let the king live" (1 Sam. 10:24; 2 Sam. 16:16) expresses the desire not only for a prolongation of the life of the king, but that he should enjoy a life in peace, prosperity and happiness; in short, a life in plenitude. Misfortune, adversity, illness, are so many signs of death or of that weakening of vital powers which leads to death.

4. We are thus led to the idea of central importance in the O.T. in regard to life. Fullness of life identifiable with man's happiness cannot be envisaged apart from God. What gives man true life in its wholeness and perfection is his attitude in face of the law of God. He who obeys the commandments of God is walking in the path of life; but he who is unfaithful to the law of the Lord is taking the road that leads to death. Life and death are a question of obedience and disobedience to the will of God (or the wisdom of God, in the Wisdom literature: Proverbs, Ecclesiastes) or again of good and evil, not in the sense of abstract morality but precisely good and evil in the sight of God. That is why happiness and prosperity imply the divine blessing. Man

does not live by bread alone but by every word that proceeds from the mouth of God (Deut. 8:3). He is confronted by a choice: "See, I have set before you this day life and good, death and evil. . . . I command you to love the Lord and to observe His commandments so that you may live and multiply and the Lord your God may bless you. . . . For that means life to you and length of days . . ." (Deut. 30:15–20; cf. also 32:47; 28:1–14; Ps. 36:9–10; Prov. 3:1–10, etc.). Life is a gift of God, a grace which He bestows freely and generously on those who love Him and obey Him.

All this is possible only because the eternal Lord God is the sovereign Lord of life. According to an expression frequent in the O.T. He is "the living God" (Num. 14:28; 2 Kings 2:2; Jer. 10:10; Ezek. 20:31; 33:11). This formula had become common whenever solemn words were uttered or oaths taken, sometimes sheer repetition which the prophets denounced (Jer. 4:2; 5:2). What does it mean? To say that God is living is to say, to an infinitely greater extent than this is true of man, that He possesses life in its unity, its energy, and its plenitude. The livingness of God is not solely what differentiates Him from dead idols (Ps. 115) but what causes Him to be an omnipresent active energy. God is life and He pours out life; He is not a passive divinity in a remote heaven: He creates the world and man, He speaks, He guides, He intervenes in history, He punishes, He delivers (Deut. 32:39; Isa. 57:14–18; 40:12–26; Neh. 9:6). All those metaphorical expressions concerned with life are to be understood only through this relation with God: the tree of life (Gen. 2:9; 3:22; Prov. 3:18), the path of life (Ps. 16:11), the source of life (Ps. 36:10), the book of life (Ps. 69:29), the land of the living (Job 28:13), the light of life (Ps. 56:14). Of course this life which God bestows can only be life in prosperity, happiness, peace, and long duration (Ps. 103:3–5).

5. In ancient Israel, since *death meant descent into the abode of shades, far from the light of God, the supreme blessing was

8*

a prolongation of man's days on the earth, before he was gathered to his fathers or his people in the tomb (Ps. 89:47-49; Gen. 49:33). Some texts of the O.T. however seem to suggest, in terms which are obstinately vague and mysterious, that the believer can know eternal life through his communion with God (Ps. 16:10-11; 73:22-28; Job 19:25-26). But these are exceptional in the O.T. as a whole. On the contrary, we normally find the belief expressed that man receives his recompense from God during the course of his earthly life and that a long life is precisely the reward of the just. But the violent and premature death of a righteous man seemed to cast doubt on the justice of God, and set a painful problem for the faith of believers. The book of Job bears poignant witness to this, and the solution to the problem emerges only very confusedly. It will require the cruel experiences of the brutal persecution and death of the most faithful under the oppression of the pagan (Greek and Roman) empires to give rise to the light of an eternal hope: the hope, namely, of a *resurrection of the dead at the end of time, and of the judgment of God which will condemn some and reward others by the felicity of *eternal life* in the Kingdom of God. This eternal life will not consist in the survival of the spiritual aspect of man's being, for the whole man passes through the experience of death. It will be a wholly new life dating from the resurrection at the last day and eternal in character. The only two texts which speak of it explicitly are Isa. 26:19 and Dan. 12:2.

F. MICHAELI

N.T.

1. The word life in our N.T. translations corresponds to one of three Greek words: *zoe, psyche, bios*. The first is by far the most common. The second, less frequent, really means *soul; like the Hebrew *nephesh*, it denotes the breath of life, the basis of life, and hence the living organism, especially that of the human being (Matt. 2:20; 6:25; 10:39; Mk. 3:4; Lk. 12:20; Jn. 10:11; Acts 2:41). The third term, which is still less frequent, is applied especially to life considered in its modes, whether it be the circumstances in which it passes away (Lk. 8:14; 1 Tim. 2:2) or the resources necessary for its maintenance (Mk. 12:44).

2. If the O.T. idea confines it generally within the limits of this world, this is no longer true of the N.T.; the *resurrection of Jesus on the one hand, the gift of the *Holy Spirit on the other, have effected a far-reaching change in the understanding of life and have shattered the framework in which it was formerly contained.

This does not prevent the N.T. writers from describing life in terms drawn from common experience. Thus with the idea of life is associated that of movement (Acts 17:28). Whatever is endowed with energy and power of effective operation is alive (Rom. 12:1; Heb. 4:12; 1 Pet. 1:3). Life is transient (Jas. 4:14), confined within a given period (Rom. 7:1-3; Heb. 9:17) of which *death is the term (Phil. 1:20). A man truly lives only in so far as he is in good health (Mk. 5:23). Life is the greatest good (Mk. 8:36-37). Man can dispose freely of the gift of life and live as he pleases (Lk. 15:13; Col. 3:7; 2 Tim. 3:12).

As in the O.T., life and death are not considered as phenomena inseparable from each other and linked together by their very nature. They are described not from a scientific point of view, but from the point of view of the relations of man with God, and against the background of faith. Thus without forgetting that one must eat to live, the N.T. affirms that life depends essentially on God (Matt. 4:4; Lk. 12:15; cf. 6:27) who gives it (Acts 17:25,28). He is in effect the living God (Matt. 16:16; Acts 14:15) and the immortal God (1 Tim. 6:16; Rev. 4:9-10) who quickens all things (1 Tim. 6:13). Likewise He can take back the life He has given (Lk. 12:20) or destroy it (Matt. 10:28). It follows that man is responsible before God for the use he makes of his life—before the God who is the Judge of the quick and the dead (Rom. 14:7-12; 1 Pet. 4:5). But the N.T., unlike the O.T., insists less on the immediate consequences of obedience or disobedience to the divine will than on those consequences which will only be disclosed at the last *judgment.

This emphasis reflects a general development in the religious thought of Israel: in proportion as the people of God saw the blessings promised by faith slipping from them as a result of the misfortunes in which they were plunged, they tended to transfer to the future the manifestation of the righteousness of God and in particular the help which He had pledged to them. The "day of the Lord" became the focal point of the aspirations of the pious, because it was the day on which, at last, life in its fullness would be their portion. Thus there emerges an idea of life liberated from all that darkens human life as we know it now; a life where *sickness, pain and death, and *sin which is the underlying cause of all these ills, are no more; a life in which man will share the glorious life of God because nothing will any more hinder his communion with the divine. Like the *Kingdom of God, with which such plenitude of life is identifiable, it may be characterized by the words *righteousness and *peace and *joy in the Holy Ghost (Rom. 14:17) and also by the word *glory (Rom. 2:7; 2 Cor. 3:11; 2 Tim. 2:10; 1 Pet. 5:1,4; cf. Rom. 3:23). In short, such fullness of life alone deserves the name of life, and often the N.T. dispenses with any further qualification for it. But at the same time it is described as life eternal. It is to be noted that this adjective suggests, rather than the infinite duration of this life, its integral connection with the *time of salvation in which it is to break forth. That is why it is called the life of the world to come (1 Tim. 4:8). As compared with it, our present terrestrial existence overshadowed by sin and death is essentially nothing but death (Matt. 8:22; Col. 2:13; 1 Tim. 5:6; Rev. 3:1).

3. It goes without saying that God alone is the Dispenser of this life as of natural life (Acts 13:48) and that men can but *inherit it (Mk. 10:17; Matt. 19:29; Lk. 10:25; Tit. 3:7; 1 Pet. 3:7) or receive it (Mk. 10:30=

Lk. 18:30). Yet the attitude which in the present we adopt with regard to God and His revelation in Christ can render us worthy of it (Matt. 25:46; Mk. 10:17,29ff.; Lk. 10:28; Jn. 5:29; 12:25; Rom. 2:7; 6:22-23; cf. Matt. 7:13-14). This life will be given by an act of God similar to the act with which He created the worlds: viz. the resurrection, which concerns not merely the soul but the entire human personality; for biblical thought, unlike the thought of Greece or the West, cannot conceive of any human existence without corporeality.

But all this would have remained on the plane of religious speculation had it not been for that event which constitutes the corner stone (Acts 4:11; 1 Pet. 2:4; cf. Rom. 10:9; 1 Cor. 15:3ff.) of the Gospel: the resurrection of Jesus Christ from the dead, by which incorruptible life has been disclosed (2 Tim. 1:10) and the hope of believers justified so that it is henceforth a living hope (1 Pet. 1:3). The first Christians greeted in this event the first decisive act in the drama of salvation. For the resurrection of Christ constitutes the beginning of a work which must finally embrace all mankind: "all shall be made alive in Christ but each in his own order" (1 Cor. 15:22-23). Thus Christ can be called the prince of life, i.e. He who walks at the head of the procession of mankind to lead it to eternal life; "the firstborn from the dead" (Col. 1:18; cf. Acts 13:33) destined to be followed by many of His brethren (Rom. 8:29).

4. We appropriate the benefits of this saving work by *faith: by believing in the saving act of God in Jesus Christ. The apostle Paul re-echoes (Rom. 1:17; Gal. 3:11) the words of Habakkuk (2:4): "The righteous shall live by his faith". He who believes will enjoy life eternal (1 Tim. 1:16; Jn. 3:15-16).

When? Here a delicate problem is posed before the reader of the N.T. In fact, here the gift of eternal life appears not only as a hope but in some passages as a present reality also. How is it that believers who still live in the *flesh (Phil. 1:22), i.e. in the conditions of life common to mortal men, and who therefore still await their resurrection or the transformation which must take its place if the general resurrection occurs before their death (1 Cor. 15:50–57; 1 Thess. 4:13–18)—how is it that such can declare that they have already risen with Christ (Col. 3:1) or write: "We know that we have passed out of death into life" (1 Jn. 3:14)? We must still consider the answer to this question.

It is easily understandable that a far-reaching change should take place in the life of the believer who knows that one day he will share in the risen life of his Lord. He sees things differently and he lives differently also. He already grasps the eternal life to which he has been called (1 Tim. 6:12) and to some extent he participates in it here and now. Hence the idea that believers enjoy here and now eternal life is part and parcel of that body of ideas which serve to characterize their present existence.

The word of God, i.e. the Gospel of the death and resurrection of Jesus Christ, is a living word (Heb. 4:12; 1 Pet. 1:23) a word of life (Acts 7:38; cf. Jn. 6:63,68) an incorruptible seed which has produced regeneration (the new birth) of believers (1 Pet. 1:23; cf. 1:3). It follows that the ministry of the Word sheds a fragrance from life to life (2 Cor. 2:16).

The Spirit quickens (2 Cor. 3:6). It is the spirit of life under the ascendancy of which man is freed from the law of sin and death (Rom. 8:1; cf. 8:13) and among the charismatic powers by which it is manifested figures that of healing (1 Cor. 12:9). This Spirit moreover is nothing and no one other than the Lord Himself (2 Cor. 3:17; cf. Gal. 2:20) who is described in 1 Cor. 15:45 as a quickening spirit. But the active presence of the Spirit in the heart of the faithful is only the first-fruits (Rom. 8:23), the *earnest (2 Cor. 1:22; 5:5) of that plenitude of life which is to be the portion of believers. Those who live in the power of the Spirit are bidden to walk also according to the Spirit (Gal. 5:25), to sow unto the Spirit so as to harvest in due time the riches of eternal life (Gal. 6:8–9).

The connection which we have just noted between the Holy Spirit and life appears again when in Rom. 6 the apostle speaks of communion with Christ inaugurated by *baptism (which Tit. 3:5 describes as the baptism of regeneration). In receiving this sacrament believers recognize that Christ died for them and that they themselves are dead in Him, so that as Christ rose again from the dead they too may live with a new life (literally: in newness of life). The apostle does not say that they have risen again but only that they are dead so as to be alive unto God, like Christ with whom they have become one seed. Hence ultimately they will have part in God's gift of eternal life (Rom. 6:23). The Epistles to the Ephesians and Colossians go further and affirm the resurrection of believers as an accomplished fact (Eph. 2:5–6; Col. 2:12–13; 3:1) without failing, however, to note that this resurrection remains for the moment hidden with Christ in God (Col. 3:3) and that the overflowing riches of the grace of God will be fully manifested only in a future aeon (Eph. 2:7). Let us observe further that such declarations as these do not imply that believers may rest content with what they have become by faith, but involve as a consequence that they ought to walk worthily of the grace which they have experienced (Eph. 4:10); the imperative immediately follows the indicative (Col. 3:2,5ff.). That is why the apostle and his companions, enduring in obedience the sufferings which their ministry involves, bear always in their body the marks of the dying of Jesus so that the life of Jesus may be manifested in them. If they do not fear this mortification, it is because they know that God who raised the Lord Jesus from the dead will raise them too and because they perceive that while their outward man is destroyed, their inward man is being renewed day by day (2 Cor. 4:10–18; cf. 6:4–10). Death has thus become a matter of indifference to the apostle, for with him to live is Christ (Phil. 1:21), and whether by life or by death he will be able to glorify the Christ from whom nothing will ever separate him (1 Thess. 5:10) just as nothing will separate him from the love of God manifest in Christ (Rom. 8:28–39). Death would even be gain to him (Phil. 1:21) since it would bring him nearer to the Lord (2 Cor. 5:6–8). But what he would much prefer is that what is mortal in him should be absorbed by life without his having to die (2 Cor. 5:4). He is evidently thinking of the consummation.

5. We have intentionally left aside for separate examination the Johannine writings, because they bear witness still more radically to the truth that in Christ we have access here and now to life eternal.

In the first place let us note that the idea of life occupies a place of fundamental importance in the Johannine outlook: thus the first Epistle ends by declaring that the God of Jesus Christ is the true God and eternal life (5:20) and the first ending of the Gospel says that the work was written so that its readers might believe that Jesus is the Christ the Son of God and believing might have life in His name (20:31). In fact, as the Father has life in Himself so He has given to the Son to have life in Himself (Jn. 5:26). The Son quickens whomsoever He wills (Jn. 5:21). He is the Bread of life (Jn. 6:35,48). He gives living water to drink (Jn. 4:10). Because He leads us to the Father and reveals Him, He is life (Jn. 14:6). It is by faith that one gains the eternal life that abides in Christ (Jn. 3:15–16; 6:40,47; 20:31; 1 Jn. 3:14). *I am the resurrection and the life; he who believes in me, though he die, yet shall he live, and whoever lives and believes in me shall never die* (Jn. 11:25–26). Faith appropriates the gift of life as we listen to the words of Christ (Jn. 5:24; cf. 6:63,68) and submit to the commandment of love (Jn. 12:50; cf. 1 Jn. 2:17; Jn. 13:34; 15:12; 1 Jn. 2:7–10). The sign that one has passed from death unto life is just that one loves the brethren (1 Jn. 3:14). This transition is likened to a birth originating in God (Jn. 1:13; 1 Jn. 2:29; 3:9; 4:7; 5:1,4,18). Again it is a question of this birth when the writer speaks of being born from above or being born of water and the spirit (Jn. 3:3–8); in these two latter expressions it is simply being connected with baptism and the gift of the Holy Spirit.

Thus, in the Johannine writings, eternal life is no longer essentially something that is future. He who believes, who listens to the word of Christ and loves with the love of Christ, has eternal life already here and now. He has not to undergo any further judgment; he has already passed from death unto life (Jn. 5:24; cf. 3:36). This life is, of course, destined to last into the world to come, the advent of which is not doubted (Jn. 4:14; 6:27; 12:25), but whatever change takes place in the new aeon, no element of any importance will be added to what believers already possess through their faith and obedience to Christ. What they are now will simply then be manifested (1 Jn. 3:1–2). Expectation is thus relaxed because it is already fulfilled; for the believer can know here and now the fullness of joy (Jn. 15:11; 17:13, etc.) and incomparable peace (Jn. 14:27; 16:33).

The striking difference which we have just noted between the teaching of Paul and that of John is not after all so considerable as it appears at first sight. It reflects only the difference of temperament between these two witnesses to one and the same Gospel. The one is a man of action bent on attaining the goal, the other is a contemplative, absorbed in the vision of being. Hence the former considers above all what will finally emerge from the prodigious saving work which God has undertaken in Jesus Christ, and in which he is himself an active participant: viz. a veritable re-creation of the world. The latter is overwhelmed by the vision of what God in Christ has already achieved, and with the eye of faith he penetrates so deeply beyond the veil of appearances that for him all things have already been accomplished.

J. BURNIER

LIGHT

1. The light of day, of the sun, of the stars (Gen. 1:4; Exod. 10:23; Job 26:10, etc.).

2. The splendour resulting from a

heavenly manifestation (Matt. 17:2; Acts 9:3; 12:7; 22:6; 26:13; Lk. 2:9; see *glory).

3. But, above all, "light" is employed in the Bible to signify the revelation of God. For the O.T. God enlightens and saves (Ps. 27:1; 36:10; 43:3; Mic. 7:8; Isa. 60:19-20); His word, His law is a light (Ps. 119:105; Prov. 6:23; Isa. 2:2-5). God turns towards man and the light of His face brings him all blessings, joy and peace. The Messiah brings light, He Himself is light (Isa. 42:6; 49:6; 51:4; cf. Lk. 2:32; Acts 13:47). Light is goodness, known and practised (Isa. 5:20), the salvation which is to come (Isa. 9:1).

By contrast, darkness signifies evil, misery, punishment, perdition (Amos 5:18; Isa. 5:20; 59:9; Job 18:6,18; Lam. 3:2; Ps. 88:7; 107:10). Light and darkness are not two worlds statically and impenetrably opposed to each other, but light comes (Ps. 43:3; Isa. 60:1-2). God inhabits inaccessible light (1 Tim. 6:16), and it is not for man to join Him there; but God comes to man in order to cause him to pass from darkness to light; it is in this that salvation consists (Ps. 18:29; Isa. 8:23; 42:7).

4. For the N.T., the light has come: Jesus is the "rising sun" (Lk. 1:78-79), the light that comes to save from darkness and from the shadow of death (Matt. 4:16), the light of the world (Jn. 8:12; 9:5; 12:46). God Himself, who is light, has become man (2 Cor. 4:4,6).

Light and *word are closely associated: Jesus, who is the light, speaks the words of God (Jn. 8:28,31; 12:46-50; Matt. 4:16-17); He is the word made flesh (Jn. 1:1,14). It is in the whole of His ministry and throughout the entirety of His work that Jesus is the light. There is no other light apart from Him, and He has come for the sake of all men (Jn. 1:4,9), in order to rescue them from "darkness", from the world of ignorance, from sin, and from death (Jn. 8:12). The condition imposed is that of following Him (Jn. 8:12), of believing in Him, of keeping His words (Jn. 12:46-47). The majority of men, in fact, do not believe

in Him (Jn. 1:5,10), preferring to remain in darkness (Jn. 3:19-21). Those who believe are made children of God, children of light (Jn. 1:12-13; 12:36).

It is not the fault of Jesus if His light is not perceived among His people, but the fault of those who voluntarily render themselves blind (Lk. 11:33-36; Jn. 9:39-41). The eye is not described as healthy or diseased, but as good or bad, which emphasizes moral responsibility; conversely, "when the light of Jesus reaches man he is placed in his entirety in the light" (Schlatter) (Lk. 11:34-36).

5. Jesus Christ makes those who believe in Him the light of the world (Matt. 5:14; Phil. 2:15; Eph. 5:8,13). They have received the light, and they ought not to hide it (Matt. 5:15; Mk. 4:21=Lk. 8:16), which they would do if ashamed of the Gospel (Matt. 10:33; Mk. 8:38; Rom. 1:16; 2 Tim. 1:8). The light is the word which has been entrusted to them (Phil. 2:15), and it is also their good *works (Matt. 5:16). It is not a matter of their bringing themselves personally into prominence, but their works will praise God because it will be manifest that they come not from them, but from God Himself (Eph. 2:10; Jn. 3:21; Phil. 2:13; Rom. 6:13).

6. The application of the antithesis light–darkness, day–night, to the conduct of believers emphasizes the contrast between their former manner of life, that of the Gentiles, and the new life in Christ. Having passed from darkness to light, they must remain in the light and bring forth its "fruits" (Eph. 5:8-9; cf. the "fruits of the Spirit", Gal. 5:22-23; cf. again, Eph. 4:1: to walk in a manner worthy of their calling). For, from the point of view of faith, darkness is without fruit (Eph. 5:11); the works of darkness exist, it is true, and the apostle cites an extreme example of them, namely, sexual perversion (Rom. 1:24-32; 13:12-14; Eph. 5:12). By condemning these works and unveiling their character of darkness, they are made to enter into the world of light; there is a victory of the light over immorality, and the sinner is called to leave

behind "death" in order to come to the light of Christ (Eph. 5:13–14).

According to 1 Thess. 5:1–7, the "day of the Lord" (Amos 5:18–20) is the day when Jesus Christ will judge the world. The mention of the thief (Matt. 24:43; Lk. 12:39–40) causes one to remember the duty of "watching in the night"; but Paul makes use of the double sense of "day" and "night": believers are the children of the day, whereas the rest of men are of the night. The night is associated with sleep and drunkenness, the day with sobriety and vigilance.

The same antithesis is found again in Rom. 13:11–14: the history of the world is enacted during the night, but the day of the Lord is at hand; Christians should live in this world as being already in the light of the Kingdom of God. In this passage, as in 1 Thess. 5:4–8, it is a question of the "armour" of light (cf. Eph. 6:13–17): faith is not a reclining, but a battle (2 Cor. 6:7; 10:4).

7. It is in this perspective of the new life given to believers and demanded of them that we should understand the declaration of 1 Jn. 1:5: "God is light". Contrary to gnostic doctrines, according to which the soul lives with God and the body does what it pleases, John affirms that God is absolute holiness, purity, truth; one cannot, therefore, be in communion with Him and live in sin. Darkness also reigns where there is no love (1 Jn. 2:8–11).

In the Johannine passages light is inseparable from *life, *truth, and *love. God has placed all these blessings, which properly belong to Him, in His Son, in order that through faith in Him men might receive these gifts and participate in the very life of God.

F. BAUDRAZ

LORD'S SUPPER

The mystery of the Lord's Supper must be understood in terms of sacred history and not of philosophy. To assume that it can be approached by an ontological theory of substances leads to an impasse. Such speculations are condemned to sterility; they suppose they can grasp by human reason what belongs to the order of faith, and they strive to submit to laboratory analysis a life which altogether defies explanation in common human terms.

On the other hand, by approaching the problem of the Lord's Supper through sacred history, the mind finds itself confronted by movement and by life. Earthly realities are lifted to the scale of the Kingdom of heaven; they are subject to the revealing light of the Holy Spirit.

The mystery of the eucharist belongs to a piece of history which has the peculiar character of being earthly and yet culminates in heaven; and from heaven, of course, it receives its true meaning. The things of the present are promised a supernatural destiny, while the realities to come are already taking shape in temporal fashions. The eschatological fulfilment finds here below an anticipation in history, an actuality which is both the presence and the promise of the *Kingdom. It will be the task of faith to recognize and to lay hold of the last things in their concrete manifestations and to nourish the hope which proceeds from the incarnation.

It is therefore easily understood why, when He was foretelling these future things, Jesus gave faith an earthly rather than a heavenly symbol, namely, that of the meal, and in order to represent the promise He had recourse to historical memory. In fact, by renewing the historical custom of the paschal meal, in the Last Supper, He succeeded in giving an image which anticipated that eschatological reality known as the Messianic banquet.

1. *The paschal meal.* The exodus from Egypt was momentous both for the history of Israel and for its great theological import; its significance was marked and the memory of it was recalled by a solemn liturgical act, the paschal meal (Exod. 12). It might have been thought a simple verbal recital of the events would have sufficed. What need of a meal? Because the ritual of

a meal would, much more successfully and in more concrete fashion than any other device, enable the guests to be intimately associated with the historical realities which were represented by what they consumed. For when they ate the lamb's flesh and the unleavened bread and the bitter herbs and drank from the cups, they were not merely recalling a past event, but were actually making it their own in a concrete way; they were placing themselves within the blessed realm of that grace of God which had once delivered the people out of the house of bondage (Exod. 13:8–9).

But even this was not all, for the past also became the pledge of the future. The actualization of the historical deliverance constituted also the anticipation of final deliverance. What God had achieved was but the sign and the beginning and the pledge of what He would do. The salvation accomplished justified His people in waiting for the glorious consummation in the Kingdom of heaven.

In this way those who shared the paschal meal shared in the history of salvation. It made them ready to await and receive the Saviour. It opened to them a vista on the Messianic meal.

2. *The Messianic meal.* Those who continue with Christ in His trials are promised the joy of eating and drinking at His table in the Kingdom (Lk. 22:28–30). This meal will be different from all that have preceded it or prepared for it on earth, for it will mark such a full state of direct communion with the Lord as no other meal could possibly have. All the elect will be gathered with Abraham, Isaac and Jacob round the living Person of Christ (Matt. 8:11). It will mark the completion of the hope of Israel, and will moreover be a fulfilment of it which is concrete, brotherly and joyful. It will be good to be in the Kingdom of heaven, because there one will sit at table, eating and drinking with the Lord. "Blessed is he who shall eat bread in the kingdom of God!" (Lk. 14:15).

It is significant that the believer's hope should take this material form of the meal-

image. Clearly it is to emphasize that the realities of the world to come, however new, are nevertheless not without analogy in the realities of this world. And while our earthly *meals are able to prefigure the heavenly meal, that in turn reflects back on earthly meals the perfect image of the absolute brotherly communion in the joy of the Lord's presence round His own table. We are instructed by what will be, since this, the objective of our waiting, is our pattern; the future is primary.

3. *The Lord's Supper.* The Lord's Supper is located midway between the paschal meal and the Messianic meal, and it acquires meaning from both of them. It is both a recalling and a hope; memorial (1 Cor. 11:24) and anticipation (Matt. 26:29). But this is not by any means to say that it finds no place in the present, as though it was merely a visitation to the past by an act of memory, or an encounter with the future by an act of hope. On the contrary, the Lord's Supper is essentially a present act, a rite of actualization. It is not necessary to isolate and ossify the different aspects, but rather to try to comprehend them in the movement of the history of salvation.

The recalling of the past must be regarded as a recalling from the past to the present life, and the proclamation of the coming of the Kingdom as the present pledge of the life to come. There is, further, no ground for separating the several elements which compose the sacramental reality (commemoration, actualization, and anticipation) into three successive stages of salvation. In the Lord's Supper indeed the Holy Spirit effects the miraculous fusion of these elements; He nourishes the present with the help of the past and the future; He actualizes the different moments of redemption.

In the life, death and resurrection of Christ, the Jewish Passover found its fulfilment and its end. The paschal lamb is replaced by the Lamb of God; to the liberation from the yoke of Egypt now corresponds the freedom from the slavery of sin. Henceforward, the very Body of Christ will be given to us for nourishment and His Blood will preserve us from the plague of the angel of extermination. "Christ, our paschal lamb, has been sacrificed" (1 Cor. 5:7). In Christ all the past is brought under His control and given life. The past, with its death, is promised life. And memory finds itself caught up into hope. "As often as you eat this bread and drink the cup, you proclaim the Lord's death until he comes" (1 Cor. 11:26).

Elsewhere the Kingdom has drawn near to us. The heavenly banquet, where the guests are seated at table with the bridegroom and share in the joy of his presence, is already anticipated on earth by a meal taken at the Saviour's table in the communion of His unseen presence and in the expectation of His coming in glory (Lk. 22:16,18). In Christ the future also is taken under control and joined to the past. The new *covenant, in virtue of which the wedding-hall is already open to us, has indeed been sealed by the blood of Christ, poured out for our sins. And in the measure in which the reality of the meal to come is present, there will also be present for us that which has constituted its price. If the Lord's Supper is received in the radiant prospect of the final redemption, it is also, and for that very reason, received in the shadow of the cross. And the stronger the shadow, the brighter will be the radiance. The more vivid the action of the Lord in glory, the more real will be the presence of the Lamb that was slain.

So the Lord's Supper must be celebrated in joy because it is a living fellowship with Him who is coming (cf. Acts 2:46). But this joy will be tempered with seriousness because it is communion with One who suffered and gave His life for us.

4. *Real Presence.* In the Lord's Supper therefore the believer is placed at once within the benefits of the redemptive death of Christ and the benefits of the blessedness to come. The "how" of all this is a secret of the Holy Spirit's working. It does not belong to us to penetrate this secret, but only to express the mystery of it. The scriptural passages, the synoptic Gospels as

well as John and Paul, all agree in conceiving Christ's presence in the sacrament extremely realistically.

The words by which our Lord defined the sacrament, the repetition of the verb "be" in the present tense in the text of the institution (Matt. 26:26-29 and parallels) clearly emphasize the realism. This *is* my Body, this *is* my Blood.

The "is" should not be made to imply an actual identity. There can be no question of identity here any more than in such expressions as "I am the door" (Jn. 10:7), "I am the way" (Jn. 14:6), "I am the vine" (Jn. 15:1), "the rock was Christ" (1 Cor. 10:4), etc. At the time when most of these statements were uttered, Jesus was still present in the flesh, which obviously excludes any confusion or any idea of one substance being changed into another.

But equally "is" must not be understood in the sense of "signifies", which some have been tempted to substitute for it in order to safeguard the spiritual nature of the Lord's Supper. This gravely weakens the close connection which Christ intended to make between Himself and the material elements which represented Him. It is as essential to avoid separating the Body and the bread, the Blood and the wine, as it is to avoid a simple identification; for Christ is not merely symbolized for us in the eucharist, but actually made present. He is not merely recalled to memory, but actually communicated to us. And His presence does not pertain only to the spiritual order, since it is linked to the material elements of bread and wine.

It is in the fourth Gospel that sacramental realism reaches its most daring expressions. "I am the living bread which came down from heaven; if any one eats of this bread, he will live for ever; and the bread which I shall give for the life of the world is my flesh" (Jn. 6:51). One can well understand the Jews who disputed among themselves saying, "How can he give us his flesh to eat?" Nor did Jesus relieve the difficulty in His reply, but rather emphasized more radically the paradox: "Truly, truly, I say to you, unless you eat the flesh of the Son of Man and drink his blood, you have no life in you" (cf. Jn. 6:52–58). Yet in the same chapter, and following upon the most absolute declarations on the material aspect of the communion, occurs this peremptory declaration: "It is the spirit that gives life, the flesh is of no avail" (Jn. 6:63). This is a warning against the temptation to rationalize philosophically about substances and, through a perverse ambition to explain, to do violence to something that ought to remain the prerogative of the Spirit. The flesh and the Spirit are the two poles between which fly the sparks of the eucharistic life. The Spirit is at work at the holy table through the material ("fleshly") elements which are laid on it, and His action is essentially directed towards the actualization and the incorporation of a presence. He not only makes the presence of Christ actual here and now, but also, because of the bread and wine, makes possible its incorporation—that is to say, the living presence—in the believer and in the Church.

The Pauline usage is perfectly in accord with this realism, and is expressed in strikingly adequate terms: "The cup of blessing which we bless, is it not a participation in the blood of Christ? The bread which we break, is it not a participation in the body of Christ?" (1 Cor. 10:16). The bread and the wine are not here, any more than in the other texts, identified with the Body and Blood. Nor yet are they symbols or even signs of the Body and Blood (that sort of reasoning would again be to drag down to the rational level what belongs to the supernatural). But, through the power of the Holy Spirit, they are in communion with the Body and the Blood; that is to say, they are, together, the medium by which the history of the salvation accomplished in the death, resurrection and ascension (with its implication of the return) is actualized in the believer and in the Church.

By this communion, the Christian is inserted into the new covenant, on an axis whose extreme points are the earthly and fleshly at one end, and the heavenly and the spiritual at the other. It is the way which leads from deliverance to promise, from salvation received to salvation expected: it is the way of the *Church.

5. *The Body of Christ.* From the beginning of the Church, Christians met at each other's houses for a meal, during which the president pronounced a prayer of thanksgiving (eucharist), broke the bread and distributed the cup to all the participants, in accordance with the Lord's command. This eucharistic meal was the central act of their worship, and of its importance in the life of the newborn Church there can be no doubt (Acts 20:7). The breaking of bread is one of the marks of the Church (Acts 2:42), and one of the essential pillars, as it were, on which she has been built up.

It is inconceivable that a Church which is faithful to its title deeds and obedient to the Word of God could minimize the vital importance of the eucharist or thrust it aside from the centre of its preoccupations. The celebration of the Lord's Supper having been made part of the *normal* life of the Church, it is the indispensable food for every Christian soul who wills to be in communion with Christ and his neighbour. In the *time which elapses between the ascension and the parousia, the eucharist is the sign of the presence and the action of Christ, the decisive focus for the life and structure of the community.

In the Church, then, the Holy Spirit actualizes the *Kingdom by even now imparting to those who gather round the Lord's table the vitality of the world to come, the power of *forgiveness and of *love. The guests are constituted a body which witnesses in this world to the reality of another world. The communion of the many in the same bread begets a human brotherhood (1 Cor. 10:16–17), to which is already given what is still promised, and promised what is already given.

J.-PH. RAMSEYER

LOVE

Whereas Hebrew possessed only a single principal verb to express the various shades of meaning of love (the particular sense being determined by the context), Greek had three words for it:

(*a*) *Eran* (which has given "erotic") chiefly denoted the love of *desire*; desire not only of man for woman but for all kinds of objects worthy to be possessed (the love of beauty, of good, etc.). This possessive love was the principal motive of the moral life (love of the virtues), the artistic life (love of beauty), the philosophic life (love of the gods, of life eternal, of immortality, etc.), in the Graeco-Roman world.

(*b*) *Philein* (which has given "philanthropy", etc.) denotes the unselfish love which cares for a man, a friend, a native land, and so on. Greek thought chiefly points it out among superior people (Antigone, for example), in whom the will and nobility of heart have mastered human passions.

(*c*) *Agapan*, much less frequent and much less colourful, was employed in the two senses given above with a preference for the second. Now it is a significant fact that it is this last verb which the translators of the O.T. into Greek preferred most often to translate the corresponding Hebrew word, and from the O.T. this Greek word passed into early Christian language and was spread throughout the Graeco-Roman world by the N.T. Perhaps no other Greek term owed so much to early Christianity.

1. *The love of God for man.* Contrary to what is often stated, the O.T. knows the idea of the love of God for man, with the following principal shades of meaning:

(*a*) The love of Yahweh is expressed and revealed principally by His *interventions in history* on behalf of His people. It is therefore an active love, addressed in the first instance to a community. "I have loved you (Jerusalem) with an everlasting love . . ." (Jer. 31:3; cf. Deut. 4:37; 10:15; Ps. 41:12). The Israelite chiefly discerned this love of God in the great deliverances of his eventful history. This is quite different from a taste or momentary interest (such as often appears in Greek myths). The love of Yahweh is "renewed" from generation to generation; it has its plan, its everlasting purpose.

(*b*) Only His interventions in history explain the bringing together of Israel; it is an *elective and creative* love; nothing in its object causes it; Yahweh creates the people whom He intends to love and save freely. "It was not because you were more in number than any other people that the Lord set his love upon you and chose you, for you were the fewest of all peoples; but it is because the Lord loves you, and is keeping the oath which he swore to your fathers" (Deut. 7:7; cf. also 4:37; 7:8,13; 10:15; Jer. 12:7–9; Isa. 54:5–8; Hos. 11:1; Mal. 1:2; Isa. 41:8; 2 Chr. 20:7).

(*c*) Finally and above all, this love is a *merciful* love: it saves (succours, restores) and pardons (Deut. 23:5; Isa. 43:25; Ps. 86:5; Isa. 63:9: "in his love he redeemed them"; Hos. 14:4; 11:7–9: ". . . for I am God and not man"). It is in this love, at the same time sovereign and merciful, that Yahweh reveals truly who He is; on this point the book of Hosea has no equal in the O.T. Of course, to these three fundamental features are often added complementary ideas: if Yahweh loves this people first He also loves "other peoples" (Deut. 33:3, an obscure text), He loves Abraham and Israel so that through them His love may reach all nations; if God loves freely and sovereignly He also loves "righteousness" or "those who practise righteousness" (Ps. 11:7; 33:5; 37:28; 146:8; Prov. 15:9) and if in the first place He loves the chosen people He also loves each of its members individually (Isa. 41:8; Mal. 1:2; Ps. 41:12; Prov. 3:12, etc.).

The N.T. takes up again, gives precision to, and develops these three intuitions of the O.T.:

(*a*) The love of God is revealed in an *historic event* which completes all the particular deliverances accorded to the fathers: the event of *Jesus Christ. In the synoptic Gospels this historic intervention of God is the approach of the *Kingdom of God inaugurated by Jesus. It cannot be too much stressed that this Kingdom opens a "period of mercy", and if repentance is urgent it is so because the possibility of it is given in the mercifulness of God actualized in the historic ministry of Jesus (this is the meaning, in particular, of the Beatitudes: *blessed!). According to Paul this historic fact is principally that of the cross and the resurrection of Christ, regarded together as the unique and sufficient revelation of the love of God (Rom. 5:8; 8:28,31ff., etc.). In the Johannine writings stress is similarly laid on Christ crucified (Jn. 3:16 where "gave" signifies delivered to death; 1 Jn. 4:9), but with particular insistence on the idea that God not only has loved (in the past) or merely loves (in the present) but that He *is* love (1 Jn. 4:8). By that the Epistle does not mean that the idea of God can be reduced to that of love, as a supreme value, but on the contrary that love can only be known by the revelation which God has given of Himself in Jesus Christ.

(*b*) That "historic" love of God is also elective and creative. God first "chose" Jesus, His only or "well beloved" son (Mk. 12:6 and parallels); He set Him apart, reserved for a special mission. The love of the Father for the Son and of the Son for the Father is thus at the basis of Johannine Christology, a love based above all on a perfect harmony between what God thinks or wills and what Jesus performs. There is no question here of a mystical confusion of the Father and the Son but of personal and active communion in the service of men (Jn. 3:35; 5:20; 10:17; 14:31; 17:23,24,26). With Paul the stress falls upon the sovereignty which chooses and calls whom He will to constitute His Church on the earth (Rom. 9:13,25): the elect are the beloved of God, which comes to the same thing (Rom. 1:7; Col. 3:12; 2 Thess. 2:13; Eph. 1:4; 2:4).

(*c*) Finally, this love of God in historic action in the person of Jesus is a love which shows mercy, which pardons. In the synoptic Gospels this love corresponds to the Messianic proclamation of the "year of grace", to the "authority" with which Jesus *forgives* sins (Mk. 2:5,10; 1:22; 11:28, etc.). Jesus does not forgive sins because He has a kind heart, nor because

He knows that God always forgives: if He forgives sins it is because He fulfils on the earth an historic ministry which corresponds to a new and final initiative of God to succour men. With Paul the references to the merciful love of God are not very numerous but are of a precision which leaves nothing to be desired. Not that the idea is foreign to him, but the apostle expresses it by other terms. It is undeniable that when Paul speaks of the *justification of man by God he is thinking above all of a work of sovereign, free, reconciling love. Paul discovers this love always in the *cross of Christ, never in an abstract definition of God. Even in Rom. 5:5 (where it is probably a question of God's love for us, contrary to St. Augustine's opinion) this love "shed abroad in our hearts" is connected with the sacrifice of the cross (v. 8), the chief characteristic of which was to have saved not the righteous but sinners ("while we were yet sinners", v. 8; cf. Eph. 2:5). But that love of God (or of Christ—the expression means the same) is not only an objective fact; accomplished in the past, it is the permanent reality by which the Church lives, which it cannot "know" once for all. That knowledge of love, which is personal communion as well as intellectual comprehension, is the "root" and "foundation" of the Christian life as its goal and fulfilment: it "fills" the believer with all the "fullness of God" (Eph. 3:18,19). It is to this knowledge of the love of God "incarnate" in Christ that the fourth Gospel consecrates some of its most impressive pages, summarized in the "ministration" described in Jn. 13.

2. *The love of man for God.* To the historic, elective and merciful love of God for men there answers throughout the Bible the love of man for God. So far as the O.T. is concerned, four main points may be stated:

(*a*) The God whom man loves is above all the deliverer. God is not loved for His perfections but for His historic acts of succour. The one the Psalmist loves (Ps. 18:2–4) is his "deliverer", his "refuge", his "strong saviour", the one who "delivers him from his enemies". "I love the Lord, because he has heard my voice and my supplications." God is loved for His "compassions". Even in a text as free from sentiment as Deut. 6:5 the command to love is preceded by a reminder of the initiative of Yahweh: the people are exhorted to love "their" god, that is to say the one who has chosen and delivered them.

(b) This love of man for God is a service, an act of obedience. The love for Yahweh, whether of the nation, a part of the nation or an individual believer, is not thought of as an emotion, as admiration or even as an aspiration towards God. To love God is to serve Him, in fact "to keep his commandments and his statutes" (Deut. 10:12ff.; in this text the various verbs which follow: fear, love, serve, keep, etc., should be understood as synonyms; cf. Jer. 8:2 where the verb to love is applied to idols). To love Yahweh and to keep His commandments are synonymous expressions (Exod. 20:6; Deut. 5:10; 7:9; 11:1; 1 Kings 3:3; Dan. 9:4; Neh. 1:5); to walk in His ways also has the same meaning (Deut. 10:12; 11:22; 19:9; etc.).

(c) This love-service of God is a personal and total (exclusive) obedience, engaging all the faculties of man. There is never any confusion between the man who loves, and God who is loved. The man's entire being is mobilized in a loving service which is his happiness and joy: all the heart and soul and strength are involved (Deut. 6:5; cf. 11:13; 30:6; cf. Matt. 22:37). There is not a spiritual principle in *man predisposed to the love of God. Man *must* love: this love is therefore ordered from him, and his "heart" is here not the seat of sentiment or emotion but of the will and of decision.

(d) Lastly, the O.T. always remains very sober and humble when it speaks of this love. It knows that the love is ceaselessly put to the test and that the test often turns to the confusion of the people of God (Hosea; Deut. 13:3ff.: "the Lord your God is testing you, to know whether you love the Lord your God with all your heart and with all your soul . . ."; cf. Jer. 2:2ff.). And the

O.T. also knows that this love, total and without shortcoming, is or will be an eschatological gift of God: "the Lord your God will circumcise your heart and the heart of your offspring, so that you will love the Lord your God with all your heart and with all your soul, that you may live" (Deut. 30:6).

The N.T. texts on the love of man for God can only be appreciated on this O.T. basis.

(a) According to the N.T. also, the love of man is a response to the saving love of God, with this decisive qualification that early Christian *faith discovers that divine love in the person and work of Jesus Christ. In the synoptic Gospels it is chiefly in the proclamation of the reign of God (a reign of mercy, a "year of grace") and in the activity of Jesus on behalf of sinners that the love of God is revealed (Lk. 7:44ff.; 6:36; 15). To that in-breaking of the Kingdom the response must be love, an unreserved dedication of man to God (Matt. 6:24ff.; Lk. 17:7ff.; Matt. 5:29; 10:37ff.; Lk. 14:26ff.). The apostle Paul has strongly accentuated the dependence of man's love for God upon the antecedent love of God: he lives "by faith in the Son of God" who loved him and gave Himself up for him (Gal. 2:20). And the Johannine writings, more than any others, have insisted on the priority of divine love (1 Jn. 3:1,16; 4:10,11,17,19: "we love, because he first loved us").

(b) Early Christian love is also, as in the O.T., more a definite service than a sentiment or aspiration of the soul. It is a voluntary engagement to a new obedience. Man is always regarded as the "servant" of a master, God or mammon. It is necessary for him now to choose between the two (Matt. 6:24; Lk. 16:13); to love God is *ipso facto* to detest, to "hate" Mammon. It is a striking fact that it is the Johannine writings, so often interpreted in a mystical sense, which refer with the greatest insistence to this characteristic of the love of God: "For this is the love of God, that we keep his commandments" (1 Jn. 5:3; cf. 2 Jn. 6; 1 Jn. 4:20).

(c) Finally, as in the O.T., love for God is a love which is "commanded". Man does not love God by nature; that requirement as well as that possibility (given in Jesus Christ) must constantly be recalled to him (Matt. 22:37; Mk. 12:30,33; Lk. 10:27).

3. *The love of man for man.* The O.T. knows all the nuances of the love of man for man. The texts can be classified into three main groups, according as they refer to love for a neighbour, love for parents, friends and co-religionists, or sexual love. In the O.T. these three shades of meaning are covered by one and the same verb; however, they often overlap and no useful purpose is served by distinguishing there a category called "profane" from another called "sacred", for the entire life of the people in all its many-sidedness is constantly referred to God and to His law, so that it is entirely religious (as will be the life of the early Christians) as well as being quite concrete, everyday, family or conjugal love at the same time.

The O.T. knows the idea of love to one's neighbour (Lev. 19:17ff.: "you shall love your neighbour as yourself: I am the Lord"; cf. Zech. 8:16f.); and the context shows that this love is something quite different from a sentiment of racial preference or personal sympathy. It is a matter of "not committing an injustice", of not spreading calumny among the people and even of reproving one's neighbour so as not to be found guilty of his sin. In the context, the *neighbour is a member of the national or religious community. Nevertheless, love is not explicitly limited by these frontiers; only it is there that it ought first to be exercised. For the O.T. also knows a love of one's enemy (cf. Exod. 23:4) and of the stranger: "you know the heart of a stranger, for you were strangers in the land of Egypt" (Exod. 23:9). It might be said that it is under the protection of this love which is respect and service for man that family and national love is expressed in innumerable shades of meaning (2 Sam. 1; 1 Sam. 20:17; 16:21; 18:3), as also sexual love (e.g. Gen. 29: the amours of Jacob; 2 Sam. 13: the

abnormal passion of Amnon for Tamar; especially the Song of Songs, a wonderful love-song which must be taken in the first instance in its simplest and most human meaning before seeing in it an allegory of the love of God for His people). There is no expression in the O.T. of any contempt whatever for the body or for sexual love as such. Man and woman, created and united by the Creator, together form a unity within which each party offers to the other the best of itself (Gen. 2:18–25, *marriage). If the Israelites had frequently to be put on guard against foreign prostitutes it was not because of their "impurity" but that their idolatrous religions ran the risk of contaminating Israel (e.g. 1 Kings 11:1ff.; in Ezra 9 and 10 it is not a question of prostitutes but of foreign wives, but the danger is the same).

Here again the N.T. can be understood only in the light of the O.T. Jesus, following the rabbis, takes up in His turn the two commandments of love to God and to one's neighbour (Mk. 12:28ff.; Matt. 22:34ff.; Lk. 10:25–27). More than the rabbis He underlines their indissoluble unity (Matt. 25:31–46; 18:23–35). In both cases to love means first of all to serve—a service of God in a renewed obedience to His will, and a service of man chiefly by such immediate help as the occasion requires (Lk. 10:29ff.). Also, more categorically than the rabbis, Jesus enjoins the love of enemies. We do not know where his listeners got the idea of hate for one's enemies (perhaps from certain Psalms?). This love of adversaries (probably in a law suit, Matt. 5:38ff.) and of enemies (probably enemies of the new people of God, persecutors, Matt. 5:43ff.) is characterized in one place as an act of *patience* (not retaliating, renouncing self-defence, thus putting an end to the conflict) and chiefly as an act of *mercy* (not to show preference for anyone, helping and favourably treating each with the royal generosity which marks the historic action of God in Jesus Christ). The divine "perfection" (Matt. 5:48) of that love does not make men who love into demi-gods, nor even into exceptional personalities; more simply, in the *acts* of love of the disciples, Jesus recognizes something of the perfect mercifulness of God (cf. the parallel text in Lk. 6:36).

In the Epistles the law of love is recalled (Rom. 13:8–10); "he who loves his neighbour has fulfilled the law" (v. 8), not in the sense that he is raised to a moral life higher than that prescribed in the Decalogue, but because by loving he submits himself at one stroke to all the prescriptions of the Decalogue (v. 10: "love is the fulfilling of the law"). Significantly enough, this requirement of love appears at the end of the Epistles (cf. chiefly Romans and Galatians), as a consequence of the *salvation of God described in the body of the letter. This love is presented as the "fruit of the Spirit" (Gal. 5:22; Rom. 15:30). The Law and the Spirit combine to demand from, and to give to, the believer this fulfilling of the divine order: by love alone the faith that has received salvation becomes active and productive (Gal. 5:6). But the Epistles lay less stress on love of the neighbour than upon brotherly love (Gal. 5:14; 1 Thess. 4:9; Col. 1:4; Philem. 5). This brotherly love, a product of active solidarity in joy as well as in suffering, already belongs to the Kingdom of God: it "never perishes" (1 Cor. 13:8) when other temporary attitudes of the Christian (including faith and hope) are fulfilled and absorbed by the final breaking-in of the Kingdom. Whilst the Epistle of James insists chiefly on the concrete character of that love—the "royal law" (2:8), which teaches the sharing of possessions with the needy (2:16), and the refusal to speak evil of the brethren (3:1ff.), and which, alone, gives life to faith (2:1ff, 2:14–26)—the Johannine writings present love (taken absolutely, 1 Jn. 3:14,18; 4:7,8,19) and particularly brotherly love (1 Jn. 2:10; 3:10; 4:20; 3:11, etc.) as the fulfilment and the one authentic seal of all Christian life (1 Jn. 2:10; 4:12). However it may appear at first sight, the first Epistle of John is primarily concerned with concrete, communal life; it reminds believers that love as the Christian understands it is neither a feeling of the soul nor an interior perfection but brotherly service:

"he who loves God should love his brother also" (1 Jn. 4:21).

It is on this basis of faith in the free and royal love of God revealed in Jesus Christ and of a brotherly love of an extremely day to day variety that what the Epistles say about conjugal love is to be understood. This latter is not absorbed or sublimated by the former; it merely receives thereby its ultimate significance and its intensity (Eph. 5:25,28,33; Col. 3:19). As the love of Christ for the Church has two essential characteristics (He gave Himself for her, and He desires her to be perfect and glorious in His presence) so a man will love his wife with a love which surrenders itself and which provides for her true destiny (for the "glory" of the spouse). In such a case conjugal love will be like a parable of the love of Christ.

P. BONNARD

MAN

O.T.

1. At the root of the O.T. teaching on the subject of man lies the assertion that he is a *creature*. As such he is characterized by weakness and mortality, while God enjoys strength and eternal life (Job 14:1f.; Ps. 103:15f.). Man was created mortal, and the fall of the first man resulted in no change in this state beyond that of making final a condition which God had possibly reserved the right to alter, had man persevered in obedience (Gen. 3:22). To look to man for salvation and life, therefore, is to delude oneself (Isa. 31:3; Jer. 17:5). This condition of creatureliness man shares with the animals: the fate of each is the same (Eccl. 3:19; Ps. 49:12). But as a being created by God, who has breathed into his nostrils the breath of life, man also enjoys an outstanding dignity. In the sphere assigned to him he is able to exert power and dominion over the surrounding nature (Gen. 1:27; Ps. 8:6ff.).

But if the bond that unites man to God is the foundation of all anthropology, man's relation to his fellows is hardly less important. According to the view that predominates in the O.T., it is not the individual that constitutes the primal reality, but the group, the enduring entity in which the individual strikes his roots and finds his immortality: individuals pass away, the people endure. At the same time, the substantial reality of the group can focus itself in a single individual, a conception that finds its highest expression in the *Servant of the Lord in Isaiah (40–55). The normal word for man in Hebrew expresses this double relationship: adam is he who is taken from adamah, the ground—a weak, ephemeral being—and this name is also regarded as the proper name of the first man (first instance, Gen. 3:17); yet, on the other hand, the sociological setting of man is expressed by the term ben adam, "son of man" or "humanity", where adam denotes the collective type.

2. Everything the O.T. has to teach about man can be found in the narratives of the *Creation. The fullest definition is that given by the Yahwist: "The Lord God formed man of dust from the ground, and breathed into his nostrils the breath of life; and man became a living being" (Gen. 2:7). This text clearly asserts that life is the exclusive possession of God, and that man exists only in so far as he receives the breath of life, which God gives him by an act of His sovereign grace (cf. Ps. 104:29f.). The body and the breath of life, both coming, as they do, from God, are not two elements that may be isolated and treated separately. The divine life penetrates the total being to such a degree that each organ of the body can express the life of the whole. Far indeed from being a covering to hide the soul, the body is, on the contrary, the indispensable expression of that immaterial reality which is the principle of life; hence the psychic and spiritual functions are always related to an organ of the body. On the O.T. view, man has no soul, but the Hebrew term (nephesh) translated "soul" in the modern versions denotes a psycho-physical totality, corresponding to that which we mean when we talk of a living being and its different modes of expression.

The term nephesh is found in the following senses:

(a) Life in general: a life for a life, in the legal texts (Exod. 21:23; Deut. 19:21), that life which one seeks to destroy or is obliged to respect (1 Kings 19:2; Exod. 4:19; Job 2:6).

(b) Life as it appears in certain bodily features most strikingly associated with the presence of life: breathing and breath (Job 41:13; Exod. 23:12; 31:17; Gen. 35:18), *blood (Gen. 9:4; Lev. 17:11,14; Deut. 12:23; Ps. 141:8).

(c) Life as it appears in certain more especially psychical functions, such as longing or desire (2 Sam. 3:21; Ps. 24:4; 41:3; Prov. 23:2; Isa. 26:8; Ezek. 24:25).

(d) Life as it appears in the totality of elements constituting a human person (Gen. 14:21; 46:18; Num. 5:6; Ezek. 33:6; when used with the first person suffix, nephesh corresponds to "I" and can be translated by the personal pronoun).

(e) Life as it appears in the corpse, before this has decomposed (Lev. 19:28; 21:1,11; Num. 6:6; Hagg. 2:13).

3. The various elements that constitute the living being have a part to play only in so far as they are animated by the principle of life.

(a) The flesh, which in mythical and poetic language is referred to as "dust", is the basic element that distinguishes man from God (Gen. 6:3; 2 Chr. 32:8; Ps. 145:21; Isa. 31:3; 40:6; Jer. 17:5, etc.), but, despite its material nature, it is capable of being the seat of functions transcending those usually implied by the word fleshly or carnal (Ps. 84:3, where the flesh longs for God; cf. also Ps. 16:9; 119:120), and the idea of the flesh as a principle in opposition to God and as the seat of sin is completely foreign to the O.T. We meet this idea for the first time, patently as the result of Hellenistic influence, in the Wisdom of Solomon (9:15).

(b) The spirit is the essential characteristic of God, and as such makes its appearance in those whom the O.T. calls "men of God". The heroes of the book of Judges are enabled to perform amazing and superhuman actions by the gift of the spirit of Yahweh: at the same time, however, they are hardly "spiritual" men, in the sense in which we understand that word (Judg. 3:10; 6:34; 11:29; 14:6; 15:14). Thus, in Samson, the spirit's activity is manifested in his extraordinary physical strength.

The king is also a man endowed with "spirit": at the time of his anointing by Samuel, Saul is seized by the spirit, which changes him into "another man" (1 Sam. 10:6–13). It is also the spirit which gives the prophet the power to carry out his mission, although the pre-exilic prophets make only occasional references to it (Hos. 9:7; Mic. 3:8; Ezek. 11:1ff.). But in other passages, the spirit denotes rather an ingredient of the human psyche and frequently overlaps with *nephesh*. We may, however, distinguish between them by saying that the *nephesh* is life tending to manifest itself in concrete form, while *ruah* (spirit) is life in its hidden and interior aspect, and corresponds more closely to what we understand by "soul" (Gen. 41:8; Judg. 8:3; 1 Kings 21:5; Isa. 25:4; Ps. 76:13; Prov. 16-32). The spirit is also the seat of thought (Ezek. 11:5; 20:32), and the supreme religious instrument by which man has communion with God: according to Ps. 51:12ff., it is the spirit in man which is capable of receiving the *Holy Spirit, i.e., the Spirit of God, and of being renewed by it.

(c) *The heart* corresponds even more than the spirit to our idea of the soul. It is the great controlling instrument, which regulates the *ruah* in order that the *nephesh* may function properly. The springs of life take their rise in the heart (Prov. 4:23), which means that the heart is, more than any other, the organ where the spirit, the source of life, can establish itself. The heart and the spirit frequently have the same functions (Exod. 35:21; Ps. 78:8), but an anthropology which seeks to regard man as an autonomous, independent entity will substitute the term "heart" for that of "spirit", which first and foremost serves to denote the power of God. The heart is the inward, hidden member: hence, it denotes the deepest level of the personality, the conscience; but equally it is the organ of understanding and knowledge (1 Sam. 24:6; 25:31; 2 Sam. 24:10; 1 Kings 2:44; Jer. 17:1; Prov. 23:12; Eccl. 7:27). "To think" in Hebrew is expressed as to say in, or to, one's heart (Gen. 24:45; 8:21; 1 Sam. 1:13; Eccl. 1:16). The individual with no heart is therefore a being with no understanding (Prov. 6:32; 7:7), and to "steal" a man's heart is to deceive his understanding by depriving him for the time being of his powers of reasoning (Gen. 31:20,26; 2 Sam. 15:6,13). The faculty of attention ("laying to heart") also has its seat here (Ezek. 44:5; Exod. 7:23) and it is the heart, too, which dictates a man's moral conduct (Isa. 57:17; Eccl. 11:9) and directs his will and affections. It is to be noted, however, that its affective rôle is secondary to its functions of intelligence. Nevertheless, so many functions are connected with the heart that, according to the O.T., it is possible to say that man's heart is the index of his whole self.

4. The author of the priestly account of the Creation defines the nature and function of man in terms of the *image and likeness of God. Although this concept is found only in the priestly stratum of the Pentateuch (Gen. 1:26f.; 5:1,3; 9:6), it sums up in one lapidary phrase the whole teaching of the O.T. on the subject of man. The "image of God" refers not to one or other of the spiritual or moral functions of man, perfection, liberty, reason, etc., but to human nature as a psycho-physical totality; for the Hebrew term translated image always denotes a tangible representation, an effigy or statue. Further, throughout the ancient East, the image was a manifestation, and, as it were, an incarnation of that which it represented: thus the image of a god or of a king expressed his veritable presence in and dominion over the place where it was set up. If, then, man is the image of God, it means that he is on earth as God's representative. This representative function man exercises by his rule over the animal world (Gen. 1:27ff.) and Psalm 8, which is the best commentary on the theme of the image of

God even though the actual word does not appear in it, also stresses the *imperium* which God has given to man, to whom He has genuinely delegated a part of His sovereignty. It is because he is the image of God that man is marked off from the animals. From the purely biological point of view they are not so very different, except that an animal has no "heart", but in the hierarchy of creatures they are on different levels, and the legal texts insist that the boundary between the human and animal worlds must always be respected (Lev. 18:23). As it forms an integral part of human nature, the image of God in man is not annihilated by the Fall and continues to exist even after the Deluge.

This aspect of man is in no way in contradiction with what the O.T. has to say about his weakness and dependence, for its effectiveness depends entirely on the degree to which the representative remains in touch with that which he represents. When man wishes to be as God, the temptation suggested by the serpent in Genesis, he steps out of his creaturely rôle and becomes a caricature. The foundation of the O.T. view of man is the assertion of his dependence on God and of his autonomy in relation to the world. Both the dependence and the dominion are expressed, for example, in that joy which is at the heart of O.T. piety, or in its positive attitude to work and culture. We may also wonder whether this theme of the image of God is not at the root of that Jewish humanism which finds its unparalleled expression in the Wisdom literature.

5. The same priestly author, in speaking of the creation of man, says: "Male and female he created *them*" (Gen. 1:27). This text forbids us to think of the creation of the first man as that of an androgyne, though this is the view of a Jewish haggadic tradition anxious to harmonize the indications of Gen. 1:27 with those of 2:18ff. According to this second story, the *woman was taken from the man, but she owes her creation to Yahweh alone, who, by plunging the man into a deep sleep, restricts him to an entirely passive rôle in the whole operation. Though this myth of the creation of woman out of the side of man is designed to explain the particular physical characteristics of the male and female, its primary object is to explain the mutual attraction of the sexes and to express by imagery that it is only in *marriage that men and women can fully realize their vocation. It is true that the woman is characterized by the submission which she owes to her husband, and that the matrimonial customs of the O.T. present the woman as a chattel acquired by the husband for money; but in leaving his father and mother to attach himself to his wife (Gen. 2:24) the man affirms that she is truly a being like himself. The mutual attraction of the sexes finds remarkable poetic expression in the Song of Songs, and the married state became, in the corpus of the prophetic tradition, the most frequent image of the covenant relationship of Yahweh with His people.

ED. JACOB

N.T.

Before trying to isolate the N.T. picture of man, a preliminary warning is necessary. The N.T. writers see man only and always as he stands before God. They take no cognisance of man in himself. The likeness of man is not to be drawn from a something called "human nature", the essence of which can be defined, its parts distinguished and its features and manifestations analysed. Man can only be surveyed and known in the history of his relations with God. Biblical anthropology is always one with theology and does not exist except as a function of the latter.

1. *The make-up of the human being.* This derivative character of anthropology is brought out when we examine the concepts that, in the N.T., define and describe the make-up of the human being. The most significant material for this examination is to be found in the writings of the apostle Paul; but if we set the indications of these texts beside those of the synoptists and the

Johannine writings, we find certain outstanding features emphasized by all.

(a) The concept of the *body*, common in the N.T., defines man as a complex organism, a whole, a unity. It is not simply the "form" of the organism, as opposed to the substance which might be its content, but a mode of being essential to and constitutive of the human person. There is no human existence which is not bodily existence (cf. 1 Cor. 15:35ff.). This corporal nature of man is most obviously expressed in his material body, that unity in which the various members are collected into a harmonious and well co-ordinated whole (Matt. 5:30; 6:25; Rom. 12:4ff.; 1 Cor. 12:12–26). But, in contrast to Greek thought, the "body" connotes a reality much more extensive than the biological unity that is a man, his visible, tangible, sensible body. It denotes man, the human person in his entirety. Thus the apostle Paul cannot conceive of a future human existence, beyond both *death and *resurrection, without a body. Nevertheless, the body is no longer to be a carnal but a spiritual one (1 Cor. 15:35–49; Phil. 3:21).

(b) Nor does the *soul*, any more than the body, denote a part of man, but the whole man in one particular aspect. To be more precise, it is—as in the O.T.—man in his character of a *living* being. Here, too, the strictly biological and naturalist sense of the word "life" is transcended. The "soul" is human life regarded as the life of an individual being with consciousness and will (Matt. 10:28; 16:26; Lk. 9:56; 12:19f.; Jn. 12:27; 2 Cor. 1:23; 12:15; Phil. 1:27; 1 Thess. 2:8). But living man does not possess the source of life and the possibility of continued existence in himself. Adam became a living soul, when God breathed into his nostrils the breath of life. It is God who determines the extent of each man's life (Matt. 6:26–30; 1 Cor. 15:45).

(c) Man as a living person is also a being with *intelligence*. He is capable of knowledge, understanding, experience and at the same time of relating himself to his environment, of willing, of adopting a particular

standpoint. The element of *will* is always involved in the intelligence of a thinking being. In the N.T., therefore, the concepts of *mind* and of *heart* denote the most inward aspects of human personality. It is the rational and conscious will of the man who experiences and evaluates, who accepts or rejects, who judges and chooses (cf. for the concept of heart: Lk. 2:19; 8:15; Matt. 6:21; 15:8; Jn. 12:40; Rom. 2:15; 6:17; Phil. 1:7; Eph. 3:17; for the intelligence: cf. 1 Cor. 1:10; Rom. 12:2; 14:5; 7:23).

But this inward "I" appears in actual human existence, especially according to the Pauline writings, as incapable of real independence. The argument of Rom. 7 demonstrates that it has no power to do the good. By itself it can conceive, it can will the good, but this process remains at the stage of imagination, of intention, of law. As soon as it becomes a question of practical performance, it becomes dependent, the agent and slave of a power not itself.

(d) In the life of the natural man, this power turns out to be what the N.T. in general and the apostle Paul in particular call the *flesh*. In Greek thought the concept of flesh denotes simply a substance, the bodily substance of man; but in the N.T., which has inherited the larger content of the O.T., this strictly physical meaning is almost always transcended. "Flesh" in the O.T. denotes man's mode of existence *vis-à-vis* God, with the accent on his natural creaturely weakness and finitude. In the same way, the N.T. writers use the term "flesh" to signify the natural man as a whole, with all the characteristics of his weak, impotent, fallen state, and—something which they stress even more than the O.T.—his close involvement with sin (2 Cor. 1:12; Rom. 6:19).

At the same time it must be made clear that the concept of "flesh" denotes not only the human being in himself, but the whole sphere of things human, everything that bears man's stamp and the mark of his dominion, the total environment and history of which he forms a part and on which he depends. This expanded sense is particularly prominent in the phrase "in the flesh" or "after the flesh" so frequently used by the apostle Paul (Rom. 1:3; 8:13; 9:5; 1 Cor. 1:26; 10:18; 2 Cor. 5:16; 11:18; Gal. 2:20; 3:3; Phil. 1:22,24). It is clear, therefore, that to know man it is not enough to describe him in terms of natural phenomena, biological development or psychological individuality. Man is a person. He must be known in his relations with others and in his particular setting in the history of humanity—that environment which reacts to his behaviour and in which he exercises responsible action. He cannot stay in isolation from the community, of which he is a part by virtue of his position both in space and time. The true perspective of the N.T. always shows man in community and in history.

2. *Man in his relation to God and Jesus Christ.* In the N.T. as in the O.T. man is considered only in the history of his relationship with God. Human existence is effective only through and in the presence of God.

If we consult the N.T. on the nature of this relationship, we arrive at the following observations:

(a) Man, being a creature, is dependent on God (Matt. 6:26–30; 10:28; Acts 17:25–28). He possesses a body and a soul and God alone sustains him in being. Moreover, he is a person, self-conscious, free, and self-determining solely because, in one way or another, he is answerable to God; because he is, by God's act, a responsible being in God's sight.

(b) But man is unwilling to acknowledge that he is bound to God. Existing only by God's will and in His presence, he has refused to accept the self-evident source of his existence. He has abused his freedom and turned from God (Rom. 1:19–21). He has spoiled his life. His existence is carnal—a concrete image to express the idea "subject to sin". The N.T. asserts the universality of this *sin, which appears both as a defect of the human race as a whole and at the same time the responsibility and fault of each individual. (In the synoptists the need for all for *repentance implies this

universal sin: cf. also Jn. 7:19; 9:34; 16:8 and Rom. 7:14–24.)

(c) The N.T. suggests a number of consequences for human life of this state of sin. They may be summed up by saying that sinful man is no longer really man, as God intended him to be. Because of sin there is no longer in the natural world a true man, whole and free. Man, turned from his Creator and in opposition to Him, is a deeply alienated being. Paul's description in Rom. 1:18–32 portrays this progressive falling away of man; because of his deviations, every aspect, every relationship of humanity is perverted, and human existence, created for life, is dedicated to *death.

When God confronts sinful man with the imperative of His *law, then man has to acknowledge that he is incapable in his own strength of fulfilling the law and so regaining life. He simply sees all the more clearly that he is no longer a free being but a divided creature, a slave—a slave to the flesh and to sin and at the same time culpable and condemned for his slavery (Mk. 14:38; Jn. 8:34; Rom. 7:14–24). The image of man as the Creator willed it has been deeply disfigured.

(d) Nevertheless, the N.T. does show us the *real man* in the person of *Jesus Christ,* He of whom Pilate testified despite himself, "Here is the man!" (Jn. 19:5).

The synoptists try to convey to us the exceptional quality of this man, which made such an impression on the majority of those around Him, and they stress the unique character of encounter with Jesus Christ (e.g. Mk. 1:17f.,22,27 and parallels). They use every effort to bring out the interconnection of the arrival of Jesus and the advent of the *Kingdom of God (cf. Matt. 12:28; 11:27; 10:32; 26:63ff.).

The Gospel of John makes it clear that Jesus, in contrast to other men, is truly *Son* of God (Jn. 8:41–47) and that a new existence is now possible for men, thanks to the work of this only Son (Jn. 3:14–16; 12:31; 6:40; 16:23).

Finally, in the writings of the apostle Paul, every aspect of man is described solely in terms of Jesus Christ. If he depicts sinful man, alienated and fallen, it is by reference to the Son of Man, for he has seen the true state of human affairs in the mirror of what we ought to be. But it is also in Jesus Christ that he sees the vision of a new life for sinful men (Rom. 8:29; 2 Cor. 3:18), the possibility of a *new man in the image of the Son of God.

Jesus Christ, then, is the typical, the representative man, but at the same time the leader, the first-born of the new humanity, conformed to the Creator's plan (1 Cor. 15:20–23; Col. 1:18; Eph. 4:15f.).

This new type of man, manifested and made possible by Jesus Christ, is the work of the *Holy Spirit, given to man to prove to him that he is no longer a slave but a child of God, no longer doomed to death but promised to the risen life of the Kingdom of God (Rom. 8:16f.). It is the Spirit of God which, in the mystery of His sovereign power, creates the new life in man, transforming him from glory to glory and setting him before the face of God in the proper place of a child and a son (Lk. 20:36; Jn. 1:12; Rom. 8:14).

To be entirely the child of God—this is the real fullness and fulfilment of human personality; and this true perfection is made possible by Jesus Christ.

H. MEHL-KOEHNLEIN

MARRIAGE

The biblical doctrine of marriage is intimately linked to the unfolding of the history of salvation. Where marriage is concerned, this history has three essential chapters: the periods of Eden, of the old covenant, and of the new covenant.

1. The Creator, in the beginning, made a man and a woman: "for this reason a man shall leave his father and mother and shall be joined to his wife; and the two shall become one. So they are no longer two but one" (Matt. 19:4–6). Marriage is not an accidental but an essential element of creation, to the extent that man is himself, complete, capable of reflecting and displaying his Maker, only if he is "male and female" (Gen. 1:26f.): it was not until the human couple had been formed that God was content with His work (Gen. 2:18). The Bible has two accounts of the institution of marriage (Gen. 1:26–31; 2:18–25), very different in form, but yet at one in affirming: (a) that it is God who wills marriage, who renders it possible, and makes it a blessing; (b) that the masculine or feminine polarity touches human existence in its very nature, with the result that one is a *man or one is a *woman in the very essence of one's person: sex is constitutive of what we are; (c) that the man and the woman are made for each other, are counterparts of each other. The first account assigns to the couple the duty of procreation (1:28); the second account shows that it is by a sort of death to himself (2:21) that the man can receive the help of the woman which God designs and provides for him, and that their encounter takes place in wonder and innocence (2:23,25). By insisting on the fact that marriage was instituted before the appearance of sin Scripture contradicts every teaching which would see in the sexuality (or corporality) of *man the disreputable or shameful part of his being, and shows that from the very first it repudiates a dualistic conception of the *world.

2. This period of innocence and joy gave place, all too soon, to the period of "hardness of heart" (Matt. 19:8), when marriage such as God intended it was spoiled by sin, and when firm and precise rules became necessary. It should not be thought, however, that, for the authors of the O.T., marriage was a hardship: if it is true that it is better to dwell in the corner of a housetop than with a contentious woman (Prov. 25:24), yet a beautiful and virtuous woman continues to be the crown (Prov. 12:4) and the happiness (Prov. 31:10–31) of her husband, and the day of their espousals fills their hearts with joy (Song of Sol. 3:11). We should also recall the sweet patience of the years of Jacob's betrothal (Gen. 29:20); the despair of Ezekiel who, through the death of his wife, loses the one who was his

strength, his joy, his glory, the desire of his eyes, and the object of his love (Ezek. 24:16–27); the purity and confidence of the betrothals of Tobit (Tob. 7:8—10:13); and the exhortation to remain constantly delighted with the love and ravished with the charms of the "graceful doe" who is the wife with whom one commenced one's conjugal life (Prov. 5:18f.). In particular, let us recall the Song of Songs, which is indeed a return to the first period, to the springtime of humanity: but the couple is no longer formed, as in Genesis, from the man (*'ish*) and from her who bears his name (*'ishshah*, Gen. 2:23); it is formed from Solomon (*Shelomoh*) and the Shulammite (*Shulammith*). The name which they bear indicates that the peace (*shalom*) and the pardon of God were necessary for the angel with the flaming sword to permit them to return to the land where, without shame, *clothes may be discarded. Their love is exposed, however, to a thousand temptations, delays, uncertainties, searchings, and yearnings which were unknown to the first couple: sin has come into the picture.

(*a*) To begin with, this is seen by the presence of *death, which restricts man. Marriage will thus become a means of compensating for this disability, of surviving in one's children. It is for this reason that procreation is now the primary object of marriage and the barren wife despairs as though she had not fulfilled her duty (cf. Gen. 30:1; 29:32, etc.). Marriage has thus become a means of ensuring a future, a remedy in the face of death, and if, by an exception particularly surprising to the Jewish mentality which expected everyone to marry (even the "monks" of the schools of the prophets: 2 Kings 4:1ff.), Jeremiah receives the command to remain a celibate, it is in order to demonstrate that Jerusalem has endangered its future (Jer. 16:2ff.). Let us enumerate several examples: (i) Abraham received the promise of a posterity, but its fulfilment is delayed to such an extent, and he becomes so old, that he wishes himself to realize the divine promise through his marriage with Hagar (cf. Gen. 16 and 21); (ii) the two daughters of Lot, who has no

son, fearing that he will be without any posterity, make him drunk and by him conceive Moab and Ammon (Gen. 19:30:37); (iii) marriage, however, was then much more an affair of the family than of the Church, a measure for the preservation of the family: thus it was a frequent practice to marry within one's own kindred (cf. Gen. 24; 28:2; Exod. 2:1, etc.), and it was necessary to define with care the degrees of consanguinity which forbade marriage (cf. Lev. 18; 20), even though there were occasions on which they were altered (cf. Gen. 20:12; 2 Sam. 13:13 and Lev. 18:6,9); (iv) it was a man's duty to marry his brother's widow—if she had no son—and to give her at least a son "so that the name of his brother should not be blotted out of Israel" (Deut. 25:6; Gen. 38; cf. Ruth 4; Matt. 22:25ff. and parallels); (v) in Judaism it was customary for a husband, after ten years of married life with a barren woman, to repudiate her and to take another wife. Most of the other regulations concerning marriage are connected with what we have just seen, and the N.T. faith in the resurrection was necessary for marriage to cease to have procreation as its primary end.

(*b*) For these varied reasons, but in a general manner, the O.T. does not take a favourable view of *marriage with foreigners*, for even though in marriage man is incontestably the master (a married woman, for example, is unable to make vows without the consent of her husband: Num. 30:11ff.), the power of love and the influence which a woman can exercise, in ways which are appropriate to her (cf. Judg. 14:15ff.; 16:4–18), over him whom she loves are recognized. As far as Israel was concerned, the danger was above all that of seduction into idolatry (cf. Deut. 7:3ff.; Gen. 24:3; 28:1,6; Judg. 3:6; Neh. 13:23ff.; Mal. 2:11), a danger which will be confirmed by the classic example of the loves of Solomon (1 Kings 11:1–8).

(*c*) Though marriage with foreigners was disapproved or even forbidden (Ezra 9–10), *monogamy was not demanded*: not only was it possible to have, beside one's wife, servants, slaves, or prisoners as concubines (cf. Gen. 16:1ff.; 25:1ff.; 30:3–13; Exod. 21:7ff.; Deut. 21:10ff., etc.), but it was possible to have two (cf. Gen. 4:19; 26:34; 29:21–30, etc.) or even more wives (cf. Gen. 28:8ff.; 1 Sam. 25:42ff.). It is stated that Solomon had as wives seven hundred princesses, and three hundred concubines (1 Kings 11:3). For economic reasons princes were in a better position to make use of this concession (cf. 2 Sam. 3:7; 5:13; 1 Chr. 3:1ff.) than were ordinary individuals, and monogamy, which was universal at the end of the period of the old covenant, was at all times more common than bigamy or polygamy.

(d) Within the marriage bond *the sexual life* was strictly disciplined and could or should be interrupted because of menstruation (Lev. 15:18ff.), confinement (Lev. 12), worship (1 Sam. 21:3ff.), war (2 Sam. 11:11ff.), etc. Extra-conjugal sexual intercourse was absolutely forbidden to the married woman, while a man could not be an adulterer towards his wife, but only towards another man whose wife or fiancée he had seduced. If the guilty were caught, they were stoned (Deut. 22:22–30; Lev. 20:10), and if a husband had doubts concerning the conduct of his wife, he could submit her to all the quirks of the law in the matter of jealousy (Num. 5:12–30). Liberty of this sort accorded to the man not only exposed virgins to violation (in which case they had the right either of being married to the man who had abused them or of receiving compensation: Exod. 22:16–17; Deut. 22:28ff.), but also encouraged the scourge of *prostitution*, that "going down to the chambers of death" (Prov. 7:27), which, despite their efforts (cf. Deut. 23:17), the people of Israel never succeeded in abolishing (cf. Gen. 38:14ff.; 1 Kings 3:16; 22:38; Hos. 1:2; Joel 3:3): at certain periods they even countenanced religious prostitution (cf. 1 Kings 14:24; 15:12; 2 Kings 23:7). On the other hand, homosexuality or degrading intercourse with animals, which were forbidden by the law (Lev. 20:13–16; 18:22–23), do not seem to have been, as was the case among the Greeks, a widespread vice.

(e) Only the husband had the right of terminating a marriage by *divorce*, or rather of putting away his wife "if she ceased to find favour in his eyes because he found some indecency in her" (Deut. 24:1–4). The Jewish doctors discussed this law a great deal and gave it interpretations which were strict or decidedly frivolous. To this law of divorce, however, there applied certain restrictions which should not be passed over in silence: the putting away of one's wife was not possible if the marriage had been contracted by consent; if the husband had been obliged to marry a young woman because he had abused her, he had no right to put her away (Deut. 22:28–29); nor did a man have the right if he had slandered his wife (Deut. 22:13–19). A woman who had been put away could be married again, but not (after being widowed or put away again) to her former husband (Deut. 24:4; Jer. 3:1ff.) nor to a priest (who was required to marry a virgin: Lev. 21:7ff., 13–15; Ezek. 44:22). These restrictions show that already the O.T. considered divorce to be fundamentally abnormal.   The prophet Malachi goes even further: it is his opinion that a man can be an adulterer also with reference to his own wife, and he asserts that God hates the putting away of a wife; he demands that every man should be faithful to the wife of his youth, to the companion with whom he has contracted an alliance (Mal. 2:14ff.).

(f) The text from Malachi just mentioned leads to a final observation on marriage under the old covenant: with ever-increasing penetration the prophets speak of the union of the *covenant between God and His people—or the holy land in which they dwell—in the perspective of a marriage (cf. Isa. 54:5; 62:1–5; Jer. 2:2; 31:32, etc.), and consequently of the infidelities of the people as though they were adulterers (cf. Jer. 3:1ff.; Ezek. 16; 23; Hos. 1–3, etc.). Within this perspective the "hardness of heart" which had given rise to the majority of the laws on marriage and divorce ought, sooner or later, to be brought into question, and human marriage, a reflection or echo of the love of God for Israel, was on the way to rediscovering the perspective of Eden: this is what will be found under the new covenant.

3. Under the old covenant of the law, marriage was endangered by the presence of sin and therefore of death. Under the new covenant of Grace marriage is governed by forgiveness and therefore by life.

Before enumerating the consequences of this preliminary observation it is necessary to make the following remark: the key-passages for the N.T. concept of marriage are found in the Epistles, and especially in 1 Cor. 7. Now this passage has, in the course of the centuries, been obscured not only by the interpretation of generations of celibate exegetes for whom marriage was a sort of fall, but also by an almost complete disregard of those to whom the Epistle was addressed, namely, men, and perhaps in particular women, excited by the irruption of the age to come, and inferring from this fact that the world of the original creation was henceforth altogether discredited; people whom the apostle calls "puffed up" and who caused him to weep. This means that in this passage St. Paul is giving not so much a catechetical instruction on marriage (he does that in Eph. 5) as intervening, as a wise pastor, in a situation where the Christian faith was being seriously endangered. Let us now turn to the implications of our preliminary observation:

(a) Marriage ceases to be a means of ensuring a survival beyond death: it is thus no longer necessary in order that our "name should not be blotted out" of the Israel of God, and procreation is no longer its primary end (in fact, in the N.T.—cf. 1 Cor. 7:1–9, for example—the sexual act is never directly connected with procreation). In other words, to die a virgin is no longer a catastrophe (cf. Judg. 11:34–39 and Rev. 14:4), and virginity and celibacy are held in honour (cf. Acts 21:9; 1 Cor. 7:25ff.) in a manner completely unknown in the old covenant. It can no longer be said without reservation that it is not good for a man to be alone, that is to say, not to take a wife (cf. 1 Cor. 7:1), for in the community of

the Church loneliness has no place. Celibacy can be, side by side with marriage, a gift of God (1 Cor. 7:7; cf. Matt. 19:12) and thus a regular and normal form of the Christian life. It matters not that the N.T. knows nothing of the very considerable depreciation of marriage which the influence of an ascetic dualism is to introduce later on into the Church; it affirms, on the contrary, that those who wish to forbid marriage spread abroad the doctrines of the devil (1 Tim. 4:1–5); it reminds us that Jesus performed His first miracle when He blessed a marriage with His presence (Jn. 2:1–12), and that as a rule not only believers (Acts 5:1; 18:26; Rom. 16:3; 1 Cor. 14:35; Col. 3:18ff.), but also ministers (1 Tim. 3:2,11; 5:9) and even the apostles (1 Cor. 9:5) were married. Especially in times of persecution, however, marriage involves responsibilities which imperil the full disposability and entire committal of the Christian (1 Cor. 7:32ff.). N.B. It would be better not to speak of the celibacy of Jesus: if He did not take a wife, it is because He is the spouse of the Church (Mk. 2:20 and parallels; Jn. 3:29; 2 Cor. 11:2; Eph. 5:23ff., etc.).

(b) Marriage is a great mystery, in the sense that it ought to reflect the union between Jesus Christ and His Church (Eph. 5:22–33); in other words, the husband ought to represent Christ and the wife ought to represent the Church. As William Farel said, God wished "holy marriage to be a mystery, a sign and a representation of our salvation, of our blessing and our triumph". This implies:

(i) The Christian couple as such have a missionary duty: they should, by their behaviour, reveal the truth of all marriage, which is to be a witness to election. But it must do so at its proper level, without defrauding, without thinking that such a vocation detaches it from the very concrete and substantial duties of conjugal life (cf. Eph. 5:29; 1 Cor. 7:3–5,33f.), and though the apostle concedes the permissibility of "conjugal vacations" (1 Cor. 7:6), he particularly advises that they should be reduced to a minimum.

(ii) Marriage is sustained by *love, a love which is not erotic in the Greek sense, but which is one of the forms of love of one's neighbour: which is not a burning out of oneself by a quest that is never fulfilled (Don Juan!), but a giving of oneself, a renunciation in favour of one's neighbour (cf. Eph. 5:25-33). It is for this reason that marriage should be contracted "in the Lord" (1 Cor. 7:39), that is to say, in the Church, or "in the name of the Lord" (Col. 3:17), as is the case with all things that Christians do: so that it may be received with thankfulness and sanctified by the Word of God and by prayer (1 Tim. 4:4f.). It follows that not every marriage is permitted to the Christian: incestuous unions are forbidden (1 Cor. 5:1-5; cf. perhaps also Acts 15:20 and 29), remarriage while the first (baptized?) partner is still alive (Rom. 7:3; 1 Cor. 7:11,39), and, probably, marriage with a heathen partner (cf. 1 Cor. 7:39).

(iii) Marriage is strictly monogamous, for Jesus Christ has and can have only one bride. In this sense Christian marriage, in advance of the reign of the law, restores the original will of God (Gen. 2 cited Matt. 19:4ff. and parallels; 1 Cor. 11:8f.; Eph. 5:31). For a second marriage to be contracted (for a reservation cf. below) it is necessary that the first partner should be dead (Rom. 7:2f.; 1 Cor. 7:39; 1 Tim. 5:11ff.). It even seems (although this matter is disputed by scholars) that ministers who have become widowers do not have the right to marry again (cf. 1 Tim. 3:2,12; Tit. 1:6).

(iv) Marriage is indissoluble as the union between the Lord and the Church: "What God has joined together let not man put asunder" (Matt. 19:6), for by the sexual act the couple have become one flesh. Paul knows and passes on the will of the Lord (cf. Mk. 10:1-12; Lk. 16:18), namely, that to put away one's partner and to marry again, which was authorized under the régime of the law, is no longer permitted under the rule of grace (1 Cor. 7:10); it is an act of adultery.

Two observations should be added here: one knows, in the first place, that the Gospel of Matthew (5:32 and 19:9) authorizes the divorce of a woman for the cause of misconduct. The majority of exegetes maintain that this must be an instance of a later addition and think that this clause reflects an ecclesiastical situation in which the full rigour of the authentic word of Jesus cannot be sustained. It will be noticed, however, that the former of these texts does not speak of a remarriage of the man who has divorced his wife, and that, in the second, it is not clear, grammatically, that he who divorces his wife has the right to marry again: the right conceded to him is that of divorcing his wife if she deceives him. The interpretation of these two passages will provide occasion for many theories yet, since they are inevitably influenced by the ecclesiastical discipline of the commentator's denomination. We may also mention that the "Bible of Jerusalem" translates the term "misconduct" as "concubinage", and supposes that here Jesus authorizes, or even recommends, the termination of unions which were illegitimate with respect to the law (it will be objected, however, that the new Christian discipline refuses precisely to recognize, in this matter, the authority of the Jewish law); we may point out, finally, that, before most of the Protestant Churches, the Eastern Church consistently saw in adultery a legitimate cause of divorce, which permits the remarriage of the divorcee, and that at the Council of Trent the Church of Rome forebore to condemn the Eastern discipline on this point.

The second observation concerns the authorization which St. Paul gives to a Christian convert to leave his (or her) partner who continues as a heathen if she (or he) demands it. This divorce, it would seem, authorizes a remarriage, since the believer ceases to be bound (1 Cor. 7:12-16): his previous marriage is now disqualified because it has not been possible to raise it to the level where salvation receives expression. One can suppose that if St. Luke is the only one of the evangelists to affirm

9

that conversion may involve divorce (Lk. 14:26; 18:29) or that the wish to continue in the married state may bring about the loss of salvation (14:20), it is because it is he alone who writes in a heathen-Christian environment.

(v) The married couple form a hierarchy, a reflection of that which binds Jesus-the-Head to His body which is the Church (cf. Eph. 5:22–33), and are besides in conformity with the creative purpose of God (1 Cor. 11:8f.; 1 Tim. 2:13). The man is the head of the woman (1 Cor. 11:3), that is to say, the one who gives her her *raison d'être*; the woman is the body (Eph. 5:28) or the glory (1 Cor. 11:7) of the man, that is to say, the one who expresses, manifests, and reveals him (as the Church gives expression to Christ). The man sustains his rôle of head in loving his wife (Eph. 5:33; Col. 3:19), for in the Bible the exercise of authority is love; the woman sustains the rôle of body in submitting herself to her husband (Eph. 5:22ff.; Col. 3:18), that is to say, in being obedient to him.

(vi) Marriage is holy (cf. Heb. 13:4; 1 Thess. 4:1–5), and in order to describe what it reflects the apostle offers an accumulation of "sacramental" terms (Eph. 5:26f.). In restoring it to its primitive purity, moreover, Jesus points out that the irruption of the Kingdom of God gives it a significance which is entirely new in comparison with that which existed under the law (Mk. 10:1–12 and parallels), a significance so holy that even the apostles view it with apprehension (Matt. 19:10). Thus in the N.T. there will be found a considerable tightening-up of the injunctions for the conjugal and sexual life: this is not only because the missionary duty of the married couple receives a more lofty emphasis, but also because henceforth the body is understood as the bearer or temple of the Holy Spirit (1 Cor. 6:19), with the result that all sexual licence is regarded as a profanation and a blasphemy. Besides a condemnation of homosexuality which goes without saying (Rom. 1:26ff.; 1 Cor. 6:9f.), a much severer

condemnation is found of relations with a prostitute (cf. 1 Cor. 6:12–20 and Gen. 38:12ff.), and adultery is no longer only intrusion into another married couple, but, for the man also, the breaking away from that which is formed with one's own partner (Mk. 19:11 and parallels). Moreover, since it is from the heart that adulteries come (Matt. 15:19), these have already commenced the moment a lustful glance is cast upon a woman (Matt. 5:27ff.; cf. Job 31:1,7ff.).

It will perhaps be objected that Jesus showed prostitutes and adulterers a gentleness which scandalized his well-disposed contemporaries (cf. Matt. 21:31; Jn. 4:1–30; 8:1–11); but to conclude from this that their sins are not so serious is a step which the N.T. never takes. It would, besides, be wrong to oppose on this point the behaviour of Jesus and that of the primitive Church. The latter also knows that *outside her boundaries* there are fornicators and lascivious persons to call to salvation (1 Cor. 5:10; Col. 3:5ff.); but, since subsequent to the ascension and Pentecost it is she who represents the Kingdom of God, it is she who is the body of Christ, such vices cannot be tolerated *amongst her members:* if they commit them, they ought to be excommunicated (1 Cor. 5:9–11; cf. Heb. 12:16) until such time as they repent (cf. 1 Cor. 6:10f.; 2 Cor. 2:1–11; 12:21; Col. 3:5ff.; 1 Tim. 1:10), for by such acts they exclude themselves from salvation (1 Cor. 6:10; Gal. 5:19–21; Eph. 5:5; Heb. 13:4; cf. 1 Cor. 10:8), and it is necessary that they should know it.

That is to say that the Church stakes its faithfulness not only on doctrine but on sexual and conjugal discipline also.

J.-J. VON ALLMEN

MARTYR, *see* WITNESS

MARY, *see* NAMES (PERSONAL)

MEAL, *see* EATING AND DRINKING

MEDIATOR, *see* JESUS

MINISTRY

O.T.

Agreement must be reached on the meaning of this word, which can be applied equally well to secular as to religious functions. Ministry comes from *ministerium*. Here we are purposely limiting its application and designating by ministry above all a religious charge, the service of holy things, God and the sanctuary. Originally it was exercised in Israel by the father of the family. Genesis shows us Abraham travelling through the land of Canaan where he sets up altars, sacrifices to his God, and calls upon His name (Gen. 12:7,8). But very soon the acts of worship are entrusted to men set apart for this function. Samuel blesses the sacrifice (1 Sam. 9). By sacrificing a burnt-offering before the arrival of the aged prophet, Saul committed an unpardonable crime. It was the cause of his rejection by Yahweh (1 Sam. 13). From the epoch of the Judges at least men were set aside for the service of the sanctuary and the altar (Judg. 17–18). The Bible recognizes three categories of men who are charged with a ministry and who can be called consecrated persons, namely, *priests* (see *Priesthood O.T.*), *prophets*, and the *king*.

1. In the O.T. the *prophetic* function does not have the character of freedom which is too often assigned to it. Like the priestly function, it is an institution which has its own distinctive traditions, in such a way that the boundary separating prophets from priests is difficult to define. The rôle of the prophets is not so much the prediction of the future, although they share with the priests the practice of divination, as to be those who speak, who announce. Exod. 4:16 and 7:1 would authorize the definition: the prophet represents the mouth of God, as also the traditional formula introducing their utterances: "Thus saith Yahweh."

From a time before the arrival of the Israelites the land of Canaan, like Mesopotamia, was familiar with the prophetic function. The prophets grouped themselves around the sanctuaries of the land (Gibeah, 1 Sam. 10:5; Ramah, 1 Sam. 19:18; Bethel, 2 Kings 2:3; Samaria, 1 Kings 22:10). They did not live in solitude, but formed brotherhoods or colleges with a common master or father who directed them in their religious exercises, whence the frequent expression "sons of the prophets", that is to say, members of one of these fraternities. They also performed the functions of diviners and depended on alms for their living (1 Sam. 10:5; 1 Kings 22:6; 2 Kings 2:3; 6:1; 9:1). They were distinguished by their *clothes, a mantle of hair and a girdle of leather around the waist, or by a special mark which they carried on the face or around the eyes (2 Kings 1:8; Zech. 13:4ff.). They had received a particular vocation and used frequently to appear as those entrusted by God with a special utterance which it was their duty to deliver, whatever the consequences might be. In the great royal temples, such as those at Jerusalem and Samaria, they were very numerous and had a clearly defined rôle in the worship, giving to the faithful the divine answer to their prayers. They practised ecstasy. For the purpose of achieving it they had a technique and made use of such means as music, singing, shouts, and dances (1 Sam. 10:5; 2 Kings 3:15; 1 Kings 22:10; 1 Kings 18:26). The O.T. also indicates the existence of a number of female prophets (Isa. 8:3; 2 Kings 22:14).

For a long time it has been sought to oppose the old Israelite prophecy of Canaanite origin to that which is attested by the prophetic books of the O.T., but it is a vain endeavour. The prophets whose writings are preserved in the O.T. are the direct heirs of the former. The reply of Amos to Amaziah of Bethel, on which the supposed opposition of these two classes of prophecy is founded—a Canaanite prophecy illustrated by the prophets of Baal (1 Kings 18) and an Israelite prophecy free from every foreign element, should be translated: "I was not a prophet nor a member of a fraternity of prophets . . . until the moment when Yahweh took me from following the flock and said to me, Be a prophet" (Amos 7:14–15).

It has been sought to make the prophets of the O.T. representatives of the nomadic ideal, of the religion of the time of Moses, who placed themselves in opposition to the religion of their own time; whereas for them as for their compatriots the land of blessing and of life was and remained Canaan, the land promised by God, and not the wilderness, the land of darkness and of death. If Hosea preaches a return to the wilderness, it is not to stay there for good, but for a period of purification (Hos. 2). The religion which they proclaimed was the religion of Israel of the royal period, a fusion of the religion of the nomadic Hebrews and that of Canaan.

Similarly it has been desired to make them enemies of the official worship and indeed of worship of any kind, purely spiritual men, condemning the rites practised in the sanctuaries—the classical prophet-priest opposition—but there has been a failure to see that a religion without worship was impossible for their epoch. Their opposition to the worship was not one of principle. It was only to a certain form of worship that they objected. What Micah 6 demands is not the suppression of the rites, but that the worship with all its practices should proceed from a sincere heart. When Amos calls for *justice* this requirement is not limited to the moral and social spheres. He desires a just worship, free of every foreign element. To practise justice is also to practise just worship, the worship of the true God and not that of idols, and to practise it from a sincere heart (Ezek. 18:5).

The Israelite did not distinguish between the representation of a thing in a spiritual manner and its fulfilment. Very much on the contrary, the latter went without saying and was of no importance. It was for this reason that the kings retained hundreds of prophets whose function was to see, to form a picture. At the time of setting out on a campaign they endeavoured to see their king under the aspect of a conqueror. These representations had as much value as the weapons of warfare and the armies

(cf. in 1 Kings 22 the part played by the prophets at the time when Ahab and Jehoshaphat set out for battle).

A difficult question is that of the true and the false prophets, for it can be asked how it is possible to distinguish them from each other. Isaiah speaks of prophets who teach falsehood and stagger in drunkenness (9:14; 28:7). Jeremiah accuses them of prophesying falsehood and of being nothing but wind (14:14; 5:13), and Hosea and Ezekiel call them stupid and mad (Hos. 9:7; Ezek. 13:3). Both true and false prophets were believers in the same God and were attached to the sanctuaries of Yahweh. It was only the verdict of history that was able to reveal the truth or falsity of their predictions and thus of the inspiration which they claimed.

If the message of the pre-exilic prophets is concentrated on the announcement of punishment, it is because of the dramatic situation of Israel of which history has made a succession of catastrophes leading up to the final calamity. The division which it has been sought to make between the prophets of disaster (= the pre-exilic prophets) and the prophets of prosperity (= the post-exilic prophets) is illegitimate. In every period the prophets have proclaimed at one and the same time both judgment and salvation. Their utterances always contained both promises and condemnations.

It is natural that those predictions which had been verified by subsequent events should have been preserved, like all those whose content had made an impression on the people. They fell into place in the main line of the religious history of the people of God. Certain prophets or prophetic circles preserved their utterances in oral form. Others committed them to writing (cf. Isa. 8:1; Jer. 36). They remained alive in the heart of the elders of the people who procured the liberation of Jeremiah by recalling the prophecy of Micah, made a century earlier (Jer. 26:18). If the books of Amos, Hosea, Micah, and Isaiah 1–39 give the impression of collections of utterances piously preserved in prophetic circles and ultimately committed to writing, Isaiah 40–66 is a literary composition made to be written. (See *Prophecy.)

The more the power of the priests asserts itself, the more the prophetic ministry, despite all that it could bring anew into a tradition ever more exclusive, loses its importance. This is a phenomenon which the Christian Church recognized. When they wished to gain a hearing the inspired men of the last centuries before the Christian era were reduced to speaking in the name of the great personages of the past, Moses, Elijah, Enoch, etc. This extremely important literature is the Apocrypha and Pseudepigrapha of the O.T.

2. Another consecrated person is the *king*. The king of Israel was not invested only with the secular functions belonging to the head of the state. He also exercised a ministry and played a separate part in the worship and before God. This fact is illustrated by the practice of *anointing with oil (Saul: 1 Sam. 9:27–10:1; David: 1 Sam. 16:12f.; Solomon: 1 Kings 1:32–40; Jehu: 2 Kings 9:7), by which the king became the property of the deity and was filled with His spirit. He passed in a certain sense into the divine sphere. To raise one's hand against him was to commit sacrilege (cf. 2 Sam. 1:14). The precursors of the kingship, such as the Judges, are described as being possessed of the spirit of Yahweh.

The question has been put whether the rite of unction did not imply that the king had a divine character, that he was god. Some have wished to derive this from passages like 2 Kings 14:17, but this conclusion seems to be forced. It is true that some of the psalms permit this interpretation (Ps. 2:7, where God says to the king: "You are my son; to-day I have begotten you", and Ps. 45:7, where the king is called "god"), but here it is a matter of formulas current in the ancient East, the object of which was to mark the distance between the king and his subjects. Were it otherwise, one would have difficulty in admitting that a deified sovereign would agree, as Ahaz did, to meet Isaiah on the highway of the fuller's

field (Isa. 7:3), would converse, as Zedekiah did, with the imprisoned Jeremiah (Jer. 37 and 38), or would go out to look for grass for his cattle, as Ahab did (1 Kings 18). If he was not deified, he held his power from Yahweh. He was king by divine right and in a manner more emphatic than that of all other monarchies of history. In Jerusalem, this characteristic also results from the situation of the palace in close association with the *Temple and enclosed within the same precincts, like the expressions by means of which he was celebrated: son of God by adoption, *'Adon*, lord, like God. He is the anointed one, the son, the servant of Yahweh.

All these expressions make it possible to assert that the king is nearer to Yahweh than any single one of his subjects. The relationship which unites him to his God has a special and unique character. Perhaps it can be said that Israel accords to its king a certain degree of divinity, but in the relationship between the king and the deity Israel discarded all ideas of identity and of physical incarnation. The king always remains a human being, "a man of the people" (Ps. 89:20), subject to Yahweh and dependent on Him. His power comes to him from a divine blessing which can be withdrawn from him, as the example of Saul shows. If he is a son of God, it is by adoption and not by nature, for it is God who has chosen him, who has elected him.

In the worship the king is never an object of adoration, but he represents the people before God, acting as an intermediary between them. He is like the channel through which the divine blessing is transmitted to the people, the point of contact between God and the community. As the intermediary by means of whom Yahweh acts on behalf of the people, the king of Israel is a proof, human and visible, a guarantee, of the covenant of Yahweh and of His active presence with His people. If in large measure he subsidizes the expenses of the worship, if he repairs the temple and undertakes a religious reform of considerable proportions, as did Josiah in 2 Kings 22 and 23, these are not the limit of his functions. As the prayer of dedication of the Temple by Solomon shows (1 Kings 8), the king himself conducts the worship and blesses the people. The place which he occupies as a consecrated person, invested with a ministry, is so important that Ezekiel, in his ideal vision of the restored Temple of which Yahweh alone is the king—the king possessing right only in the title of prince—is obliged to reserve for the sovereign a particular place and rôle in the worship (Ezek. 46). In a mysterious passage of Zechariah two golden crowns are prepared, one for Joshua, the high priest of the returned exiles, while the other is no longer assigned to any particular person in the present text. It should be Zerubbabel, a descendant of David, whose person aroused hopes which subsequent history did not fulfil (Zech. 6). The promises that are made to him illustrate well the sacred character of the kingship in ancient Israel (Zech. 6:13).

In the attempts which have been made to reconstruct the festivals of the Temple of Jerusalem several authors have put forward the hypothesis that the great moments of the history of the past, such as the exodus from Egypt celebrated in the festival of the Passover, formed not merely the subject of a recitation of the sacred texts, but also of enacted representations in which the king would have taken the rôle of God. If this theory is correct, one can understand more easily how expressions such as that of Ps. 45:7, expressions apparently reserved to God, could have been transferred to the person of the king.

Since the *Messiah* was the king of the future, it is not surprising that the formulas used in the worship and at court for extolling the person of the sovereign had also been employed for the Messiah. Thus the relationship between passages like Isa. 9 and 11 and the royal psalms cited above would be explained. It is natural that after the Exile, when Israel no longer had a king, the hopes attached to the person of the sovereign should have become concentrated on that of the Messiah.

G. PIDOUX

N.T.

1. *Service and ministries*. By the general term "service" (*diakonia*) the N.T. designates the charges and functions which are exercised in the Church. This general term is applied to the ministry of an apostle, to the various offices of particular believers, and to the duty of all believers to be at the service of their brethren in the community. It is not because of poverty of language that the N.T. in this way uses the same word in three different connotations. It is for the purpose of emphasizing that the Church is the living body of Christ and that each member of this body is active, in his own proper rôle, with a view to giving its completeness to the common life. "To serve" is the vocation and the duty of everyone who belongs to Him who "came not to be served but to serve", and who has made service the norm of all greatness in His Kingdom: "Whoever would be great among you must be your servant" (Mk. 10:43–45). This exhortation is a reminder that service is contrary to the natural tendency of the human heart. Only those can serve with all their heart whom Christ transforms by His Spirit and who then place all their gifts at the disposal of the Church. At this level there is no longer any distinction between natural capacities and the gifts of grace.

It is for this reason that the terms "service" and "charisma" (a gift of divine grace) are complementary and not opposed to each other (cf. 1 Cor. 12:4–5; 1 Pet. 4:10). The Spirit has been given to the Church; He manifests His presence there by the gifts distributed among the believers, in the same way as—to adopt St. Paul's comparison—the various properties and activities of the human body belong to its members, inevitably differing from each other and yet harmoniously interdependent (1 Cor. 12:18).

If all believers are in service in the Church, the Church none the less profits from the special services or ministries of particular believers. It is necessary that this fact should be explained before the various ministries are described.

The work of salvation was accomplished by Christ at a given moment of history; it is not repeated. It is therefore needful that the men chosen by Christ—the *apostles— should proclaim the Gospel to the world in order that it may believe and be saved. In their capacity as witnesses of the Risen One the apostles have no successors, since fresh appearances of Christ are no longer granted. The foundation of the Church has been laid once for all by the work of Christ and by the apostolic witness. But the construction or edification of the Church must be pursued until the return of Christ. This work requires ministries other than the apostolate, in order, in the first place, to assist the apostles and afterwards, when the first witnesses have disappeared, to ensure its continuance. These ministries are just as indispensable to the life of the Church as the apostolate. It is for this reason that Paul regards them as a divine institution. It is God (1 Cor. 12:28) or Christ (Eph. 4:11) who gives to the Church "apostles, prophets, teachers". The ministries of the *word always have pride of place in the lists of ministries (cf. also 1 Tim. 5:17), for the Church is nourished by the apostolic word, preached, expounded, and applied by men capable of doing so. There would no longer be any Christian life without the knowledge of the revelation which has occurred in history and been transmitted by *tradition, of which the apostles are the first links. The Church, besides, is called to be a "building" and not a heap of materials, a "body" and not an amorphous mass of believers. These metaphors of the building and the body, which commonly designate the Church in the N.T., show that the Church is unable to dispense with ministries of order and government.

The different ministries came into being very early, even during the lifetime of the apostles, in Jerusalem as well as in the places reached by St. Paul's missionary journeys, both as a normal growth and as the necessary expression of the life of the Church.

2. *The Church at Jerusalem.* According

to the book of the Acts, the Twelve were assisted, at Jerusalem, by the Seven, and later by the presbyters or elders. The rapid growth of the Church led to "the service of tables"—the celebration of the Lord's Supper and of the common meals, together with the distribution of supplies to all according to the need of each (cf. Acts 2:42f.)—being entrusted to the Seven, in order that the Twelve might be able to devote themselves "to prayer and to the ministry of the word" (Acts 6:1–4). Among these Seven there are two who play an important rôle, in the capacity, to be sure, of preachers and missionaries: Stephen (Acts 6–7) and Philip (Acts 8; cf. 21:10). Without doubt the author of the Acts regards the Seven as the forerunners of the deacons, who are not mentioned in Acts, but who are introduced especially in the pastoral Epistles as entrusted with a ministry of assistance.

The presbyters or elders appear a little later at Jerusalem, although the author of the Acts does no more than mention them. He says nothing of their appointment to office nor of their functions. It is into their hands that Barnabas and Paul place the collection made at Antioch on behalf of the brethren in Judea (Acts 11:30). In this incident the apostles are not mentioned; no doubt they were occupied abroad on their missionary travels (cf. 1 Cor. 9:5). Thus it seems that the presbyters direct the Church in the absence of the apostles, and in collaboration with them when they are present. This is the case at the time of the council of Jerusalem (Acts 15) and later when Paul arrives for the last time in the holy city (Acts 21:28).

According to the book of the Acts there are also presbyters in the churches founded by Paul (Acts 14:23) and notably at Ephesus (Acts 20:17). Paul himself never uses this title in his Epistles—the pastorals excepted —but he speaks of ministries equivalent to that of the presbyters. There is as well an echo of this equivalence of titles in the Acts. The presbyters of Ephesus are also called overseers or bishops (Acts 20:28) and the text indicates that their mission is to be shepherds or pastors of the Church. Again, the church at Philippi, founded by Paul, has bishops (Phil. 1:1) and in Eph. 4:11 teachers or doctors are also designated by the term shepherds or pastors. Thus an almost certain identity is established between the terms and the functions of presbyters (elders), bishops (overseers), and teachers (doctors). To feed the flock of God (Acts 20:28) is to defend it against the peril of erroneous teachings by providing for it the good nourishment of the truth (Acts 20:29–31), that is to say, instruction in harmony with apostolic thought. It is therefore the primary ministry of the word and of instruction that is performed at Jerusalem by the presbyters and in the Pauline churches by the teachers and the bishops.

Presbyters are mentioned again in the Epistles which tradition attributes to the apostles of Jerusalem. According to 1 Pet. 5:1–4 presbyters are charged with the task of feeding the flock, thus of instructing it faithfully. According to Jas. 5:14 presbyters ought in particular to pray for the sick and to place their hands upon them.

3. *The Pauline Churches.* The apostle has the care of organizing the churches which he founds. The living hope in the return of the Lord is not regarded by him as an excuse for neglecting the order which ought to reign in the household of God (cf. 1 Cor. 14:33), any more than this expectation ought to encourage believers no longer to provide for their needs by engaging in *work (cf. 2 Thess. 3:6–12). The apostle, however, does not devote a special epistle to the question of the ministries; he contents himself by giving each church injunctions in harmony with local circumstances. At Philippi, he salutes, with the church, "the bishops and deacons" (Phil. 1:1), without stating the nature of their functions. The "bishops" are, according to all the evidence, those who watch over the church, that is to say, those whose concern it is that she should persevere in the instruction received from the apostle; their ministry seems to be the same as that of the "teachers" (doctors)

of Corinth and the "presbyter-bishops" of Ephesus. The deacons are without doubt subordinate to them, since they are named in the second place. These two functions which are brought into association in this way are not mentioned elsewhere, apart from the pastoral Epistles, but this text in Philippians is sufficient to establish "the existence of a ministry that is already stabilized at the time of Paul" (M. Goguel). The apostle alludes to an equivalent ministry when he writes, in Gal. 6:6: "Let him who is taught the word share all good things with him who teaches." This text also testifies to the primary importance accorded from the very beginning to the teaching ministry, since this ministry, like the apostolate, has a right to remuneration (1 Cor. 9:6–15).

At Corinth, on the other hand, the necessity to combat anarchic and illuministic tendencies constrains Paul to remind the Corinthians that God Himself has instituted a variety of ministries and orders. "God has appointed in the church first apostles, second prophets, third teachers, then workers of miracles, then healers, helpers, administrators, speakers in various kinds of tongues" (1 Cor. 12:28; cf. 12:29–30). In this passage the apostle enumerates two series of ecclesiastical functions which he is careful not to place on the same level: first of all the three ministries of the word and of instruction, which are numbered in order to emphasize their importance. These ministries, moreover, are found in all the churches under different names, for they are indispensable to the life of the Church. The apostle is at the head because the Church is founded on his testimony given to the Risen One and because his is, at first, the only ecumenical ministry; the commission of the apostle is to go everywhere preaching the Gospel and, as the churches are brought into being by his preaching, to ensure by his letters, by his visits, and by his representatives who speak and act in his name, the unity of the various churches. The other ministries, on the contrary, are local. *Prophets are without doubt inspired preachers, who express themselves with clarity and not in incomprehensible language like the *glossolaletes* who "speak in tongues" (see *Language) and whose word is lost, unless an interpreter, equally inspired, is found to give the translation. The task of teachers would appear to be the interpretation of the Christian message in the light of the O.T. and to cause the significance to be appreciated of the truths which the believer has grasped by faith. (See *Teaching.)

In the second section of his catalogue Paul gives a list of "charismata", gifts. He designates them by terms which are abstract and not personal, for they are beyond doubt spontaneous and sporadic manifestations of the Spirit, which do not possess the permanence of a ministry. He does not enumerate them, for they are too free to form a complete series; they escape all classification. In the recapitulation of verse 28, which we have in verses 29–30, Paul sets out a slightly different list of charismata, while he gives pride of place once again to the three ministries, and in the same order. Briefly, the apostle emphasizes that the Spirit makes use on occasion of certain believers as bearers of charismata which enrich the life of the Church, whereas on the contrary the three ministries of the word are indispensable to the very existence of the Church. Because of the capacities and culture which they presuppose on the part of those who exercise them these ministries have a character all their own of permanence and authority.

In Eph. 4:11 there is a list of ministries almost identical with that of 1 Cor. 12. "His gifts were that some should be apostles, some prophets, some evangelists, some pastors and teachers." The two terms last mentioned designate the same men; by their instruction teachers feed the flock of Christ; the term *shepherd or pastor is only a metaphor occasioned by that of the flock, which is frequent in the N.T. for designating the *Church. The only new term with reference to the text from Corinthians is that of evangelist. The evangelist has the same function as the apostle: to spread abroad the Gospel, but without the title of apostle, for he is not, like him, a witness of the Risen One. The N.T. gives the title of evangelist only to Philip, one of the Seven (Acts 21:8) and Timothy, Paul's faithful fellow-worker (2 Tim. 4:5).

In Rom. 12:6–8 the apostle names the following charismata, speaking first of functions and then of the men who perform them: "prophecy, the diaconate"—here the ministry in a general sense (cf. 1 Thess. 5:12)—"he who teaches, he who exhorts, he who contributes, he who directs"—that is to say, who exercises spiritual rule (cf. 1 Thess. 5:12)—"he who does acts of mercy". The list is less precise, no doubt on purpose because Paul is not well informed of the particular circumstances of the Church at Rome. But this list also gives a prominent place to prophets and teachers. The Acts (13:1; cf.11:27–28; 15:32) attest that prophets and teachers exist at Antioch, the point of departure of St. Paul's great missions.

4. *The post-apostolic period.* The Epistles to Timothy and Titus (the pastoral Epistles) are our source of information here. They were probably composed by a disciple of Paul, perhaps using notes of the apostle or drawing inspiration from his oral instruction. They depict a situation distinctly more advanced than that which is found in the Pauline Epistles and in the Acts. The apostle is no longer there to be the living bond between the churches. If he has not passed from the scene, he is in prison and separated from his converts among whom he is represented by his commissaries Timothy and Titus, who are entrusted with the supervision of the good organization of the Church. To this four ministries should contribute:

(a) *Deacons* (1 Tim. 3:8–13), in whose number deaconesses are without doubt included (cf. 1 Tim. 5:3–13), ought to be endowed with solid moral and practical qualities. It may be concluded that their functions, which are not precise, are those of assistance and administration.

(b) *Presbyters* or elders (1 Tim. 5:17–22; Tit. 1:5–6) ought to be men of irreproachable character. Of their number, those who

9*

work at preaching and teaching deserve "a double honour", which probably means a double stipend (honorarium). From this it follows that the functions of presbyters are varied, but that the ministry of teaching maintains the first place. It is evident, moreover, that presbyters are remunerated, which indicates that they devote a great part of their time, if not the whole of their time, to their ministry.

(c) *The bishop* or overseer (1 Tim. 3:1–7; Tit. 1:7–9) is always mentioned in the singular. It is therefore very likely that at the time when the pastoral Epistles were written there was only one bishop to each church. The bishop has a rank and fulfils duties which distinguish him from the presbyters. He should be hospitable—that is to say, he should welcome believers who come from other churches—and ought to enjoy the respect of non-Christians. In other words, it is he who represents the church to other churches and to outsiders. Further, he does not limit himself to teaching, like the presbyters; he must also defend the teaching handed down by the apostles against the distortions which it may suffer. This demands of the bishop a more extensive knowledge and a more intelligent understanding of the difficulties which the church may encounter. In brief, the bishop appears as the head of the local church.

(d) *Timothy and Titus* are the delegates of the apostle at Ephesus and in Crete. Like the apostolate, their ministry extends beyond the local church and ensures the bond of unity between the different churches in one region. In this respect the functions of these apostolic emissaries are distinct from those of the bishop, the presbyters, and the deacons. This ecumenical ministry must be perpetuated in the Church (2 Tim. 2:2).

In bringing this survey of the ministries known to the N.T. to a conclusion, three facts stand out prominently:

(i) The necessity for the ministry of men set apart to preside over the essential functions of the life of the Church.

(ii) The diversity and the plurality of the ministries, which, however, are dominated throughout by the ministry of the *Word (preaching and teaching).

(iii) The existence of an ecumenical ministry which expresses the unity of the many local churches.

5. *The ministries and the Church.* We have little information concerning the organization of the Church in the period of the N.T. It is far from being the case, however, that the apostles were indifferent to this question because they were living in the expectation of Christ's return. On the contrary, the hope of the parousia, which impelled believers to live in the most careful watchfulness, also urged the apostles to expand the Church by missionary endeavour and to strengthen it by organizing it. The choice of the Seven at the time when the church at Jerusalem is increasing in size, the existence of presbyters around the apostles, St. Paul's anxiety concerning the ministry and order in the Church, and the existence of the pastoral Epistles all disclose care that the Church should be organized and that it should not be left without leaders at the time when the apostles are disappearing from history.

Christ Himself chose His apostles and endowed them with His Spirit in order to render them capable of fulfilling their task. Subsequently it is the apostles, inspired by the Spirit, who preside over the choice of the men of whom the Church has need (Acts 6:2–6; 14:23), and then, in the place of the apostles, their delegates, such as a Timothy and a Titus (2 Tim. 2:2; Tit. 1:5; cf. 1 Tim. 5:22). The believers are invited to give their assent.

This system has its foundation in the theology of the Church. Christ is the head of the Church which He governs by His Spirit. The sovereignty resides in Christ or in the Spirit. The authority comes from above. It passes to those whom Christ has designated, namely, the apostles, and through them to those whom they summon to support them. In a word, the Church is, according to the N.T., a Christocracy, and, more precisely, an apostolic Christocracy.

PH.-H. MENOUD

MIRACLE

O.T.

1. The conception which we have of miracle depends on the manner in which we understand the world. For a modern individual who considers that nature is governed by a certain number of laws the problem of the relationships between "natural" laws and miracle raises great difficulties of a scientific and philosophical order. The O.T. ignores questions of this sort; for it the concept of nature does not exist. The *world does not lead an autonomous existence, it is not a machine which has been set in motion once for all by its inventor, but it was *created by God and remains in a state of continuous dependence on Him. The universe exists and subsists only by the divine will; God remains its master and manifests Himself in it ceaselessly. Nature even participates in the drama of redemption; it suffers and rejoices with man and because of him. The Creator is constantly in relationship with His creation as with His creature.

2. Miracle therefore does not appear in particular as an event of the supernatural order, it is not characterized by the fact that it suspends the laws of nature: it is extraordinary because it manifests, generally in an unexpected manner, with a special intensity, the presence of God here below. Yahweh reveals His care for Israel by His miracles and prodigies, but there is also something upsetting about His solicitude, for it provokes dread as much as admiration. It is noteworthy that the terms employed in Hebrew for speaking of the exploits of Yahweh call forth His power, His creative activity, His lofty deeds, but above all the astonishment, the stupefaction, and the fear which they arouse.

In the eyes of the men of the old covenant therefore it is characteristic of a miracle that it reveals the presence of God. Wonders, in the O.T., manifest the intervention of Yahweh in the midst of His people, whether or not they are accompanied by unusual phenomena. It is true that Scripture re-counts the extraordinary acts performed by God: the earth opens its mouth and engulfs the family of Korah who rebelled against Moses (Num. 16:30); hailstones fall upon the Gibeonites and the sun stands still in the middle of the day in order to ensure the victory of Joshua (Josh. 10:10ff.); the shadow turns back ten degrees at the request of Hezekiah (2 Kings 20:10); the creation itself is hymned as one of the most prodigious acts of the power of Yahweh (cf. Ps. 89:6; 106:2; 139:14; Job 5:9f.). But simple occurrences like the blowing of the east wind, a meeting with a young girl, and the defeat of an enemy are miraculous for Israel because they would not have taken place apart from the divine intervention (cf. Exod. 14:21f.; Gen. 24:12ff.; 1 Sam. 14:23 and 45).

3. For the O.T., miracle is never an isolated fact. It is linked with other events. The object of God's extraordinary interventions is precisely to say something, to warn, to announce, in brief, to reveal the divine intention. Miracle, writes W. Eichrodt, is like a finger pointing towards God; it calls attention to Him, it manifests His power and His will, it is a Word of God. The miraculous has significance and it is its significance that is much more important than its material setting. Confronted with a fact which seems to be wonderful, Israel does not ask: "Is this occurrence possible? Is it true?", but "What is its meaning? What is its message?"

4. Miracle is thus, for Israel, a sign that Yahweh grants, but this sign does not possess absolute value; it is valid only for faith, and all the more so because there are such things as false signs, pseudo-miracles, or, more exactly, prodigies performed by powers that are opposed to the true God. The Egyptian magicians rival Moses in the matter of "enchantments" (cf. Exod. 7:11,22; 8:7,18, etc.); false prophets can seduce the people by their extraordinary acts (cf. Deut. 13:1ff.). Mere miracle therefore is not adequate as a proof of the divine intervention; it must be related to

other events and explained and interpreted by the biblical revelation as a whole. True miracle harmonizes with the information which believers already possess concerning God; it is thus addressed to faith and to faith enlightened by the knowledge of Yahweh.

There is a close connection between faith and miracle; in the incidents of daily life or in the great affairs of state of the Middle East the unbeliever does not notice the hand of the God of Israel. He is unable to read the signs of the times, he fails to hear the numerous warnings which Yahweh gives, he has eyes but does not see, and ears but does not hear. To those who do not believe in God miracle reveals nothing; it even seems that it hardens them. Thus Pharaoh continues obstinate in his determination to keep the people of God, despite the more and more extraordinary plagues which come upon his land (cf. Exod. 7:3,9; 11:10, etc.); thus Ahaz and the authorities of Jerusalem are unwilling to see in the strange names which the children of Isaiah have been given the message which Yahweh sends them (cf. Isa. 8:18; 20:3; 7:11). On the other hand, the God of Israel gives Gideon a sign in order to strengthen his faith before he sets out to rescue his country from the oppression of the Philistines (cf. Judg. 6:17, 36ff.).

5. Miracle is thus a means which God employs for directing history until the time when He has established His rule over the whole universe. It has its place in the biblical revelation; it is neither indispensable nor superfluous. The reading of the O.T. leads us to assert that the extraordinary interventions of Yahweh are concentrated in particular on three periods of Israel's history which seem, in each case, to be decisive turning-points where it is not only the destiny of a nation that is involved, but even the future of God's plan of salvation. There is, in the first place, the deliverance from Egypt, when behind the men who are taking part, Moses and Pharaoh, Yahweh is confronting the demoniacal power of the Egyptian idols (cf. Exod. 5ff.).

Then, at the time of Elijah and Elisha, when the Israelites, led astray by the cults of Baal and Astarte, a kind of deified natural forces, call in question the continuity of the work of Yahweh (cf. 1 Kings 17ff.). Finally, on the occasion when the Assyrians are encamped outside the holy city and threaten not only to destroy the throne of David and the Temple of God, but also to annihilate the elect people (cf. Isa. 6ff.; 36ff.).

6. Miracles in the O.T., far from being intended to satisfy the desire of the human heart for the marvellous or its longing for security, are addressed to believers at the crucial hours of their history, in order to strengthen them in their faith in Yahweh and to reveal to them the power of a God who does not leave the world to itself. But at times when faith is weak the search for the sensational flourishes, and the need for strengthening a vague religiosity by fantastic occurrences makes itself felt. As it is, certain passages of the O.T. (cf. the book of Chronicles) and especially the whole of the apocryphal literature testify to this falling off of faith in Israel. The miraculous then becomes an end, it is sought for its own sake, and prodigies appear as a decisive and necessary proof to a people who no longer have a living contact with their God and who cling to the extraordinary and the marvellous. Jesus commences His ministry at the moment when the Jews, like the people of the Middle East, are running after the workers of miracles and are expecting to experience sensational happenings; but from the beginning of His ministry, and even on the cross, He rejects the temptation to be a wonder-worker (cf. Matt. 4:1ff.); He performs miracles only for the purpose of testifying to the nearness of the Kingdom (cf. Matt. 11:2ff.) and in particular to those who ask Him for a sign to prove His Messiahship He offers only the experience of Jonah (cf. Matt. 12:38–41 and 27:39–44). But is there a more astonishing story than that of Jonah lived again by the Son of God?

R. MARTIN-ACHARD

N.T.

1. The evangelists and the apostles used three different terms for speaking of miracles: *miracle, sign,* and *wonder.*

(*a*) A *miracle* is an act of power. He who performs it is the possessor of a certain power, whether it be divine, conferred by the Holy Spirit or by God, or whether it be demoniacal. It is not limited to being an extraordinary act which is otherwise inexplicable (by science, psychology, etc.). Every action and every intervention by God in the life of the world and, in particular, of men is a miracle. This action may take place equally well in the spiritual realm (conversion, encouragement, knowledge of the Gospel, etc.) as in the material sphere (see *sickness). From this point of view the cessation of illness, its complete cure, is regarded as miraculous equally with the battle waged against it spiritually and brought to a victorious conclusion. Thus the apostle Paul receives from the Lord the power to fulfil his apostleship despite his illness (2 Cor. 12:9f.). It is not only the healings performed by Jesus before His death and resurrection that are miraculous, but also the power and the encouragement which He communicates to those who live in communion with Him (2 Cor. 12:7–10). Thus in the N.T. the significance of the word miracle is often wider than in our modern usage.

(*b*) A *sign,* the outward form of which may offer nothing extraordinary, has a double object: firstly, to announce what is about to take place: in this respect it often constitutes an anticipation of the world to come; secondly, to proclaim or to reveal Him who is active even now in the world: by drawing attention to Jesus, the sign reminds us that God is at work in Him and through Him.

(*c*) A *wonder* departs from the ordinary course of events: it is contrary to the natural laws known to man. It reveals a power that is divine (or sometimes demoniacal) in a manner which is impressive and wonderful as well as incomprehensible (cf. Acts 2:19–20).

2. Without going into the details of the chronological sequence of the various Gospel writings, there are certain characteristic traits which should be noted:

(*a*) The *Pauline literature* displays the widest usage of the word miracle. All the senses mentioned in the preceding definition are found there. The *synoptic Gospels,* on the contrary, frequently describe miracles without, however, using the term itself. It is only when it is wished to depict the activity of Jesus in a general manner that it is found: reading the Gospel of St. Mark is instructive in this respect.

(*b*) In the *synoptic Gospels,* signs are demanded by the Scribes and Pharisees (Matt. 16:1–4; 12:38–39; Mk. 8:11–13; Lk. 11:16) and consist especially in heavenly phenomena. As far as we know, Jesus performed miracles, but no sign. On one occasion only is this term placed in his mouth: "This generation," he said, "shall have no sign other than that of Jonah" (Mk. 8:11–21 and parallels), and on one occasion only is it applied to His person: "He shall be a sign that is spoken against", declares the aged Simeon (Lk. 2:34; Lk. 2:12 also in a sense).

It is a distinctive mark of the *fourth Gospel* that it never speaks of miracles, but always of signs. The multitude is satisfied with the signs (6:2,14,26; 12:18,37) which are seen by them as marvellous events, but they fail to comprehend their meaning. Jesus remains for them an extraordinary being, but He is not the Son of God. In His acts they see the effect of a mysterious power, without discerning the true author of them: God acting in Him whom He has sent (5:19). His signs astonish and fascinate these curious spirits who are eager to gain some profit from them (6:26) without, however, leading them to faith (12:37).

Those only come to faith who, beyond the occurrence, grasp, perceive, see the presence of God and the glory of the Lord (2:23; 3:2; 10:41). A sign therefore remains an event whose significance is not at first apparent and whose meaning may be discerned by faith alone: instead of making it an autonomous act resulting from an extraordinary power, in it faith sees God at work announcing prophetically that which is to be: resurrection and life (2:18; 11:47; 12:18), healing (4:54; 6:2), the transformation of nature (2:11). Conversely, a sign may also anger and further harden the adversaries of the work of God (2:18; 6:30; 9:16; 11:47; 12:37).

The disciples will have the power to perform signs (14:12–14; 15:5) some of which will surpass those of Jesus in their scope and power. Yet their significance like their origin will be identical with that of the signs performed by Jesus.

(c) In his description of the church at Jerusalem the editor of *the book of the Acts* has committed himself to reproduce faithfully a source (cf. Lk. 1:1–4) of which one of the characteristics was the simultaneous usage of the two words signs and wonders. We find them used for speaking of the work of God in the last times (the prophecy of Joel: Acts 2:19), of the work accomplished by Jesus on the earth (2:22), as well as for describing the power which God or Jesus Christ confers on Moses, on the disciples, on the apostles, and on Barnabas or Paul (2:43; 4:30; 6:8; 7:35; 15:12).

3. We see therefore that the various writers of the N.T. literature employ quite different words for expressing a common reality. It is true that this variety of terms is not fortuitous. Frequently enough it even has an importance which is not negligible in the expression of certain nuances of thought. All, however, present a significant unity of outlook throughout this diversity of terms: miracles, signs, and wonders always result from a divine intervention. Their supernatural character resides precisely in this divine origin and not in the astonishment, more or less considerable, which they are capable of producing in the human spirit. It should be said again and again: a divine action of quite ordinary appearance, visible only to the believer, is a miracle. On the contrary, a phenomenon which is extraordinary, amazing, inexplicable, but unrelated to faith, is not one. Our habitual conceptions cause us to

admit as miracles only certain astounding and scientifically extraordinary wonders. The writers of the N.T. think very differently: in a world which is separated from God every occurrence which reveals His active presence is something outside of the natural course of events or of habitual notions. This occurrence, even though it may resemble certain human actions, differs from them none the less by its meaning and by its object, since by it God or Jesus Christ overcomes the indifference or hostility of men in order to reveal Himself to them and to show His power and His love. It is this that constitutes what is "marvellous" in a miracle and not certain features which might render it acceptable to our natural incredulity by the effect of surprise which they could produce, by the fascination which they would not fail to exercise, by an attractive originality.

M. CARREZ

MONEY

Ideas of money, gold, possessions, riches, Mammon, are closely associated in biblical thought. Possessions or riches is the term with the widest denotation. The term gold or silver does not signify on all historical levels of the Bible the symbolic realities which we designate by these names: they are often material things, precious in themselves and not as objects of exchange (cf. Gen. 2:11–12 and Hagg. 2:7–8: "the treasures of all nations shall come in, and I will fill this house with splendour, says the Lord of hosts. The silver is mine, and the gold is mine, says the Lord of hosts").

1. Possessions, riches, gold and silver constitute the *splendour and the glory of the creation*, and as the creation is never regarded as independent of the Creator that splendour and that glory belong to Him (Ps. 24:1). He disposes of them, He promises them and gives them to those He loves, freely, gratuitously, even when man in no way deserves it. So God promises to Moses for His people "great and goodly cities, which you did not build, and houses full of

all good things, which you did not fill, and cisterns hewn out, which you did not hew, and vineyards and olive trees, which you did not plant" (Deut. 6:11). Thus riches are above all a sign of the blessing of God, of His free grace and His free election. They testify to the faithfulness of God, and the faithfulness of men to God is paid in return by means of possessions (Ps. 34:11; 36:9; 65:10–14; Isa. 1:19: "If you are willing and obedient, you shall eat the good of the land"). Even when given by God, possessions and riches must always still be regarded by man as belonging to God (Ps. 105:24; Hagg. 2:7–8). He who inherits the promise must not forget that it is the Lord alone who promises and who gives and that He alone guarantees and assures the continuance of the possessions which He gives. It is not possible to dissociate the act of giving from the thing given, as Ps. 16:5–6 shows:

> "The Lord is my *chosen portion* and my cup; thou *holdest* my lot.
> The lines have fallen for me in pleasant places; yea, I have a goodly heritage."

All the history of Israel, so long as the people remain faithful, testifies to this concern of not appropriating in an absolute manner the gifts of God. He who continues to dispense them can take them back, as the book of Job clearly shows.

2. In addition, these goods and riches are regarded much more as *sustenance which God gives* to satisfy men who are hungry and thirsty (and to the degree in which they are hungry and thirsty) than as possessions to accumulate. The O.T. stresses less the proprietary rights of man than the fact that man can enjoy what is given to him (see e.g. Eccl. 5:17–19). Man has the usufruct of creation, he is not its proprietor in the full sense of the term. God has created him to joy and rejoice in the good things of this earth. Doubtless this statement must be related to the kind of civilization and the mode of existence of ancient Israel: nomads or semi-nomads, they did not seek to accumulate

possessions, they sought food, and the story of the manna with which God fed them in the desert left a profound memory in their tradition (Exod. 16), since Paul can refer to it as a piece of fundamental teaching (2 Cor. 8:15). But that explanation is not sufficient, because Israel became a settled, property-owning people and yet even then the accumulation of goods and wealth was not accepted without difficulties or scruples. At all events, such accumulation was always made the object of reprobation, especially by the prophets (cf. Ezek. 27 and 28: the city of Tyre is accursed because of the accumulation of its riches and its trade). This accumulation calls forth the judgment of God, who will withdraw that which is His own (Zech. 9:4). Furthermore, Deuteronomy shows us that Israel was conscious of the spiritual danger attached to sedentary life, to the possession of a soil and a kingdom: and so the accumulation of horses, of wives, of gold and silver is clearly forbidden to the king (17:16–17), and in spite of all his wisdom and piety King Solomon will be blamed for having made "silver as common in Jerusalem as stone" (1 Kings 10:27), and the downfall of Solomon's kingdom is connected with that policy of accumulation made worse by his successor (1 Kings 12). In the eyes of the O.T. it is the unique lordship of God, the Creator and Father, which is challenged by any policy of accumulation or avarice: these things represent mistrust of God.

3. The N.T., which underlines less strongly than the O.T. the idea that earthly goods are the sign of God's blessing, takes up with much energy, on the other hand, *the forbidding of the appropriation of goods which belong to God only* (cf. Lk. 15:12ff., the parable of the prodigal son, in which one sees that the claim and the appropriation signify separation from God). This appropriation marks our intention of dispensing with God (the parable of the rich fool, Lk. 12:15–21), or our inability to follow Jesus Christ (cf. the story of the rich young man: the young man "went away sorrowful; for he had great possessions", Matt. 19:22).

James stresses that there is no appropriation of riches which is not associated with some injustice (5:1–6). Similarly, 1 Jn. 3:17 establishes an incompatibility between the possession of goods and brotherly love. A veritable duty of improvidence is recommended by 1 Tim. 6:17–19: spiritual foresight consists, on the contrary, in generously distributing one's goods, by putting them at the disposal of those in need. So the final worth of all riches is to meet the needs of those who are hungry. The good things of creation are not intended to be accumulated or to insure the power of a man; they are indeed "consumer goods". The rich man who egotistically keeps his possessions to himself is accursed, whilst the poor man is called happy (Lk. 6:20). This explains the attitude of the first Jerusalem community: the sharing of all the money after the sale of their possessions (Acts 2:45 and 4:32). The possessions are for the *poor, not in order that they may become rich in their turn, but that their misery may cease; and it would not conform to the spirit of the Bible to take these words of the Magnificat only in a spiritual sense: "He has filled the hungry with good things, and the rich he has sent empty away" (Lk. 1:53). This collection of texts must not be regarded as a eulogy on poverty itself; the condition of misery is not agreeable to God. On the contrary, God wishes it to cease, and that is why He forbids the accumulation of possessions in the hands of the rich. That accumulation announces the ruin of the rich man, who puts his confidence not in God but in his riches themselves.

4. The idea that these constitute a *favour of God and a blessing* is not lost sight of in the N.T., but it is connected with the idea of *renunciation*. A man must lose his life to gain it: "Truly, I say to you, there is no one who has left house or brothers or sisters or mother or father or children or lands, for my sake and for the gospel, who will not receive a hundredfold now in this time, houses and brothers and sisters and mothers and children and lands, with persecutions, and in the age to come eternal life" (Mk. 10:29–30). It will be observed, however, that earthly blessings do not constitute an absolute and unequivocal sign of divine grace: in the middle of all these possessions persecutions also find a place. The O.T. had already shown that possessions are not an absolute criterion, and unimpeachable proof of the favour of God, for "better is a little that the righteous has than the abundance of many wicked" (Ps. 37:16), and Job struggled for a long time to arrive at the certainty that his wretchedness and misery were not proof of his abandonment by God.

5. Whilst it is true that the concept of possessions includes that of money and that all that has been said about the former could be repeated of the latter, nevertheless *money* merits a study of its own because more than other possessions it represents a menace to man. "The love of money is the root of all evils" (1 Tim. 6:10). The token of money, by the facilities which it offers a man, enormously increases his power and excites in him a passion without limits: "He who loves money will not be satisfied with money; nor he who loves wealth, with gain" (Eccl. 5:10). In a certain sense it is the opposite of a good thing meant to supply a need: it does not satisfy, but multiplies the will to power. It constitutes for man a permanent source of bondage. That is why the Mosaic legislation was so concerned to limit the power of money: the prohibition of the taking of interest on loans and of usury in so far as the relations of Israelites between themselves and of Israelites and strangers living in their territory are concerned (Deut. 23:20; Lev. 25:35,36; Exod. 22:25f.). Very properly the O.T. fears that money might intrude itself between a man and his neighbour and impair their relationship. One could compare all these prescriptions with those which deal with wages (Deut. 24:14–15; Jer. 22:13; cf. Jas. 5:4), for they also testify to a concern not to let money acquire a power of oppression. James (2:1–4) reminds us that the consideration given to people because of their wealth and the external signs of wealth leads to discrimina-

tions which ruin all brotherliness. But it is Jesus above all who throws into relief the demonic power of money and possessions.

By a kind of fatality, a man places his confidence in them and it is then impossible for him to enter into the Kingdom of heaven (Mk. 10:23–25). Jesus will therefore demand a radical renunciation of the power of money: "Sell your possessions, and give alms; provide yourselves with purses that do not grow old, with a treasure in the heavens that does not fail, where no thief approaches and no moth destroys. For where your treasure is, there will your heart be also" (Lk. 12:33–34). It must be observed that this precept of Jesus is inserted in a sequence on eschatological expectancy of the *Kingdom: money, and the cares which attach to every form of possessions, deprive us of that openness of mind and that liberty which are necessary in the search for the Kingdom. Money alienates us both from the Kingdom and from hope. There lies its omnipotence. Contrary to what modern man thinks, the power of money does not come solely from an inward passion which may devour us. That inward passion, the reality of which Jesus never disregards, corresponds to an outward and objective reality. Money is not a neutral thing which may offer itself for the good or bad use which we may make of it. In the eyes of Jesus, money takes its place among the demonic powers which enslave man. That is why He gives it a demonic name, *Mammon* (Matt. 6:24; Lk. 16:13). "It is known," writes J. Ellul, "that it is a question here of an Aramaic word which means in general money, and which can also signify wealth. Here Jesus personifies Money and regards it as a kind of god. Now, this is by no means derived from contemporary usage. Jesus has not taken a denotation current amongst the people He was addressing, for it does not seem that a god of this name was known amongst Jews and Galileans or amongst the neighbouring Gentiles. Jesus does not seek a pagan deity to show that one must choose between the true God and a false god. He certainly does not refer to a current superstition which He

might have more or less shared. This personification of money appears to be a creation of Jesus Himself, and, if such it is, it means that He reveals to us something exceptional, since Jesus does not customarily use these deifications and personifications" (*L'argent*, p. 31, in "Etudes théologiques et religieuses").

What Jesus shows us is precisely that supernatural power which money exercises over men, a power which, within the limits permitted by God Himself, can hold God in check, a power which can be put alongside that of God. Hence the dilemma: "No one can serve two masters. . . . You cannot serve God and mammon" (Matt. 6:24). Only the lordship of Him who "disarmed the principalities and powers and made a public example of them, triumphing over them by the cross" (Col. 2:15) can set a limit to the lordship of Mammon, just as it puts a limit to every care and every anxiety. The O.T. had already noticed where this power of money could lead. Amos (2:6) denounces the crimes of the children of Israel who "sell the righteous for silver, and the needy for a pair of shoes". Micah (3:11) describes in these terms the perversion of the house of Israel: "Its heads give judgment for a bribe, its priests teach for hire, its prophets divine for money." The same phenomena are described by the N.T.: it is the lust for money which drives men to transform the house of prayer into a house of trade (Jn. 2:15). Ananias and Sapphira break the fellowship of the Church through the love of money (Acts 5:2); Simon the magician—and it is not without importance to underline that he is a man who has dealings with demoniacal powers—believes that the gift of God is acquired by money (Acts 8:20); Felix expects from Paul, not the word of salvation, but money merely (Acts 24:26). Finally, and above all, the word of Amos becomes a kind of prophecy which is fulfilled in Judas (Mk. 14:11) and in the soldiers whose false witness against the resurrection is achieved by money (Matt. 28:12–13). It is very striking that amongst all the demonic *powers which joined together so that the Son of God should die on the cross, money had its place and even played a decisive part. For He who was crucified is the Righteous One, but money is designated by Jesus with the name of "*unrighteous* mammon" (Lk. 16:11). There could be no compromise there between the Righteous One and Mammon. This is why Jesus refused to protect with His authority the power of money: it is necessary to render to Caesar (i.e. to another power) the money which belongs to him (Matt. 22:21). Money as such cannot be put at the service of God.

To the constraining power of Mammon there will then be opposed the gratuitousness of the Word and of the Kingdom. The liberation of man is not gained by payment of money: "Come to the waters; and he who has no money, come, buy and eat . . . without money and without price" (Isa. 55:1–2). The Twelve will be sent on a mission without money (Mk. 6:8). Paradoxically, men will be fed, revived and saved by the Poor One: "For you know the grace of our Lord Jesus Christ, that though he was rich, yet for your sake he became poor, so that by his poverty you might become rich" (2 Cor. 8:9). The servant of Christ will therefore be a man who, without possessing any of the riches for which men thirst, will nevertheless enrich them (cf. the healing of the lame man at the Beautiful Gate by Peter: "I have no silver and gold, but I give you what I have: in the name of Jesus Christ of Nazareth, walk" (Acts 3:6)).

However, it is not permissible to conclude from these indications that the N.T., repudiating the affirmation of the O.T. according to which riches are a sign of the blessing of God, has forbidden believers to have any contact with money and has sanctioned an ethic of contempt for money: it is necessary to render to Caesar the money which belongs to him and Caesar must use it to accomplish a mission which, though transitory, is none the less in conformity with the will of God. To him who truly recognizes the lordship of Christ, money has lost its power. It could be said that the teaching of Jesus tends to devalue money: what counts is not money as such,

its mere bulk, but the ability to dispose of it freely. Then money can become the object of an offering made to God Himself (cf. Mk. 12:41–44: the widow's offering). Money can become the token of brotherly fellowship, as it is seen in the "communism" of the early Church and as it is confirmed on the occasion of the collection for the Jerusalem church, a collection which was one of the chief signs of the Church's unity. It is in the degree that money is freely given, and not amassed, that it is a blessing of God (1 Tim. 6:18–19).

Contempt of money is by no means recommended. It is simply that money as a power must vanish before the power of Christ, that it must cease to be a power in order to become the sign of brotherly love. Paul gives a very concrete maxim which characterizes the new state of things: money as a power led to the enslaving of man by man, now it is going to lead to the re-establishment of equality between men. "I do not mean that others should be eased and you burdened, but that as a matter of equality your abundance at the present time should supply their want, so that their abundance may supply your want, that there may be equality" (2 Cor. 8:13–14).

But it is above all the singular parable of the unfaithful steward (Lk. 16:1–13) which clearly shows this dethronement of money as a power and its use for displaying the free salvation of God: the steward, although unfaithful and dishonest, is praised by Jesus and presented as a pattern because he took no account of the sacredness of money, but in the first place he regarded the distress of the debtors. Money is subordinate to man (in so far as it is subordinate to Jesus Christ) and it is better to make friends than to follow the religion of money. The point of this parable is therefore to proclaim that the money king is dethroned. Similarly in the parable of the workmen hired at different hours of the day, the master shows that he cares less about respecting the laws imposed under the reign of money than of doing good to those he loves (Matt. 20:1–16).

Far from recommending an ethic of

abstention with regard to money and other forms of wealth, the Bible invites man, during the absence of the Master (Matt. 25:14) to use them, make them bear fruit (parable of the talents, vv. 14–30), and to use them to sustain men (Matt. 24:45–47). But manifestly they can only do this if money has ceased to be a power, that is, if they themselves are Christ's (1 Cor. 3:22). If they act thus their works will not be destitute of meaning. God will one day take, in a form which they cannot at present know, those works achieved by "unrighteous wealth" and they will be included in the Kingdom (Rev. 21:24). For these works belong to the Lord, and God's declaration (Hagg. 2:8), "the silver is mine, and the gold is mine" has essentially an eschatological meaning.

R. MEHL

MOSES, *see* NAMES (PERSONAL)

MOTHER, *see* FAMILY

MOUNTAINS, *see* NAMES (GEOGRAPHICAL)

MULTITUDE

The multitude is the collection of men, gathered in groups by chance circumstances, which the preaching of Jesus and the apostles (and therefore the love of God) is searching out and reaching for, and to which it responds. From the ethnic, social, religious and theological points of view its extent is fortuitous, scarcely possible to define. The written narratives of the N.T. (Gospels, Acts, Revelation) constantly make mention of it as being the daily accompaniment, loved and welcomed, of Jesus and the apostles, and, in the kingdom of Christ's glory, the innumerable company of the redeemed (Rev. 7:9; 19:1). The Epistles on the other hand do not speak of it: their more exact theological language makes them see sharply defined collectives in place of the multitude, such as *Israel, the *Gentiles, the *Church, believers, unbelievers, etc.

The multitude is not the Jewish people as such, although most often in the Gospels it very nearly approaches so being. It is this people in so far as it has remained spontaneous, independent and irresponsible, with direct and personal reactions. It is not what John calls "the *Jews", the party of well-informed but culpable critics who through their blindness are the representative voices of their people and the "world" (from which however they would carefully distinguish themselves, Jn. 7:49). Neither is the multitude the mass of unbelievers. It embraces everyone—Pharisees (Lk. 19:39), tax-collectors (Lk. 5:29), disciples (Lk. 6:17), the able-bodied and the sick, credulous and incredulous, the faithful and those without grace. In the heathen environment where Paul and Barnabas worked, it was not a typical heathen multitude, but simply a collection of human beings. Where it was formed of Christians, the fact is expressly noted ("the multitude of the disciples" or "of believers"): for while the Church may be undefined in number, its allegiance cannot be undefined.

Jesus loves the multitude; He has compassion upon it because He perceives that God's people has become a flock without a *shepherd and which is therefore going astray and will perish. Always the crowd was round Him, so that He even made efforts to escape from it; when He avoided villages, the multitude followed Him in desert places and on the shores of the lake. Jesus summons them and sends them away; He teaches them with a hope which is yet without hope (Matt. 13:13), and before their eyes, though with immense discretion, He performs the miraculous signs of the coming of the Kingdom; while He gives explicit instructions to those He has healed to keep silence, the multitude learns of them and very soon they are retailing them on all sides. Over against the Pharisees of Galilee and the personages in Jerusalem, the multitude is a witness of the Messianic authority of Jesus, just as before Herod, who holds it in respect, the multitude is a witness to the righteousness of God (Matt. 14:5). Similarly, after Pentecost, the "multitude of those who believe" are witnesses before the people and the established powers of the fulfilment of the prophecies of the O.T. in Jesus Christ.

But the testimony of the multitude is not reliable in every situation; it is itself specifically human, inclined to doubt or to denial, giving way before secular coercion. The multitude does not always understand (Jn. 7:20; 12:34). Before Pilate they give evidence against Jesus on behalf of their recognized spiritual leaders (Matt. 27:15. Note a curious detail: at the decisive moment, in verse 25, the crowd is called "people", as if its murderous verdict gave it back its character as a culpable people, as denounced by the prophets). So also, in the Acts, starting with chapter 14, the multitude at Lystra, Philippi, etc., bear witness against Paul and Silas and in favour of the diverse forces by which they are enslaved (Jewish agitation, love of money, devotion to the empire, local religious traditions). The multitude is at all times an unpredictable witness, divided within itself (Jn. 7:43), never indifferent where Jesus and the apostles are concerned.

When they speak of the multitude, the Gospels, the Acts and Revelation are describing men such as Jesus met, as they actually are, without any antecedent theologizing, and such as are called to adore one day the Lord of glory. The multitude represents what is unknown; it represents what is risked and what is promised from one's "*neighbour", when these are confronted with Jesus.

CH. BIBER

MYSTERY

1. We are familiar with the amazing part played by the word mystery in the Hellenistic religions, that feverish effort of an epoch intent on the conquest of the secret of the gods. It is not our task here to determine what may have been their influence on biblical thought. But we ought at once to define the frontier which separates them: in the Bible this term refers far less to the revelation of the divine Being than to that of His redemptive plan. When, for example,

St. Paul speaks of "the deep things of God" (1 Cor. 2:10) he is not concerned with the secrets of the divinity, which were the object of the mystic initiations, but with the depth of the wisdom of God (cf. Rom. 11:33ff.) which is revealed through the dispensations of His plan of salvation for the whole world. This already explains a certain mistrust of this ambiguous term which appears only very late in the O.T.; its use is restricted to the Hellenistic period and is found to be definitely associated with the development of apocalyptic in later Judaism. Among the canonical books Daniel alone makes use of it, following the LXX, in 2:28,29,30 (there is in fact no exact equivalent of the term mystery in Hebrew): "There is a God in heaven who reveals mysteries, and he has made known to king Nebuchadnezzar what will be in the latter days." These mysteries therefore are ultimate events, delayed by God from all eternity, to which He holds the key, and which His Spirit alone is able to disclose in advance.

2. In the N.T. the word mystery is encountered almost exclusively in those writings which are directly or indirectly Pauline (especially in the letters addressed to the Churches which are surrounded by gnostic influences: those at Corinth, Colossae, and Ephesus. In this way the N.T. frequently adopts from heathen speculations their own distinctive terms in order to increase the thrust of the Gospel); elsewhere it is found once in the synoptic Gospels and four times in the book of Revelation. The term can be understood in its widest sense: the mystery of *God* (1 Cor. 2:1, but the reading is contested; Col. 1:27; cf. Rev. 10:7); the mystery of *Christ* (Eph. 3:4; Col. 4:3); the mystery of *the Kingdom* (Mk. 4:11 and parallels—the parallel passages have the word in the plural: mysteries); the mystery of *the Gospel* (Eph. 6:19). In these cases the term mystery designates in general the fulfilment and the revelation in Jesus Christ and in the Church of the grand redemptive plan of God, or its reference may be to particular dispensations

of this plan (when this is so it is sometimes used in the plural): the temporary hardening of Israel (Rom. 11:25), the glorious transformation of believers at the parousia (1 Cor. 15:51; in these passages the apostle states that he has received these things, not by a tradition that goes back to Jesus, but by a personal revelation: a more profound insight into the purposes of God has been granted to him); the intimate relationship between Christ and the Church (Eph. 5:32). Finally, mystery may be given a sense analogous to that which it has in Daniel for pointing by means of veiled imagery to ultimate events, in apocalyptic texts: the mystery of iniquity (2 Thess. 2:3,7), or of the seven stars (Rev. 1:20).

A consideration of these various usages leads us to the following conclusions:

(*a*) We have a series of events which may seem to be submerged in the history of mankind, without any particular importance or consequence, and yet it is precisely here, in this world, that God has chosen to intervene. He is present in the midst of men, and yet accessible to faith alone. He gives Himself, and yet He remains the Lord; this is the heart of the New Testament mystery. These events are successively: according to Mk. 4:11, *the hidden presence of the *King- dom of God* in the person of Jesus of Nazareth, His words, His acts; a mystery, for some welcome in Him the arrival of a new world, whereas for others, those who are without, "everything is in parables" (they understand nothing!); according to 1 Cor. 2:7, it is the supreme victory of the *cross* where all the power and the wisdom of God are concentrated, but where, again, the powers of this world, despite their knowledge, have failed to recognize the Lord of glory; according to Col. 1:27, there is a mystery once more in *the presence of Jesus Christ in us*, poor "Gentiles", in whom others discern nothing extraordinary, and who yet bear within ourselves all the hope of glory, the earnest of the world to come; according to Eph. 3:4, *the constitution of the *Church*, in which it is possible to see only one religious sect amongst many others, and yet which is in reality the body

of Christ, the germ of a new and reconciled humanity; according to 1 Cor. 2:13ff., *preaching* itself constitutes an integral part of the mystery; it is a word stripped of all grandiloquence and of all charm, and yet it is the very *Word of the living God; and finally, according to Rev. 17ff., the *parousia* also participates in the mystery: through the chaos of the final convulsions of history faith descries the vivid signs of the approaching advent of the Son of Man.

Thus the mystery indicates the *choice* of God. At the same time that He comes and reveals Himself, He is hidden. He has chosen the weak things of the world to confound the strong, and things that are not to bring to nothing the things that are. In order to manifest eternity He has chosen time; to reveal His Spirit He has chosen flesh; to reveal His divinity, man; to cause His sovereignty to shine forth, the cross; for His own presence, our own lives; He has chosen the Church, to unite all men; the stammerings of His servants, to make His voice sound forth; the catastrophes of the history of the nations, to lead us on the way to the new Jerusalem. In view of each of these declarations, it is striking to see the recurrence of the term mystery in St. Paul.

(*b*) The mystery has been prepared from the creation of the world (1 Cor. 2:7), it is hidden in God (Eph. 3:9), veiled through the ages (1 Cor. 2:8; Eph. 3:9; Rom. 16:25; Col. 1:26). But God has purposed to reveal it now, in Christ, to His elect in order that they may participate in it "for their glory" (1 Cor. 2:7). The understanding of the mystery (Eph. 3:4) is in particular associated with Paul's apostolic consciousness: he regards it as a stewardship (1 Cor. 4:1); his mission is to preach it (Col. 1:25f.; Eph. 3:8f.) and the great conflict in which he must engage concerns it (Col. 2:1). In connection with it he requests the prayers of the Churches (Col. 4:3; Eph. 6:19).

(*c*) In conclusion we should notice that the plan of God, even when revealed to the saints, and even when announced to the world, continues to be a mystery in so far as the last judgment has not brought it to its final disclosure and fulfilment, and in so far as it has not made plain the secret of history, vindicated the wisdom of God, and confirmed the truth of prophecy.

In 1 Tim. 3:9 (the mystery of the faith) and 3:16 (the mystery of godliness) the association with the term mystery does not seem to have effected a modification of the meaning of the words faith and godliness; here it serves to accentuate all the more its objective character.

To sum up: mystery in the N.T. concerns the wisdom of the Father in accordance with which He decides, prepares, and executes His redemptive purposes, the aim of which is to "unite all things in Christ" (Eph. 1:9f.), and in accordance with which He reveals Himself by His Spirit to His elect and more particularly to His apostles and prophets who are its stewards.

M. BOUTTIER

NAME

O.T.

1. *Name, a profound reality of being; name, a living person.* In the O.T., far from being a mere label, just an external description, a name expresses the profound reality of the being who carries it. That is why the creation is not completed until the moment when everything brought into existence has received a name. In this respect two passages are significant: Isa. 40:26: ". . . see: who created these (stars)? . . . He who calls them all by name", and Gen. 2:20; after having formed the animals of the field and the birds, Yahweh causes them to pass before Adam in order that he may name them and perhaps thereby discover their companionship: "Adam gave names to all cattle and to the birds of the air . . .; but for Adam there was not found a helper fit for him." Is it necessary to recall that at the end of each day of the account of creation God gives a name to the creatures? The proper names of the O.T. therefore possess a significance which discloses the essential character of the person: "Adam" is a "human" being, for having been made from the "humus" his reality is earthly (Gen. 2:7); contrariwise, *God is "Yahweh", that

is to say "HE WHO IS", for His reality is that of everlasting being (Exod. 3:13–15). For all these reasons to cut off a name is to suppress existence (1 Sam. 24:22; 2 Kings 14:27; Job 18:17; Ps. 83:5; Isa. 14:22; Zeph. 1:4).

The true nature of the name is clearly seen in the following examples: God causes His name to rest in a particular place (Isa. 18:7; Jer. 7:12), and a temple is built for the divine name (1 Kings 3:2, etc.), for the name of Yahweh is like Himself: where His name is, there He is present ("Behold, the name of the Lord comes from far . . .", Isa. 30:27; cf. also Exod. 20:24; 23:21; Mic. 5:3). Likewise human names are something living and hold from God the power of continuing existence (Isa. 66:22); also a person whose name is asked frequently refuses to give it, for otherwise he would surrender a part of himself (Gen. 32:29; Judg. 13:18). It goes without saying that this realistic notion respecting names sometimes lost its importance, since a name could pass from someone possessing certain characteristics to a descendant with different characteristics; hence the necessity occasionally arose for explaining the underlying reality of a name, as was indicated in the case of "Nabal"= "Fool" when it was said "as his name is, so is he" (1 Sam. 25:25).

2. *Name, a possibility of knowledge.* By reason of its nature a name imparts knowledge (Exod. 33:12; 1 Chr. 4:41; Ezra 10:16; Ps. 9:11; 91:14; Isa. 52:6; Jer. 48:17) and by one's name one makes oneself known to others (Isa. 64:2); in so far as one does not know a person's name one does not know him who bears it (Judg. 13:6).

3. *A change of name signifies a change in the reality of being.* The custom existed of giving a new name to a person who was called to a new dignity or function: Abram becomes Abraham (Gen. 17:5); Jacob becomes Israel (Gen. 35:10); Mattaniah becomes Zedekiah (2 Kings 24:17). In the course of their history cities did not escape these changes (Num. 32:38; Judg. 1:17). In eschatological times the renewing of Zion

will be marked by a new name, assigned by God (Isa. 62:2), and the elect will receive a name different from that which they have hitherto borne (Isa. 65:15; see *Garment).

4. *Name, a token of continuity of being.* In the O.T. the individual forms a solidarity not only with his ancestors, but also with his people and with God who presides over the destinies of the people; a name expresses in its own manner this sort of psychic dimension in which the person is only a local and temporal aspect of an organic whole: God, people, family.

(*a*) The name of God is the name *par excellence* (Zech. 14:9), so much so that God is called by religious dread simply "the name" (Lev. 24:11; 2 Sam. 6:2; His name is *holy,* Lev. 20:3; Ps. 103:1; Ezek. 20:39, etc.; *glorious,* Neh. 9:5; Ps. 72:19; *great,* 1 Kings 8:42; Jer. 44:26; *honoured,* Deut. 28:58; *exalted,* Ps. 148:13; *terrible,* Ps. 99:3; 111:9), the invocation of which produces terror among the people (Mal. 2:5) and provokes the fear of the enemy (Deut. 28:10; Ps. 102:16). The name of God is Yahweh, "HE WHO IS", the eternal name (Exod. 3:15), on which the reality of all other names depends (Isa. 56:5).

(*b*) The people of God is composed of those who are called by the name of Israel (Isa. 48:1) and upon whom the divine name has been pronounced (2 Chr. 7:14; Dan. 9:19). Every offence to the name of the people is an offence to the name of their God (Josh. 7:9). The visible place where the two realities of God and the people, united by covenant, meet is the *Temple of Jerusalem which has been called by the name of Yahweh (Jer. 7:11; Dan. 9:19).

(*c*) Each tribe of the people has its name (Num. 17:3), and likewise each family which wishes to perpetuate itself in the midst of the people, whether by its male descendants (Num. 27:4; 2 Sam. 14:7, whence the law of the levirate: Deut. 25:6,7; Ruth 4:5,10; see *Marriage), or by a monument for the sake of those who have no children (2 Sam. 18:18; Isa. 56:5), or by the founding or the capture of a city (Gen. 4:17; 11:4; Num. 32:37–38,42; Judg. 18:29;

2 Sam. 12:28). A name given to a place can also perpetuate the family or tribal reality because of the occurrence which it calls to mind (Num. 11:34; 21:3; Josh. 5:9; 7:26; Judg. 1:17; 2:5; 2 Sam. 5:20; 1 Chr. 14:11; 2 Chr. 20:26).

5. *To speak or act "in someone's name" is to participate in the reality expressed by that name.* People speak in the name of David (1 Sam. 25:9), of Ahab (1 Kings 21:8), of strange gods (Deut. 18:20), but above all in the name of Yahweh (Exod. 5:23; Deut. 18:22; Jer. 11:21). Because a formula involving the name of Yahweh is employed, Yahweh is invoked (Gen. 4:26; 12:8, etc.); people bless in His name (Deut. 21:5; 2 Sam. 18); curse in His name (2 Kings 2:24); take oaths in His name (1 Sam. 20:42; 1 Kings 22:16); trust in His holy name (Isa. 50:10; Ps. 33:21; cf. Ps. 9:11); there is aid in His name (Ps. 124:8); refuge is sought in His name (Zeph. 3:12); people walk in His name (Mic. 4:5); an altar is built in His name (1 Kings 18:31f.); the priest ministers in His name (Deut. 18:5,7). The realism of the expression "in the name of Yahweh" is shown in the account of the battle of David against Goliath; the artful shepherd says to the Philistine who is advancing heavily armed: "You come to me with a sword and with a spear and with a javelin; but I come to you in the name of the Lord of hosts . . ." (1 Sam. 17:45).

6. *A name is also renown and fame* (Gen. 6:4; 11:4; Num. 16:2; Deut. 32:3, etc.).

7. *Metaphorically,* the name of the day is the date, Ezek. 24:2.

H. MICHAUD

N.T.

1. The N.T. speaks at first of the name of God *in the same sense as the O.T.,* and all the more so as the expression is frequently found in textual quotations from the O.T. A name is a programme: the name of God reminds all those to whom it has pleased

God to reveal Himself who He is, what He has done, and what He requires. His name implies a certain revelation and a certain knowledge of God: the consequence is that God is no longer one who is "stronger than we" nor "Providence" (although He is that!), but the Father of our Lord Jesus Christ (Matt. 11:25; Jn. 20:17; Rom. 8:15; Gal. 4:6). The name of God is found at the head of the petitions of the Lord's Prayer (Matt. 6:9) so that he who prays commences by accepting and acknowledging the revelation of God, and the salvation and commandments which are involved in it: it is by this act of acknowledgment that he will associate himself with its sanctification. Since the N.T. provides a completing preciseness to the revelation of the O.T., in it the name of God acquires a more glorious significance. Hence the N.T. is not silent about this name (Matthew, however, observes Jewish prudence by writing "Kingdom of heaven" for "Kingdom of God"), and in speaking of it throws into relief all the implications of the revelation which, though generally unknown, are a delight to believers. As for the prophetic expression "in the name of God", it also becomes more precise: the one who has been sent with a definite mission from God is in fact reduced to a single person, namely, Jesus Christ (cf. the salutation of Palm Sunday, Matt. 21:9).

2. The general reduction of the bearers of the name of God to a single one, to Him who has received "the name which is above every name", confers on the name of this sole bearer a distinction that is unequalled. The great novelty of the N.T. in the use of the supreme name is that *the name of Jesus Christ* comes to be subordinated, substituted, and joined to the name of God: subordinated, because the name of Jesus is only the explanation, the effective development, of the name of God; substituted, because it is the integral and authorized manifestation of all the mysteries which the name of God contains; joined, because henceforth the sacred authors will delight to mention in the same breath the two names, in the unity of the two covenants. (The joining of the two names is not done without the realization of their profound unity. A third name will be joined to them with the same significance, that of the Holy Spirit: their relationships will be defined later on in the dogma of the Trinity.) Thus, to be clear when speaking of God, the N.T. uses the name of Jesus. To acknowledge the full revelation which God has granted in Jesus is to accept the name which sums it up and describes it; a name that is human and historical and apparently fortuitous, but chosen of God and to which all the prophecies are related. Forthwith the name of Jesus is found in association with all the prophetic names of the Messiah of Israel and the divine titles of the Greek mysteries (see *Jesus Christ); "Jesus" is really a personal name; "Christ" and the others are titles, but several of these titles become names because they could not designate any one other than Jesus. The highest name of all—a title, which becomes precisely the personal characteristic of Jesus—is that of "Lord" (Phil. 2:9; Heb. 1:4), which in the Greek O.T. is the name of God Himself.

3. Henceforth the name of Jesus is used: that indicates the acceptance pure and simple, astonished but confident, persevering and audacious, of the manifestation of God in Jesus Christ (Acts 4:10 and 12; 5:40–42). In this name one believes, and that indicates the entrance into the ways of God (Jn. 1:12). This name is invoked (Acts 9:13; 10:14; 2 Cor. 12:8), but that has nothing in common with the religious practice which consists in providing oneself with influential names in order to create an impression on the divinity. One confesses this name (1 Cor. 12:3), impelled by the Holy Spirit. By this name one acts, one bears testimony to it, one suffers because of it. It conveys a wonderful blessing (Lk. 9:49); on the other hand, a mercenary utilization of this name will result in a curse (Acts 19:13—a curse full of blessings! —vv. 17–19).

The whole life of the Church, the whole life of Christians, has its place under this name; whence the frequency of the expression "in the name of Jesus", or "for", "by", "because of" His name (in Greek there are eight different styles). This name is the efficacious sign of the lordship of Christ. Every believer bears it, having been baptized "in the name of Jesus" (Acts 2:38: a variant of the trinitarian formula, Matt. 28:19); it is the "new name" which will distinguish the elect at the last day (Rev. 2:17; 3:12). By this name (=by Him who faithfully answers to this name) the elect are delivered from the powers of sin, are pardoned (Acts 10:43; 1 Jn. 2:12), washed, sanctified, justified (1 Cor. 6:11). In this name the disciples receive power to cast out demons, who have never upheld the lordship of Christ, and the power to heal the sick (Mk. 16:17; Acts 3–5). It is in the name of Jesus that His disciples gather together (Matt. 18:20), that is to say, in His spiritual and real presence, and it is in His name that they pray, for this gives their prayers the effectiveness of those of Christ Himself (Jn. 16:26). In His name the apostle exhorts the Churches (Rom. 12:1; 1 Cor. 1:10; 2 Thess. 3:6), which indicates that it is the Lord who commands through His apostle (cf. 1 Cor. 7:10). The whole life of believers is to be lived in the free obligation of Christ, for this is the heart of all "morality" (Col. 3:1ff.; Mk. 9:37).

This powerful bond with the Lord will not fail to disturb the world, whose evil lords will consider themselves injured in their absolute demands: the believer, however, continues to confess the name of Jesus, even though it leads him to suffering. This name speaks much more of glory to him than of shame or suffering (1 Pet. 4:14–16; Matt. 19:29). Finally, since the whole new existence of the believer is marked by this name, the proclamation of the Gospel is called the good news of the name of Jesus (Acts 8:12) and to persevere in the faith is the same as to keep His name (Rev. 2:13).

CH. BIBER

NAMES (GEOGRAPHICAL)

Although the elect, that is to say, "those who have been redeemed from the earth" (Rev. 14:3) have no permanent *city here below (Heb. 13:14; cf. 11:13; Phil. 3:20), yet that does not prevent them from living in a world which has God for its *Creator (Gen. 1:1) and Lord (Matt. 11:25, etc.).

While it is true that this world has been corrupted by sin, it none the less remains, in the expectation of a new world (2 Pet. 3:13) and for those who have eyes to see, the theatre in which God manifests Himself (Rom. 1:19f.) and in which He may choose particular places so that He may be worshipped there (cf. Gen. 22:3; Exod. 3:5, etc.): whether it is a question of the Promised Land (Gen. 12:1; Num. 33:51; Ps. 105:11, etc.) on which God's eyes are continually fixed (Deut. 11:10ff.) and which the prophets will even call His bride (Isa. 62:4), or whether it is a question of other places which bear the *name of God's manifestations (cf. Gen. 28:19; 35:5ff.,15; 32:30; Exod. 17:7; Num. 11:3,34; 21:3; Josh. 5:9; 1 Sam. 7:12; 2 Sam. 5:20; 6:8; 2 Chr. 20:26, etc.), there is in the Bible what may be called a "sacred geography" just as there is a "sacred history", that is to say that certain geographical terms and places are governed by a theological coefficient apart from which it is impossible to understand their significance. The rapid survey which follows is far from being exhaustive: it is our wish simply to provide several instances of the constant biblical presupposition that there is no place which God cannot reach and set apart for the manifestation of His presence, His wrath, His forgiveness, or His promises. It should, however, be noted that God remains free in His association with these "sacred places" (in the wide sense of the term): He is able to bless His people even in Egypt or in Babylon, and He is able to desert His Temple in Jerusalem (cf. Jer. 12:7; Ps. 80:15 and 9–20).

1. *The "fertile crescent"*. This is the name given to the territory where almost the whole of biblical history is enacted; it comprises, to the east, the valley of the Tigris and of the Euphrates (Babylon), to the west, the valley of the Nile (Egypt), and between the two the

valley of the Jordan (Canaan). The topographical situation of CANAAN, the land chosen by God for His people, is typical of the theological situation of Israel: schematically, to their right and to their left Israel have the "*world" from which God has called them (Gen. 11:31–12:1) or saved them (Exodus), and which constantly remains for them a threat or a temptation. Thus the history of Israel will be a conflict, more or less well conducted, to establish themselves in their vocation and in their salvation, that is to say, to remain, although surrounded by the "world", yet free from the "world" (hence the polemic of the prophets against alliances with the East or with the West). It is true that Canaan also used to be the "world" with its *idols which were so difficult to eradicate; but God wished, through Joshua, the Judges, and those of the kings who were obedient to Him, to plant His *vine there, and for this purpose He drove out the nations and cleared the soil for it (Ps. 80:8f.).

On its right, to the east, Canaan has—an elastic term!—BABYLON, the great city which, at the very commencement of history, wished to dethrone God (Gen. 11:6–11). This Babylon, land of exile and sorrow (Ps. 137) where the choicest of God's people suffer, pray, and hope after the fall of Jerusalem in 586, this Babylon whose end Isaiah proclaims with so much joy (21:8ff.) will assume, moreover, an almost mythical attraction, and will become, in the Revelation, the antitype of the heavenly Jerusalem, the city of God: she is not one espoused, but a prostitute (Rev. 17:1,5; 19:2), she is not the place where the elect gather together, but the place from which they must flee (Rev. 18:4; cf. Isa. 52:11; Jer. 50:8; 51:6), and their hope and expectation is, not that she will endure, but that she will perish (Rev. 18:1–19:3). That the apocalyptic appellation of Babylon the Great involves a theological notion rather than a geographical entity is demonstrated by the fact that this name designates Rome, "the great city which has dominion over the kings of the earth" (Rev. 17:18) and which is seated on seven hills (17:9). In all proba-

bility Rome should also be understood by the Babylon of 1 Pet. 5:13. The fact that the new-born Church was able to give the name of Babylon to Rome shows, on the one hand, that in the Roman Empire she felt herself to be not at home but in exile, and, on the other hand, that she was aware that Rome, having pronounced (through Pontius Pilate) sentence of death on Jesus, had at the same time pronounced sentence of death on herself.

On its left, to the west, Canaan is bordered by EGYPT, the land from which God rescued His people (Exod. 13:9,16; Num. 20:16; Deut. 6:21, etc.) by the might of His arm: a land of slavery (Exod. 20:2), but also a land of flesh-pots and bread (Exod. 16:3), of such a kind that, if Babylon is to be the symbol of the world which threatens the people of God, Egypt would be the symbol of the world which tempts and would seduce the people of God: a land of which the people dream when entry into the land of salvation appears to be too difficult and doubt overmasters faith (cf. Num. 13:1–14:23, etc.): the land with which the people seek to form culpable alliances when the threat of the East is too strong (cf. Isa. 36:6,9; also Ps. 20:8; 33:17 which speaks of the horse, an animal particularly associated with Egypt, cf. 1 Kings 10:28; Isa. 31:3). This attraction of the West is not only a sign of lack of faith, of a desire to be no longer responsible and free, a desire, that is, to return to slavery: if it is the West rather than the East that was the great political temptation of the people settled in Canaan, this may perhaps also be because of the memory that the West has been a land of refuge (cf. Gen. 12:10ff.; 42:1–47:12; Jer. 26:21; 41:17; Matt. 2:13ff.; cf. however Jer. 42:13–22) and because it is the only place where a representative of the people of God, Joseph, was truly able to make his home and to govern the "world" (Gen. 41: 37–44; 45:9,13, etc.). Salvation, however, comes neither from the West nor from the East, but from God (Ps. 75:7).

2. The DESERT or wilderness is, paradoxically, one of the most fertile geo-

graphical concepts of Scripture. We draw attention here to its more important aspects:

In a general manner it can be said that the term "desert" immediately reminds the Israelite, by an association of ideas, of the exodus from Egypt and the forty years spent in the desert (Deut. 29:5). For the prophets, this was the fullest and most significant period of sacred history (cf. Hos. 2:14; 13:5f.), and it was not by chance that, in order to prepare the people for the eschatological advent of the Lord, it was precisely in the desert that John the Baptist's ministry was located (cf. Matt. 3:1 and parallels; 11:7 and parallels); it is here that the people of God were able (by means of *baptism, which answers to the crossing of the Red Sea) to be gathered together and re-formed.

The desert is territory that is frightening (Deut. 1:19), desolate (Ezek. 6:14), and murderous (Jer. 2:6). But, precisely because man cannot by himself live there, it is a place where faith is tested: it is in the desert that the people have to choose whether they will put their trust in God (who has so often proved His might) or whether, grumbling and impatient at having to depend only on His grace, they wish to return "to Egypt". It is understandable, therefore, that both O.T. and N.T. should have regarded the history of the forty years spent in the desert by Israel, when they were guided, protected, and provided with food and drink by God, as affording us an example (1 Cor. 10:6): as the passion and resurrection of Jesus Christ are, for the Church, the governing reference of her faith and life, so also the exodus is, for Israel (and, by reason of its fulfilment in Christ, for the Church also), the governing reference of their faith and life.

But because the desert is above all else the place where faith is tested, it is also the place of Christ's *temptation, the place where, in a certain sense, the conflict between God and the Devil respecting the future of man can be staged in a scene free from all admixture foreign to the essential debate (even if in the desert it is possible to be transported in a moment to the very heart of religion—to the pinnacle of the Temple in Jerusalem—or be confronted with all the grandeur of human civilization on a high mountain whence the perspective includes the world, Matt. 4:5ff. and parallels). Thus it is "to be tempted by the devil" that Jesus is led by the Spirit into the desert (Matt. 4:1 and parallels). The desert is, in a sense, the "*world" in its essential state, and it is for this reason that it is regarded as the resort of demons (Matt. 12:43; Lk. 8:29; 11:24): if God leads His people and His Son there, and later on anchorites and hermits, it is not to cause them to flee from the world, but on the contrary to bring them to its heart so that there, in the hardest place of all, they may manifest His victory and His rights. It may be supposed, moreover, that when Jesus withdraws into the desert, generally after having performed a miracle (Mk. 1:35; Lk. 4:42; 5:16) it is not only to seek privacy (cf. Matt. 14:12f. and parallels; Mk. 1:44; Jn. 11:53f.), but rather to betake Himself to the place where He ought to give all the glory to God.

The desert, however, is not only a place of temptation and thus of proving one's faith: it is also a territory of expectation and pilgrimage, the place which leads from the pledges of salvation to *rest in salvation: it is the place to which, for Israel, the crossing of the Red Sea and, for Jesus, His baptism (Mk. 1:9–13 and parallels) leads; the place where salvation has already given pledges of its reality, but where it has not yet been manifested in its completeness. For the Church (cf. 1 Cor. 10:1–13) therefore the desert becomes the image of the situation in which she finds herself between Pentecost and the return of Christ: salvation is there already, baptism has already effected participation in the death and resurrection of Christ, and the *Lord's Supper makes it possible to taste already the heavenly gift and the powers of the world to come (Heb. 6:4f.); but the Kingdom in its completeness, the Promised Land, is not yet there: salvation can yet be lost (only what you have been given can be lost!). Thus the desert becomes an image of the *time in which the Church is now placed, the situation in which she must believe and love and hope, and which could be called a "sacramental" situation. This is the theme of the Epistle to the Hebrews.

Finally, the desert is an image of the world in the sense that it is awaiting the time when it will no longer be the desert, when it will be delivered from that which makes it formidable; for the world awaits, with an ardent expectation, the cosmic baptism of the last day when it will be transformed into a *new world (2 Pet. 3:13; cf. Rom. 8:18–23): the desert awaits the time when God will make it into a garden (Ps. 107:35; Isa. 32:15; 35:1–7; 41:18f.; 43:19f.; 51:3).

3. JERUSALEM (=foundation of peace?) or ZION (=the fortified hill? the eastern hill of the city on which the Temple was built) is, since the time when David made it the capital (2 Sam. 5:6ff.) and brought the *ark to it (2 Sam. 6:1–23)—for which Solomon built the Temple (1 Kings 5ff.)—at the heart of the history of the old covenant: a city chosen by God (1 Kings 11:13; 2 Kings 23:27) to cause His *name to rest there (2 Kings 21:4; 2 Chr. 33:4; cf. Ps. 132:13; Isa. 31:9; Joel 3:17, etc.), a holy city (Isa. 52:1), God's throne (Jer. 3:17), a place of salvation (Isa. 46:13), God's holy mountain (Ps. 2:6, etc.), Jerusalem is supremely the place where the history of salvation is enacted. Essential *ministries are performed there: the *kings* of the line of David rule and die there (cf. 2 Chr. 9:31; 16:14; 21:1, etc.), the *priests* carry out their duties in the *Temple there, and the *prophets* do not cease to declare that the fortunes of Jerusalem and of the people of God are bound up together: that is why the deliverance of the city at the time of the siege of Sennacherib in 701 B.C. (2 Kings 18:17–19,37), its destruction by Nebuchadnezzar in 587–586, its reconstruction under the Persian Empire at the end of the sixth century (Ezra, Nehemiah), then its fortunes under the Greeks (destruction of the city in 167) and under the Romans (capture of the city by Pompey in 63), affect the people in what they hold most sacred. One has only to remember what Jerusalem means to the psalmist! (cf. Ps. 87; 122; 125; 128; 137;

147, etc.). If, despite His tremendous love for this city (cf. 1 Kings 11:36; 15:4, etc.), God sends His prophets with their threatenings against it (cf. Jer. 9:11; 13:9,27; Ezek. 5:1ff., etc.), if He punishes it and appears to abandon it, it is because He cannot endure that, through its sins and idolatries, it should depart from its vocation which is to be the centre of the world (Ezek. 5:5), the place from which the law goes forth (Isa. 2:3) and towards which not only the people of the Exile turn, for the great final assemblage (cf, Jer. 50:5; Joel 3:1, etc.), but all the *nations of the world (cf. Isa. 2:1ff., etc.). It is understandable therefore that, especially at the time of the Exile when the so-called second Isaiah was preaching, Jerusalem should have become almost synonymous with the eschatological Kingdom of God (cf. Isa. 52:1ff.; 62:1ff.; 65:17ff.; 66:10ff., etc.)—the city which the rabbinical and apocalyptic literature is to call the heavenly Jerusalem, the bride of the Lord.

In the Gospels Jerusalem preserves its right to be the theatre where the fortunes of the people of God and, accordingly, the fortunes of the world are enacted: this city which kills the prophets (Matt. 23:37; Lk. 13:34) is like a lover who attracts Jesus in order to murder Him there (Lk. 9:51; cf. Matt. 16:21 and parallels; 20:17 and parallels; Lk. 9:31; 13:13). The question may be put whether Jesus, when going up to Jerusalem with the *Twelve, who are the representatives of the people of God, did not bring to fulfilment—in secret, like all the promises which He fulfilled at the time of His first coming—the great eschatological gathering together to the holy city, in such a way that after Palm Sunday (in association with His words concerning the temple which He would rebuild and which is His body) the holy city, in so far as it was the centre of the world, was superseded by His own person. For it is He who is from then on the light of the nations (Lk. 2:32; cf. Matt. 12:21; Jn. 8:12; 9:5; 12:46 and Rev. 21:24): it is He who takes over the rôle of Jerusalem and its Temple. This seems to be confirmed when we find Jesus announcing the destruction of Jerusalem as well as of the Temple (Matt. 24 and parallels: it took place in A.D. 70).

A further indication might be the fact that since Palm Sunday (and the activity of St. Paul, cf. below) Jerusalem has no further theological importance as a geographical place, and that it is no longer to this city, but to Jesus and His body, the *Church, that the prophecies of the O.T. concerning "the city of the great King" (Matt. 5:35) must be referred. This in itself is sufficient to invalidate Jewish Zionism (it should not be forgotten that Jerusalem is, in fact, essentially "the city of David", that is to say, the Messianic city—and even the city of the Messiah after the order of Melchizedek, since this mysterious personage was king of Salem (Gen. 14:18): Jewish Zionism is, of course, when pushed to its logical conclusion, an assertion that the Messiah has not yet come). Before answering this question we must examine the rôle which Jerusalem plays after Pentecost (which, like the death of Jesus, was to take place in this city, Acts 1:4, thus manifesting once more its position at the centre of the world: Acts 2:5-11): it is from there that the Gospel goes forth (Lk. 24:47; Acts 1:8) and even— something that is too easily forgotten—the mission of St. Paul (cf. Rom. 15:19).

It is also possible to discern in the life of St. Paul an attraction towards Jerusalem, analogous to that which marked the last part of Jesus' life (cf. Acts 20:16,22; 21:4,13); but if Jesus, by going up to Jerusalem, ful- filled the prophecies of the gathering together of the people of Israel to the holy city, St. Paul by going up to it fulfils, in secret also, the prophecies of the gathering together to the holy city of the "nations" and their riches: it is in fact because of his mission to the Gentiles that he goes there after his conversion, whether to learn there the apostolic *tradition which he will hand on to the nations (Acts 9:26ff.), or in order to assure the Gentile Christians of their right to citizenship among the people of the new covenant (Acts 15:1ff.; Gal. 2:1ff.), or above all to take to Jerusalem the collection (the glory and riches of the nations!) which

he has made among his Churches (cf. Rom. 15:25-31).

It seems, therefore, that from now on the prophecies concerning Jerusalem have been fulfilled and that St. Paul will be able to turn his back on a city which is no longer the holy city, the guardian of the future, but, like Hagar in relationship to Sarah, an outcast (Gal. 4:35). If, however, the earthly Jerusalem seems from henceforth to be disqualified, the theological concepts con- veyed by the name of this city do not dis- appear: they are attributed to Jesus Christ, to the Church, or to the heavenly Jerusalem, which is free and the mother of Christians (Gal. 4:26), which is kept in reserve so that it may appear at the end of the world (Rev. 21:1-22:5; cf. 3:12) and to which it is already possible for us, in Christian wor- ship, to draw near (Heb. 12:18-24). It therefore seems possible to conclude that since the occasion when Jesus went up to Jerusalem with the Twelve (who represent the twelve tribes dispersed and gathered together to the holy city) and when St. Paul went up there with the collection (the sign of the gathering together to the holy city of the nations and their riches) Jerusalem as a topographical locality surrendered its theo- logical significance to Jesus and His body, that is to say, it lost the rôle which had been assigned to it during the period from David until the advent of Him who is pre- eminently the Son of David. It will, how- ever, be noted—without any specific instruction having been given—that the ascension of Jesus from the mount of Olives proclaims a return which will take place in the same manner, and perhaps in the same place, according to the prophecy of Zech. 14:3-4 (cf. Acts 1:11f.), and that St. Paul introduces two O.T. quotations which speak of Zion into what he says con- cerning the future of Israel after the flesh (cf. Rom. 9:33; 11:26).

4. Of the rivers to which Scripture attri- butes more than a topographical significance the JORDAN is certainly the most important.

Even though the tribes of Reuben, Gad, and half the tribe of Manasseh received as their share territories to the east of the Jordan (cf. Num. 32; Josh. 13:8ff.; 22:1–34), it none the less forms the true boundary of the promised land, "the good land beyond the Jordan" (Deut. 3:25; cf. 11:31). The land to the west of the Jordan will therefore be "the side that belongs to the people of Israel" (Josh. 22:11) or "the land of which the Lord has taken possession" (Josh. 22:19), whereas the east will be—in spite of the Israelite tribes settled there—"the territory of the Gentiles" (Isa. 9:1; cf. Matt. 4:15). Accordingly it is not surprising that this river should have been regarded as a last obstacle to the entry into the Promised Land, and that the crossing of it should have been effected as miraculously as that of the Red Sea (Josh. 3–4; cf. Ps. 114:5): the Promised Land is a country which cannot be taken in one's own power, but which can only be received through the grace of God.

No more should it occasion surprise that this river, which borders the holy land, should have been the scene of miracles, especially at the time of Elisha when there was an accumulation of miracles (cf. 2 Kings 2:7–14: the miraculous crossing of the Jordan; 5:1–19: the healing of Naaman the leper; 6:1–7: the axe-head which came to the surface of its own accord from the bottom of the river), and doubtless it is not by chance that the Jordan should have been the river in which John baptized (Matt. 3:6 and parallels; 3:13 and parallels). The fourth Gospel even states that John was ministering beyond Jordan (Jn. 1:28; 3:26; 10:40), that is to say that he had left the Promised Land in order to cause those who repented to enter it anew through *baptism: he repeated, in a sacramental manner, the history of Joshua for them. It is thus understandable that reference to the Jordan in the tradition of the Fathers of the Church should have been associated with baptism, linking with it Psalm 42 where, far from Jordan (v. 7) the Psalmist is "like a thirsty hart panting for flowing streams" (v. 1). The biblical atmosphere of so many of the negro spirituals which sing of Jordan will also be appreciated.

5. When the passages which relate to the SEA are examined it is remarkable to find that the book of Revelation (21:1) declares, as a promise and a victory, that in the world to come there will be no more sea. The reason is that, for the Bible, the sea is a place suspected of harbouring enemies of God, and the impression is received that in speaking of it one is assured on each occasion that God is the stronger: it is so dangerous with its tempests (cf. Acts 27:14–44; 2 Cor. 11:25f.) and with its monsters (cf. Job 3:8), and it also plays a similar rôle in the cosmogonies and mythologies of the Near East, so that it is important to state, with expressions of thankfulness, that God is its master: He is its creator (Gen. 1:10; Neh. 9:6; Jon. 1:9; Acts 4:24; Rev. 10:6, etc.), He assigns it its place (Job. 38:8; Prov. 8:29) and it is obedient to His will (Isa. 50:2; Jer. 31:35; Amos 5:8; cf. Matt. 8:23–27 and parallels), as are also its monsters (Jon. 2:1,11). It is so submissive to Him that He can cause it to recede or to become dry (Exod. 14:15ff.; cf. Ps. 106:9; 136:13; Isa. 11:15; Nahum 1:4, etc.), and He tames it so that it is possible to walk over it on foot (Job 9:8; cf. Matt. 14:25ff. and parallels): He causes it to fear (Ps. 114:3). Thus it cannot be separate from Him (Ps. 139:9; Jon. 1–2), and, before God, the sea and all that it contains have only one thing to do, namely, to renounce themselves, to adore God (cf. Ps. 148:7), and to acknowledge that all life and all sustenance come from the Lord (cf. Ps. 104:25 ff.). The fact that Solomon has a fleet and that he can travel across the seas (cf. 1 Kings 2:26ff.; 10:22) is the most striking proof that God is his protector: Israel is not a nation of seafarers.

6. Somewhat like the sea, and without doubt for the same reasons of implicit opposition to the pagan mythologies (cf. the opposition of the prophet to the worship in the "high places" after the centralization of worship on mount Zion: 1 Kings 11:7; 14:23; 2 Kings 18:4; 21:3; Ps. 78:58; Jer. 7:30f.; Ezek. 20:27ff.; Hos. 10:8; Mic. 1:5, etc.), MOUNTAINS are seen first of all as a

place which God, in His omnipotence, can reach and rule (Judg. 5:5; Ps. 65:7; Isa. 40:12; Mic. 1:4, etc.), despite the power which they symbolize (cf. Dan. 2:34; Jer. 51:25; Zech. 4:7). It is for this reason that Scripture repeats so often that the mountains have no right to be placed where they are (Matt. 17:20; cf. Lk. 17:6; 1 Cor. 13:2; Job 9:5; Ezek. 38:20) and that, to prepare for the coming of His Kingdom, they will be levelled or uprooted (cf. Isa. 40:4=Lk. 3:5; Isa. 41:15; Rev. 6:14; 16:20, etc.), with the exception, however, of mount Zion which, according to certain prophetic texts, will become the summit of the earth (Mic. 4:1; Isa. 2:2). This is also the reason why the mythical "everlasting hills" or "mountains of the gods" (Gen. 49:26; Deut. 33:15; Ps. 36:7; 68:16; Isa. 14:12ff.; Ezek. 28:16) have no autonomous right with reference to the Lord.

Mountains, however, are also places specially reserved for the revelation of God and His worship (was He not regarded as a God of the mountains?—1 Kings 20:23,28f.): it is on a mountain that Abraham must sacrifice his son (Gen. 22:2), it is from a mountain that the people of God can most suitably be blessed (Exod. 17:9ff.; cf. Num. 22:4–24:14), it is on the mountains that sacrifices were offered in primitive times (cf. 1 Sam. 9:12ff.; 1 Kings 3:4; 1 Chr. 16:39), it is on a hill that the ark of God is placed (1 Sam. 7:1; 2 Sam. 6:3; cf. 1 Chr. 21:29), and it is on the heights again that the schools of the prophets are situated (1 Sam. 10:5; cf. 2 Kings 1:9; 4:25). Above all, it was on a mountain, Sinai, that God gave the law to His people (Exod. 19ff.), and Sinai (or Horeb), together with mount Zion where the Temple is situated, will continue to be pre-eminently the "mountain of God" (cf. Exod. 3:1; 1 Kings 19:8, etc.), the "holy mountain" (cf. Ps. 2:6; Isa. 8:18; cf. Jn. 4:20).

It is without doubt within this perspective of the place of worship and revelation that the frequent mention of mountains in the life of Jesus must be understood: while Jesus likes to withdraw Himself to a mountain for prayer (cf. Mk. 6:46 and parallels; Lk. 6:12;

9:28 and parallels, etc.), it is also on a mountain that He gathers together and chooses the Twelve, who are the representatives of the new people of God (Mk. 3:13 and parallels); it is on a mountain that He appears in the glory of His transfiguration (Matt. 17:1ff. and parallels: the "holy mountain" according to 2 Pet. 1:18); it was a mountain that he appointed as a meeting-place for the Eleven after His resurrection (Matt. 28:16ff.). Above all, it is on a mountain, *the* mountain, that Jesus delivers His "sermon on the mount", according to Matthew (5:1–8:1), which beyond doubt must be interpreted—cf. the allusions to the Decalogue, 5:17ff.—as the counterpart, for the new *covenant, of what Sinai was for the old covenant: the charter of the people who are not only saved by Moses from the servitude of Egypt, but by Christ from the servitude of sin. (In Lk. 6:17–49 Jesus delivers His sermon after having *descended* from the mountain; the perspective is different, and here Christ's discourse contains maledictions as well as beatitudes. It is a word which separates and judges, and it should probably be understood as an anticipation, in the life of Jesus, of the last judgment which will take place when Christ will descend no more from a mountain only, but from heaven.)

7. In listing these few examples—which could be multiplied—of geographical concepts with a theological connotation, mention may also be made of the enigmatic *Har* (=mountain) *Magedon* of Rev. 16:16, when the "kings of the whole world" are gathered together, under the incitement of demoniacal spirits, for the "battle on the great day of God the Almighty" (vv. 13f.). The exegetes of the Revelation find it difficult to know what to make of this high place where the enemy forces assemble together against God. It seems impossible to identify it with the town of Megiddo or to see it as an alteration of the hypothetical Har-Moed (=mountain of assembly). One must be content to admit that the author, by retaining this Hebraic term in his book written in Greek and omitting to interpret

it, remains faithful to the mysterious style of all apocalypses.

J.-J. VON ALLMEN

NAMES (PERSONAL)

O.T.

1. ABRAHAM. As he is presented in the accounts of the book of Genesis (and our interest in him here is confined to these limits) Abraham is the prototype of the people of Israel. The following elements, in fact, characterize his person and his destiny:

(a) He is *chosen by God* without there being anything to justify the choice of his person among so many other descendants of the line of Seth and of Noah, which was the line of the divine promise (Gen. 12:1).

(b) God made a *covenant with him and with his posterity, and, by sealing this covenant with a sacrifice (Gen. 15:7–12; 17–18), He indicates that Abraham and his descendants will stand before Him in a particular relationship. Henceforth God will be the "God of Abraham", bound to Abraham by His promise.

(c) The sovereign initiative of God places Abraham on trial, not only at the time of his calling, but throughout the whole of his life (Gen. 15:1–6; 22:16–18, etc.). By His covenant God *calls Abraham to faith* and to the consequences of this faith: separation from his heathen setting and trustful obedience to the declared will of God.

(d) The election of Abraham concerns not only his own person and his posterity, but *all the nations of the world* (Gen. 12:3); hence the change from Abram, a simple proper name, to Abraham which means "father of the peoples" (Gen. 17:5). It is through Abraham that all the nations will participate in salvation. Thus the covenant makes Abraham an intercessor (cf. Gen. 18:22–32).

In conformity with its general tendency, which is to put the Israelites on guard against the illusion of a salvation automatically resulting from the fact of the covenant, classical prophecy speaks little of Abraham. When it does speak of him (for example

Isa. 29:22–24; Mic. 7:20) it is to call to mind the freeness of the pardon which God grants to the repentant Israelite. The Exile focuses the attention once more on the divine promise (Isa. 41:8; 51:2; Ps. 105:9; Neh. 9:7). For the sake of His covenant God will remain faithful to His people.

In later Judaism the perspectives are distorted. Abraham is praised for his merits, as though the covenant had not come into being by the sovereign initiative of God, and to belong to the race of Abraham is regarded as a guarantee of salvation.

The N.T. shows how the promises made to Israel in Abraham are fulfilled in Jesus Christ:

(a) The election of Abraham is confirmed (Matt. 8:11; Mk. 12:26; Lk. 16:22; 19:9), but it is now evident that in reality it testifies to Jesus Christ and His work (Jn. 8:51–59).

(b) The covenant which by God's will rests on the "rock" Abraham (as he is sometimes called in Judaism, following Isa. 51:1–2) will henceforth rest by the will of Christ on *Peter (Matt. 16:18).

(c) In opposition to every notion of an automatic salvation, the N.T. reminds us that the faith of Abraham, which involved the works of faith, continues at all times to be the sole means of participating in the covenant of salvation (Rom. 4:1–25; Gal. 3:6–29; Jas. 2:21–23; Jn. 8:39–40; Matt. 3:9).

(d) The world-wide perspective is fully in evidence: every believer can become, by faith, a "child of Abraham" (Gal. 3:7,29).

2. JACOB. Taken as a whole, the accounts in the book of Genesis concerning Jacob show that he, like Abraham, is a prototype of the elect people. None the less, from the point of view of the history of salvation, a distinction is made between these two patriarchs. In Abraham the election was placed in a manner that was as yet very general. In Jacob its particularities are given definition.

(a) Jacob has *twelve sons* (Gen. 35:23–26) who, according to the biblical accounts, are the ancestors of the twelve tribes which God liberated from the Egyptian captivity and with whom He will make a covenant at Sinai (cf. Gen. 49:28–29; Exod. 24:4, etc.; see *Twelve under *numbers).

(*b*) In Jacob God displays *the unpredictable freedom of His *election*. He chooses the younger and rejects the elder (Gen. 25:23; cf. Mal. 1:1–3). His grace is not automatically conformed to nature (cf. Cain and Abel, Ishmael and Isaac).

(*c*) The divine election, moreover, is manifested *in the midst of the worst human unreliability*. Jacob is the "supplanter", for such is the force of his name (Gen. 25:26; 27:36) and his behaviour, from his birth onwards, illustrates only too clearly the aptness of this name (cf. Gen. 25:26–34; 27:1–45). Not only does human sin not impede God in the achievement of His purposes, but in a mysterious manner God makes use of sin in the fulfilment of His holy will.

(*d*) A rebel against God and at the same time an instrument of God, Jacob the supplanter is inextricably bound to God. In constant conflict with God, he will bear the new name of *Israel* (*Israel=one who strives with God, Gen. 32:28).

It is therefore not surprising that Jacob represents the elect people very distinctively (in their entirety, Deut. 32:9; Isa. 9:7, etc., or in one of their sections, Jacob=Ephraim, Hos. 10:11,=Judah, Isa. 65:9), with their sin (Hos. 12:3–5; Mic. 3:8; probably also Jer. 9:3–4) and with the promises attached in spite of everything to their election (Isa. 10:21; Mic. 5:6–8).

Apart from certain usages taken over from the O.T. (the God of Abraham, of Isaac, and of Jacob, the House of Jacob, etc.), the N.T. scarcely mentions Jacob except to illustrate the freedom of divine election (Rom. 9:6–13).

3. MOSES. Moses occupies a unique place among the personages of the O.T. He is not only a political leader, a priest, a worker of miracles, or a prophet, but he is all these things at once and much more also: the single mediator between God and His people, superior to all the prophets (Exod. 4:16; 7:1; 33:11; Num. 12:1–8;

Deut. 5:24–28). A mission of this sort reveals the essential elements of the covenant of God with Israel.

(*a*) From the time of the departure from Egypt the relations between God and His people are founded on a single individual, whose presence manifests at the same time both *the insuperable distance* between man and God and the will of God *to communicate Himself to man* (Exod. 20:18–21; 33:5–11; 34:9,29–35; Num. 11:2; Deut. 5:2–5, etc.). The covenant of God is thus inscribed in a unique *history*, on which all subsequent history will depend.

(*b*) This will, communicated by God to Moses, is at all times the *sole original source* whence the Israelites will draw the knowledge of God and of His promises and demands (cf. 1 Kings 2:3; 8:9, etc.).

(*c*) The unique mediation of Moses makes of Israel a *people*, a holy nation, a community bound to God by the covenant and whose members are also bound to each other by the same covenant (cf. Exod. 6:7; Deut. 4:20, etc.).

(*d*) Moses, however, is *only an instrument*. The work which God entrusted to him will be accomplished without him: he will die without entering into the Promised Land (Deut. 34:5–8).

After the perversions of later Judaism, especially that expressed in Greek which turns Moses into a perfect man, a man of genius, and not a simple mediator, the N.T. confirms the original vocation of Moses and shows that it is fulfilled in Jesus Christ.

(*a*) The law which God gave to Moses *remains valid* (Matt. 23:1–2; Acts 7:38, etc.), but Jesus shows its *new significance* (Mk. 10:1–12; Matt. 5:11–48; see *Law).

(*b*) The N.T. emphasizes *the prophetic character* of Moses. He announced the coming of Christ (Lk. 24:27,44; Jn. 1:45; 5:46; Acts 3:22, etc.), the resurrection of the dead (Lk. 20:37), the evangelization of the Gentiles (Rom. 10:19), and the sovereignty of God's grace (Rom. 9:15).

(*c*) In his person Moses is himself *a prototype of Christ*, particularly of the suffering Christ (Acts 3:22–33; cf. Deut

18:15,18; Acts 7:37; 1 Cor. 10:1–2; Heb. 11:24–26; Matt. 2:1–15, etc.).

(d) Christ the new mediator, however, is *superior to the old*, the whole of whose reality resides in the future now at last accomplished (Jn. 6:32; Heb. 3:1–6).

To sum up: the typology between Moses and Christ is one of the points at which the difference and the unity of the two covenants is displayed in the majority of the New Testament writings (cf. Jn. 1:17).

4. DAVID. David, king of Judah, at Hebron, and then of all Israel, at Jerusalem (beginning of the 10th century B.C.), is one of the most celebrated and best known figures in the history of Israel. Many of the psalms are attributed to him.

In David the covenant of God with Israel takes its precise form which will be maintained even in the new covenant. According to the biblical texts, and particularly the two books of Samuel, this covenant is characterized by the following elements:

(a) To the charismatic covenant (that is, the covenant constantly renewed by sudden interventions of the Spirit of God), of which Saul, in succession to the Judges, had been the representative, there is henceforth added *a covenant of a dynastic and institutional order*. The Spirit of God is given once for all to David (1 Sam. 16:13). God will remain unconditionally faithful to David and his descendants (cf. the divine charter prophetically given to David and his dynasty, 2 Sam. 7:4–16 and 23:5).

(b) This in no way indicates that the charismatic aspect of the federal covenant of the twelve tribes had been suppressed. Much rather, David united in his own person as dynastic monarch and one charismatically elect *the two currents of the divine work in Israel:* the inheritance promised to the posterity of Abraham (Gen. 38:29; Ruth 4:18–22) on the one hand, and the guidance of the people of Israel by God Himself, under the form of prophetic interventions, on the other (2 Sam. 12:1–23).

(c) The two elements indispensable to the fullness of Israel that were united in David and in Solomon are separated from each other from the time of the *disruption* between Judah and Benjamin on the one hand and the ten tribes of the north on the other (1 Kings 12:1–19). The salvation of the ten tribes of the north will, however, continue to be joined to the promises made to David and his house (Hos. 3:5; Isa. 9:6; Jer. 30:9). And the house of Judah will need to be admonished by the prophetic warning which describes the ruin of the tribes of the north (Isa. 28:7–22; Jer. 3:6–13).

(d) Despite the punishments imposed on David and his descendants because of their unfaithfulness, *the promise will remain indelibly associated with the house of David* (Isa. 11:1; 55:3; Jer. 33:14–26; Ps. 89; 132, etc.), the successive sovereigns of which will continue on the throne until the Exile, in contrast to the sovereigns of the north who never succeeded in constituting a dynasty; and for this reason, that it was to the Davidic dynasty alone that the promise of perpetuity had been made.

In the N.T. these perspectives are preserved. *Jesus is the "son of David" (Matt. 1:1; Rom. 1:3, etc.), but, typically, He is conceived by the Holy Ghost outside of the Davidic line (Matt. 1:18,20,25; Lk. 1:34–35), a sign that the latter cannot bear the fruit of the promise—which, however, it retains—apart from the miraculous intervention of God in Mary. None the less, it is indeed the "kingdom of David" which Jesus comes to inaugurate (Mk. 11:10; Acts 13:34; Rev. 5:5; 22:16, etc.).

5. SOLOMON. Solomon, David's son and successor (middle of the 10th century B.C.), despite the profound transformations which he brought about in the kingship in Israel, left behind him such a reputation for wisdom that many writings were attributed to him as a result (Proverbs, Ecclesiastes, the Song of Songs, certain canonical Psalms, and, outside the canon, the Odes and Psalms said to have been written by Solomon). The following elements characterize his person and his work:

(a) The son of David and Bathsheba (2 Sam. 12:24–25), he demonstrates in his person that *the faithfulness of God to the*

Davidic covenant is fulfilled despite human sin, which, indeed, it causes to work in with the divine plan.

(*b*) God's faithfulness, however, is not automatic. For having *transformed the Davidic kingship into an absolute monarchy*, in imitation of the sovereigns of the surrounding peoples, Solomon will incur God's punishment, which, moreover, will be completed after his death (1 Kings 11:1–40). God, it is true, will remain faithful to the house of David, but not without testing it by the disruption of Jeroboam.

(*c*) The *building of the Temple*, in accordance with God's will (2 Sam. 7:11; 1 Kings 6:11–13), yet leads Solomon into temptation. To it he joined his palace (1 Kings 7:1–12) and thus encouraged a sort of caesaro-papism against which the majority of the Israelites were soon to rebel.

(*d*) In making Israel *a great power*, in forming an alliance with Egypt and other neighbouring nations (1 Kings 3:1; 9:11–16; 11:1–8, etc.), in adopting the culture of the surrounding peoples (1 Kings 5:9ff.; 10:1ff., etc.), in replacing the voluntary co-operation of the confederate Israelites by a royal levy (1 Kings 9:15–21), and in making the army a personal guard (1 Kings 9:22), Solomon—without, however, completely succeeding in any of these matters— opposed himself to the specific tradition of Israel, when at the same time they were beginning to commit to writing the anonymous authors of Israelite history, as is witnessed by the most ancient portions of the Pentateuch.

It is only occasionally that the N.T. refers to Solomon, and generally in an unfavourable light. Matt. 1:6,7 typically declares that he is the son of David and of the wife of Uriah. The glory of Solomon is inferior to that of the lilies of the field (Matt. 6:29; Lk. 12:27). Christ is superior to Solomon (Matt. 12:42; Lk. 11:31), and if a Gentile, the queen of Sheba, came to listen to Solomon, with how much more reason should the present generation listen to Christ! Stephen criticizes the temple of Solomon (Acts 7:46–48). Certain passages that refer to "Solomon's Porch" have no theological significance (Jn. 10:23; Acts 3:11; 5:12).

6. ELIJAH. The prophet Elijah (9th century B.C., cf. 1 Kings 17:1—2 Kings 2:12) is the only one of all the figures of the O.T. to possess in combination the following two characteristics: (*a*) He did not die, but was taken up into heaven (2 Kings 2:1–12. The same was the case with Enoch, Gen. 5:24). (*b*) His return to earth was foretold (Mal. 4:5).

Later Judaism developed at length these two themes which it found in the canonical Scriptures. In post-canonical (and even post-Christian) Jewish literature Elijah appears as a protecting angel of the elect people, the precursor whose coming announces the day when God will accomplish His judgment, and even, more precisely, the precursor of the Messiah Himself. It is therefore not surprising that, after Moses (mentioned 80 times), Abraham (73 times), and David (59 times), Elijah should be the character of the O.T. most often mentioned in the N.T. (29 times and perhaps 30, if, following certain manuscripts, Lk. 9:54 should be added).

Apart from a number of passages that refer to various episodes in the life of the prophet (Lk. 4:25–26; Jas. 5:17; Rom. 11:2–5) and a passage that attests the Jewish faith in the intercession of Elijah (Mk. 15:35–36 and Matt. 27:47–49), there are two groups of verses which are particularly significant from the theological point of view:

(*a*) Those which attest the expectation of the return of Elijah as precursor of the Messiah (Matt. 16:14 and parallels; Mk. 6:15; Lk. 9:8; Matt. 17:10–11 and parallels; Jn. 1:21,25). Whatever John the Baptist's attitude may have been in this connection (cf. Jn. 1:21,25), one thing is certain: Jesus Himself considered that the prophecy of the return of Elijah was fulfilled in John the Baptist (Matt. 11:14; 17:12–13; Mk. 9:13; Lk. 7:27; cf. Mk. 1:2; Lk. 1:16–17,76). John the Baptist is thus *the last of the prophets*, immediately preceding the coming of the Messiah.

(b) Those in which Elijah appears as the representative *par excellence* of the prophets, side by side with Moses representing the law (Matt. 17:3–4 and parallels). Moses and Elijah, the law and the prophets, *bear witness to Christ* at the time of the Transfiguration, as they will do again at the end of the age (Rev. 11:3–6). Thus the unity of the two covenants is attested and also the fulfilment of the old by the new.

J.-L. LEUBA

N.T.

1. JOHN THE BAPTIST. The birth, life, and death of John the Baptist are too well known to need repetition here (cf. Lk. 1:5–25,57–80; Matt. 3:1–17 and parallels; 14:1–12 and parallels). We shall draw attention only to two theological aspects of his person and work. For the rest see *Baptism.

(a) *The ministry of John the Baptist is indissolubly bound to that of Jesus,* and it is impossible to understand John the Baptist except as the one who prepares the way for the coming of Christ (cf. Matt. 3:11ff. and parallels; Jn. 1:26–39; cf. also the close bond between the annunciation and birth of John the Baptist and of Jesus, in Lk. 1–2). It is for this reason that John does not wish rivalry to spring up between his disciples—who were subjected to a certain spiritual discipline, Matt. 9:14f. and Lk. 11:1—and the disciples of Jesus (cf. Jn. 3:22–36). It is for this reason also that, after Pentecost, the disciples of John were brought to the Church (Acts 18:25ff.; 19:1–7). After his imprisonment a certain doubt seems to have assailed John the Baptist concerning the Messiahship of Jesus, a doubt which was all the more understandable because *Jesus was a Messiah so much less glorious than the one the Jews had pictured (*Kingdom of God): now if Jesus were not the Messiah, the whole of John's ministry would have been in vain, and vain also would have been his imprisonment and its ultimate outcome. The "calculated" reply which Jesus sent back to him ought to have made it possible for John the Baptist to die

in peace: Jesus is indeed "he who is to come" (Lk. 7:18–23 and parallels).

(b) *John the Baptist is the last of the prophets and the first to be foretold;* he forms the link between the old and the new *covenant; he comes on the scene at the point where the present age and the age to come begin to coincide (*Time). Like all God's messengers (cf. Jn. 1:6; Matt. 21:25 and parallels) under the old covenant, he announces the coming of the Messiah: he is on this side of the Messianic era, unworthy in his own eyes—although, according to Jesus, the greatest among men: Lk. 7:28 and parallels—to perform for the Messiah the most humble services (Matt. 3:11,13ff. and parallels). And yet he appears on the threshold of the Messianic era, being the Elijah *redivivus* foretold by the prophet (Mal. 4:5ff.; cf. Lk. 1:76ff.; Matt. 17:10–13). In this sense John the Baptist is typical of the manner in which the N.T. embraces the O.T.: past and yet present, and oriented in such a way towards the Messiah that it is by Jesus and in Him alone that the *Scriptures become comprehensible and take on significance.

2. MARY, *the mother of our Lord.* Within the confines of the N.T. the mother of Jesus shows a reserve and humility which cause one to think that she also would have been able to say concerning her son: "He must increase, but I must decrease" (Jn. 3:30). Nothing is known of her birth or of her death, and almost nothing of her life. Even though, with the majority of Protestant scholars, we are unable to identify her under the description of the woman "clothed with the sun, with the moon under her feet, and on her head a crown of twelve stars", of whom the 12th chapter of Revelation speaks, that does not alter the fact that, from the theological point of view, Mary plays a unique rôle in the history of salvation.

(a) This rôle is not stressed in the synoptic material of the first three Gospels. Here Mary is introduced either to assign a place to Jesus (Mk. 6:3 = Matt. 13:55) or to indicate—for she does not seem to admit the Messiahship of her Son—that "a prophet is not without honour except in his own country *and in his own house*" (Matt. 13:57; cf. Mk. 3:21): Jesus, in fact, seems to have broken with His family who were not willing "to do the will of God", and to have found a mother and brothers and sisters elsewhere than amongst His own people (Mk. 3:31ff.; Matt. 12:46ff.; Lk. 8:19ff.). Thus the Gospel relates a tradition according to which Jesus Himself was familiar with the harsh wrenches which attachment to the Kingdom of God can bring about (cf. Matt. 19:29 and parallels; Lk. 14:26). The severe word which Jesus spoke to Mary at the time of the wedding at Cana (Jn. 2:4) should not be interpreted in the same light, for the fourth Gospel presupposes that the mother (and the brothers?) of Jesus were always aware of His Messiahship (cf. Jn. 2:12; 19:26f.; cf. however 7:4f.), thus allocating to the life of the Lord what is attested by Luke to belong to the period that follows the resurrection (Acts 1:14).

(*b*) The mother of Jesus, however, plays an important rôle in what are called the "Gospels of the infancy" (Matt. 1–2; Lk. 1–2), which state that the Virgin Mary "was found with child of the Holy Spirit" (Matt. 1:18; Lk. 1:26–38) in accordance with the prophecy of Isa. 7:14. Even if the Hebrew word used by Isaiah makes it possible to hesitate between "virgin" and "young woman" as its translation, it is evident that Matthew did not hesitate to translate it by "virgin". It is no less evident that the fourth Gospel presupposes the virgin birth of Jesus—although it does not relate it explicitly—since allusion is made to it in speaking of those who "are not born of a mixing of bloods (plural!), nor of the will of the flesh, nor of the will of man (the *male*), but of God" (1:13). The theological significance of the virgin birth is as follows:

To begin with, it declares that in *Jesus Christ the first creation is renewed; it is He who becomes what St. Paul calls (making allusion to the virgin birth?) the last Adam, the new man, He in whom God is going to recapitulate all His work: He is born of a

woman like all other men (Gen. 4:4) and thus He is truly man, but at the same time He interrupts the human line in order to bring into being, by the power of God, a new human line (cf. Jn. 1:13; Eph. 2:15). He is thus born at once on a level to which other men will be raised only by *baptism (which is, for them, parallel to the virgin birth of Jesus), the level of regeneration. Therefore, despite what has been said, the virgin birth of Jesus does not imply any diminution in His true humanity; on the contrary, it emphasizes it. In the next place, the miraculous conception of Jesus—He whose name, given in advance, means "God saves"—indicates that men were unable themselves to fulfil the promises of God or themselves to produce their Saviour, and thus to find in themselves the source and the power of their own salvation: all they can do is to receive and embrace it. With reference to salvation, therefore, they are in exactly the same position as Joseph, Mary's betrothed, before the Saviour Jesus (cf. Matt. 1:19ff.; Lk. 1:34): at first excluded as incapable of being its authors, and then called to acknowledge and receive it and to make it truly their own salvation.

(*c*) What we have just seen makes it possible for us to evaluate, as worthy of acceptance or rejection, a number of opinions and traditions which are connected with the person of the Virgin Mary.

Firstly, the question as to whether Mary had children other than Jesus is of no interest to the N.T. Although Scripture provides examples of the attraction of a special veneration for things closely associated with the bearers of salvation (Acts 19:12; cf. Matt. 9:21; Mk. 5:30; Acts 5:15), the Virgin Mary remains outside this sphere in which pious legends originate: even if she is never called the mother of any but Jesus, there is no hesitancy in speaking of the Lord's brothers and sisters (Matt. 12:46ff., 13:55 and parallels), without specifying whether these are His true brothers and sisters or children of Joseph by a former marriage (Joseph seems to have died before the commencement of our

Lord's ministry) or again cousins (which is exegetically defensible because of the elasticity of the terms of relationship in the Jewish world). Thus the N.T. provides no explicit support for the later tradition, which was also upheld by the Reformers, according to which Jesus was Mary's only child.

Secondly, the N.T. is also entirely ignorant of an assumption of the Virgin into heaven: St. John, to whom Jesus when on the cross entrusted His mother (Jn. 19:26f.) and who consequently would have been best able to preserve the memory of so miraculous an occurrence, writes—certainly after the death of Mary—"no one has ascended into heaven but he who descended from heaven, even the Son of Man who is in heaven" (3:13).

Thirdly, the virginity of Mary has been given a meritorious significance: this is to prefer thought governed by Greek dualism to the Semitic setting of biblical thought. If there had been anything meritorious about her virginity, Mary—who was so surprised at being chosen to become the mother of Jesus! Lk. 1:34—would have wished to preserve it and would not have continued her betrothal to Joseph. It should be said that the virginity of Mary is emphasized especially because she is "new" and thus able to be at the service of the great renewal which is coming with Jesus. At the risk of being over-bold, we can place the virginity of Mary on a level with the new tomb in which Jesus will be laid (Matt. 27:60; Lk. 23:53; Jn. 19:41; cf. also Mk. 11:2; Lk. 19:30).

Fourthly, it has been thought that the object of the virgin birth of Jesus was to provide an explanation why, in distinction from all other men, He was without sin (Jn. 8:46; 2 Cor. 5:21; Heb. 4:15; 1 Pet. 2:22; 1 Jn. 3:5, etc.). This suggestion implies that sin is essentially transmitted by sexual intercourse, and thus that the seat of sin must be located in sexuality. The biblical doctrine of *man and of *marriage contradicts this ascetic view.

Fifthly, no doubt under the influence of the dubious profundities of certain Asiatic cults of a mother-goddess, the very precise limits taught in the N.T. between the mother and the bride of Christ have been forgotten and Mary has been envisaged as the new Eve. But if Jesus is the new Adam, it is not Mary but the *Church who is the new Eve: it is she who is born of the water (baptism) and the blood (eucharist) which flow from the side of the crucified One (Jn. 19:34), as the first Eve was formed from the side of Adam while he experienced a death-like sleep (Gen. 2:21ff.).

Sixthly, assuming a conception of original *sin that is much more moral than juridical, it has been imagined that in order to become the mother of the only Son of God the Virgin Mary was miraculously exempted, from the womb of her mother, from the sinfulness to which man is subject prior to regeneration. This is the doctrine of the immaculate conception of the Virgin which is too often confused with the biblical affirmation of the virgin birth of Jesus. Such a doctrine could not have occurred to the N.T. authors, for it contradicts the true humanity of Jesus and overthrows the good news of salvation: in fact, if Mary is found to be outside the "camp" where humanity is held captive by the Evil One, then the child which she has miraculously conceived will Himself also be born outside this camp: and then neither He nor His work will have relevance for men. Consequently it is essential that Mary—whether or not, on the "moral" level, she has committed sins—should be under the "juridical" servitude of sin, so that Jesus may not become a dream of salvation, but that He may indeed be the Saviour.

(d) Thus the N.T. speaks of Mary with an extreme reserve; it also takes great care to shield her from the legends and errors which would so easily find in her a motive for setting aside in her favour the absolutely central person of Jesus. This, however, in no way hinders us from admiring her as "the mother of the Lord" and as the one whom "all generations shall call blessed" (cf. Lk. 1:39–56). She is not comparable to any other woman, and her vocation was as unique and unrepeatable as that of her

Son. If she is "blessed among women" (Lk. 1:42), it is not because she is a mother or because she should be the ideal example of maternity, but because she becomes the mother of the eternal Son of God and is the means whereby His incarnation becomes a reality. Moreover, her obedience makes her the very picture and example of the vocation or responsibility of the Church and of each of its members. From the very first it is she who receives the Lord with submission (Lk. 1:38,48) and at the risk of endangering her reputation (cf. Matt. 1:19ff.). Then it is she who carries Jesus Christ within herself; but she does not wish to keep Him to herself, for it is she, finally, who brings Him into the world: in this sense she has a share—like the Church—in what might be called the "conspiracy" of God for saving the world, and she can be celebrated as the one who secretly introduced among men the Christ in whom the Kingdom of God is present. As far as the world is concerned, she was what the Church will continue to be until the return of Christ, namely, the "smuggler in" of heaven.

3. PETER. For a profound investigation of the historical and theological problems posed by the person and work of the apostle Peter, Oscar Cullmann's book *Peter: Disciple, Apostle, Martyr* (S.C.M. Press) should be consulted. Within the limits of a brief article we shall draw attention only to the following points:

(*a*) Simon, the fisherman of Bethsaida by the lake of Gennesareth (Jn. 1:44) is certainly the best known and the most prominent of the *Twelve. He is presented as the first disciple whom Jesus called to Himself (Matt. 4:18 and parallels; cf. however Jn. 1:40ff.); it is also known that he was married (1 Cor. 9:5; cf. Matt. 8:14 and parallels). There is no account of his death in the N.T., except under the form of a veiled prophecy which suggests a violent death (Jn. 21:18f.). One can, however, accept the tradition according to which he died as a martyr at Rome in the sixties of the 1st century. There are in the N.T. two circular letters which are attri-

buted to him (the authenticity of the second is dubious). Simon is a living illustration that those whom Jesus takes into His service *do not suffer any violation of their humanity through this vocation:* agitated (Lk. 5:7f.), daring (Matt. 14:28ff. and parallels), quick to understand the injunctions of the Spirit, but also quick to oppose them (Matt. 16:16f.,22f.), sure of himself (Matt. 26:33), courageous (Jn. 18:10), faint-hearted (Matt. 26:69ff. and parallels), anxious (Lk. 24:12), humble (Jn. 21:7), fearless (Acts 4:8ff.), able to maintain his position when he is in the right (Acts 11:1–18), and yet easily influenced (Gal. 2:11), he shows that it is not necessary to be a hero before one can come to the faith and service of Christ. To this very human person Jesus gave the unexpected name of "rock" (Peter=Cephas in Aramaic: Jn. 1:42; Mk. 3:16; Lk. 6:14; cf. Matt. 16:18), and it is under this new *name, which became for him both a promise and a programme, that he has taken his place in the history of salvation.

(*b*) *This place is the first among the Twelve:* in the lists of the apostles he regularly appears at the head (Mk. 3:16 and parallels; Acts 1:13) and Matthew even emphasizes the fact that he is "the first" (10:2). Together with James and John he has a place in the inner circle of Jesus' disciples, and in this connection also he is always mentioned first: he was present with them at the raising of the daughter of Jairus (Matt. 5:37 and parallels) and at the transfiguration (Matt. 17:1 and parallels); together with them and Andrew he heard Jesus speak of the destruction of Jerusalem and of the signs of the end of the world (Mk. 13:3), and together with them he should have supported Jesus in His agony at Gethsemane (Matt. 26:37 and parallels). During the life of Jesus it is Peter who, of the Twelve, regularly addresses Jesus, generally as their spokesman (cf. Matt. 17:4; 18:21; 19:27; 26:33–35; Mk. 8:29; Lk. 12:41, etc.), and to such an extent does he seem to be the first among them that it is possible to speak of the "disciples *and* Peter" (Mk. 16:7; cf. 1:36). Conversely, it is frequently Peter personally that Jesus addresses when He is speaking to all the Twelve (cf. Matt. 8:33; 14:37; Lk. 22:31).

St. Peter continues to maintain this leading position in the apostolic college after Pentecost, and still more strongly so since he was fulfilling a function which Jesus Himself had assigned him (cf. Lk. 22:31ff.; Jn. 21:15ff.): he is the spokesman of the new-born Church (Acts 1:15; 2:14; 3:1ff.; 4:8ff.; 15:6ff.), it is he who is singled out in the persecutions (Acts 12:3ff.), it is he who undertakes the visitation of the Churches which are dependent on Jerusalem (Acts 9:32ff.; cf. 8:14ff.; Gal. 2:7), it is his acquaintance which St. Paul wishes to make in order to establish contact with the mother-church of Jerusalem (Gal. 1:18), it is he who enforces discipline (Acts 5:3ff.). And even if, for the purpose of devoting himself to the missionary work among the Jews (Gal. 2:7), he seems to have recognized James, the Lord's brother, as the head of the Church at Jerusalem and consequently as the leader of the Church to which he, Peter, was responsible for the new aspect of his ministry (cf. the order of the names in Gal. 2:9; cf. also Gal. 2:12), he none the less continues to be a person of such importance that certain Christians at Corinth wished to associate themselves with him, without doubt because they entertained misgivings concerning the validity of St. Paul's apostleship: their connection with Peter was, according to them, a guarantee of their connection with the only true Christian Church; cf. 1 Cor. 1:12; 3:22. (Concerning the question of the possible subordination of Peter to James, it is symptomatic that on the only occasion when James speaks of him he does not call him Peter or Cephas, but Simon, Acts 15:14.)

The fourth Gospel, while with the rest of the N.T. it recognizes the pre-eminence of Peter (1:42; 21:15-19; cf. also 6:66ff.; 13:36), has, however, a tendency to insinuate the "beloved disciple" between Jesus and the chief of the Twelve: he must without doubt have followed Jesus before Peter (cf. 1:38-42, contrary to Matt. 4:18 and parallels); it is he whom Peter must ask concerning the meaning of Christ's announcement of the betrayal (13:24), it is by him that he is introduced into the court of the high priest (18:15ff.), it is he who reaches the tomb first (20:2-9), it is he who is the first to recognize the Risen Lord (21:7). It may be inquired whether it was not the intention of the author of the fourth Gospel to give preference to "meditative faith" over "ecclesiastical title". But even if that were the case, it would not invalidate the unanimous testimony of the N.T. concerning the primatial rôle played by St. Peter; on the contrary, if it was his intention to estimate the place of this apostle, his verdict is that it was important. Moreover, other sources of the apostolic tradition, those which St. Luke utilizes, associate and couple St. Peter and St. John (cf. Lk. 22:8; Acts 3:1ff.; 4:1ff.; 8:14ff.; cf. also Gal. 2:9). It is no longer possible to discover a tendency to disparage St. Peter in the somewhat ridiculous rôle which Jn. 13:6f. makes him play: none of the other Gospels fails to draw attention to discreditable or cowardly aspects of St. Peter's character, and yet they do not dispute the unique rôle which is his.

This prominent rôle is also recognized by St. Paul. It is true that he does not hesitate to resist him, but he does so (Gal. 2:11ff.) not because St. Peter laid claim to too high a position, but because by giving an example of sectarianism he was endangering his rôle as leader. The disagreement at Antioch was governed neither by jealousy nor by a "democratic" structure as opposed to a "monarchic" structure of the Church, but—on the part of St. Paul who brought it to a head—by the desire to maintain the unity of the Church in the truth, a desire which should have been close to the heart of St. Peter in particular (cf. Lk. 22:32). Besides, the opposition which it has at times been sought to establish between St. Paul and St. Peter is artificial: they are different from each other, it is true, and are entrusted also with different missions (Gal. 2:8), but St. Paul knows himself to be one with St. Peter before Jesus Christ (cf. 1 Cor. 1:12; 3:22; 15:3ff.) and it seems very likely that he had no stronger advocate at Jerusalem than St. Peter himself (Acts 15:7ff.). It is possible that the prominence given in the book of the Acts to the conversion of Cornelius (10:1–11,18) is intended to prevent the ministry of St. Paul to the Gentiles being disqualified in favour of that of St. Peter to the Jews: it is safeguarded by the example of St. Peter who no longer demanded *circumcision as the condition of admission to *baptism.

(c) This unique and leading position in the apostolic college was acquired by St. Peter neither by ambition nor by election: *it was accorded to him by Jesus*. St. Peter is the rock upon which Jesus will build His *Church, and those who turn to this rock for refuge have no need to fear the claims of the grave. It is to him also that Jesus entrusts the keys of the Kingdom of God and consequently the right to admit to or to exclude from the Church, which is the courtyard of this Kingdom (Matt. 16:16ff.). To-day Protestant scholars are coming more and more to agreement in acknowledging that this rock on which Jesus wishes to build His Church is not the faith of St. Peter nor the confession of the Messiahship of Jesus (though it is these things also), but the very person of St. Peter. It is also St. Peter for whom Jesus prays that, when he has been converted, he may be able to strengthen his brethren (Lk. 22:32). It is to him, finally, that the Risen Lord, after having cleansed him of his triple denial, entrusts His flock, that is to say, the Messianic people (Jn. 21:15–17). Therefore the position which he held in the new-born Church had not been usurped by him.

During the Church's history few biblical texts have been examined more closely than those we have just cited, and, since the Church is divided, their examination is almost inevitably conditioned by the denominational allegiance of the commentator. The debate is no longer so much concerned with their meaning within the structure of the N.T. (we have seen that the latter, in reporting the rôle of Peter in the new-born Church, already indicates in what sense these texts should be evaluated) as with their significance for the subsequent history of the Church—in other words, with the question as to whether St. Peter has had successors, at any rate as far as his ministry in the foundation of the Church is concerned. Perhaps it could be said that to assert, with Rome, that this ministry of the rock of foundation is perpetuated through the centuries is to assert that the Church is founded anew on each new pope (the Church then is always beginning again, which is more of a "Protestant" concept!), whereas to assert, with the Gospel, that this rock has been set by Jesus once for all is to assert that the Church never begins again, but endures (which is more of a "Catholic" concept!). In so far as he is the Church's foundation St. Peter cannot have successors: like the other *apostles, he exercised a ministry as unique as the earthly ministry of Jesus. The apostles, in fact, are a part of the work of salvation performed "once for all", and to wish to multiply their number as time passes is to run the risk of denying at the same time the uniqueness of the revelation and the redemption which came with Jesus.

4. PAUL. The person of the apostle Paul appears as an element of disharmony in the picture of the new-born Church: before preaching Jesus he persecuted Him (Acts 7:58; 8:1; 9:5–21; 22:4; 26:11; 1 Cor. 15:9; Gal. 1:23; Phil. 3:6; 1 Tim. 1:13), and he is an *apostle (Rom. 1:1; 1 Cor. 1:1; Gal. 1:1ff., etc.) without, however, being one of the *Twelve. This altogether unique situation makes of him *the one who prevents the Church from being turned in upon itself*. It should not occasion surprise, therefore, that in this respect certain Churches had been threatened with schisms (when he more than anyone else laboured for the unity of the Church) (cf. 1 Cor. 1:10–16; 3:1–12), or that those who had most difficulty in understanding the scope of the renewal effected by Jesus—namely, the Judaizers—should have distrusted him (cf. Acts 15:1–29; 21:15–26; Gal. 2:1–21, etc.). By preventing the Church, through his presence alone, from becoming self-satisfied he constantly confronts it with the question of its faithful-

ness, and his witness will become the most important standard of all the tests of reform: it can be said that in a certain sense he disturbs the Church. In one respect, it will try to absorb him, to break the force of his message; but in another respect it will misuse him in order to make him the patron of numerous divisions and heresies. St. Paul, however, refuses as much to lose his originality as to depart from the tradition of the Church.

(a) *The Church cannot be set in opposition to St. Paul.* Yet it is no more permissible to integrate the two in a manner that would bring his ministry down to an ordinary level. The N.T. has no knowledge of a Church whose apostle to the Gentiles may not be at one and the same time its disturber and also its defender. St. Paul, it is true, will go very far to prove that he is in the Church: following a revelation of God, he will go up to Jerusalem in order to gain recognition of the validity of his apostleship to the Gentiles, knowing that without this recognition his ministry would be vain, that is to say that the Churches founded by him would not be apostolic and thus not Christian (Gal. 2:1ff.); he will not hesitate to make the greatest concessions to the Judaizers (cf. Acts 16:3; 21:18ff., etc.); he will never fail to recognize the precedence of those who have been apostles before him (cf. 1 Cor. 15:8f.; Gal. 2:9), and the manner in which he cites the apostle Peter in 1 Cor. 9:5 (it should be translated: "and even Cephas") shows that he does not dispute with him the rôle which he plays in the newborn Church. But the trouble which he takes to gain recognition of himself before the Church in Jerusalem as "the least of the apostles" (1 Cor. 15:9) does not prevent emphasis being placed also and all the more vigorously on the unique and specific character of his apostleship: it is not by the will or the intervention of the members of the Church that he is an apostle, it is directly "through Jesus Christ and God the Father, who raised him from the dead" (Gal. 1:1; cf. 1:8–24; 1 Cor. 9:1–27; Rom. 1:1, etc.). It is, moreover, for this reason that, on the occasion when he finds St.

Peter making common cause with the sectarians, he will not be afraid to oppose him in order to call him back into the Church and to the place which he ought to occupy in it (Gal. 2:11ff.).

By defending his apostleship against those who disputed it (cf. 1 Cor. 9:2) he defends, on the one hand, the apostolicity and therefore the authenticity of the Churches he has founded. On the other hand, and all the more so, he defends the special rôle which has been assigned to him in the history of salvation. This rôle consists in assuring the Gentiles also, by their incorporation into the Church, of their right to "the commonwealth of Israel", of their participation in "the covenants of promise", and of the possibility of their being "fellow citizens with the saints and members of the household of God" (Eph. 2:12,19f.; cf. Acts 9:15; 15:1–29; 22:21; 26:17f.; Rom. 1:5; Gal. 2:7, etc.). This is what he calls the *mystery of his apostleship (Eph. 3:3ff.; 6:19; Col. 1:25ff.; 4:3, etc.).

By his mission to the Gentiles St. Paul (and without doubt those who are to succeed him in this task) protects the Church against a too rapid appearance of the Antichrist, he delays the development of the events which will mark the end of the world, and he makes possible the realization of our Lord's announcement that His return would be postponed until the Gospel had been preached to all nations (Mk. 13:10). In all probability the one that restrains the mystery of lawlessness (2 Thess. 2:7) is in fact St. Paul in his ministry as apostle to the Gentiles. As for those who are afraid of seeing the *nations granted accession to the promises made to *Israel, he refers them to this other mystery (Rom. 11:25), namely, that by their conversion (of which he is the agent) the Gentiles will not deprive of salvation the people for whom it was in the first place intended, but, on the contrary, that this conversion is the condition of the conversion of the Jews (Rom. 9–11).

(b) *St. Paul cannot be set in opposition to the Church*, and those who wish, on the pretext of the vigour with which he defends the original and specific character of his ministry, to make him independent of the Church of the Twelve and in some sense to find in him the founder and head of another Church, or even merely an anti-clericalist or anti-traditionalist, simply show that they fail to understand him. Even when humanly speaking it would have been excusable for St. Paul to reply in a spirit of independence to the cavils and annoyances which certain groups in Jerusalem devised against him, he does not presume to say that the whole of his person and work should be accepted when he says that he is a man who belongs essentially to the *tradition of the Church. This tradition is the normative standard of his message, and he does not hesitate to identify it with the "Lord" (cf. 1 Cor. 7:10; 11:23; 15:3ff.): he makes Jerusalem the point of departure (Rom. 15:19) and the terminus (Rom. 15:25,31) of his mission; he does not cease to say that the Churches founded by him are part of the same Church as that of the "saints" of Judea (Rom. 10:12; 15:25ff.; 1 Cor. 16:1ff.; 2 Cor. 9:12ff., etc.), and he will prefer to jeopardize his later missionary projects (Spain!) rather than withdraw from carrying himself to *Jerusalem the collection made in his Churches, a token of their unity with the mother-church of the holy city (cf. Acts 20:22ff.; 21:4,11–14).

We have already pointed out other aspects of the care which he took to remain in unity with the Church of the Twelve, the Church which preceded him. He takes the same care to make preparations for the continued existence and faithfulness of the Church which will succeed him: he provides for this through Timothy and Titus, "genuine sons", that is to say, successors (1 Cor. 4:17; 2 Cor. 8:6; 1 Tim. 1:2; Tit. 1:4; cf. Phil. 2:19ff.; 2 Tim. 1:6), to whom he entrusts the handing on of the good deposit of the Gospel (2 Tim. 2:2; cf. 1 Tim. 6:20; 2 Tim. 1:14). St. Paul is not only aware that he has a ministry that is specific and as unique as his vocation: he sees himself also as one courier among others at the beginning of the course which must link together, on earth and in history, the moment of Christ's departure and the moment of His return.

Besides, how could he have held himself independent of the Church into which he had been incorporated by baptism (Acts 9:18, in contrast to the other apostles who without doubt had not been baptized with water), he who intervened so strongly against the Corinthian Christians who were "puffed up" (1 Cor. 4:19; 5:2, etc.) and who, no doubt fortified by calling themselves members of the "Christ party" (1 Cor. 1:12), believed that by associating themselves with the Lord (vertically) they could dispense with the link (horizontal) with the apostles? Nowhere more than in his Epistles to the Corinthians does St. Paul show that to detach oneself from the apostolic tradition is to detach oneself from the Church, and thus to endanger one's salvation.

(c) In spite of suggestions that have been made in recent times, *it is no more possible to set Jesus in opposition to St. Paul*; the opposition between Jesus and the last of His apostles is as empty and artificial as the opposition between Paul and the Twelve. This imaginary opposition has resulted from a failure to understand both Jesus and the Church: there has, in particular, been a failure to understand that, if apostolic theology, and especially Pauline theology, implies, for example, a moral severity which seems to be absent from the preaching of Jesus, it is because since Pentecost it is the *Church which is the body of Christ and thus His representative on earth: she ought therefore to be holy and perfect like her head. Though she ought to maintain the same welcoming generosity towards sinners *from without* (cf. 1 Cor. 5:9ff., and the missionary narratives of the Acts), yet she cannot tolerate that sinners *within* her ranks, that is, saints, should be slack in conducting themselves in a manner worthy of their vocation (Eph. 4:1; cf. Col. 3:1–14), in view of the fact that obedience and *holiness are part of the missionary task of the Church.

It is here above all that the difference of "climate" between the Gospels and the Epistles has its explanation. Moreover, St. Paul "completes in his flesh what remains of Christ's afflictions for the sake of his body, that is, the church" (Col. 1:24; cf. 2 Cor. 1:5). In a mysterious manner his life is, so to speak, a copy of the life of Christ: he is an imitator of Christ (1 Cor. 11:1) who wishes even by his *death to reproduce that of his Lord (Phil. 3:10f.). As Jesus was unwilling to take advantage of His divine rights, but humbled Himself in order to serve (Phil. 2:6ff.), so St. Paul renounced all those things which could have caused him to place confidence in himself in order that he might serve Christ (Phil. 3:4–11); as Jesus was, from all eternity, committed to a unique and particular course, so St. Paul is conscious that he has been set apart from his mother's womb for the unique and particular work which it was God's will to entrust to him (Gal. 1:15); like Jesus, he preaches the Gospel—but to the Gentiles—performs miracles, and gathers together the Messianic people (cf. Acts 13–20); as was the case with Jesus, the end of his journey draws him irresistibly towards Jerusalem, even though he knows that his life will be in danger there (cf. Mk. 8:31; 9:31; 10:32f. and parallels; and Acts 20:22ff.; 21:4,11–14), but, like Jesus, he is ready to die for the unity of the people of God (cf. Jn. 11:52). His death, however, did not take place at Jerusalem, but—according to ancient and unanimous tradition—at Rome. Yet none the less his death conforms to that of Jesus: Jesus, in fact, died in the capital of Israel, while St. Paul, in conformity with his specific apostleship, died in the capital of the nations. It has even been suggested—though it is only a conjecture—that the N.T. has preserved a legendary tradition according to which St. Paul, three days and a half after his death, was restored to life and ascended into heaven; in fact, that he and St. Peter are the two witnesses of whom the eleventh chapter of Revelation speaks.

J.-J. VON ALLMEN

NATIONS

O.T.

To denote the peoples or the nations the O.T. uses a number of words, according as it wishes to indicate their genealogical, linguistic, or geographical character (Gen. 10:31). The two most frequent nouns ('am, goy) originally designate a certain group of men or of animals (Joel 1:6) without any specific differentiation. Gradually, however, the custom became established of reserving the noun *people ('am) for Israel, the elect people of God, the People par excellence; and of designating other peoples by the word nations (goyim), with a depreciative nuance. It is thus that the Psalms often speak of the nations and the wicked in parallel (Ps. 9:6). The distinction between the two terms is clearly brought out in a text like 1 Chr. 17:21: "Israel, the only nation on the earth whom God went to redeem to be his people." In our English versions this distinction was preserved by the use of the term Gentiles (from the Latin gentiles, from gentes=tribes) in contrast to the Jewish people.

In the O.T. this distinction is not a matter of race, as is shown by the assertion that all the peoples so variously spread throughout the world have sprung from Noah (Gen. 10 and 11), but a matter of divine election and revelation (Deut. 7:6ff.). And even when they speak of a perverse and crooked race (Deut. 32:5) or an elect race (Isa. 41:8) the biblical authors envisage the children of Israel in their relation to God and not in the racial characteristics which distinguish them from other peoples.

The attitude of Israel towards the heathen evolved in the course of the history of the O.T. in the setting of a twofold affirmation of faith: God made a *covenant with Israel, His people—God is the only God. In a general way three phases may be distinguished:

1. Religious nationalism. Originally, it is the worship offered to the same divinity which makes an ethnic group into a people. Thus the covenant concluded at Sinai (Exod. 24) and later at Shechem (Josh. 24) between Yahweh and the twelve tribes of Israel made them the people of Yahweh and Yahweh the God of Israel. It is, besides, possible to offer worship to Yahweh

only in the land of His people (cf. Naaman taking back some of the soil of the land in order to be able to worship Yahweh in Syria: 2 Kings 5:17), and it is only in exceptional cases that the God of Israel protects His faithful servants on foreign soil (cf. Joseph in Egypt, Gen. 39; or Elijah at Zarephath, 1 Kings 17:9); for in other lands other national divinities reign (Judg. 11:24). Every *war is a holy war in which Yahweh necessarily intervenes in order to bring succour to His people and to destroy the nations and their divinities (Num. 10:36).

Thus faith in the covenant made with a jealous God leads ancient Israel into religious nationalism: the nations are alien to God and the outpouring of His wrath is invoked upon them (Amos 5:18).

2. *Prophetic universalism.* The prophets rose against this religious exclusivism. Amos was the first to proclaim that the judgment of God would overtake the unfaithful people of Israel as well as the heathen nations (1 and 2), for *election is a gift concerning which Israel has no right to boast before the nations (9:7–8), but which is, on the contrary, the basis of their responsibility (3:2). In the name of the holy God Isaiah declares that punishment is going to descend upon hardened Ephraim and Judah. For the punishment of His people God makes use of heathen nations, especially Assyria, "the rod of his anger" (10:5–6). It is God who controls the nations according to His purposes and when they boast of their providential mission God punishes them in turn (10:12–16). The destiny of the heathen nations therefore depends upon God in the same way as that of Israel, even though they are not aware of it. Thus through the crises of the world's history the judgment and the pardon of God are revealed (Jer. 18:6–10). It is in this prophetic perspective that the most ancient historic traditions (the Yahwistic and Elohistic sources of the Pentateuch) have been committed to writing, showing the constant interventions of the sovereign God in the history of Israel and the nations.

But after the punishment and dispersion of Israel the prophets announce the return to Jerusalem of a faithful remnant and the establishment of Messianic *peace (Isa. 10:29ff.; 11:1ff.). The redeemed of the elect people will come from the most distant lands, and the nations themselves, acknowledging the vanity of their *idols (Jer. 16:19–21), will gather together at Zion in order to worship the God of Jacob (Isa. 2:2–5; Zeph. 3:9–10).

At the same time as this first extension of salvation to the nations, which is the result of faith in the one sovereign God, Deuteronomy emphasizes afresh the gravity of the covenant of grace whereby God has bound Israel to Himself and has made them, in the midst of all the nations of the earth, a holy people, set apart for the service of their God (7:6). Israel must be radically separated from the foreigner (7:3) and keep from all contact with the nations (7:16). Similarly, Ezekiel raises before the people who are in exile and deprived of their worship the vision of a city of priests, of a temple from which the uncircumcised is rigorously excluded (Ezek. 44:9).

This apparently contradictory attitude with respect to the nations was adequately surmounted only by the second Isaiah (Isa. 40–55), towards the end of the Exile. With a vigour never equalled the second Isaiah proclaims the sovereignty of the only God (44:6), God the Creator (45:12) and universal providence (40:25ff.), the sole God of all the peoples (45:22–24). But at the same time he recalls the unshakeable faithfulness of God to the election of His people (41:8–10; 54:10). In fact—and here we have the central message of the O.T. concerning the nations, which the N.T. takes up—God has elected a special people and is going to deliver them so that they may be the witness of His glory in the world (42:10–12; 55:4–5), the instrument of His salvation which is to be known to the ends of the earth (52:10), the Servant who will be the light of the nations (49:6). By Israel, the people of God, all the nations will be called to salvation (51:4–5) and the whole creation will be renewed (40:4–5; cf. 65:17ff.).

3. *Jewish particularism.* On the return of the exiles to Palestine conflicts with the neighbouring populations and foreign domination bring about a revival of Jewish particularism. The restoration of the worship and the putting of the *law into force again set up once more an insurmountable barrier between Israel, the holy people (Lev. 19:2), and the heathen nations. All contact with the uncircumcised must be stopped (Neh. 10). and in particular marriages with foreigners (Ezra 10). It is true that the last prophets announce once more that the nations will gather together at Jerusalem to call upon God in His temple (Hagg. 2:6–9; Zech. 8:20–23) and will proclaim His glory (Isa. 66:18–20), but on the condition that they observe the Jewish worship and submit scrupulously to the law (Zech. 14:16ff.): the nations must be incorporated into the holy people, becoming their slaves (Isa. 61:5–6), or be wiped out at the time of the great massacre of the peoples (Joel 3:12ff.). The account of origins which the priestly code gives strongly emphasizes the right of primogeniture of Israel, son of Shem, with respect to the other peoples of the earth (Gen. 10), and the interest of the chronicler is concentrated on the worship and the one kingdom of Judah (cf. 1 Chr. 17:21). In his apocalyptic visions Daniel sees the great heathen nations under the guise of formidable animals whose power will be taken away so that they may become subject to the people of the saints of the Most High (Dan. 7). Exclusivism goes so far as the hatred of all who are not Jewish, as the spirit of the book of Esther shows (Est. 9).

It is in opposition to this summary judgment passed by Judaism on the *massa perditionis* of the nations that the book of Ruth, the Moabite believer, was written, and especially the book of Jonah, in which the divine mercy shown to the heathen multitudes confounds the fanatical pride of the Jews (Jon. 4:10–11). The Psalter, which is not unfamiliar with hatred and imprecations against the nations (Ps. 9; 59; 137), also gives expression to the hope of a great assemblage of the nations before God, their Creator (Ps. 86:9; 102:22f.), the King of all the peoples (Ps. 97), whose glory must be proclaimed by the entire creation (Ps. 96).

Thus the judgment which the O.T. pronounces on the heathen nations is always ambiguous: on the one hand the election of Israel excludes the nations from the covenant of redemption, while on the other hand the nations in no way escape the universal sovereignty of God the Creator and Saviour. In the secular history of the old covenant each of these affirmations providentially had its periods of preponderance, but without ever eclipsing the other. They are, in fact, complementary: Israel will not be saved without the nations, and the nations will not be saved apart from Israel. It is within this perspective, depicted by the second Isaiah, that the mystery of the destiny of the nations will be fully revealed in Jesus Christ.

S. AMSLER

N.T.

1. The N.T. uses four words to designate the "nations": *ethnos* (people in a general sense), *laos* (political unity), *glossa* (linguistic unity), and *phule* (tribal unity). The first of these terms is much the most frequent. When used in the singular it keeps its general neutral sense, whereas in the plural (apart from rare exceptions) it assumes a precise technical sense, taken over from the O.T. (which is often cited in this connection) and designates the "nations" which do not know God, the "Gentiles", in contrast to the elect people. These numerous citations from the O.T. show the extent to which the primitive Church discerned a fulfilment of the Messianic prophecies in the participation of the nations in salvation, and accordingly also in its missionary activity. It is, moreover, striking to see that this collective way in which the O.T. designates the "Gentiles" is also found in the N.T.: Jesus and the apostles address themselves to "peoples"— whether it is Israel or the "nations" or in other respects the Church that is in question —as much as to individuals; it is the nations in so far as they are collective personalities

that are called to bring their riches into the new Jerusalem (cf. Matt. 12:18,21; 21:43; 24:14; 28:19; Acts 13:46-47; Rom. 1:5,16; 3:29; 1 Pet. 2:9; Rev. 14:6; 21:26). Paul's missionary method is characteristic in this respect: he is "content" to found Churches in the main cities of the countries through which he is passing and then to move on further (Acts 16:6-12). From this the importance, in the perspective of the Acts, of Rome—the capital of the nations—can be gauged.

2. ". . . Separated from Christ, alienated from the commonwealth of Israel, and strangers to the covenants of the promise, having no hope and without God in the world" (Eph. 2:12), such is the situation of the heathen, the "heathen who do not know God" (1 Thess. 4:5). Not that God has no interest in them: it is He who has created the nations according to His purpose, and who determined their "allotted periods and the boundaries of their habitation" (Acts 17:26-28; Lk. 21:24; Matt. 5:45; Acts 14:16-17). According to Rom. 1-2 a certain revelation of God has even been given to them through the works of the Creator (1:19-20), the law written in their heart (2:14-15), and a conscience of good and evil (2:9-10,15). But this knowledge, so far from protecting them, will be the principal witness against them on the day of judgment (2:9-10,16): it will render them inexcusable in their threefold blindness toward God (1:19-23,25), toward themselves (1:24-28), and toward men (1:29-31). The situation of the heathen is therefore catastrophic: they are under the wrath and judgment of God, delivered up to their sin, the fruits of which they must experience.

The whole of the N.T. shares in this severe judgment upon the heathen (Matt. 5:46-47—this text, like Matt. 18:17, puts them on a level with "tax-collectors" whom the Jews regarded as hardened and lost sinners—6:7,32; Lk. 12:30; 1 Cor. 5:1; 10:20; 12:2; Gal. 2:14; Eph. 4:17; 1 Thess. 4:5; 1 Pet. 4:3). Revelation goes so far as to affirm that their corruption, of which Babylon is the type, is due to the sway which is exercised over the nations by the Beast (13:7) or Satan (20:3,8). This judgment pronounced on the nations is in no way a judgment of value pronounced on their civilization, the degree of their culture, etc.; their situation is described only as before God in the perspective of the history of salvation, and not in itself; that is why the word Greeks can become, under Paul's pen, a synonym of Gentiles (Rom. 1:16; 1 Cor. 1:22,24; Gal. 3:28). This may be severe, but it does not involve contempt (cf. the contempt of the Greeks for the "barbarians"); on the contrary, it arouses missionary zeal. Moreover, to the extent to which the Jews fail to perform the will of God and do not receive Christ the N.T. puts them on the level of the heathen; this, indeed, is the great innovation of the N.T. in relation to the O.T., and the great *stumbling-block for Israel. The very judgment which they pronounce on the heathen becomes the instrument of their own condemnation and renders them equally inexcusable (Rom. 2:1-29; Matt. 5:47; 6:7,32). Gentiles or Jews, all are guilty (this culpability culminates in the condemnation and crucifixion of the Messiah in which both take part, Matt. 20:18-19; Lk. 23:12; it is continued in their opposition to the new-born Church, Acts 4:25-27; 14:1-5, and in their contempt for the Gospel, 1 Cor. 1:23); all come short of the glory of God (Rom. 3:9-20,23; 5:18; 11:32); all are responsible before the tribunal of God and are judged according to their works (Rom. 2:16; Matt. 25:32).

In this situation from which, apart from the grace of God, there is no escape, they evince no inclination to receive the Gospel, which continues to be a stumbling-block and foolishness to them (1 Cor. 1:23); it is their condemnation alone that can be the way of salvation. (We should note that it is without doubt for this reason that John, in the prologue to his Gospel, places Gentiles and Jews on the same plane where their attitude to Christ is concerned, and includes them both in the concept of the "*world", although he does not employ that of the "nations" in a technical sense.

3. In their inexcusable situation and their condemnation the nations are not abandoned; on the contrary, they have been universally and at all times included in the plan of God: "In thee shall all the nations of the earth be blessed" was the Gospel proclaimed to Abraham (Gal. 3:8,14; Rom. 4:16–25). In Christ this promise has found its fulfilment: He is the "light of the nations" (Lk. 2:30–32; Matt. 4:15–16; 12:18,21 = three quotations from the O.T.), and "repentance and forgiveness of sins" can be "preached in his name to all nations" (Lk. 24:47). The attitude of Jesus during His ministry seems to contradict this affirmation: He enjoins His disciples not to go to the Gentiles with the Gospel and confirms this by His own example (Matt. 10:5; 15:21–26; Lk. 4:25–27 says the same thing, though it does so in an indirect manner). While He persists in this extreme detachment towards the Gentiles, it is not because of indifference. As the Messiah He knows that His person and His work concern them in the highest degree. But His vocation as a suffering, humiliated, and non-political Messiah demands secrecy if He wishes to avoid all confusion concerning His person. The time is not yet ripe for the mission to the Gentiles and He is able only to give preliminary indications of it (Matt. 8:5–12; 15:27–28; Jn. 4:7–30; Matt. 10:18; 21:33–43; 22:1–10; 24:14).

After His resurrection from the dead it is no longer necessary for Christ to conceal His Messiahship: linked for ever to the *cross, it can be revealed without equivocation. From then on the great "invitation to repentance" (Acts 17:30) and to salvation may be sounded out: "Go and make disciples of all nations" (Matt. 28:19; Lk. 24:47; Acts 1:8). All have a full right to be admitted into the Messianic community (Rom.15:27; Eph. 2:19; 1 Pet. 2:9–12). All are called upon to rejoice (Rom. 15:9–12) for Christ is henceforth their riches (Rom. 11:12). Pentecost is the sign that this universality (one would like to say here this internationality) of salvation fore-ordained by God is being fulfilled (Acts 2:1–13, 16–21) and that henceforth all can, through the apostolic preaching, participate in it. The primitive Church quickly became aware of its mission to the Gentiles. It was assisted in this on the one hand by the rejection of the Gospel by the Jews and the persecution which obliged them to leave Jerusalem (Acts 8:1–25; 13:46–48; 18:5–6) and on the other hand by visions and commands from its Lord (Acts 8:26–27; 9:15; cf. 22:21; 26:20,23; 10:9–28; 23:11). In the name of the Messiah who has been raised from the dead the "everlasting gospel" is proclaimed to the whole world (Rev. 14:6), and the entire book of the Acts bears testimony to the fearful and joyful astonishment of the Christians as they are confronted with this new fact: the Spirit, that is to say, the Risen Lord, working among the Gentiles (Acts 10:45; 11:1,17–18,23; 13:48; 14:27; 15:3,7–9,12–14; 19:26; 21:19–20).

Without doubt it was *Paul who led the Church to an appreciation of this great *mystery of the calling and the *reconciliation of the nations (Eph. 3:1–6; Col. 1:26–27; 1 Tim. 3:16). As an apostle, his election has no other reason and no other object than to make this mystery known (Eph. 3:7–8; Rom. 1:5,14–15; 11:13–14; 15:16; Gal. 1:15–16; 2:2,8–9), and his Epistles bear witness to his missionary activity and his preaching, the purpose of which was that the body of Christ might be edified, this body in which all separation between Gentiles and Jews is abolished, in which they are united in a common salvation (Eph. 2:11–22; 3:4–6; Gal. 3:28), forming henceforth the *Church, this new "nation" (1 Pet. 2:9; Matt. 21:43) that witnesses to the universal grace and calling of God. From now on the vital importance of the *unity of this "holy nation" and of the behaviour of Christians in the divided world of the nations (1 Cor. 1:10; 1 Pet. 2:12) is understood. But this admission of the Gentiles to the new *covenant did not come about without opposition, as is shown by the conflict which soon arose between the apostle Paul (and Peter) and the Judaizers: the latter did not dispute the fact that the Gentiles had been called to salvation, but were opposed to their immediate acceptance into the Church without any conditions other than faith and baptism (Acts 11:1–4,18; 15:1–29; Gal. 2:3–16; cf. Rom. 14:1ff.; 1 Cor. 8; 11:18–19).

4. The universality of salvation proclaimed by the Church, and based on the Messiahship and on the cross of Christ, is not in fact automatic. The rejection of Israel, already announced by Jesus (Matt. 8:11–12; 21:41–43; 22:8–9; Lk. 21:24) and realized in the early days of the mission (Acts 13:46; 18:6; 28:28) is typical in this respect. In Rom. 9–11 Paul shows that it is not a question of mere resistance to the divine plan, but a new "mystery" of God (11:25): both the election and the rejection of a people are in the end only the means of proclaiming the Gospel to the furthest corners of the earth in order that all, Jews and Gentiles, may be reunited in God's mercy (11:31,33). That is why "the gospel must be preached to all nations" (Mk. 13:10) so that they may pass from the servitude of Satan into the service of Jesus Christ through judgment (Rev. 12:5–9; 14:8; 19:13–15). "Then the end will come" (Matt. 24:14), the sudden bringing of all things into the light and the ushering in of the new time when the Messianic expectation will reach complete fulfilment, the time when the whole world will worship the "Lamb" and the "King of the nations" (Rev. 15:3–4) and will "walk in his light" (Rev. 21:24–25).

The primitive Christian Church, since she sees the "nations" in this way as before God and not in themselves, regards their ignorance neither with complacency nor with contempt. On the other hand she has had a clear conscience to live, until the return of Christ, in the time of missionary activity realizing that the destiny of the "nations" depended upon her witness as the "holy nation" and upon her apostolic fidelity.

S. BICKEL

NEIGHBOUR

O.T.

The Hebrew terms that our English Bibles translate as "neighbour" sometimes simply designate "another" (Jer. 23:27, "their dreams which they tell one another"), but in general, the term neighbour means a member of God's people and becomes a synonym for brother (cf. Lev. 19:17–18).

The term brother is applied primarily in the Old Testament to the children of the same father and, by extension, to the members of the same tribe, of the same people. In the Mosaic law, the bond is less that of blood-relationship than that constituted by the *covenant. The term brother or neighbour comprises all those who share in God's covenant. This covenant brings well-defined moral obligations (Exod. 20:16,17; Lev. 25:14; Deut. 15:7–11). Certain of these obligations are clearly limited to members of the covenant; thus the cancellation of debts in the seventh year: "Of a foreigner you may exact it; but whatever of yours is with your brother your hand shall release" (Deut. 15:1–3); or again the treatment of slaves (Deut. 15:12; cf. Lev. 25:39–46). All the commandments relating to one's neighbour are summarized in this one: "Thou shalt love thy neighbour as thyself" (Lev. 19:18). Note that the Levitical writer extends this commandment to the stranger who settles in the land (Lev. 19:33,34).

Exceptional use is made of the term brother when a pact is concluded between an Israelite and a non-Israelite, as in the case of Solomon and Hiram, King of Tyre (1 Kings 9:13).

N.T.

1. *Literal sense*. On several occasions reference is made to the brothers of Jesus, in the literal sense (Mk. 3:31,32 and parallels; 6:3 and parallels; John 2:12; 7:3,5,10; Acts 1:14). Those who, for dogmatic reasons, accept the tradition of Mary's perpetual virginity invoke the Jewish custom by which the term brother or sister can mean near relatives, half-brothers or cousins. This is the interpretation of the Roman Church particularly.

2. *Religious sense*. The term brother con-

tinues to be applied in the New Testament to members of the Jewish community (Acts 2:29; 3:22; 7:2; etc.). But very soon it refers essentially to the members of the Christian community. It appears as many as 130 times in St. Paul's writings.

(a) Jesus looks on His disciples as His real family: "Who are my mother and my brothers? And looking around on those who sat about him, he said, Here are my mother and my brothers! Whoever does the will of God is my brother, and sister, and mother" (Mk. 3:32–35). This fundamental passage shows that what makes us brothers is our obedience to God, the fact that we behave as sons of the same Father. But that Father is the one who "makes his sun rise on the evil and on the good". Hence the commandment to love not only one's "neighbour" but one's enemy (Matt. 5:43–48). Here Jesus decisively breaks the bounds of the Jewish notion of one's neighbour. In the parable of the Good Samaritan (Lk. 10:25–37), the neighbour is not, as might have been expected, the man who receives help, but the Samaritan who helps him, who behaves in a neighbourly way.

(b) Jesus, by coming to seek and to save that which was lost, *constituted Himself as the neighbour of all men* and in this sense the ancient Church was right to see in the Samaritan of the parable a picture of Jesus Christ. To follow Him means to act from that time onwards as a neighbour not only towards brothers in the flesh, nor even to brothers in the faith, but to all men.

(c) Jesus did even more: by dying upon the cross He took upon Himself the sickness, the suffering and the sin of all men and of *each man*. That is what allows Him to say to the "*nations*" (that is, to the Gentiles) who surround Him in the scene of the last judgment (Matt. 25:31–46) that what was done to the least of His brethren was done to Himself. Traditional exegesis generally considered that these "brothers" were the disciples, in view of the usual sense given to this term in the New Testament. We think (with Th. Preiss, cf. *Le Fils de l'Homme*) that this is to narrow the thought

of Jesus in a peculiar way: "He *substituted* Himself for all these wretches. Not only on a book-account, holding that the smallest acts of love and service and the smallest sins of omission of love and service were done to Him, but in reality, in flesh and blood, He substituted Himself for the least, for the last of His brothers."

(d) Jesus emphasizes that the two commandments of *love of God and love of one's neighbour are inseparably linked (Matt. 22:35–40). The Old Testament was already aware of this. What is new is the extension of the very idea of one's neighbour, one's brother, and the quality of that love (Jn. 13:13–34). God calls believers to be conformed to the image of His Son, in order that He may be "the first-born among many brethren" (Rom. 8:29). It is by love for the brother that the authenticity of the faith is recognized (1 Jn. 2:9–11; 3:12–17; 4:20,21). The "strong" will have to help the "weak" along because brothers for whom Christ died are involved (Rom. 14:13–15; cf. 1 Cor. 8:9–13).

In Jesus Christ there is neither Jew nor Greek, bond nor free, man or woman (Gal. 3:28–29; cf. Col. 3:11); the slave becomes a "beloved brother" (Philem. 16); every Christian woman becomes a "sister" (Rom. 16:1; 1 Tim. 5:2), sharing the same mercies and the same service.

Thus the act by which the Son of God made Himself our neighbour, our brother, and assumed our human lot, becomes the foundation of the whole Christian ethic, of all our conduct towards our fellows.

S. DE DIÉTRICH

NEW

1. The term *new* can have the following meanings: *not yet used:* cloth (Mk. 2:21), sepulchre (Matt. 27:60); *change:* of the moon (Isa. 1:13), of the year (2 Chr. 36:10); *annual produce:* wine (Mk. 2:22), the first-fruits of the harvest as offerings (Lev. 23:16); *still unknown:* gods (Judg. 5:8), doctrine (Mk. 1:27; Acts 17:19); *recent:* newly converted (1 Tim. 3:6), new-born (1 Pet. 2:2); *unpublished,* signifying a special effort or joy: song (Ps. 33:3; 40:4; 96:1).

2. There is a renewal of beings and things, thanks to the faithfulness of God, who by His repeated gifts causes all His creatures to live (Ps. 104:30), and in particular men who trust in Him (Isa. 40:31; Lam. 3:23; Ps. 51:12).

3. "New" relates principally to what is hoped of special revelation and to that which it brings; it emphasizes the fullness of the salvation in Jesus Christ with reference both to the Jewish religion and to paganism.

The new covenant (Jer. 31:31–34) is realized through Jesus Christ who gives His life for the remission of sins (Matt. 26:28; 1 Cor. 11:25). It is no longer the *covenant founded on the law, but that of the Spirit who places the knowledge of God in men's hearts (Jer. 31:33–34; 2 Cor. 3:3,6). The covenant of which Jesus Christ is the mediator takes the place of the old covenant, since it is founded upon the oath of God (Heb. 7:20–22), since it is superior with respect to the person of the high priest, the priesthood, and the sacrifice offered (Heb. 8–10), and since it is eternal (Heb. 13:20).

The *wine which Jesus will drink new in the Kingdom of heaven (Matt. 26:29; Mk. 14:25) is a promise of the celestial banquet to which Jesus invites all men (Matt. 22:2; Lk. 13:29). The incompatibility of the new cloth and the old garment, of the new wine and the old skins (Mk. 2:18–22), signifies that the new things which Jesus brings cannot be accommodated to the old manner of thinking and living, namely, that of the Jews and of John the Baptist.

4. The end of the work of God is a new *world, a new creation: new heavens and a new earth in which righteousness dwells (Isa. 11:9; 65:17; 66:22; 2 Pet. 3:13; Rev. 21:1). In this connection "new" occurs in the book of Revelation like a refrain: new Jerusalem (21:2), new name (2:17; 3:12; cf. Isa. 62:2), new song (5:9; 14:3), all things new (21:5).

This renewal of all things is still to come (Matt. 19:28; 22:30; Jn. 6:39; Acts 3:21; Rom. 8:18–25; 2 Pet. 3:13); it will coincide with the *resurrection and the *judgment of the last day. Until then the work of God is being accomplished in the setting of the old world in which good and evil and the revelation of Jesus Christ and the works of the Devil exist together (Matt. 13:24–30, 36–43; 1 Jn. 5:19).

5. Though the new heavens and the new earth are not yet a reality, yet God has already accomplished through Jesus Christ the major part of His work of salvation (Rom. 5:10; 8:32–39; Jn. 5:24) by creating through Jesus Christ the new *man: on the one hand, Jesus Christ reconciles by His death both Jews and Gentiles, making of them a single new man, the *Church which is a new humanity (Eph. 2:15; 1 Cor. 12:13); on the other hand, the believer is a new man, liberated from the power of sin and living by the *Holy Spirit (2 Cor. 5:17; Gal. 6:15).

It is *baptism which causes the old man to become the new man (Jn. 3:3,7; Rom. 6:4; Col. 2:12; 3:1; Tit. 3:5). The baptized person is born from above, born anew; he is dead and risen with Christ. Baptism is the sign and the gift of a new situation.

But this gift of Christ is also an action in which Jesus Christ, the Holy Spirit, and the believer are active. The new life is received, but it is also demanded; it is necessary that the conduct of the believer should testify to the work of Jesus Christ and of the Spirit within him (Eph. 4:24; Col. 3:10; 1 Cor. 5:7). The marks of the new man are righteousness and holiness (Eph. 4:24), purity and truth (1 Cor. 5:7). The standard of the new man is the *image of God in Christ (Col. 3:10); for *Jesus Christ is the new man, the "last Adam" (Rom. 5:14–15; 1 Cor. 15:21–23,45–47; Jn. 19:5).

The life of believers is new in contrast to the life according to the *flesh (Rom. 8:1–17), the Gentiles (Eph. 4:17–24), or the old man (Col. 3:9). The means of the new life are the Holy Spirit (Rom. 8:1–17), the knowledge of God (Col. 3:10), the truth (Eph. 4:24), and "existence in Christ"

(2 Cor. 5:17). In this way the renewal for which the prophets hoped finds fulfilment (Jer. 4:3; Hos. 10:12; Ezek. 11:19; 18:31; 36:26). The Spirit of God causes men to live again (Ezek. 37:14; Rom. 7:6; cf. 2 Cor. 3:6).

The new man is constantly renewed (Rom. 12:2) by receiving new life from Christ (Eph. 4:23; Col. 3:10–11). For those who do not persevere in this renewal there is no hope (Heb. 6:6). The daily renewal of the inner man—by the Holy Spirit (2 Cor. 5:5) —is consolation to Paul for the destruction of the outer man by the sufferings and hardships of this earthly life and of the ministry (2 Cor. 4:16).

6. The new commandment (Jn. 13:34) is new in that it bases love of one's fellowmen (Mk. 12:31; cf. Lev. 19:17–18) on the love which Jesus has shown to His own (Jn. 15:12–13), the love of God (1 Jn. 4:10–11). This commandment is also called "old" (1 Jn. 2:7; 2 Jn. 5) in order to exclude the novel demands made by heretics.

The new tongues (Mk. 16:17; see *language) are the phenomenon of *glossolalia* (Acts 2:4) which was regarded as the heavenly language (1 Cor. 13:1; 14:2).

The new *way (Heb. 10:20) signifies the free access obtained into the presence of God through the death of Christ, who makes priests of all believers (1 Pet. 2:9; Rev. 1:6).

F. BAUDRAZ

NUMBERS

It seems that in primitive times numbers did not have a religious significance, but that they were used only for counting. In all religions, however, certain numbers have assumed a symbolical force and have afforded opportunity for speculation or for complicated enigmas. Both the O.T. and the N.T.—especially in certain books, such as Revelation—recognize, form, or return to arithmological symbols; but it is difficult to know how to explain them. One is in fact reduced to conjectures both concerning the number of figures with a symbolical

value and concerning the interpretation of these symbols. Therefore the list which follows does not pretend to be exhaustive: its sole aim is to show that the Bible makes use of this marginal procedure in order to emphasize matters that are central. It is plain that in a list of this kind it is difficult to avoid a somewhat artificial character, particularly for the modern mind.

1. The fact that the Bible often combines *2* with *3* (Deut. 17:6; 2 Cor. 13:1; 1 Tim. 5:19;—Matt. 18:20; Jn. 2:6, etc.) leads one to think that the latter number does not have the importance for Scripture which it is to have in the Church following the formulation of the doctrine of the Trinity; and it may even be asked whether this number—like the number *2* as well—does not often appear for the purpose of "contradicting calculation", that is to say, so that it may disappear in favour of the number *1* (*One): thus it is that there are three who bear witness that is unanimous (1 Jn. 5:7f.), that the Father and the Son and His people are one (Jn. 17:20 ff.), or that husband and wife are "no more two, but one flesh" (Matt. 19:6; Gen. 2:24; Eph. 5:31). It will be observed, however, that in the case of blessings (cf. Num. 6:24ff.; 2 Cor. 13:13), cursings (Gen. 9:25ff.), and in baptism (Matt. 28:19), that is to say, on occasions when God Himself is at work, a triple invocation or repetition occurs spontaneously. Besides, God frequently manifests His power and His glory "on the third day": He descends on the burning Mount Sinai (Exod. 19:11), He heals His people (Hos. 6:2), He saves Jonah (Matt. 12:40), and He raises His Son from the dead (1 Cor. 15:4). But to conclude from this that the number 3 is the number of God is a step which even a summary survey of a biblical concordance shows to be unjustifiable.

2. Because it was let down by its *4* corners, the sheet which St. Peter saw in his famous vision (Acts 10:11) could be held without losing any of its contents. And in fact it often happens that this number is

found in the Bible in a context which indicates that nothing is lost and that all is achieved: the 4 corners of the earth (Rev. 7:1; 20:8), whence come the 4 winds (Jer. 49:36; Ezek. 37:9; Dan. 7:2), bound the world and embrace it; the 4 rivers which flow out of paradise (Gen. 2:10ff.) water the whole earth; the Jews recognize 4 archangels who govern the whole angelic world (Jub. 1:27); the 4 extraordinary creatures of the vision of Ezekiel (1:4ff.), which provided the symbols of the 4 evangelists, contain, retain, and convey all the glory of the divine presence; it seems also that the book of Daniel (chapters 2 and 7) is influenced by the idea, which is frequent in other religions, that all history is embraced by 4 kingdoms. Moreover, the number 4 plays a considerable rôle in apocalyptic (cf. Daniel, Ezekiel, Zechariah, Revelation).

3. It is on the *6th* day that God created the human couple (Gen. 1:26ff.), and there are 6 days out of 7 which man may use for the performance of his own work (Exod. 20:9; 23:12; 31:15; cf. Lk. 13:14, etc.). From here it is only a step to conclude that the number 6 is the number of man. This theory is of interest because of the importance, in the Bible, of certain multiples of the number 6.

4. The number *7* (with some of its multiples) is one of the most important in biblical numerology. This number indicates, in the first place, totality or plenitude, of evil as well as good: Mary Magdalene, for example, when possessed of 7 demons, had been completely possessed (Lk. 8:2; cf. Matt. 12:45); and if 7 men have had the same wife (Matt. 22:25ff. and parallels), if 7 women have been bound to a single husband (Isa. 4:1), if a mother of 7 sons is desolate (Jer. 15:9), if a stepdaughter like Ruth is preferable to 7 sons (Ruth 4:15), the number 7 indicates, in all these passages, a maximum, the limit, rather than a real number. The Evil One also, in order that he may the better deceive the saints, has recourse to the number 7 (cf. Rev. 13:7; :7ff.), for this number—that is, in

its second symbolical application—spontaneously expresses the *divine* plenitude and totality (especially in Revelation, where it is very frequent): it is the number of God's creative work (cf. Gen. 2:2f.) and redemptive work (cf. Exod. 12:15,19 which shows the importance of this number for the Passover rites). Mention may also be made of the *Sabbath, the 7th day of the week and thus the day of worship, and of the preponderance of this number in the ritual laws of purification (Lev. 12–15; cf. 2 Kings 5:10). With reference to Acts 6, it is usual to speak of the 7 deacons. It should be noted, however, that the author of the Acts never calls them "deacons": they are the "Seven" (cf. Acts 21:8), just as the apostles are the "Twelve" (*Ministry N.T.). When the text of Acts 6 is compared with the ordination of the "Elders" in Num. 11 one is disposed to think that Acts 6 recounts the institution of the presbyterate rather than the diaconate in the Church.

5. *8* persons entered into the ark at the time of the flood (1 Pet. 3:20). The Bible, however, betrays no knowledge of the speculations on the number 8 (in particular with reference to baptism and eschatology) which the Fathers were to develop.

6. The number *10* appears above all as a round number (cf. Lk. 15:8; 19:13; Rev. 2:10, etc.): there are 10 patriarchs before the flood (Gen. 5), 10 plagues before Pharaoh grants Israel their freedom (Exod. 7–12), 10 commandments expressing the will of God (Exod. 20), 10 powers that are powerless against the love of God (Rom. 8:38f.), and 10 vices which exclude from the Kingdom of God (1 Cor. 6:10).

7. The number *12* is in particular that of the Israel of God, the number of election: Jacob-Israel had 12 sons (Gen. 35:23; 42:13,32; Acts 7:8), and in order both to vindicate his claim to be the Lord of all the people and also to show that with him a new *Israel was commencing, Jesus chose 12 *apostles (Matt. 10:1ff.; Mk. 3:14; Lk. 6:13; Jn. 6:70) as the foundation of the

Church (cf. Rev. 21:14; Eph. 2:20). So it is that the people of God is composed of 12 tribes, historically for the old covenant (Gen. 49:28; Exod. 24:4; 28:21; Josh. 4:9, etc.) and symbolically for the new covenant (Matt. 19:28; Jas. 1:1; Rev. 21:12). This number 12 seems to be absolutely constitutive of the Church, and it is apparent that the replacement of the traitor Judas, one of the Twelve (Matt. 26:14, etc.), by Matthias *before* Pentecost (Acts 1:15–26) took place because the Church needed to be complete *in nuce* in order to receive the Holy Spirit and to undertake the mission with which Jesus had charged it.

It is in general assumed that the origin of the importance of the number 12 should be sought in the development of the 12 months of the year. But, given the link between this number and election, it may be asked whether, at least for theological reflection, 12 is not rather a multiple of the number 6, the number of man: the Church, in fact, is the place where man cannot be alone, where he is both limited and consoled by the presence of his neighbour.

8. At the time of the flood it rains for *40* days (Gen. 7:4); Israel wanders in the desert for a period of 40 years (Exod. 16:35; Num. 14:33; 32:13; Deut. 29:5; Josh. 5:6—indeed, the whole history of the exodus is governed by the number 40: Exod. 24:18; 34:28; Deut. 9:9; Num. 13:25; cf. Acts 7:23,30,36); Saul (Acts 13:21), David (2 Sam. 5:4), and Solomon (1 Kings 11:42) each reign for 40 years over Israel; Elijah journeys for 40 days to escape from Jezebel and reach the mountain of God (1 Kings 19:8); Jesus is tempted in the desert for 40 days (Matt. 4:2 and parallels), and after His resurrection He was seen during a period of 40 days also (Acts 1:3). This simple list shows that Scripture spontaneously has recourse to the number 40 when a new chapter in the history of salvation is beginning: the covenant with Noah, the deliverance from Egypt, the kingdom, the era of the great prophets, the coming of the Messiah, the origin of the Church. In so far as one is able to say that it has a theological signifi-

cance, this number is that of the history of salvation. Is it too speculative to see in it the number 42 ($=7 \times 6$) in round figures, that is to say the number resulting from (and the history of salvation is just this!) the encounter between the fullness of God's purpose and man? (According to Matt. 1, the genealogy of Jesus is composed of 42 names.)

9. The number *70* is generally understood as signifying universality: the descendants of Shem, Ham, and Japheth who repopulate the world after the flood are 70 in number (Gen. 10); it is with a company of 70 persons that Israel comes down into the "world" which is Egypt (Gen. 46:27; Exod. 1:5); and it is for a period of 70 years that Israel will be exiled in that other aspect of the "world" which is, for the O.T., *Babylon (Jer. 25:11; 29:10). Because of the discontent of a "rabble of foreigners" who had joined themselves to the people of the exodus, God gave Moses the command to choose 70 elders to assist him in his duties (Num. 11; cf. the parallelism between this text and Acts 6, where the 70 elders are reduced to 7; cf. above). It will also be recalled that when on Samaritan territory, and thus in what was for the Jew a semi-heathen land, Jesus chose 70 disciples to whom He gave instructions similar to those which, according to Matthew, He passed on to the Twelve (Lk. 10). In view of the fact that there is no further mention of these 70 disciples, it is probable that the object of this account is in particular to show that Jesus wished not only, by choosing the Twelve, to lay claim to the lordship over Israel, but also, by the choice of the 70 (which is reported by the only non-Jewish author of the Bible!) to the lordship of all the nations. There is, finally, the familiar legend which recounts that 70 scribes provided, without any collaboration, an identical translation of the O.T. (the translation called the Septuagint): the purpose of this legend is to prove that the Jewish Bible when prepared for the mission to the Gentiles and to the synagogues dispersed in Gentile lands is inspired of God no less

than the original Hebrew or Aramaic text.

From the viewpoint of its theological interpretation it may perhaps be inquired whether the number 70 is not 72 ($=6 \times 12$) in round figures: at any rate this interpretation, which brings together the number of man and that of the Church, would have the effect of emphasizing the universal scope of the call of God.

10. In this necessarily fragmentary survey of numbers that are of importance for biblical theology it remains for us to draw attention to some precise figures and to an account in which numbers play a particular rôle: here, too, one is reduced to offering hypotheses:

(a) When Jesus commands His disciples to forgive up to 7 times a day (Lk. 17:4), or even up to 70 times 7 (Matt. 18:21ff.), it is in order to emphasize that *forgiveness has no limits and that it is impossible to forgive too much.

(b) The Gospel of John recounts that the miraculous catch brought in *153* large fish without the net being broken. This account has given rise to many interpretations, for it is apparent that the number has a symbolical significance. St. Jerome makes reference to a zoologist subsequent to John (whom, however, as we now know, he misread) according to whom there were 153 species of fish. Thus the purpose of the text is to declare that in the Church (=the net), without its losing its unity, there is room for all the races of mankind. Others of the Fathers used their imagination in seeking an explanation of this number in the sum of a certain number of letters; it is in fact known that in ancient times letters had a numerical value. It was a question therefore of finding words the total of whose letters would amount to 153. Thus Origen succeeded in finding in this number the symbol of the Trinity, and Cyril of Alexandria the symbol of God and the Church (Gentiles= 100, Jews=50, the Trinity=3). To-day the explanation is sought rather in the fact that 153 is the triangular number of 17 (153 is the result of adding $1+2+3+4 \ldots$ up to 17). St. Augustine had already sought to find the

key to this passage in the number 17 and it was his opinion that it constituted a symbol of the Gospel (Law=10+Spirit=7).

Ph.-H. Menoud has communicated the following interpretation to me, and it seems to me very attractive: it is necessary, he says, to join the net to the fish, that is to say, to add 1 and 17. In this way the number 18 is obtained, the equivalent in alphabetical transposition of the first two letters, in Greek, of the name of Jesus (IH). Now, as the result of the discovery of papyri and from the Epistle of Barnabas, it is known that since the earliest times the name of Jesus was shortened to these two letters. The sense, then, would be as follows: the preaching of Jesus (=the casting of the net) and the believers which it gathers in, in other words the Church, appear in the world as the same saving power as Jesus was during the time of His incarnation. The Church, in its unity and in its catholicity, is, between the ascension and the parousia, the very sign of the presence of Jesus on earth—His body, as St. Paul would say.

(c) The *144,000* men who were sealed, of whom the book of Revelation speaks (7:4ff.; 14:1ff.) certainly do not represent a crowd that has been meticulously counted. This number is symbolical. It is the number of election, 12, carried to its ultimate point: $12 \times 12 \times 1000$ (the coefficient of immensity). In other words, this number indicates that all the elect, without exception, are kept under the protection of God.

(d) Another text of Revelation (13:18) invites the intelligent reader to discover under the number *666* a man who ought to be recognized. But who is this whom this number or the symbol of the "other beast" (verse 11) conceals? St. Irenaeus, at the end of the 2nd century, admits that he has no inkling, and no one has discovered the secret since his time. Should a solution be sought in the fact that 666 is the triangular number of 36, which is the triangular number of 8, and thus that an identity can be established between 666 and 8? Now, this number 8 is found in Rev. 17:11 as a symbol of the Beast. Others apply the method of gematria, that is to say, giving the figures the value of corresponding letters. It is undoubtedly due to this procedure that, in certain manuscripts, the number 666 has been changed to 616, in which the name Gaius Caesar may then be found, that is, the brutal emperor Caligula. But he ruled too late (37–41) to be taken into account. It has also been thought that this number conceals a *Nero redivivus*, and, indeed, by reading Neron Qesar in Hebrew letters one arrives at the famous number. But the book of Revelation (1:8; 21:6; 22:13) uses the Greek alphabet. The name which the author of Revelation veils under this number seems to be quite indecipherable. Looking back, it has been possible, by the same method of gematria, to identify the number 666 with the names of the majority of the tyrants who in the course of history have persecuted the Church. Thus, since this number remains living throughout the course of history, one is tempted to seek consolation for our ignorance by suggesting that it signifies a threefold repetition of the number 6, and therefore a refusal, in counting, to go as far as 7: the number of man who is unwilling to enter into the plan of God and who glorifies himself.

(*e*) Finally, mention must be made of the account of the miracle of the loaves and fishes, in which numbers play an obvious part (Matt. 14:13–21; Mk. 6:30–44; Lk. 9:10–17; Jn. 6:1–15). It tells how Jesus feeds a great multitude with 5 loaves + 2 fishes (=7) and 12 baskets of fragments are gathered up. The symbolical sense of this account seems to relate to three points: firstly, Jesus is the one from whom the fullness of God's grace comes (5+2=7), and this grace is inexhaustible: sufficient remains over for the Church in all places and at all times (12); secondly, these 5 loaves + 2 fishes are a symbol of Jesus Himself, in whom the fullness of the Godhead dwells bodily. In breaking His body on the cross He produces an effect absolutely disproportionate to the poverty of His person: not merely His contemporaries, but the whole Church will be satisfied and blessed for ever through His death. This interpretation of the miracle of the loaves and fishes is supported by the fact, thirdly, that the account is given with the very clear intention of inviting the reader to think of the supper which the Church celebrates (this is especially apparent in the fourth Gospel).

The second miracle of loaves and fishes (Matt. 15:29–39; Mk. 8:1–10) is governed by the number 7 and points to Jesus as to the one who fully satisfies, in the name of God, those who live by His gifts.

J.-J. VON ALLMEN

OATH

1. Oaths and vows throw into relief the solemn seriousness, power, and efficacy with which the word of man becomes endowed when it is brought into vital connection with God. Once uttered, oaths and vows are irrevocable and bind the person who utters them by determining his future and that of others. To perjure oneself is not merely an act of infidelity but an act of madness because implying a contradiction of the future already created by the spoken word, a sin against the very nature of that future, producing an impossible situation from which the only issue is death.

2. *The Oath.* (*a*) O.T. The aim of the oath is not to increase the solemnity of a statement by calling on God to witness it. The function of the oath is rather to release the action of God. To invoke the divine *name by one of the usual formulas (1 Sam. 14:39,44; 20:23) meant, according to the probable etymology of one of the two terms employed, to put one's promise or one's deeds under the influence and agency of the divine number "7". By means of the oath one committed to God the duty of taking action against the perjured or false man. (Zech. 5:3ff. and Num. 5:21ff. show us how God gives effect to the curses of the perjured.) Thus oaths were taken in serious or obscure cases; when, for example, an investigation was impossible (Exod. 22:7ff.; Num. 5:11ff.; Matt. 26:63) and whenever because of his weakness man would be taking risks in perjuring himself (oaths of alliance: Josh. 2:17,20; Gen. 21:23; oaths

of submission: Ezek. 17:13ff.). Perjury was punishable by death (Ezek. 17:15ff.), even if the oath had been taken in ignorance (Josh. 9; 2 Sam. 21:1ff.).

The joyfulness of the oath of fidelity to God (2 Chr. 15:13ff.) shows that such a solemn engagement, if held, guaranteed the help of God ("and he was found by them", v. 15). Finally let us note the comforting effect psychologically upon the man to whom the oath has been made: God will surely act since the oath has been taken in His name (1 Sam. 20:42). The oath of God Himself sometimes accompanies the promises He makes (Gen. 22:16–18). Such an oath made the promise inviolable and unalterable, by guaranteeing that neither God nor any man could ever revoke the promised future, even in the face of sin (Heb. 6:13ff.; Ps. 110:4; Num. 23:19; Rom. 11:29; Lk. 1:73).

Jesus Christ is the "yes" to the promises of God, He is their goal and the basis of the guarantee offered by the oath of God; He is the Word given by God (2 Cor. 1:19–20; cf. Rom. 15:8).

(b) N.T.   Far from denying the efficacy of the oath, Jesus confirms that view of it by emphasizing the infinite worth and potency of human words (Matt. 12:36–37; cf. Jas. 3:1ff.). That is why He accepts the imprecatory oath required by the high priest (Matt. 26:63ff.); that solemn oath will bring about His redemptive death at the very moment when Peter will be mortally perjuring himself (cf. 1 Tim. 1:10). Similarly the opposition of Jesus to oaths in general (Matt. 5:33ff.; cf. Jas. 5:12) is directed against the casuistical system of certain Jews who established a hierarchy of value in regard to oaths. Paul, again, will not fear to swear when the honour or truth of his ministry and preaching is at stake (2 Cor. 1:23; 11:11,31; Phil. 1:8; Gal. 1:20).

3. *Vows.*   Vows were perhaps originally a prayer reinforced by the promise of a gift intended to incline the deity to answer the petition. They have been much criticized on the grounds of the element of bargaining they seem to imply. Let us note in the first place that they show a degree of disinterestedness far greater than that of the simple prayer of petition and that certain vows are at times made after the granting of the request (Ps. 76:12; Jon. 1:15ff.). The vow is not a bargain but a devotional exercise, thanks to which the believer will act conformably with the granting of his prayer, since he asks only in order to be able to give back and can rejoice in the thought that through the accomplishment of his vow he has not forgotten the gift as soon as it was received.

Hence there is nothing surprising in the fact that the Psalms so often allude to votive sacrifices publicly celebrated in the Temple at Jerusalem (Ps. 22:26; 50:14; 56:13; 116:14; cf. Deut. 12:11,12 and Ps. 61:8; 65:2).

The believer is not obliged to make a vow. He decides freely to offer goods (Gen. 28:20), persons (1 Sam. 1:11; Num. 21:2) eventually redeemable (Lev. 27), or sacrifices (Judg. 11 and numerous Psalms). But once he has uttered it aloud, man cannot revoke his vow (cf. Judg. 11:35) nor cheat about it (Mal. 1:14). Hence vows must not be made lightly (Deut. 23:21–23; Eccl. 5:3–6; Prov. 20:25).

In Acts 4:34–5:11 the N.T. mentions the vows of the first Church; all who transgress them die; the sacrificial communion meal is replaced by the common surrender of private property.

4. *Nazirite vows.*   Parents sometimes dedicated their children to the service of God for the whole of their lives (Samson, Judg. 13:7; and Samuel, 1 Sam. 1); adults were similarly consecrated for a limited period. The Nazirite's consecration to God was symbolized by his hair, the supposed seat of the strength and vitality he received in consequence of his being dedicated (Judg. 16:15ff.). He was forbidden to profane that sacred vitality by cutting his hair. For the same reason he must not approach a dead person (Num. 6:6–7). Abstention from wine (Num. 6:3–4) expressed his opposition to the establishment of Israel in Canaan (cf. the Rechabites, Jer. 35).

The Nazirite thus expressed his faith that the believer is a stranger and pilgrim on this earth, who looked back towards that period in the desert when God alone was the guide of His people and who looked forward to the Kingdom that was to come. This Nazirite attitude of faith, where the believer lives already under the inspiration of a hope as yet unrealized, has its place in the life of the Church: thus Paul twice adopted it (Acts 18:18; 21:23) and James the Just (*Hist. Eccl.* Eusebius 2,23,3).

A. LELIÈVRE

OBEY

Etymology gives a clear indication of the significance of this term: to obey is to hear, to listen to the voice of someone, with ears and heart open to the words which he speaks. To obey is not to conform to a moral or sacrificial code, nor is it to listen to oneself (Jer. 7:24; Ps. 81:12–14; Matt. 15:19). Obedience is the *living* response of one being to the words of another.

1. *Obedience, relationship of the creature to the Creator.* The biblical equilibrium of the relationships between God and the world is that God is He who speaks, and the creation that which listens and obeys. By speaking God creates His hearer (Gen. 1; Ps. 33:9). In His *Word was life (Jn. 1:4). There is no possibility of existence for creatures apart from this divine Word (Deut. 8:3; Amos 8:11–13; Jn. 4:32ff.): man in the garden of Eden (Gen. 2:17), the heavenly beings (Ps. 103:20), and the natural elements (Job 38:10ff.) exist only in so far as they are conformed to God's will for them. In Eden man obeys freely in the double sense that he is not obliged mechanically to obey, and that he has a variety of ways of obeying, but only one manner of disobeying.

2. *Destruction of the relationship.* In Gen. 3 the disobedience of man consists in having "short-circuited" the life-giving relationship with God by listening to the voice of another (v. 17), doubting the good-ness of God, and proudly seeking life and happiness in an autonomy opposed to the Word of God. Disobedience is similarly defined in the O.T. as the refusal of man to listen to God by preferring voices other than His (false prophets, nations, himself). It is natural that disobedience should produce physical suffering since it destroys the only life-giving relationship (Deut. 28). "Sacred" history is also the history of the disobedience of men who are unwilling to obey (Zech. 7:11–13) and then can no longer obey (Jer. 6:10; Rom. 8:7).

3. *The attitude of God to disobedience.* (*a*) On the one hand, this rebellion of men does not foil God; those who are disobedient do not escape from His control. God takes their disobedience seriously; He does not abandon them to themselves. He hardens the disobedient man (Exod. 7:3; Jn. 12:40), He gives him up to sin (Rom. 1:24), not permitting him to rebel in isolation. But, much more, God makes use of this disobedience, which instead of counteracting His salvation works in with it by making this salvation "gracious". By it God proves His love towards us (Rom. 5:6); thanks to it God can be merciful (Rom. 11:32). He is more than one who administers just retribution; He is able to manifest fully the secret of His essence, which is *love.

(*b*) On the other hand and in a parallel manner, God is preparing the way for the coming of a new obedient humanity. He chooses Abraham, elects Israel, gives His law in order to create a *"remnant" of obedient men, through whom He will pardon others (Gen. 18:24ff.; Jer. 5:1). This faithful remnant is reduced to a single person entirely turned towards God, namely, Jesus, who performs not His own will but the will of the Father (Jn. 6:38), and who is obedient even unto death (Heb. 5:8; Phil. 2:8). By His obedience alone is *righteousness extended to all (Rom. 5:18–19). His obedience is imputed to the disobedient (1 Cor. 1:30).

4. *The obedience of the Christian.* Hence-

forward man no longer needs to seek to establish a personal obedience founded upon his works, even in imitation of Jesus Christ. It is necessary for him to be found clothed with the obedience of Jesus Christ (Phil. 3:4ff.). In Rom. 6:1ff. Paul explains how disobedient men have become obedient in Christ. Plunged into the death of Christ by *baptism, the old disobedient man is destroyed and the obedient life of Christ is given to man. *The obedience of the Christian is faith in Jesus* (Rom. 1:5), faith which in this exchange and this gift accepts for its life no longer that which man supposes he can give himself, but that which God gives him in Jesus Christ (Col. 3:3ff.). Everything is given in this obedience of faith; and without it man remains with his disobedience under the wrath of God (2 Thess. 1:8).

The obedience of the Christian is no longer like that of the Jew, regulated by a law composed of rules and prohibitions. It is expansive, as in Eden: "Everything is lawful. Everything is pure. You have been called to freedom." The setting for the exercise of this Christian liberty, which is characteristic of the obedience of faith, is the recognition of the work of Christ in one's neighbour (Rom. 14:13ff.; 1 Cor. 8 and 9) and of the life of Christ in one's own life (Rom. 6:3). It is for this reason that the love of Christ for us and the humility of His obedience even to death lead the believer along the road of brotherly love (1 Jn. 4:12) and of mutual submission (Eph. 5:21ff.): in particular submission of the wife to her husband, of children to their parents, of servants to their masters, of believers to the political, juridical (Rom. 13:1ff.), and ecclesiastical (Heb. 13:17; cf. Deut. 17:9–13) authorities.

A. LELIÈVRE

OIL, *see* ANOINTING

ONE

The words grouped in the following study are not integrally connected with each other nor do they form an absolutely coherent

whole. Both in English and in the Hebrew or Greek original they stem from very different roots and cover ideas which are neither quite equivalent nor exactly complementary or opposed. However, they present among themselves such a degree of kinship that it is more convenient to expound them together than to devote to each of them a special article.

1. *Oneness, the attribute of God and the characteristic mark of His self-revelation.* In many passages, among which we cite Deut. 6:4; Mk. 12:29,32; Jn. 8:41; 17:3; Rom. 3:29–30; 16–27; 1 Cor. 8:4; Gal. 3:20; Eph. 4:6; 1 Tim. 1:17; 2:5; Jude 25, Holy Scripture affirms the oneness of God.

But to be properly understood these declarations should not be taken abstractly as so many philosophical propositions. For God has revealed Himself and has explicated His oneness in a particular history, the history of salvation.

(*a*) In the story of this saving history— which is moreover entirely dependent on divine *election—the idea of oneness plays a part of capital importance and may be described under the two following categories:

(i) Men, nations and even in a more general way, animate or inanimate beings, whatever they are, have significance only to the extent in which God makes of them instruments of His saving work and consequently means of His revelation. But in so far as they become such they have universal significance. Israel alone has been chosen by God (Amos 3:2). But in her all the nations of the earth will be blessed (Gen. 12:3; cf. Jn. 4:22). It is the same with every divinely inspired vocation: one accomplishes the destiny of all and the destiny of all is fulfilled in that of one (cf. Gal. 1:15–16; 1 Cor. 15:9–10; Rom. 9:3; 2 Cor. 1:4–6; 4:11–15; Col. 1:24, etc.). Such an idea transcends the familiar antithesis between collectivism and individualism.

(ii) Similarly the history of salvation is the sphere where the drama of universal history is enacted in epitome. Further: the history of salvation itself depends on decisive and unique moments in which the whole of the past and the whole of the future are implicated. One single event, one single occasion (Heb. 6:4; 9:26–28; 10:2,12–14; 1 Pet. 3:18; Jude 3) a once-for-all (Rom. 6:10; Heb. 7:27; 9:12; 10:10) crystallizes the whole past and determines the whole future. Such an idea transcends the antithesis between the "contingency" (for one single occasion determines in effect all other occasions) and the "necessity" (for this single occasion attributable to the sole freedom of God was necessary to determine all the others) of historical evolution.

In the light of this one can understand the high significance of such declarations as Mk. 10:21; Lk. 10:42; Matt. 5:18–19; Jas. 2:10; Gal. 5:14; Mk. 14:37; Rev. 17:12; 18:8–10. One single thing is necessary to human life, the law of God can be reduced to one commandment, one single transgression makes guilty, one single hour is decisive.

(b) This notion of oneness such as we have defined it is essentially applicable to two fundamental aspects of the N.T. witness.

(i) *Adam and Christ.* Humanity as a whole flows from one man (Acts 17:26). Now, in this one man the destiny of the whole of humanity was at stake and the stake was lost (Rom. 5:12). In accordance with what we have urged above, the fall of Adam is neither the necessary cause nor the contingent example of the sin of humanity. It transcends this insoluble opposition. On the one hand, certainly, it determines the future once for all, since one time is determinative of all times. But on the other hand it sums up the whole future, for the whole of later history repeatedly confirms and is reflected in this single occasion. Not only then are men sinners because Adam has sinned, but Adam sinned because men are sinners. Such is the burden and the dead weight of human history. What emerges in one single situation—but the decisive situation, and in one single moment—but the decisive moment, is revelatory of the whole process.

But the weight of historical oneness which caused the ruin of mankind in Adam (1 Cor. 15:22) will be used by God for the salvation of men and for His glory (Rom. 5:12–17; 1 Cor. 15:21–22,42–49). To the once-for-all of Adam there succeeds by the power of God the once-for-all of Christ. To Adam, the first man, summing up all men, there succeeds He who is literally the second, He who alone is the second, all men from Adam to Christ being absorbed in the oneness of Adam. One for all had sinned once for all. And again in one unique event one will save all mankind from sin (cf. Jn. 11:50–52; 18:14; 2 Cor. 5:14–15; Heb. 10:11–18).

(ii) *Christ and the Church.* Just as objectively as all men were in Adam, so since the coming of Christ all mankind is summed up in Him. But there is an essential difference between the way in which we are partakers of the nature of Adam and the way in which we are partakers of the nature of Christ. Man is one with Adam naturally, whereas he shares in the saving life of Christ by *faith (Eph. 2:3–8). It should be emphasized, however, that this difference by no means implies that the comprehensive oneness of Christ is less real than that of Adam. On the contrary it is more real since it supersedes the unifying reality of Adam (Rom. 5:15–21; 1 Cor. 15:45–49), and makes it obsolete, for it is itself the sole ultimate reality.

Christ is the new man embracing the life of all men, whose destiny, being at stake in Him and in Him alone, is now finally determined by His victory. All are literally in Him, not in virtue of some non-temporal mystical relation, but by the decisive power of the historical uniqueness of the saving work of God. Those who believe are only recognizing what all men will one day be forced to recognize (Jn. 5:24–30; 1 Cor. 15:23–28). They have recognized by faith that their existence—and that of all men—is indissolubly bound up with the reality of Christ. Hence the very frequent use of the preposition or prefix "with"—"with Christ"; in the case of such verbs as the following: live (Rom. 6:8; 2 Cor. 7:3), suffer (Rom. 8:17), be crucified (Rom. 6:6; Gal. 2:19), die (Rom. 6:8; 2 Cor. 7:3; Col. 2:20), be buried (Rom. 6:4; Col. 2:12), rise again Col. 2:12; 3:1; Eph. 2:6), inherit (Rom. 8:17), reign (2 Tim. 2:12; cf. also Col. 2:13; Eph. 2:5; Rom. 8:32; 2 Cor. 4:14; 13:4; Phil. 1:23; Col. 3:3–4; 1 Thess. 4:14; 4:17; 5:10).

The Church, the Body of Christ, sharing in the life of Christ and wholly committed to Him, partakes of His oneness and of all His other attributes (Eph. 4:4–6). Communion with Christ as it is realized essentially in the *Lord's Supper implies necessarily the recognition of His sole sovereignty (1 Cor. 10:14–22).

2. *The unity which results from participation in the uniqueness of the work of God in Christ.* All believers representing in hope all men (1 Cor. 15:22–23) are one in Christ. By the Spirit they are one with Christ (1 Cor. 6:17) and they are one with each other (Rom. 12:5; Gal. 3:28; Jn. 11:52; 17:23, etc.).

Their unity with Christ does not at all mean that because their life is embraced in the reality of Christ, their person is as a consequence confounded with His. They will never form anything other than the Body of Christ of which Christ alone is and always will be the Head (Eph. 1:22–23; Col. 1:18). Just as the unity of the Father with the Son does not imply the confusion of their persons (Jn. 17:20–23) so the unity of believers with Christ does not imply their fusion with Him.

Similarly the unity of believers among themselves, their brotherly fellowship, far from making them monotonously resemble each other as models cast in the same mould, is realized precisely through their diversity. What is more, their communion together gathers its deepest meaning from the very fact of this diversity. The Body of Christ has differentiated members and the differences not only do not compromise the unity but are the condition of it. Christian unity contrasting with uniformity is organic and structural. It does not obliterate but rather confirms and hallows the difference between man and woman (1 Cor. 11:3–6; 14:34–35), between rich and poor (2 Cor.

8:9–15), between the free and slaves (1 Cor. 7:17; Col. 3:22), between Jews and Gentiles (1 Cor. 9:20). This is also the meaning of the fellowship between Jewish and Gentile Christians, and Paul at times uses the same term, fellowship, to indicate the collection in favour of the Jerusalem Christians (Rom. 15:26; 2 Cor. 8:4). The new dispensation even creates new differences between men in order the better to unite them. The communion of the apostles and the faithful is in fact not unconnected with the specific differences which distinguish them (Acts 2:42; 1 Jn. 1:1–4). The same is true of the fellowship of the apostles among themselves (Gal. 2:9). The same note of unity in diversity characterizes the various forms of ministry (1 Cor. 12:4–30) and the distinction between the strong and the weaker brethren (Rom. 14:1—15:13). The unity of the Spirit is manifested in the love of men for other men who are precisely dissimilar. Communion does not spell confusion or fusion but participation in the life of a being different from oneself. (*Marriage would become absurd in this new order if we had to understand otherwise such passages as Gal. 3:28. The same is true of the other differences.)

3. *Division, the sign and the consequence of sin.* Since the oneness of Christ is the foundation of the unity of the Church and of believers, any division in the Church or among believers will be the symptom of the fact that the oneness of Christ is being compromised and His Lordship called in question (cf. 1 Cor. 1:10–13). Hence the clearness with which the N.T. condemns all party strife, schism and heresy among believers (Rom. 16:17; 1 Cor. 11:18; 12:25; Gal. 5:20; Phil. 2:3; Tit. 3:10, etc.). For all division among believers is symptomatic of the fact that their differences—legitimate in their place—have taken precedence of obedience to the Spirit of the only Lord. Union without confusion, differences without separation; such is according to the N.T. the character of the unity given by Christ to His own and founded in His own relation to the Father (Jn. 17:10).

J.-L. LEUBA

PARABLE

1. A parable is a *comparison*, developed in the course of an account, between two deeds or events of different spheres, the purpose of which is to explain an unknown fact by a known fact.

What we understand by a *proverb* (Lk. 4:23) or a simple comparison (Mk. 13:28) is also called a parable in the N.T. It is for this reason that the biblical parable cannot be defined as precisely as is possible in rhetoric.

In general, the teaching given by a parable relates to a single point: e.g., the importance of the Kingdom of God, for which every sacrifice should be made (Matt. 13:44), and the joy of finding again what was lost (Lk. 15:8-10). But there are also cases of parables which convey several lessons: eg., Lk. 15:11-32: the joy of God in forgiving, the repentant sinner, the man who is upright but self-righteous.

For a long time the Church interpreted all the parables as *allegories*, in which it is no longer the unity of the account but each of its elements which becomes figurative; in Lk. 10:30-35 the wounded traveller represents sinful man; the Good Samaritan, the Lord; the oil and the wine, the sacraments; the inn, the Church, and so on. In reaction against the arbitrariness of these interpretations it was claimed that the allegorical elements had been added to the parables by the primitive Church. But some parables are allegories, interpreted as such by Jesus (Matt. 13:4-9,18-23,24-30,36-43,47-50; 21: 33-41); and others have allegorical characteristics which cannot be overlooked (Matt. 22:2-14; Lk. 13:25-30; 10:11-27).

2. In the O.T. several parables are found: the rich and the poor (2 Sam. 12:1-4), the vine (Isa. 5:1-6), the thistle and the cedar (2 Kings 14:9), the ploughman (Isa. 28:23-29). The prophets also indulge in "parabolic actions" (Isa. 20:1-4; Jer. 13:1-7; 19:1-2,10; 18:1-4). Figurative passages and visions occupy an important place in the apocalypses (Ezekiel, Daniel 4, Esdras, Enoch).

The rabbis contemporary with Jesus delighted to teach in parables. They made use of them for commenting on the law; Jesus gave them a new content corresponding to the object of His ministry. But, like the rabbis, He brought into use what He saw around Himself, in nature and in human life: habitual experiences, the leaven, the lamp (Mk. 4:21), the sowing of seed (4:26-29). There were also occasional experiences, the unjust judge (Lk. 18:1-5), the importunate friend (Lk. 11:5-8), the children who refuse to play (Matt. 11:16-17). Sometimes the story is improbable; it is governed by the reality which has to be grasped: the labourers in the vineyard (Matt. 20:1-15), the wicked husbandmen (Matt. 21:33-40).

3. Jesus makes use of parable for the purpose of *announcing the Kingdom of God:* how it is heralded, the success and the failure of this message (Matt. 13:4-9,18-23); the certainty of its coming (Matt. 13:31-33; Mk. 4:26-29); its importance for men (Matt. 13:44-46); the threat which it brings because of the last judgment (Matt. 13:24-30,36-43,47-50); the grace of the Kingdom, the same for all (Matt. 20:1-15); the invitation (Matt. 22:1-14; Lk. 14:15-24); the suddenness of its coming, the watchfulness necessary and what it involves (Matt. 24:45-51; 25:1-13,14-30; Lk. 16:1-12; 19:11-27; 12:35-40).

Jesus also expresses His own situation in parables, with respect to the reaction of men to His ministry: sinners rejoice in the grace of God, the "righteous" fail to understand it (Lk. 15:1-32); the people of God reject the Son of God (Matt. 21:33-44).

Some parables are concerned with love of one's neighbour (Lk. 10:30-37); with the danger of riches (Lk. 12:16-21; 16:19-31). Perseverance in prayer (Lk. 11:5-13) is also placed in relationship to the coming of the Kingdom of God (Lk. 18:1-8).

4. Jesus speaks with *the purpose of making Himself understood* (Mk. 4:21ff.,33); by means of figures or parables He adapts Himself to the capacity of His hearers.

The meaning of parables can, however, remain hidden, and it is necessary for them to be followed up with an explanation or application (2 Sam. 12:7; Isa. 5:6–7). It is possible for the hearers not to be in agreement and to reject the revelation which the parable contains (Mk. 12:12; Matt. 21:45). The Kingdom of God does not come in the way that the Jews expected (Lk. 17:20–21); it must be grasped by faith, together with the fact that Jesus is the Christ. The parables participate in the mystery of Christ; one understands them if one receives and believes in Him.

According to Mk. 4:11–12 the parables may be a means of hardening with a view to the last judgment, following Isa. 6:9–10. But these words of Jesus, which are also cited in Jn. 12:40 and Acts 28:26, concern the result of the whole of His ministry: for those who do not believe "everything takes place in parables", that is to say that they rely upon earthly signs and fail to see the divine reality to which these testify; they do not discern who Jesus is and what He brings. It is for the evangelist Mark, and not for Jesus, that the parables are a means of hardening.

5. The Gospel of John contains no parables, but declarations by Jesus concerning Himself, frequently in the form of figures: the *shepherd, the *door, the *way, the *light. According to Jn. 16:19,25, Jesus spoke to His disciples not plainly, but in a figurative manner; when the Holy Spirit is in them they will know truly what it is that Jesus had to reveal to them. The revelation of the Spirit is nothing other than that of Christ (Jn. 16:13–15; 14:26; 15:26).

F. BAUDRAZ

PARADISE, see DEATH, LIFE

PATH, see WAY

PAUL, see NAMES (PERSONAL)

PEACE

At times it is difficult, if not impossible, to distinguish between the numerous texts which speak of peace, those in which it is a question of the peace *of* God or *with* God and those which speak of peace with men or between men. Biblical realism makes no separation between internal (or spiritual) and external peace: the latter is symptomatic of the former and the first proclaims and conditions the second (e.g. Ps. 122:6–7). Theologically, peace is a gift of God (Num. 6:26), and as a sign of His blessing it is most often associated with the *grace by which God establishes or re-establishes His covenant (Isa. 54:10; Ezek. 34:25; 37:26); hence it becomes a synonym of *reconciliation; but it is also sometimes synonymous with tranquillity and *rest as opposed to a state of *war between individuals or peoples, and men have to seek it, to ask for it, and to "make" it (Matt. 5:9; Mk. 9:51; 2 Cor. 13:11; Prov. 17:1; 1 Tim. 2:2; Rom. 12:18, etc.). This double sense of the word peace must be taken into account if the majority of the texts where it occurs are to be understood.

(*a*) The Messianic promises are frequently accompanied by the announcement of peace: Melchizedek, in whom the Epistle to the Hebrews sees a type of Christ, is "king of Salem" (=king of Peace, Gen. 14:18; cf. Heb. 7:2). Solomon is also a peaceful king and reigns in Jerusalem, "the place of peace", the "quiet habitation" (Isa. 33:20). The Messiah will be called "Prince of Peace" (Isa. 9:5) and his coming will inaugurate an age of peace for the entire creation (Isa. 2:2–4=Mic. 4:1–3; Isa. 11:1–9; 32:15–20), of which the peace of Jerusalem, the reconciliation of the two kingdoms of Israel, and the submission of all nations are the signs (Isa. 49:8–12; 60:17–18; Zech. 9:9–10; Mic. 5:4). The echo of this hope is found in the Gospel of the Nativity (the songs of Zacharias: Lk. 1:79; of the angels: Lk. 2:14; and of Simeon: Lk. 2:29).

(*b*) But the announcement and proclamation of peace is accompanied by the declaration of its *conditions*, of which the principal one is the observation and fulfilment of the *righteousness of God: no peace without righteousness! (Ps. 72:3–7; 85:9–11; Isa.

32:17). It is for this reason that, at a time when the final defence of Jerusalem is being contested, the prophets denounce the false hope held out by the words of peace spoken by false prophets (Jer. 6:14; 8:11,15; Ezek. 13:10; Mic. 3:5). Jesus likewise is to denounce the false security of men in view of the imminence of judgment (Lk. 17: 26–36; 19:42–44; cf. 1 Thess. 5:3). That is why "there is no peace for the wicked" (Isa. 48:22; 57:21).

(c) Strange to say, the subject of peace occurs very rarely in the Gospels: if the seventh beatitude says that "peacemakers" are the "sons of God" (Matt. 5:9), it is certain that Jesus neither brings nor promises His disciples peace as the *world sees it; He Himself declares that He has not come "to bring peace on earth, but division" (Matt. 10:34; Lk. 12:51). Thus He removes all equivocation regarding His Messianic rôle: the peace which He gives is *His own*, that is to say, the peace of which He is the author and mediator (Jn. 12:27; 16:33). It is not the result of human enterprises or transactions, but it is *received*, in faith by the Holy Spirit (Jn. 20:19,22). The peace of Jesus Christ exists for him to whom Jesus gives the command to go in peace (Mk. 5:34; Lk. 7:50; 8:48, etc.).

It is this peace which constitutes the message that the apostles will have to proclaim, not as an ideal, but as a reality given and fulfilled in Him and by Him; just as love of men for each other is founded upon the love which God has for them in Jesus Christ, so peace between men is founded upon the peace which God grants them in Jesus Christ.

(d) Apostolic preaching consists in proclaiming "the *Gospel of peace by Jesus Christ who is Lord of all", declares Peter (Acts 10:36), and the salutation with which most of the Epistles open—"grace to you and peace from God our Father and the Lord Jesus Christ"—is not a stylistic device. It is an affirmation that now, in Jesus Christ, peace is granted by God to all men and that they are called to live in this peace. Here therefore we find the double sense of the word which was pointed out above:

(i) As grace which is offered, the gift of God, peace is Christ Himself: "He is our peace" (Eph. 2:14–17). "Since we are justified by faith, we have peace with God through our Lord Jesus Christ" (Rom. 5:1). He has made "peace by the blood of his cross" (Col. 1:20). The redeeming work of Christ, which is to *reconcile "all things" to God, to *justify sinners freely by the mediation of the new covenant, is entirely contained in this word: Peace. By Christ and in Christ we know that God is a "God of Peace" (Phil. 4:7,9; Col. 3:15; 2 Thess. 3:16).

(ii) But this peace of God which is received by faith in Jesus Christ is a peace which we have to manifest in our lives (just as the *love which God has for us produces in us love for our brethren); like love, peace is a fruit of the *Spirit (Gal. 5:22). That is why the preaching of the Gospel of peace carries with it also the exhortation to "live in peace", to "be in peace", to "seek peace with all" (Rom. 12:18; 14:19; 2 Cor. 13:11; 2 Tim. 2:22; Heb. 12:14; 1 Pet. 3:11; 2 Pet. 3:14). The zeal which the Gospel of peace gives (Eph. 6:15) cannot be a "bitter zeal", for the wisdom from above is "peaceable" and "the harvest of righteousness is sown in peace by those who make peace" (Jas. 3:14–18).

Does the teaching of Scripture permit the definition of a Christian attitude to *war and peace between nations? Adhering to what is said about peace, it is necessary for us to bear in mind two affirmations:

(i) The coming of universal peace is bound to the coming of the Lord and to the manifestation of the unity of His Church. Wars continuing to the end of the age will remain as one of the signs of the world in its fallen state.

(ii) On the other hand, it is this world in which, already, Jesus Christ has come "to reconcile all things" and to manifest His victory over sin and death. Therefore to live in this hope and in this faith commits the Church and Christians to manifest, in this domain as in all others, the reality of Christ's finished redemption and of His coming reign. It is just as impossible to take refuge in a purely spiritualized conception of peace when taking part in war as it is to confuse the peace which is promised as a result of the reign of Christ with that which is sought or desired by men, whatever the ideologies or the interests by which they are motivated. It is the responsibility of the Church, inasmuch as she knows herself to be the announcer of "the good news of peace by Jesus Christ, who is *Lord of all*" (Acts 10:36), to show, on the one hand, that no war is able to disturb her faith or break the "bond of peace" which exists between her members, whatever their national or racial connections (for in Christ there is no longer Greek or Jew, etc., Col. 3:11); and, on the other hand, that no peace can be desired or imagined by men which has not as its condition the acknowledgment and acceptance of the righteousness of God. Only "righteousness will bring forth peace" (Isa. 32:17). There is never any place for saying hypocritically: Peace—when there is no peace! (Ezek. 13:10).

H. ROUX

PEOPLE

O.T.

The O.T. possesses a number of words related to the ideas of *gathering, community* and *totality* to translate what we express by people and nation. In very many instances, these words are used parallel to each other (Gen. 27:29; Ps. 2:1; Prov. 14:28; Isa. 34:1; Jer. 51:58; Hab. 2:13). They often signify the whole of the peoples or of the nations of the earth (Deut. 32:8; Ps. 9:8; 44:2,14; 57:9; Isa. 41:1; 43:9; 49:1; 60:2; Mic. 1:2), or they represent the peoples and nations over against the peoples of God (Gen. 49:10; Deut. 14:2; Ps. 7:8; 33:10; 47:3; 67:5). But when God speaks and says "my people", it refers of course to the Chosen People (Isa. 51:4; Zeph. 2:9). A close study of the above references brings out the clear distinction made in the O.T. between a people set apart and all the other nations of the earth.

1. *The people to whom the Promise is given.* They are the people of Yahweh (Judg. 5:11; 1 Sam. 2:24), just as the Moabites are the people of Chemosh (Num. 21:29). They are the people of God (2 Sam. 14:13) who belong to Him by right (Deut. 14:2; 26:18), who are His own possession (Deut. 4:20). The king of Egypt called them "the people of *Israel" (Exod 1:9), recalling their ancestor Jacob-Israel. A passage in the book of Deuteronomy gives the clearest expression of this relationship between God and His people: "For you are a people holy to the Lord your God: the Lord your God has chosen you to be a people for his own possession, out of all the peoples that are on the face of the earth. It was not because you were more in number than any other people that the Lord set his love upon you and chose you, for you were the fewest of all peoples; but it is because the Lord loves you, and is keeping the oath which he swore to your fathers . . ." (Deut. 7:6–8). Indeed, the divine *election is shown by a promise, made in the first instance to Abraham, that he will become a great nation (Gen. 12:2; 18:18); this promise is made effective through a *covenant (Gen. 17:1–15), for the keeping of which the loyalty of both parties is required, the loyalty of God springing from His very nature. The love of God for His people is shown in history, in the events which bring about the unity of the people: the deliverance from Egypt, the desert wanderings, the conquest of Canaan, the formation of a state.

Of all these events, that which was most significant for the welding together of the chosen people and that which undoubtedly has left the most lasting impress upon Israelite literature, was the sojourn in the desert under the leadership of *Moses. The work of Moses was great and permanent: Moses regrouped in the desert tribes which previously had been enslaved, gave them a code of law which covered every phase of their life, united them in the worship of Yahweh and so formed them into a people who lacked only a land in which to settle. The nomadic period lasted scarcely more than a generation; then followed the invasion of Canaan, which proved disastrous to the unity of the people since it gave rise to such a revival of tribal particularism that frequently the word "people" was used to denote one of the tribes (Zebulun: Judg. 5:18). The judges, local chieftains who were anxious to prevent the fusion of a tribe or of a group of tribes with the Canaanites and to reawaken in the Israelites the feeling that they belonged to Yahweh, did their best to mitigate the growing anarchy. They achieved but little success if we are to believe the rather resigned statement in Judges: "In those days, when there was no king in Israel" (19:1).

In the period of the kings, and especially under David and Solomon, some degree of national unity was attained within the confines of the land given to them by Yahweh. All the requisites of a permanent unity seemed to be available; the unity achieved at such cost was, however, of brief duration, as though Yahweh were afraid that familiarity with an earthly fatherland would be injurious to the quest for Himself who was the only true principle of unity. After the glorious reign of Solomon, the chosen people split into two kingdoms whose inhabitants were to be known henceforth as the people of Judah and the people of Israel (cf. 2 Sam. 19:41); but the feeling of national unity did not disappear from the consciousness of these two peoples; they knew that they were brothers and freely used Israel as the common name (Isa. 5:7). Even the various deportations did not extinguish this feeling of national unity and, when the exiles returned to Palestine, their national life was formed anew around the reconstructed Temple and the law of Moses.

The different ways in which the occupied territories were dealt with led to a greater ethnic and religious mixture in the north than in the south (2 Kings 17:24–27 describes the settlement in the former northern kingdom of pagan people) and may account for the fact that the people of Judah realized the responsibility which fell upon them of safeguarding the national unity. Now that national independence was no more than a memory—the Persians were undisputed masters of the Near East—the

kingship of Yahweh was emphasized and the unity of the people was of an essentially religious nature.

To understand the difference there was in the conception of the "people" before and after the Exile we must give consideration to the evolution of the expression frequently met with in the Bible: "the people of the land". In pre-exilic times it denoted all the inhabitants without exception, apart from the king (2 Kings 16:15), and the priests (Jer. 34:19), what we would call to-day "the common people". After the Exile, the expression refers to the population of Palestine, to those inhabitants of the country who do not rigorously observe the regulations of the Mosaic Law (Ezra 4:4; 10:2,11; Neh. 10:31). The discrimination is no longer, as formerly, on historical or political grounds; it is now on religious grounds. The "people" has become the community of those who belong to Yahweh through their obedience to the law. The tragic history of the chosen people led to the centring in Yahweh of all their energies and all their hopes.

In the community, before and after the Exile, only men were taken into account, as was the case with most of the Semitic people (see Nahum 3:13). This is the reason why Judaism is primarily a masculine religion.

2. The *Nations. The genealogical table found in Genesis 10 is ample proof of the interest taken by the Chosen People in their neighbours and in the peoples inhabiting the then-known world. Yahweh Himself was not unconcerned with the destiny of the nations and several of His prophets received messages intended for them. Elijah's actions are calculated to extend the influence of Yahweh beyond the frontiers of Israel (1 Kings 19:15); in 2 Kings 5 we see the healing power of Yahweh through the instrumentality of Elisha reaching out to Naaman the Syrian; the prophecy of Amos opens with a collection of oracles concerning the nations; Isaiah warns Damascus, Egypt and Assyria (Isa. 17:1–11; 20:1–6; 37:33–35); the title conferred upon Jeremiah is "a

prophet to the nations" (Jer. 1:5). The title bestowed on the youthful prophet makes it clear that, while he follows the tradition established by his illustrious predecessors, there is something which sets him apart from them, a genuine message addressed to the nations (Jer. 12:14–17). This preaching of Jeremiah prepares the way for the latter days when many nations shall join themselves to the Lord and shall become His people (Zech. 2:11), when the least member of the Chosen People shall become a mighty nation (Isa. 60:22).

Until the moment when these predictions shall come true, the Chosen People and the nations possess in the spiritual world their guardian *angels whose struggles on the spiritual plane are mirrored in terrestrial history (Dan. 10:13, 20; 12:1).

H. MICHAUD

N.T.

In the N.T., the terms "people" or "people of God" are applied to the *Church which unites Jews and Gentiles in the unity of those who believe in Christ. Indeed, the condition which must be fulfilled before one can be accepted into the people of God in the new *covenant is neither the call formerly addressed to Abraham, and through him to the race of which he is the ancestor, nor *circumcision, the rite through which a man is assimilated into Israel, but *faith in Jesus, Israel's Messiah and Lord of all the world. By definition the people of God in Christ comprises men of every race and every tongue. It is an essentially spiritual reality and consequently universal.

According to Lk. 1:17, the mission of John the Baptist is "to make ready for the Lord a people prepared", and in the thought of the evangelist this people extends beyond the confines of Israel, since the Baptist declares that "God is able from these stones to raise up children to Abraham" (Lk. 3:8). That is precisely what the apostolic preaching brings about. The conversion of the centurion Cornelius proves that "God visited the Gentiles, to take out of them a people" (Acts 15:14). At Corinth, the Lord

encourages Paul by declaring to him in a nocturnal vision that He has "many people in this city" (Acts 18:10) and this people embraces the Jews and the Gentiles (Acts 18:4–8).

In his Epistles, Paul constantly stresses the unity of the people of God, formed from Jews and Gentiles, united by faith in the same Lord (cf. Eph. 2:11–22). That the Gentiles should become the people of God on the same terms as believing Jews was what had been foretold by the prophets (Rom. 9:25; 2 Cor. 6:16; Tit. 2:14). On the other hand the Church acknowledges Jesus as the Christ foretold in the old covenant. It is the Church then which lives in theological continuity with the past—and not the unbelieving Jews who, by their very unbelief, have for the time being strayed from the path of salvation. Since the Church is the people of God she inherits all their titles. She is "the *Israel of God" (Gal. 6:16), the true Israel (Rom. 9:6), the true offspring of Abraham (Gal. 3:29; Rom. 9:7f.), the true circumcision (Phil. 3:3), the authentic temple of God (1 Cor. 3:16).

1 Pet. 2:9f. declares that the title of "people of God" and all the privileges attached thereto have passed over to the Church.

Briefly, the title "people of God" borne by the Church underlines three essential characteristics of the Church.

1. The Church is in unbroken continuity with the old covenant which finds its fulfilment in the faith of believers and not in the rejection of Jesus by the Jews.

2. The Church constitutes a purely religious unity in which ethnic and social distinctions are superseded. Doubtless the Church of Jews and Gentiles does not form a third race, any more than a man or woman who are one in Christ (Gal. 3:28) are a third sex. But the natural differences, which continue as long as this present world lasts, are overcome by faith. This victory finds its clearest expression in the celebration of the Supper which unites all believers at

the same table, the table of the Lord from whom their unity is derived.

3. The Church, by its very existence and composition, is a reminder that Christian redemption is a collective and communal work. God desires the salvation and the unity of the human race, and not merely of a few men or of Jews alone or Gentiles alone. Certainly the call comes to individual believers, for divine calls are always personal. But the new life of the faithful can only be developed by their incorporation into the people of God.

PH.-H. MENOUD

PERDITION, see GEHENNA, JUDGMENT

PERFECT, see GOOD

PERSECUTION

1. The O.T. gives an account of how God's chosen people, despite the promises of blessing made to them, encountered, as a community or as individuals, the violent hatred of men and of other nations. On their way to the Promised Land the Israelites aroused the envy of other tribes at the land which had been allotted to them (Judges); the life of David, the anointed of the Lord, was threatened by a Saul from whom God had withdrawn the royal authority; the prophet Elijah had to flee (1 Kings 17); Amos was driven out of the royal sanctuary at Bethel (Amos 7); Jeremiah was imprisoned and condemned to death as a traitor (Jer. 38). These facts are stated with a passionless objectivity and in complete faith in the justice of God. The grief and despondency of the prophets (1 Kings 19:14; Jer. 15:15–21) are always set over against the sure promises of God (1 Kings 19:15–18; Jer. 1:8,17–19). The same balance is to be observed in the Psalms (35; 79; 130): persecution will not last for ever, God will execute justice (Ps. 126; Isa. 40–55). And, better still, persecution is even a test of expectation which enables the man who undergoes it to share in the fulfilment of the hidden purposes of God. The profound

significance of persecution is apparent in Isaiah 53, where the persecution of the "*servant of the Lord" is set forth as the ground of the redemption of many sinners. The poor "servant" of his own free will atones for the sins of the guilty; his future triumph will not only bring him a personal reward, but will show that his life's work was effective in reconciling many to God.

2. At the beginning of the N.T., Jesus proclaims: "Blessed are those who are persecuted for righteousness' sake, for theirs is the kingdom of heaven" (Matt. 5:10). Persecution is no longer the exceptional experience, it has become one of the authentic marks of belonging to the Kingdom. Whence comes this paradox?

It comes from the course which the ministry of Jesus took: contrary to general expectation, He had to be rejected and put to death. Despite this He is still the Christ: raised from the dead, faithful and humble in the midst of His undeserved *sufferings, such as the prophets had foretold that He would be. But the rebellion of men against their Creator is now condemned, their hatred is shown up. Every disciple must bear this in mind (Lk. 14:26–33) and not imagine that he can be above his Lord (Matt. 10:24f.).

Since the *cross, an instrument of agony, has become, in defiance of human expectation, the sign of the mercy of God who dwells in the midst of His own even if this involves being rejected by them, blessed will be that cross, the instrument of "martyrdom" (which means witness), and blessed will be persecution, affliction and tribulation by means of which the love of God is revealed to triumph one day in the resurrection and in the judgment.

Who can understand this? He to whom much has been forgiven, who in consequence will love much and will follow Christ closely. This love will far outweigh the hatred of the "*world". Feeling within itself a foreign body, "a growing, acute, deep-seated tumour", the world will do its best to get rid of it either by assimilation (artful temptations) or, if it proves to be irreducible, by persecution. When that arises, the disciple will follow with confidence the way of his master (Matt. 5:12; Acts 14:22; 1 Pet. 4:13f.).

In the N.T. period persecution emanates almost exclusively from the Jews (Acts depicts Roman justice as the protector of Paul), but, later on, the whole world with the entire structure of the Roman Empire is to be ranged against the Christians. (Is this already happening at the time of the composition of "Revelation"?)

Through the persons and the goods of the Christians persecution is really aimed at the living, the too living person of the Risen Christ. It is Jesus whom Saul persecutes at Jerusalem and Damascus (Acts 9:5); it is His Body, the Church, which is attacked in the person of His apostles. The Church is on trial, not primarily because of what she is, but on account of her preaching of Christ. So Christians should not be ashamed of these tribulations, at least if these are not caused by their own sin (1 Peter 4:15f.). At the same time they are aware that her persecutors are not in conflict with the Church but with the omnipotent Lord, whom they reject to their own hurt. Christians will therefore pray for their persecutors (Matt. 5:44; Rom. 12:14) and will be ready to welcome them into the Christian fellowship without being afraid of them and without gloating over them (Acts 9:10-17). Since persecution has no merit in itself, the disciples will avoid running into it as far as possible (Matt. 10:23; Acts 13:51; 16:37). Persecution is simply an essential element of the history of the age between the cross of Christ and His final appearance (1 Thess. 3:3f.). Through it God is glorified (Rev. 17:14) and the Church is built up (2 Cor. 4:16; Col. 1:24).

3. Persecution appears in the form of "*tribulations*". The Jews expected these tribulations at the end of the ages, but the Christians claim that they began from the moment of the Crucifixion of Jesus: the end of the *ages has already come then! By their persecution of Christ and His Church the Jews and the pagan world are only hastening the fulfilment of the prophecies. These final tribulations are of various kinds (2 Cor. 11:23-28), but they have in common the relentless power of death (2 Cor. 4:10), which strikes man in his personal existence (2 Cor. 7:5f.), body and soul. They give rise to a sustained temptation (1 Thess. 3:3; Rev. 2:10), but they reveal the perseverance, the hope, the consolation, the joy which issue from faith (Rom. 5:3f.; 1 Thess. 1:6; 2 Cor. 8:2), because the world has reached the end of its power.

4. In the face of tribulations, the Christian —who is still in the world—feels *affliction*. He knows that this is only temporary (Rev. 21:4; 22:12), but also that for the time being it forms an integral part of his existence as a Christian. He feels grief (2 Cor. 7:9-11), but he knows that affliction is a sign of his deliverance from the world, of the life force which makes him grow (Phil. 3:10). The present solitude of the disciples (Jn. 16:20-22), the result of their union with the invisible Christ, is also the beginning of their joy.

CH. BIBER

PETER, *see* NAMES (PERSONAL)

PHARISEES, *see* JEWS

PIETY

Although the word itself is found only once in the A.V. (1 Tim. 5:4), the spirit which it represents is to be found throughout the Bible and especially in the Psalms, having a much wider connotation than "piety" has in English including, as it does, ideas expressed by other names: faithfulness, *love, *fear, etc.

1. In the O.T., piety (*ḥesed*) implies a relationship: it is loyalty to the one towards whom one has a certain obligation which arises from kinship, friendship or service.

In its most general meaning, piety is the faithful and sincere respect for the duties which are involved in every human relationship, for example the relationship between father and son (Gen. 47:29), with a relative (Ruth 2:20), a guest (Gen. 19:19), a friend (1 Sam. 20:8), or with anyone who has rendered one a service (Judg. 1:24). The word implies equally the condescension of the superior to his subordinates as the devotion of the subordinate to his superior (2 Sam. 9:1; 16:17); this accounts for the different ways in which the word is translated. Scarcely any of the original meaning of the word has survived except in the expression "filial piety" (cf. 1 Tim. 5:4).

In the religious sense *ḥesed* is the manifestation of the loyalty and goodwill of God towards His people; it is often translated *goodness* (Ps. 33:5 A.V.), *mercy* (Ps. 136:1ff.; Exod. 20:6 A.V.). But, just as in the secular meaning of the word, it indicates the attitude, compounded of respect, love and obedience, of the faithful towards God, or that which we properly call *piety*. Thus Hosea, the prophet of faithful love, blames Israel whose piety is sporadic and superficial: "Your love is like a morning cloud, like the dew that goes early away. . . . For I desire steadfast love and not sacrifice" (6:4,6), or Jeremiah who recalls the days of Israel's first love for her God (2:2). Later, the adjective *ḥasid*, which in the plural readily turned into a noun *ḥasidim*, became the special term to denote those pious Jews who, out of loyalty to God, opposed every compromise with pagan and Hellenistic civilization. It is they who are so frequently depicted in the Psalms as the *godly* (4:3), the *saints* (85:8). Their piety springs from an intense spiritual life, from love and prayer, but also from certain "acts of piety": vows (Ps. 76:11), sacrifices (2 Chr. 32:32), offerings and alms (Neh. 13:14), *fastings. When, under the pressure of various influences, the group of the *Ḥasidim* tended to form a rigorist sect (Essenes) or a politico-religious party (Pharisees), the most humble among them, despised and often persecuted, abandoned this name in favour of the title of "*the poor". In the N.T. a term corresponding to *ḥasid* is applied to Elizabeth and Zacharias (Lk. 1:6), Simeon (Lk. 2:25), Anna the prophetess (Lk. 2:37),

Ananias (Acts 22:12) or to proselytes such as Cornelius and one of his soldiers (Acts 10:2,7).

2. A considerable body of teaching on piety is found in the N.T., in the Gospels (Matt. 6:1–18; Lk. 18:1–14, etc.) as well as in the Pauline Epistles (Rom. 12; 2 Cor. 8–9; Phil. 4, etc.). The word itself, however, never appears. In the later texts of the N.T., the pastoral Epistles, the Epistle to the Hebrews and 2 Peter, its synonym "godliness" is found. In these later writings can be discerned a reaction against the rising danger of the intellectualization of the faith and a warning against those teachers, "puffed up with conceit", who hold not "the teaching which accords with godliness" (1 Tim. 6:3; cf. Tit. 1:1; Heb. 12:28). This is what inspires the urgent exhortations addressed to Timothy "aim at godliness. . . . Train yourself in godliness" (1 Tim. 6:11; 4:7). On the other hand, piety is frequently associated with moral virtues such as honesty (1 Tim. 2:2), justice (1 Tim. 6:11; Tit. 2:12), holiness (2 Pet. 3:11); it involves, therefore, the whole spiritual life of the Christian (adoration, prayer, meditation) with reference to his moral life. Piety penetrates the very mystery of the faith: the revelation of God in Jesus Christ (1 Tim. 3:16; 2 Pet. 1:3); it is the "great gain" (1 Tim. 6:6), even if its possession leads you into being persecuted (2 Tim. 3:12).

But, just as Jesus attacked the pious hypocrisy of the Pharisees (Matt. 23), so the Epistles warn us against interested piety (1 Tim. 6:5) and superficial godliness (2 Tim. 3:5). At the time of the healing of the impotent man (Acts 3:12ff.), Peter disclaims that this miracle has been effected through his personal *piety* (v. 12) and declares: "and his name, by faith in his name, has made this man strong" (v. 16).

True piety, then, is sincere, steadfast and completely humble. It is of piety that the claim is made: "godliness is of value in every way, as it holds promise for the present life and for the life to come" (1 Tim. 4:8).

S. AMSLER

POOR

1. (*a*) The O.T. has two terms for designating the poor: the poor man is, in the first place, the slave of men, one whom necessity places in a subordinate position, or who is obliged to beg (Deut. 24:14–15; Ps. 22:69); then, in the second place, he is one who, in relation to God, finds himself in a state of dependence, who obeys God as a slave obeys his master (Ps. 25:9; 34:2–3), who is responsive to his will (Ps. 25:15).

In the N.T. the poor are, on the one hand, those who are dependent on others, that is to say, beggars (Matt. 19:21; 26:11; Mk. 12:42–43; Lk. 14:13–21; 16:20–22; Jn. 12:5–6; 2 Cor. 6:10; Gal. 2:10; Jas. 2:2–7), and, on the other hand, those who, because of their situation, are in particular need of God's help, those who count only on Him (Matt. 11:5; Lk. 4:18; 7:22). The N.T. also has certain terms which can be translated as "poor" and which express more particularly the ideas of "meekness" (Matt. 5:5) and "humility" (Lk. 1:52).

Oppressed, reviled, mocked, despised, "without political abilities, without commercial aptitudes, the poor is unarmed and powerless before his adversaries" (Causse). "There is no resource remaining to him in the world in which he can trust. He is completely destitute, in fact and in awareness, in means and in spirit; it is this double destitution which makes him poor" (Ellul). His material destitution turns him to God and in this way a close connection is established between material poverty and faith: "It is at one and the same time an external and an internal situation. The poor are men whose situation is such that they must expect everything from God and from Him alone, and their internal dispositions are such that they really do expect everything from Him" (Schniewind); ". . . who, being chastened and subdued by afflictions, submit themselves entirely to God, and, being inwardly humbled, come to Him for succour" (Calvin).

In Scripture, therefore, we find two correlative senses of poverty: *material* poverty and *spiritual* poverty, of which the latter ought to be the consequence of the former.

(*b*) The presence of the poor in Israel was the result of a historic evolution. At the time when the people entered into Palestine the land was divided between all the families. All enjoyed plenty and there were no poor people (Deut. 8:6ff.). In the course of the years the situation changed. In particular after the Exile (587 B.C.) there appears in the midst of the people a class of poor persons composed of those who have been plundered by unscrupulous compatriots. The book of Psalms is especially the voice of these "poor of Israel". Because they have no more possessions, because they are despised and reviled, they await the vengeance of the Lord (Ps. 58:11–12) and the justice which they know can come only from God (Ps. 40:18; 109:31; 69:34). It is these concerning whom the N.T. tells us that they were awaiting "the consolation of Israel" (Lk. 2:25). Simeon, Anna, Joseph, and Mary are of their number. It is in the midst of these poor persons that the Messianic hope was particularly alive (Lk. 1:51–53; 2:8–14, 25–38). Whatever the nature of their claims, often very earthly, may have been, they were the ones most disposed to welcome Christ. Hence we can understand the affection and tenderness which Jesus showed them and how it was that He was able to say to them: "Blessed are you poor, for yours is the kingdom of God" (Lk. 6:20). This word of Christ concerning poverty is of fundamental importance and we must examine it more closely.

2. Let us look, first of all, at the famous divergence between Matthew and Luke. While Luke says: "Blessed are you poor . . .", Matthew adds: "Blessed are the poor *in spirit*, for theirs is the kingdom of heaven" (Matt. 5:3).

Numerous interpretations have been given of the Matthean addition. Some commentators regard the text of Luke as authentic, and thus more ancient. Matthew added "in spirit" in order to cause the Aramaic expression employed by Jesus to be better understood. He places the emphasis on the spiritual character of poverty, which becomes a privilege. It is then synonymous with openness to the Gospel, with inward renunciation; it is to this kind of poverty that the Messianic promises are made. Calvin also observes that the text of Matthew expresses the intention of Jesus more clearly, for material poverty by itself can be accompanied by the greatest pride. The words "in spirit" apply to a poverty that is fully acknowledged: "St. Matthew, by adding the qualification, limits the beatitude to those alone who under the discipline of the cross have learnt to be humble."

Poverty in spirit, however, is not stupidity, as was sometimes thought; much less is it a want of the Holy Spirit, or an entirely "spiritual" detachment from wealth (see *Money), but an inner emptiness, an expectation, which requests satisfaction from God. Thus the "poor in spirit" are those who have a full realization of their own indigence and who look to God for everything. "Jesus is here describing . . . human situations which arouse in those who experience them an expectation and a hope, and which create in these same individuals a manner of existence, an attitude which is both inward and practical, resulting from that which is lacking to them" (H. Roux). Thus the two redactions of Luke and Matthew express simply this double character of poverty, which should be "inward and practical". This double sense can help to prevent false interpretations: in itself material poverty is of no value whatever unless it serves to turn a man towards God. But, on the other hand, the spirit of poverty, spiritual poverty, can be a snare if it is not associated with a true material poverty. In the N.T. the rich are always in a very perilous situation (Matt. 19:21–23).

Evangelical poverty, therefore, cannot be the privilege of a class of society, nor a virtue, nor a merit; it should be "an agreement of the spiritual life with the material condition" (Ellul).

3. Let us examine further a number of important texts of the N.T. regarding poverty:

(a) ". . . the deaf hear, the dead are raised up, and the poor have good news preached to them" (Matt. 11:5). The proclamation of the Gospel to the poor indicates that the Kingdom of God is at hand. The deliverance of the poor thus becomes one of the signs of the *Kingdom, like the *healing of the sick. Cf. in the same sense Acts 2:45, etc. St. Paul's collection for the poor at Jerusalem (cf. Gal. 2:10; Rom. 15:26, etc.) should rather be interpreted in the context of the *unity of the Church.

(b) ". . . you always have the poor with you, but you will not always have me" (Matt. 26:11). This text has frequently been misunderstood. It has been used to make Jesus an enemy of social progress. Jesus is not here condemning every loyal attempt to battle against pauperism; He simply wishes to emphasize that while He is present the truly essential thing is to draw near to Him. Afterwards the Church will have plenty of time for attending to the poor, and Jesus, while emphasizing that the poor will always be a question which God poses to the Church, has given the commandment of charity.

(c) Jas. 2:2–7: The Church should be the place above all others where all social distinctions are abolished. The primitive Church was already familiar with rich persons who were an offence, and this Epistle stresses the privilege of the poor.

(d) ". . . not knowing that you are wretched, pitiable, poor, blind, and naked" (Rev. 3:17). The believer should never regard himself as spiritually rich and prosperous; he should always be "one begging for grace".

4. The great perspective of the last judgment (Matt. 25:31–46) shows that the poor do not confront the Church in an abstract fashion with "the social question", but with a far more serious question: the Church is asked whether she can recognize in the poor man someone in whom, mysteriously, Christ Himself is present calling her to the *love of her *neighbour.

A. PÉRY

POSTERITY, *see* FAMILY, GENERATION

POWER, *see* AUTHORITIES

PRAISE, *see* HYMN, PRAYER

PRAYER

To write a theology of prayer would involve writing a complete theology. But it has often been treated only as an "appendix". It has certainly been stated that "it was the central phenomenon of the religious life" (Heiler), but even the most realistic theologians have not taken sufficient account of this central place which prayer, even in a formal manner, occupies in the Bible.

Now, what according to the Bible is the most important work of the man who has been saved, what is the principal work of the Spirit in us, if it is not prayer? Prayer is the extreme limit of the grace of God toward us (cf. K. Barth, *The Lord's Prayer*). It is characteristic that St. Paul, e.g. in Gal. 4:4-7 where he touches briefly on the history of salvation, sets as the crown on the story of redemption the cry of *Abba*=Father (cf. also Rom. 8:12-15).

The very definition of prayer has been uncertain. Sometimes it has been regarded as speech addressed by man to God; this is too indefinite unless the "operative" value of the *word in the Bible is kept in mind. More often it has been thought of as a communication, a communion of man with God (provided one does not abandon the theological for the poetical plane and look upon prayer as the exhalation of the soul). There again it is not clear; God enters into communion with us before we pray (it is His Word and not ours which is the source of this communion). These definitions, which are far from being untrue, make the mistake of artificially linking prayer to the salvation God has granted to us, even if they do not turn it into a natural response. Now quite clearly the Bible pays scant attention to these "natural responses" except to oppose them (Jn. 3:6; 1 Cor. 1:7—2:16), and indeed affirms that God desires that *His people* should pray in a particular

manner, either in a formal way (the Psalter is the collection of the prayers of Israel) or, above all, in a profound way (Isa. 29:13; Amos 5:24). Yahweh does not listen to every prayer offered by every man. He is not to be addressed as any god might be addressed.

Our definition of prayer then is: "*the voluntary sharing on the part of God with man of His will, His power and His love* (the secret of this sharing being in Christ which makes the prayer specifically Christian) *through the medium of human speech*" (cf. K. Barth: "In prayer God invites us to live with Him", *ibid.*).

In the Bible prayer is described as having power over all that over which God Himself has power (our lot, the Psalms; the demons, Mk. 9:29; sickness, the Psalms; other people, Acts 12:5; God's decisions, Gen. 18, etc.).

In prayer through God's grace man becomes *subject*, he is admitted to a share in causality. Primarily prayer will be a furthering of God's Kingdom, and by our share in this advancement it will be an anticipation of the *Kingdom where God will be all in all. This is why the pivotal petition of the Lord's Prayer is "Thy Kingdom come" and the prayer of the Church is: "Come" (Rev. 22:17,20; cf. 1 Cor. 16:22). It is for this reason that it is so important and so vital to pray and to pray *aright*. Having become children of God by adoption, we must learn to live and therefore to speak as children of God.

Prayer is the medium which God has given us to induce Him to desire what we desire; but it must also be that by which we ask Him to induce us to desire what He desires. "Thy will be done" (Matt. 6:10; cf. 26:39ff.). All those who try to reduce this ambiguity to a unity, or to suppress either of these affirmations, destroy the nature of prayer.

The latter is lost sight of by those "parishioners" who often use prayer as a kind of magic. The former is ignored by a large number of theologians who are eager to avoid anthropomorphisms; their point of departure is a definition of God and His immutability, and the only function they can attribute to prayer is that of spiritual education. Now it is the biblical conception of the Living *God which is the background of prayer, and prayer must be studied as the second phase of the relation of the Living God to a living person, that is to say in a dynamic way; one might dare to say, in an existential way. We must always remember that one prays before reflecting on prayer, certainly before having a theology of prayer.

To sum up: prayer is the proof that the believer is *truly* saved, and that he can *really* live out this salvation. It is and must be his chief activity, the main expression of his faith (cf. the episode of the ten lepers where the act of thanksgiving is hailed by Jesus as the chief expression of faith, Lk. 7:11ff.).

O.T.

The numerous expressions used to denote prayer are for the most part derived from: "to sacrifice", "to cut" (to cut oneself?), "to caress" (the divine image?), "to prostrate oneself" or even from "to leap". Let us simply stress this close relationship of prayer with gestures which, etymologically at least, appear to have preceded oral prayer (gesture has speech value).

1. There is in the O.T. one book which was the canon of Israelite prayer (where and when are of little importance to the present issue): *the book of the Psalms*. After Balla had done justice to the collectivist interpretation of the Psalms and had shown that, for the most part, they had been written by individuals to depict individual troubles, scholars to-day are giving due weight to the older interpretation, that the Psalms had also a cultic intention, and that, therefore, although personal, they cannot be separated from the community which heard and used them.

In the Psalms the Israelite is not speaking to a God who is either defined or undefined in Himself, but to the God of the *covenant, that is to say such as He has defined Himself with reference to Israel. It is then in the great context of the covenant that the Psalms must be understood. But this in no

sense prevents the Psalmists from understanding that the God who has made a covenant with Israel is the God of the universe (Ps. 8; 19; 104; even if Pss. 19 and 104 have been borrowed, this only corroborates this affirmation, all the more because these borrowings have been amended). "If Yahweh, the creator of the universe, is for us, who can be against us?" Such is the reasoning both in the collective psalms and in the personal psalms, where "us" refers to the godly, i.e. those who cling only to the covenant of Yahweh and in consequence to His law alone. This explains why in the Psalms prayer reveals great audacity. The writers speak as heirs of the covenant who have remained faithful to its obligations. They feel bound to share their feelings with all the faithful, i.e. with all those who took part in the worship of those days (the great congregation: 22:25; 35:18; 40:10).

What the individual member has endured is made known. This disclosure has a two-fold origin: in the first place there is the desire to make the experience of the psalmist intelligible to the minds of all; further there is a firm conviction that God does not want to hear of abstract, anonymous troubles. God does not understand those who speak to Him in hints, and He remains deaf to those who speak too low. For this reason men cry aloud (an expression which is to be taken literally as an outcry), they roar even. Prayer in a quiet voice was unusual (Eli thinks that Hannah is drunk because her prayer is not audible, 1 Sam. 1:14). When they have managed to make themselves heard, God answers their prayer. Then they give thanks to Him. The most frequent causes of distress were sickness, which was the result either of sin (Ps. 32) or of sorcery (Ps. 59), false accusations, or doctrinal disputes. Few of the troubles could be described as purely spiritual; but material distress always leads to a profound spiritual distress. Sometimes they pray as guilty men (Ps. 51 and 32, a remarkable psalm in which the chief crime which the author acknowledges is that of not having confessed his sin earlier).

The covenant has been broken, the guilty man asks God to cover his sin and to bring him back into the covenant relationship. This prayer presupposes that God is willing to listen to the sinner. Sometimes it is as a "just" man that one prays; but in every case it is quite clear that the author is justifying himself in the face of some particular charge which would merit death or an exemplary punishment for him, if it were established (Ps. 7–17, etc.). It is a gross error to discern in the book psalms of "natural justice" in the sense which this expression acquires later. They are nothing more nor less than defences, often courageous, of men who are accused but are persuaded that God will confound the false witnesses.

2. There are in the O.T. many other prayers, in particular the book of Job, which often resolves itself into a sustained prayer. What must be stressed here is the astounding sincerity and the slow unfolding which leads to harmony between Job's will and God's will. And if we may be allowed to suggest a theory concerning this book, it is our opinion that therein lies one of the book's principal themes. "Whoever ponders over difficult problems will only obtain an answer after a long and sincere struggle with the Creator, but at the same time he will stop disputing." Prayer is the most important answer. The book of Job then supports this thesis at the point where it touches the most delicate problem: how is it possible for an upright man to suffer so much?

3. Again there are the great prayers of Moses (Exod. 32:11–13,31–32; 33:12–16; 34:9; Num. 11:11–15; 14:13–19; 21:7; Deut. 9:18–21; 10:10 and Deut. 33), that of Abraham for Sodom (Gen. 18:22ff.), and those of David. It should be noted that in these prayers intercession, which is little in evidence in the Psalms, is much more clearly attested (Job 42:8,10; Isa. 37:14–20), but it seems to have been confined to exceptional men who played the part of advocates with God: prophets, priests and kings. With Moses this intercession was a real ministry.

It is, moreover, interesting to observe that almost invariably the intercessor uses an argument which to-day surprises us: "Because You are what You are, forgive; otherwise You will let it be said of You that You are unjust, or that You have forsaken Your people. It is for Your sake that I intercede and You must answer, for in ourselves there is no good ground for intercession and still less for an answer." This is the explanation of the expression "in the *name of" "in Thy name". It means to cover oneself with the name and therefore with the personality of God when one speaks; it means in addition to be sure that one's prayer corresponds to a specific promise (Dan. 9:11–19). Through this promise, God has ranged Himself on the side of those who pray, even though they be sinners.

4. It must be remembered, too, that prayer was often accompanied by a *sacrifice* (Ps. 66:13ff.; 54:6), so that one may wonder whether prayer was the oral part of the sacrifice. There were certainly prayers without a sacrifice (Ps. 50; 51; 69:31), but in these last two "anti-sacrificial" Psalms (51, 69) note must be taken of the fact that Jerusalem had then been destroyed; it is sacrifice outside Zion which is condemned, while the Temple is still not rebuilt, for sacrifice is invalid apart from the objective presence of Yahweh, i.e. outside the *Temple. There are no doubt sacrifices without prayers (Leviticus has very little to say about prayer). One can sometimes be a substitute for the other. But while affirming their "concurrence" at certain periods, it must also be clearly stated that each has its own place and that prayer and sacrifice may be complementary: prayer being a safeguard against any magical conception of sacrifice, and sacrifice making prayer objective (and perhaps rendering it valid).

*Fasting and humiliation in sackcloth and ashes often accompanied prayer.

5. With regard to *the practice* of prayer, this doubtless varied from place to place and from age to age. It should be stressed that

there was at one and the same time freedom and rule. *Attitude:* prayer was sometimes offered standing, with the worshipper's hands open and uplifted (to receive something?) (Ps. 28:2; 134:2; 1 Sam. 1:26; 1 Kings 8:22), sometimes kneeling (1 Kings 8:54; Ezra. 9:5; Dan. 6:10), perhaps also sitting or with the worshipper's head between his knees (1 Kings 18:42). Often the hands were lifted towards the altar, or towards heaven (1 Kings 8:54; Lam. 3:41; and in many of the Psalms). The worshipper turned towards the Holy Place if he was in the Temple, or towards the Temple if he was in some other place. He would make every effort to go to the Temple as often as he could to pray there, for prayer offered in that place was more "effective": Deut. 12:11; Dan. 9:3,20 which should be rendered *towards* the holy hill. In the same way, whilst he could pray at any *hour*, there were also fixed hours (Dan. 6:10; Ps. 55:17). There were also set *formulas*, as is proved by the Psalter, but the Psalter shows that there were also private prayers, which the community could adopt. There was then a framework, but also a freedom which prevented the worshipper from being imprisoned in it. But why was there increasing insistence on the necessity for a special place (or orientation) with set hours and a formulary? To see in this process a regression from spirituality and to mobilize the prophets in support of such a criticism seems a mistake. Apart from a certain academic solicitude, it must be recognized above all as a sign of a growing awareness of Israelite reality and unity and of the will to manifest them if not to realize them.

As for the *subjects* of prayers, they covered the whole of human existence; note should be taken, e.g., of the beautiful prayer of Eliezer (Gen. 24:12–14,27) firmly "anchored" to the promise made to Abraham. Finally, due attention should be paid to the great wisdom of Eccl. 5:1–6.

N.T.

The N.T. has some ten terms for "to pray".

1. Here, too, we have a canon of prayer: not indeed a collection of prayers but a very brief prayer, the *Lord's Prayer*, which Christ gave as a model for every Christian prayer in answer to the request of His disciples "teach us to pray" (Lk. 11:1–4). If the request of the disciples is authentic (there are hardly any reasons for doubting its genuineness), it teaches us, apart from the desire of the apostles to imitate the disciples of John the Baptist, on the one hand that Jesus must have possessed a "characteristic" prayer, and on the other hand that they felt either as Jews (in possession of the Psalms) or as mere men their inability to pray in a Christian way. Jesus confirms this when He says: "When you pray, say . . .", attesting by these words that we have to learn the art of prayer and learn it from Him. The Lord's Prayer instructs us concerning the range, the meaning and also the limits of prayer. It has not been recognized sufficiently clearly that this prayer constitutes our main share in the three principal demands. In effect it is the hallowing of God's name, it advances His Kingdom, it is also the fulfilling of the will of God. Through our prayer God hastens His Kingdom, through prayer we also work therein. In prayer we bring ourselves into line with what we ask, we take our part in it, which means that prayer, far from being an attempt to avoid a more precise "commitment", actually demands it.

It is God's will to need us, in the very things which, however, belong entirely to Him. Indeed the final petition of every prayer (and rather as a corrective to an overweening human ambition) is the third petition—the will of God; but it is not thought of *in abstracto*: what God wills first of all is that we should pray. The will of God is "open"; it is favourable and it can, and sometimes does, take up and include our will. There are, however, occasions when it diverges from our will; then our will must conform to His (2 Cor. 12:8ff.), but this may be also because we have been irresolute (divided, or more exactly double-minded: Jas. 1:6–8). Prayer, then, is effective not by its own virtue and not immediately: there will often be a delay between the visible answer and the petition, and this delay must be filled in with sustained prayer (Lk. 18:1ff.; 11:5–9). During this delay, moreover, the requests may vary so as to coincide with the answer. A prayer has a *history*; it is composed of "prayers" which must be considered as a whole and in their unfolding (cf. the prayers of Christ in Gethsemane). The first essential quality of prayer, then, is perseverance, the second is confidence. Perseverance enables us to continue to the end, i.e. until we reach harmony between God's will and ours, while confidence enables us to know that this issue is sure. Jesus assures us that on the plane of the invisible this harmony has already been realized (Mk. 11:24; cf. 1 Jn. 5:15).

Further concerning the prayer-life of Jesus it should be noted: (*a*) Jesus does not appear to have greatly used extempore prayer when praying with His disciples but in these instances to have used liturgical prayers; (*b*) He used to withdraw into a hidden place for His private prayers (cf. Matt. 14:23; Lk. 5:16; 9:18, etc.); (*c*) at least during the time of the Passion He made extensive use of the Psalms (cf. Matt. 26:30; 27:46; Lk. 23:46; Jn. 19:28); (*d*) the Lord's Prayer seems to have been the résumé of His own way of prayer which intrigued the disciples; (*e*) Jesus begins His prayers by "Our Father" rather than by the usual "Lord" and appears thus to inaugurate a new age of prayer; (*f*) the vital theme of great High Priestly Prayer (Jn. 17) was the unity of the Church.

2. For the *apostle Paul*, prayer was the word of the Holy Spirit uttered by a member of the body of which Christ is the head. Without saying it in so many words, he shows that prayer is the formulation of love, or its commonest vehicle: it culminates in the cry *Abba*=Father, and in reminding his readers of his love for the Churches, he stresses on every occasion that he intercedes on their behalf. Moreover, prayer is considered by him as a word of Christ (cf. 1 Cor. 1:4ff.; 2 Cor. 1:3ff.; Col. 3:17, etc.).

Much might be said on the subject of this prayer: the word of the Holy Spirit in so far as it "rises", and the word of Christ in so far as it edifies and is normative. It was quite possible that Paul was afraid that the Holy Spirit might be regarded as a rival of Christ; in any case history would have decided in his favour. Let us simply stress that Paul puts on the same plane the prayers of the Church of his day and the words of Christ; these prayers are the living Word of Christ who through them is building up His Church.

The apostle speaks of the Holy Spirit praying (cf. Rom. 8:15f.,26f.) in this respect, that Christian prayer is inspired by the Holy Spirit. But let us remove at once any such fallacy as: spontaneous prayer= spiritual prayer. When the apostle speaks of "sighs too deep for words", he intends to convey the idea that we cannot express them even in tongues. The Spirit comes to our help by a kind of parallel prayer, for we do not properly know what we ought to ask, all the more because we are dealing with what is inexpressible. Does this mean that we ought to be silent and leave it all to this intercessor? No, for there are inexpressible sighs which are also spiritual prayers (but in Paul, as in John, spiritual is the opposite of natural) and which possess certain external signs which guarantee their inspiration. Among these signs are to be noted the cry *Abba*=Father, the acknowledgment of Jesus as Lord (cf. 1 Cor. 12:3), the approval of those who have the gift of discerning spirits (cf. 1 Cor. 12:10f.), but above all the consensus of the community which, if the prayer is genuinely Christian, is bound to acknowledge itself edified thereby (1 Cor. 14:12ff.). For this reason he makes extensive use of the hymns and prayers of the period.

Thus, when our prayer is truly Christian, there is a kind of interchange between the Spirit and the Father: we speak but it is chiefly the Spirit whom the Father hears.

3. The Spirit is not our only intercessor. Christ also intercedes for us (Rom. 8:34). It is the author of the *Epistle to the Hebrews* who builds this truth up into a system. Christ is the mediator of our prayers which

He transmits and transfigures (4:14ff.; 7:25). It is, of course, clearly understood throughout the Epistle that the first thing that Christ offers is His sacrifice, but this work, accomplished once for all, is "completed" to-day by Christ's intercession, which, even if it adds nothing to the sacrifice, enables us to receive its benefits.

4. For John, the essential element in prayer, in order that it may be answered, is that it should be offered in the name of Jesus (Jn. 15:16; 14:13; 16:23f.). The expression "in my name" is to be understood in two ways: it implies first "covering you with what I have been", referring to His past mediation: Christ has "saved" our prayers; it means further "having recourse to what I am now, to my present mediation" (cf. 1 Jn. 1:9; 2:1). In the book of Revelation, where we have a description of the worship of the Church Triumphant (in close connection, moreover, with worship on earth, which means then that our prayers are not independent of the prayers of the Church Triumphant), the saints and martyrs praise the Lamb or ask for vengeance (6:9ff.). Clearly they are celebrating a liturgy. There is room to believe that, if they are really praying (the book of Revelation thinks so), there is nothing to prevent them from interceding for the living.

On the question of intercession, to which the apostles (St. Paul especially) paid so much attention, because in the Lord they had the example of it (Stephen echoes Christ's intercession on Calvary, Acts 7:58–60; we have here the prayer-type of the martyr) a special study needs to be made: does it not presuppose a kind of osmosis of grace? Is it not the sharing of one of Christ's essential ministries? His priestly office as intercessor is transmissible.

5. In the N.T. men pray without ceasing, but Jesus recommends short prayers. Christians pray for bread, for the forgiveness of sins, to return thanks, to abase themselves, for the authorities (cf. 1 Tim. 2:1ff.), for the brethren, for the other Churches, for enlightenment when any important decision has to be taken, for faith, for wisdom, for perseverance, for vigilance, and—this is something new—for their enemies and those who put them to death (Matt. 5:44; Lk. 6:28; cf. Lk. 23:34).

As for the mechanics of prayer, from the outset Christians followed Jewish usages (Peter and John went up to the Temple at the hour of prayer, Acts 3:1), and made use of Jewish prayers. But Jesus issues a warning against prayers which are too external or offered to acquire merit, and against mechanical prayer (cf. Matt. 6:5ff.; 7:21). Similarly Paul urges that in prayer our intelligence should be wide awake (1 Cor. 14:14). However it is quite certain that from the beginning there were in existence liturgical prayers (Jewish prayers, the *Maranatha*, the *Abba*, the *Amen*; cf. also the doxologies in the Epistles and Revelation). And without withdrawing this privilege from the ordinary Christian, it was understood that one of the essential apostolic functions was prayer (Acts 6:4). It should be noted, too, that prayer accompanied the *laying on of hands and *healing. Finally, communal prayer was regarded as being more powerful than private prayer (Matt. 18:19).

6. What, then, is *the new element in Christian prayer*? It is that it is offered in direct relationship with the prayer of the Lord. That is why it is offered in the name of Jesus with a new certainty concerning its fulfilment: because in Him whose name is used all is fulfilled, prayer demands that the fact that "all is accomplished" should be made manifest. Thus prayer relates not merely to a divine promise nor to a past act of no permanent validity nor to a simple announcement of an act in the future, but it relates to the great work of the incarnation, of which prayer is the outcome. It can be affirmed that to-day prayer is one of the most important mediums of action or of the transmission of that which, during His lifetime, and before His resurrection, Jesus accomplished "once for all". It seems to us, as Oscar Cullmann has emphasized, that the

Gospel of John has given a pre-eminent place to prayer (especially in the later chapters) as being, alongside the sacrament (without being on the same plane) the means through which Christ grants to His people what He did for them during His earthly ministry. The answer to prayer is the transmission. It is also interesting to observe that the acts of thanksgiving, the benedictions or the doxologies are very often in close relationship with the saving Gospel.

Christian prayer, then, is not simply prayer which is more rationally profound than Israelite prayer, i.e. having a deeper knowledge of its object and its meaning; but prayer is the movement of the members towards the Head: it is the edification of the Church, it is the perfect realization of the work of God in us, the chief expression and formulation of love. Through prayer Jesus Christ continues His work in us and through us. In addition, prayer brings about the union of the present and the future: "Thy Kingdom come"—"Come quickly".

A. MAILLOT

PREACHING

1. The verbs to preach, to proclaim, are only imperfect renderings of the original expressions. *To preach*, especially, has lost for us its primitive meaning, since it suggests a discourse more or less personal, more or less doctrinal and theoretical, addressed to a closed group of convinced believers within the precincts of the church, and that is the very opposite of what it ought to suggest and indeed of what the original word means: a proclamation made by a herald, by the town crier, in the full light of day, to the sound of a trumpet, up-to-the-minute, addressed to everyone because it comes from the king himself. But *to announce* also is often too weak a term. In the majority of the cases where a message coming from God is involved, it is the translation of verbs taken from the same root (that from which "gospel" and "angel" come) which signifies a solemn public proclamation, and in the R.S.V. that word is used: "you proclaim the Lord's death until He comes" (1 Cor.

11:26); "that which we have seen and heard we proclaim" (1 Jn. 1:3); "as for you, go and proclaim the Kingdom of God" (Lk. 9:60).

These obvious remarks have a very profound significance; they underline the public and universal nature of the *Gospel, which is not to be thought of as another system of teaching, a body of truth or one solution among many others from which we can choose according to our own personal preferences, but which is a proclamation coming from the king, addressed to all, and from whose authority no one can escape. He who preaches the Gospel must preach it to all, since it is valid for all.

2. "Preacher" means herald; to preach is *to act as a herald*. Of a herald the chief requirement is absolute fidelity; he does not have to express his own ideas, but to deliver a message laid upon him; he is not asked for his opinion on the questions at issue, he is merely the mouthpiece of him who has commissioned him. By this very fact he is invested with the authority which he represents and his speech is endowed with an unquestionable prestige. The herald is nothing in himself; he speaks as representative of the one who has sent him and on behalf of the message which has been entrusted to him. So the Twelve do not go of their own accord to proclaim the Gospel; they proclaim it because they are sent: "And preach as you go, saying, The kingdom of heaven is at hand" (Matt. 10:7). They are *agents*, simply spokesmen; their mission is based not on the strength or the sincerity of their convictions, but on Him who sends them, on what God has done in the very event of the coming of Christ, and precisely for this reason they are invested with the *authority* of Him who sends them. Paul says similarly: "How can men preach unless they are sent?" (Rom. 10:15) expressing the idea that preaching is not the outcome of the believer's initiative, but an element in the very purpose of God, in that movement through which God draws near to man to save him: God is the author of the work of redemption and at the same

time of the preaching which proclaims this work (cf. 2 Cor. 5:18).

The preacher does not preach himself; he is not a virtuoso of religion, performing by means of a kind of contagion and imposing his personality upon his audience, but the servant of those to whom he speaks for the sake of Jesus (2 Cor. 4:5). Paul goes so far as to say that it matters little whether the motives from which Christ is preached are pure or impure, provided only that He is proclaimed (Phil. 1:15–18). That certainly does not mean that the life lived by the preacher does not matter. It does matter both to the preacher, for by living after the flesh he lays himself open to the danger of being himself rejected after having preached to others, and to the message which his life can confirm or contradict (1 Cor. 9:27; 1 Tim. 3:1–7; 2 Tim. 4:5).

Since preaching is an act of divine initiative and has as its object the work of God and its manifestation in Jesus Christ, it is *the word of God Himself* and must be received as such: "He who receives you receives me and he who receives me receives him who sent me" (Matt. 10:40); "He who hears you hears me, and he who rejects you rejects me, and he who rejects me rejects him who sent me" (Lk. 10:16). Jesus makes this claim concerning both the preachers and those who will hear their message, so that the preachers may be set free from all doubt, not about their own qualifications—for "who is sufficient for these things?" (2 Cor. 2:16), and the preacher does not preach about his own qualifications—but about the truth of their preaching and its absolute necessity, since through it the world is set in the presence of God Himself. The hearers, too, must learn that it is not a matter of personal convictions which can be discussed, expounded to them by human personalities who are also subjects of discussion, but the truth which determines their salvation or their perdition (2 Cor. 2:14–16). As Christ came into the world, not because the world was psychologically and spiritually ready to receive Him, but because it needed to be saved, so preaching comes to man not as the expression of what

he can already see and think by himself, but as the challenge which wrests him from himself to bring him into submission to God and His purpose. That is why Paul writes: "Preach the word, be urgent in season and out of season" (2 Tim. 4:2): do not let yourself be deluded by what you think to be favourable circumstances, nor paralysed by psychological conditions which you deem to be unfavourable; times and circumstances are certainly not to be ignored —they form part of the human situation in which Christ must be preached—but it must be made clear that God alone creates and knows the opportunity (Col. 4:3–6).

3. *The object of preaching*, which never varies, is designated in a variety of ways and described more or less explicitly. Jesus and His disciples preach the *Gospel of the *Kingdom (Matt. 4:23; 9; 35; Lk. 8:1; Acts 20:25; 28:31), the advent of God for man's salvation and the end of the reign of the Evil One. Preaching is accompanied by *miracles, healing of diseases, and particularly the expulsion of evil spirits; these are not two parallel activities, but two aspects, united in their very essence, of the same event: the Kingdom is coming, the bonds which enslave man are beginning to fall away. The word of Jesus is not simple teaching, but the proclamation of a deed, the decisive intervention of God in history (Matt. 10:7f.). Where John the Baptist, Jesus or His disciples preach *repentance (Matt. 3:1; Acts 10:37; Matt. 4:17; Mk. 6:12), they are not setting forth a high moral standard, but again, explicitly or implicitly, they are proclaiming salvation, the work of God: they are announcing the time of repentance, because the Kingdom and salvation are imminent, already even present, though hidden. The Kingdom of God is not a reality which is distinct from Jesus Christ, it is in Him that the Kingdom comes and must be recognized (Matt. 11:5f.; Lk. 7:22f.; 11:20).

This is why Christian preaching can be described simply as to preach *Christ* (Acts 8:5; Phil. 1:15), which means that the preaching proclaims that Jesus is the Christ, the Son of God, the fulfilment of God's promises (Acts 9:20). This, too, is why in the Gospel of John, *Jesus Himself appears as the sole object of the preaching. The death and resurrection of Jesus are the central facts in the event of salvation and the essential objects of the preaching (1 Cor. 1:17–25; 15:12–20; Rom. 4:25). To express this systematically, it might be stated that the former event, showing as it does the inevitable end of the man who has rejected God and whom God abandons, is the proclamation of the judgment and death of man: in dying for me, the Son reveals my death, the barrier which God's judgment erects against my desire to live; in the second event it appears that Jesus, whose death entails man in death, is also the one in whom the life given by God, the life of the world to come, commences for man (2 Cor. 5:14f.; Gal. 2:20; Rom. 6:5). So that the preaching may be summed up thus: "proclaiming in Jesus the resurrection from the dead" (Acts 4:2), which means not merely that the apostles announced that Jesus was risen, but that in Him, whom men crucified, the life of the age to come has made, for dead men like us, its appearance in the world (1 Cor. 15:20).

4. To preach is *to proclaim the word* (Mk. 2:2; Acts 4:29,31; Phil. 1:14; Heb. 13:7). Nowhere in the Bible do we encounter the modern deprecation of speech as opposed to deeds, or the romantic distrust of speech as compared with feeling and mystical silence. This springs from the very idea of *God and of *revelation. God is neither feeling, nor enthusiasm, nor the irrational (any more than He can be equated with reason): He is the one who is face to face with man and who speaks to him, the sovereign "I" addressing man personally. God reveals Himself to man through speech, which is not, as sentimental romanticism would have it, a derivative, lifeless, inferior reality, but the manifestation of the essential nature, the very reality. It is speech which creates and establishes relationship between persons; through it an I communicates with and thus makes itself known to another, the divine I to the human I. Thus speech is inseparable from reality, it is an integral part of the event of salvation, like the death and resurrection of Christ: "God was in Christ, reconciling the world to Himself . . . entrusting to us the message of reconciliation" (2 Cor. 5:19). God saves through Jesus Christ; but it can also be said, for the meaning is just the same, that He saves through preaching (1 Cor. 1:21), for it is by this means that the saving act is proclaimed: it is the unveiled and actively present manifestation of salvation.

Preaching is *the word of faith* (Rom. 10:8). This is not to say that the preacher reveals in his message his own personal faith in order to carry conviction through his sincerity or his fervour; it means the setting of the Christian message over against the law, which might be called the Word of Works (cf. Rom. 3:27). Christian preaching reveals nothing other than the work accomplished by God in Jesus Christ, a work which is the foundation of preaching and faith (1 Cor. 15:14); it declares that in order to be saved a man must confess that Jesus is the Lord and believe that God raised Him from the dead (Rom. 10:9).

CHR. SENFT

PREDESTINATE, *see* ELECT

PRIESTHOOD

O.T.

Although the narratives concerning the patriarchs, Abraham, Isaac, and Jacob, do not allude to priests, it may be assumed that from the very beginning Israel like other nations possessed a priesthood. According to the Pentateuch a very complete priesthood existed at the time of Moses; but such evidence must be used cautiously, for the priesthood and the cultus described in Exodus and Leviticus clearly reflect those of the Temple at Jerusalem. Moses however is presented to us as combining in his own person the threefold functions or ministries of king, priest, and prophet. On their arrival in Canaan the Hebrew people found themselves confronted by a large number of sanctuaries served by priests. Quite naturally they took these over. The task of the priests was to regulate the sacrifices and to give answers to those who came to inquire of God. For this purpose appropriate means were used, among which were the Urim and Thummim, a sort of dice carried by the priest in the pocket of an apron, called the ephod (1 Sam. 23:9, which must not however be confounded with the linen ephod, a short garment worn by David when he danced before the ark: 2 Sam. 6:14, or with the ephod of Gideon which is an idol: Judg. 8:27). The decision thus obtained was called *torah*.

The priest was the intermediary between the people and the divinity to whose sphere he belonged, since like the king (*Ministers O.T.) he was *anointed with oil. The priestly office was hereditarily transmitted. The O.T. is familiar with families or dynasties of priests like that of Eli at Shiloh (1 Sam. 1–4) or that of Ahimelech at Nob (1 Sam. 21). When David took Jerusalem he found himself master of a town which had its established sanctuary, cultus and clergy. Certain indications would lead us to suppose that he retained these and that by the side of Abiathar, who was a descendant of Aaron, Zadok represents the Canaanite priesthood.

As a sacred person, the priest had to observe numerous rites in order to safeguard his holiness. He had to submit to many ceremonies of purification. This is easily understood since he was specially connected with the supremely holy God. He must have no physical defect or infirmity (Lev. 21:16). He was forbidden to shave his head or beard (21:5), or to touch a corpse (21:1). The special *garment he wore is described with a wealth of detail (Exod. 28). Each part of which it was composed served to distinguish him from the common and profane and to announce what was indicated by the golden plate attached to his turban: "Holy to the Lord", i.e. the property of Yahweh (Exod. 28:36). The ordination of priests was the occasion of a solemn ceremony, the object of which was to confirm that they belonged to a special domain,

that of the holy (Exod. 28:41; 29:7; 30:30; Lev. 8:12,33).

The priesthood of which the Bible usually speaks is that of the Temple of Jerusalem. It was headed by the high priest whose prototype was presumed to be Aaron. He had in his entourage a subordinate priest, a superintendent of the Temple, doorkeepers and a large number of priests pure and simple. The supreme authority in matters civil and religious rested in the hands of the king, to whom the Temple belonged. If we are to judge by the census taken of the Jews who returned to Jerusalem after the Exile, the priests would have numbered several thousand (Ezra 2:36ff.). They are divided into a number of classes beginning with the priests, strictly so-called, who were grouped in families. The Levites fulfilled subordinate functions. That is why they show less eagerness to return. In Babylon, owing to the absence of the Temple, they had acquired an importance which they would lose on their return to Jerusalem. Only 74 of them desire to see again the walls of Zion (Ezra 2:40). The question of their origin is difficult to determine. If the existence of a tribe of Levi is indisputable, it is no less true that the word Levite is used as a common noun. It has been suggested that they were perhaps the descendants of the Canaanite priests dispossessed by the Israelites—a supposition which is confirmed by their association with the stranger, the *ger*, who represents the old native Canaanite population (Deut. 26:12). It is possible also that the Levites were those priests who after the reform of Josiah in 621 (2 Kings 22–23), which suppressed the local sanctuaries to the advantage of the royal Temple, were assigned accessory functions at Jerusalem in compensation for the local offices which they had lost. Such a hypothesis would explain the fact that the distinction between priests and Levites, unknown to Deuteronomy, was introduced by Ezekiel. In addition to the Levites Ezra also mentions singers, doorkeepers, and nethinim (Temple servants: 2:41ff.).

It is a well-known fact that after the Exile the number of priests attained enormous dimensions. Ezra reckons 6,000 (2:36–39) and the Chronicler mentions 24,000 Levites, 4,000 singers and 4,000 doorkeepers (1 Chr. 23:4–5). Fanciful as such figures may appear, they none the less explain why it was impossible for the priests to inhabit Jerusalem, and their division into 24 classes (1 Chr. 24:7–18) which functioned in turns in the Temple for the space of one week and resided outside the capital; hence the existence of villages for priests in the neighbourhood of Jerusalem.

The priests had charge of the cultus, by which is to be understood the whole complex of words and symbolic actions of which the object was to maintain and safeguard holiness. One special feature which should be mentioned is the religious *feasts, which must have been extremely elaborate, since the twenty-four classes of priests took part in them. Moreover in October the great Day of Atonement was celebrated, on the occasion of which the high priest (called Aaron in Lev. 16) entered the Holy of Holies to sprinkle blood. The sabbath also gave rise to ceremonies in which the priests played an important part. The central point of the cultus was *sacrifice, which is to be understood as a gift offered to God. Individuals could offer such gifts as an expression of their gratitude, to perform a vow, to obtain forgiveness, and to support a petition. Such gifts consisted of animal or vegetable offerings, oil, wheat, salt, or incense.

More important were the sacrifices offered in the name of the people and the expense of which was borne by the king or defrayed by the Temple tax. In Lev. 1–7, a section which is of capital importance for sacrificial laws, the sacrifices are divided into five groups according to the intention with which they were offered and their characteristic ritual. The latter, according to the witness of the Bible, is so elaborate that it required for the service of the altar the collaboration of many priests who were specialists in the manipulation of holy things. Every day on the Temple altar was offered the daily sacrifice, called the continual burnt offering (Num. 28:10,15,24,31,

etc.). In the time of Ezra this consisted in an unblemished lamb offered every morning and evening (Exod. 29:38–42; Num. 28:3–8). This oblation was accompanied by a vegetable offering and libations. When the sacrifice was offered the Levites began to sing and to play on their stringed instruments, while two priests sounded the trumpet (2 Chr. 29:26–28; Num. 10:1,2,10) and the people who were assembled in the Temple for prayer prostrated themselves. Some of the psalms, such as Pss. 24; 48; 81; 82; 92; 93; 94, were sung by Levites on various days of the week. It is understandable that a ritual so highly developed should have required the functioning of numerous priests, Levites, and a large number of minor officials whose duty it was to keep watch over the many parts of the Temple. Another of the offices of the priests was to give replies to those who came to seek in the Temple the will of God for them. The O.T. contains many examples of such priestly oracles.

From the beginning the priests constituted the educated class of the nation. It was the sanctuaries which safeguarded the traditions forming the basis of the biblical writings. *Traditions were developed and enriched, theologies were formulated and moulded in priestly circles. We owe to the priests the successive editings to which the biblical writings were subjected in the course of centuries. Further, the period of residence in Babylon, far from the Temple, was the occasion of a considerable development in the activity of the Scribes, whose importance is so great in the time of Jesus Himself.

Whereas before the Exile the Temple and the priesthood were subject to the authority of the king, the disappearance of the kingship brought about a radical change in the situation. The clergy assumed an ever-increasing importance which was both political and religious, and the Temple became their special property. In the time of Jesus the priesthood constitutes an aristocracy whose head, the high priest, is the equivalent of a sovereign.

However painful may be the impression caused by the conflicts between Jesus and the Temple priesthood, we must note the essential part played by the priests in the formation and preservation of the sacred writings. It may be said in fact that without them we should not have the Bible.

G. PIDOUX

N.T.

The position of the N.T. with regard to the priesthood may seem curiously paradoxical. Jesus Christ enters into the very heart of the cultic life of His people and without criticizing the legitimacy of the priestly institutions of the old covenant, and a few months later no member of His Church will any longer maintain his connection with the Jewish cult; never before did God come so mysteriously close to men and yet never was the very word holy so carefully eschewed; never in Jewish history was such a sacrifice offered, of such incalculable significance, and yet it appeared rather in the light of a surprise, as if the result of flagrant criminal injustice, and in a life where attention seemed concentrated on the prophetic consciousness; henceforth there will be no more clericalism and yet now all believers are priests! To elucidate this tension we have only a few texts at our disposal in which a specific priestly vocabulary is employed. They can easily be grouped around two centres: on the one hand the Epistle to the Hebrews and the figure of the high priest, and, on the other, certain passages of the Epistles which throw some light on what is meant by the royal priesthood of the Church.

1. *Jesus Christ, our high priest.* The author of the Epistle to the Hebrews bears witness to our redemption in the light of the priestly institutions of the O.T. He shows how the latter culminate in the unique and perfect sacrifice offered by *Jesus Christ once for all upon the cross. In His supreme function of high priest Jesus Christ showed Himself to be in fact the perfect Mediator, priest, and victim. He is the perfect Mediator because He is the Son of God and also true man; He is the Son of God from

all eternity (1:1–4) and yet it is especially on earth that He confirmed that Sonship and carried it to its perfection by His total and victorious obedience (5:8–10); He was truly man because He manifested His solidarity with the human condition by sharing our flesh and blood (2:14–18), by submitting to the trial of temptation (4:15), by entering into the very depths of suffering and death with strong cries and tears (5:7). He is the perfect priest because He is so according to the order of Melchizedek, i.e. by exercising His priestly function eternally and without needing to embody it in the framework of an earthly institution (7:1ff.), because it was established by an exceptional divine oath (7:20ff.), because He is eternally alive and thus has no need of a successor (7:23–25) and is holy, innocent, and sinless (4:15; 7:26). He was under no necessity to offer daily sacrifice for His own sins: He was utterly devoted to the service of others (this is the very meaning of the baptism of Jesus). Finally He offered no victim other than Himself; in Him office and offering, priesthood and sacrifice, perfectly coincide. Hence He is the perfect victim of the new covenant; He who voluntarily offered Himself (7:29; 9:27; 10:4–10) to expiate the sins of the people (2:17), who was consecrated by the eternal spirit (9:14) in such a way that His sacrifice is truly final and irrevocable as death itself is irrevocable (9:27); this sacrifice is no longer involved in a liturgical cycle but in the successiveness of time which cannot move back; Christ died on the cross "once for all" (9:12,26; 10:10,14) and by the grace of God the benefits of this death may henceforth be extended to all mankind (2:9).

But the priesthood of Jesus Christ does not stop there: for the author of Hebrews the "chief point" (8:1) is that in offering His own blood our high priest entered once for all into the most holy place, beyond the veil. As though they formed one single supreme action, the death on the cross and the majestic entrance of Christ into the heavenly sanctuary are intimately connected. He is truly our king, clothed in splendour at the right hand of God, and at the same time our high priest who has prepared the way for us and who before the throne tirelessly intercedes on our behalf (6:19–20; 7:25; 8:1ff.; 9:11; 10:11ff.; 12:25). Thus the priesthood of Jesus Christ is presented as the royal way which leads to life, in contrast to the law and the sacrifices of the old covenant which lead to death. Christ has gone before us and is now our intercessor—that is the ground of our hope!

2. *The royal priesthood of the Church.* Thus as believers in the new covenant we are now and once for all sanctified and brought into the way of perfection (Heb. 2:11; 10:14,29). By faith we have been made participators in the life of Christ and have been led by Him into the *rest of God (4:10) since we no longer have to shoulder the desperate burden of sacrifices ever to be renewed, and which can only serve to remind us ever afresh of our constantly accumulating sins (10:3). Just as the law had multiplied transgressions, so the Levitical priesthood strengthened the bondage of sin and confined Israel within a materialistic purity: just as now we have been justified so as to be able to live in obedience, so we have been freed from the necessity of offering all further sacrifice— Christ is our only priest and our only expiatory victim—freed so as to live in praise and thanksgiving as the children of God, so as to be entirely surrendered to the service of witnessing and giving thanks (13:15).

It is within such a framework of ideas that we should view the various passages which speak to us of this new priesthood. Jesus Himself in His word about the Temple of Jerusalem had declared that He would build it again: on the ruins of the Levitical priesthood He did in fact rebuild in the three days between His death and resurrection His Body, the Church, the temple of the living God (2 Cor. 6:16), a spiritual house (1 Pet. 2:5). And if we find nowhere in the N.T. the smallest allusion to a special sacerdotal ministry (to maintain a distinction between priests and believers, to reconstruct a clergy or to repeat the redemptive sacrifice, would be to make void the cross and to deny the continual intercession of Our Lord), it is just this text of 1 Peter which declares "Be yourselves built up into a spiritual house to be a holy priesthood to offer up spiritual sacrifices acceptable to God. . . . You are a chosen race, a royal priesthood . . ." A text to which we find the counterpart in the celestial liturgy of the book of Revelation: "He has freed us from our sins by his blood, he has made us a kingdom, priests unto God his Father . . ." (Rev. 1:6; 5:10; 20:6).

By offering Himself as a pure and spotless victim, the Lamb of God who takes away the sins of the world has made of the people of believers a people of sacrificing priests. But why this people of priests if henceforth there is no redemptive sacrifice to offer? In order to bear witness before the world by praise and preaching to the sacrifice accomplished once for all and the eternal presence before the throne of God of the Lamb that was slain. But why this spiritual temple on the earth if Christ has entered into the heavenly sanctuary? Because the service of intercession in the heavens must also be rendered on earth until the end of time. Why this royal priesthood? Because the Church is the sacerdotal body attached to the person of the King, with the duty of proclaiming to the world the mediation and the Lordship of Christ.

Jesus makes intercession and sanctifies Himself for His own (Jn. 17:19): in union with Him the Church prays, intercedes and is called to sanctify itself for the world. Jesus has offered Himself in sacrifice: in Him the Church's function is to offer itself in sacrifice (it has now nothing to offer but itself) and that is the living and holy sacrifice of our bodies which is our reasonable service as members of the new covenant (Rom. 12:1). Jesus on Golgotha took upon Himself all redemptive *suffering: in union with Him the Church shares in His suffering, not to complete it, for all was completed on the cross, but to know in its fullness the suffering proper to the body of Christ by which we are assured of our part in the pains of the last time, in the birth pangs of the new world, in the suffering of witness-bearing, of the apostolate and of martyrdom (Col. 1:24). Jesus alone could shed the *blood of the new covenant: but in communion with Him His apostle can also shed his own blood as a libation which consecrates the faith of the believers (Phil. 2:17). Even in respect of the collection in favour of the Church at Jerusalem the sacrificial terms of the O.T. recur. St. Paul sees in this a double symbol—both of the offering of our lives and of the communion of the saints, and all this is ranged under the standard of the service of the Church: mutual help and the diaconate, in the same way as adoration and intercession, constitute this new priesthood.

Thus while gradually the rupture between the nascent Church and the old Jewish cultus is becoming ever more complete (the apostles now go up to the Temple at Jerusalem only to pray), while all clericalism markedly disappears from the *ministries of the new Christian community, there reappears throughout the N.T. a sacerdotal vocabulary which concerns the edification of the Church as well as its missionary endeavour, but which receives from Golgotha quite a new significance. Moreover this priesthood, peculiar to the Church, will never wear an institutional aspect; for it sprang from the action of the Holy Spirit Himself. It is the Holy Spirit who makes of this Temple, rebuilt in three days, His dwelling-place, and the word spiritual constantly recurs in all the texts like a *leitmotiv* to describe this house as well as the priesthood, the sacrifices and the offerings, the *worship (in spirit and in truth), the praise, the *hymns and the *prayers of the Church: all is the work of "that one and the selfsame Spirit".

M. BOUTTIER

PROCLAIM, *see* PREACHING

PROMISE

O.T.

1. Accustomed to N.T. vocabulary, we think that the notion of promise by God

to His people, in the old covenant, occupies a central place in the theological thought of Israelite writers. If reference is made to the vocabulary itself, it is nothing of the kind: the Hebrew language has no word corresponding to the noun promise, or to the verb. Silence of this kind does not give us authority, however, to assert that the idea of a promise is absent from the books of the O.T. On the contrary, although the word is lacking, the idea itself is to be found everywhere without its being necessary to use a special term, for ordinary verbs like say, speak—which have lost so much of their force in our modern languages —were sufficient to make it understood that a word pronounced, especially by God, had the value of a solemn promise. This indeed is what is noticed in the texts where our translations use the word promise. The original text in Hebrew uses only the verbs to say ('*amar*) or to speak (*dabar*), and that is enough. This evidence is rich in theological significance: it stresses the importance of the expressions which occur time after time in biblical pages: *God speaks; thus says the Lord; word of God*; etc. The *word of God does not need to be reinforced by special terms, by oaths, by exceptional pledges; when it is pronounced, it is true, and God keeps His word, which has for mankind the force of the most solemn promises. It was later, in Hellenism and in Rabbinic Judaism, that writers were no longer content to use the verb to speak to give full significance to a word, but created a stronger word, like the one meaning to promise (the Rabbis used a word derived from the root: to have confidence, *batah*).

2. It is pointless to pick out passages where man speaking to man makes a promise, often confirmed by an *oath (Neh. 5:12). In such a case, it would be necessary to study the verbs: to swear, make an oath, make a vow, etc. The same words are used when man addresses God and makes a vow to Him (Deut. 23:23). On the other hand, a point which gives us particular interest is the promise that God gives to man when he speaks to Him.

Certainly the promising is reciprocal, as is shown especially in Deut. 26:17,18: "You have declared this day concerning the Lord that he is your God . . . and the Lord has declared this day concerning you that you are a people for his own possession, as he has promised you. . . ." However, if the circumstances are sought in which the word of God implied more especially the character of a promise, it seems to be in the two following cases: the promise made to *Abraham* and the promise made to *David*.

(*a*) At the beginning of Israel's history, God's solemn word to Abraham (Gen. 13:14–17) reproduced by the various traditions which make up Genesis (15:18; 17:3–8; 22:15–18), repeated to Isaac (26:3) and to Jacob (28:13–14) indubitably marks a triple promise of God to the ancestors of the people. When reference is made, in other texts, to one or other of these promises, the reference is really to Abraham whether it be explicit or not: it is firstly the announcement of a posterity as numerous as the stars of heaven or the dust of the earth (Neh. 9:23; 1 Chr. 27:23), but it is especially the gift of the land of Canaan, "flowing with milk and honey", to be Israel's land and the Lord's dwelling place among His people (Deut. 1:21; 6:3; 19:8; 31:20–23; Exod. 12:25; Num. 32:11; Neh. 9:8,15,23). Lastly it is the announcement of a blessing by God of His people who will receive from Him prosperity and the material goods necessary for their happiness and peace (Lev. 26:3–13; Deut. 11:13–17; 28:11–14; Num. 10:29).

(*b*) Concerning the promise made to *David* that he would always have a descendant on his throne, we find it referred to in 2 Sam. 7:12,16,28–29, and it is repeated several times because of its importance in the people's destiny (2 Kings 8:19; 1 Chr. 17:26–27; 2 Chr. 1:9; 7:18; 21:7; Ps. 132:11–12). David's kingship was considered as the ideal period of the people's past in Canaan, and the memory of that promise in later tradition was to remain alive when people thought about the future of God's people and about the king who was to reign over them.

3. We could indicate other texts where the words of God have the special force of a promise, but we believe that no other was to play the part taken by these two promises made to Abraham and David. It is enough to recall how important among the eschatological and Messianic preoccupations of the O.T. was the place occupied in Israel's hope by these two elements: God's kingdom will be like the gift of the real promised land to the people (Jer. 32:37–38; Ezek. 28:25–26; 37:25–28) and the king that God will give to His people for ever will be a new David or a descendant of David's (Jer. 23:5; Ezek. 34:24; 37:24–25).

F. MICHAELI

N.T.

1. (*a*) In *classical Greek*, the word promise often has a juridical sense: it means a decree promulgated by the State, or the deposition of a complaint. In everyday language, to promise is to give prior notice of what one intends to do. With hardly a single exception, it deals with declarations made by a man to one of his fellows or to a god, and not with a pledge by the deity to men.

(*b*) O.T. *Greek* (Septuagint Version) does not contain the words to promise and a promise. However, these two terms appear in texts dating from the *Judaic period*. When they have a religious sense, they refer to statements that God makes to men. The question debated by the rabbis was to know what conditions the faithful must fulfil in order to be beneficiaries of the divine promises.

2. The promise holds a central place in the N.T. It may be said that the N.T. is based on the idea that the promises made formerly by God to the patriarchs and to the people of Israel are fulfilled in Jesus Christ, that "all the promises of God find their Yes in him" (2 Cor. 1:20). They had already been partially carried out in the old covenant: for example, Abraham lived in the promised land; but it was only an imperfect and temporary dwelling-place,

where he lived as a stranger; he was waiting for the definitive city built by God Himself (Heb. 11:8–10,13). It is only in Jesus Christ that God's promises receive their perfect fulfilment (Acts 13:23,32–33; Rom. 15:8; Gal. 3:14). And the Gospel, the good news that the Church must publish in the world, consists in proclaiming that the promises formerly transmitted through the prophets are fulfilled in the person of Jesus of Nazareth (Rom. 1:2–3).

The prophets had foretold that, in the last days, the Spirit of the Lord would be shed on every creature (Joel 2:28–29). Jesus Christ made this a reality at Pentecost (Lk. 24:49; Acts 1:4–5; 2:16–21,32–33). The time of waiting has passed then, the coming of Christ has opened the latter *time, the time of fulfilment. The consummation of all things is imminent (Heb. 10:25,37). It is true that it has not yet taken place, and mockers hold a strong position when they accuse the Christians' hope of foolishness (2 Pet. 3:3–4); that is why believers must be encouraged to persevere in the faith, for they can still fall back into unbelief and cut themselves off from the promise (Heb. 6:11–12; 10:36; 4:1–2). But let them take courage: if their Lord delays the carrying out of His promise, it is not through weakness, it is through His patience, in order to give all men an opportunity to repent (2 Pet. 3:9); and the day will certainly come when He will give to His own what He has promised, for He undertook it on oath (Heb. 6:13–20). For the rest, God has given a guarantee to believers, a tangible pledge of the fulfilment of His promise: He has affixed to His promise the seal of His Spirit, which constitutes the first-fruits, the *earnest of the final consummation (Rom. 8:23; 2 Cor. 1:22; 5:5; Eph. 1:13–14).

3. The N.T. writers use various images to describe the *content* of God's promises: they say that believers will be raised to the dignity of the children of God (Rom. 9:8; Gal. 4:28), that as such they will one day receive an *inheritance (Gal. 3 : 18, 29), which is defined by the terms *kingdom (Jas. 2:5) and eternal *life (Tit. 1:2; Jas. 1:12; 1 Jn. 2:25). In a word, the promises concern the salvation brought by the Messiah at the end of time. These promises are better than those on which the old covenant rested, for nothing now stands in the way of their fulfilment (Heb. 8:6).

4. But who are the *beneficiaries* of the divine promise? The promise is addressed to Abraham and his posterity (Rom. 4:13), that is, primarily, to the people of Israel (Rom. 9:4). In the old covenant, the Gentiles were excluded from the promise (Eph. 2:12). That is why Christ first exercised His ministry among the members of His nation, the circumcised (Rom. 15:8). But the new *covenant is new because among other things it excludes nobody. Abraham's real posterity are not his blood descendants, but those who live by the same faith as his, whatever their origin may be (Rom. 4:16). Properly speaking, only Jesus Christ deserves the title of child of Abraham (Gal. 3:16). But those who belong to Him, that is to say, those who are united to Him by faith—and by *baptism which is its seal—become members of Abraham's posterity, and, consequently, heirs of the promises (Gal. 3:26–29).

God has the power to perform what He has promised; to doubt it is to cast a slur on His glory (Rom. 4:20–21). That is why the inheritance is reserved for those who through faith take as their own the word of the Gospel (Heb. 4:1–2). The fulfilment of the promise depends on God alone, and not on the efforts of man (Rom. 4:16). Whoever tries to obtain the inheritance by observance of the law, in fact nullifies the promise, since he behaves as if it were valueless (Rom. 4:13–14; Gal. 3:18). The inheritance has been guaranteed by testament. The *law, which only supervened after the event, can change nothing in the latter's dispositions: God gave the law so that man may discover his sin and his inability to save himself, and so that he may be thus led to the faith (Gal. 3:15–29).

This does not contradict 2 Cor. 7:1; indeed, in this text, the Christian's duty of sanctification is not presented as a condition to be fulfilled in order to receive the promised good things; on the contrary, it is because they have received outstanding promises that believers are invited to sanctify themselves, in order to honour the Lord who grants them the promises. The divine promise is then the foundation of the Christian's obedience as well as of his hope.

A. GOY

PROPHECY

O.T.

1. The O.T. testifies to an expectation, a waiting for the coming of God. A great hope, based on what Israel's God did and said in the past, animates its pages. The O.T. lives as a consequence of a promise, the fulfilment of which it does not yet see, it looks forward to the future. The O.T. thus looks beyond itself, it aims at a goal which is out of its reach: left to itself, it would remain incomplete. In one sense the entire O.T. is prophecy, since it announces, foreshadows, prepares a future event. It has real meaning only by virtue of an act of God which will mark its completion and its crowning at the same time. The O.T. is only a rough sketch of what will one day be a reality.

It is striking to discover, even in the seemingly most unprophetic writings, the importance of this waiting for the "Day of Yahweh". History, like the cult, only has meaning in Israel because of the hope of the *Kingdom of God. Thus the historical books are arranged among the prophetic writings—a significant fact; they are just as much concerned with the future as with the past of God's people. The psalmists testify to a passionate waiting for the God of Israel, without whose coming their faith and the struggle which it imposes on them become absurd. The Israelite *feasts give regular reminders of Yahweh's great deeds in order to strengthen the hope of the faithful. The Pentateuch itself looks beyond Moses, the Exodus and Sinai, towards the time when Israel, freed at last from all bondage, will be the holy nation of the holy God. In short the O.T., in its totality, proclaims, sings and summons the coming of its God.

2. Naturally it is in the really prophetic books that this aspect of the message finds its clearest expression. But nowhere do we have to deal with a systematic teaching on the future of God's people. The prophecies always remain fragmentary, and to some extent occasional; they are scattered from Genesis to Malachi and it is not possible to summarize them, all the more because they are very diverse, even when they do not openly contradict one another.

The prophets did not have in general the intention of giving a complete picture of future events. They must not be confused with the apocalyptic writers who dream of writing the history of the last days down to the most minute details and often lose themselves in fanciful and ambiguous lucubrations; the prophets are primarily preachers (*Ministry O.T., *Revelation O.T.).

Prophecy then is not a simple prediction; it is a proclamation of God's intentions with regard to His people and the world, it is a message spoken before somebody just as much as before such and such an event. Prophecy presupposes a certain audience, it is addressed to a particular public, it answers to a precise situation. There is nothing vague or abstract about it; it implies a well-defined time and place. It is a prediction spoken at a particular moment in Israel's history and this history must be known in order to understand the prophecy. It is not a message of general application, valid in all circumstances; it varies with the destiny of God's people, and its diversity was already a source of surprise to the contemporaries of Isaiah who reminded them that there was a time for each thing: to plough, as to sow, to announce salvation as to predict judgment (cf. Isa. 28:23–29).

It is then important to be thoroughly conversant with the historical character, and in a particular way for each case, of each of the O.T. prophecies. Amos, Isaiah, Jeremiah, Ezekiel appear at different stages of

Israel's history and are themselves aware of the ever-changing circumstances to which their preaching must be adapted.

3. But prophecy is not limited to any particular event, it is part of a history: the history of God's people. It presupposes a *covenant between Yahweh and Israel, it depends on a contract which unites God to a particular people, it even has the mission of confirming the validity of this agreement and of giving reminders of its implications. Prophecy transmits to each Israelite generation the Word which God gave in former times to the patriarchs; it makes it a thing of the present, it reassesses it in the light of the varying situations in which the elected people finds itself. In one sense, prophecy makes no innovations; it limits itself to reforming. Prophecy in effect intervenes at the critical points of sacred history where Israel is definitely turning away from Yahweh and succumbing to all the temptations which the world offers. Prophecy corrects and sets God's people right again, it sets the people squarely before the divine Word without which they would be nothing; it calls the people to the faith and asks them to take without delay decisions which involve their future. Time after time prophecy reacts against Israel and goes counter to the evidence of human history. It announces, in happy times, unthinkable disasters, it promises unforeseeable liberation to the desperate; at all times it testifies to God's extraordinary faithfulness to His promises.

4. As its object prophecy has God Himself and not a certain number of precepts on future events. It does not state some truths, it bears witness to the Truth. It does not speak of judgment or of salvation but of the God who comes to punish or to pardon. It places Israel in front of Someone and not in front of something, it reveals to the elected people its covenant partner, the God who is at hand, the God who goes out to meet His own and intervenes in the affairs of the world.

So prophecy is in God's service, and He is its master. He is not bound by the prophets' oracles; He depends only on Himself, and on His *word which is eternally living, concrete, personal. The O.T. prophecies must not be placed above the God of Israel; even the prophets must always receive afresh the oracles that they have to transmit to the people; they are not exempt from surprises (cf. Jer. 28).

Prophecy does not depend on the forms in which it is expressed, but on God; it announces, in a form always adapted to the historical situation, the God who personally makes an approach to men.

5. The O.T. is then eager for its realization. Of course, it is already aware of a certain fulfilment, for the word of God does not remain ineffectual. Events confirm it, history carries it out, but at the same time it is clear that all that happens to God's people refers to a future when the divine promise will receive full consecration. In the O.T. there exists a curious dialectic of prophecy and fulfilment. The promise is made real from time to time in history, but in its turn history becomes prophecy: each fulfilment of the word of God announces a still more decisive event for the world, each fulfilment is charged with a message concerning the future of the elected people. Thus the judgments of God that fall upon Israel foreshadow a judgment which will be the final point of human destiny; similarly the successive liberations from which the elected people profit suggest a more complete deliverance; the Davidic kingdom as well evokes an image of a sovereign who will be more fully the faithful servant of Yahweh. History reveals by what has come to pass that it has not yet reached the objective indicated by prophecy which, stage by stage, is renewed, is made more precise and more profound.

In one sense the O.T. is being fulfilled all the time, but neither does it stop prophesying; in announcing the coming of God among men, a coming whose mystery is greater and whose grace richer in proportion as it meditates on the divine promise, the O.T. testifies that "it did not obtain what had been promised, God having something better in mind in order that it should not reach the objective without us" (cf. Heb. 11:40).

R. MARTIN-ACHARD

N.T.

In the N.T., this term designates firstly the declarations by the prophets of the old covenant (Matt. 13:14; 2 Pet. 1:20) as they are recorded in the O.T. (and not only in the prophetic books properly so-called) and even in other writings which were in the end not included in the Bible (cf. Jude 14). It is also applied to a new prophetic activity characteristic of the Christian Church.

1. *The old prophecy*, constantly recalled and quoted in the N.T., is old from the point of view of its *fulfilment in Christ and in the Church. Jesus Himself turns to it to suggest that He is the Messiah (Lk. 4:16–21; cf. Matt. 11:4–6). It enlightens the disciples after the crucifixion and the resurrection of their master (Lk. 24:25–27, 44–47), as at Pentecost (Acts 2). It serves as a basis for the proving of the Messiahship of Jesus to the Jews and other readers of the O.T. (Matt. 1:22; 2:6,15,17–18,23, etc.; Jn. 1:45 f.; Acts 13:27,29; 17:11; Rom. 1:2; 16:26; 1 Pet. 1:10–12). Note that interpretation of prophecy could not be left to the arbitrary whim of individuals: a product of the Holy Spirit, it cannot be truly understood without the help of the same Spirit (2 Pet. 1:20–21; cf. Lk. 24:45; 2 Cor. 3:14–16; 2 Pet. 3:2,16). O.T. prophecy is not restricted to enlightening the Christian present in which it is made real. As all that it announces is not yet fulfilled, it still helps to nourish the hope of believers, in cooperation with the new prophecy, which moreover takes up the themes, the images and the very declarations of the old (cf. Mk. 13 and parallels; 2 Thess. 1 and 2; 2 Pet. 1:19; Revelation).

2. *The new prophecy* appears then as the resumption and continuation of the old in the light of saving events to which the N.T. bears witness. After greeting the Christ who is to come, through the lips of the priest Zacharias who performs the exceptional act of prophesying on the day of his son's birth (Lk. 1:67–70); after preparing the ways of the Lord by the ministry of John the Baptist, consecrated as a prophet before his birth (Lk. 1:15–17; 76–77; 3:1–17 and parallels; Mk. 11:32; Matt. 14:5; 21:26); after recognizing the expected Messiah in the child of Joseph and Mary, through the declarations of the inspired believer Simeon (Lk. 2:25–35) and the prophetess Anna (Lk. 2:36–38), it was not to disappear: the life, death and resurrection of Jesus, by fulfilling the old prophecies, but without exhausting them, were on the contrary to strengthen the expectation of their full realization and to evoke, as well as to allow, new insight into the fulfilment of God's plans now and at the last day.

(a) Let us note that it is inaccurate to have called *Jesus a prophet (Mk. 6:15; 8:28 and parallels; Matt. 21:11,46; Lk. 7:16; 9:8; 24:19; Jn. 4:19; 9:17). It is true that He did not scorn to designate Himself as such (Matt. 13:57 and parallels; Lk. 13:33): did He not bring the revelation of the mystery of God's *Kingdom (Matt. 11:25–27; Mk. 4:11 and parallels) and did His look not penetrate the future (Mk. 13,14:62 and parallels)? Like John the Baptist, He was even identified with one of the old prophets (Lk. 9:19): indeed, He did not withhold upon occasion the imparting of a divine revelation; the supernatural knowledge that He had of God's plans led Him into a many-sided ministry (Lk. 24:19) which absorbed His whole being. However, the N.T. sees more than a prophet in Jesus; nor does it ever say that Jesus prophesies, any more than it speaks of the prophecies of Jesus. Indeed, for Christians, the word of Christ rises above any prophetic word of the old or the new covenant, for empirical prophecy knows only in part (1 Cor. 13:9), while Jesus knows the Father as a person (Matt. 11:27; Jn. 14:6–11): He is the very *Word of God (Jn. 1:14; cf. Matt. 24:35), He is the Lord. The current idea of prophecy seems inadequate then when we wish to speak about Him, unless He is called the *Prophet* in the absolute sense, as is done in the fourth Gospel (Jn. 6:14; 7:40), in reference to the prophecy of Mal. 3:1; 4:5-6 (cf. also Deut. 18:15), according to which at the end of *time a prophet was to come, responsible for preparing Israel for the last judgment. Then it is understood that Jesus is the supreme and perfect revealer of God.

(*b*) In contrast, the question of prophet and prophecy in the usual sense of the terms arises when the N.T. expresses itself on the subject of the early Church. Except for the prophecy of the two witnesses of Rev. 11, which, in the manner of O.T. prophecy, appears as the public revelation of judgments which are to strike the earth and a call to repentance, the new prophecy is in a more or less narrow relationship with the cult. It is an internal function of the Church. New converts who receive the Holy Spirit *prophesy*, when they confess their faith and share with their brethren the revelation which has just enlightened them (Acts 19:6). In this sense, prophecy can be the lot of all believers (Acts 2:17). Similarly any believer, man or woman (1 Cor. 11:4-5; but cf. 14:34) may be called to pass on to the community a revelation given by the Lord in the course of worship (cf. 1 Cor. 14:30). Yet prophecy also appears, and especially so, as the gift that God grants only to certain Christians (Acts 11:27-28; 15:32; 21:9) for the common good (1 Cor. 12:7-11), with a view to edifying the Church (1 Cor. 14:5). This gift is at the origin of a recognized *ministry and one that is held in high esteem, that of prophet, which Paul places immediately after that of apostle (1 Cor. 12:28; Eph. 4:11; cf. 2:20).

"He who prophesies speaks to men for their upbuilding and encouragement and consolation" we read in 1 Cor. 14:3. Prophecy is distinguished from *teaching (*Ministry) by its character of a direct message in relation to the situation of the brother or of the community to which it is addressed, and by its reference to a particular divine revelation (cf. 1 Cor. 14:30). This revelation may also be a prediction concerning the future of a member of the community (Acts 21:10-14) or of the whole community (Acts 11:27-28), a deeper knowledge of the Gospel (1 Cor. 14:6; 13:2; cf. 2:7-16), the answer to a problem born of the faith (1 Cor. 15:50-57) or a series of visions concerning the end of this world and the appearance of the new world, as is the case in the Apocalypse (= Revelation) of St. John. Eph. 3:2-7 is typical of the language that an apostle may use before a community when he is the recipient of a prophetic revelation. Prophecy also plays a decisive part when the question arises of recognizing the ministry that the Lord entrusts to a brother (1 Tim. 1:18; 4:14; cf. Acts 13:1-3; 9:10-19). Interventions like those suggested by 1 Cor. 5:3-5 or Acts 5:1-11 and 8:20-23 also have a prophetic character.   From what goes before we may assess the all-important rôle of prophecy: it is through it that Christ reigns over His Church.

Like every good thing, prophecy is threatened: it can be supplanted, as at Corinth, by ecstatic and unintelligible speech (1 Cor. 14); a prophet may venture outside what is permitted to him by the measure of faith that has been granted to him (Rom. 12:6). The faithful must beware then of false prophets (Matt. 7:15; Mk. 13:22 and parallels; 1 Jn. 4:1). Our concern is not so much to despise prophesyings, as to prove all things and hold fast that which is good (1 Thess. 5:20-21; cf. 1 Cor. 14:29; 1 Jn. 4:1; Rev. 16:13, etc.). The gift of prophecy recalls then the complementary gift of discerning of spirits (1 Cor. 12:10).

J. BURNIER

PUNISH, *see* JUDGMENT, REWARD

RACE, *see* NATIONS

RANSOM

An idea characteristic of the Bible and especially of the O.T., where, as expressed by various Hebrew terms, it plays a part of considerable importance in the social and religious life of Israel.

O.T.

1. The idea first emerges in connection with ancient family law, according to which a man could ransom the property and persons of his nearest kinfolk from one who had obtained possession of them (Lev. 25:23–55; cf. Ruth 2:20; 4:1–8). The one who was entitled to exercise this privilege—called in Hebrew *go'el*—was also, as our translations say, the avenger of blood: it was his duty to avenge in some way the blood of his kinsman by shedding that of the murderer (Num. 35:10–28; Deut. 19:1–13; Josh. 20).

In Second Isaiah the term is applied to the God of Israel Himself (Isa. 40ff.). Our versions translate by such words as Saviour or Redeemer (Isa. 41:14; 43:14; 44:24; etc.). The description suggests the close ties which bind the Eternal God to His people: the fact of Israel's *election links the Eternal God to her and creates for Him obligations toward her as strict as those of the ties of blood (cf. Isa. 41:8). "The holy one of Israel is your Redeemer" means: your God who, because of His holiness, has punished you and sold you as a slave (Isa. 50:1) is nevertheless your *go'el*. Hence He ransoms you from bondage (Isa. 43:1–3). If in the latter text it is stated that Egypt, Ethiopia and Seba are given as a ransom for Israel, the phrase cannot be understood in the sense of a literal transaction; the prophet is simply applying to God and to the liberation of Israel—and only in so far as that is possible—the image of ransoming.

When the religion of Israel became individualized, the idea of God as Redeemer was transferred from the national to the individual plane. For example, in Job 19:25 we find that the unhappy man in some sense appeals from the God who strikes him down and causes him to die, to the God who is his Ransomer, his *go'el*, and who, after his death, will vindicate his righteousness.

2. The O.T. attaches to the idea of ransom another characteristic meaning, denoted by the root *kpr* from which on the one hand comes a noun of more or less secular usage corresponding to our word ransom (literally, covering) and on the other hand a verb belonging almost exclusively to religious terminology and, in particular, to the language of sacrifice, and denoting the idea of expiation, generally by means of a bloody sacrifice. Every time it is a question of the offering of compensation in order to rescue from death or from an unhappy fate a human life which has thus been struck down in consequence of a sin against man or God (Exod. 21:30; 30:11–16; Num. 35:31–32; Job 33:24; Prov. 6:35; 13:8; Isa. 43:3–4). In the former case, the ransom generally consists in the payment of a sum of money: in the latter, God in His mercy accepts the blood, i.e. the life, of an animal in exchange for that of the guilty man whom He regards in consequence as acquitted. (See *Sacrifice.)

3. Lastly, Israel had a number of terms parallel to our words to ransom, ransom, redeemer, and which had no special connotation beyond the implication that the object of the redemption was living beings only. These terms formed from the root *pdh* are thus used to denote the ransom of a slave (Exod. 21:8) as also the ransom of a human or animal first-born which as such was dedicated to the Eternal (Exod. 13:1–16; 34:19–20; Num. 3:46–51). They are also applied to God to signify that He is the Liberator of His people (Deut. 7:8; 13:5, etc.; 2 Sam. 7:23; Neh. 1:10; Ps. 25:22; 44:27, etc.) or of certain members of His people (2 Sam. 4:9; 1 Kings 1:29; Ps. 144:10; Jer. 15:21, etc.). It should be noted that the O.T. offers us only one text in which it is a question of God redeeming men from their sins (Ps. 130:7–8). This fact is to be explained by the regular practice of institutional expiatory sacrifice. On the other hand it is expected that God will redeem the soul (i.e. the life) of His servants from the death which threatens them (Ps. 34:23; 49:16, etc.) as from all other tribulations (Ps. 26:11; 31:6, etc.). This divine redemption, it has already been pointed out, does not imply the payment of a ransom: for God disposes of all things in accordance

with His sovereign transcendence. One further point should be noted: while the verb studied in section 1 denotes particularly a deliverance which God grants out of His fidelity, flowing from that act of election by which He has made Himself responsible for His people, the verb at present under consideration suggests rather that God intervenes in complete freedom, by sheer grace.

N.T.

The idea of ransoming, so common in the O.T., occurs less frequently in the N.T. Nevertheless it does play a part of considerable importance. On the one hand, it is used to illuminate the meaning of the death of Jesus; on the other, it indicates the deliverance which will be effected for believers at the Second Coming of the Lord.

1. "For the Son of Man also came not to be served but to serve and to give His life as a ransom for many" (Mk. 10:45; Matt. 20:28). This is a text of capital importance which is echoed at many points in the apostolic writings (1 Cor. 6:20; 7:23; 1 Tim. 2:6; Tit. 2:14; Heb. 9:12; 1 Pet. 2:18–19; Acts 5:9) as it is also reflected in one of the fundamental articles of the Church creed (1 Cor. 15:3; cf. 2:2). In this declaration Jesus explains the meaning of His Messianic vocation (see *Jesus, Son of Man): the whole meaning of His life is to serve, even to the point of sacrificing His life for those whom He serves. This death, says Jesus, will be a ransom for many: in sacrificing His life He will liberate other lives. From what will He liberate them? According to the Gospel of St. Mark it can only be that He will rescue them from their alienation from God, from the sin which subjugates and enslaves them. He will effect this liberation by undergoing in their stead the death which was meant for them, death in stark loneliness and abandonment by God. It is clear that Jesus will pay this ransom to no one but God, whose holy and righteous anger weighs on sinners. Jesus does not tell us why God requires of Him just this: He simply indicates the meaning of His death without telling us why it must be so. It would be useless to seek an explanation of this mystery in the speculations of mediaeval theology on the nature of God (e.g. the relation between His mercy and justice, and the offence to His honour which required satisfaction) for in so doing we should be leaving the plane on which the thought of Jesus moves: this thought is controlled solely by the fact of the unique fellowship with His Father in which He lives and by His mission to reconcile man with God. It is against this background that Jesus declared to sinners the forgiveness of God. But if He was not to cause them to minimize the gravity of sin and to blunt their sense of the divine demand, He must at the same time give them proof of His own utter loyalty to the will of the holy God to whom the sinner is odious and who perforce pronounces on him the sentence of death. Hence Jesus could only deliver men from the enslavement of sin by undergoing in their presence the punishment which was their due. Nothing less was necessary to bring us to a new life in joyous and entire obedience to God.

As regards the apostle Paul's theological amplification of this theme, we would single out in particular such passages as 1 Cor. 6:20 and 7:23 where he affirms that, having been redeemed, Christians no more belong to themselves or to other men but solely to God, and also Gal. 3:13 and 4:5 where the apostle shows, by a rabbinical argument which is difficult for us to follow, the effects of the sacrifice of Jesus from the standpoint of our relations with the law of Moses: Christ born under the *law has become in our place the object of its curse, with the result that our obligations toward it are now cancelled and we are free to live outside its dominion as the sons of God who are dependent only on Him.

2. We have seen emerge in the language of the O.T. an idea of redemption which in effect leaves aside the meaning of ransom and retains only that of emancipation and

deliverance. In Judaism already, but especially in primitive Christianity, under the influence of belief in the imminent advent of the Kingdom of God, this idea gained special emphasis and acquired a note of peculiar fervour reflected for example in Luke 1:68; 2:38; 21:28. This is because deliverance is understood to be total and final. Yet when the apostle Paul speaks of redemption, it is at times in reference to something which believers are still awaiting (Rom. 8:23; Eph. 1:14; 4:30) and at other times in reference to something which they already possess in Christ (Rom. 3:24; 1 Cor. 1:30; Eph. 1:7; Col. 1:14). In fact, for Christians, redemption is already at least partially realized and present through the *Holy Spirit whom they have received. Their expectation of what is still to come (the redemption of the body, emancipation from the present structure of our life, etc.) is in consequence more assured and fervent.

3. We might also mention a meaning of the word redeem which is unrelated to the foregoing and which is to be found in the two parallel texts Eph. 5:16 and Col. 4:5: "Redeem the time." The Greek verb here means "buy up", exhausting every possibility. *Time in this phrase means opportunity, the auspicious moment. Hence the meaning is: make full use of your opportunities (Masson), learn how to take advantage of every opportunity (Goguel) so as to bear true witness to Christ by your conduct (Ephesians) and your speech (Colossians).

J. BURNIER

RECONCILIATION

1. Among the terms which describe the new situation of mankind subsequent to the death of Jesus on the cross, that of reconciliation occupies a special place: if in meaning it is very closely related to words like *salvation, justification, *peace, in form it is distinguished by the peculiarity that it derives from no word in the O.T. nor in Hellenistic religious language. The event of redemption brought about so radical a change in the situation of man, and was of such special significance religiously, that a new and original word was needed to denote it. Moreover, the word was destined to play a part in Christian thought which curiously far surpasses the place which it occupies in the N.T. itself: in its theological sense it is met with in 5 passages only, all of Pauline origin (Rom. 5:10–11; 11:15; 2 Cor. 5:18–20; Col. 1:20,22; Eph. 2:16): 5 passages only but 5 passages which are of vital importance. The root of the Greek term means other or different. The first derivatives normally mean to change (e.g. the accusation brought against Stephen at the time of his trial in Acts 6:14: "For we have heard him say: that this Jesus of Nazareth will *change* the customs which Moses delivered to us"). By the addition of another prefix classical Greek had created a second term whose primary meaning remained "to change" with the double implication "transform" and "exchange", hence by derivation arose the ordinary secular meaning "reconcile" (reconcile adversaries or reconcile a husband and wife, etc.). The noun undergoes the same evolution from exchange to reconciliation.

2. We have already emphasized the fact that the word reconciliation has no exact equivalent in Hebrew (the LXX as we shall see uses it only in the Maccabees). But it is evident that we might assemble a whole body of O.T. texts or ideas which more or less precisely foreshadow its use. For example, reference can be made to those passages which allude to the restoration of the rebellious people to the favour of Yahweh. In particular we should be justified in invoking the propitiatory *sacrifices, the ceremonies of the great day of expiation in the sabbatical year, the Day of Atonement (Lev. 16:17,25). Did not the Day of Atonement mean for Israel a new departure, a transformed situation, in which the commercial transactions and debts, the faults and impurities, the weight of the past no longer sullied relations with Yahweh nor of men with each other? Appeal has also been

made to the death of the 7 martyrs which according to Macc. 17:1 inaugurated a new epoch in Israel. Further, reference can be made to various prophetic texts, that of Isaiah 11, for example, where the reign of the Messiah brings about a sort of cosmic reconciliation of the creatures, and that of Hos. 2:23 cited by Paul in Rom. 9:25: "Those who were not my people, I will call my people, and her who was not beloved, I will call beloved." Finally we must remember all the prophecies and prayers which foretell and appeal to the great intervention of God in favour of His people at the end of time, that restoration of Jerusalem which often seems like the signal for a universal reconciliation. Such possible antecedents could clearly be multiplied.

To conclude this O.T survey we will come to the only passages where the word is specifically employed in the LXX: viz. 2 Macc. 5:20; 1:5; 7:33; 9:20 (e.g. 2 Macc. 1:5; "May God hear your prayers and be reconciled with you"). It is important to note that for the Jewish piety of this period a return to grace seems inevitably bound up with human initiative: pray, repent, offer sacrifices and the Lord will be moved and will turn away from you His anger (cf. the "Return to me and I will return to you"). This point will enable us better to understand what is so extraordinary in the Gospel.

3. In order to understand the meaning which the word assumes in the N.T., let us note the affirmations of the various texts which mention reconciliation and infer from them its subject, object, circumstances, and consequences.

(a) The Subject. In Rom. 6:11; 2 Cor. 5:18ff., the subject is God. In Col. 1:20,22 it is the pleroma, i.e. God Himself, likewise expressed in terms proper to this Epistle. Only Ephesians refers to Jesus Christ as the subject, but it should be noted that Christ is mentioned here simply as the one who fulfils the plan of God concerning Israel and the heathen. Thus there is complete agreement: without doubt it is God alone who is the sole initiator of this movement of reconciliation, which is unaffected by the attitude of His creatures. It is He who has decided upon this action and who unceasingly fulfils it: "All this is from God" (2 Cor. 5:18).

(b) The Object of reconciliation. According to Rom. 5, this is ourselves, the enemies of God (and not ourselves as believers); according to Rom. 11, it is the world, here understood in its technical sense, i.e. the heathen peoples who so far had been deprived of citizenship in Israel, who were strangers to the covenants and promises, without hope and without God (Eph. 2:12). For 2 Cor. 5, it is once more the world, understood here in a wider sense; mankind as a whole, the creation which is subject to sin (v. 19). In Col. 1:20, it is "all things, whether on earth or in heaven", it is "you who were once estranged" (note that this term has precisely the same root as the verb reconcile) "hostile in mind, doing evil deeds". For Eph. 2:16, it is "the two stems of humanity", the Jews and the Gentiles, both resting under the wrath of God (see the opening of the Epistle to the Romans) and who were mutually opposed and separated by the wall of partition. Two features stand out as characterizing all these passages: the reconciliation has a universal bearing; its beneficiaries had manifested up till then only hostility whether towards God or towards each other.

(c) The circumstances. The texts are unanimous in affirming Jesus Christ to be the mediator of reconciliation, as the Son (Rom. 5), the first-born of all creation (Col. 1:15) and still more precisely as the one who died on the *cross. Here the terminology varies according to the context; one finds: through the cross, through the *blood of the cross (blood does not necessarily mean the blood of cultic sacrifices but utter self-surrender to the point of death), through the body of His flesh; each expression confirms in its own way this essential witness, viz. reconciliation is bound up with an event which happened at a specific point in place and time and which consisted in the accursed death of a man tortured on the gallows; it has to do not with psychology, religion, cultus or rite, but with history. The meaning of this death is likewise specified: Christ died for us (Rom. 5:6), i.e. in our place; for all (2 Cor. 5:18–21). On Him our offences have been laid. He has undergone the judgment of God and the condemnation of the law (Eph. 2:13ff.). He was crushed by that which caused enmity among men, between Israel and the Gentiles; He succumbed to it and abolished in His death all enmity (Eph. 2:15); His rejection prefigured the rejection of Israel, as a result of which grace became accessible to all (Rom. 11). 2 Cor. 5:21 sums up all this in an unforgettable formula: "He was made sin for us."

(*d*) *The consequences.* It is at this point above all that we must investigate the special bearing of the term reconciliation. So far the same analysis applied to justification, redemption, salvation, would have yielded similar results, and it is difficult to discriminate between these terms, which often appear almost equivalent. It has been said that justification concerns the individual aspect of redemption while reconciliation has to do with its universal character. But this would be restricting too much the bearing of justification, which in its connection with the last judgment has a universal implication. It has also been maintained that reconciliation is the consequence of justification. This may be more accurate, but it seems difficult to establish a sort of chronology between these various themes by which the N.T. tries to impress upon us the fullness of the saving work accomplished in Jesus Christ. If justification triumphs over the law, redemption over sin and disobedience, reconciliation presupposes the hostility and chaos which has shaken to its depths the creation of God. All the passages mentioned declare with the same decisiveness: now everything is different; by His sovereign intervention God has transformed the cosmic situation. While, of course, creation has not yet received its new shape which will be given to it at the last day, yet here and now every creature is irradiated by the breaking forth of light as the earth is irradiated by the sunrise. The cross has

had the effect of a death sentence cancelling the past and inaugurating something wholly different: "If any man is in Christ he is a new creature; the old has passed away; behold, the new has come" (2 Cor. 5:14–17).

This peace extends to the entire cosmos in its celestial as well as its terrestrial spheres, both of which find in Christ the principle of their renewal (Col. 1:20). This new creation is rooted in Christ, in the new man, the body of Christ, in which are incorporated without distinction Jews and Gentiles (Eph. 2:16). The grace of the new covenant is applicable henceforth to all nations (Rom. 11). We have become the righteousness of God (2 Cor. 5:21), we have access to the Father (Eph. 2:18), we are brought into His presence, holy and spotless (in the cultic sense), blameless (in the juridical sense, at the last judgment) (Col. 1:22). Reconciliation gives us the pledge of our final redemption: it is for us a new point of departure and we can go forward to the last day with the certain promise of salvation, and the assurance of participating in the life of Jesus Christ (Rom. 5 and 11). Hence we are filled with joy and gratitude because of the grace which has been vouchsafed to us in Jesus Christ (Rom. 5:11).

Yet the work of reconciliation is not completed; inaugurated in Christ, it must be continued on the earth until the final resurrection which it foreshadows (Rom. 11:5). Hence God has chosen ambassadors to exercise the *ministry of this reconciliation. Through them the exalted and glorified Lord continues His service on the earth and exhorts all men: "Be ye reconciled to God" (2 Cor. 5:20).

4. In order to complete our survey of the consequences of reconciliation brief mention must be made (even though the precise term does not appear in the texts) of the many passages which show how reconciliation transforms human conduct. The preaching of Jesus in the Sermon on the Mount marks out the way in advance. All the fruits of the law of retaliation, all hatred and malediction having been borne by Christ in His suffering, cursing and hatred,

vengeance and retribution in human relations are now done away ("you have heard . . . but I say unto you . . ."—cf. Matt. 5:38–45; Lk. 14:12–14 or the parable of the unforgiving servant, Matt. 18:23–35). The amazing attitude of God must be reflected in the amazing attitude of the Church towards men, and it is to this end that the new man of whom Eph. 2:16 speaks has been created in the present age. Finally we should note the striking parallelism between the idea of reconciliation as expressed in the Pauline texts and the Johannine idea of love (cf. moreover Rom. 5:8: "God has manifested His love", and 2 Cor. 5:14: "The love of Christ controls us"): "In this is love, not that we loved God but that He loved us" (1 Jn. 4:10).

The whole of the N.T. resounds with the theme of reconciliation, that sovereign and triumphant initiative of God which through the cross has opened up the way of *love and has succeeded in reconciling unto Himself a world which had simply not given the faintest indication of love. In this respect the N.T. is aware of standing in radical opposition to all the religions of humanity, past and future, and of being in an absolute sense the Gospel of sheer divine grace.

M. BOUTTIER

REDEMPTION, *see* RANSOM

REGENERATION, *see* BAPTISM, LIFE, WORD

REIGN, *see* KINGDOM

REJECT, *see* ELECT

RELEASE, *see* FREEDOM, SALVATION, SIN

REMNANT

Four Hebrew words with various shades of meaning render the word remnant: two of them denote those who escape a danger; a third indicates the existence of a remaining quantity; the fourth suggests what remains after a process of selection and purging. Such words are frequently used in their current meaning without the theological associations of "the remnant of Israel". Lastly, this theological idea is often present in spite of the fact that the terms themselves are not employed.

1. *The remnant as the work of divine judgment.* In the O.T. "the remnant of Israel" nearly always springs from some catastrophe which has brought destruction on the people as a whole. The crisis may be of a physical kind as in the case of the flood, but more often it is a military defeat such as the capture of Jerusalem in 586 B.C. The absence of a remnant among the Philistines (Amos 1:8; Isa. 15:9) and the existence of a remnant for Israel are facts which have their origin not in the accidents of history but in the truth that God exercises through history His judgment on mankind.

To mention the remnant of Israel at the time of the great military defeats of the 8th and 9th centuries B.C. is to suggest at once the anger of God against the sins of His people. The smaller the remnant the greater the destruction, and the more serious the sin. God condemns this sin by destroying the people as a totality. What remains therefore stands as a witness to the wrath of God which has revealed itself against the people as a whole. "Only a remnant remains." This remnant by its very existence constitutes in some sort the proof that a destructive catastrophe has struck down the whole (Amos 3:12).

This remnant may even bear witness not only to the condemnation of the others but also to its own (Ezek. 14:21–23). Thus it fulfils the function of being a vessel of wrath manifesting the righteous judgment of God on sin. Hence the images by means of which it is described: namely the process of grape-gathering, gleaning or sifting after the harvest, or the vintage of the judgment of God (Amos 9:8ff.; Isa. 17:5–6; Jer. 6:9).

2. *The remnant as the work of divine grace.* "A remnant nevertheless does exist." But this is not the result of forces immanent within history which might be regarded as tending to preserve minorities, nor is it that

the resourcefulness or strength of the few enables them to escape the disaster by their own initiative and to form a reserve (Amos 2:14ff.; 9:1ff.).

The fact that some few should survive is a miraculous event of which God alone is the author. He alone grants this unforeseeable and essentially gracious favour, that some should be allowed to survive from the thick of the most terrible catastrophes.

Those who thus survive do not owe it to the purity of their life or to their repentance or to any other sort of worth. The remnant cannot be defined in advance by institutional criteria. It reveals rather the charismatic aspect of the people of God in hours of crisis. §§ 3 and 4 below will show that this aspect, far from being opposed to the institutional basis of the people, is a manifestation of the latter.

Thus the remnant is the work of God (Isa. 1:9). Its existence bears witness to the dual revelation of His righteousness and grace in the history of mankind. The O.T. cannot conceive of this twofold attitude of God as implying inwardly contrasting impulses at the heart of divinity. It is not that He pours out His wrath on some and His favour on others. It is rather a question of the two facets of a single work, of the two ways in which God manifests the eternal love which He bears towards His people. Thus He remains faithful to His promises by making their fulfilment possible in spite of sin (Jer. 31:2–3).

3. *The relations of the remnant with the destroyed section of the people.* The remnant is not essentially different from the majority which has suffered destruction. Through it the old Israel prolongs its life, and by its means the life of the people is safeguarded through the crisis of the catastrophic judgment of God. The remnant represents the persistence of the old body of the people. It is not a new community superseding the former (cf. Isa. 6:13). It canalizes, as it were, the life of the ancient people and the promises once made to the totality are focused within it.

This numerical reduction of God's elect introduces nothing new. The elect people still exists; its extent, magnitude, identity and qualities are of little importance—such factors are embarrassing to human wisdom and foresight; thus it is not the tribe of Joseph, the most remarkable of the sons of Jacob according to Genesis, nor Ephraim the most populous of the kingdoms which will constitute the remnant in the period of the monarchy, but the tribe of Judah. Nor is it a moral criterion which decides the choice of those who are to belong to the remnant and differentiates them from others: no doubt one could point to 1 Kings 19:18 and the prophets who sometimes emphasize the righteousness, faith and obedience (Zeph. 3:12–13) or the social insignificance of those who are to constitute the remnant (Jer. 23:3; Isa. 7:22); but these particular features are far from characterizing the remnant as a whole. It can no more be equated with a certain human group, naturalistically delimited, than with a moral or social category. We should judge rather in the light of Ezek. 14:12–23 or the incident of the fall of the tower of Siloam (Lk. 13:1ff.) which affirm not only a physical solidarity but an identity of conduct as between the totality and the remnant (cf. also passages in the prophets where we are reminded that this impious remnant will have to repent and be converted, Isa. 4:3; 10:20; Exod. 11:18ff.; Jer. 24:6ff.).

The composition of the remnant is a mystery rooted solely and utterly in the free *election of God. God alone chooses among His people those who will constitute the remnant (cf. 1 Kings 19:18).

4. *The relations of the remnant with the people of the future.* The remnant surviving from the catastrophe which has swept away the people of old is closely bound to the people of the future. It forms in some sort a bridge between the two moments in the history of the people of God: the moment of promise and foundation, and that of fulfilment. The remnant exists for the sake of the eschatological community that is to come. It will become a great multitude (Exod. 32:10; Num. 14:12; Isa. 60:21ff.).

The life of the ancient people which in a hidden form has been transmitted to the remnant is one day to blossom forth in the people of the future (Mic. 4:6–8; Isa. 37:31ff.).

In addition to this conception of the remnant as a rallying point for the future (Isa. 30:17), other texts emphasize a very important function which the remnant is called on to fulfil: it is the instrument of the grace of God toward others, the narrow channel through which God will mediate His grace (Gen. 18:26; Jer. 5:1; Mic. 5:6). The office which devolves upon Israel in so far as its significance for the Gentiles is concerned (Gen. 12:2; Exod. 19:6) becomes the special task of the remnant in its relation to the other members of the people of God, and of the *Servant of the Lord in the Second Isaiah (49:5,6; 53).

5. *The relations of the remnant with the Messiah.* The remnant of the people, sometimes compared to a new shoot bursting forth with new life from an old trunk (Isa. 6:13) must be considered in close connection with the Messiah, who is also sometimes compared to a new branch (Isa. 4:2; 11:1; 53:2; Ezek. 17:22; Ps. 80:15ff.).

The central and life-giving element in the remnant is the Messiah. The remnant can only exist in so far as it revolves around Him, in so far as all its other members are grafted on to Him and share in His life (Jer. 23:3–6; Mic. 2:12–13; 5:1–8).

If we imagine in geometrical terms the rhythm of the history of revelation, we might compare its movement to a cone, the base of which—symbolizing the exodus from Egypt—becomes ever more narrowed in the course of centuries to an ever-decreasing remnant until its apex is constituted by the sole "remaining" One Jesus Christ, who "remains" triumphantly through the death on the cross and the resurrection.

In Him the twofold work of God is fulfilled in judgment and grace (cf. above, §§ 1 and 2).

The same pattern may be noted in the Gospels: the infant Jesus alone escapes the slaughter of the innocents; the circle of His followers progressively diminishes: during the Galilean ministry He is acclaimed by the multitudes, then He is abandoned in turn by several disciples (Jn. 66:6), by Judas, and finally by the eleven, until He remains alone and desolate hanging on the cross.

The Greek word rendered "many" in Matt. 20:28; 26:28, etc., indicates the rest of mankind in contrast with Jesus, as the sole representative of the remnant.

After the resurrection, the culmination of the history of salvation precludes the principle of the remnant. In this respect, the Acts is especially clear and significant in its allusions to ever-increasing numbers (1:13,26; 2:41,47; 5:14) and in its geographical design which emphasizes the extension of the Christian community on the earth. There can no longer be this movement of reduction in the case of the new *covenant, for it is a movement which is entirely characteristic of the O.T.: it is a pattern inherent in the process by which the coming of Christ is prepared. The Christian Church is not the remnant, but rather the new humanity of the future springing from the remnant which Jesus Christ embodied in His own person. The geometrical design now contrasts with that which was typical of the old covenant. From the apex common to both it develops downwards by way of increasing extension. If in certain crises of history it is brutally reduced in size as a result of persecution, for example, in that case we see not a radical modification of the movement but a temporary narrowing of its scope which will later give birth to an even greater expansion.

6. *The remnant and the preparatory unfolding of the history of salvation.* We have seen in the preceding paragraph that the essential co-ordinate of the remnant is the *time during which God is preparing His work of salvation. The temptation always existed in the course of the history of Israel (and in that of the Church too) to seek to determine the composition of this remnant, even to create it by fixing its lines of demarcation.

This is in effect to deny the "instantaneous" or empirical character of the existence of the remnant. The fundamental characteristic of all sectarianism is precisely to negate history and to substitute for it an idea, or a preconceived criterion, according to which discrimination is made among men.

The sect constitutes itself deliberately: it defines its frontiers by criteria of a moral, theological, or social kind; it delights to be separated from others whom it abandons to perdition, keeping jealously for itself the monopoly of spiritual life; its *raison d'être* lies in itself; it has ceased to be an organ for the transmission of divine life and grace; its principle is self-conservation. Hence arise its characteristic features: pride, egoism, and lack of brotherly love.

The prophets Jeremiah and Ezekiel sometimes describe to us men whose aim it is to transmit to the future the existing remnant and to make its continuity depend on something other than the free initiative of God. Thus, after the destruction of the northern kingdom, some wished to see in the kingdom of Judah the true remnant (Isa. 28:5) while, between the two deportations of the inhabitants of Jerusalem, the remnant was identified now with those who had remained in the holy land, or in the holy city, now with those who were in the entourage of the last petty kings of Judah. After the destruction of the sanctuary itself the remnant is sought in the circle of Gedaliah; then, when the flight to Egypt takes place, the Israelites wish to assure themselves that they constitute the remnant by insisting on the presence of Jeremiah (Jer. 24; 40:15; 42; 43). Mention should also be made of the closed circles of Essenes in the time of Jesus who took refuge in the Judean desert, or again of the Pharisaic party isolated in its self-righteousness and sense of racial purity, and of a certain section of the Jews in our own time who call themselves the remnant.

In contrast to these anthropocentric conceptions of a remnant which men wish to define or create, biblical history seems full of surprises: Jacob the younger son, Judah, the remnant of Judah, rather than the great and notable; nor again is it those who remain in the Promised Land after 597, but the first emigrants, those who will capitulate before the armies of Nebuchadnezzar, the unfortunate, the *poor of the Psalms.

In the N.T. the "remnant of Israel", which mysteriously subsists during the time of the Church, is composed of the Jewish Christians; they are the first-fruits of the ultimate conversion of all Israel (Rom. 11:1,5).

A. LELIÈVRE

RENEW, *see* NEW

REPENTANCE

The Greek word which our translations usually render "repent" means literally: to think again or to change one's mind, hence to regret, to repent, to be converted. It signifies less a state of mind which could become permanent and in which one might delight, or which might reduce one to despair, than the transition from one state to another. In biblical thought repentance is not a static but a dynamic notion.

1. *The two aspects of repentance.* The biblical idea of repentance includes two aspects, one negative, the other positive, the former existing only for the sake of the latter.

The negative aspect of repentance has to do with the past, and presupposes the realization of an abnormal state of affairs, a wrong direction, a state of sin. He who repents begins by recognizing that he is on the wrong road. He regrets this, he acknowledges his mistake, he detests his sin.

The positive aspect of repentance has to do with the future and opens up to the repentant sinner a new way of life in which he can walk only as the result of conversion, that is, a radical reorientation of life. To be converted means that, after recognizing his mistake and the dangers of his false situation, by a redirection of his whole being he enters into a new and right path of life.

Thus repentance means on the one hand the acknowledgment of and the cessation from sin, and on the other hand the resolution to accept the challenge of a new life. It is poised between the state of sin and the state of salvation.

It is a great mistake to confine repentance within the limits of its negative aspect. To see in it nothing more than remorse, regret, morbid and fruitless brooding over the faults of the past, is to deprive it of all vital and liberating power. It is to block it at its point of departure, which is of course a necessary point but a transitory one. One cannot live in a state of repentance, regret, or remorse. One enters into that situation only to emerge from it; and if one lingers in it, one does so only in so far as it is a transient phase of development. It is not merely necessary to regret one's sins and their consequences, it is chiefly necessary to get out of one's sinful condition.

Hence in Scripture the word repentance is usually accompanied by some term or expression emphasizing that according to the will of God repentance always issues through conversion in salvation. "Godly grief produces a repentance that leads to salvation, and brings no regret" (2 Cor. 7:10; cf. Lk. 13:3; 15:7). Repentance and conversion are linked together (Acts 3:19; 26:20) just as are repentance and forgiveness (Mk. 1:4; Lk. 17:3; 24:27; Acts 2:38; 5:31; 8:22), repentance and faith (Acts 20:21), repentance and knowledge of the truth (2 Tim. 2:25), repentance and healing (Mk. 6:12–13), repentance and new life (Matt. 3:8; Acts 11:18; Heb. 6:1; Rev. 2:5; 16:9).

2. *Repentance and the Kingdom of heaven.* Since repentance is poised at the transition point where one state passes into another, it marks a moment of tension between two mutually exclusive realities. Repentance must be placed at the point where the Kingdom of God and the kingdoms of this world stand over against each other.

In this respect the position assigned to the preaching of John the Baptist at the very threshold of the N.T.—a preaching founded essentially on repentance—is extremely characteristic. John takes up the old message of the prophets: "Repent and be converted: return to God." But the message is this time delivered more emphatically than by any prophet of the old covenant. It has a more piercing sound, a higher note of urgency. The fact is that the appeal is now situated on the very verge of a new world, in the expectation of the imminent advent of the Kingdom, and is thus moulded by the pressure of momentous eschatological events. Here we are at the very point where two worlds meet. In such a context the sole attitude required and fitting is repentance, i.e. a disposition to be humble (symbolized by baptism) and a readiness to renounce the powers of the old world and to await the one to come. Thus the sinner is urged to turn towards God because God is turning towards man.

3. *The causes of repentance.* In the outlook of the Bible repentance generally speaking does not arise from the fault itself, as if the gravity of the sin inevitably involved sooner or later its detestation. The sinner becomes aware that he is on the wrong road and accepts conversion only under the challenge of an eschatological message and revelation. It is the nearness of the Kingdom which brings to bear on every situation a judgment and promise, and which arouses repentance. "Repent, *for* the kingdom of heaven is at hand" (Matt. 3:2).

Repentance is thus the object of an appeal from without, of preaching (Mk. 1:4–15, etc., 6:12; Matt. 12:41 and parallels; Lk. 5:32; 24; 47; Acts 2:38; 3:19; 17:30; 20:21; 26:20), of an order, a command, for the imminence of the Kingdom no longer permits tergiversations or prevarications: the cry is "repent" (Acts 8:22; Rev. 2:5, etc.). Repentance also may be aroused by the mere manifestation of facts which bear witness to the advent of the Kingdom (Lk. 5:8).

Thus repentance is the gift of God. It is the sign of a grace which is still external to the sinner but already operative within him. It represents an impulse coming from the Holy Spirit which, while not yet dwelling within the sinner, urges and incites him, illuminating him with a light which reveals to him the shadow of death in which he lives, and brings him finally to the sphere of salvation. This is why repentance, far from being a harassing demand of God, is rather a fruit of His love. "Do you presume upon the riches of his kindness and forbearance and patience? Do you not know that God's kindness is meant to lead you to repentance?" (Rom. 2:4).

4. *Repentance and sin.* If repentance is not primarily the result of auto-accusation or introspective scrupulosity, this is because it is not inherently bound up with external manifest sins such as are openly condemned by received ethical opinion. It is true that grace always exercises its effects upon a sick man, but the sick man may be apparently well, may be living an honest life and behaving irreproachably from the point of view of the law. Here again the preaching of John the Baptist is extremely revealing, for he addresses himself not merely to notorious sinners, but also to the Pharisees and Sadducees. Nothing less than the power of the Holy Spirit and the revelation of the love of God is needed to convince man of sin. Hence the preaching of repentance and conversion, in spite of its pitiless severity, is never suggestive of legalism. It never results in the idea of salvation by works, but in a joyful acceptance of grace. It causes us to take sin seriously because first of all we have taken God seriously. Thus in the state of repentance the despair into which we might have been cast by the realization of our sins is overcome by our trust in the mercy of a God who condemns only to save. "Godly grief produces repentance that leads to salvation and brings no regret, but worldly grief produces death" (2 Cor. 7:10).

The summons which sounds throughout the long history of salvation, inciting men to acknowledge and turn aside from their sins, ought not therefore to be understood in a legal sense or as an irrevocable decree of condemnation. Rather in Jesus Christ it becomes a Gospel, i.e., good news.

Thus the repentant sinner, on whom already the grace of forgiveness rests, will wish to express his gratitude and to bear witness that in the light of the Gospel all things have become new (2 Cor. 5:17). Henceforth he will live in conformity with the laws of the Kingdom of heaven, producing fruits worthy of repentance (Matt. 3:8), and showing by his works that every gift of God calls forth the obedience of man.

5. *The Repentance of God.* Repentance is not confined to created spirits. In certain passages of the Bible we find an allusion to the repentance of God (e.g., Exod. 32:14; Jer. 26:13; Jon. 4:2). It goes without saying that the word used in this connection (which moreover as applied to God is not the same as that which is used for human repentance) should be understood in a radically different sense from that which we have just been considering. If it is the case that God repents of the evil which He had determined to do (in one single passage God repents of the good which He had resolved upon, Jer. 18:10) it is because He is not a God of the philosophers, a prisoner of His eternal immutability, but a living and personal *God, ceaselessly watching the conduct of His children and ready, when they show serious repentance, to revoke from motives of love the sentence of condemnation which He had decreed. For God does not desire the death of the sinner but rather that he should turn from his evil and live (Ezek. 33:11).

                                    J.-PH. RAMSEYER

REST

1. When the words "rest" and "to rest" are used in a theological sense they must be understood against the background of the history of salvation with its tension and trials. Rest signifies the sphere to which God is leading His people; it is the land promised by God to those whom He has delivered from bondage in Egypt (Deut. 12:9; Josh. 21:44; cf. Ps. 95:11); it is the homeland to which the exiles will return (Jer. 46:27); it is the consummate and eternal felicity of the Kingdom of God (cf. Heb. 3:7–4:10)—a fulfilment which so

far had only been anticipated—it is the advent of the *sabbath rest of God, i.e., the rest of all things in God who rests from His labours (cf. Gen. 2:2ff.; Exod. 20:11; Heb. 4:3ff.).

2. Just as a woman when she marries finds rest, an easing of the tensions of her being through its imminent fulfilment (cf. Ruth 1:9; 3:1), so the Church is moving towards the time when its labours, its trials and its sufferings will come to an end. For the moment the people of God do not know —any more than their Lord, Matt. 8:20; Lk. 9:58—this security and appeasement so much desired (Ps. 55:1–7) and woe to the man who is lulled into a false sense of security! (Zeph. 1:12ff.; Lk. 12:16–21). For the present time is one when there is no respite, obedience requires such constant vigilance and readiness (cf. Acts 5:42; 20:31; Col. 1:9) and to such an extent does God desire our co-operation in the work of salvation which brooks no ease (Jn. 5:17; cf. Isa. 62:7).

3. And yet the rest which God has promised His people (cf. Zeph. 3:13) finds already certain anticipations (which may be reflected in human history itself, Exod. 23:11; Lev. 25:4ff.): for example in the deliverances which punctuate the history of salvation (2 Sam. 7:11; 1 Kings 5:4; 2 Chr. 14:5; Isa. 14:3ff. etc.)—but this rest may become a temptation (Neh. 9:28); again in the period of Solomon's reign (cf. 1 Kings 8:56–61; 1 Chr. 22:9) or in the temple which he built (Ps. 91:1) and which is for God Himself a place of rest (cf. Ps. 132; but also Isa. 66:1; Acts 7:49) and especially in the sabbath (cf. Exod. 31:17; 23:12; 34:21; Lk. 23:56, etc.). Doubtless a similar anticipation of the eschatological rest may be seen in the times of retreat to which Jesus invites His disciples (Mk. 6:31) and which moreover prepare the way for the miraculous feeding of the multitude (Mk. 6:34–44 and parallels) a fulfilment of rest promised by Ps. 23:2 or Ezek. 34:14ff. Finally *death itself when irradiated with hope can be the prelude to the great and ultimate rest (Dan. 12:13; Ps. 16:9ff.; Acts 2:26; Rev. 14:13); yet it is still not the fullness of this rest (Rev. 6:9–11).

4. Since Jesus in His incarnate life embodies the very power and richness of the Kingdom of God (Matt. 12:28), in His person is concentrated the peace which God had promised His people; that is why He chooses so often the sabbath day to pour out His benefits on men and to give respite to the poor and wretched (cf. Isa. 14:30); that is why He calls unto Himself all those who are weary and heavy laden that He may lighten their sorrows and give rest unto their souls (Matt. 11:28). Doubtless it is in the perspective of this idea of Jesus our peace (cf. vv. 66–69) that we should read John 6.

N.B. For a description of the antithesis of rest, cf. Lev. 26:34–39; Deut. 28:63–68.

J.-J. VON ALLMEN

RESURRECTION

To express the idea of resurrection, the Bible, both Hebrew and Greek, uses several verbs which have all a commoner and more extended meaning than our own term resurrection. Such verbs denote "to waken", "to raise up", "to construct", "to heal", etc., or in the intransitive form "to rise up", "to appear", "to manifest oneself". In the Bible there is no word which expresses exclusively the theological notion of resurrection. In the N.T. the verb most frequently used (*egeirein*) in the main presents the resurrection of Jesus and the dead as an act of power on the part of God, while another verb (*anistanai*) meaning literally "to rise", "to stand up", suggests rather the notion of a victory of life over death; but by means of such rather vague terms, the meaning of which should not be pressed too literally, the theology of the Bible expresses ideas which are certainly not lacking in precision.

1. In comparison with the many doctrines of resurrection which characterized the ancient religions of the Near East (Osiris in

Egypt, Tammuz in Babylon, Attis in Asia Minor) the O.T. is marked by its astonishing sobriety on this. The fact is that in the O.T. God is not conceived as a divinity immanent in the fecundity of the vegetable world and thus linked to the rhythm of the seasons; it is rather that He rules the world of vegetation and of the recurrent seasons. He does not participate in the "becoming" of nature; He has established and ever controls that process. Thus He has not to be reborn each year at the beginning of the season of rains, and men have no need to participate in or even further this cosmic drama by means of magic, seasonal feasts, mysteries and rites. On the other hand, in the religion of the Parsees we do find some of the leading ideas of the Bible with regard to resurrection, for there it is connected with the idea of a judgment on persons at the end of time and with the expectation of a process of universal purification culminating in the total restoration of humanity and the world.

In Israel it was not until the time of the Exile that the idea of resurrection was developed and it was then first applied to David, the resurrected shepherd of Israel (Ezek. 34:23–31; 37:24–28) and later to Israel as a whole, restored to life by the sole power of Yahweh: "I will put breath in you and you shall live. . . ." (Ezek. 37:1–14; in Hos. 2:16ff. and Jer. 3:19ff.,31:1ff., 29:10ff., it is not a question of the resurrection of Israel but of its restoration; though it should be noted that in Ezekiel the idea of resurrection is made subordinate to that of the restoration and ultimate prosperity of Israel); in Isa. 53 it seems indeed that a resurrection is visualized for the Servant of Yahweh (vv. 10–12); in the book of Job (19:25) the idea assumes a more individual character and merges in that of ultimate and enduring communion with God: "I shall see God." Finally, in some of the later Psalms, the notion of a personal resurrection appears here and there, but is always expressed with extreme reserve (Ps. 16:10ff.; 49:16; 73:26; 17:15—and moreover the meaning of all these passages is debated). It is only in Jewish apocalyptic literature (Isa. 26:19; Dan. 12:1ff.) that we find more precisely formulated the idea of a double resurrection, of the righteous and wicked, and here it is associated with the notion of a last judgment and a total restoration of humanity (4th Esdras, Apoc. of Baruch). In the time of Jesus Himself the opinion of Jewish doctors was divided on this point; it would seem that the Sadducees, unlike the Pharisees, rejected the very idea of a resurrection (Mk. 12:18ff.; Acts 23:6–8, texts which are supported by the evidence of Josephus, *Jewish War*, II,8.14).

2. When we pass to the N.T. we are at once struck by the fact that the idea of resurrection suddenly takes on an importance and a precision in formulation which at first sight seem inexplicable. The fundamental insight presupposed is unquestionably that of the O.T. and of Parseeism: the resurrection of Jesus and of the dead is understood not as a cyclic (seasonal) and cosmic victory of life over death but as an eschatological and gratuitous act of God who thus ultimately shatters the reign of *death. Thus the latter is interpreted not as a temporary eclipse of life but as a complete annihilation of man from which only the power of God the Creator can rescue him. But, above all, the N.T. is characterized by the fact that all its affirmations about the resurrection are connected with a historical event which is quite recent; the death and the resurrection of Jesus. Against the background of this threefold perspective which forms the originality of early Christian thought on this subject, the following special points may be elucidated:

(a) The most ancient evidence for the fact of the resurrection of Jesus is to be found not in the Gospels but in the Epistles and certain ancient texts of the Acts of the Apostles (1 Cor. 15:4,12; 6:14; 2 Cor. 4:14; 5:15; Rom. 1:4; 4:24ff.; 6:4,9; 7:4; 8:11,34; 10:9; Gal. 1:1; Eph. 1:20; Phil. 2:9ff.; Col. 2:12; 1 Thess. 1:10; 4:14; 2 Tim. 2:8; 1 Pet. 1:21; Acts 3:15; 4:10; 5:30; 10:40; 13:30,37).

The most striking feature of these texts is that the resurrection of Jesus is not so much described as affirmed and that it is affirmed as an act of divine power which could neither have been foreseen in advance nor subsequently explained. The apostles do not attempt to prove the resurrection of Jesus; it is for them an object of faith, in fact it is even the fundamental certitude of their faith (1 Cor. 15:12). Yet on the other hand it is never attenuated to a spiritual assurance cherished by the believer; first, Jesus rose according to the Scriptures (1 Cor. 15:4); that is, at a particular moment—foreseen by God—in the history of salvation; but also the risen Christ appeared to men who can still, at the moment when Paul is writing, bear witness to what they have seen. The *apostles are by definition the witnesses of the resurrection of Jesus, and they are so in the sense which we attach to the word "eyewitness". Yet, according to these same texts, Jesus appeared only to His disciples or to those who were about to become such; thus the witness rendered to the resurrection of Jesus is not understood as a compelling and "objective" proof but as a deposition of faith in view of the faith of the hearers.

(b) In spite of the confusion which characterizes the N.T. texts in regard to the appearances of the risen Christ (chiefly as concerns the locality and the number of these appearances and also their time with reference to the ascension of Jesus) it should be noted that the Risen Lord is not described as "pure spirit" but as a living person clothed with a "body" (Mk. 16:6; cf. vv. 11,12,14; Matt. 28:6ff.; Lk. 24:34, cf. v. 39; Jn. 20:17,19,26–29) which at times seems to be identified with the mutilated body of the earthly Jesus and at other times appears to be that "spiritual body" of which the idea often emerges in the N.T. (Matt. 22:30 and parallels; 1 Cor. 15:50–52; 2 Cor. 5:1; Phil. 3:21). What the N.T. wishes to emphasize in all this is above all the identity of the person of Him who "suffered" and Him who now has been "raised". This suffering and this glory shed light upon each other. If we are to be faithful to the N.T. we must neither confound them nor dissociate them.

(c) In fact the resurrection of Jesus according to the N.T. is not merely a historical fact in the sense which we have just explained; it is a judgment of God which "now" vitally affects every human being. No N.T. formula expresses that more clearly than Rom. 4:25; Jesus was "put to death for our trespasses and raised for our justification". What God has done in raising up Jesus He has done for our sakes and our salvation. Therefore the resurrection of Jesus expresses the particular will of God who after destroying sinful man miraculously summons him to enter a new life. By *His* resurrection we are thus restored to life, and that quickening takes place here and now although as yet in a hidden manner (Rom. 6:4–11; Gal. 2:20; Col. 2:12ff.; Eph. 2:1,5; 2 Cor. 4:10ff.; 1 Pet. 1:3). Man is not magically or spiritually transformed into a celestial or immortal being, but by the power of the preaching of the Gospel, which applies to him personally the judgment of God embodied once for all in the resurrection of Jesus, he becomes reconciled to God already in this earthly life and already shares in the victory of Jesus Christ over death.

(d) Yet it is only in the last days that the effects of the resurrection of Jesus both for individual believers and for humanity as a whole will be seen in their full scope and extent. The stories of the resurrection of individuals narrated in the Gospels show us the premonitory signs of this last and general resurrection: they bear witness to the fact that the times are fulfilled, that Jesus is the Founder of the *Kingdom (provisionally hidden) and that the reign of death will be succeeded by the triumph of *life (Mk. 5:41 and parallels; Lk. 7:11–17; Jn. 11; cf. 5:21; 12:1,9,17). We must also interpret in this eschatological sense the synoptic predictions of the passion and resurrection of Jesus; they present the death and resurrection of Jesus as foreseen stages in the stream of saving history and as pointing to the final reconstitution of humanity under the authority of the Risen Lord (cf. Matt. 16:21; Lk. 9:22; Matt. 17:9,23; 20:19; Mk. 14:28). The Gospels make a few allusions to this general resurrection of the dead (Mk. 12:23ff., 14:25 and parallels; Matt. 8:11; Lk. 13:22–30; Matt. 25:31–46; Jn. 5:28ff; 6:39ff.,44; 17:24).

The indications of the Epistles on this theme are more precise: (i) The general resurrection is absolutely dependent on the resurrection of Jesus. *Man is not made to rise again; he has no intrinsic principle of immortality (soul or spirit), but the Risen Christ is the first-fruits of them that sleep (1 Cor. 15:20,23; 1 Thess. 4:14). (ii) The resurrection at the last day will signalize the final victory of Christ over His enemies, especially over death (1 Cor. 15:26). (iii) If in the main it is a question of the resurrection of believers, the resurrection of the "unjust" for judgment is often implied or even affirmed (Acts 24:15; Jn. 5:28ff.; Matt. 11:24; Rev. 20:4ff.,12ff.; 1 Thess. 1:9ff.; 2:12). (iv) Exactly as we have seen to be the case in regard to Jesus, the resurrected will not be "pure spirits"; they will be clothed (by the agency of God, 1 Cor. 15:38, and not by virtue of a process of spiritualization) with that same spiritual and incorruptible body which the glorified Christ was clothed with before them (1 Cor. 15:50–57). (v) It has sometimes been thought that the eschatology of the apostle developed from that expectation of a future resurrection which he owed to his Jewish origins, to the more spiritual conception of an individual communion with Christ fulfilled immediately after death—a conception he is supposed to have derived from surrounding Hellenistic mysticism (cf. 1 Thess. and 1 Cor. 15 with 2 Cor. 5:1ff.; Phil. 1:23). It is not probable that this was the case; we can say at most that when he wrote Philippians Paul no longer expected to see the return of Christ in his own lifetime; but if he hopes to be with Christ after his death (Phil. 1.23) it does not mean that he has ceased to expect the ultimate consummation of God's saving work in history in accordance with the eschatological hope which governs the whole of his thought (cf. Phil. 3:10ff.; 20ff.; 2 Cor. 1:9; 4:14).

P. BONNARD

REVELATION

O.T.

God is both the subject and the object of revelation. Man can know God only in as far as God communicates Himself to man; that is why the God of the O.T. is the hidden God (Isa. 45:15) who can be known only in so far as He discloses Himself (Deut. 29:28). The fact of revelation is expressed in such terms as the following: God is revealed (Gen. 35:7), He appears (Gen. 12:7), He makes Himself known (Exod. 6:3; Num. 12:6), He makes known His will or events which are about to happen, and even more generally God speaks. In the face of such initiatives on the part of God, the attitude of man is expressed by such terms as seeing, looking for, listening and knowing. God discloses Himself to man and man must respond by coming to know God—these are two affirmations which sum up the whole theology and piety of the O.T. The knowledge of Himself which God vouchsafes is unified as regards its object, but variable as regards the means used, for God being the Lord of all things can make use of the whole of creation for the purpose of His self-disclosures, although no single one of these means is capable of expressing revelation in its fullness.

1. God can appear *personally*. The O.T. is especially rich in episodes where God appears and acts as a man: thus, God shuts Noah into the ark (Gen. 7:16). He visits Abraham and Lot and in their presence behaves like a normal human being (Gen. 18–19). He wrestles with Jacob (Gen. 32:22ff.). He confronts Moses and tries to kill him (Exod. 4:24). He Himself puts to flight the Egyptian army at the crossing of the Red Sea (Exod. 14:25ff.). But it should be noted that even in passages relating a theophany proper, such as Exod. 24 and 33 and Ps. 18, the self-revelation of God is shrouded in mystery and the dazzling effulgence of the divine majesty is hidden behind a cloud (Ps. 18:12ff.).

2. In general, *the direct vision of God is*

reserved for certain beings specially chosen to this end. Moses was permitted to *see the face of God, but only on certain conditions. The prophets declare that they have seen God, but even in prophetic visions He remains the hidden God: in the vision of Isaiah (6:1ff.) God's face is veiled by the seraphim who veil their own faces also so as not to be annihilated by the glory of His majesty. Nevertheless the prophet is someone who has received a personal revelation of God.

3. *The *Dream*, although very different from prophetic visions which do not involve loss of consciousness, can also be a medium of revelation; it is of frequent occurrence in this connection in the patriarchal traditions (Gen. 20:3; 28:12; 41:1ff.; 46:2) and is recognized as a medium of revelation in the tradition of Israel as a whole (Num. 12:6; Deut. 13:2; 1 Sam. 28:6,15; Job 4:13ff.; Joel 2:28; Dan. 2:1ff., 7:1ff.); it is criticized by the prophets who emphasize its illusory character especially when practised by prophets of deceit (Jer. 23:25–32; 27:9; Zech. 10.2).

4. *God reveals Himself by means of *angels*. In Genesis the commands of God are often communicated by an angel (Gen. 16:9; 22:11) who sometimes takes the place of God. Besides this angel of Yahweh who is a manifestation of the divine the O.T. is familiar with an order of angels who as messengers are entrusted with the execution of divine commands (Ps. 103:20) and who constitute an army of auxiliaries at the disposal of God (Josh. 5:13ff.; 1 Kings 22:19, etc.). After the Exile, when as a result of the increased emphasis on divine transcendence direct revelation becomes more rare, the angels assume the office of necessary mediators between God and man (cf. Job 4:18; 33:19–23; Zechariah and the whole body of apocalyptic literature).

5. *The *Name* which expresses the essence of a being or a thing also constitutes a revelation. It is by the name that a living being becomes self-conscious and free and capable of entering into relations with another. The beginning of the history of salvation is marked by the revelation to Moses of the name of Yahweh—an act which implies a revelation of the divine being and also an invitation to man to enter into relation with the God who thus discloses His name; to utter the name of God is equivalent to declaring that one belongs to Him and intends to place oneself under His protection (1 Sam. 17:45; 2 Sam. 6:18; 2 Kings 2.24; Amos 6:10). In certain texts the name becomes a reality in some way independent of Yahweh, a mode of apparition similar to that of the angel or the *face; in such passages as Exod. 23:21 and Isa. 30:27 the name is a substitute for Yahweh.

6. Like all religions, the O.T. is aware of the revelation of God in *the world of nature*. The heavens declare the glory of God (Ps. 19:2; Isa. 40:26). The whole of *creation is a revelation of God and texts such as Gen. 1 and Ps. 104, by their detailed account of the works of creation, aim to bring out the fact that God creates each thing at the right time and places it where it should be. Thus nature becomes the mirror of the God who is one and sovereign; but (as O. Procksch says very aptly) nature is only the garment and not the body of God, whereas, in most of the religious cultures surrounding ancient Israel, the gods are often identified with the forces of nature. Among the various elements of nature, God chooses certain ones in preference to others in order to make of them the vehicle of His revelation: the wind (2 Sam. 5:24), the thunder which is called the voice of God (Ps. 18:14; 29:3), earthquake (Hab. 3:6), and especially fire which because it is luminous best symbolizes the essence of the divine, for God is light. But it should be appreciated that such natural phenomena are rather a concomitant of the divine presence than in themselves a manifestation of it; in the well-known incident of Elijah at Mount Horeb, the storm, the earthquake, the fire and even the still small voice are merely signs which foreshadow the revelation of Yahweh, which itself consists solely in His word (1 Kings 19:9ff.).

7. It is *in the *word* that God is accustomed to reveal Himself most completely. The word of God may assume the form of the law, the prophetic oracle or the apothegm of the Wisdom school.

(*a*) The most ancient laws are called words (*debarim*); they were short statements formulating either a command or a prohibition. The Decalogues, both Yahwist (Exod. 34) and Elohist (Exod. 20) are "words" (Exod. 20:1; 34:1,27,28). These words are uttered by God Himself and are not connected with concrete cases like most legislative texts; their scope surpasses any particular occasion. Now such commands of God are in the first instance a revelation of God. The preamble of the Decalogue of Exod. 20 begins by recalling the revelation of God to Moses and God's deliverance of His people from their bondage in Egypt. The laws of the holiness code (Lev. 17–26) are in general motivated by the event of Yahweh's self-disclosure: "I am Yahweh" (Lev. 19:32,34,36,etc.). The *torah*, a term which eventually came to denote the codified *law of the Pentateuch, was originally the pronouncement of the priest in answer to a consultation about some particular case (cf. for an example Hagg. 2:11ff.). The priest made his decision either after consulting the sacred lot, the Urim and Thummim (Deut. 33:8–10) or by having recourse to a kind of traditional law of which the sanctuaries were the depository.

(*b*) The word is the characteristic mark of the *prophetic office (Jer. 18:18). Associated with other phenomena such as ecstasy, sacred frenzy, at the beginning of the prophetic movement, it will become the sole distinctive criterion: Nathan and Elijah, the first of the line of prophets, are presented to us as men of the word (1 Kings 17:2,8; 18:1; 19:9; 21:17,28). But the word is not a permanent possession of the prophet; it may even be refused him (cf. Jer. 42:6ff.). Thus he speaks only when God has spoken to him and has given him a message which he is to deliver. It is interesting to notice that the formula which usually introduces the oracles of the prophets: "Thus saith the Lord", is met with in secular speech to designate a royal message which the messenger must deliver faithfully and without introducing any changes (Num. 22:16; Judg. 11:12; 14–22; 1 Kings 20:2ff.; 22:27; 2 Kings 18:28; the same turn of phrase is also found among the neighbours of Israel). The divine word is placed in the prophet's mouth (Jer. 1:9) or spoken in his ears (Isa. 5:9); having been present at the council of God (Jer. 23:18,22) he faithfully delivers what has been confided to him, even when this message is likely to arouse the hostility of his hearers, to whom he is often obliged to say that because they have failed to accept the revelation they will be deprived of all revelation: those who have hardened their heart will find that ultimately God will harden their heart completely.

The prophet is the man of his message, his person is subordinate to his mission, but as the latter wholly absorbs him it influences his personality itself, so that the very person of the prophet can become a revelation of God. The mere sight of the man of God, even before the delivery of his message, could make his hearers tremble with anxiety and hope (cf. for Elijah, 1 Kings 17:18); by means of his eccentric costume and certain symbolic actions—for example the nakedness of Isaiah (Isa. 20), the yoke of Jeremiah (Jer. 28), and the marriage of Hosea (Hos. 1–3), the prophet illustrates his message and enhances its effectiveness. At times the word could seize a prophet with such power that it would cast him into an abnormal psychological state, as in the case of Ezekiel (3:15, etc.).

(*c*) The maxims of the Wisdom literature are less directly revealed by God than the oracles of priest and prophet. They are counsels based both on revelation and experience; but the term *mashal* by which these words are generally indicated and which is applied to an oracle whose content is mysterious and secret (Num. 23:7; 24:3) suggests that the element of revelation was its main feature. The teachers of wisdom were organized into corporations like the priests and prophets (Isa. 5:21; Jer. 9:23; 18:18 and Ecclus. 38:24–39:11); around them were grouped disciples eager to learn how to live well. At the basis of this teaching, so lay and humanistic in appearance, lies the affirmation that the fear of God is the beginning of wisdom (Prov. 1:7) and that true wisdom is to be found in God alone (Job 28).

8. *The revelation of God in history* is the distinctive mark of the religion of Israel. Certain outstanding events were, for those who witnessed them, the occasion of touching the very nerve of the activity of God; certain miracles such as that of the Exodus and the flight of the Assyrian armies before Jerusalem in 701 B.C. were the proof of the direct intervention of God in the shaping of events—an intervention believed to be so real that even the phenomena of nature were subject to it; the staying of the sun by Joshua (10:12) and the return of the shadow on the sundial of Ahaz (Isa. 38:8) show to what an extent God's self-revelation in history took precedence of His self-revelation in nature. But the action of God in history is not confined to a few spectacular miracles. As their Hebrew name suggests, the latter are but signs of a divine sovereignty which is far more extensive. God exercises His sway over the historical process in a continuous manner; His activity resides in the direction of events according to a plan formed in view of a determinate end, namely, the establishment on earth of the Kingdom of heaven. It is the prophet Isaiah who spoke with the greatest precision of this plan of God (Isa. 7:7ff.; 8:10ff.; 14:24–27; 19:12; 23:8–9). Yahweh is not indifferent to or aloof from anything that happens on earth, and through the apparent confusions of earthly history it is His own work which He accomplishes (Isa. 5:12,19; 10:12; 28:21). God fulfils this plan according to His own wisdom in which opposites are resolved (cf. the parable of the ploughman, Isa. 28:23ff.) and in which to build and destroy, to judge and to save are the normal ways in which He sets up His Kingdom.

Other writings likewise emphasize this redemptive plan of God; the great historical work of the Yahwist narrator presents the history of humanity and that of the chosen people up to its entrance into Palestine as the effect of God's saving action towards men who, although incurring punishment by their disobedience, yet are assured of salvation by the operation of divine grace; and the book of Daniel, the latest in the O.T., offers us in the vision of the statue a striking summary of universal history culminating in the establishment of the Kingdom of God (2:26). But the revealing character of history is conveyed only through the word of the prophet: God makes known to His servants the prophets the secret plan which inspires His action (Amos 3:7). The almost uninterrupted succession of the prophets secures the permanent presence of the revealing word, and the Deuteronomic redaction of the history of Israel tries to show that history is the fulfilment of the prophecies; according to the Hebrew conception the word of the prophet is designed not merely to interpret events, but is efficacious in creating them.

9. Revelation in the O.T. is never in any special way dependent on the *written word*. At an early date, however, reverence for the word of God began to be shown by writing it down. The reform of King Josiah in 621 B.C. marks the beginning of the idea of Holy *Scripture (Deut. 30:11–14) and the post-exilic writings are often based on older documents which they regard as constituting a norm. However, the scriptural argument properly speaking, implied in the phrase "It is written" and suggesting the fixed authority of the letter, is not used in the O.T.

ED. JACOB

N.T.

Revelation is the event by which God discloses Himself to man. This event is the coming of Jesus Christ into the world.

1. *The knowledge of revelation.* In revealing Himself to men God concedes to their powers of apprehension, but He

remains the Initiator and the Master of His self-revealing activity. In making Himself the object of human knowledge He remains its active, free, and mysterious subject. He does not submit Himself passively to human investigation; He does not place Himself at the disposition of man that the latter may undertake religious or metaphysical research into the character of the divine. He has revealed Himself and will not disavow His revelation; but this revelation is offered only to him who is prepared to receive it as a creature humbly conditioned by space and time, and who gratefully recognizes that the revelation is a saving action. Hence the point of view from which N.T. authors speak about God's self-revelation is not that of men who can consider and judge the process of revelation in a detached and aloof manner, but is rather the only objective point of view possible in such a case: that of men for whom the grace of God was intended and who have benefited by it, that of witnesses to redemptive events and of confessors who have entered into communion with the almighty and holy God. Apart from this point of view there is nothing but darkness and illusion, there is nothing but a hidden God.

The N.T., standing in the light of God's self-revelation, gives to the Church and the world its witness to the events in which God has drawn near and made Himself known to men. The theoretical possibility of revelation has no longer to be discussed; it is already decided by facts and its authenticity can be experienced by anyone who is willing to receive it. Every one is invited to receive this revelation, for in telling the story of God's self-disclosure in Jesus of Nazareth, the Christ of Israel, the N.T. resolutely invites all those who hear the news to adopt the attitude of obedience and faith (Rom. 16:26; Jn. 20:31; Lk. 1:2; the eyewitnesses became ministers of the word).

2. *The author of the revelation.* Its author is God at every stage. First it is God who takes the initiative in revealing Himself. Things hidden from man both in consequence of his creaturely condition (1 Cor. 2:9,14) and sinful condition (Rom. 1:18) can be discovered by him neither as a result of planned investigation nor chance (the angels themselves moreover cannot find out such things; 1 Pet. 1:12); they become known only by the decisive will of God. Having determined His plan God accomplishes it, and at a moment of His own choosing, by revealing Himself to the world in *Jesus Christ.

Jesus Christ, the emissary of God and one with Him, reveals to us the Father and becomes with Him the subject of revelation (Lk. 10:22–24; Jn. 17:6–8). Through the Son, God is revealed to the world, but God is not content to have made the revelation once for all and for all men. It is God also who by His ceaseless activity makes men capable of receiving the revelation (Matt. 16:17; Gal. 2:15–16; 1 Thess. 2:13): He gives His *spirit to men so that they may be able to understand Him (Matt. 11:27; 1 Cor. 2:10ff.; 12:3). His revelation becomes effective with those who enter into the sphere of His fellowship and recognize His sovereignty; with others it remains without effect or even arouses rebellion. Thus God is the revealer in a twofold sense: objectively in Christ, subjectively through the Holy Spirit given to men. Finally, the ultimate and universal revelation is likewise subject to the sole decision of God (Mk. 13:32); it is not an event to be brought about by a metaphysical conjunction of circumstances, but by God alone, the sovereign of all times.

3. *The contents of revelation.* It is Himself whom God reveals to mankind, He whom no man can see (Jn. 1:18) and whom the sinner must even fear to encounter (Lk. 5:8; Rom. 1:18). This self-revelation is total; God does not impart to men simply a body of information with regard to subjects which surpass their natural capacity, such as the hidden things of eternity or the future unfolding of time. Nor does He deliver over to them a knowledge which would give them the illusion of becoming divine or semidivine and capable of doing without Him. He reveals His person to them by revealing His primal secret, namely, that He loves

them (1 Jn. 4:9), and that this *love, derided by sin and made ineffective since the entry of death into the world (Rom. 5) has impelled Him to give His only Son for the world's salvation (Rom. 3:21: the "righteousness of God"). It is in this Son that God makes Himself known, as the One who forgives sin and triumphs over death, hence it is the Son Himself who forms the explicit content of the revelation (Jn. 14:9; Gal. 1:16; Mk. 1:1 has simply as its title "Gospel of Jesus Christ"). And since Jesus Christ does not remain an external reality to be contemplated but in revealing Himself He lives and reigns among believers, His life which circulates in the body of the Church is the concrete form in which He is manifested in the world. Hence the life of Christ in the members of His body becomes equally an object of revelation (our life, says the apostle, 2 Cor. 4:10; Christ in you. Col. 1:27; faith, Gal. 3:23). Hence it is not the human aspect of Jesus considered separately (His character, His virtues, His opinions) which reveals God to us, but rather what He says as coming from God (His word); what He does for us on behalf of God (His self-humiliation and triumph); His life within us as Lord of the Church (His present authority, the authority of God); what He is and will be for the whole world as the vicegerent of God (His ultimate advent). Finally at the last day it is this same total revelation, neither more nor less, which will be manifested to the whole world: God will be all in all (1 Cor. 15:28), the *glory of God and of His children (Rom. 8:18–19; Col. 3:4; 1 Jn. 3:2). From beginning to end it is God Himself, His person, which is revealed, and with Him all the treasures of wisdom and knowledge (Col. 2:2–3).

4. *Those for whom the revelation is intended.* It is destined for all men (Lk. 2:31; 3:6; 1 Tim. 2:4) and it is for this reason that it is addressed in the first instance to those to whom it was promised, the children of Israel. Now, it is clear that as soon as it is presented to Israel who hopes for it and rejects it at one and the same time, it comes also within the reach of the world where it

is welcomed by men who are not or are no longer members of the covenant: the "children" (the people who are ignorant of theological subtleties, Matt. 11:25–27), the Gentiles (Matt. 8:10–12; 15:24–28, to the surprise of Jesus even; Acts 10–11). Israel's rejection and crucifixion of Christ (in which the world in its blindness has part) and the victory of His resurrection are events which give a universal significance to His coming and thrust revelation outside its historical grooves. Henceforward the Gospel will be preached to all creatures (Mk. 16:15; Matt. 24:14; 26:13; the ministry of *Paul). Preached but not universally received, for it could only be received in the act of *faith. But faith is not a universal attitude (2 Cor. 4:3–4). That is why Paul in his apparently exclusive summaries says that God has manifested Himself to those who believe (Rom. 3:21), to "those who love" (1 Cor. 2:9), "to his saints" (Col. 1:26). Similarly John emphasizes the fact that the *world does not know God because it does not accept His self-revelation and that Jesus Himself refuses to become known except through faith (Jn. 7:4). The intended scope of revelation nevertheless remains universal, both with regard to men and to creation as a whole (Rom. 8:19–22) and will find its fulfilment at the last judgment and the new heaven and earth (Rev. 20–22).

5. *The time of revelation.* Since the revelation of God is mediated through a historical event, the coming of Jesus Christ, it is situated within the time process. The whole history of mankind is controlled by it. Before that event there is the time of expectation (the old covenant and the prophecies: Lk. 10:24; Heb. 11:1; 1 Pet. 1:10–12; this O.T. God is not a different God from the God of the N.T., it is one and the same God whose mystery is simply made transparent in Christ), the time of obscurity and groping for the *Gentiles. The revelation of God in Jesus Christ occurs at the end of the times (1 Pet. 1:20) and marks the entry not into another time span of the same nature but into ultimate time ("eternal life", cf. Jn. 3:36). The N.T. says in-

differently that the revelation has taken place at the end of time or in Jesus Christ, for Jesus Christ marks the end of world time. With the preaching of the apostles and the edification of the Church, this ultimate time becomes of critical importance for the whole world, for all nations. Now the hour strikes when salvation is imminent (Rom. 13:11–12; 1 Jn. 3:2), it is a time calling for vigilance and careful recollection (1 Cor. 11:24–26 and "until He come"), and for supplication (Rom. 8:19; 1 Pet. 4:13; Rev. 6:10; 22:17,20). Since the intervention of Christ the glorious manifestation of a creation lost and saved is the climax that is preparing, the time of ultimate disclosure has begun; if there is delay, it is simply to give the world the chance of repentance and faith (2 Pet. 3:9ff.). The urgent character of the revelation of Jesus Christ distinguishes it from all speculation and excludes arid sceptical indecisiveness.

6. *The revelation strikes home to men in different ways.* There are no special media reserved for the fulfilment of God's self-revelation. Jesus Christ has been manifested in the flesh and has risen again; everything that makes up life, including death, is therefore affected by this event. The apostles and especially St. Paul (Gal. 1:12; 2:2; 2 Cor. 12:1) were the first to receive the revelation. Since, it has been through the sense of the word of the messenger and the action of the Holy Spirit in the Church that the revelation has penetrated to the ends of the world, whatever the external forms it has used to promote its effectiveness. God employs every means so that men should come to the free knowledge of His self-revelation in Jesus Christ.

7. *The writings of the N.T.* (Gospels, Acts and Epistles, Revelation) *are not the revelation itself but the witnesses to it,* the narration and proclamation of it. Unique and of irreplaceable worth because of their place in history and their quality as informed witnesses (the so-called apocryphal writings are differentiated from the canonical ones not only by their later date, but also by

their more ambiguous spiritual value), unanimous in their declarations without however having been designed to form a literary unity, they are the source from which the Church takes its knowledge of Jesus Christ (Holy *Scripture). They are the guarantee and the judge of the Church's fidelity and apostolicity. They proclaim Jesus Christ and do not claim any other infallibility but that of being the authorized messengers regarding His coming into the world. God revealed Himself through Jesus Christ and not through a book, but the writings of the N.T. are the "ministers by means of which you have believed" (1 Cor. 3:5), which indeed it is essential to consider and to study down to their very details. But faith, like obedience and honour, is reserved for the Master Himself.

CH. BIBER

REWARD

The Greek word which our translations usually render by such terms as reward, hire, recompense, means literally the wages due to the workman for his work (Lk. 10:7; 1 Tim. 5:18; Jas. 5:4; Matt. 20:8) or the recompense for a service rendered (cf. Acts 1:18 and 2 Pet. 2:15; the reward of iniquity is the pecuniary profit which Judas and the false teachers have derived from their sins). We have the same sense figuratively in Jn. 4:36 and 1 Cor. 9:17–18. In most of our texts the idea of recompense, without any essential change of meaning, is used to denote the reward which God grants to those who have accomplished His will (cf. Matt. 6:1,4,6,18; 1 Cor. 3:8, 14:2; Jn. 8, etc.), and even exceptionally divine retribution or punishment (Acts 22:12; 2 Pet. 2:12–13; in the latter text the hire of wrongdoing forms a pun on the same expression understood literally in 2 Pet. 2:15, and means the just punishment of sin). The N.T. took over from the O.T. not only the language of recompense but also the fundamental outlook which required its use.

Retribution in the O.T. In its oldest parts the O.T. presents the idea of divine retribution in an essentially negative manner: God punishes men who, behaving contrary to the spirit of the *covenant, exclude themselves from it. Thus it is with Adam and Eve (Gen. 3:16–19; cf. Gen. 2:17), with mankind in the days of Noah (Gen. 6:5–7) with the inhabitants of Sodom (Gen. 18:20–21) etc. This is still more clearly the case from the time of the founding of the covenant of Sinai. When the Israelites show by their actions that they do not remain within that covenant, God gives free course to His righteous *anger against them (Num. 25:3; Josh. 22:20, etc.). Once the alliance of God and man has been founded in Adam, in Noah, in Abraham, in Moses, once God has united men to Himself by His sovereign initiative, the conduct of man becomes of decisive importance: he remains within the alliance or he leaves it, he remains faithful to it or he becomes unfaithful. God, having set up for ever this alliance, must thenceforward react to the deeds of men. The task of the first writing prophets is to develop this fundamental essentially negative aspect of retribution (negative because reflecting the positive divine creation of the covenant). The Israelites are wrong to suppose that their election ensures their salvation whatever their conduct. On the contrary, that election invites them to live within the framework of salvation and to maintain themselves within it by their actions, thus escaping the divine wrath, and protected by a covenant which alone can give them life (Amos 3:2; 5:6,14–15; Hos. 6:7; Isa. 5:1–30, etc.).

Classical Greek thought, having nothing corresponding to the Israelite idea of the divine covenant, can conceive of no other terms of reference for human life than those of the sovereign good. From such a point of view retribution has no meaning. The good is its own reward. But for the Israelite the value of actions is not intrinsic, they derive their worth solely from the fact that they are the means by which man remains within the covenant founded by God.

In Israel the idea of retribution became gradually enriched and quite legitimately so, at least in the early stages of this develop-

ment. On the one hand the influence of Ezekiel brought about a transition from the collectivist idea of retribution to the individualist idea (Ezek. 18). On the other hand its positive aspect was developed. Just as by leaving the covenant one becomes exposed to the anger of God, so by remaining within it one shares in its blessings which moreover are understood in an essentially materialistic way. Deuteronomy gives typical expression to this development, both in the book which bears its name as also in the editing which the deuteronomists imposed upon other earlier books, such as that of Judges (cf. Deut. 28:1–68; 30:1–20; Judg. 2:6–22).

Yet these developments, legitimate in themselves, could lead and did in fact lead to a falsification of the true conception of retribution. On the one hand, individual retribution, conceived too rationally and in too temporal a guise, provoked insoluble problems (Job and the sufferings of the pious man of which we hear in certain Psalms). Hence the scepticism of Ecclesiastes (8:14). On the other hand retribution gradually became divorced from the idea of the covenant; it was established as an independent dogma and hence distorted. Thus the idea arose that human actions *ipso facto* gave their authors the right to salvation, as if the covenant were no longer of any abiding and essential significance. In opposition to original Israelite thought, Jewish legalism as eventually formulated ended by linking together two concepts which in the perspective of the Bible are diametrically opposed: that of retribution and that of merit.

Recompense in the N.T. In this respect as in many others, the N.T., ignoring late Judaism, renews contact with the O.T. whose ideas it confirms and brings to their culmination. Generally speaking it will be noted that the ambiguous idea of retribution is superseded by the clearer notion of reward. As in the genuine thought of Israel itself, reward and punishment in the N.T. are not two opposite facets of one and the same thing. Rooted once again in the thought of the covenant, they show themselves to be specifically different from each other.

1. First of all it should be noted that outside the covenant, i.e., (in terms of the Gospel) outside the Kingdom of God proclaimed by Jesus Christ or (in Pauline terms) outside the new humanity of Christ, man, whatever his condition, is exposed to the righteous anger of God (Matt. 3:7; Rom. 1:18). Man can be saved only by means of *faith, by self-surrender to the mercy of God manifested in Jesus Christ. It is impossible to merit this salvation, since it has been given (Lk. 19:9–10).

2. Does this mean that human actions are of no consequence? Not at all. On the contrary, they become more decisive than ever; for they now show whether men have real faith. For what matters is not what man says but what he does. He has only one means of proving his faith and assuring himself that he really has faith: and that is precisely his *works (cf. Matt. 21:28–32; 25:14–30; 25:31–46; Rom. 2:6–11; Jas. 2:14–26).

3. Yet, no believer can ascribe to his works the power to secure his salvation. In themselves they are useless (Lk. 17:7–10; Rom. 3:27–31) and the Christian has no reason to glory in them. Why so? Because it is not to be assumed as a matter of course that good works are rewarded. That is the case only because God has so willed it in His mercy. It is by grace that the work of man is counted to his credit. Such is the meaning of the parable in Matt. 20:1–16; hence also the significant formula of Rom. 4:4. To refuse to do the good works which God requires would therefore be tantamount to man's showing that he does not wish to live by the Spirit of God (Gal. 5:16–25).

4. In these circumstances reward is not really distinguishable from salvation itself. For the reward is salvation not now merely offered but appropriated. Hence it could not form the basis of a self-interested motive

since salvation is granted only to those who deny themselves (Mk. 8:34–35). From this point of view the reward is in heaven (Matt. 5:12; 6:20; 19:21) without however being completely future, since believers receive the first-fruits of it already in this life (2 Cor. 5:5; cf. Mk. 10:28–30).

5. Hence it is neither faith nor works which saves man. It is God in Jesus Christ. But by faith man approves and accepts the divine plan of salvation and its realization in Jesus Christ, and by works he shows that this faith is sincere. The statement "God will reward believers for the works which their faith inspires", amounts therefore to this: "God really gives man by faith the opportunity of living in the Kingdom which He has established in Jesus Christ." This precludes all possibility of lapsing into legalism, since only he who abides in Christ bears fruit (Jn. 15:5). Hence the venture of faith does not issue in the void. It is wisdom itself (Matt. 7:24–27; 25:1–13) but a wisdom founded in God Himself (1 Cor. 2:12–14) and leading man to the rich fulfilment of God's promises (Gal. 6:7–10).

J.-L. LEUBA

RIGHT HAND

1. The O.T. writers show no marked predilection for anthropomorphisms; but the expression the "hand" or the "right hand" of God is the only concrete way in which men can speak of the living, active God who creates, who actively maintains, who attacks and defends, who judges, punishes and saves. It is very rarely used to convey the sense of hands which enfold and comfort (Isa. 40:11) like the hands of a mother (Num. 11:12). Rather the hand of God is spoken of as the hand of the Deliverer (Exod. 13:3), of the sovereign Lord of the universe (Ps. 95:4), of the Shepherd who keeps watch over his flock (Ps. 95:7), of the gracious and mighty Protector (Isa. 40:2; Ps. 63:8), of the King who instructs his messengers (Ezek. 3:22; 37:1), of the Creator (Ps. 104:28), of the

Judge exacting punishment (Isa. 5:25), of the invincible Adversary (Deut. 32:39; 2 Sam. 24:14), of the Judge beyond whom there is no appeal (Ps. 31:5,15). The "avenging" (not "vengeful", but literally "hand of justice", Isa. 41:10) hand of God establishes justice for the relief of the oppressed and for the vindication of His own honour (*Judgment, *Righteous). The "arm" of the Lord is spoken of in the same sense. To the people of God it is a source of great consolation and of great hope to know that His right hand is active, that is to say, that He is the Lord of world history and that His watchful providence is at work in the life of nations as well as in the life of each individual believer.

2. The N.T. rarely speaks of the hand or of the right hand of God (Lk. 1:51; Heb. 10:31; 1 Pet. 5:6). Rather the active intervention of God is thought of in terms of the coming of Jesus; henceforth it is expressly of Him that the N.T. speaks. By contrast, the expression "at the right hand of God" (from Ps. 110) occurs some 20 times. In the old dispensation Psalm 110 was a solemn song which formed part of the enthronement ritual; the accession of the king to the throne of Israel, although an action of a political character, was carried out under God's authority. The king became "lord next after God" of the people and assumed the highest authority, for which he would be at all times responsible to God. The N.T. applies this enthronement psalm to Jesus, whom God has made to be both Lord and Christ (Acts 2:26) and to whom He has handed all His powers (Matt. 28:18). Therein lies the significance of His "ascension", related at the end of Mark and Luke and at the beginning of the Acts, but just as forcefully preached in the two passages quoted as well as in numerous passages in the Gospels and Epistles, where it is referred to explicitly or implicitly.

The "ascension" expresses a real assumption of power, not a miraculous journey (the accounts of this event are couched in very sober terms, cf. the texts); the words "He ascended into heaven" express a political rather than a meteorological ascent (W. Vischer), for *heaven is the place where God reigns and which will always be higher than any human authority. "God exalted him" (Acts 5:31), "he sat down" (Heb. 1:3) or is "standing" (only in Acts 7:55–56) "at the right hand of God" means that Jesus, after His ministry, His death and resurrection, has been installed by God as King in the sense of Ps. 110, that is, as victor over all His foes (v. 1), as King of Israel (v.2), acting at the same time as eternal High Priest (v.4, cf. Heb. 7), and extending His victorious rule over every kingdom and nation (v. 5–6). All the N.T. writers proclaim this kingship of Jesus. (Other important passages are: Matt. 26:64 and parallel passages; Eph. 1:20; Col. 3:1; Heb. 8:1; 10:12; 12:2 and 1 Pet. 3:22, a very significant verse.) While John does not use the expression "at the right hand of God" and makes no reference to Ps. 110, his testimony supports that of the other writers in a different way (e.g., *Word). For all of them, it is through Jesus that God acts, reigns, creates, maintains, attacks, defends, judges, punishes and saves.

CH. BIBER

RIGHTEOUS

1. During the first century of our era the adjective *righteous* was common in the Greco-Roman world in three main spheres of thought. The man was said to be righteous whom we to-day would call correct in his dealings with his fellow-men, also the citizen who was faithful and submissive to the laws of the state (political and juridical loyalty), and, above all, the man who was virtuous according to the standards of popular stoicism. This doctrine of virtue was characterized by a fundamental moral optimism: man finds in himself and in "nature" the principle and the possibility of this righteousness conceived as a moral equilibrium, a personal achievement, rarely attained, it is true, but definitely entering into the possibilities of the person who is willing to apply himself seriously to it. The noun *righteousness* corresponds to this

general orientation of thought; as for the verb to *justify*, we come across it much less often, and by it is understood the idea of righteousness describing in the main a state or a quality. In Hellenistic mysticism, which was influenced by the Oriental religions, to justify signified to make righteous, to make sinless and perfect in the sense of a religious quality acquired once for all. We will cite here the following passage, which is perhaps opposed to the Christian idea of imputed righteousness at the last judgment: "This stage, my child, is the seat of righteousness: see how, *without trial*, it has driven out unrighteousness. We have been *made righteous*, child, now that unrighteousness is no longer there" (*Corpus Hermeticum*, XIII, 9).

2. In the O.T. the orientation of the idea of righteousness is very different; basically, the conviction is found that Yahweh alone "judges" concerning what (or who) is righteous; the verb to justify is most often passive; man is not righteous in himself, he is justified, that is to say, *declared righteous* by God, and it is this divine approval which he seeks above all: "In the Lord shall all the seed of Israel be justified and shall glory" (Isa. 45:25, A.V.). Even in human relationships the notion of righteousness retains the juridical and forensic (declaratory) emphasis: Woe to those . . . who "justify the wicked for reward, and take away the righteousness of the righteous from him" (Isa. 5:23, A.V.). In this conception God is presented primarily as a judge; but not at all like a modern judge who seeks only to apply the requirements of a code in the most equitable manner possible, but like an ancient king sovereignly exercising his right of life over his subjects (Ps. 7:12; Jer. 12:1; Judg. 5:4; Ps. 5:9,11; 18:26ff.; Isa. 42:41). The biblical, and in particular the Pauline, notion of the righteous and righteousness will not be understood unless it is seen in this O.T. perspective of the king-judge. Here the righteous is no longer the virtuous man, far less the man who has been inwardly transformed or deified by some mystical initia-

tion; it is essentially the man who is *approved by his king*. This approval contains two nuances: it can be an explicit approval of the subject's life; but it can also be an approval that is a liberation, delivering the subject either from the oppression or violence of his enemies or from the oppression of his own errors.

The O.T. displays all the nuances of this "juridical situation" of man before his king. The most profound is undoubtedly that of the man who does not even dare to present himself before his king-judge: "Hear my prayer, O Lord; . . . answer me in thy righteousness. Enter not into judgment with thy servant; for no man living is righteous before thee" (Ps. 143:1–2). In this same Psalm, 143, it is remarkable that man at one and the same time fears and yet seeks the juridical verdict of his God; the fact is that he knows that this righteousness is fundamentally a righteousness of mercy and goodness: "In thy righteousness bring me out of trouble; and in thy steadfast love cut off my enemies" (vv. 11 and 12). And this righteousness not only liberates; it is righteousness in action which, after having humbled man under its royal authority, lifts him up and assists him to live better: "Teach me the way I should go. . . . Teach me to do thy will; for thou art my God" (vv. 8 and 10; cf. Ps. 19:10ff.; Mic. 7:9, which one cannot refrain from quoting: "I will bear the indignation of the Lord because I have sinned against him, until he pleads my cause and executes judgment for me. He will bring me forth to the light; I shall behold his righteousness" (A.V.). Here we see both the trepidation and the confidence of man before his judge-king (see *Judgment O.T.)).

3. The N.T. with its very appreciable nuances is dominated by these same O.T. conceptions. In it, it is true, we come across several texts where *righteous* signifies respectable, virtuous, honest, as in surrounding Hellenism (Matt. 27:19; 27:24; Phil. 1:7; 4:8; Lk. 12:57; 2 Pet. 1:13); but even in this group the tendency is for this "respectability" to be constituted "before God"

(Acts 4:19; 2 Thess. 1:6; Eph. 6:1, according to the original text).

God is righteous in the same sense as in the O.T. He exercises sovereignly his right of life and death, of approval and disapproval, over His subjects who comprise all men (whether they know it or not; Rev. 16:7; 19:2; 1 Pet. 2:23; Jn. 17:25; Rom. 7:12), with this decisive qualification that this righteousness of God is not considered in itself, but in the historic verdict pronounced in the death and resurrection of Jesus Christ (Rom. 3:26; 1 Jn. 1:9; Rom. 1:17; 2:2). God is thus conceived as a king *who has pronounced a verdict* which entirely alters the condition of man (and even of the whole universe) before Him.

But before describing what this condition is (that is to say, what is the content of the judicial declaration of God in Jesus Christ) we should notice that the N.T. recognizes a righteousness, in a much broader sense, which does not result directly from the work of the cross; in a very general sense, the righteous are all those whose conduct is approved by God: Abel, Matt. 23:35; Heb. 11:4; Lot, 2 Pet. 2:7; cf. Matt. 13:17; 23:39; Lk. 1:6; 2:25. Jesus seems to have taken seriously the current distinction of His day between the righteous (the practisers, those who remain faithful to the law and to its main religious exercises: almsgiving, prayer, fasting) and sinners or the unrighteous (the great mass of the indifferent, those who are detached from the religious life and its practices: Mk. 2:17; Matt. 5:45; Lk. 5:32; 15:7; cf. Rom. 5:7; Matt. 23:28; Lk. 14:14; 20:20). It is in this same sense that the noun *righteousness* designates the sum of the concrete practices of the faithful Jew's religious life (Matt. 3:15); those who "hunger and thirst for righteousness" are those who long for a life finally approved (and set free from all oppression) by God (Matt. 5:6; 6:33; 5:10,20). This righteousness is not internal or spiritual; it is always understood as a concrete, human, historic way of life (Matt. 6:1; Lk. 1:75; 1 Pet. 2:24; 1 Jn. 2:29; Jas. 3:18).

As for the distinctively Pauline terminology, it is completely dominated by the O.T. conceptions, with the qualification already mentioned that the verdict of God, accuser *and* liberator (cf. Ps. 143), is no longer expected or recognized in some particular event of national or personal destiny, but in the unique fact of Christ "dead and risen". Confronted with this event, the apostle Paul is like a man who, having received the sentence of a judgment which has just taken place, applies himself to its clarification and to the examination of its unforeseen consequences.

(*a*) The verdict of God has not only been pronounced once for all in *Jesus Christ; it is now "revealed" to all men by the preaching of the Gospel (Rom. 1:17). It is not sufficient for Paul that a work of salvation should have been accomplished in the past; it is necessary, in addition, that man should give attention to it and live by it. The righteousness of God, "accomplished" on the cross, is now "revealed" by the apostolic preaching, and will finally be "manifested" at the last judgment. At one time the apostle emphasizes the fact of the past event, at another the possibility which man "now" has of living as the "justified" person which the cross has made him, and at another on the ultimate consummation of this righteousness accomplished on the cross and already received by faith.

(*b*) Man's condition is not defined by his need of immortality or of perfection, but by the divine curse which rests upon him (Rom. 5:18; Gal. 3:13). Because God loves man and intends to re-establish him in his dignity as a freely obeying son, he does not cease to curse him and to "impute" to him his sin (Gen. 15:6; Rom. 4; 5:13; 2 Cor. 5:19). His curse, which is subservient to His purpose of love, thus finds its accomplishment in the *cross of Jesus. And because His righteousness is a liberating righteousness it must close with and condemn sin once for all (1 Cor. 15:3; Rom. 14:15; 1 Cor. 8:11; Gal. 2:20; Rom. 4:25; 8:32–34, etc.). It wins at the cross a decisive victory over all the "powers" which held man and the universe completely enslaved (the law, sin, angels in the service of Satan, etc.).

(c) It is a matter, then, on God's part, of a new act of liberation; but it is, above all, a matter of a new dispensation of His eternal love. Since the creation of the world God has had in view the new creation in Jesus Christ; all the history of mankind converges on the cross (Rom. 5:12ff.; 1 Cor. 15:20ff.). The cross is not a last human attempt to appease the divine wrath; it is the work of God, the decisive "ceremony" of reconciliation, long since prepared, as was the Levitical sacrifice (Lev. 16) in the old covenant.

(d) It is God's intention that man should respond to this act of reconciliation. This response could not be anything other than an unconditional surrender to the verdict of God pronounced in Jesus Christ. Man can do no more than surrender, than believe; the mention of *faith is in the first place restrictive; but man is able truly to believe (when the Gospel is preached to him). Paul intends that this submission of faith (Rom. 10:17) should be the *only* possibility left to man as the *only* condition of his entry into the Church (Rom. 3:25,26; 8:3; 5:6,7; Phil. 3:12,8). Thereafter the believer, relying only on the work of God accomplished in Jesus, renounces all claims to a righteousness of his own (the righteousness of [= resulting from the works of] the *law); he is a man justified "by" faith, not that his faith is for him a new meritorious work, but because he does not cease to rely on the sole righteousness "of God" (Phil. 3:9, the clearest text on this subject).

(e) This righteousness "imputed" to the believer by God, let it be noted, is a real righteousness. The man to whom God, for Jesus' sake, no longer imputes his sins *is* righteous (before God, which is all that matters); he is a "pardoned sinner", really pardoned, and thus really righteous. Just as in Ps. 143 the God who has condemned and caused to die is also the God who raises up and opens to man the concrete possibility of a better life (Rom. 6); set free from sin, man becomes "the slave of righteousness" (Rom. 6:18). In this text we find the word righteousness used in its current Jewish sense of a life approved by God; the

man who has been pardoned can and must lead a righteous and truly new life.

(f) Finally, if righteousness has been accomplished at the cross, revealed by the Gospel, and lived in the "service of righteousness", it will be fully manifested only at the last judgment. It therefore remains, as well, an object of hope and the believer lives as one who hungers and thirsts after this full righteousness (Rom. 3:6; 2:3–10,16; 2 Cor. 5:10; 1 Cor. 4:4–5; Rom. 8:38,39; 5:9,10,11; Gal. 5:5: "For through the Spirit, by faith, we wait for the hope of righteousness"=righteousness hoped for).

P. BONNARD

SABBATH, *see* FEASTS

SACRIFICES

O.T.

1. The offering of sacrifices to the deity is not a custom peculiar to Israel. Under various forms almost all primitive peoples were accustomed to this practice. It would be no use trying to attribute the use of sacrifice to one single originating cause; several ideas have certainly contributed to its genesis and development. In the oldest period which our documents allow us to reach—and in the case of Israel this is not very old—we can establish the co-existence of very diverse types of sacrifice: some are a joyful gift to the deity (Exod. 23:15; Deut. 16:16); others are intended to seal an alliance between men (Gen. 31:44–54) or between the latter and God (Exod. 24:9–11); others again are genuinely aimed at nourishing the god (cf. the shewbread, 1 Sam. 21:1–6). The phrase "bread of God", often so rendered in our translations, is frequently used in the priestly code to denote sacrifice (Lev. 21:6,8,17). In other cases the aim of sacrifice is to expiate sin which has been committed (cf. Lev. 16:11).

Faced by this diversity it is impossible to say whether a transition took place from one type of sacrifice to another or to trace any movement of organic development. Sacrifice in its various forms does not originate in any single factor, and must have had very varying aspects from the start. The same also seems to be true of peoples much older than the Israelites. A theoretical reconstruction of any supposed line of evolution would correspond more to our own logic than to any thoughts of primitive peoples; what is still done to-day among the peoples of Australia or Africa is no guarantee that the same development took place in ancient Israel. When we are dealing with sacrifice we must never lose sight of the fact that there were bloodless as well as bloody sacrifices: in ancient times both types seem to have had equal importance and often the same theoretical value is assigned to them.

2. According to some of our texts, sacrifices existed from the most ancient times: Cain and Abel already offer sacrifices (Gen. 4:3,4). But according to the priestly theory the rules of sacrifice were first revealed to Moses, and the most precise directions were given from the start. This theory of course completely denies the sacrificial activity of the patriarchs, of which, however, we have information in much older texts. In the story of the Flood (J source) Noah on leaving the ark hastens to offer a sacrifice to the God who has saved him (Gen. 8:20–22); but in the priestly version of the same story there is no mention of such an incident. The prophets tell us indeed that even in the desert the Israelites did not offer sacrifice (Amos 5:25) but our old documents show clearly that sacrifices were offered in this period and that on this point the view of the prophets was wrong.

In the history of sacrifice in Israel we see that the Babylonian Exile forms a very sharp line of demarcation. For on the one hand this event had a profound repercussion on the religious conscience of the people and on their cultic habits, and, on the other hand, it was only after the Exile that extensive cultic legislation was drawn up and a systematic account given with indications of the particular sacrifices to be offered in given circumstances. Before and after the Exile we find the same sacrifices,

but their relative importance underwent a change; certain types, such as expiatory sacrifices, now assume great significance while others are less frequently practised.

For the pre-exilic period it is solely on the basis of the accounts which we have that we must try to reconstruct the sacrificial system in use. The circumstances in which the various sacrifices were offered are made quite clear but nowhere are we given the underlying theory. It would seem indeed that the original sacrificial customs of Israel were very similar to those of neighbouring Semitic peoples; and for a still older period the Ras Shamra texts of Northern Phoenicia give us very valuable information. The O.T. stories do not provide a picture in the least systematic, but their main features seem convincing enough.

3. All the circumstances of daily life, both sad and joyful, may be the occasion of the offering of sacrifices. On feast days sacrifices are celebrated with great rejoicing (1 Sam. 20:6) while a yearly family pilgrimage gives the opportunity of celebrating them in more intimate fashion (1 Sam. 1:3). When the harvest is gathered in—corn, wine or oil —part of the produce is offered to the deity as a token of gratitude. If this feeling of gratitude was predominant at a very early stage, it is no less clear that originally the object of the offering of the first-fruits was to give to the deity the part which he could rightfully claim of all the products of the soil so that the remainder could be consumed without fear by his worshippers. It was, so to speak, a sort of de-consecration of the harvest so as to make it safely utilizable in common life. If these rites had been omitted wittingly or unwittingly the fertility of the earth would have been seriously affected (cf. Hos. 9:3ff.). When a child was weaned (Gen. 21:8) or a wedding celebrated, or it was desired to honour a distinguished guest (Gen. 18:6) all those concerned assembled to partake of a joyous feast and the ceremony began by a sacrifice, whether expressly mentioned or not; it was always an integral part of the feast. More-

over, before Deuteronomy it would have been inconceivable to slay an animal without ritual, and meat was the basis of every serious feast. If a treaty was negotiated it was finally sealed by a sacrifice (Gen. 31:54). When man begins an important undertaking he offers sacrifice in order to invoke the aid of the deity. On the battlefield, sacrifice is meant to help in discovering the will of God and in obliging God, so to speak, to come and succour His worshippers (1 Sam. 7:8ff.; 13:8ff.).

At other times the worshipper is more cautious; he simply makes a vow: "If Yahweh will grant me this or that I will offer Him such and such a sacrifice" (Gen. 28:20ff.; Judg. 11:30ff.). It would seem that there was felt to be hardly any difference between fulfilling a vow and offering a sacrifice of thanksgiving. In the oldest periods it appears that the worshipper was under the distinct impression of sharing his food with the deity, whence the expression "food of God" used at times to denote sacrifice. If the deity is justly angry with his people, it is obvious that he must be appeased by a sacrifice before one shares food with him (cf. 2 Sam. 24:15ff.; 1 Sam. 26:19). In certain circumstances the sacrifice is wholly burnt on the altar, the supreme means of conveying it to the god: this is the whole burnt offering, which is less frequent than other types of sacrifice.

4. Apart from the sacrifices offered by pious individuals there are also of course the sacrifices which are regularly offered in the various sanctuaries on behalf of the community as a whole, and which presuppose a more advanced stage of development with an organized clergy. Such is the implication of the shewbread (1 Sam. 21:4). Later still in the Temple at Jerusalem there was offered every day a burnt offering in the morning and a meal offering in the evening (cf. 1 Kings 18:29,36; 2 Kings 16:15).

5. The biblical accounts also give us such slight information as we possess about the way in which sacrifice was offered. The sacred stone is anointed with the oil (Gen.

28:18) while the water and wine are poured out on the ground before Yahweh (1 Sam. 7:6). The loaves are placed in the sanctuary (1 Sam. 21:3ff.); in the Temple at Jerusalem there is a special article of furniture for this sort of offering. But sacrifices of that kind are not the most frequent. More often fire is used, whether it be a case of bloody or bloodless sacrifices (cf. Judg. 6:21). We see that cakes are not only placed before the deity but burnt (Amos 4:5). Thus the food is more effectively conveyed to him.

Sacrifices do not imply secret rites which only a priest would be qualified to carry out. Originally anyone could offer sacrifice; the king as head of his people, but also any head of a family. Very soon however a class of qualified specialists arose to fulfil this office (Judg. 17:1-13). They gradually grew in importance and soon to offer sacrifices was a privilege that was reserved to them (see *Ministry O.T.: *Priesthood O.T.). Every local sanctuary must normally have had its special customs regarding sacrifice, but we are only informed of the system embodied in the priestly code, which no doubt reflects the practice of the Temple at Jerusalem—the sole authentic sanctuary since the Deuteronomic reform. It is not likely that this code introduced any important innovations; it would rather systematize what had for long been the practice, but we have no formal proof of that. Yet this systematization must have occasioned some changes reflecting the feelings predominant at that time and which had not previously been to the fore.

6. In the sacrificial system a distinction must be drawn between the whole burnt offering and the sacrifice of thanksgiving—a distinction based on the portion of the sacrifice assigned to the deity. It is a distinction in quantity rather than quality. The whole burnt offering is that in which the victim, generally an animal, is entirely burnt on the altar (1 Sam. 7:9; Deut. 33:10); the word holocaust suggests this well (Gk. *holos*=all, *kaio*=burn) but the Hebrew word normally used does not make clear the nature of the sacrifice. In the

sacrifice of thanksgiving, only a small portion of the victim is burnt on the altar; the remainder is eaten by the priests and communicants. This type of sacrifice is the one most frequently practised in pre-exilic times. It gave rise to joyous feasting and banqueting such as must easily have degenerated into licentiousness, and it is the fact of this too customary excess which caused the prophets to condemn it so severely (cf. 1 Sam. 1:14). Often indeed to denote the act of sacrifice the Hebrews spoke of eating and drinking before Yahweh (Deut. 12:18; 14:26; 15:20; Exod. 32:6; Judg. 9:27; Amos 2:8, etc.). We learn also that near to the altar was a chamber intended for feasting (1 Sam. 9:22; Jer. 35:2).

In order to offer a sacrifice the worshipper must be in a state of ritual *cleanliness. The regulations with regard to this must have differed fairly considerably from one sanctuary to another and we know little of them in detail. No doubt they must have followed the same general lines, however much they varied in detail.

We should also mention for the oldest periods the fact of human sacrifice, which seems to have been always the exception and to have been essentially repugnant to Yahwism (Gen. 22:1–18; Judg. 11:29–40; 1 Kings 16:34; 2 Kings 16:3). In the time of Manasseh child sacrifices which had been practised by the Canaanites once again came into favour, no doubt under foreign influences.

7. The return from the Exile marks a new period because we possess from then onwards more systematic texts: the laws of Ezekiel and the priestly code in its various stages. But it is especially the case that a different spirit animates the whole religious life of the nation, and this fact has immediate repercussions on the prevalent ideas of sacrifice. The systematization of sacrifice is important because the new codes are to remain in force until the destruction of the Temple in A.D. 70, and this new system corresponds to what we see reflected in the N.T. Even if we cannot positively affirm

so much owing to lack of precise information, the ritual changes do not seem to have been very important. We hardly find any until the later strata of the priestly code. Thus it is only at the climax of this long process of evolution that the high priest (the sovereign priest as so many versions clumsily put it) is assigned a special dogmatic position (Lev. 21:10–15).

The Deuteronomic Reform by its centralization of the cult at Jerusalem had already completed the separation of sacrifices from everyday life; this tendency was strengthened after the Exile. But the Exile modified especially the general idea of sacrifice. Sacrifice now ceased to be essentially an act of thanksgiving aimed at celebrating the blessings of God. Under the influence of retributory punishment such as the prophets foretold the consciousness of sin was enormously heightened, and as a natural consequence the part played by expiatory sacrifice was considerably developed. The latter was by no means an innovation (cf. 1 Sam. 3:14; 26:19), but previously it had not at all the same degree of importance. Whatever be its true origins, expiatory sacrifice is an instrument which God places at the disposal of sinful men in order to enable them to become reconciled with the deity who in strict justice should remain angry with their sins. To expiate is in a sense to pay the ransom price; but the idea of vicarious satisfaction is never met with in the theory of expiatory sacrifice, although it is found in other contexts in the O.T. (cf. Isa. 53:4ff.). The victim is not laden with the sins of the guilty and offered as a substitute, for in that case it would have been unfit to become a sacrificial victim. That does happen in the case of the goat for Azazel, which is laden with all the sins of the people; but it should be noted that it is not sacrificed, it is sent away into the desert (Lev. 16:20–28).

The idea basic to expiatory sacrifice is rather that the sacrifice represents something precious, and so much the more precious because it is bloody. Only at this time are sacrifices somewhat systematically grouped into bloody and bloodless ones; but these two categories are often found in the same ceremonies. The bloodless sacrifices, incense and libations, were not in former times of great importance; in the prophetic writings they are seen to be characteristic of foreign cults or strongly influenced by foreign ideas (cf. Jer. 7:18; 32:29). In the priestly code the libation of water or wine accompanies bloody sacrifices, while oil is reserved for bloodless ones (Lev. 2:1ff.). At this time the term *Minḥah* becomes the technical term to describe bloodless sacrifices, whereas in former times it had been applied to all sacrifices, bloody or not. It implies the offering of first-fruits of cakes and baked flour and shewbread. These gifts accompany bloody sacrifices (Num. 15:1ff.). They may even be used for expiatory purposes when they are offered by the poorest of the people. Incense was usually burnt by the Canaanites, but the oldest texts do not mention the Israelites as having used it. It may be surmised, however, that the latter did make use of it but it did not assume any importance until the formulation of the priestly code. Incense accompanying other offerings has probably the significance of something very precious.

In regard to sacrifices of thanksgiving one may distinguish sacrifices of praise, sacrifices performed in fulfilment of a vow, and purely voluntary sacrifices, i.e., those not prescribed by the law in given circumstances (Lev. 7:11–21; 22:17–25; Num. 15:1–16). In the priestly code the holocaust becomes of the utmost importance and often acquires expiatory significance. It is so important that, in the case of the very poor, the immolation and burning of very small animals is accepted, such as turtle doves or pigeons. As regards the circumstances in which a holocaust is to be offered, only certain special cases are mentioned: Lev. 12:6–8, after childbirth; Num. 6:14, on the expiration of the Nazirite vow. When several sacrifices are combined in one ceremony the whole burnt offering must never be missing. Thus in the daily sacrifices, which expressed the prayer of the community and which were intended to cover the sins of the people so that they

should not be exposed to the divine wrath, holocausts played a great part. These sacrifices made on behalf of the community were also intended to operate in favour of the authorities, and—we know this with certainty from the Greek period onward—foreign powers bore a part of the expense, which was quite considerable.

Sin offerings and guilt offerings are not always clearly distinguishable. The latter are used when injury has been done to the property of others and accompany the restitution of stolen goods. The sin offering is made whenever someone has involuntarily violated one or other of the commandments of God. In the latter case the offerer places his hands on the head of the victim, not in order to transfer to it his own sins (this would only be to make it impure and hence unsuitable for sacrifice) but in order to be more effectively identified with it.

In the whole of this period expiation, and especially expiation by *blood, plays an important part; but at times (or at least in certain texts) forgiveness is granted quite apart from any sacrifice. There seems to be not only a difference but a radical opposition between the two conceptions. To make this clear we should distinguish with certain authors between the sphere of the law, where the worshipper acts as a member of the community and where he must repair the damage done to the community by his sin, and on the other hand the sphere of the interior life, where man enters into direct contact with the divine. It is essentially for sins against the covenant that sacrifices are efficacious, since they can restore the harmony which has been disturbed by an infringement of the law. In this matter it is of course entirely a question of unwitting faults. For voluntary sins, sins with a high hand as the Bible says, there is no reparation possible; death alone can expiate the offence. But it should be realized that for the doctors of the law the area of involuntary sins was very extensive, certainly far more extensive than we should expect. As regards the sphere of personal communion with the deity, the idea of *forgiveness is not at all dependent on sacrifice, although in post-exilic theology sacrifice and expiation should always be considered as interconnected. In the Psalms for example we often see a very definite contrast drawn between these two modes of obtaining forgiveness (Ps. 32:5; 50:7–15; 51:18–19; 69:30–32; 103:8–14). In other passages forgiveness is connected with a change in the way of life and not at all with sacrifice (Mic. 6:6–8; Prov. 21:3; Dan. 4:27; Isa. 55:7; 58:6–9). In all these cases it is a question of individual sins which normally sacrifices should have expiated, but there is expressed a very marked consciousness that forgiveness is possible apart from all sacrifice.

To reconcile these two ideas, which seem conflicting, it should not be forgotten that at the basis of both lies the notion of the love and *grace of God, expiatory sacrifice being a gift of God exactly like direct forgiveness. No right conscience could be satisfied with sacrifices alone, for they always remain disproportionate to the gravity of the offence committed. In order to find peace one must obtain, over and above sacrifice, the grace of God, and one must bring to God true *repentance and the fervent desire to make amendment of life. The external and internal action do not by any means exclude each other and the second should always accompany the first and bestow upon it its true value. With the most pious souls the rite eventually takes second place. The sacrifice was allowed to function normally but the soul committed itself entirely to the grace of God.

The destruction of the Temple in A.D. 70 brought to an end the operation of sacrifices at the very moment when in many circles they had come to seem superfluous, although the pious had not had the courage or the will to abolish them. When, by the inevitable trend of development, sacrifices and especially expiatory sacrifices were nothing more than memories which could be idealized, the theology of them was sublimated. Since the practice of them had ceased, contradiction was no longer possible. The same development took place among the Christians where the O.T.

sacrifices, because they were no longer practised, became the symbol of higher realities.

G. NAGEL

N.T.

1. Jesus never declares Jewish sacrifice as it was offered in the *Temple at Jerusalem devoid of meaning. But for Him it belongs to the dispensation of the old covenant. What Jesus specifically rejects is the erroneous idea of those who consider that they have satisfied the demands of the will of God by the simple offering of a sacrifice, however costly (Matt. 12:7; 9:13; 23:23). In fact, what at best might prove a partial means of becoming reconciled to God thus becomes a means of further hardening of the heart under the deceptive appearance of a good conscience. For these two reasons Jesus is not interested in the sacrifices of the old covenant.

This superiority of the new *covenant to the old is further brought out in certain words where Jesus stands forth as the Messiah inaugurating the new covenant: "I say unto you that one greater than the temple is here" (Matt. 12:6), or again "Destroy this temple and I will build it again in three days" (Matt. 26:61; 27:40; Jn. 2:19; 4:21, etc.).

It is clear from these declarations (a) that Jesus is greater than the Temple, and that in His person God is present as He was never present even in the sanctuary at Jerusalem; (b) that Jesus is the Founder of the new covenant (cf. the three accounts of the Last Supper, Matt. 26:26–29; Lk. 22:15–20; Mk. 14:22–25) and that His mediation surpasses in every way that which was only partially and temporarily realized through the sacrifices (the author of the Epistle to the Hebrews will take up and amplify this theme). Jesus is the living expression of the will of God which the sacrifices never were.

2. (a) Paul, the apostle of the Gentiles, certainly knew all about the Jewish form of sacrifice, but he hardly ever speaks of it. On the other hand he examines closely the

pagan form of sacrifice. The problem raised by Christians' consuming meats sacrificed to idols, and the stir caused in the first Christian communities by a conflict of views on the subject, bear witness to a certain background of ideas on sacrifice. The apostle himself seems to have hesitated between two ways of understanding pagan sacrifice: (i) The consumption of the flesh of a victim sacrificed to an idol creates a certain communion with the latter. The Christian need not fear on this score, since Christ has overcome all the principalities and powers, which are henceforth subject to Him; nevertheless he should abstain from such meats (1 Cor. 10:20). (ii) The demon world is unreal (1 Cor. 8:4: "an idol has no real existence and there is no God but one"), hence the consumption of meats sacrificed to idols is a matter of indifference; the only possible reason for abstention is consideration for weaker brethren.

(b) These two attitudes of the apostle with regard to pagan sacrifice are however very close, since, in both cases, the victory of Christ is clearly affirmed. This victory of Christ of which we are at present concerned to analyse only one aspect is twice compared by the apostle to a sacrifice of unique value and efficacy. To the Corinthians he writes (1 Cor. 5:7): "Christ our paschal Lamb has been sacrificed"; and to the Ephesians (5:2): "Walk in love as Christ also loved us and gave himself up for us, a fragrant offering and a sacrifice to God." Christ is not a victim offered against His will; He offered Himself deliberately. The spontaneous character of His sacrifice is very important: it confers upon it universal significance, since the victim, instead of being offered by those in whose favour it was sought to restore communion with God, offered itself voluntarily. Such a sacrifice is therefore valid for all and at all times. Its meaning is not merely negative, as was the case with the offering of the old covenant; it does not merely efface sins, it does not merely overcome the barrier which separates man from God, it introduces sinners into a new way of life of which the resurrection of Christ marks the point of departure.

(c) Similarly the apostle uses various words and phrases all connected with the sacrificial idea to speak of his own life or that of believers in general: (i) If he dies as the result of a sentence consequent upon his loyalty to Christ, which the imperial tribunals would consider sacrilegious, he will "be poured as a libation upon the sacrificial offering of the Philippians' faith". Such an issue will be for him and the Philippians a subject of rejoicing (Phil. 2:17). This declaration is of the same order as "for me to live is Christ and to die is gain" (Phil. 1:21). (ii) The apostleship of Paul makes him a priestly servant of Jesus Christ. The converted Gentiles are the offering which he brings to the Lord (Rom. 15:16). In the same circle of ideas, believers are exhorted to offer their whole being as a living and holy sacrifice acceptable to God—which will be for them a service that is reasonable (Rom. 12:1). This same approach to sacrifice is found in the First Epistle of Peter (2:5). (iii) The only Pauline text where the term sacrifice is applied to a money offering is that of Phil. 4:18; Epaphroditus in the name of the Philippians has come to the help of the distressed apostle and has handed over to him a certain sum of money. Overwhelmed, the apostle declares that he has received the gift as a "fragrant offering, a sacrifice acceptable and pleasing to God".

3. The Epistle to the Hebrews, although it contains the word sacrifice but rarely, is nevertheless of all the N.T. writings the one which amplifies the theme most elaborately. It contains in fact a systematic comparison between the sacrifices of the old covenant and that of Christ who founds and inaugurates the new covenant.

(a) The sacrificial system of the old covenant was instituted by God but it is now superseded and surpassed by the sacrifice of Christ. It was merely an adumbration of the true and uniquely efficacious sacrifice which has been offered by Christ who is both high priest and victim (Heb. 7; 8; 9; 10:1–8); (b) the former was temporary and subject to constant repetition, but the second is eternal and unique (9:25,26); (*c*) the priest was a mortal and sinful man whilst Christ is the Son of God, without sin (7:11–8:6); (*d*) the *blood of Christ cannot be compared with the blood of animals (9:12); (*e*) the sanctuary of the new covenant is heaven and no longer an earthly temple (9:1,11,24).

The unique value of the sacrifice of Him who "has appeared once for all to put away sin by the sacrifice of himself" (9:26) inspires in the believer such confidence that he can now approach God. But for him who openly scorns the sacrifice of Christ there no longer remains any sacrifice for sins but "a fearful prospect of judgment" (10:27).

4. The author of the fourth Gospel is the only evangelist who does not speak of sacrifice in connection with the death of Jesus Christ. For him Jesus is either "lifted up" (cf. 3:14) or else He "ascends to the Father" (20:17) or else He is "glorified" (12:16, etc.). These three phrases describe the total action accomplished by Jesus between the cross and the ascension. The former sees this action as centred in the cross, the second insists rather on the transition from earth to heaven; the third throws into relief the result of the ascension; all three are concerned with the ascension in its point of departure, its fulfilment, and its result. Certain aspects of the thought of the Epistle to the Hebrews recur here, though it is never a question of the sacrifice of Jesus. The sacrificial value of His death seems to be assumed.

To sum up; all the N.T. writers, except the fourth evangelist, assign an important position to the death of Jesus Christ understood as a sacrifice (see *Cross). But at the same time they are conscious of the inadequacy of this affirmation: thus Jesus Himself emphasizes the realization through His sacrifice of the will of the living God, the apostle Paul presents the new life (flowing from the resurrection) as a consequence of the forgiveness of sins (flowing from the death on the cross), the author of the Epistle to the Hebrews declares the entrance

of Jesus Christ into heaven as into an eternal sanctuary into which we in our turn will enter, and lastly the author of the fourth Gospel sums up the whole work of Christ in His death (3:14) which is accompanied by a return to heaven—an event making heaven accessible to believers.

M. CARREZ

SADDUCEES, *see* JEWS

SALVATION

O.T.

As is the case with many biblical notions, it is somewhat difficult to combine into a synthetic view the very varied ideas which revolve around a single theme such as that of salvation. The idea of salvation is not quite the same in all the books of the O.T. and varies considerably from one prophet to another. Hence what we propose to say here will remain in broad terms and we shall not analyse in detail the complex aspects of the problem.

1. Several words in the Hebrew vocabulary are connected with the idea of salvation. Let us quote three main ones. The verb *padah* is often met with and means initially "to acquire an object or a person as one's possession by giving something in exchange" (money or the equivalent). It is a word which may be translated "buy" or better "buy back" (Exod. 13:13; 34:20; Job 6:22–23). When it is a question of God ransoming His people there is no exchange conceivable: God acts purely from grace and requires nothing in exchange. It is thus that He saved His people from their bondage in Egypt (Deut. 7:8). One other verb is used with the same sense: namely, *ga'al*. In the early days this word is applied to the fact of vengeance, when an offence or crime was committed against the member of a tribe or clan. The nearest kinsman of the victim had the duty of avenging the blood that had been shed: such a one was the *go'el* or avenger of blood. But the same word is used in the much wider meaning of ran-

soming, liberating a slave, delivering, saving, and is also used of God (Exod. 6:6). The *go'el* is the redeemer (see *Ransom).

But the verb which means more precisely to save is *yasha'*; especially when used in the passive voice or as a causative (cause to be saved). Originally this root seems to imply the idea of space and breath: to be in a spacious environment or to be at one's ease. Its opposite is the verb *sarar*, to be confined, hence to be in discomfort, distress, or anguish. From the original sense we pass to a more current sense connected with some deliverance or other: e.g., from an illness or danger, from war or death or bondage, etc. The word then takes on according to the context a special meaning: to be cured, to be successful, to be victorious, to live, to be freed. Later the scope of its meaning may be widened and may concern the salvation of man or of a people, at the last judgment at the end of time. By that development it becomes linked with eschatological and Messianic notions.

A noun derived from the verb means saviour (*moshia*). This is applied to men who have delivered Israel from an oppressor (e.g., the Judges, Judg. 3:9,15). There may be several saviours at one and the same time (Obad. 21). However, the word is generally applied to God Himself. It is He who is the saviour of man or of the people; there is no other but He (Isa. 45:21). It should also be pointed out with regard to this verb that it is the root which has given rise to the expression Hosanna (*Hosha'-na'*) the meaning of which is "Save now!" (Ps. 118:25 and Jn. 12:13), and that several of the best known proper names of the Bible are formed from it: Isaiah, Hosea, Joshua, and Jesus. Finally the word which corresponds to our own word "salvation" (*yecha'*) has a much wider meaning than is the case in our language. In addition to salvation it may mean deliverance, victory, wealth, happiness, prosperity, peace (it sometimes corresponds to the word *shalom*: peace).

2. As we have just seen, the idea of salvation in the O.T. includes certain features which we may now try to disentangle under the following heads:

(a) Salvation suggests first of all a material and concrete deliverance: it concerns the life of man or of the people in the many circumstances in which they are engaged and threatened. To be saved means to emerge safely from a perilous situation in which one risks disaster, defeat or death. Whether it be the Israelite on the field of battle (Deut. 20:4) or the believer who is a victim of illness or moral anguish (Ps. 6:5; 69:2, etc.) he turns to his God for deliverance and salvation. To save then is to help in the most material sense, as a friend who nurses a sick person, or as a company of troops who come to the help of another menaced by a superior enemy.

(b) In the O.T., salvation appears much more often as a collective and national deliverance than as an act of liberation towards an individual. Doubtless the salvation of the individual plays an important part too, especially in the prayers voiced by individual piety which are so often reflected in the Psalms. But even there it is not always easy to discriminate between the concern of the individual and that of the community. The liturgical character of the Psalms forbids us to make that radical distinction which we are tempted to make. Generally speaking, it is usually a question of the immediate or imminent salvation of the people or nation as a whole. Salvation is bound up with those political circumstances which constitute the thread of the history of Israel. It is hardly possible to speak of salvation in the abstract but only of salvation of the people in certain particular contexts: the bondage in Egypt, the oppression by neighbouring tribes, the threat of Assyria, the conquests of the Babylonians, captivity in Babylon, and the cataclysm of destruction which will herald the end of time and the coming of the Kingdom of God. The Messianic hope of Israel was always coloured, so to speak, with national and political shades: it was assumed that salvation would be marked by the beginnings of national restoration and the re-establishment of the throne of

David in Jerusalem, together with the reconstruction of a kingdom, free, prosperous, victorious, and eternal.

(c) Such a salvation can only be the work of God. It is God who is the saviour of the people as of the individual. The verbs which we have been discussing above have for the most part God as subject. Even when men are sent as saviours, it is God who sends them and guides them to enable them to effect the deliverance of the people. The prophets, whatever be the differences in the individual delivery of their message, are all at one on this point: that it is neither the kings of Israel and Judah nor the alliance with the Assyrians and Egypt nor national military power which can ultimately save the people. God alone saves (Hos. 5:13; Isa. 31:1; Ps. 33:16–17, etc.). More precisely, the divine work of salvation can be described under the following aspects. God has acted in the past: He has saved His people from bondage in Egypt. In biblical tradition the exodus was engraved as the supreme act of salvation wrought by God. In the present God saves His people in the circumstances which threaten them, for He is faithful to His *covenant and *promises. In particular, if He has permitted His people to go into exile as a punishment of their disloyalties, He will deliver them from that trial in His own time, and will bring them back into the land of promise. But that opens up the perspective of the future broadening out unto the end of time: God will save His people at the moment when the prophecies are finally fulfilled.

(d) It is in this eschatological sphere that ideas are perhaps the most varied. Although there is a risk of being too schematic we may perhaps suggest that there is a two-fold notion of salvation at the end of time. Firstly, a prophetic notion which describes the events of the end with reference to the return from captivity and the restoration of the elect people in Palestine. This restoration will be the prelude to the inauguration of the eternal Kingdom of God on the earth: the reassembling of the two kingdoms of Israel and Judah, the purification and sanctification of the people, the foundation of a new covenant with God, the judgment of the nations by the Messiah who will ascend the throne of Jerusalem and will be a descendant of David or a new David, the establishment of an eternal reign of peace, love, and righteousness, where nature itself will be renovated and the wolf will dwell with the lamb (Isa. 11:1–10; Jer. 31:31–34; Ezek. 37:21–28, etc.).

A second idea also emerges in the O.T., but it is in the extra-canonical literature that it is especially developed: this is the apocalyptic idea of salvation, which is to follow a universally destructive catastrophe; after such a cataclysm the judgment of God will take place for which the dead will be raised up; finally there will be the advent of the Messiah for the establishment of the eternal Kingdom with new heavens and a new earth (Isa. 65:17; Dan. 7 and 12).

(e) The notion of an interior personal salvation in the sense of a deliverance from sin and the joy of forgiveness, is not alien to the O.T. but it appears only rarely (e.g., Ps. 51:14).

The pages of the O.T. which contain the richest expression of the idea of salvation in the most complete sense of the word, as being both national and universal, immediate and future, collective and individual, are perhaps those of the great prophet of the Exile, Isa. 40–55.

F. MICHAELI

N.T.

The verb to save and the noun salvation together appear no less than 150 times in the N.T. Of these 150 texts the greater number (more than 100) give the *verb* whether in the active or the passive voice. The noting of this fact is not without its value; it means that the N.T. is concerned not so much with the idea of salvation in itself as with the fact of a historical salvation accomplished in *Jesus Christ, and soon to be manifested in its consummation.

1. But the N.T. uses the word primarily in a simpler sense, already current in classical Greek; to save is connected with salvation

in the sense of health: it means to restore health to one who has lost it, to restore safety to one who is threatened by a danger, to snatch from death someone who is about to perish (Matt. 8:25; 14:30; 27:40,42,49; Mk. 3:4; Lk. 6:9; Jn. 12:27; Acts 27:20; 4:9; 14:9; Heb. 5:7).

With regard to this first series of texts it should be noted above all that here Jesus often appears as the author of this immediate and tangible act of deliverance. He saves the disciples from the storm, He rescues Peter from drowning; and in parallel circumstances He does not save Himself from the cross. The fact is that the N.T. does not distinguish between a spiritual salvation of the *soul and a salvation, which might be considered less important, of the body. It envisages the person as a whole and considers that a sick or drowning man is totally threatened and that such a one would not hesitate to invoke the aid of Jesus (in many O.T. texts the saviour or deliverer is the one who brings decisive help quite simply). On the other hand if Jesus has come to help man who is threatened by all sorts of immediate perils, the help given, according to the mind of the N.T., assumes quite a special significance; its function is to declare and already to fulfil in a limited area of life the final and universal salvation which is generally awaited; to bear witness that the aeon of eschatological salvation has arrived and that now God is coming to the help of humanity as never before (Matt. 11:2–6). In this respect one often finds in the Gospels a phrase which is characteristic in its very ambiguity: "Thy faith hath saved thee" (Mk. 5:34; Lk. 8:48; Mk. 10:52; Lk. 7:50; 17:19; 18:42). The context shows that here salvation consists in the first place in the physical healing of the person to whom Jesus is addressing Himself; one might equally well translate (as has sometimes been done): "Thy faith hath healed thee"; but elsewhere the same phrase is found in stories which are not stories of healing (Lk. 7:50 where salvation is explicitly the forgiveness of sins; cf. also Lk. 17:19 which shows that salvation cannot be confined to mere physical healing).

2. We may now pass to the second series of texts where the specific character of N.T. thought is more clearly expressed.

(a) What we note first of all is that salvation is no longer understood as a particular or provisional deliverance but as a total and ultimate deliverance; there are many texts where the noun salvation is used in an absolute sense without any qualification (Acts 4:12; 13:26; 16:17; Rom. 1:16; 10:1,10; 11:11; 13:11; 2 Cor. 1:6; 7:10; Eph. 1:13; Phil. 1:28; 2:12; 2 Thess. 2:13; Heb. 1:14, etc.). These texts show that the primitive Christian faith soon acquired an idea of salvation in itself (especially in the school of the O.T.) and that it was more concerned to proclaim salvation as an accomplished or imminent event (as we shall see) than to define it.

(b) Salvation in the N.T. is always understood as a deliverance or a liberation and not as an accession to a higher or more spiritual life. The transition from the situation of man lost or enslaved to that of man in a state of grace is not effected by a process of development or spiritualization, but as the result of a sharp break, a reversal of values, a death through which salvation is achieved; this revolution in the condition of man is often described by means of verbs in the passive; man is saved (it is understood —by God; Matt. 9:21; 10:22; 24:13; 19:25; 24:22; Lk. 8:12; Jn. 3:17; 5:34; 10:9; Rom. 5:9,10; 10:9; 11:26; 1 Cor. 1:18; 3:15; 2 Cor. 2:15; 1 Eph. 2:5; 2 Thess. 2:10; 1 Tim. 2:4, etc.).

(c) But from what is man saved by God in Jesus Christ? On this point the N.T. uses various formulas which together, however, express a unified coherent conception. In the infrequent texts which define the matter, it becomes clear that man is saved from his sins (Matt. 1:21; Lk. 1:77; Acts 5:31; Lk. 7:50; Jas. 4:12), from condemnation (Jn. 3:17; 12:47; Mk. 16:16; 1 Cor. 5:5; 3:15; 1 Pet. 4:18), from perdition (Matt. 16:25; Mk. 8:35; Lk. 9:24; 1 Cor. 1:18; 2 Cor. 2:15; 2 Thess. 2:10; Matt. 18:11; Lk. 19:10), from *death (Jas. 5:20; Lk. 6:9; 2 Cor. 7:10), from the wrath of God (Rom. 5:9; 1 Thess. 5:9ff.). These various suggestions are

13

coherent in that they all reduce the peril with which man is threatened and from which he must be saved to the divine condemnation; no threat for biblical man is so serious as the disapproval of God. For this reason also the N.T. gives us a very sober description of the salvation attained; whether it speaks of it as joy, *life, the *Kingdom, etc., the essential presupposition is always that salvation will consist in a communion or *peace with God that has been recovered.

(d) With regard to the event or operation of salvation, the N.T. uses various formulas again. We have already found the phrase "Thy faith hath saved thee", which makes the event of salvation coincide with the act of *faith itself. Of course, if there is coincidence, there is not a relation of cause and effect here; it is Jesus who saves (or heals) and not faith; in such texts salvation or healing are presented as a fact realized in the past but still effectively present (the Greek verb is in the perfect). In a similar way the Epistles often speak of Christians as persons who are saved (literally those who are in the process of being saved, 1 Cor. 1:18; 2 Cor. 2:15; Eph. 2:5,8, etc.); it is not that the believer already possesses salvation as an inner religious security, but through apostolic preaching he is the object of the saving action of God; it is in this sense that the apostle can speak to the Ephesians about the "gospel of your salvation" (Eph. 1:13, i.e., the Gospel which not only speaks to you of salvation but which makes you enter into your salvation); it is in this sense also that the apostle affirms that he is not ashamed of the Gospel "because it is the power of God for salvation to everyone who has faith" (Rom. 1:16; cf. further 1 Cor. 15:2; Jas. 1:21). Such texts show us then salvation as a present reality, a new relation with God made effective by the preaching of the Gospel and its reception in faith.

(e) But we cannot remain there. In fact it soon becomes clear that these very texts which seem to make of salvation a quite immediate reality imply that while inaugurated of course it is nevertheless to some extent future; only in the *Kingdom, *after* the last *judgment, will man be definitely and completely saved. In this connection we should recollect those verbs in the future tense of the synoptic tradition (Matt. 10:22; 24:13; Mk. 13:13; 16:16; Lk. 8:50) of the Johannine (Jn. 10:9), of Acts (Acts 2:21; cf. Rom. 10:13; Acts 16:30ff.) and especially of the Epistles (Rom. 5:9,10; 9:27; 10:9; 11:26; 1 Cor. 3:15; 10:33; 1 Tim. 2:15; 2 Tim. 4:18); all these verbs imply that salvation is the ultimate accomplishment, after the last judgment, of the redeeming work of God in Jesus Christ. In the strict sense of the Greek terms believers *are* not saved but are in process of so being, yet have still to confront the pitfalls of this life and especially the last judgment of God. In this respect the most important N.T. texts are certainly Rom. 5:9 and 10, where we see that the apostle bases his certitude of ultimate salvation not on any present experience of partial salvation but on the fact that "Christ died for us"; Rom. 8:22,25 where we find that believers too are said to "sigh and groan" while waiting for their redemption, since they have been saved only by hope (v. 24), whence the necessity of the help of the Spirit granted to the believer until the final consummation of the work of salvation; and Rom. 11:25 where it is clear that salvation is not yet completed, and that not only as regards the life of the individual but in respect of the life of mankind, since all Israel will be saved after the multitude of the Gentiles has been brought into the fold of the Church.

P. BONNARD

SANCTIFY, *see* HOLY

SATAN, *see* DEVIL

SAVE, *see* JESUS, SALVATION

SCRIPTURE

The verb to write and the noun writing are frequently found in the N.T. First in the natural sense (Jn. 8:6,8; Jesus wrote with His finger on the ground; Lk. 1:63; Rom. 16:22; 2 Thess. 3:17, etc.), of a letter written (lit. engraven), of the work of writing or of a letter written and despatched, of written evidence or statements (Jn. 20:30f.; cf. Rev. 1:11,19 etc.), of legal provisions or written ordinance (Mk. 10:4f.; Lk. 20:28, etc.; and in a derived sense, Gal. 3:1).

The expressions "what is written" or "everything that is written" (*sc.* in the law or some collection of regulations) were common in the ancient world. In the Gospels they refer always to the O.T. Luke especially uses them a number of times to give expression to the idea that the *whole* of the O.T. (lit. "all the written things") witnesses to Christ Jesus (Lk. 18:31; 21:22; 24:44, etc.). The same anxiety to emphasize the unanimity of the O.T. witness to Christ is apparent in Paul's use of the word scripture (lit. writing), Gal. 3:8; 3,22; cf. Rom. 11:32. In the two Galatians passages Scripture is personified by the apostle; though not, as in Hellenistic-Jewish speculations, by way of hypostasizing the O.T. (as happened to Wisdom in late Judaism): rather, Paul speaks of Scripture as a person because he sees behind it, controlling it and alone giving to it its meaning and authority, the "Lord" or "the Spirit of God": in fact, as the comparison of Gal. 3:22 with Rom. 11:32 makes clear, it is God who has handed all men over to sin (by means of scripture, in particular by means of the written *law) in order that one day He might have mercy on all.

It is only comparatively rarely that the word *scripture* refers to a particular text of the O.T. (Mk. 12:10; Lk. 4:21; Jn. 19:37; Acts 1:16; 8:32; possibly also, but not certainly, Mk. 15:28; Jn. 7:38; 13:18; 19:24,36), and this indicates that primitive Christianity was not so much concerned to demonstrate the correspondences between particular texts of the O.T. and items in the story of Jesus as to bring out the fundamental correspondence between the whole of the O.T. and the events of the new covenant. It is of fundamental importance to analyse the terms of this correspondence as it was then conceived.

1. Jesus and the earliest Christians shared the same notions about the O.T. as their Jewish contemporaries: it was the sole authority for religious doctrine and practice. The N.T. is indeed incomprehensible unless this primary fact is recognized. The O.T. canon had not been finally fixed by the time of Jesus; but the hesitations, in particular with regard to the books of Daniel, Ezekiel and the Song of Songs, are of no consequence. The division given in Lk. 24:44 (the Law of Moses, the Prophets and the Psalms) was the most usual; little distinction was made between the several books in the collection, all admittedly being invested with unquestioned authority. (Serious divergences only emerged in the realm of interpretation.) This authority of the O.T. had by this time found its apologists, both among the Jews of Alexandria, who based their theory on a Greek idea of inspiration regarded as "ecstasy", an invasion of the sacred writer by the spirit of God, and among the doctors of Palestine who attached a greater importance to the idea of tradition, which embraced both the sacred text itself and also the commentaries given on it. This doctrine of the inspiration of the O.T. (and even of the Greek translation of it, the LXX) was apparently adopted by Jews and the first Christians without reservation (Jn. 5:39; Matt. 22:43; Mk. 12:36; Acts 1:16f.; 28:25; 1 Pet. 1:11; 2 Pet. 1:21; Heb. 3:7; 9:8; 10:15; 2 Tim. 3:16 especially, etc.). It has also been observed that the N.T. mentions the authors of the O.T. books less often than the rabbis were accustomed to do; possibly because the N.T. is more sensitive to the historical and human character of the O.T. witness than the Jewish doctors.

2. Upon the basis, however, of what they had in common with Judaism, the first Christians erected a doctrine controlled by the relationships between the old and the new *covenant. This could be illustrated in three ways:

(*a*) The overruling conviction is that Jesus and the community of His disciples *fulfil the O.T. According to Matt. 5:17 Jesus began to say: "Think not that I have come to abolish the law and the prophets

[=all the O.T.]: I have come not to abolish but to fulfil": cf. Mk. 14:49; 15:28; Matt. 26:54,55; Lk. 4:21, etc. This verb to fulfil cannot be understood in the modern sense of *perfect*, or *bring to its most noble expression*. Jesus did not come "to make improvements" to the law of God preserved in the O.T.: He was sent by God to give it concrete realization in history, that is to say, in order to inaugurate the *Kingdom of God which was promised in the O.T. (for the fulfilment of the promises, see e.g., Lk. 4:21); and to remind men of the meaning of the law of God, to summon them to unconditional obedience (Matt. 5–7); and to submit to it Himself (the fulfilment of the law). Thus the first Christians were able to find predicted in the O.T. not merely certain words and actions of Jesus but the whole career of Jesus and all the events which marked the foundation of the first Christian community (e.g., Acts 2:14–41; 3:19–26).

(*b*) But this idea of fulfilment evidently imposes a definite limit to the authority of the O.T.; for the decisive event of history is no longer the exodus from Egypt, the reign of David, or the figure of Elijah, etc. The decisive event has now just occurred and the name of *Jesus Christ completely sums it up. This Jesus has come forward specifically as the Messianic interpreter of the law (Matt. 5–7); in appealing in the Sermon on the Mount from the O.T. improperly interpreted to the O.T. understood by its fundamental affirmations (Matt. 5:31; Gen. 2:24 against Deut. 24:1) He swept aside both the rigid literalism of the rabbis and the allegorical and far-fetched commentaries beloved at Alexandria. His loyalty to the O.T. is fully expressed in His perfect understanding of its essential message. With Paul equally the O.T. is used as a witness to Jesus Christ, who died and was raised "in accordance with the scriptures" (1 Cor. 15:3,4); the object of faith is not the O.T., but Jesus Christ. Above all Paul finds types in the O.T., not particularly of Jesus Christ Himself, but of the condition of the new people of God. The narratives of the Israelites in the *wilderness (1 Cor. 10:1–13;

cf. Num. 25:1–9; Exod. 32:6) "were written down for our instruction, upon whom the end of the ages has come" (v. 11). According to Paul, the O.T. and the whole history contained in it only reach their destined end, their final series, in the new *Church of God; Abraham (Rom. 4; Gal. 3:8ff.; cf. Jas. 2:14–26), Sarah and Hagar (Gal. 4:21–31), and the Israelites in the wilderness are presented not as examples to be followed or not followed, but as the events of the old covenant which illustrate those of the new, as type to antitype.

The events and the situations of the two covenants are not merely repetitive, for the history of salvation ever moves forward to its destined end; but, from their place in history, their proper rôle is both to enlighten and warn those who stand within the new covenant. This is precisely what the Epistle to the Hebrews declares: its terms may recall the speculations of Alexandrian allegorizing, but its argument is rooted in history and is fundamentally Christocentric —it searches the O.T. purely to find "figures" or "types" (Heb. 9:9; 11:19) which bring into relief the superiority and uniqueness of the work of Christ.

(*c*) The Pauline antithesis of letter (Gk: *gramma*) and *spirit (Rom. 2:27; 7:6; 2 Cor. 3:6,14–16) is often much misunderstood. Paul does not there extol private inspiration or some "spiritual" conception of truth as against the adherents of "the religion of the book and its legalistic regulations". What he means is that the era of the old covenant with its subservience to the Mosaic Law (engraved on tables of stone) has been succeeded by Jesus Christ— the era of Christian faith and freedom made possible by the preaching of the apostles and the eschatological gift of the Holy Spirit. This apostolic preaching, soon embodied in the collection of canonical *scriptures* (writings) will, with the help of the Holy Spirit, always remain in the Church as the source and the guarantee of true freedom. (In 2 Pet. 3:16 the Pauline Epistles are already named alongside the "other scriptures" of the O.T.)

P. BONNARD

SEA, *see* NAMES (GEOGRAPHICAL)

SEAL

The seal has been in use from the most ancient times and often makes its appearance in the Bible. The matter, imprint, engraving, the mode and form of it are variable, but its use can usually be brought under a two-fold heading: it serves to secure a thing (to make it firm and keep it secret) or to confirm it (by the use of the *name, since the seal implies the witness of its possessor). It took the place of the many procedures which to-day go by the name of certificates of authenticity, identification papers, signatures, judicial seals, marks of ownership or of guarantee, rubber stamps, official stamps, commercial labels, etc. Many examples can be cited: thus a stone is sealed so as to make it inviolable (the den of lions, Dan. 6:17; the stone of the tomb, Matt. 27:60; the abyss into which Satan is cast, Rev. 20:3); a signature is sealed at the bottom of a document of alliance (Neh. 9:38; 10:1); the royal seal is affixed making a decree enforceable (Est. 3:10; 8:2–8; cf. 1 Kings 21:8, where the order is written in the name of the king); a deed of sale is thus legalized (Jer. 32:10), or a sign of identity given (Gen. 38:18).

However, the very importance of its function in everyday life soon made of the seal a theological symbol to which we must give our primary attention. In this respect we find the two principal meanings: (1) to fix under seal; (2) to attest, which are combined in a third expression which we shall study last: (3) to seal with the Holy Spirit.

1. *To secure under seal and keep secret.* This meaning appears principally in apocalyptic writers, for the seal is one of their favourite symbols (as we shall see, they also use the word in its second meaning). Thus in Dan. 8:26; 12:4 and 9, or in Rev. 10:4, the seer is commanded to keep secret the vision which has just been granted him: "these words will remain hidden and sealed until the time appointed". God wishes to reveal His plan to His servant but

the revelation must be kept hidden until the time of its fulfilment; it is in a sense rather like a staff secret which must studiously be prevented from reaching the ear of the enemy. Nevertheless God intends both to reveal and secure the secret and its witness so as to enlighten the faith of the latter and also so that the prophecy, divulged at the appointed time, should be there to show the foreknowledge and the omnipotence of Him who has inspired it. Accordingly we read in Rev. 22:10: "Do not seal the words of the prophecy of this book, for the time is at hand"; in this case it would be useless to keep the prophecy hidden, for the events are imminent and it is too late for the enemy to be able to forestall their realization. In Isa. 29:11 it is said that the visions of the prophets have become as the words of a book that is sealed; in fact as a result of their faithlessness the prophets have become unworthy to know the plans of God; they would only betray them. Isa. 8:16 suggests again in this sense that there is a kind of esoteric teaching among the prophets.

In the famous passage of Rev. 5 and 6 it is the prophetic book itself which is considered to contain the future events held under seal; to each of the seven seals corresponds an act in the drama of history; to break the seals would be to unleash the course of events and to put in motion those convulsions which are the prelude to the parousia. No one is found worthy to bring in the Kingdom, no one except the Lamb who is alone capable of leading history to its conclusion; it is He who keeps the keys.

Finally let us note Dan. 9:24: "sins are sealed up", i.e., enclosed as in a sealed bag so that no one can find them any more. The seal here is the divine *forgiveness. On the other hand in Job 14:17, by a curious reversal of the meaning, the same expression ("You have sealed up my transgression") denotes the wrath of God which publicly confirms through all the misfortunes of Job the memory of his sin: here we come to the second meaning, that of attest.

2. *To attest, confirm.* This meaning is found throughout the Bible and in the most

varied contexts. To seal is connected with the great biblical ideas of *witness and the sacramental sign. Thus the covenant of the promise made between God and Abraham is confirmed by the mark of *circumcision which Abraham receives in his flesh and whereby God is the first to commit Himself with regard to Abraham: He makes Himself the guarantor of the righteousness of Abraham (Rom. 4:11); similarly the *covenant of Sinai is sealed by blood (Zech. 9:11); the misfortunes of Job are, as we have seen, the speaking attestation of his sin; the presence of the beloved and his embrace are presented in the Song of Songs as the very seal of love (8:6). Further, in Jn. 3:33 the man who receives him whom God hath sent and accepts his witness "sets his seal to the fact that God is true". It is thus clear that the believer is invited by faith to confirm the Word of God—and here more especially the Word of God made flesh—but inversely in Jn. 6:27 it is the Father who marks Christ with His own seal. In this case the seal is the miracle of the feeding, one of the signs by which God attests the Messianic status of the Son of Man. For Paul the Church of Corinth is the sacramental seal of his apostolate; the authenticity of his vocation receives from those whom he has engendered into the Christian life a decisive and divine attestation (1 Cor. 9:2). By coming to Jerusalem to bring the offerings intended as a gift to that Church (Rom. 15:28) Paul seals the fruit of the Macedonians, i.e., he confirms the gift of their generosity which has witnessed so powerfully to the unity of the Church: his arrival in Jerusalem is the outward sign of this unity in love and the spirit. Finally, in 2 Tim. 2:19, the unshakable foundation of our salvation carries the seal of two words of God which confirm each other: the one deciding our justification (the election of God), the other our sanctification (the order of God).

There remain to be examined two series of texts where the meaning of our word is enlarged:

(a) The passages Exod. 28:11,21,30 and 36 in which sacerdotal vestments are described. The breastplate and the ephod, the girdle and the headdress of the priests will be sealed with the names of the children of Israel. The seal is at once a memorial and a consecration. When the priest advances towards the altar he truly presents himself before God in the name of the whole people; the names inscribed on each part of his garments are the unforgettable witness of this; (b) Those texts in which is mentioned what has been called the eschatological seal, the seal which designates and protects the elect through the vicissitudes of the last times; recognized by this sign they will emerge conquerors from the trial of the last judgment. In this connection already we might allude to the great Passover document where the blood of the lamb preserves the Jewish houses from the last plague of Egypt. We must also cite Ezek. 9:4 where in a Jerusalem destined to punishment and destruction the faithful receive on their foreheads the sign of salvation (cf. Isa. 44:5). But Rev. 7:2 and 9:4 are especially well known: there the angel is represented as holding the seal of the living God and with a gesture which is a prelude to the launching of apocalyptic tribulations he marks with it the forehead of the servants of the Lord. In this context the seal is at one and the same time a sign of recognition, protection, and divine seizure: since believers no more belong to themselves, they are confirmed in their faith and have received from the hand of God the assurance of their salvation. It is interesting to note that Revelation uses another word to denote the mark of the beast (Rev. 13:16; 14:9; 16:2; 19:20; 20:4)—and to note also that the mark of the beast is the result of succumbing to a pressing allurement, whereas the seal of God is received in virtue of an eternal election. Finally we may note the kinship of the latter expression with the one currently used in connection with baptism: "in the name of Jesus Christ".

3. *Sealed with the Holy Spirit*. All that has just been said with regard to the eschatological seal explains the origin of this expression and throws a vivid light on

it. But here the sense is much further expanded and the symbol finds its fullest meaning: in order to appreciate this we should think simultaneously of all the various uses of the seal which were described at the beginning of this study. The phrase occurs in three passages: 2 Cor. 1:22; Eph. 1:13 and 4:30.

"By the Holy Spirit we are sealed for the day of our redemption." The Holy Spirit, the Paraclete: the faithful defender, He who assists us every day as He will assist us at the last day, He who intercedes for us with sighs and groans that cannot be uttered, He who beyond all the vicissitudes and lapses of the Christian life and in the teeth of all the accusations of the adversary indefatigably bears witness to our minds that we are children of God, He whom we have received as a baptism—He is within us, the true seal of the living God, the seal of eternal life, the unequivocal "yes" of the God who is faithful (2 Cor. 1:22), the *earnest of our inheritance (Eph. 1:13), the pledge of our ultimate redemption, the guarantee that we are putting off the old man and that the new man recreated in the image of Christ is springing to life within us (Eph. 4:22ff.). Yet it always remains the gift of God to us; the Holy Spirit does not belong to us; while witnessing to and guaranteeing the new life, the fruit of the new covenant, the Holy Spirit secures and seals it, withdrawing it from our introspective scrutiny and from injury by us, as though it were some great secret, a wonderful surprise which God snatches from the power of the enemy and keeps mysteriously until the last day. The new man is already within us, we have the irrefutable pledge of it, but we know that this treasure of abundant life is sealed, for our life is hidden with Christ in God (Col. 3:3); when Christ appears the seal will be broken and then "I shall understand fully even as I have been fully understood" (1 Cor. 13:12).

One last problem: does the seal of the Holy Spirit specifically indicate *baptism? We may bring forward imposingly the passages which associate baptism and the gift of the Spirit (Matt. 3:11; Acts 1:5; 8:17; 19:6; Tit. 3:5, etc.) and among the Fathers of the Church it very soon comes about that the seal is quite simply equated with the sacrament of baptism. As we see then the seal is rapidly assimilated to the sacramental symbol of baptism. Whatever justification there may be for this association, it suggests a development which is very revealing of the process of transformation which the Christian faith undergoes; in the N.T. itself in every passage it is the Holy Spirit itself which is symbolized by the seal of redemption and that without any explicit allusion to baptism. It is clear then that very soon the assurance of salvation is made to depend on the reception of baptism, whereas originally it was determined by the outpouring of the Spirit.

M. BOUTTIER

SEDUCE, see TEMPTATION

SEE

1. This verb will be examined here only to the extent in which it has God (and Jesus Christ) as subject and object. In point of fact "to see" in the language of the Bible expresses a very precise theological meaning: it indicates a mode of relation and revelation in which the original and underlying visual sense becomes merged in direct spiritual perception. The relation is that of an immediate confrontation of God with man and man with God in which nothing at all any longer separates the Creator from the creature, in which the Father and His child stand face to face. This type of revelational experience suggests that man can attain a direct and extraordinary knowledge of God related either to our sensuous and terrestrial being or to our ultimate and eternal being, and one which may precede or accompany that other form of knowledge by *faith which is provisional but alone decisive in this life, and which in the Kingdom of God will be replaced by the former.

To have immediate awareness of the being of God is the most tenacious of the religious aspirations of humanity. In particular the whole effort of Hellenistic piety is aimed at this immediate vision of the sacred, the realm of the divine there becomes a "spectacle", the object of initiation is to introduce the aspirant into the secrets of contemplation (the Homeric hymns declare "Happy is he who has seen"). Of course gnosis later develops the theme of the invisibility of God (this will be an inexhaustible source of later mysticism which will always find its climax in divine "darkness"). But at the same time—and this will be the objective of gnosticism—the divinization of man himself enables all obstacles to be overcome and contemplation of the divine to be attained.

There is a classic contrast between the ever unappeased desire for vision, which is the driving force behind the mysticism natural to man, and the prophetic faith characteristic of Israel which consists in the evidence of things not seen (Heb. 11:1), that faith which comes by hearing (Rom. 10:17). This antithesis would seem to be almost precisely a reflection of that between eros and agape (love as desire, and love as self-giving). Like eros, vision appears as the supreme enjoyment within the reach of man, as the temptation to take possession of the living and "invisible" God (1 Tim. 1:17; 6:16) surrendered in this moment of ecstasy to man's inner gaze, and divested, not of the mysteries in which He would wish to be clad, but of His holiness. On the other hand, hearing, which is bound up with the word, engenders the stark obedience of faith on the part of the man who has heard the good news of the grace of God. Visionary elements are however not altogether excluded from biblical thought; on the contrary—dialectically by relation to faith—vision constantly plays a part in the course of the history of revelation.

2. God sees all things; such is the primary truth of revelation which the Bible discloses. The scope of the divine vision covers the whole universe (Job 28:24), penetrates the being of each individual (Ps. 33:13) tries the heart and the reins. If the wicked cast doubt on the reality of this divine omniscience and reject it, the believer is unwaveringly assured of its truth (Ps. 94:9). This all-comprehensive vision of God is in the first place the perfect expression of His care and *love; love of His creation when from the very first morning He beholds His creative handiwork (Gen. 1:4); love of His people whose sufferings in Egypt He sees (Exod. 3:7) and which He will not cease to watch attentively; love of each individual (cf. Ps. 139) and especially of the meek (Ps. 138:6), of those who are plunged in misery (Ps. 25:18), of those who secretly invoke Him (Matt. 6:4). Of all these the expectation and the hope and the certitude that God will ultimately intervene to save them, rest upon the presupposition of the all-embracing divine vision. The glance of God appears in fact to be alike the sign of His omnipotence (Ps. 104:32), the pledge of His righteousness (cf. Job 24:23; Gen. 6:12, etc.), and at times the very proof of His anger (Job 7:19). The first chapter of the Book of Ezekiel, considered in Israel to be the supreme revelation, by its description of the wheels of the chariot which are filled with eyes bears witness to this decisive declaration of faith: God sees all things!

3. But man, can man see God? No, proclaims the O.T. Not because God is essentially invisible but because He is the thrice holy. Since the fall of man He is the hidden God; man has been driven from His presence. It is by His *word that God will graciously reveal to the people that listen to Him His abiding presence. Henceforth it is by His word that His deliverances will be wrought. Henceforward there weighs on sinful man this interdict: "No man can see the face of the Lord and live" (cf. Exod. 19:21; 33:20; Judg. 13:22; the reaction of Elijah in 1 Kings 19:13. In 1 Sam. 6:19 it is clear that there is danger even in casting a look at the ark). And yet the O.T., tremblingly as it were, gives us a glimpse of those lurid moments when some have been admitted to the terrible vision of the Lord face to face. We leave aside the frequent expression: "The Lord appeared to such a one and said . . ." (cf. Gen. 17:1): the verb here simply marks the presence of the

eternal God who is about to manifest Himself by His word to His servant. Moreover, many passages tone down the scandal of this divine confrontation by the use of such phrases as: see the *angel of the Lord (Judg. 6:11ff.) or see the *glory of the Lord (cf. Ps. 27:4; 96:6). We have even this curious example of the LXX translation of Exod. 24:10: "Moses and the elders of Israel saw the God of Israel", as "they saw the place where the God of Israel was".

Yet some texts go further and affirm the impossible: men have seen God, have beheld His majesty, astonished still to be alive and the witnesses of His grace. So it is with Jacob on his return journey at Peniel (Gen. 32:30), or with Moses in those recurring passages of Exodus (cf. also Num. 12:6–8) where we see him ascend the holy mountain and in fear and trembling there encounter his God face to face. Nowhere do the texts show such intensity and depth of religious emotion; nowhere do they affirm more uncompromisingly the human impossibility of confronting the holiness of God, and nowhere do they allow a man to penetrate more deeply into the shrine of His presence. Perhaps all these implications are well summed up in the astonishing passage of Exod. 33:17ff. where we see Moses admitted to behold the "back" of the Lord: while the glory of the Lord is passing by, the divine hand covers the sight of this friend of God. The same type of experience is accorded the prophets: Micaiah (2 Chr. 18:18), Isaiah (the famous vision of chapter 6), Ezekiel (chapter 1). All these visions have the common characteristic that they are not deliberately sought after by the "men of God" and for their own sake. They flow from free divine initiative. Like all the spiritual experiences recorded in the Bible, they do not form the supreme objective of piety and faith, the summit of the ascetic and mystical life; they are on the contrary only a point of departure: they are not the goal of human striving, but the mark of the initial intervention of God who thus powerfully reveals Himself in order to draw His people into the stream of saving history. Here we find the great moments marking the signal stages in the life of the elect people: Jacob becoming Israel, Moses receiving the law, the prophets on the threshold of their ministry. This visionary experience lies at the very heart of the revelation flowing from the "law and the prophets".

The exceptional character of these visions as affording a glimpse of what lies beyond the veil (Job 19:26 is the most moving text in this regard) is strongly suggested, and in later Judaism above all there emerges from the eschatological point of view the expectation of an ultimate intervention of God manifesting Himself in the sight of all the nations of the earth, justifying the faith of some and confounding the unbelief of others, and setting up a new heaven and earth. Finally this hope takes on a special form in the piety of the Psalms, where the manifestation of the glory of God is realized —in advance, as it were—through the beauties of liturgical worship and the contemplation of the Lord in the *Temple at Jerusalem (e.g., Ps. 63:3; 27:4).

4. In fulfilment of this hope there sounds on the threshold of the Gospel the apostolic proclamation: "No one has ever seen God; the only Son, who is in the bosom of the Father, he has made him known" (Jn. 1:18), a proclamation which is only the echo of that declaration of Jesus Himself: "He who has seen me has seen the Father" (Jn. 14:9; 12:45). But this appearance of the Son of Man, foretold by Daniel, in whom God reveals Himself unto the world which He loved so greatly, is divisible into two phases: the double advent of Christ, in the incarnation and the parousia, to which correspond two modes of seeing Him.

(a) *The incarnation.* This first coming is wrapped in mystery; as Pascal wrote, "when the moment came for God to appear on earth, He hid Himself still more by taking the form of humanity". For the synoptics this mystery is centred in the *Kingdom; for John it is centred in the person of Christ. "Blessed are your eyes, for they see" (Matt. 13:16; cf. Matt. 11:4) and at the same time "the Kingdom of God is not coming with signs to be observed" (Lk. 17:20). Only the fact of divine election enables men to discern this reality by faith (cf. Mk. 4:11,12). The same truth is expressed in characteristically different terms in Jn. 9:35–39. The tension between faith and sight is more acute than ever. The presence of Jesus and the observation of His miracles is not enough to enable anyone to discern in Him the revelation of the Father: the gift of God—faith—is also necessary. Far from being the privileged, the eyewitnesses of the incarnate life of Jesus have greater difficulty than ourselves in estimating its incalculable momentousness: they have not yet received the Holy Spirit. Nevertheless they are the necessary agents in the genesis of our own faith, because they alone are in the position to describe to us the events of that earthly life. Such is the scope of the mysterious task which the *apostles must accomplish for the whole duration of the life of the Church, since they are the witnesses of these saving events, of the cross, the resurrection and the ascension of the Lord (Lk. 1:2; 1 Jn. 1:1). In this respect the appearances of the risen Lord play a decisive part. The one encounter on the Damascus road is sufficient to qualify Paul as an apostle (1 Cor. 9:1: "am I not an apostle? have I not seen Jesus our Lord?"). It has often been pointed out how carefully he distinguishes this vision from all those which were granted to him subsequently. Can one forget the cry of joy which resounds on Easter morning: "We have seen the Lord!"?

(b) The parousia. To see the face of God in His Kingdom is to share in the divine glory. Certain of the angels already know this privilege (Matt. 18:10). In order to describe the inheritance of the Kingdom promised to the pure in heart, the beatitudes declare that these latter shall see God. The Epistle to the Hebrews reminds us that in this respect sanctification is necessary (Heb. 12:14; cf. Ps. 17:15). But all of us together will only be brought to this supreme climax of the ultimate vision of God through the heavenly coming of the Son of Man. His second coming, by annihilating sin and death, will put an end to the trials of faith and the struggles of hope (Rom. 8:18–27), will abolish all distance and separation and will reintroduce the whole of creation to the very presence of the Father. Then Christ will appear, no longer wrapped in mystery, but in an effulgence of light "on the clouds of heaven". "Every eye shall see Him" (Rev. 1:7). Then we shall see Him as He is and "we shall be like Him" (1 Jn. 3:2; cf. 2 Cor. 3:18); we shall see face to face and shall know—"as we have been known" (1 Cor. 13:12). The world will have God for its light; "there shall no more be anything accursed, but the throne of God and of the Lamb shall be in the city and his servants shall worship him: they shall see his face" (Rev. 22:4). Such are the supreme promises and hopes. Hence, "we groan," writes Paul, for, "walking by faith and not by sight we still dwell far from the Lord" (2 Cor. 5:1–8), we "love Him, not having seen Him, and we believe in Him though now we see Him not" (1 Pet. 1:8), and we thus live in burning expectation of this ultimate revelation of glory.

5. But the joy of the Church is already explicit in the cry: "Blessed are those who have not seen and yet believe" (Jn. 20:29). Poised between the two visible appearances of the Lord, the Church is called to experience the joy of faith. It is as it were liberated from the ambiguity of the time of the incarnation, it has above all received the gift of the *Holy Spirit, the witness which enables it to apprehend the fullness of what was seen and greeted from afar by the prophets and beheld by the apostles. The time of the Holy Spirit is an aeon in which the disciples of Jesus are promised the full vision of their Master (Jn. 16:16,19,22; cf. 14:19).

The Holy Spirit gives us the power of apprehending the person and presence of Jesus although He is at the moment invisible to the world. The Holy Spirit illuminates for us that mirror given us in the word of God where we can see, as in a reflection (cf. 1 Cor. 13:12; 2 Cor. 3:18) the life of Christ as it will twice break forth in history:

Jesus treading the *via dolorosa*, and the Lord returning on the clouds of heaven. Our faith, like a spark flashing in the night of time, is poised between those two poles. Looking out into the darkness, but illuminated thus by the Spirit, the Church cherishes the vision of the Son and already has eternal life (Jn. 6:40). That is why, even if we no longer regard Christ "from a human point of view" (2 Cor. 5:16) Paul does not hesitate to describe Him to the Galatians (Gal. 3:1). That again is why the Epistle to the Hebrews exhorts us to "look to Jesus", the author and the consummator of our faith (12:2). Clinging to the person of Jesus, the Christian faith is henceforth, in an unforgettable way, vision and contemplation. And in order that this vision may not get lost in the mists of a discarnate mysticism, Scripture constantly seeks to keep it anchored in those visible and immediate signs which are given us of the presence of the Lord, those pledges which confirm for us the reality of His life, namely, our *neighbour in whom we now encounter the Son of Man, and all the more so, the more despicable and lowly that neighbour is (Matt. 25:31–46; cf. 1 Jn. 4:20); the commonalty of the *Church, the visible body of Christ, the water poured over our heads in baptism and the bread and wine set out upon the table.

M. BOUTTIER

SEEK

This frequently used verb touches the very heart of the biblical message. It characterizes indeed three aspects of the relationship of God with men and of men with God.

1. God comes to His creatures to *seek*, that is to say, to *demand* that which He has a right to expect from them: the Lord seeks obedience (Mic. 6:8), genuine adoration in spirit and in truth (Jn. 4:23), and faithfulness (1 Cor. 4:2), in the same way as a landowner comes to seek for fruit from the tree which he has planted (Lk. 13:6–7). This search of God, demanding but just, turns to the confusion of sinful man who flees

before God (Gen. 3:10). In vain does God seek the man who responds to His expectation (Ps. 14:1–3).

2. So God has resolved to come in His Son to *seek* men in order to *save* them and to bring them back to Himself. As the *shepherd seeks his lost sheep until he finds it and brings it back to the fold (Lk. 15:4), so the Son of Man has come to seek and to save that which is lost (Lk. 19:10). This saving search of God, far from sheltering man from divine requirements, makes legitimate more claims by the Lord for service (Lk. 12:48).

3. Most frequently, in the O.T. particularly, to *seek* describes the attitude of man before God. It is indeed one of the signs of God's love that He allows Himself to be sought by men (Isa. 65:1; Ezek. 36:37), just as it is a sign of His anger that He hides Himself from their search (Hos. 5:15; Amos 8:12; Ezek. 20:3).

(*a*) Left to himself man seeks God, but gropingly (Acts 17:27), by the various means that he can think of for himself. He consults idols, considered as the visible manifestation of the invisible deity (2 Kings 1:2; Isa. 19:3; Rom. 1:23), he conjures up the dead (1 Sam. 28), he questions the stars (Jer. 8:2), diviners and magicians (Lev. 19:31), etc. All these practices are absolutely condemned by Scripture, not only as illusory but as attacks on the liberty of God who reveals Himself only when and where He pleases (Deut. 18:10). It is also a disastrous search for a man who wishes to reach God by his religious or moral merits (Rom. 9:32) dispensing with repentance and conversion to Jesus Christ.

(*b*) But in order that He may be sought and consulted God has put certain means at the disposal of His people. One of the most ancient means of consultation was the *drawing of lots*, practised by the chief (Josh. 7:14), and soon a prerogative of the priest indicating the judgment of God by the Urim and Thummim of the ephod (Num. 27:21). This ancient means of consultation seems to have been practised anew in the sacerdotal era (Ezra 2:63; cf. Acts 1:26). Often the people of Israel consult God by *prophets* whom He sends to them (Exod. 18:15; 1 Kings 22:8; Ezek. 14:4); and so, after them, God is sought in His written word (Isa. 34:16; Ps. 119:2). In a similar way the *sanctuary*—altar, tabernacle, *Temple—the sign of the presence of the invisible God among His people, is the place where the Lord is sought and consulted (Exod. 33:7; Deut. 12:5; 2 Chr. 1:5). The search of the pilgrim who goes to the sanctuary is mainly fulfilled in prayer, from which comes the very frequent use of the verb in the Psalms, where, dissociated from any allusion to the sanctuary, *to seek God* or *seek His face* becomes synonymous with praying (Ps. 24:6; 27:8; 40:17; 2 Chr. 7:14). It is likewise the sense which Jesus gives to it in the famous passage: "Seek . . . and ye shall find" (Matt. 7:7). To seek God or to approach Him (Heb. 11:6), is to have access to Him by the prayer of faith. All these ways of search are summarized and fulfilled in Jesus Christ, the Way by which any man who seeks may find (Matt. 7:8).

(c) In a more general way this verb describes the attitude of the faithful man who maintains himself in obedience and receptiveness before God (Ps. 34:11; Rom. 10:20; Acts 15:17). The "seeker after God" is the one whose life is completely directed by Christ and the coming Kingdom (Matt. 6:33; Col. 3:1) and who is not afraid to sell all that he has to buy that pearl of great price (Matt. 13:45).

Thus, to *seek* marks the very particular tension which has existed since the Fall between God who comes to us and sinful men, who, renouncing flight, turn to Him. The search of the faithful is the response given to God's initiative. The man who seeks God enters immediately into real communion with Him through the medium of Jesus Christ. In this sense he has already found the one whom he is seeking (Matt. 13:44). But in contrast to philosophy which examines its object, or to mysticism which loses itself in God, this search is a communion of faith and of expectation which will be fulfilled only in the Kingdom. Then only will the search give place to full and complete possession (1 Cor. 13:12).

S. AMSLER

SEND

1. In the O.T. as in the N.T. certain personages send messengers to other persons or other kings in order to acquaint them with decisions or to communicate certain information to them. The person of the envoy therefore disappears beneath that of the sender; and this kind of commission is important, since it allows a real meeting between two men in spite of their physical separation. The only conditions demanded from the side of the envoy are his fidelity, obedience and submission. The Bible is unaware of any mission which could have an exclusively religious character. Moreover, when the term *send* is used with God as the subject, less emphasis is, as it happens, put on the religious aspect of the mission which is entrusted to someone than on his being fully and completely at the service of his master (Jn. 13:16).

The kind of welcome which such an envoy receives is a true indication of people's feelings towards his master. "I have persistently sent all my servants the prophets," the Lord of Hosts declares to Jeremiah (7:25), "yet they did not listen to *me.*" Rejecting God's servant is equivalent to rejecting God Himself. Later, Jesus was to say this too: "He who receives you receives me" (Matt. 10:40). The missionary is what he is simply in virtue of his mission, of his being sent. The importance he has he owes only to the Master who gave him his orders in the first place. Apart from Him, the envoy is nothing, and his activity signifies nothing.

In the fourth Gospel all that Jesus does, all that He says, all that He Himself is, has reference to God, "the Father who sent him". "This is the work of God," He asserts, "that you believe in him whom he has sent" (6:29). But Jesus alone is able to know God and to make Him known, since it is God who sent Him (7:29). Hence loving God must imply loving Jesus too

(8:42). In short, the envoy cannot be separated from the one who sends. The purpose of the mission is the salvation of the world (3:17), and in order that it may be preached to all men, Jesus sends also His disciples (20:21).

But this union between the Father and Jesus is of quite a different order from that which used to exist between God and the prophets: in the person of Jesus God is actually present. This is very clearly brought out in some of the prayers of Jesus: thus, "this is eternal life, that they know thee the only God, and Jesus Christ whom thou hast sent" (17:3). *This envoy, Jesus, is unique and must not be compared to any other.*

He is the word of God, He is the authority, the will of God. He does not merely bring the word: he *is* the word and the will of God. In Him the messenger's person is *not* effaced behind that of the master who sends; it is fused with it.

The author of the Epistle to the Hebrews alone qualifies Jesus as an apostle, one sent (3:1); but his use of the expression is quickly followed by a comparison with Moses, which effectively brings out the difference: Moses was a mere servant (v. 5), Jesus is the Son of God (v. 6).

Jesus, the only real envoy of God in the full sense of the word, can act on His own account to manifest His sovereign power: He will send on behalf of the Father the Spirit of truth, who comes from the Father (Jn. 15:26). Thus He demonstrates His divine authority to the disciples.

While Jesus is the envoy *par excellence*, He in turn proceeds to make envoys of His disciples. Going out as sheep in the midst of wolves, without money, without food, without sandals, without a change of clothing, they set out in pairs to proclaim the Kingdom of God. Some passages mention the set-backs which the envoys received when they were heedless of the terms of their mission (Mk. 9:14–29), or describe how the Master admonished and corrected their outlook: "Do not rejoice in this, that the spirits are subject to you; but rejoice that your names are written in heaven" (Lk.

10:20), which is equivalent to saying: "Your power is given you from above: never forget it!"

We do no more than mention here, by way of reminder, the rôle of the *apostle; this would demand a study of the development of apostleship from the resurrection of Jesus until the primitive communities began to be organized. We remember how Paul declares that he was called to be an apostle (or envoy) of Jesus Christ by the will of God (1 Cor. 1:1, etc.).

The Churches too have their own envoys (Acts 13:2; 2 Cor. 8:23). Their mission, though sometimes temporary and limited, has nevertheless no little importance, for the apostle calls them "the glory of Christ".

2. All the above shows that in the N.T. it is not the case that a Church happens to undertake a mission (for the envoy and the mission are the same thing). *The Church is herself missionary.* She is made up of men who all know themselves to be in their several ways sent by the Lord. It is her nature to radiate out in every direction and thus she expands throughout the ancient world. She has received freely, that she may give freely (Matt. 10:8). The Gospel is not to be kept to itself; it transmits itself. The Church does not possess an autonomous existence; she does not live for herself; she is sent, she transmits. She has been sent by God; she proclaims the Kingdom of God. She does not absorb into her own inner life the strength of those who are sent by God; she in her turn sends them out (Acts 13:2). In the N.T. there is no problem of Church and Mission: in the N.T. there is simply the missionary Church. Because she has welcomed the Christ, who was sent by God, she longs for others to welcome Him as well (Rom. 15:7), and she sends to them her servants that they may preach the Gospel.

3. But we must not lose sight of the profound significance of that succession of envoys (prophets, Son of God, Spirit, apostles) by means of whom God wills to reach out to every individual of His people,

and, later, of all peoples: the people of Israel or the Church must be gathered together in the name of God. All men who welcome the envoys are by the same token welcoming the Lord and are added to the people of God. It can therefore be said that God sends His servants to gather together and bring to Himself many people who then constitute His true "Israel according to faith", or His Church.

This image of calling together was frequently used to describe the end of the Exile and the reconstitution of the people of Israel on the soil of Palestine. It had previously been more or less transposed in expectation of another order, in the hope of seeing the Kingdom of God inaugurated and the assembly of all mankind at the end of time either for judgment (in the case of heathen nations, Zeph. 3:8; Joel 3:2) or for participation in salvation (Isa. 56:7,8).

Jesus will Himself, as the envoy of God, gather them. But while His being sent refers to His coming on the earth at the beginning of our era, the gathering together will refer primarily to His last action at the time of His return (Matt. 22:10: "The servants went out into the streets and gathered all whom they found, both bad and good; so the wedding hall was filled with guests"; Matt. 25:32: all the *nations). Here again there is a double intention, that of allowing genuine believers to be marked out, and making them enter into possession of the Kingdom of God (Matt. 25:34; 13:30: gather the wheat into my barn) or even to exclude the others (Matt. 25:41; 13:30; the weeds are to be burned). Yet it must not be forgotten that if in His day Jesus speaks of the two possibilities open to men at the time of the final assembly, it is just to warn them and to bring them to repentance from that time onward so that they will escape the final punishment. Again we find here, therefore, that joyful and positive aspect of the act of sending: such a man is sent to save sinners and to make of them a redeemed community.

It is for this reason that between Jesus' first coming and His return, between the sending of the Son of God and the great gathering at the end of time, there is inserted the mission and the gathering of the Church, God's people, sinful and redeemed.

To sum up, we see that sending and gathering together are two aspects of the same action: that of bringing salvation to mankind.

M. CARREZ

SERVANT

The term "servant" or the verb "to serve" (in Hebrew 'ebed or 'abad) implies the twofold idea of work and submission. According as to whether the one or the other of these notions is predominant, we have the meaning of "worker" or "*slave", and the same verb can be translated by "act" or "obey". These different meanings are found both in the application of the words to everyday life and to the sphere of religious life.

1. As applied to the domain of everyday life, the word servant can be used in the various contexts where the idea of service is involved. Normally it denotes a slave and especially a male slave (for women other terms are used implying often other ideas than the work of a servant, for example concubinage, Gen. 16:1–3; Exod. 7–11). Elsewhere the servant is a person who is subject to a superior: in political life, he is the subject of a king or some other chief (1 Sam. 8:17; 2 Kings 10:5) and in military life he is the man who is bound to a life of service, i.e., a soldier or an officer (1 Sam. 17:8; 22:17; 2 Kings 18:24). The same word indicates also an important official with large responsibility although always subject to his king: for example the minister (which means servant) or the messenger (Gen. 40:20; 2 Kings 22:12; Est. 1:3). Finally, in formulas of politeness and greeting, the use of the word servant is understandable as a term of respect and submission: "I am your servant" (Gen. 32:4; 33:5), and it often replaces the personal pronoun "I" (2 Kings 19:19–20).

2. It is in the sphere of religious life that the word gathers its richest meaning: the

servant is he who is surrendered to God and works in the divine service. The "service of God" has therefore in the first place a cultic and liturgical significance which has remained to the present day: divine service is the Church office or *worship. The servant of God is thus the people who celebrate the cult, i.e., the community of Israel in its liturgical life (in connection with the foundation of the *covenant, the celebration of *feasts, assemblies in the *Temple, etc.; Ps. 113:1; 134:1; Exod. 7:16; Ezek. 20:40). Of course the servants of God are in the first instance those whose function it is to officiate at the cult, the priests and the Levites (Num. 18:7; Neh. 11:3; Ezra 6:18).

But it would be incorrect to restrict the religious meaning of service to the purely ritual and liturgical domain; the service of God is essentially a moral attitude of the people or the individual in regard to God and in obedience to His commandments: Israel is the servant of God (1 Kings 8:23; Ps. 69:37; 102:15; Isa. 41:8–9; 43:10; 44:1–2, etc.). In this very affirmation the whole essence of the relation between God and His people is expressed: God describes Israel as His servant because He has chosen her and exacts from her exclusive obedience to His will, fear of Him and faithfulness to Him, love and trust. God is jealous of His people and will not allow them to serve other gods. Moreover, the people receive from their God the blessings and promises specially reserved to them: numerous progeny, protection, deliverance, grace and pardon. Chapters 40–55 of Isaiah emphasize particularly this relation of God to His servant Israel or Jacob and draw out most fully all its implications.

In several contexts of the O.T. the term is applied not to the people as a whole, but to one part of the people only, to a minority in contrast to the collective. This is the group of the faithful existing at the heart of the majority who allow themselves to be enticed away from the true service of the eternal God (Ps. 34:22–23; 35:27; Isa. 65:8–14; Mal. 3:17–18). The servants are the righteous, while the others are the wicked. Lastly, the word may assume an individual connotation and denote one person only: Abraham (Gen. 26:24), Moses (Exod. 14:31), David (2 Sam. 3:18). The Psalms offer many examples of this individualization, even though anonymous; this is seen above all in the lamentations and complainings of the righteous man who cries to God to gain deliverance from the hands of his enemies (Ps. 19:12–14; 31:17; 109:28; 119:17,23,38; 143:2, etc.). Yet if the servant is the just man in the eyes of God, he is especially the man whom God entrusts with a precise mission: whether as king (Isa. 37:35; Jer. 33:21), whether as prophet (1 Kings 14:18; Jer. 7:25), or even as a provisional instrument of the will of God, even though such a one is not part of the elect people: a Gentile may be a servant of God (for example "my servant Nebuchadrezzar", Jer. 25:9; 27:6).

3. In conclusion we must note the special use of the word servant in the four well-known passages of the book of Isaiah called the songs or poems of the Lord's servant (Isa. 42:1–7; 49:1–6; 50:4–9; 52:13–53:12). Who is the figure thus described in these poetic sections, the contents of which are so rich in suggestiveness for Christian thought? This is one of the most vexed questions of O.T. scholarship and scholars have formulated many hypotheses in interpretation. It is impossible for us to review them in detail here and we must be content to mention them in general outline. For many critics, the servant of the Lord in these chapters must portray an individual person in contrast to the people as a whole (thus in Isa. 49:6 the servant has a part to play in regard to the people, as also in Isa. 53:3–8) whereas in the rest of the book the servant certainly designates the people (e.g., 44:21). But disagreement begins when it is a question of identifying this figure: is it some historical character (Moses, David, or one of his descendants), or some contemporary person (a prophet, perhaps the author himself), or some figure of the future (the Messiah, a glorious king who is to reign at the end of the age)? This

difficulty is not a modern one; it appears already in the N.T. itself: "About whom does the prophet say this? about himself or about someone else?" (Acts 8:32–35).

Other scholars insist on understanding the poems in a collective sense and refuse to see in this servant anyone but the people of Israel itself, who are in question in the other passages of the same book. It is the people who will be the light of the Gentiles, and who will have to suffer persecution and death for the salvation of other nations. The most they would concede is that perhaps it is a question of a small group of believers in the midst of the people, that tiny *remnant which remains faithful to the Lord and which is to serve as a witness to the rest and to the Gentiles. Or again it is suggested we have here a personification of the people, in a prophetic perspective.

Confronted by such different theses, it seems probable, as many are now emphasizing, that this idea of the Servant of the Lord is a fluid conception passing readily from the collective to the individual life, or from the present to the future, and that we should not expect it to show the rigorous logic which the modern mind requires. What is essential is to realize that Jesus Christ saw in these passages the description of His own mission and that the humiliated servant suffering for the sins of his people is, from the point of view of the Christian Church, the prophetic foreshadowing of Christ crucified for the salvation of the world.

Just as the person of Christ is a well-defined individuality while at the same time the body of Christ is the reality of the Church (1 Cor. 12:27) so also the servant of the Lord denotes the community of believers in the old covenant as well as the particular person to whom God will entrust the mission of saving the Gentiles. Jesus in His incarnation will actualize this latter figure. This interpenetration of the individual and collective personalities corresponds perfectly, moreover, to the thought of the biblical writers, who never separated the individual from the community in the religious life of Israel.

F. MICHAELI

SERVE, *see* WORSHIP

SHADOW

This term can signify a threat, or a protection, or an inadequacy in relation to the full reality.

1. The shadow of death (Matt. 4:16; Lk. 1:79; cf. Isa. 9:1; Ps. 23:4) expresses the fear and suffering of sinful men over whom death reigns and whom the divine light will visit and save by Jesus Christ (see *Death, *Light).

2. A beneficial and protective shadow: of a tree (Mk. 4:32); of a house (Gen. 19:8); the divine protection which is powerful and reliable (Ps. 91:1; 121:5). People hope that the shadow of Peter will heal those on whom it falls (Acts 5:15; cf. the power of the *clothes of Jesus, Mk. 6:56, and of Paul, Acts 19:11–12); it is not, however, the garment or the shadow which heals, but God through faith (Acts 19:11; Mk. 5:25–34).

The shadow of the Highest (Lk. 1:35) recalls the cloud at Sinai (Exod. 19:9,16,18) when God was present and at the same time hidden: God acts by His creative power, while preserving His secrecy.

3. "Shadow" designates Israelite and Jewish institutions and customs which had a provisional significance and for whose existence there is no further justification after the advent of Jesus Christ.

Col. 2:16–17: to abstain from certain foods, probably from meat and wine, and to observe certain Jewish *feasts was regarded as a means of separating oneself from the world and winning the blessings of God. But the good things hoped for in the world to come, forgiveness (v. 13), liberation from the flesh and from evil powers (vv. 11, 12, 15), resurrection (v. 12; 3:1), and the life and glory to come (3:4), are in Christ, and believers partake of them in His body, which is the Church. "The shadow has no more worth for him who is part of the 'body' " (Ch. Masson).

The Israelite worship was the image and shadow of heavenly things, of which the reality is Christ (Heb. 10:1). The true sanctuary is that which Christ has set up in heaven, of which the sanctuary of Moses is only an imperfect reproduction (Heb. 8:2,5). The same is the case with the *sacrifices: the true sacrifice is that which Jesus Christ has completed by offering His own life (Heb. 9:11–14; 10:1–10).

4. Jas. 1:17: God is the father "of lights", that is to say, of the stars. The latter experience astronomical variations, periods of obscurity; but it is not so with God: in Him there is no shadow, He is faithful to Himself (1 Jn. 1:5). His gifts are like Himself, free from all evil, fitted to save us perfectly.

F. BAUDRAZ

SHEPHERD

1. Very often in the O.T. we find that God is the shepherd of His people (cf. Gen. 49:24; Ps. 23:1; 28:8; 78:52; 80:2; Isa. 40:11; Jer. 31:10; Mic. 7:14; Zech. 10:3, etc.), and that the latter is God's flock (cf. Ps. 79:13; 95:7, etc.; cf. also 2 Sam. 24:17; Jer. 13:17, etc.). In the N.T., this double declaration is made concerning Jesus and the Church (see below); and in both Testaments the ministers of God or of Christ are called Shepherds (cf. Isa. 63:11; Jer. 17:16; Jn. 21:16; Acts 20:28, etc.). The use of this comparison arises at the same time from the fact that at the beginning of its history at least the chosen people was a people of nomadic shepherds (cf. Gen. 46:32; 47:3; Exod. 12:38, etc.), and from the fact that many of the heroes of their history were shepherds (cf. Exod. 3:1; 1 Sam. 16:11 and Ps. 78:70f.; Amos 1:1, etc.). From the theological point of view, this comparison has some importance because it bears on the doctrine of *Jesus Christ, of the *ministry, and of the *Church.

2. Jesus is the Good Shepherd (Jn. 10:1–16). He has come to gather God's flock (Mk. 6:34; 1 Pet. 2:25; cf. Matt. 15:24; Jn. 10:16), to count it (Lk. 15:3–7; Matt.

18:12; cf. Jn. 10:3,14), to lead it (Jn. 10:4), to guard and defend it (Lk. 12:32; cf. Jn. 10:11f.), to lead it to the pasture of salvation (Matt. 2:6; Jn. 10:9; Rev. 7:17; cf. Ps. 23:2), to judge it, that is, to purify it and distinguish it from other flocks (cf. Matt. 25:31–46; 1 Pet. 5:4). To have Jesus as shepherd is to have peace, rest (Matt. 9:36) and life (Jn. 10:10): it is to have found one's place again, to be brought back, to be directed to one's purpose. There is a striking parallelism between Jesus the Shepherd and Jesus the Head who sums up and sets all things in order (cf. Eph. 1:10), inasmuch as Jesus is not only the shepherd of the Church, but of the whole world (cf. Rev. 2:27; 12:5; 19:15). If one wishes to understand this pastoral ministry of Christ the prophet (Jn. 10:3), priest (Jn. 10:11,15) and king (Rev. 2:27), one must get rid of the pious imagery which so readily creates the belief that the calling of a shepherd is an attitude of the effeminate and that belonging to a flock is an invitation to bleat like a gentle lambkin.

3. Jesus is the "great shepherd" (Heb. 13:20), the "chief shepherd" (1 Pet. 5:4): He sums up in Himself all the pastoral ministry (Jn. 10:11). But before His coming, as after His ascension, He delegates the exercising of it to His ministers (=servants).

(a) It means that no minister is—to make further use of what is an image rather than a well-defined activity or title—a shepherd of himself or by the will of the flock: he is a shepherd by grace, through the calling and command of the Lord of the flock. As it was God who, under the old covenant, appointed the shepherds of His flock (Jer. 3:15; 23:4; Ps. 78:71, etc.), under the new covenant it is Jesus (or the Holy Spirit: Acts 20:28) who entrusts his flock to the apostle Peter (Jn. 21:15–17) or who appoints shepherds in the Church (Eph. 4:11; cf. Matt. 10:6). The pastoral ministry derives thus from the Lord, and it is to Him that the shepherds are responsible for the flock that is committed to them (cf. as a contrast Jer. 23:2; Ezek. 34:10; cf. also 1 Cor. 4:1–4).

(b) The pastoral ministry requires not

only courage (cf. 1 Sam. 17:34ff.; 25:7; Isa. 31:4; Amos 3:12; Jn. 10:12), but also a sense of responsibility (Matt. 18:12; Lk. 15:6), love and patience (Isa. 40:11; Ezek. 34:4), competence in the calling (Prov. 27:23), joy in the work and self-abnegation (1 Pet. 5:2–3), order (cf. Jer. 33:13; Jn. 10:3), humility (Ezek. 34:4; 1 Pet. 5:3), judgment (cf. Ezek. 34:17; Matt. 25:32; Gen. 30:31ff.). If this ministry was badly exercised or not exercised at all, it would be the ruin of the Church (cf. Isa. 13:14–16; Jer. 50:6f.; Ezek. 34:4ff., etc.): shepherds are indispensable to the Church.

(c) Although they are *in* the Church (Acts 20:28), the shepherds are, however, distinct from the flock for which they are responsible: they are its leaders (cf. Num. 27:12–23; 2 Sam. 5:2; 7:7f.; 1 Kings 22:17; Jer. 25:35f., etc.), that is to say they are its guardians, they should lead it to pasture, defend it against its enemies, maintain it in unity and peace (cf. as a contrast, the picture of bad shepherds in Ezek. 34; Jer. 23:1–4). If it is forbidden for them to grow rich at the expense of their flock (cf. Ezek. 34:2f.; 1 Pet. 5:2), they have the right to draw from it their subsistence (1 Cor. 9:7).

It is easy to link up with the biblical doctrine of the ministry this comparison of the minister with a shepherd or a pastor.

4. On the level of the Church's doctrine, the biblical image of the shepherd and of the flock has the following aspects especially:

(a) The Church has a Head, a pastor, Jesus Christ (cf. Jn. 10, etc.); it must also recognize those to whom Jesus has delegated the everyday exercise of His pastoral ministry; if the Church tries to upset the ministry, it loses its way, loses its cohesion and falls into error (cf. Matt. 26:31). But having a Head should not be a trial for the Church; it is on the contrary a pledge of security, of peace and of comfort, a pledge that loneliness is henceforth conquered and that communion is possible (cf. 1 Kings 22:17; Ps. 119:176; Isa. 53:6; Mic. 2:12; Matt. 9:36, etc.): that is why the picture of a flock well led by a good shepherd is one of

the essential promises on which the O.T. hope is fed (cf. Jer. 31:10; cf. also 1 Pet. 2:25), a sign of the awaited *rest.

(b) The Church is an assembled people: even though each member of this flock has his name (Jn. 10:3) and the number of the sheep is known (Jer. 33:13), it does not prevent anyone who leaves the flock, who tries to weaken its unity, who wishes to live as a "lone sheep", from exposing himself to the danger of death, and salvation is only found again when the flock is rejoined: what saves is not simply to be found by the shepherd (cf. Matt. 15:24), but to be restored, by him, to the rest of the flock (Matt. 18:12f.; Lk. 15:3–7; Jn. 10:16). In other terms, the Church is a community outside which there is only the threat of perdition and death.

(c) The Church is one, for it has only one shepherd. In this sense the dispersion, the division of God's flock by the schism which followed the reign of Solomon, has been experienced as a falsification of the chosen people, as an affliction whose end is awaited and hoped for. Also the promise of a gathering of the sections of the flock and their return to unity is one of the great hopes of the old covenant (cf. Ezek. 37:15–28), fulfilled in the coming of the only shepherd (Jn. 10:16).

J.-J. VON ALLMEN

SICKNESS

1. Sickness and healing are never approached in the Bible from the medical or scientific point of view, but always from the religious point of view, that is to say, from the viewpoint of the particular relationship which they create or make apparent between the sick person and God. It is not the nature of the sickness, its development or its treatment, which receives attention, but the fact itself envisaged as an event significant of man's destiny or condition within the general perspective of the history of salvation.

The terms used to designate the various sicknesses are frequently vague and do not permit of classification, and if the Bible alludes to fevers, skin complaints, haemorrhages, and a diversity of infirmities, or again to mental illnesses or nervous troubles attributed to demon possession, it also speaks in a general manner of "evils", "afflictions", "weaknesses", "debilities", and "sufferings", and these different expressions designate the normal and ordinary state of fallen humanity, physical *suffering and pain and finally *death having been introduced as a consequence of the Fall (Gen. 3:16–19). Bodily sicknesses, infirmities, and accidents are thus the ordinary lot of sinful man; in their acute form they are the characteristic signs, direct or indirect, of *sin and the curse or of the punishment which they bring. The direct relationship between sickness and punishment, however, is rarely mentioned (Num. 12:10; 2 Chr. 21:11–19; Acts 12:20–23), and Jesus refuses to discuss the question of personal responsibility in connection with the man born blind (Jn. 9:2f.). Likewise when sickness comes upon an individual or a group or a class of men or a people, it makes apparent the *common* fate of sinful man before God.

It should also be observed that, even when it is attributed to the intervention of *Satan (Job 1:5–6), sickness is connected with God's intention or will, whether secret or clearly expressed. This is plainly seen in the setting of the Mosaic covenant: Israel is a people that is spared, saved, healed (Exod. 15:26). As such, the people are called to live under the judgment and grace of God; if they persevere and remain faithful to the *covenant, they will be blessed and will prosper, and sicknesses and calamities will not overtake them; but if they violate the covenant, they will be visited with the same evils as those which smote the Egyptians (Exod. 23:25; Deut. 7:15; 28:16–22; Lev. 26:16). Thus not only health, prosperity, and fertility, but also sickness, sorrow, and sterility are equally in God's hands the signs of blessing or of cursing, for the Lord "kills and brings to life" and it is at His hand that we receive both good and evil (1 Sam. 2:6–7; Job 2:10; Isa. 45:6–7; Lam. 3:37–39).

That is why a relationship has been established, not in a superficial manner but in a very serious and deep sense, between the notions of *holiness and health and also between *wisdom and health: this does not mean that the wisest or most virtuous person will be the healthiest, but that the people who are holy (= set apart, sanctified) are blessed, protected, healed, and that the knowledge and practice of the Wisdom of God is productive of life (Prov. 3:8; 4:22). It is the same notion of holiness that inspires the Mosaic legislation concerning leprosy (Lev. 13 and 14). This legislation forms part of the "laws of holiness" founded upon the distinction between the clean and the unclean. It is the priest who by a ruling, a judgment, pronounces the exclusion or the reinstatement of lepers within the community of the holy people, for nothing unclean can belong to this people "consecrated to the Lord". Likewise and for the same reasons men affected with infirmities were excluded from the priestly functions (Lev. 21:16–23). The same notions of judgment and of grace are found again in the case of the sickness and healing of Hezekiah (Isa. 38 and 39). Hezekiah is sick "unto death" as a consequence of God's judgment. He humbles himself and implores deliverance. His healing is then the sign of the grace which God bestows upon him in his capacity as *king of His people*, a sign therefore of the covenant of righteousness and mercy ("I will deliver this people and this city", 38:6). Later on, because he has failed to understand the meaning of the extension of grace which was granted him, Hezekiah will undergo punishment (Isa. 39:1–8). This incident also emphasizes the didactic character of sickness (2 Chr. 32:24–31). It reminds man that his life is in God's hands; it tests his faith.

2. If sickness is a sign of condemnation and cursing, *healing* is seen in like manner as a sign of grace and blessing. God's will is not the death of the sinner, but his conversion and his life (Ezek. 18:23). That is why sickness, like death which follows it, is

destined to disappear! It is a reality, characteristic of a state of sin, destined to be conquered together with it. The Messianic promises witness that the coming of the "King of righteousness" will be marked by the liberation of captives and the healing of the sick (Isa. 42:1–2,7; 61:1–2). The "Sun of righteousness shall rise with healing in his wings" (Mal. 4:2). When that time comes, no one will say in Jerusalem, "I am sick" (Isa. 33:24). This salvation promised as a work of righteousness is not going to be accomplished by the "death of the wicked" but by that of the Just. The Messiah will heal by Himself bearing sickness (Isa. 53:4–5). He will be smitten, bruised, humbled in taking the place of the guilty. Healing thus appears as the sign of the redemption obtained by grace; it is parallel with *forgiveness (Ps. 103:2–3).

The earthly ministry of Jesus marks the fulfilment of these promises: the presence and the multitude of the sick around Him testifies to the profound significance of His coming (Matt. 9:12–13). He heals in order to add to the authority of His word the visible sign of the power which it possesses; but also in order to give assurance that He is indeed the one who should come (Matt. 11:4–5) and who comes to fulfil the word of Isa. 53:4–5 (Matt. 8:17). The healings of demoniacs have a prophetic import in that they illustrate the victory of God "by his Spirit" over the spirits, and the appropriation of the whole realm of creation subjected to Satan. Similarly, the healings of lepers proclaim the end of the separation between the clean and the unclean: Jesus touches lepers; they are no longer excluded, but reinstated in the covenant of grace. The fact that the healings performed by Jesus are in harmony with the publication of the good news of the Kingdom, of the forgiveness of sins, and that they are addressed to faith, removes from them every note of publicity. They are not designed to inaugurate in a dazzling manner an era of happiness on earth, but to set up signs of the presence of the Son of Man and of the nearness of His reign. It is "the power of the Lord" that enables Him to perform miracles of healing (Lk. 5:17).

But in the end the Lord is the rejected and the crucified one. It is not the healing of sicknesses which is the decisive "sign", but "the sign of Jonah" (Matt. 12:38–40), that is to say, the cross and the resurrection. Jesus heals, but He does so by Himself "bearing the sickness", by refusing "to heal himself" (Lk. 4:23), by Himself becoming the sick one (Matt. 25:36). One must not lose sight of this close link between the healing of sickness and redemption by the expiatory sacrifice of the cross, if the scope of the ministry of healing and the significance of sickness in the Church and the Christian life are to be grasped. The apostles receive from Jesus the command to proclaim the Gospel and the power to heal "by the *laying on of hands" (Mk. 16:18), "in the name of Jesus" (Acts 3:6). Can it be concluded from this that the ministry of the Church purely and simply follows on that of Jesus? If the testimony of the Acts alone is to be taken into account, one would be tempted to say yes (Acts 4:30; 5:16, etc.). But this does not indicate that Pentecost inaugurates a kind of reign of the Holy Spirit characterized by glorious signs of which the miraculous healing of the sick was to be the most certain. If it is true that the healing of the sick, connected with the ministry of intercession, continues to be promised and given to the Church (*Ministry), and that no restriction can be placed upon the promises of the New Testament related to prayer and the assurance of faith (Matt. 17:19–21; 21:22; Jas. 5:14–15), that does not mean that the sickness and suffering involved have only a negative character and should be regarded only as an evil to be suppressed. By the ministry of Jesus Himself, identifying Himself with sick and fallen humanity, sickness continues to be, for the Church and in the life of the Christian, the sign of this human condition, the state which Jesus Christ wished to assume in order to be "God with us". Thus at the present time not only healing but also sickness can be signs of grace and mercy.

H. ROUX

SIGN, *see* MIRACLE

SIN

O.T.

1. The Israelites drew no distinction between an act and the one who performs it. An act is always the expression of the nature of the agent. It constitutes, therefore, a verdict pronounced upon his character. To understand the O.T. conception of sin we have to go right back to the source of the action, i.e., to the man who acts. A good action is the normal action, performed by a healthy, normal being. The Bible always thinks of man as an entity (cf. Gen. 6:9: Noah was a righteous man, blameless in his generation). Over against the normal and good action, which reveals the normal and well-balanced personality, is set the evil action, performed by one who is inwardly divided and lacking in real health and vitality. This action is a sin.

On the other hand, the Israelite view of the world is marked by its optimism. The world of men is the dwelling-place of light and life, and happiness is man's heritage. God created and guaranteed this happiness. Every attempt to jeopardize the life of the world which God made and to threaten the full development of the forces of life is evil. Sin, then, is defined in relation to God, the guarantor of life and happiness. Life and death, however, like good and evil, are not considered as two opposites. One reality alone counts; life, light and blessing. Experience drives us to admit the existence of other forces hostile to the first: sin, evil, malediction and death. When sin enters the heart of a man, it acts like a disease which saps the life forces.

2. A great variety of words is used in the Bible to denote sin. Although in the O.T. they are frequently used interchangeably (cf. Deut. 19:15, "for any crime or for any wrong . . . any offence"), it is interesting to go back to their primary connotation which reveals to us the inward meaning of the biblical conception of sin. The word most frequently used comes from a root which connotes "*to get lost*", to miss the mark. It implies that the action is worthless because it achieves no result (cf. 2 Kings 18:14: Hezekiah, who admits that he has gone astray in revolting against Nineveh, cries: "I have acted without discernment" or "I have gone astray", i.e., "I have sinned"). The good action is the one which leads to a positive result by contrast with the sinful action which leads to no result. There are in the Bible many sinners whose actions may be defined as "straying". Another word which is commonly used for sin comes from a root which denotes something distorted and twisted. Here the sinful action is thought of in contrast to the right or straight action. Another very common expression comes from the verb *to rebel*, which is used with a secular as well as with a religious connotation (cf. 1 Kings 12:19: "So Israel has been in rebellion against the house of David to this day"). Sinners are also called *evil-doers* (see *Wicked*), a term which presupposes a judgment, the evil-doers being those who have been declared guilty before a tribunal, in contradistinction to the *just*, who have been declared innocent.

3. Sin, then, is on the one hand a departure from the normal and from the divine order, and the very antithesis of life. Now in the Bible man is never thought of as an isolated individual, for the O.T. always takes cognizance of man in the situation where he is in life, and that life is only real when man is considered in his relationship to other men, i.e., in the community. The Bible expresses this by the idea of *covenant. Sin is precisely that which damages the community or the covenant, that which threatens their solidarity. In other words, when one sins, that sin always affects another person, be it a man or God, Israel and her God being united in the covenant. Sin, then, like justice, is interpreted in terms of relationship. It impinges upon others and is the violation of an accepted duty. Hence the common expression "*to sin against someone*", an expression which takes for granted the existence of obligations which have been broken. God, who vouch-

safes life and order, has settled the laws which safeguard normal life. To transgress them is to rebel against God (cf. 2 Sam. 12:13: "I have sinned against the Lord", Ps. 51:6). It is evident that the idea of sin embraces the whole life of the individual, as well as that of the nation, the religious life as in the failure to observe some particular rite or institution, such as the sabbath, as well as the moral life: sin of a sexual nature, or sin which touches the possessions of one's neighbour, the widow or the orphan. The fact that the life of the whole people is closely linked to God, who sustains that life, gives to the O.T. conception of sin a profound significance.

4. Like all her neighbours, Israel possessed a highly developed legal system which regulated the life of the community and the personal conduct of its individual members. Whatever may be the origin of these laws, many of which are common to the Semitic peoples, they are all attributed to Moses and by him to God who taught him. To infringe these laws is to commit a sin, to act in opposition to life, to behave as a fool (1 Sam. 26:21), to work against God, to sin against Him. There is therefore no real distinction between religious and other sins. All are an offence against God.

5. *Every sin brings its punishment*, for it is vital that order and life should be kept intact. In His capacity as the guardian of life, God takes upon Himself to inflict punishment. This He does by sending misfortunes: cosmic catastrophes, military disasters, disease and death. This idea led on to another, namely that every disaster is the outcome of sin. The dramas which marked the history of Israel explain the increasingly large place which the consciousness of sin occupied in the life of this people, with its corollary: an ever-growing need of expiation. Herein lies the significance of those agonized questions in the penitential psalms (Ps. 3; 5; 6; 7; 13; 17; 22, etc.) and in the sustained debate in the book of Job. Not only was Israel keenly aware of the problem of the sufferings of the innocent,

but the cultus made special provision for involuntary sins, such as sins of which one was unaware and for which forgiveness was craved (Ps. 19:13; Lev. 4). Once a year, on the great Day of Atonement, the high priest made atonement for the sins of the people, and a he-goat, laden with these sins, was driven out into the desert (Lev. 16).

6. What, according to the O.T., is *the origin of sin*? While it affirms the reality of sin in the life of man, the O.T. also mentions men who claim to be free from all sin (Ps. 18:24; Job 33:9). Such claims would leave room for us to suppose that man is not a sinner by nature. Other passages, however, insist on the universality of sin (Gen. 8:21; Job 14:4; Ps. 14:3; 130:3; 143:2). How can two such contradictory teachings be reconciled? The Israelites did not possess what to-day would be called an ontology of sin. They were concerned not with the ultimate origins of sin but with its undeniable existence all around them. They could affirm the fact of the universal diffusion of sin without being unduly concerned to know whether or not man was a sinner by nature. It is in this sense that the expression in Ps. 51:5 must be taken, "in sin did my mother conceive me": which amounts to saying: like the rest of men, I have been a sinner since my birth. This, too, is how the great chapter 3 of Genesis must be understood. The purpose of the story of the Fall is, indeed, to explain the self-evident fact that all men are sinners, that the world has fallen away from the perfection which it possessed at the time of the *creation. If there is a relation of cause and effect between the sin of Adam and the sin of men, the O.T. neither says so nor even gives the slightest hint of this idea. We have to go to a writing of 200 B.C., the Wisdom of ben Sirach, to find the doctrine of original sin, which St. Paul later develops (Ecclus. 25:24). This silence must not, however, be too strictly interpreted, for the Pauline doctrine of the involvement of the human race in the sin of Adam may well be implicit in the story of Genesis 3 without the Israelites being concerned with the problems which it raised.

7. The nature of Adam's sin has always given rise to many discussions. Men have speculated on what lies behind the account of the Garden of Eden, the tree of life and the tree of the knowledge of good and evil. The account in Gen. 3 is undoubtedly a parable which teaches that, when man put forth his hand to take the forbidden fruit, he broke a divine command and committed a sin. If, as the writer holds, to know good and evil really means to be master of good and evil, a meaning which is implied in the Hebrew verb "to know", then to know good and evil may mean to be like God. The sin of man consisted, then, in his desire to become God's equal, the only privilege which man did not enjoy. What, then, are we to think of life and death? Was the first man mortal or immortal by nature? The sin resulted in denying man access to the tree of life whose fruits would allow him to nourish the life force. Man was not created immortal. He had to return to the earth whence he had been drawn, but his earthly condition was suspended during the period when he was able to live near to the tree of life.

To the question of the origin of sin is linked that of the first cause of sin. The O.T. gives no uniform answer on this point. In 1 Sam. 18:10, it is a divine being who is the agent of the homicidal madness of Saul; in 1 Kings 22:21, a divine spirit drives the kings of Israel and Judah to defeat. The ills of Job are attributed to Satan (Job 1:6), the sin of Adam and Eve to the serpent. These are attempts to explain the mystery of *the origin of evil*. In Judaism, where the omnipotence of the law is so clearly stressed, sin is defined as the violation of one or other of the commandments. One of the signs of the legalism of the contemporaries of Jesus was that the rabbis sought to base on the text of Gen. 8:21 the doctrine of man's inclination to evil.

G. PIDOUX

N.T.

1. All the N.T. writers assume that sin, in the final issue, rests upon the misunderstanding of God's will. They do not, however, hold that blind obedience to the divine commandments is the aim of piety. Man's heart needs to be purified so completely that he comes to hate evil: he will then shun evil because he detests it. The obverse side of this truth is that *goodness must be motivated by love for God and for one's neighbour.

The Epistle to the Hebrews even speaks of the faculties of the soul, which, when developed by exercise, enable the believer to distinguish for himself between good and evil (5:14). It is for this reason that the Gospel warns us against *legalism*, i.e., the attitude which ensues when the heart is not engaged in the fulfilling of the commandments. It is out of love and pity that one must help the unfortunate, forgive one's neighbour, and, if the need arise, give one's life for one's brethren.

Jesus also denounces *hypocrisy* as a particularly dangerous vice, for hypocrisy leads to the performance of actions deemed to be good with the intention of being "on the right side" of God and to acquire merit. In the wake of hypocrisy follows *vanity*, another sin which lies in wait for the pious and which prompts them to make themselves seen and praised by men for the "good" they do (Matt. 23; 6:1ff.). It is easily understood that the Gospel viewpoint is radically at variance with the pharisaic conception of sin: to the Pharisee the breaking of the laws concerning the sabbath or ablutions was a greater sin than lack of love. They failed to understand that it is what comes out of man's evil heart that defiles him (cf. Mk. 7:15 and parallel passages).

In reference to these ideas attention must be called to the particular importance of the confession of the Publican (Lk. 18:13). After the enumeration of meritorious deeds recited by the Pharisee, one would have expected the Publican to give a list of his sins. But we have nothing of the sort. What he confesses is his sinful *condition*, and that is the only thing that matters in the sight of God. It is true that the fourth Gospel and the Epistles of John frequently identify the absence of sin with the fulfilment of the commandments. But these commandments are deliberately reduced to the supreme commandment of love (Jn. 15:12; 1 Jn. 3:18f.; 4:7f.; 5:1f.). The legalism of the Pharisees has been left far behind.

2. This subordination of all the moral precepts to *love does not prevent the N.T. from warning us against a whole series of particular sins. The biblical writers knew that in practice the Christian is not always at the level of his ideal and that, in consequence, he will always need a moral code as a fence to keep him from falling. For this reason the apostle Paul, whilst he sums up the commandments in the one law of love (Rom. 13:9f.), gives us several lists of vices to put us on our guard against the snares of the Devil. 1 Cor. 5:9–11 and 6:9f. remind us that the unchaste, robbers, slanderers, drunkards, thieves and, of course, idolaters cannot enter the Kingdom of God (cf. also Eph. 5:5; 1 Pet. 4:15). The pastoral Epistles add to the list other sins which the Christian must especially flee: jealousy, the spirit of controversy, base suspicions (1 Tim. 6:4f.), avarice, pride, inhumanity, enslavement to the love of pleasure (2 Tim. 3:1–7), sins which are particularly odious when they are found in bishops, "elders" or "elder women" (Tit. 1:7–12; 2:2–5).

It is genuine Christian love which will safeguard the Christian against these sins. According to 1 Cor. 13, love is far removed from fanaticism, tactlessness, pride, egoism, anger, revenge (this is the meaning of the quotation from Zech. 8:17 in 1 Cor. 13:5), as well as from the wicked habit of rejoicing over the evil which others suffer (*Schadenfreude*). This healing virtue of love constitutes the originality of the N.T. teaching on vices and virtues, as the lists of these found in the N.T. do not differ appreciably from those which are to be found in the Greek philosophers of the period, e.g., in the Stoics.

3. Another quite original aspect of the N.T. doctrine of sin is deserving of emphasis: it is the relationship between sin and the more or less developed conscience of the faithful. Jesus, according to a text preserved in the MS. of Theodore of Beza and given in the notes in certain modern translations (after Lk. 6:5), said to a man who was working on the *sabbath day; "If you know what you are doing (i.e., if you understand that the sabbath was made for man and not man for the sabbath), you are blessed. But if you do not know (i.e. if in your conscience you still feel bound by the letter of the law concerning the sabbath rest), you are accursed as a transgressor of the law."

The apostle Paul develops the same idea in the famous passages on the "strong" and the "weak". There are indeed some who are weak in the faith who have scruples about eating meat, whether from the fear of being involved in the eating of flesh of an animal which has been sacrificed to *idols or on the ground of vegetarian principles. Some even feel scruples about drinking wine. In these circumstances, the apostle teaches that, if one who is "weak" acts in violation of his conscience, he commits a sin (1 Cor. 8:7–13; Rom. 14). On this account those who are "strong" will take care not to cause those who are "weak" to stumble, while the latter on their side will refrain from judging their stronger brethren. These considerations lead the apostle to give a definition of sin which is perhaps the most evangelical of all: *whatever does not proceed from faith is sin* (Rom. 14:23). We should note in passing the function of the religious conscience in the Epistle to the Hebrews, without laying too much emphasis upon the developments found there, since they concern the problem of *forgiveness, which does not enter into the scope of this article (Heb. 9:9–14).

4. Another particularly fascinating aspect of the Pauline doctrine of sin consists of his teaching on its origin. The principal references to this are in the passages Rom. 1:18–2:11 and chapter 5. The latter recalls the fact that Adam's rebellion has brought about the fall of the whole human race. It must be stated categorically that the question of original *guilt* is not implied.

Every man is responsible for his own sin. What is hereditary is the corruption of the whole of humanity, a corruption which brings in its train a degradation of our nature and its involvement in death.

The other passage is more detailed. Paul gives a brief dissertation on the moral history of the pagan world. Its initial sin consisted of men's refusal to give glory to God (1:18f.). They chose rather to worship idols and animals. The first result of this apostasy was of an intellectual nature: the minds of men were darkened (1:22f.), this led to moral disorders (1:24f.). We are here brought face to face with a progressive conception of the Fall, which evidently at the time of the appearance of the Gospel had not brought all men equally low.

Nevertheless, this Fall was universal. "All have sinned and fall short of the glory of God" (Rom. 3:23). "None is righteous, no, not one" (Rom. 3:10). It must be noted that the thought of original sin as a real defilement may explain why it is not merely the mind of man which is actually responsible for the different acts of sin. Human nature (that which to-day we call the "subconscious") is involved. There is "in our members" a law which rebels against the law of God (Rom. 7:21–23; 6:13f.), and this fact must be firmly grasped in order to understand the duality of the term *flesh in the thought of the apostle. It denotes, on the one hand, the very principle of sin, revolt against God (there is also a "carnal, earthly, wisdom", 2 Cor. 1:12), on the other hand contaminated human nature, the very stronghold of sin which is the adversary of God and of the human race and which is frequently almost personified (Rom. 5:21; 6:6,12,14,16,17, etc.). It must be borne in mind that all creation longs to be set free from its bondage to decay (Rom. 8:19–23), for human nature is inseparably bound up with the whole of the natural world.

For this revolt of the "flesh", 1 John has discovered a classic expression: it speaks of "the lust of the flesh and the lust of the eyes and the pride of life" (1 Jn. 2:16). The best commentary on this theme is found in Nietzsche (with this difference, however, that Nietzsche exalts what the N.T. condemns). In this same Epistle is found the statement: "The world passes away, and the lust of it; but he who does the will of God abides for ever" (2:17).

5. But is it possible for the Christian to be really sinless? The apostle Paul denies the possibility. The Christian must wait to be delivered from "this body of death" before he can share in "glory", i.e., in sinlessness (Rom. 7:24f.). 1 John, however, seems to suggest that sinlessness is a possibility; none of those who abide in Him (i.e., in Christ) commits sin (3:5f.). "He who commits sin is of the devil" (3:8), whilst he who is "born of God" knows not sin (5:18f.). The same Epistle describes the man who claims to be without sin as a liar (1:9f.). It has been claimed that the first chapter is speaking solely of sin in the past before conversion. But it is also possible to believe, with the Venerable Bede, that chapters 3 and 5 contain a sketch of the Christian ideal, whereas chapter 1 takes account of empirical reality. The meaning would then be: "In so far as we abide in Christ, we sin no more."

6. We must come back to the link between sin and *death (Rom. 5:12f.; 1 Cor. 15:26). Modern thought rightly sees in death the operation of a natural law. The N.T. does not deny this. But it adds that the "nature" of "our world" does not conform to the original purpose of God, who did not desire the death of living beings. There is scope to enlarge on this problem: to what degree are the sufferings of humanity the result of sin? The Gospel rules out belief in *karma* in the sense that particular misfortunes (the fall of the Tower of Siloam, the massacres ordered by Pilate (Lk. 13:1–5), congenital blindness, Jn. 9:1–3) could be either the result or an indication of exceptionally grave sins. Nevertheless there is a general connection between sin and misfortune: it is because men have surrendered themselves to the *Devil that he has the power to afflict them (e.g., Lk. 13:16). The fact that in the account given in Mk. 2:1–12

and parallel passages healing is accompanied by forgiveness adds weight to this. It is for this reason that the victory of Christ over the hostile powers stimulates the hope that the power of the Evil One will be completely broken.

7. What is the significance of the "sin against the Holy Ghost" (Mk. 3:29 and parallel passages)? The context admits the interpretation that this is blasphemy against God by those who are deemed to know Him. Nor is there any doubt that, when 1 Jn. 5:16f. refers to "mortal sin", the writer has in mind the sin of *blasphemy, probably a particularly odious form of this sin, namely apostasy and the worship of idols. The same reason prompts the writer of the book of Revelation to warn us against the temptation to worship "the Beast".

J. HÉRING

SLAVE

1. Slaves seem to have been less numerous in Israel than amongst other peoples of antiquity (Neh. 7:67 mentions one-sixth of the population). The greater part of them were of foreign extraction, having been either bought commercially or acquired as prisoners of war (Gen. 17:12; Num. 31:11). Their status was no different from Israelites who had fallen into slavery, except in one single matter: the length of their servitude, which, in their case, could only be terminated by death. Emancipation, though possible, was not an obligation and was rarely offered.

On the other hand, the condition of Israelites who had become slaves through stealing or falling into debt or perhaps voluntarily in order to escape extreme poverty (Exod. 21:7ff.; 21:2; Amos 2:6; 8:6) was in theory a great deal milder. Their lot was progressively improved and legislation after the Exile aimed at abolishing slavery. The most ancient laws stipulated that a man had to be set free six years after he had lost his liberty (Exod. 21:2). Later this measure was extended to include women (Deut. 15:12). In face of the wide disregard of these legal statutes, post-exilic legislators instituted the year of jubilee, which came round every 49 years (Lev. 25:8–10). In that year all Israelite slaves, whatever may have been the date of their enslavement, regained their liberty.

As the word slave is used both of the servant of a private individual and of an ordinary citizen bound to the person of the king (1 Kings 9:27), it sometimes bears the sense simply of "servant". It is then a polite word for the submission of a free subject to his sovereign (Gen. 20:8).

By an easily understood extension of meaning, "to *serve" can also translate the faithful submission of a believer to God (e.g., "David, my servant", Isa. 37:35). But from this point of view, Israel's slavery in Egypt had a double character, for besides the deprivation of freedom it involved their being unable to "serve" God. Egypt is, par excellence, the land of "servitude" (Exod. 1:13; 2:23, etc.).

2. Before considering the attitude of Jesus and the primitive Church to slavery, it should be noted that the literature of the N.T. makes a distinction between several kinds of "services" and uses different words for each of them. Slavery or servitude implies the deprivation of one's self-determination in virtue of being the absolute property of a master (Matt. 6:24—no one can serve two masters). To serve in a religious context signifies at once to honour, to work for, and to be dedicated to (Rom. 1:9; Phil. 3:3; Lk. 2:37). It can equally well be used of an official service, whether civil or religious. In this case the function of a servant is to minister to his king or his God (Rom. 13:6; 15:16). Finally, service can be personal and voluntary (whether or not any payment is made: Matt. 8:15; 20:28; Rom. 15:25).

While Jesus was not indifferent to the well-being of slaves, since He alludes in several of His parables to the despotism of masters, He did not come forward as the champion of only one type of man, or of a particular social class. He proclaimed in everything the absolute will of God. He

Himself came "to serve" and to give His life a ransom for many (Matt. 20:28). The mission of the Son of Man is to deliver all men, whoever they may be, and to save them. It was He who, for the first time, imparted a peculiar dignity to the person of the slave. "Whoever would be first among you must be your slave" (Matt. 20:27). So it is that the Son of Man came not to be served but to serve (Matt. 20:25–28; cf. 23:11; 23:8; Lk. 22:24–30). The slave ceases to be an inferior creature, an intermediate being between a beast and a man; he is a man, a human soul, worthy of the salvation of God with as much right as his master. Immersed in an equal state of perdition, he can and must be saved from it.

The first communities were faced with some very delicate problems. Some slaves had become Christians, while their owners had remained pagans: what should be their proper attitude? Some Christians owned pagan slaves: what were they to do?

For the apostle Paul, "Christ died for all, that those who live might live no longer for themselves but for him who for their sake died and was raised" (2 Cor. 5:15). The end of life is communion with Christ (Rom. 10:10–13). Emancipation remains secondary. "For he who was called in the Lord as a slave is a freedman of the Lord. Likewise he who was free when called is a slave of Christ. . . . In whatever state each was called, there let him remain with God" (1 Cor. 7:22,24). In Christ there is no longer master or slave (Gal. 3:28). Let each master remember his heavenly Master. Let the slave have always before his eyes the example of Christ, the true *servant (Phil. 2:5–11). It is not indifference to social questions, since both the slaves and their owners are exhorted to live in Christ (cf. Col. 3:22 to 4:1; Eph. 6:5–9), but rather of a translation into the terms of social existence of the love of the Father (the only true Master) for the Son (the only true servant) and *vice versa*. The apostle Paul does not lay down general instructions, but gives encouragement. He was not, in the modern sense of the word, a revolutionary, still less a traditionalist. He sought to emphasize that what had to be worked out in daily life was the extraordinary fact that in Christ all men, masters or slaves, were one. But this is a far larger reality than any simple claims on the human level: these are not overlooked, but they are relegated to their proper station: they belong to a transitory order (1 Cor. 7:31).

The author of the first Epistle of Peter shares Paul's point of view.

M. CARREZ

SOLDIER, *see* WAR

SOLOMON, *see* NAMES (PERSONAL)

SONG, *see* HYMN

SOUL, *see* MAN

SPIRIT, *see* HOLY SPIRIT

STUMBLING-BLOCK (SCANDAL)

1. In the O.T. this word means a trap or an obstacle which causes you to fall and die (it is used in the literal sense in Lev. 19:14; Amos 3:5. It is rendered in various ways in our translations, the word scandal no longer giving the original meaning). It is used figuratively to denote a means of ruin (Josh. 23:13; 1 Sam. 18:21; Ps. 106:36), especially in the realistic language of the prophets where it is an allusion to the retributive intervention of God (Isa. 8:14). God places an obstacle or a trap in the way of those who violate His covenant to baffle their designs and work their undoing.

2. In the N.T. Jesus Christ is described as a stumbling-block in conformity with the prophecy of Simeon (Lk. 2:34). In fact, far from responding to the Jewish and human desire for national and world redemption (and yet it is He alone who can respond to it) Jesus comes into the world of men as a gift which seems to them utterly unacceptable, and thus He produces in their midst a deep, painful, fierce division. His advent stands revealed as a divine judgment on the self-centred thoughts and imaginings

of mankind. His ministry of the word and of acts of power, greeted by the faith of some as the expected Messianic deliverance, stumbles against the reprobation of others who see in it only blasphemy and begin to hate Him with a fury of holy indignation (Matt. 13:57; 15:12; 17:27). Jesus knows that each one of His hearers by not surrendering to Him fully in faith is exposed to the possibility of turning away from Him in an apparently religious and righteous anger, and He warns them of this several times (Matt. 11:6; 21:44; Jn. 6:61; 16:1–3). His Messianic claim, at the very moment when it is about to be realized most authentically through His rejection by Israel and the nations, through His loneliness and desolation, and His triumphal recognition by God alone, will encounter condemnation (Matt. 16:23) and will cause the dispersion of even His most enthusiastic disciples (Matt. 26:31). No one will come to Jesus the Messiah without at first falling, without being mortified by the contingent and contemptible aspect of His appearance on earth (cf. Matt. 16:25 and *cross).

Jesus Christ as a stumbling-block is not merely the purely historical result of a struggle between two conflicting ideas of Messianism within Judaism (and throughout the O.T.). The same effect persists in the preaching of the Gospel to the nations: it is inevitable in a humanity which can now boast only of itself and its own achievements. If the cross is for the Jews a fatal obstacle to their salvation, for the non-Jews it is "folly" (1 Cor. 1:23); the Church itself will be constantly tempted to make it vain (1 Cor. 1:17), to ignore the obstacle constituted by the historical apparition of Jesus, to abandon faith for works, or ethics: hence the apostles feel obliged in their letters many a time to remind it of the reality of the Christ which transcends all human thinking and is accessible only to faith (Rom. 9:33; 16:17; Gal. 5:11; 1 Pet. 2:8. These texts cite Isa. 28:16 and Ps. 118:22). Rom. 11:9 (cf. Ps. 69:23) shows the relative but essential place of the irreducible "scandal" in the economy of God's plan of salvation.

3. Stumbling-block also connotes *sin, a natural pitfall which causes the downfall of the unbeliever, and also implies the external causes of this sin. We should read in this sense Matt. 5:29ff.; 13:41; 18:7ff.; 1 Jn. 2:10. And further 1 Cor. 8:13 and Rom. 14:13, where the strong in faith are exhorted not to lead the weak into temptation.

CH. BIBER

SUFFERING

Human suffering occupies a place of considerable importance in Holy Scripture. From the figure of Cain to that of Job, from Golgotha to the visions of the book of Revelation, there are few pages of the Bible which do not either touch upon or come to grips with this harsh reality of human life. And yet, because it is not a philosophical system, Scripture nowhere gives a definite and rationally satisfying explanation of the fact. In the context of the biblical message, suffering remains what it is in earthly life; an open problem of which faith alone can pierce the secret through the vision of the sufferings of Jesus Christ—that supreme manifestation of the disorder of the creation and the redeeming love of God.

If in the language of the present day the idea of suffering suggests primarily the physical pain of the sick or wounded, in Holy Scripture the term has a much deeper and more existential meaning. The Bible is aware of physical suffering, for example the pains of childbirth (Gen. 3:16; Jn. 16:21) of sickness (Job 7:5; Ps. 102) or of martyrdom (Matt. 27:27–30). But without minimizing it after the manner of the Stoics or the Christian Scientists, the Bible in speaking of suffering never emphasizes the aspect of physical pain. Often suffering is moral; it is the suffering aroused by scorn, calumny, desolation or the hardness of heart of others (Ps. 55; Jer. 15:18; Matt. 27:39–44; Gal. 4:19). But, far from being considered simply as a physical evil or a moral evil, suffering has always in Scripture a spiritual character: it represents a mortification in the presence of God, it is a sign of His reprobation and anger (Job 10:2; Ps. 107:12,39; Matt.

27:45,46; 2 Cor. 12:5–10). That is why the opposite of suffering is not so much health and well-being (Job 42) as consolation (2 Cor. 1:5–7) and *glory (Rom. 8:18; 1 Pet. 1:11), i.e., rehabilitation in the sight of God by divine grace.

It is above all the spiritual or theological implication of suffering which is revealed in Scripture:

In the early chapters of Genesis, suffering appears only after the Fall (Gen. 3:16). By contrast the original creation is "very good" (Gen. 1:31), harmonious and coherent, free from all suffering. The new world which is the object of hope throughout the Bible is a world in which there will be no more suffering (Isa. 65:16ff.; Rev. 21:4). This means that suffering is not eternally inevitable but that it is bound up with the condition of sinful man; it is one of the signs of the confusion and chaos in creation which are the direct consequence of man's revolt against God. In the present age the hold of *sin is such that none can escape it. Hence, in order to assume fully the condition of man, the Christ must suffer (Heb. 2:14–18).

Does this essential nexus between suffering and sin imply that suffering is proportionate to the degree of personal disobedience among nations and individuals? The O.T. often presents misfortunes as the collective punishments which God sends to faithless peoples (Amos 1–2). It is in this sense that the prophets interpreted the history of Israel and the nations. But for them the agonies of punishment have the value of inciting to repentance (Jer. 18:11), while in Deuteronomy (chap. 28) and certain Psalms (49:52, etc.) and in Proverbs suffering has become a final and operative punishment reserved for the wicked and which the righteous are spared. Finally, in late Judaism and thence in certain strands of tradition in the N.T., the punishment of sin by suffering is carried over to the after life, to that place of torments known as *Gehenna (Lk. 16:24; Rev. 20:10).

It is against this doctrine of direct retribution which connects the operation of divine justice to human deserts, and which

is thus confronted by the scandal of the suffering of the righteous, that the book of Job protests: in reply to his friends who infer from his suffering that he is a sinner, Job declares his innocence (chap. 31) and, after the phase of revolt (chap. 7), Job humbly submits himself to the sovereign Lordship of God (39:37ff.). Apart from the speech of Elihu, who sees in suffering a divine discipline (36:15) the book leaves unsolved the mystery of the suffering of the innocent which is the cause of distress in so many Psalms (7:44, etc.) as also in several passages of the prophets (Jer. 15:18).

In the O.T. itself only the pages of the Second Isaiah suggest to us that the suffering of the righteous has expiatory value for others: "A man of sorrows and acquainted with grief . . . he was wounded for our transgressions and bruised for our iniquities . . ." (Isa. 53:3–5).

The sufferings of Jesus Christ the Servant of God and the Son of Man lie at the very heart of the message of the N.T. The Gospels relate this passion while giving us to understand that it is the image of the whole life of Christ from Bethlehem (Matt. 2:13ff.) to Gethsemane and Golgotha. In Him physical and moral suffering culminates in the spiritual suffering of the innocent who feels rejected by God: "Why hast thou forsaken me?" (Mk. 15:34). We see here not the glorious and deliberate martyrdom of a hero but a humble obedience to the inscrutable will of God: "The Son of Man must suffer many things" (Mk. 8:31). Although they are at pains to emphasize the divine necessity of the sufferings of Christ (cf. Jn. 12:27), the Gospels merely suggest the expiatory character of this suffering (Mk. 10:45; cf. Jn. 12:24). It was left for the apostles explicitly to declare its substitutionary and expiatory function by summing up all the suffering of Christ in that of His *cross.

The sufferings of the Son of Man are complete and final in so far as in the sight of God they are the concentrated expression of all human sorrow and pain. This is why St. Paul sees in his sufferings as an apostle the prolongation of the passion of Christ

(Col. 1:24) and links with Jesus Christ all the suffering of believers (Rom. 8:17); humiliation and persecution freely accepted by the believer cause him to share in the destiny of his Lord who through suffering entered into His glory (2 Cor. 1:5ff.; Phil. 3:10; 1 Pet. 4:1–2; 5:1). Whether it speaks of the suffering of bodily *sickness (Matt. 17:15; Jas. 5:13) or of moral temptation (Heb. 2:18; Jas. 1:12) or, as so often, of persecution (2 Tim. 3:10f.) the N.T. proclaims that suffering has been overcome by Christ but not yet done away; through the life of faith it becomes a state of grace in which the believer can rejoice here and now, for it is the pledge of future glory (Acts 5:41; Rom. 8:17ff.; Phil. 3:10; 1 Pet. 4:13).

It is clear that this conception of suffering by losing its Christocentric character could lead the early Church to meritorious courting of martyrdom—a paradoxical relapse into the Jewish doctrine of retribution.

S. AMSLER

TEACHING

In Greek, the terms which our English versions translate by the words doctrine, teaching, to teach, doctor and master (this last word being used in addition to translate an entirely different Greek word which approximates in meaning more to the English "lord", e.g., Matt. 6:24) all come from the same root. It must be further noted that, in certain passages, (e.g., Matt. 23:7–8; Jn. 1:38; 11:8, etc.), the term "rabbi", the Aramaic equivalent of "master", has passed into Greek just as it stands and that the English versions have sometimes retained and sometimes translated it. The general effect of the N.T. references to teaching is, therefore, to present a unity, a coherence and a precision much greater than the English text of the N.T. would lead us to suppose.

1. *Greek and Jewish Teaching.* In the Greek world, teaching implies the communication to one's pupil of knowledge of an intellectual or technical order, for example, reading, music, fencing and riding. So considered, teaching comprises two aspects. (*a*) It consists, on the teacher's part, in awakening and developing the aptitudes which the pupil possesses by furnishing him with a certain number of rules. (*b*) The subjects taught are addressed to the particular human faculty which is involved: to reason in the case of intellectual exercises, to the body in the case of sport, to manual dexterity in the case of art or technics. Teaching does not envisage man's whole personality.

The O.T. writers are familiar with a pedestrian form of teaching analogous to the above: instruction in the art of war, for example (2 Sam. 22:35) or in singing (Deut. 31:22). In the majority of instances, however, the verb to teach refers to something altogether different: to the communication by God, by the father of a family, or by some pious man, of the "laws and precepts" of the law, of the will or of the "way" of the Lord (cf. Exod. 18:20; Deut. 4:1; 11:19; Ezra 7:10; Ps. 25:4; 51:13, etc.). Teaching of such a nature differs radically from the Greek conception. (i) Its aim is not to develop certain human faculties, but to bring the pupil into contact with a reality outside himself, the divine reality. (ii) It is, by its very nature, directed towards the will of a man, who is summoned to submit himself to the authority of the divine message. Here the man's whole personality is involved. It is in no sense different—at least with regard to the aim and the form of the teaching—in later Judaism. The aim of the Jewish religious teacher, the rabbi, is not to develop the intellectual and practical faculties of his disciple, but to acquaint him with the will of God by laying stress (and this is to become one of the distinctive features of Christian teaching) on the authority of the sacred texts on which he is commenting.

2. *Jesus as teacher.* Judged by its external form, the teaching of Jesus is identical with that of the Jewish rabbis. Like them, He teaches in the synagogues (Mk. 1:21 and many parallels); He sits to teach (Matt. 5:1;

Lk. 5:3; Mk. 9:35). Like them (and like John the Baptist, also a rabbi, Lk. 3:12; Matt. 9:14; Lk. 11:1; Jn. 3:25), He has His *disciples. Like them, too, He comments on Scripture (Lk. 4:16–21; Matt. 5:17–48; 9:13; 19:16–20, etc.). As distinct from the titles reserved exclusively for *Jesus, such as Christ or Lord, the title of teacher may be applied, without any sense of infringing the position of Jesus, to persons other than Him, before (Lk. 2:46), during (John the Baptist and Nicodemus) and after His ministry (Christian teachers), and that in spite of Matt. 23:8 (on which see below).

The teaching ministry of Jesus possesses, nevertheless, an absolutely unique character. In teaching *Scripture, Jesus is in reality speaking of Himself, for Scripture bears witness of Him (Jn. 5:39,45–47). It is this testimony of Scripture which supplies the foundation of the absolute authority which He claims (Jn. 5:31–38) and which so impresses His hearers (Mk. 1:22; Matt. 7:29; Lk. 4:32). The Jewish teachers were content to comment on the law and to place before their hearers the abstract requirements of God. When Jesus teaches, it is the very will of God which is present in His person. He does not say as the prophets said: "Thus saith the Lord", but "I say to you" (Matt. 5:22,28,32, etc.). In Him the will of God confronts the will of man so directly and so imperatively as to leave no time for discussion or for delay. He is the living commentary on the Scripture which He is teaching. If the law was given by Moses, it is through Jesus that have come that grace and that truth to which the law bore testimony (Jn. 1:17) and which summon men to faith.

3. *The teaching ministry of the Church.* The unique character of the teaching of Jesus does leave room, however, in the Church for "teachers" endowed with gifts for a specific ministry, that of teaching (*Ministry N.T.). On this issue, as on many others, the absolute uniqueness of Christ does not exclude, but on the contrary, demands the exercise of ecclesiastical functions which derive from this very

uniqueness. In other words, Matt. 23:8 can only be understood by laying alongside this verse such passages as 1 Cor. 12:28–29; Eph. 4:11; Acts 13:1. If Matt. 23 rules out all independent teaching, it is with the intention of anchoring all the more firmly "in Christ" the ecclesiastical ministry of teaching. This ministry, indeed, has its origin in one of the "charismata" bestowed by Christ (Eph. 4:11) through the medium of the Spirit (1 Cor. 12:1,4–11).

4. *Teaching and preaching.* Based as it is on Holy Scripture and having as its aim the exposition of Holy Scripture, the teaching ministry differs specifically from the *preaching of the Gospel message.

Jesus, in fact, both preaches and teaches. The two verbs used together in Matt. 11:1 do not constitute a pleonasm, any more than they do in Acts 4:2; 5:42; 15:35; 28:31, where the same pair of identical or analogous terms is found. When they preach, Jesus and His apostles announce the Gospel, the incredible "good news"; the Kingdom of God, a present and accomplished fact in Jesus Christ. In this proclamation Scripture plays no decisive part. On the contrary, when they teach, Jesus and the apostles demonstrate from Scripture the agreement of contemporary events with the sacred history of Israel which lights up their range and their wealth. The natural process of development is that to the O.T. Scripture there come to be added the words of Jesus (Matt. 28:20) and even, eventually, those of the apostles themselves (1 Cor. 4:17; Col. 2:7; 2 Thess. 2:15; 1 Tim. 6:2). The earlier canon of Scripture is completed by the new canon which supplies the final and perfect commentary upon it. From that time onwards the Old and New Testaments constitute the sole source of all Christian teaching.

Consequently, it is not surprising that two-thirds of N.T. passages where the verb to teach occurs are found in the Gospels and in the first half of Acts, and that out of 59 references to teacher (or doctor), the Gospels alone contain 49. Teaching, being such as we have been led to define it, could at the outset be addressed only to Jews. Pagans had to be brought to Christ through preaching before the full richness of that same Christ could be revealed to them in Scripture and in the commentary given thereon by Christ and the apostles.

The general experience was that as soon as pagans came into the Church, teaching and doctrine became necessary for them, too, as the stress placed on (sound) doctrine in the Epistles to Timothy and Titus testifies. This renewed interest in doctrine, after the first missionary period in which preaching predominated, confirms the testimony of the N.T. as a whole: Christian teaching can be addressed only to men already brought into the faith through preaching.

In other words, more general but still valid in the Church, theology, which is the attempt to make explicit the wealth of the divine revelation, can only follow in the train of preaching. A window, however small, must first be thrown open on to the vast horizon of the Kingdom of God, before biblical and catechetical teaching, based on the two Testaments, can, with the aid of the Holy Spirit (Jn. 14:26), undertake an intelligible description of the inexhaustible resources of that Kingdom.

J.-L. LEUBA

TEMPLE

O.T.

1. When the Israelites entered Canaan at the close of the 13th century B.C. they found themselves in a country of numerous shrines. Far from destroying them, they took them over and dedicated them to their own god Yahweh. The evidence of the Bible is at this point corroborated by that of archaeological discovery. The old Canaanite sanctuary was generally to be found on an eminence. Besides the altar there were stelae of stone in which the divinity was thought to dwell (cf. Gen. 28:18) and a building for the meals which followed the sacrifices (1 Sam. 9:22). It was to such sanctuaries that worshippers brought the first-born of their flocks and the first-fruits of the harvest and crops. By making these offerings to the deity they brought a blessing on the flock and the products of the soil.

At Jerusalem, as in other towns, there was a sanctuary which was dedicated to a local deity. It had its clergy and liturgy. Gen. 14:18ff. might justify us in concluding that this god was called 'Elyon, which means the Most High—a term which often occurs in the Psalms (cf. 18:14; 21:8; 47:3; 57:3; 78:56, etc.). When David took possession of the city he used the holy place of Jerusalem for the service and worship of his God, who became Yahweh 'Elyon. In 2 Sam. 7, the Bible has preserved a story relating to the building of the Temple. David is here concerned in fact with replacing the tent which housed the ark of the covenant by a building more worthy of it. This tradition above all reflects the admiration that was felt for the Temple of Solomon, the splendour of which surpassed all that had previously been seen and which therefore impressed the imagination as a monument of extraordinary novelty and magnificence.

2. During the course of its existence the Temple at Jerusalem knew three successive periods: the first Temple or the Temple of Solomon, which was to last from the year 960 B.C. until the destruction of Jerusalem in 587; the second Temple constructed by the Jews on their return from Babylon in consequence of the edict of Cyrus (539) and the splendour of which was far inferior to that of the first (Ezra 3:12; Hagg. 2:3); finally the third Temple built by Herod the Great and known to Jesus (see below, N.T.). The latter monument, the building of which lasted from 20 B.C. to A.D. 60, excelled its predecessors in magnificence.

The Temple of Jerusalem, called the house of the Lord, the house or that house (Ps. 23:6; 1 Kings 8) because Yahweh was present there, is described in 1 Kings 6; Ezek. 40–42; 2 Chr. 3. Several of the passages of the Pentateuch relating to the tabernacle of the desert period were directly inspired by familiarity with the later building. There can be no doubt as to its site. It rose on the hill to the north-east of the town, occupied to-day by the mosque of Omar, a holy place of Islam after being the holy place of the Jews—and a circumstance which makes it impossible to-day to carry out archaeological excavations there. To-day it is a large flat surface in the form of a trapezium, the longest sides of which measure approximately 1480 × 1570 ft., the others 900 × 1020 ft. To-day the esplanade is occupied by various buildings, but the outstanding feature of its middle portion is the famous sacred rock (57 × 42 ft. approx., height 6 ft.) which bore the altar of sacrifices.

The principal building of Solomon's Temple had modest proportions. Its interior measured 60 cubits by 30 (the cubit being about equal to 18 inches) and included two chambers of unequal size, the *hekal*, or holy place (40 × 20) and the *debir*, most holy place, (20 × 20). They also were 30 cubits high (according to the Greek text 25 cubits). It is probable that the *debir* was 5 or 10 cubits higher than the *hekal* and that there was a staircase leading up to it. Whereas the holy place was lit by windows, the most holy place was plunged in total darkness in conformity with the command of Yahweh (1 Kings 8:12). The walls of the house were lined with cedar wood and cypress wood, with golden carvings and ornaments. In front of the edifice was a vast vestibule (10 × 20), the entrance of which was flanked by two pillars of bronze, called Jachin and Boaz (1 Kings 7:15–22). On the north, south, and west the Temple itself was surrounded by a secondary construction containing a large number of rooms intended to house objects connected with the cult. A courtyard surrounded the whole group of buildings; Ezekiel says it measured 100 × 100 cubits, whereas the 1st book of Kings does not mention its dimensions. This is the inner court, in contrast to the great court which enclosed all the royal buildings including both palace and Temple. There were doors, in describing the ornamentation of which the Bible is inexhaustible, leading into the various parts of the sanctuary.

In the most holy place was kept the *ark of the covenant—visible sign of the presence of Yahweh. This was the nomadic sanctuary *par excellence*, which it was easy to transport according to the hazards of migration. Its shape was that of a small wooden box and it contained originally the sacred stones. Exod. 25:10 gives its dimensions in cubits: 2½ × 1½, height 1½. Above the ark there rose the two great cherubim of olive wood overlaid with gold. Their outspread wings, 10 cubits long, touched the walls of the *debir* on each side. These cherubim were four-footed winged beasts with human heads, in imitation of those genii who were guardians of the temples of Mesopotamia. The golden slab which formed their base was the mercy seat where Yahweh was especially to manifest Himself in His glory (Exod. 25:17).

In the holy place were ten tables of cedar wood. They were shaped like altars and received the shewbread. Ten gold candlesticks, five on each side, served to illuminate the sanctuary whose latticed windows gave only insufficient light. The great altar for sacrifices was set up in the inner court on the site of the sacred rock still visible. There was also the famous molten sea, an immense reservoir resting on twelve oxen of bronze. According to the 1st book of Kings its capacity was 16,000 gallons. In it was kept the water necessary for the service of the altar. Also it may be that the water as such played a certain part in the cult, the aim of which was to secure the fertility of the soil (cf. the words of Jesus in Jn. 7:38). To convey the water of the molten sea to the altar there were again ten stands with chariot wheels and metal basins. Lastly, the 1st book of Kings is alone in placing in the *hekal* the altar of incense made of gold (7:48).

3. This immense wealth in construction and ornamentation accumulated in the course of ages did not fail to arouse covetousness. Already under Rehoboam the Pharaoh Shishak plundered the house of the Lord (1 Kings 14:25) as did the Babylonians in 587 (2 Kings 25) and the

Romans under Titus in A.D. 70. When the kings of Judah were wanting money, they knew how to draw on the reserves of the Temple (cf. Ahaz in 2 Kings 16:8, Hezekiah in 2 Kings 18:14). On several occasions also the Bible records works of embellishment or restoration undertaken in the Temple by various kings (cf. 2 Kings 22).

4. Absorbing the cults of the local sanctuaries, which never completely disappeared, the royal Temple at Jerusalem eventually gathered to itself the great mass of Jewish worshippers. The attempts to create a rival sanctuary in the northern kingdom did not succeed (cf. 1 Kings 12:26ff.). Crowds came to worship there at the three great *feasts of the year: the Passover or spring festival, the Feast of Weeks or Pentecost, and the Feast of Tabernacles in the autumn, to which was added later, in February or March, the Feast of Purim of which the book of Esther alone speaks.

Apart from the major feasts the Temple possessed a very elaborate ritual. Sacrifices of very many kinds were offered there (cf. Lev. 3–7), corresponding to the various aspects of human life: joy, sadness, grief, illness, healing, thanksgiving. As their description suggests, several of these sacrifices are an inheritance from the Canaanite period. The Psalter, which contains the songs sung on the occasion of the feasts and various types of divine service, constitutes in a sense the liturgy of the Temple. We should also insist on the important part played by the *king, who, in the royal sanctuary which belonged to him in a special sense, conducted the worship in which he represented or more accurately personified the people face to face with God. The kings were liberal in maintaining the *worship. Their liberalities, added to those of the people and the revenues from the land belonging to the Temple, assured a very considerable income for the latter.

5. In the course of time the Temple assumed ever-increasing importance. After the return from Exile it became the centre of the whole national and religious life of the country. The more Israel became conscious of sin, the more was felt the pressure of the need for expiation. In the idealized description of the Temple in Ezek. 40ff. the underlying thought is that the Temple is an immense institution for the expiation of sin. The belief that the God of Israel had His dwelling there also created the supposition that the rock of Zion, on which it was built, was inviolable. No human undertaking could be risked against that fortress. This conviction was reinforced in 701 B.C. when the armies of Sennacherib for mysterious reasons raised the siege of Jerusalem (cf. the taunt song of Isa. 37:22). The mere presence and existence of the royal sanctuary constituted for the Jews the guarantee of salvation. Hence their reply to the plea of Jeremiah that they should repent is "This is the temple of the Lord" (Jer. 7:4).

This belief received a terrible blow when in 587 B.C. the Temple was destroyed; but it would seem that in the time of Jesus it existed anew. Around the many priests and singers whose functions were indispensable to the service of the cult, there gravitated officials of various capacities, some of whom had the duty of establishing order in the sanctuary and its precincts (cf. Jer. 20; see *Priesthood) as also a large number of prophets attached to the royal sanctuary (*Ministry O.T.). There was easy and frequent communication between the royal palace and the Temple, as is clear from Jer. 26:10; 2 Kings 11:13.

G. PIDOUX

N.T.

1. Leaving aside the Temple of Ezekiel which we have fullest knowledge about but which never existed, we recall the fact that there were three successive Temples at Jerusalem: that of Solomon, that of Zerubbabel, and that of Herod. It is the third of these which concerns us here. It was in 29–20 B.C. that Herod began to demolish the previous Temple, relatively modest, in order to replace it by an edifice rich in

marble and gold, and intended to be a worthy successor to the Temple of Solomon. The essential part of the building was quickly finished, but in the time of Jesus work was still going on at the accessories (Jn. 2:20) and it was not until A.D. 62–64 that the whole building was completed, not long before its destruction.

THE TEMPLE OF HEROD:

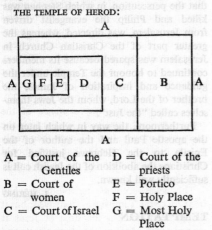

A = Court of the Gentiles
B = Court of women
C = Court of Israel
D = Court of the priests
E = Portico
F = Holy Place
G = Most Holy Place

According to the historian Josephus the Temple of Herod occupied the site of a square stadium, i.e., about an area of 30-odd acres. On the south side it projected beyond the hill of Zion; that is why it was widened by a sort of platform resting on arches. Once the outer enclosure, formed by high walls with four doors, was crossed, one entered a courtyard open to everybody and known as the court of the Gentiles. The inner enclosure of it was furnished with porches and many ancillary buildings. Near to one of the entrances (probably the eastern gate) was situated Solomon's porch, so-called, where, as certain traditions assert, the remains of a door of the first Temple had been embedded (Jn. 10:23; Acts 3:11; 5:12). On the western side was to be found the room used for meetings of the Sanhedrin. It was in this outer court that the sellers of animals and the money-changers plied their trade (Mk. 11:15–17 and parallels). After crossing this outer court one came to a further gateway which the Gentiles were not allowed to pass through. An inscription

which has been found expressly forbids them to pass through on pain of death. This interdict was respected even by the Roman soldiers, and it nearly cost St. Paul his life, for he was accused of having taken un-circumcised Gentiles into the inner precincts (Acts 21:27ff.).

The inner precincts, somewhat raised and also surrounded by rooms and sanctuaries, were divided into two parts of unequal size: to the east was a space accessible to all Jews and for that reason called the court of women. It must have been there that the treasury mentioned in Mk. 12:41–44 (and parallel passages) was situated. The other and larger part, described as the court of Israel, was reserved for male Jews. This court was entered by a richly decorated gate called "the beautiful gate" (Acts 3:2). Within this court of the Israelites was erected the sanctuary strictly so called; it was in fact situated within an inner section of it called the court of the priests. It was here that the animals for sacrifice were slaughtered and the altar for whole burnt offerings was placed. Rather more to the west, still in the same section but on a higher platform, rose the building which housed the holy place and the Holy of Holies.

It was through an eastern portico that the priests entered the holy place to offer the daily sacrifices (i.e., those without blood; cf. Lk. 1:8–10). Here were the table for the shewbread (northern side), the altar of incense (in the middle) as also the seven-branched candlestick, which was no doubt lit during the daytime, owing to the absence of windows. The holy place was separated from the most holy place (which was more to the west) by a veil. The Epistle to the Hebrews (9:3) knows of two veils; the first would be the veil which separated the holy place from the outer parts (as is indicated in the text of Josephus, *Jewish War* 5:5,4–5). The veil which was rent in two at the moment of the death of Jesus, according to Mk. 15:38 and parallel passages, was probably the veil of the Holy of Holies (cf. Heb. 6:19). Only the high priest could enter the latter and then but once a year. In theory he had to sprinkle the lid of the ark with blood. But the latter had long ago vanished; at the latest, at the moment of the plunder of the Temple by the Babylonians (587). The Holy of Holies in the Temple of Herod (and already in that of Zerubbabel) was empty and the duty of the high priest consisted merely in placing the censer on a stone which stood in the middle of it. As for the data of the Epistle to the Hebrews in regard to the contents of the most holy place, they reflect certain rabbinical speculations as to what should have been there and are without any historical value.

2. As for the religious importance of the Temple and the cult in the eyes of the Jews, it was always of course very considerable. But in practice, especially for the Jews of the Dispersion, it was the observation of the commandments regulating the life of every day which had become the essential point. Furthermore, the preaching of certain prophets tending to question the value of the sacrificial cult was by no means forgotten and the negative attitude of the Essenes with regard to it is well known. It is also significant that the evangelists never suggest that Jesus took the slightest interest in the sacrificial cult, with the exception of the rite of the paschal lamb, and this in point of fact had nothing whatever to do with the Temple. Nevertheless He loved the Temple; but according to His statements (Mk. 11:17 and parallel passages) it ought to have been a place of prayer. He went even further in His teaching: *prayer in spirit and truth had no need of a Temple (Jn. 4:21–24); and that is why He announced, not as a catastrophe but as an achievement, the imminent disappearance of the Temple and its replacement by a spiritual edifice which according to the fourth evangelist (2:19–21) as according to the apostle Paul (1 Cor. 12:27 and elsewhere) is the body of the risen Christ.

The first theologian who deduced from the preaching of the prophets and also from the attitude of Jesus conclusions which were frankly anti-ritualist was Stephen (Acts 7, and especially vv. 48–50) who opposed to the Aaronic cult the declarations of 1 Kings 8:27 (= 2 Chr. 2:6) and of Isa. 66:1–2. He certainly was not the only one to think on these lines. But there is reason to believe that at that time only the Hellenists among the Jewish Christians took up this attitude. For it was against them alone that the persecution, in which Stephen was killed and Philip the evangelist driven from Jerusalem, was directed, whereas the greater part of the Christian Church in Jerusalem was spared because its members continued to honour the Temple under the guidance and inspiration of James, the brother of the Lord, whom the Jews themselves called "the Just".

Furthermore, the way in which later on the apostle Paul and the author of the Epistle to the Hebrews justified for Christians the abolition of the Jewish cult is sufficiently well known.

J. HÉRING

TEMPTATION

In the Bible this word has an essentially religious meaning; its moral implications are secondary, contrary to present-day usage. Hence let us not try to impose on the word our modern concepts but let us rather listen to the teaching of Holy Scripture.

Temptation, trial and seduction are not synonymous. Trial, which is an exclusively positive notion, is often united to purification; seduction, which is exclusively negative, means surrender to disobedience. We must first understand these two terms in order to grasp the meaning of temptation in the Bible.

1. *Trial—to try.* When someone or something is tried, this is always done with a positive favourable and good intention in view. Thus God is often described as He who tries the reins and the heart so as to shed light upon the secret recesses of thought and emotion (Ps. 7:10). To try is often a doublet of to purify (see *Clean), the image of the crucible and the fire being more or less explicit—an image which fully

elucidates the meaning of the Hebrew and Greek words. (The Greek word for trial means strictly speaking the touchstone by which a coin is tried.) It goes without saying that if you put auriferous ore into the crucible you know that you will inevitably get much waste and dross, but you hope to gain a little pure gold: that is your sole real intention (Zech. 13:9; Job 23:10; 1 Pet. 1:7; 1 Cor. 3:13). To be sure, trial can be severe and painful (sickness, war, the "trials of life" as we say) but nevertheless it is always good and inspired by favourable and beneficent purposes, since it leads to a purification and sanctification of the tried. The positive connotation of the term is proved by the fact that the simple adjective "tried" has the meaning of "capable of standing up to any trial", whereas its opposite, "reprobate", is one of the most sinister terms in Scripture. Trial might be associated with correction, which always indicates a reformatory purpose (1 Cor. 11:32; Rev. 3:19; Heb. 12:4-11).

It is said that man tries or tempts God when the people of God or the Christian seek to verify the goodness of God or to receive a sign of His favour (Mal. 3:10,15; Ps. 95:9; Rom. 12:2). When Scripture invites us to try ourselves, that can only be in order to discover the image of God within us, and the merits, the fellowship, or the person of Christ (1 Cor. 11:28; 2 Cor. 13:5).

2. *Seduction—to seduce.* Seduction is always willed and determined by an enemy who is actuated by evil designs. Eve declares that she has been seduced by the serpent (Gen. 3:13; 1 Tim. 2:14). The purpose of seduction is to cause us to deviate from the way of obedience to God (Deut. 13:6; Eph. 5:6). One can deceive oneself (Jer. 37:9) and allow oneself to be led astray by one's own heart, by the love of money, covetousness and pride, etc. (Jas. 1:26; Matt. 13:22; Heb. 3:13; 1 Jn. 1:8). Seduction should be connected with *covetousness, occasions of *stumbling, scandals; the implication of all these words is the fall and the ruin of the man who is thus attacked. The seducer disguises himself as an angel of light (2 Cor. 11:14; Matt. 24:4,24). The expression "to deceive God", to attempt to lead Him astray, means that the Devil imagines he can treat God thus (Job 2:3). Thus John calls the Devil the deceiver (Rev. 12:9; 20:10). How shall we explain the idea that God Himself deceives men (2 Sam. 24:1; Jer. 4:10; 20:7; Ezek. 14:9)? The Chronicler's correction shows that such an idea shocked him (1 Chr. 21:1). Yet Jeremiah accuses God of having deceived him (cf. 1:8; 15:18 and 20:7): such words which recall the sorrows of Job (Jer. 20:14-18 and Job 3) were wrung from a soul engaged in the battle of faith, and are devoid of any doctrinal pretension. But a passage such as Jer. 4:10 teaches that nothing escapes the divine omnipotence (cf. Rom. 9:17; 8:38).

3. *Temptation—to tempt.* The idea of temptation in the Bible expresses the spiritual tension in which every man is destined to live and die. Two contrary urges make themselves felt at one and the same time in the soul of the tempted person, and force him to decide one way or the other. Thus Eve, torn between the promise of God (Gen. 2:16ff.) and the beguilements of the serpent (3:5); Abraham between the covenant promise (Gen. 21:12; Heb. 11:18) and the sacrifice which he has been commanded to make (Gen. 22:1ff.); Job between his God (2:10; 27:11) and Satan working through his wife (2:5,9); David between the purity of his heart (Ps. 51:12) and his weakness (2 Sam. 11:27); Israel between the trials of faith (Ps. 81:8) and the murmurs of unbelief (Exod. 17:1ff.); the Christian between the love of the Father and the Evil One (Matt. 6:13).

Thus temptation is always both good and bad, since it voices an appeal to faith and at the same time expresses the counter-attractions of sin. We might define every temptation as a seductive trial and a purifying seduction, if usage permitted us such associations of words.

God wills our temptation, since He wills us to be free. "I have set before you life and death; therefore choose life" (Deut.

30:15–20): these words express precisely the fact that God requires of us a free adoration; such is the order of creation which will endure from the beginning to the end in all tempting.

Who is the author of temptation? God or Satan? We must reply fearlessly: God *and* Satan. Satan is described not only as the seducer, but also as the tempter (Matt. 4:1,3; 1 Cor. 7:5; 1 Thess. 3:5). Thus Satan tempts only in order to seduce. God not only tries us (which is never said of Satan) but He tempts us (Gen. 22:1; Deut. 8:2,16; 13:3; Judg. 2:22; Exod. 15:25–26; 16:4; 20:20; Ps. 26:2; Matt. 4:1; 6:13; 1 Cor. 10:13). Thus the Devil both tempts and seduces, but he does not try us; he is subject to the divine permission (Job; 1 Cor. 10:13; Matt. 4:10); God beguiles, God tempts, God tries. Jas. 1:12–16 does not contradict this. It is clear that, for James, God is working through temptation, since temptation causes a trial of faith which obtains for the victor the crown of life; that is what the believer must know and confess (1:2,12). But as for the unbeliever, let him not allege this as an excuse for his sin. There is only one thing he must know; in temptation he is drawn away and enticed simply by his own lust which, when sin is conceived and consummated, brings death (1:13–16). The unbeliever is wrong to plead the excuse of God's evil intentions towards him; evil is in the heart of the unbeliever and nowhere else! In God there is nothing but perfect good (1:17–18). This assurance gives man force and strength to resist the Devil (4:7).

The temptation of Jesus. This event sheds light on our own experience of temptation. Jesus was tempted in all points like ourselves except that He was without sin: such is the explicit apostolic witness recorded in the synoptic Gospels (Matt. 4:1–11; Lk. 22:28; Mk. 8:27–33; Matt. 22:18; 27:46) and in the Epistle to the Hebrews (2:18; 4:14ff.), while it is implicit in John (12:20–32) in Paul (Phil. 2:5–11; Gal. 4:14; 2 Cor. 5:21) and in Peter (1 Pet. 4:1ff.). Jesus was tempted as man, as the One called by God to be the suffering Messiah—a vocation proclaimed at the time of His baptism by the heavenly voice (Matt. 3:17): Jesus is the royal Son (Ps. 2) but He will have to fulfil His office by becoming the *Servant of the Lord (in accordance with the prophecy of Second Isaiah). Throughout the course of His ministry the Lamb of God was obedient to His vocation, hence victorious in temptation; renouncing the easy way of an earthly and glorious Messiah, Jesus proceeds from renunciation to renunciation until He reaches the final humiliation of death and the desolation of the *cross. The anguished cry of Golgotha: "My God, my God, why hast thou forsaken me?" expresses the tensest moment in the Lord's life of temptation: at that supreme moment God and Satan both made their appeal to Jesus with maximum power and energy. Satan was never so strong as then since Jesus was surrendered to his power. But at the same time God was never so close to His Son, since the prayer of Jesus signified that God was hidden in the very heart of the crucified and abandoned One. In the midst of temptation Jesus was manifested as our Christ, our Saviour, and our Lord. Through the triumphant endurance of temptation, redemption completes creation. This thought gives us a measure of the importance of temptation in the life of Jesus.

The victory of Jesus illuminates every human life. It is through the agency of the Holy Spirit within us that we can exclaim: "Father, lead us not into temptation but deliver us from evil!" In fact, corresponding to the order of creation with its characteristic note of temptation securing the freedom and responsibility of our worship, and to the order of redemption which assures of the love of the Father, there must be the work of our sanctification, the life of the children of God lived under the sign of the triumphant obedience of Christ.

This Christian life is the life of *faith. Faith has been the essence of the spiritual life of believers in all ages (Heb. 11; Jn. 8:56ff.; Matt. 13:17; Phil. 2:8–11). Like his Master, every believer must know the experience of temptation, but he is supported by the assurance which the triumph and the grace of Christ give him. In many diverse forms—personal, social, political, moral and religious—temptation forms the very climate in which faith must develop and expand (1 Cor. 10:3).

The N.T. very clearly directs our thoughts to the successful conclusion of temptation and the glorious coming of the Kingdom of God. The spirit of the beatitudes should inform the Christian's experience of temptation: the tempted Christian is blessed, since through his faithfulness he will receive the crown of life (Jas. 1:2ff,12ff.; 5:11; 1 Pet. 1:6; 4:12ff.; Acts 14:22; Heb. 10:34). Temptation is no trivial matter, but a struggle against the powers of the Devil (Eph. 6:12). We are submitted by the word of God to the serpent of old (Gen. 3:15) with all the risks, dangers, and wounds which that entails (Gen. 32:25,31; 2 Cor. 12:7). But the unconquerable hope which the victory of Jesus brings to birth in us must fill us with all fullness of joy (Jas. 1:2).

It remains for us to make clear the sixth petition of the Lord's Prayer. First of all it is important that it should be correctly translated. The most literal translation will be the clearest, and one wonders why so many paraphrases have been attempted which only render part of the original meaning: "Snatch us not away in the hour of temptation but deliver us from evil." The idea "carry off" is in line with the idea that God in His providence is guiding our footsteps to the goal of His kingdom. The locative sense of temptation (as though one should say "go to Massah"—cf. Exod. 17:7),—as one says "go to Canossa"), giving the meaning: "lead us not to the point of murmuring against You and doubting Your grace", is altogether too limited in scope. It is rather that the petition should be seen against the background of the contemporary apocalyptic ideas of Jesus (Matt. 24 and parallel passages; Rev. 3:10). Just as the life of Jesus developed in ever increasing tension up to the point of His death on the cross, so the world will go from crisis to crisis in ever more intolerable tension to culminate in the great temptation of the end and the last judgment, in which connection we

should note that temptation and *judgment are the two biblical terms expressing essentially the paradoxical and transitory character of this present aeon. According to the very definition of the word temptation, how is it conceivable that we should ask God not to lead us into temptation since we are already plunged and immersed in it? In fact we are prisoners of the Devil and we pray to God our Father to deliver us: the state of temptation consists precisely in this—that we have God as Father and the Devil as our stepfather and wicked tyrant (Rom. 8:20ff.; Jn. 8:44; 14:30).

Jesus thus exhorted us to pray, looking forward in faith and hope so that the great temptation of the end of time will not mean for us our final perdition as it will for the Devil and his abettors, but on the contrary will mark our ultimate liberation and entrance into the fullness of life of the kingdom (1 Cor. 15:28). When the end thus comes the world will pass away and the Devil and death will be destroyed. Temptation will vanish with the old creation. In the new heavens and earth, faith will pass into sight. In the meantime there is no remission from the exacting life of faith, but in Jesus Christ and in the struggle with temptation there is peace *in* faith and the life of waiting for the manifestation of Our Lord Jesus Christ (1 Cor. 1:7).

P. VALLOTTON

TERAPHIM, *see* IDOL O.T.

THRONES, *see* AUTHORITIES

TIME (TIMES)

1. The biblical idea of time nowhere reaches the level of abstract thinking. We like to make of time a universal idea including all existing schemes of chronology. The biblical authors never do this and do not give this meaning to any of the words they employ.

Plato has taught us to contrast time with eternity. Such an antithesis is alien to biblical thought in so far as the contrast rests on a philosophical conception of either term.

Modern science has accustomed us to consider time as a dimension of the universe, uniform and measurable. In the Bible chronological ideas still have a certain vagueness; the hour, the day, the year, the century are somewhat variable units of measurement. Rather than of a time, the Bible speaks of times which are ill co-ordinated and hardly commensurable. Each of these times corresponds to a life to which it remains inseparably linked. God, the creation, the people of Israel, the individual, have each their characteristic time, constituting one of the dimensions of their existence.

2. The time of God is *eternity*. This word is not of frequent occurrence in the biblical writings: we find it hardly more than 20 times and then almost always in expressions of an adverbial nature such as "for ever", "from everlasting to everlasting" etc. In the only passage where the word might have a philosophical implication (Eccl. 3:11) the context shows that the author considers all speculation excluded from the outset: "He has put eternity into man's mind, yet so that he cannot find out what God has done from the beginning to the end."

Furthermore, N.T. Greek has no word to express the notion of eternity; it speaks only of "ages" or "seasons". But on the other hand the adjective eternal and adverbs and adverbial expressions meaning eternally are frequently connected with the name of God, His reign, His throne, etc.; (cf. for example, Dan. 6:26; Ps. 29:10). Thus when some modern translations of the Bible render the sacred name of *God by "the Eternal", they are not by any means unfaithful to the thought of the original.

The eternity of God is first manifested in the fact that He was and acted *before* all things and all life: before the individual life (Jer. 1:5), before the people of Israel, before the created world (Ps. 90:2). Likewise He is the One who will be after all created existence. He is the "alpha and the omega, the beginning and the end" (Rev. 21:6; cf. 22:13). His divine time overflows,

holds together, and envelops all other times. He is God "from everlasting to everlasting".

But this "before" and this "after" are only the two ends of a chain. The eternal life of God does not of course cease to have its specific dimension within the period between the *creation and the last *judgment. God is "He who is and was and is to come" (Rev. 1:4; 4:8) and His Son remains the same "yesterday and to-day and for ever" (Heb. 13:8). He is not affected by the vicissitudes which mark the time of His creatures, for on the contrary He remains the absolute master of time: "With the Lord one day is as a thousand years and a thousand years as one day" (2 Pet. 3:8; cf. Ps. 90:4).

3. As contrasted with the eternity of God, the days of the individual have a very precarious character.   Many are the biblical texts which emphasize their transitory, limited and always fragile note. "Our years come to an end like a sigh . . . their span is but toil and trouble: they are soon gone and we fly away" (Ps. 90:9–10). "As for man, his days are like grass" (Ps. 103:15; cf. Isa. 40:6). The fact is that *man has to endure the chastisement of his *sins, that he has aroused the wrath of God (Gen. 3:22). Yet God has not punished him as he deserved. He has given him the gift of time which he may organize as he pleases, ordering all things in human existence. "To everything there is a season under the heaven. . . ." (Eccl. 3:1–8). In the life of every man God fixes certain decisive hours when death threatens and which form the "hour", "the time", "the end" of this individual (Gen. 6:3; Job 6:11; Eccl. 7:17; Jn. 16:21; cf. all those texts in the fourth Gospel which speak of the hour of Jesus).

4. Will the time of the history of Israel, the people chosen by God for the purpose of His redeeming work, form a more stable time than that of the individual? Hardly. Certainly in that history time is counted by generations, no longer by days. Further, God sets His mark upon that time by the institution of holy days (Neh. 8:9) and

*feasts, the first and most important of which is the sabbath.

But this time of the people of God remains strictly limited and ceaselessly exposed to dangers. It had a beginning (Isa. 40:21), the day when God called Israel out of Egypt. But above all it is ever menaced by a brutal termination. In fact the prophets announce to the people who look forward with confidence to the day of the Lord the message that that day will bring about their ruin, for their sins have provoked the divine anger (Amos 5:18-20; Isa. 13:6-11; Ezek. 7:5ff.). No doubt this catastrophe is not always considered final; the post-exilic prophets do indeed promise a day of the Lord which will signalize the triumph of Israel (cf. for example Zech. 12-14). But such words of hope remain mingled with threats and already imply a transcendent time beyond that of creation.

5. This time, the time of creation, is, so to speak, time *par excellence*. It had a beginning, creation (Gen. 1:1, with which should be connected Jn. 1:1-2; Matt. 19:4-8; Heb. 1:10). It is organized by God into days (Gen. 1), into seasons (Gen. 8:22), etc. It moves towards its appointed end (Matt. 10:22; 24:13; 28:20; Mk. 13:13; 1 Cor. 1:8, etc.) to which the biblical writings give various names: "the latter days" (Isa. 2:2; Jer. 23:20; Ezek. 38:16, etc.); "that day" (cf. e.g., Zech. 12ff.); "the day of the Lord" or "the day of our Lord Jesus Christ", these two expressions amounting to much the same (cf. e.g., Acts 2:20; 1 Cor. 1:8; 5:5); "the last day" (Jn. 6:39ff.; 11:24; 12:28); "the day of judgment" (cf. e.g., Matt. 10:15), etc. (The expression "last judgment" is not found in the Bible.) This end depends solely on the will of God. Men cannot foresee it: "No one knows the day nor the hour" (Matt. 24:36), for the day of the Lord will come like a thief in the night (1 Thess. 5:2). In the N.T. this day is conceived as a cosmic catastrophe accompanied by the *resurrection of the dead and followed by the last judgment (Mk. 13 and parallel passages; Rev. 6ff.).

6. The idea of judgment and of the *reward granted to the righteous involves inevitably the question: what will happen after the last day?

The answer of the post-exilic prophets and of late Jewish tradition was accepted by Jesus and the first Christians: this was in effect the proclamation of the eternal reign of God established on a new earth, or the Kingdom of God, as our translations call it. On the temporal plane this means that a new time will be created by God for His new creation. It is this new time which the authors of the N.T. call the world to come.

Corresponding to this expression are the phrases "the present age", "this age", designating the period between creation and judgment. "Present age" is sometimes replaced by "ages", especially in the expression "the end of the ages" (1 Cor. 10:11; Heb. 9:26); once we find "coming ages" in the same sense as the singular (Eph. 2:7). The word age is likewise used in various semi-adverbial phrases such as "before the ages" (1 Cor. 2:7; 2 Tim. 1:9; Tit. 1:2—before the creation) or "unto all ages" which means "for ever" and is usually so translated, or as "eternally". The contrast between the present age and the age to come is very emphatic. The present age is in effect the reign of Satan and sin, and is destined to disappear (Rom. 12:2; 2 Cor. 4:4; Gal. 1:4; 2 Tim. 4:9) whilst the age to come is the Kingdom of God which will be endless. Moreover, the Greek adjective which our translations render by the word "eternal" could be translated whenever it is applied to the gifts of God as "life (inheritance, glory etc.) of the world to come".

7. The Jewish scheme of the two ages was, as we have said, accepted by Jesus and the first Christians. But in the sphere of Christianity it underwent an important change. The fact is that Jesus established a close connection between His own Person, His death and resurrection, and the advent of the Kingdom of God (cf. e.g., Mk. 14:62 and parallel passages). His resurrection followed by the gift of the Holy Spirit to

His disciples gave to the latter the conviction that the reign of Christ—the first phase of the Kingdom of God—had already secretly begun, and hence that the world to come was being mysteriously embodied in this present world. Thus instead of being clearly separated in time, the two ages are as it were intermingled during the period between the resurrection of Christ and His return. The "present age" apparently continues, but for anyone who can read the "signs of the times" it is clear that, in sending His Son and raising Him from the dead, God has inaugurated the "age that is to come". In fact the resurrection of Christ marks the beginning of the general resurrection (1 Cor. 15:20,23). The gift of the Holy Spirit bears witness to the fact that the "last days" have already begun (Acts 2:16–17). Christians are delivered from the present evil world (Gal. 1:4) and already enjoy a foretaste of the powers of the world to come (Heb. 6:5; cf. 2 Cor. 1:22; 5:5). Their life is thus a perpetual tension between a present which is potentially closed and a future which is already present. They must live in the present age without giving their hearts to it (Tit. 2:12; cf. 2 Tim. 4:10). It remains for them to *hope and to await the day when the world to come will be visibly established at the second coming of Christ (see *Advent).

Hence the coming of Jesus Christ into the world has marked the close of one age and the beginning of another. The use by European nations of the Christian era spells their largely unconscious recognition of this state of affairs.

E. TROCMÉ

TONGUES, see LANGUAGE

TRADITION

This word and the idea it implies are unknown to the O.T. In the N.T. the word is applied either to Jewish tradition or to Christian tradition. Tradition means that which is handed on. For Judaism this refers to the explanations given by the authorities in regard to the interpretation and application of the law. As far as Christianity is concerned, it refers to the facts of the life, death, and resurrection of Jesus and the theological significance of those facts on which the new faith rests. This means that tradition is closely concerned with the *revelation which it hands on and with the scriptures which bear witness to the latter.

1. *Jewish tradition* is mentioned twice in the N.T. In Gal. 1:14 St. Paul recalls that before his conversion he was full of zeal for the traditions of his fathers. It is clear that Paul after becoming an apostle no longer assigns any theological value to these traditions, since in another passage he describes the zeal which formerly consumed him as a zeal without knowledge (Rom. 10:2).

The second passage is that relating to the controversy of Jesus with the Pharisees about the law and tradition, which arose from their criticism of Jesus for allowing His disciples to sit down to table without washing their hands according to the tradition of the elders (Mk. 7:1–13; Matt. 15:1–9). In this case tradition means the whole corpus of the interpretations of the law and of the prescriptions relating to cases not foreseen by the law, handed down from one master to another and recognized by the Pharisees as having the same binding force as the law itself.

But there were other sections among the Jews, in particular the Sadducees, who did not feel themselves bound by tradition to this extent. Jesus as a matter of fundamental principle is opposed to the attitude of the Pharisees. He recognizes only the Law of God as valid and refuses to attribute any validity to tradition which springs not from God but from men. This is to say that for the mind of Jesus men are not capable of completing the divine law. When nevertheless they insist on trying to do so, they succeed only in destroying the law, as is shown by the example of the *corban*. This Hebrew word means "offering" as Mark says and especially an offering made to God. By this subterfuge, a certain amount of money was set aside in consideration of which a man would excuse himself from assisting his aged parents in their need, since the money which this elementary duty would have absorbed was in advance consecrated to God, if only by way of vows and quite theoretically. The Pharisees took it upon themselves to elaborate regulations for the scrupulous observance of such vows which, in reality, as Jesus emphasizes, had the effect of annulling one of the ten commandments. The tradition of the Pharisees is indeed a very human tradition which, under the pretext of completing the law of Moses, destroys it.

Jesus on the contrary refuses to recognize in this matter any other authority than that of the law of Moses, and by the sovereign way in which He sets aside the Pharisaic interpretation He substitutes for tradition His own judgment as alone qualified to interpret this law. Jesus alone has power to modify the law, as He lets it be understood on other occasions. In the debate on divorce (Mk. 10:1–12; Matt. 19:1–12) He declares that Moses' concession to the husband of the right to put away his wife does not express the primary will of God, which is that man must not put asunder what God has joined. When on the other hand Jesus Himself deviates from the letter of the law it is in order to restore in its plenitude the original will of God. It is with this in view that He develops the antitheses of Matt. 5: "You have heard that it was said by Moses and the elders . . . but I say unto you . . ." (Matt. 5:21 etc.). In short, Jesus does not confine Himself to repudiating the tradition of the Pharisees. For this tradition of men He substitutes the tradition of God, i.e., His Person and His message which have come into the world to perfect and crown the law.

2. *The Christian Tradition.* According to the N.T., the apostolic testimony to Jesus and the body of Christian teaching which flows from it are the object of a tradition (Lk. 1:2; 2 Pet. 2:21; Jude 3).

It is St. Paul who gives fullest scope to the idea of tradition. According to the apostle, the faith of believers and their manner of life are determined by tradition (Rom. 6:17; 1 Cor. 11:2; Col. 2:6ff.; 2 Thess. 2:15; 3:6), in other words, by the faith and the life of the witnesses to Christ, among whom St. Paul himself figures (1 Cor. 15:8; Phil 4:9). The central core of this tradition consists in the witness to the decisive acts of the redemptive work of Christ: the institution of the Lord's Supper (1 Cor. 11:23) and the resurrection appearances to the disciples (1 Cor. 15:3ff.).

The existence of Christian tradition and its theological importance are not an artificial fabrication. They are the consequence of the form which God gave to His soteriological intervention. The Gospel is an act of God accomplished in Jesus Christ at a given moment in the course of world history and in a specific geographical locality. Jesus lived in Palestine under the reign of the Emperor Tiberius and was crucified under Pontius Pilate; the witnesses of His resurrection lived in the Roman Empire about the middle of the 1st century of our era. This act, or more precisely this series of acts, of revelation and redemption were accomplished once for all and are not to be repeated. Since they are situated in the past, they can only be known through the attestation of those who witnessed them, an attestation which must be handed on after the death of the first witnesses, so that the work of divine salvation may continue to be proclaimed to the world and that the world might believe and be saved. Thus God's redeeming work in Jesus Christ and the apostolic tradition which transmits it to all generations have the same value. Were it not for the tradition which declares it unto the end of the ages, the work of redemption would soon be lost in the sands of time and would be robbed of its saving effects; it would cease to have that universal validity in time and space which makes any fresh incarnation superfluous. It is for this reason that the N.T. writers feel authorized to make, without any sense of contradiction, either Jesus Christ (1 Cor. 3:10–11), or the apostles (Matt. 16:18; Eph. 2:20) the foundation of the Church. The faith of believers in all ages rests both upon the work of Christ and the apostolic witness which proclaims it to them.

Furthermore, the heavenly Christ, in communion with whom the apostles live, secures by His living *Spirit the authenticity of tradition. The Spirit which the Son pours out from the Father upon His own bears witness to the life and mind of Jesus (Jn. 15:26), instructing the apostles in all things and reminding them of what Jesus taught them during the time of His incarnate life (Jn. 14:26). By thus recalling to the apostles the teaching of Jesus and disclosing to them those depths of meaning which had escaped them during His earthly ministry (Jn. 2:22) the Spirit leads them into all truth (Jn. 16:13). By the work of the living Spirit, Christ remains the source and the guarantor of the tradition which concerns His redeeming work effected once for all in history. That is the ultimate meaning of St. Paul's affirmation that tradition flows "from the Lord" (1 Cor. 11:23).

3. *Tradition and revelation.* The idea of tradition is unknown to the O.T., as we said at the beginning. In fact the old dispensation consists in a sequence of acts of God, co-ordinated in advance so as to converge upon the central act which God is to accomplish in Jesus Christ at the foreseen moment of time. To set up a tradition within the framework of the covenant of promise would be equivalent to introducing accretions of human opinion into that saving history of which God has fixed the plan and foreordained the development, i.e., it would be adding arbitrarily to a datum whose sole legitimate completion is Jesus Christ Himself. But from the moment of the coming of Jesus Christ the tradition which concerns Him is the very expression of divine revelation, as we have just seen. That is why the tradition of the apostles is the only valid one, not only by contrast with the tradition of the Pharisees but also by contrast with every addition which men might presume to make to it (Col. 2:8).

The ideas of *revelation and tradition are

organically connected. There is no contradiction between them. This is the consequence of what we said above. In this respect no historical example is more instructive and significant than that of the apostle *Paul. No one more than St. Paul makes appeal to the direct revelations which were granted him. It is God Himself who stops him on the Damascus road to reveal to him His Son (Gal. 1:15ff.). From that moment the apostle lives in a state of mystical communion with the Son of God, characterized by exceptional visions and revelations (2 Cor. 12:1ff.). At the same time, no one knows better than St. Paul that the Lord who has been revealed to him is Jesus Christ, already believed in and preached by those who were apostles before him (Gal. 1:17). Hence he is not called upon to found a new religion. But by the call and summons of God he takes his place in the tradition of which the Lord Himself is the Author and the Source. Paul, who of all the apostles has most frequent resort to his private revelations, is also the one who relies most firmly on the authority of tradition; as we have seen, it is in his Epistles that the latter is most often cited and invoked. For no one better than St. Paul realized and expressed the truth that the Gospel is at one and the same time and, as it were, by definition, both revelation and tradition. Moreover, John grasped this just as clearly. When he warns his readers against false prophets, he gives as the criterion to distinguish the truly inspired from the false, whom the Church must not follow, the fact that the true prophets confess that Jesus Christ has come in the flesh, that is to say, they preach Christ conformably with the revelation transmitted by apostolic testimony (1 Jn. 4:1–3).

4. *Tradition and *Scripture.* The work of God in Christ gives rise to an apostolic tradition stamped by the divine seal of revelation, and in consequence a valid tradition rather than a human one. After the death of the apostles this tradition is crystallized in writing. It is already being thus fixed fragmentarily in the Epistles of

Paul. We now find the tradition enshrined in Holy Scripture. Just as the apostolic tradition alone is valid because it alone bears on the work of God in Christ of which it is the authentic commentary, so Scripture, which contains the apostolic *depositum*, is for the Church the sole authorized expression of tradition.

PH.-H. MENOUD

TRANSFIGURATION

The three synoptic Gospels have preserved for us an account of the "transfiguration" of Jesus (Matt. 17:1–8; Mk. 9:2–8; Lk. 9:28–36). This modern word renders imperfectly the sense of the Greek word which figures in Matthew and Mark (Lk. 9:29 simply notes that "the appearance of His countenance was altered"). This word (cf. again Rom. 12:2 and 2 Cor. 3:18) connects the story with the Jewish apocalyptic theme of the glory of the Messiah and of believers in the latter days, a glory betokened by radiant whiteness of colour (see Rev. 1:14; 2:17; 3:4,5; 4:4; 6:11, etc., and already Zech. 1:8; 6:3,6; Dan. 7:9). Thus the aim of the passage is not to describe the metamorphosis of a man into a god, nor the divinization of an initiate in the Hellenistic sense, nor even a stage in a process of progressive spiritualization as though "Jesus was now ripe for immediate entry into eternal life" (Godet) but, as the voice of Mk. 9:7 and parallel passages declares, to affirm that Jesus *is* (not becomes) the well-beloved Son, i.e., the Messiah (cf. the same voice in the account of the baptism of Jesus, Mk. 1:11 recalling Ps. 2:7). Jesus is "clothed" with glory by God; the mention of His shining garments (and of the countenance in Matthew and Luke) is not restrictive or external; the *garments denote the whole Person of the Christ considered in His historic mission and the significance with which God endows Him. Thus the account of the transfiguration may be included among those passages in which Jesus is shown as appearing to His most intimate followers (here Peter, James and John) clad in His eschatological glory, but

without for that reason losing anything of His humanity: such passages as those narrating the baptism, the confession of Peter at Caesarea, the incident of Gethsemane, the appearances of the Risen Lord, etc. Thus our particular narrative expresses a note which is sounded throughout the Christology of the Gospels.

But the theme of Messianic revelation to the disciples (anticipating the final manifestation) is not the only one struck by this extraordinary text. Recent exegesis has seen in it sometimes the recital of a dream or vision on the part of the disciples, sometimes a notable stage in the progressive spiritualization of Jesus, or again a misplaced resurrection appearance, or the foreshadowing of Christ returning in glory on the clouds of heaven, or a scene representing the enthronement of Jesus in His Messianic dignity, in terms of the traditional Jewish scenario of the New Year feast when the king of Israel, symbolizing Yahweh, was invested with supreme dignity. All these hypotheses, and especially the last, stress elements that are incontestably present in the text; which, however, calls for more precise elucidation.

1. The situation of the narrative in the plan of the ministry is the same in the three Gospels; the event is placed between the two first predictions of the Passion. Immediately after the scene (cf. Mk. 9:12 and parallels) we see the disciples questioning among themselves what the rising from the dead should mean, while Jesus draws their attention to the prophetic sufferings of Elijah. If the narrative of the *baptism showed that Jesus, although identifying Himself with the sin of His people, was none the less the well beloved Son, the story with which we are concerned seems to wish to resume this theme but with the reverse meaning: the One who has been endowed with Messianic glory is now advancing towards death: in the plan of God this glory does not preclude but rather includes the ignominy of the cross.

2. The appearance of Moses and Elijah

can hardly mean that the heavens are opened above Jesus and that He is temporarily assumed there: these two figures represent respectively the law and the prophets. Only the O.T. can make first Jesus, then the disciples, understand the necessity of the Passion; v. 31 of Lk. which is peculiar to him, gives an explicit interpretation of this confrontation of Jesus by the O.T. dispensation: Moses and Elijah spoke with Jesus about the departure (i.e., death, cf. 2 Pet. 1:15) which He was about to accomplish. Furthermore the appearance of these two personages was to mark the inauguration of the Messianic era (cf. Mal. 4:5 and Rev. 11:13).

3. The "sleep" of the disciples mentioned by Luke (and in v. 7 of Matt.) as also the suggestion of Peter that they should build three tabernacles (probably an allusion to the huts of leaves characteristic of the Feast of Tabernacles) emphasize the spiritual blindness of man in face of the Messianic glory. This blindness and inability to understand is especially indicative of impatience, i.e., refusal to accept the idea of a suffering Messiah. To make of this narrative a vision or a religious experience on the part of the disciples thus runs contrary to its deepest intention, which is to suggest that the glory of the transfiguration can belong of right only to the Crucified.

4. The cloud, which is common to the three accounts, signifies the presence of God, like the cloud which rested on the tabernacle. This is as much as to say that the chief actor in this drama is not Jesus but God, invisible but omnipresent; the mystery emphasized by the story is not that of the transformation of Jesus into a more or less divine being but rather that of the active energy and presence of God resting on the humble destiny of the Son of Man.

However we interpret what happened on the mount of transfiguration (identified by some with Tabor, by others with Hermon) it is important to grasp the central affirmation of the story, which is in unison with one of the major themes of evangelical tradition; namely, that the disciples of Jesus (but only the disciples) who were witnesses of the sufferings and the shame of the cross, witnessed also, although rather late and not without a certain dullness of spiritual understanding, the glory of the Christ (Jn. 1:14, a text which however is not an allusion to the transfiguration but, conformably with Johannine Christology, refers to the whole destiny of the Son of God).

P. BONNARD

TRIAL, *see* TEMPTATION

TRIBULATION, *see* PERSECUTION

TRUTH

1. In the Bible, in so far as we are concerned with the context of Hebraic thought, the word truth suggests fundamentally the ideas of solidity, security, faithfulness, steadfastness (see *Amen). The idea which in our own customary mode of thought attaches primarily to this word, as for example in the phrase "to speak the truth", i.e., to give an exact statement, becomes in this perspective only a special and derivative aspect of the basic notion. In Hebrew we speak of a man of truth (Exod. 18:21; Neh. 7:2); i.e., a man of integrity and reliability; of a way of truth (Gen. 24:48) which will certainly lead to the goal; of a seed of truth (Jer. 2:21) from which one has a right to expect good fruit; of a peace of truth (Jer. 14:13) which means that it is lasting and secure. Thus true riches are opposed to false, i.e., to those which offer only a fallacious security (Lk. 16:11); the grace of God is true (1 Pet. 5:12) and offers secure foundations. To judge according to the truth (Ezek. 18:8) means not merely to establish, objectively, the facts, but in doing so to bring to light the true relationship between the parties concerned and to restore to a threatened life a solid basis (cf. Prov. 14:25).

In several writings of the N.T. it happens that the notion of truth corresponds not to the Hebrew but to the Greek word, which does not so much suggest solidity and faithfulness as express the fact that something stands disclosed, that instead of being concealed it becomes explicit and freed from the appearances which falsify it. This connotation is found sometimes in the Epistles of Paul and is frequently and systematically employed in the Gospel and Epistles of John. It is easily seen, however, that the two ideas are not mutually exclusive, but rather complementary and convergent, and that it is sometimes difficult to decide between them.

2. The word truth, in one or other of these meanings, has quite naturally entered into religious and theological vocabulary. As meaning what is stable and secure the word is often used to express the attitude of God towards man, and the characteristic of His presence and activity in human life. Our modern versions say almost indifferently "God of faithfulness" (Exod. 34:6) or "of truth" (Ps. 31:6); such variations clearly showing that these modern words only partially express the original idea. "Thou hast redeemed me, Thou God of truth" (Ps. 31:6). God, faithful to Himself and to His promises, allied to the believer, by His intervention rescues the latter from the insecurity which threatens, gives new foundations to his existence and opens up for him a future. This whole Psalm is one long description of the truth of God in its contrast (v. 7) with the vanity of *idols, which offer a fallacious support to their worshippers. The whole word of God and its very essence is truth (Ps. 119:160); the second part of the verse shows the meaning of this; the divine word is ultimately valid and irrevocable, it establishes life for ever on its true foundations. "Thy words are truth" (2 Sam. 7:28): the promise of God is a reality on which one can rely, and by trusting in which one can advance boldly towards the future. "I walk in Thy truth" (Ps. 26:3) means: I run the risks of life by trusting in Thee, with all the religious and moral consequences which this involves. "The works of God are faithful and just: His precepts are trustworthy (immutable) they are performed with faithfulness and uprightness" (Ps. 111:7ff.); they are the expression of the covenant grace which is the eternal basis of God's relations with His people (cf. Ps. 93:5). Christ is the servant of the circumcised to manifest the truth (faithfulness) of God, in order to confirm the promises made to the fathers (Rom. 15:8). The meaning of the word truth appears clearly in the conjunction of the two phrases: does their faithlessness nullify the faithfulness of God? (Rom. 3:3), and if through my falsehood God's truthfulness abounds to His glory (Rom. 3:7); it becomes apparent that the truth of God is none other than His faithfulness to the promises He has made towards Israel, just as the falsity of man consists in not putting his trust in God. If Jesus Christ is called the True (Rev. 3:7,14; 9:11) it is that He accomplishes, with regard to the Church and the world, the purpose of God in salvation and judgment.

It is natural also that truth should refer to the written word, by which God is present in the midst of His people: true law (Neh. 9:13; Mal. 2:6) true testimony, true judgments (i.e., precepts of the law, Ps. 19:8,10); or true doctrine, the Gospel; the word of truth (Eph. 1:13; Jas. 1:18; cf. Tit. 1:9); to proclaim the truth is to preach the Gospel (2 Cor. 4:2), to obey the truth (Gal. 5:7) is to believe in the Gospel. The *Gospel is also called truth by contrast with heresy (1 Tim. 6:5; 2 Tim. 4:4; Tit. 1:14; 2 Pet. 2:2) just as God is called the true by contrast with idols (1 Thess. 1:9; 1 Jn. 5:20).

3. Mainly in the Gospel and Epistles of John, where they are of very frequent occurrence, the words true and truth are used almost constantly in their Greek sense to denote the manifestation of the reality and the very essence of a thing. In this case truth is not primarily understood as what gives a secure foundation to imperilled human existence but as the light which is shed on it; it is revelation, divine reality unfolding itself for man to deliver him from the falsehood of which he is the prisoner

and to enable him to know God and hence himself; the Word Jesus Christ is the true light, i.e., the light of God Himself which enlightens every man (Jn. 1:9). When Jesus says: "I tell the truth, I bear witness to the truth" (Jn. 8:40,45f.; 18:37) this does not mean merely that His words are in conformity with reality but that they are the manifestation of God Himself, the sovereign event in which God approaches man to expose the lie in which he lives, and this lie is that man does not listen to God, wishes to slay Jesus in whom God speaks to him, wishes to live independently of God and thus himself becomes the victim of the murderer (Jn. 8:37,40,44). But in the words of Jesus God calls man to submit himself and thus to find life: truth is the grace which frees man from sin by restoring him to God (Jn. 8:32,34). Jesus is the Word, full of grace and truth (Jn. 1:14): the divine reality, the grace vouchsafed to man is fully disclosed in Him. Jesus can say also: "He who sent me is true and I declare to the world what I have heard from him" (Jn. 8:26; cf. 7:28); thus He declares that He acts and speaks in utter dependence on God whose authentic representative He is; God is with Him and does not leave Him, He acts and speaks in Him; man must not seek God apart from or outside of Jesus. Jesus seeks glory from Him who sent Him, that is why He is true (Jn. 7:18; cf. 5:31): He is not like man who seeks his own glory, who seeks only his own interests, and whose whole thought and life thus become a lie; Christ seeks God alone and wishes the encounter of God and man: thus He is the truth and it is truly God whom we encounter in Him. But His enemies do not believe in Him because they derive their honour from each other, they seek their foundations in themselves, in the approval of their fellowmen; they do not love God nor do they seek His sanction (Jn. 5:41–44).

Jesus is the true bread of heaven, the true vine (Jn. 6:32; 15:1). His flesh and His blood are true (not "indeed" as the translations say) meat and drink (Jn. 6:55). Thus He is opposed to the bread which perishes (Jn. 6:27) in which man seeks life and which cannot however secure him against death; to all those trees of life which are the dream of humanity and which are only the expression of man's greed: Jesus alone, being the manifestation and the very presence of God for man, saves life; the branch that is cut off withers. Because in Jesus God Himself confronts man, this encounter implies a divine judgment on man. The judgment of Jesus is true because the Father who has sent Him is with Him (Jn. 8:16; cf. 5:30). This does not mean so much that Jesus judges men equitably because God gives Him an intimate knowledge of man, but that in the encounter with Himself who is the representative of God there takes place the decisive and ultimate discrimination between those who are saved and those who are lost; man is judged on his attitude towards Christ. All that Jesus says about Himself here is well summed up in His affirmation: "I am the way, the truth and the life" (Jn. 14:6), where each is illuminated by the two others: Jesus is the way, the approach to God, because He is the truth, the very presence of God for man shedding the true light on human life; thus He is the life, i.e., that whoever believes on Him is restored to the place which God has destined him to fill, and where life is no longer an object of greed but the divine gift.

4. Since truth is the reality of God to which man has closed his eyes, it escapes the attention of man who is the prisoner of himself, and it cannot now be recognized from the standpoint of natural insight; this fact is illustrated by the misunderstandings ceaselessly aroused by the witness of Jesus (e.g., Jn. 3:4;4:15). Sin, the revolt of man against God, has as a consequence the fact that man sees falsehood or sin in the revelation of God itself (Jn. 8:48ff.; 9:24). The disciples themselves cannot bear what Jesus tells them; the Spirit of truth must lead them into all truth, must reveal Jesus to them by taking His treasures and unfolding them to their gaze (Jn. 16:12–15); He will recall to them what Jesus has said, i.e., He will impart divine reality to them (Jn. 14:26; cf. 1 Jn. 2:20,27; the same thought occurs in

different terms in Paul: 1 Cor. 2:6–16). The Holy Spirit like Jesus Himself is called the truth, showing that He is the divine reality, active within the revelation itself, enabling men to recognize its truth, the divine illuminating power of the word itself. Perhaps it is not superfluous to point out here that by the worship in spirit and truth which God requires (Jn. 4:23ff.) is certainly not meant a purely "spiritual" cult without Bible or sacraments, without church or temple, springing only from the sincere thoughts of the heart, but rather worship in conformity with the revelation of God in Jesus Christ made effectual in the present by the power of the Spirit.

5. The knowledge of the truth is not theoretical, but "existential", a living reality rooted in the self-committal of the whole man. The knowledge which the Spirit imparts is the truth that Jesus is the Christ (1 Jn. 2:20–22; cf. 1 Cor. 12:3); in spite of the apparently academic theological formulation, this knowledge is something essentially practical, implying an illumination and a conversion: implying that I recognize in Jesus the life, the truth, and the way, and that I abandon my revolt against God. To know the truth is to be sanctified by it (Jn. 17:17,19), to be delivered from the enslavement of falsehood and rooted in God. Man can know the truth only in so far as he abides in Jesus Christ (Jn. 8:31ff.) through the continuous life of faith. To put it still more concretely: this knowledge is sincere and real only in so far as we live in submission to the commandments of God. "He who says: I know him, but disobeys his commandments, is a liar and the truth is not in him; but whoever keeps his word, in him truly love for God is perfected" (1 Jn. 2:4ff.; cf. 1:6). In this context commandment and word are synonymous: the word or the Gospel is only understood if we see in it a challenge to obedience, and if we respond to that challenge by walking as Jesus Christ Himself walked (1 Jn. 2:6), i.e., by basing our whole life on the revelation of God which is Jesus Christ.

CHR. SENFT

TWELVE, *see* APOSTLE, MINISTRY N.T., NUMBERS

UNBELIEF, *see* FAITH

UNITY, *see* ONE

VICTORY

1. The whole drama of the redemption of the world in Jesus Christ is presented throughout the Bible as the victory of God over the adversary. Strictly speaking it is the eternal Lord God of Hosts, the Most High, the Omnipotent who is the conqueror. Victory necessarily belongs to the eternal God just as the kingdom, righteousness, holiness, glory are His; these qualities are not attributes, but disclose rather His manner of being, of manifesting Himself, of becoming an active energizing force in the world. The struggle which precedes the final victory is not a doubtful struggle between two equal powers or powers of the same nature; there is no hint of dualism in the Bible, for, as a foregone conclusion and from the very first moment of the incursion of the adversary into the world, *Satan is crushed: victory is promised to the posterity of Eve (Gen. 3:15), and Cain receives both the command and therewith the possibility of overcoming sin ("but you must master it!" Gen. 4:7). That is why, from Abraham to Jesus Christ and throughout the course of saving history by which the triumph of God is manifested in the world, this divine victory is at every moment associated with the victory *of faith*. It is in the light of this and in the light of God's covenant with His people that we must understand the many stories of victory achieved by the patriarchs, by Moses, Joshua, the Judges and the Kings (Gen. 14:13–14; Exod. 14:13–14; 15:1–27; 17:8–16; Josh. 6ff.; Judg. 6–7; 1 Sam. 17:45, etc.). All these victories are so many signs of the presence of the eternal God *with* His people or with His anointed, His elect.

It is always by the powerful arm or the right hand of God or in the name of the Lord of Hosts that victory is gained. Sometimes there enters on the scene the "*angel", or "the prince of the armies of the eternal God" (Josh. 5:13–15; Dan. 10:13–20; Isa. 37:36) or again the Lord Himself (Exod. 14:14). Conversely the defeats and reverses which Israel suffered in the course of her history manifest likewise the victory of the Lord, but this time *against* His people, for the revelation of His righteousness and holiness; if the Lord God marches at the head of His people to crush their enemies (Ps. 68) He can also declare war and march to victory against this same people when they by their idolatries or unbelief are unfaithful to the covenant and come to behave as the enemies of God (Judg. 2:10–21). Thus it is that Jeremiah announces the disaster and ruin which are about to overtake Jerusalem and sees in the victory of Nebuchadnezzar the servant of the Lord (Jer. 27:6) the means whereby the great judgments of God upon His people are being executed (Jer. 15:1–8, etc.). In such ways the mysterious destiny of Israel is played out—that destiny which ever since the strange combat of Jacob with the angel of the Lord (Gen. 32:24–32) had called her to be both victor and vanquished in her struggle both for and against God as the witness to His righteousness.

2. The same relation between victory and righteousness is found again on the plane of the personal life of the believer, who, in Ps. 51:6, recognizes his defeat and guilt under the blows of the righteousness of God ("You will win in your judgment", i.e., your lawsuit). This juridical character of the victory of God is again emphasized in the preaching of the prophets, who announce the ruin and chastisement of Israel and Judah as the righteous verdict of a lawsuit which the Eternal God will ultimately win as against His people (Hos. 4:1–4; 5:1,11; Mic. 6:1–16). Finally the Messianic promises closely associate the coming of the Messiah, the Lord's Anointed, expected as "the King of glory" (Ps. 24:7–8) with the triumph of righteousness, embodied either in the victory of Cyrus the liberator of oppressed Israel (Isa. 45:1–8,22–25) or in

the ministry of the Servant of the Lord who will not be discouraged until He has "established justice in the earth" (Isa. 42:4,21), or again in the humble and pacific king of Jerusalem "just and bearing victory" (Zech. 9:9).

3. The note of Messianic and eschatological victory is struck again in the N.T., first of all in subdued fashion in the synoptics. The *miracles of Jesus, and especially the healing of demoniacs, are the signs which foreshadow the coming decisive victory over Satan implied by the parable of the strong man (Lk. 11:21–22), and prophesied by Jesus at the time of the return of the 70 disciples (Lk. 10:17–20). The *advent of the Son of Man in glory is described as that of the Judge of all nations (Matt. 24:30–31 and 25:31–33). But it is the Johannine writings which amplify this theme by identifying the ultimate victory of Christ, as conqueror and judge of the prince of this world, with the triumph of Jesus on the cross and in the resurrection (Jn. 12:31; 16:33). The victory in question is that over the world, sin, death, Antichrist—a victory in which believers by faith already share (1 Jn. 2:13–14; 4:4; 5:4–5). Paul too in his teaching about justification by faith makes the struggle and the triumph of faith in the Christian life closely dependent on the unique and decisive victory of the all-conquering Christ, a victory won through the cross and the resurrection. By virtue of the free grace of God and the decree of His justice, the triumph has been achieved once for all. Christ *is* the conqueror of sin and death; *faith consists in seizing this victory already won and living in the strength of it (Rom. 5:1–5; 6:3–11; 1 Cor. 15:57).

But if the decisive victory of Jesus Christ is already won, it remains nevertheless yet to come and will be fully manifested only at His second coming. Hence the Christian life remains always a struggle; conquered sin must still be fought and overcome (Rom. 12:21). And finally that is why the book of Revelation, which proclaims the ultimate manifestation of the Conqueror (5:5; 6:2) and the victory of the Lamb

(17:14) is of all the books of the N.T. the one which contains most exhortations to persevere in the faith and gives the most emphatic promises to him who overcomes (2:7; 3:5,12, etc.).

H. ROUX

VINE

O.T.

The tree of life was doubtless a vine (see *Wine). In any case it is the tree of the Messianic country, together with the fig and olive trees (Mic. 4:4; Zech. 3:10). For the surrounding religions the tree has a sacred if not divine character (there is an echo of this in Deut. 22:9 where an agrarian observation is given a sacral implication).

1. *The sign of ownership.* The vine is a sign of ownership; it is often merged with territorial possession. It is one of the most precious goods that a man can have: parallel with a wife or sons. The injury that Ahab did to Naboth is comparable with that done by David to Uriah, not merely because of the murder but also because of the theft. To abide under one's vine symbolizes the enjoyment of perfect *rest: the rest characteristic of the Messianic land (Mic. 4:4).

2. *The vine as Israel.* Further, the vine means Israel regarded as the property of God. This theme of Israel the vineyard of God, constantly occurring in the prophets, shows first of all the precious value of Israel in the sight of God, the peace which He desired to find there and the fruit He hoped to gather from it. Here we are faced by the mystery of the *election of Israel and of the covenant which God established with this people rather than any other, a covenant of which He is the sovereign Lord. It is a veritable epithalamium which Isaiah strikes up at the beginning of chapter 5 with the description of the hope and the anger of the husband (we find in the O.T. a triangle, Israel-bride-vine). Psalm 80 shows how the vine was snatched away from Egypt; Isa. 5, note that it is a precious plant (cf. Jer. 2:21)

but Ezek. 15:2ff. carefully recalls that the vine is of worth only as a result of the fruit it bears; in itself it is no more than wretched wood, fit only for burning. All the texts emphasize the fact that Yahweh hoped for good fruit from it. In order to secure this He planted it in fertile soil (Ezek. 19:10 and Isa. 5:1), put far from it all that was hurtful, and faithfully nursed it. Yahweh was ever a good and faithful gardener to it, such was His steadfast love. Only Hos. 9:10 and perhaps Ps. 80 (but if the prophets express the point of view of Yahweh towards His vine Ps. 80 expresses the point of view of the vine itself) affirm that Yahweh was once refreshed by it, namely in the desert period. All, however, agree that in the prophetic period the fruits are bad, and are such as give rise to Jeremiah's wondering question: "How can it be?" Here we are faced by the incomprehensible disobedience of Israel and the mystery of iniquity. The good vine planted by the good owner who surrounded it with every care and attention has brought forth bad fruit. Hence Yahweh will destroy His vineyard; for His vine was not a sound plant—its health was illusory and ephemeral only, like the dew of morning (Hos. 6:4). Another plant will be required, but a plant of Yahweh's own creation. That is why Jesus will come before Israel as the true vine that will never degenerate into something alien and wretched.

N.B. It should be pointed out that in Mesopotamian religions, the king who is the guardian of the tree of life (often a cedar tree) was sometimes identified with it. This assimilation of a king and a tree is found also in the O.T. (Isa. 11; 53:2-8, and especially Ps. 80).

N.T.

In Matt. 21:28-46, we find again this theme of another people who shall be raised up to bring forth the fruit of the vineyard, but the vine itself remains the same: it is the Kingdom of God which, entrusted to the Jews, will now pass into the hands of the Church.

But the great text is that of Jn. 15 where

Christ presents Himself as the true vine, whether we are to understand this as a replanting of the former or as the vine which the former merely foreshadowed; in any case as the fulfilment of the intention of God in the planting of His vine (perhaps Jn. 15 is inspired by Ps. 80:15ff. where the vine and the Son of Man are parallel). Here Christ presents Himself as the true people of God and not merely as the support of this new people—as is suggested by the translation which in our opinion is faulty: the true vine. We are here confronted by a conception of Christ as essentially the people of God. As for the branches or shoots, they cannot be fruit-bearing as long as they remain outside the vine; they can but wither, for (cf. Ezek. 15) they are of use only in proportion as they bear fruit. Further, there are three possible positions for the branches: (1) to be in Jesus, but this is static and must quickly be reduced to one of the two following, (2) to *abide in Jesus: i.e., to bear fruit and be pruned, (3) to be separated from the trunk, because they are not fruit-bearing; to wither and be burned.

To be in Jesus doubtless means to be baptized, whereas to abide in Jesus means to love Him and to keep His word and commandments (cf. v. 9: abide in my love).

A. MAILLOT

VIRGIN, see MARRIAGE, MARY

VOCATION, see CALL

VOW, see FAST, OATH

WAIT, see HOPE

WALK

The figurative sense is much more frequent in biblical language than the concrete sense. Thus in general to walk signifies either simply *to live* (Ps. 23:4; 2 Cor. 10:3) or more precisely *to behave, to conduct oneself.* The figure of walking is, in fact, very suitable for expressing certain aspects of our existence, especially our religious and moral existence. It is appropriate, in the first place, for indicating that life has a meaning and

that this can be given to us by God when He has become our companion in the way in order to guide and strengthen us. To walk is thus applicable also to God when He intervenes in men's journey through life. In connection with this latter usage the following expressions may be noted:

To walk before, which is said of the leader or king whom God has chosen to walk at the head of his people into battle (Deut. 3:28; 1 Sam. 8:20), but also of the angel of the Lord (Exod. 23:23) and of the Lord Himself (Num. 14:14), who is the true leader of Israel and whose presence is the guarantee of victory. Similarly in the parable it is the shepherd who walks before his sheep (Jn. 10:4): "No one shall snatch them from his hand" (10:28).

To walk in the midst: Moses entreats the Lord (Exod. 34:9) and the Lord promises (Lev. 26:12) to walk in the midst of His people. This provides a further expression of the presence of the Lord, thanks to which Israel is assured of triumphing over her enemies (Exod. 34:11; Deut. 23:14). Likewise, "he who walks among the seven golden candlesticks" (Rev. 2:1) is the strength of His Church, to whom He will give the victory.

It is also said in the same sense that the Lord *walks with* Israel (Exod. 33:16; Deut. 20:4).

In all these expressions to walk occurs as a specific religious term indicating the advance to battle in the setting of the holy war. Cf. also Mic. 4:5 and perhaps even Isa. 6:8 and 9, where God takes up arms against His own people.

To the walking of the Lord at the head of His people there corresponds, for this people and for each individual member of the people, the duty of *walking with God* (Mic. 6:8), or, as is also said, *before His face* (Gen. 17:1), *in His presence* (1 Kings 8:25), or simply *before Him* (Ps. 116:9). All these phrases indicate the same attitude of obedient piety: God is followed as a captain by His soldiers; during the battle care is taken never to lose sight of Him in order to be able to comply with the least signal which He may give; in brief—to leave the metaphor—one's whole life is centred in Him. The religion of Israel is not, in fact, limited to the setting of the holy war, to which several of the terms of its vocabulary seem to apply; it did not hesitate to embrace the whole of life. The texts cited at the beginning of this paragraph afford evidence of this.

In a more precise manner the O.T. also makes use of the formula: *to walk in the *way or ways of the Lord* (2 Kings 21:22; Deut. 10:12), which refers to the instructions which God has given and particularly to the commandments of the law (Deut. 8:6; 28:9). Similarly there are expressions such as *to walk in the paths of uprightness* (Prov. 2:13) or simply *in uprightness* (Prov. 14:2), *to walk in truth* (Isa. 38:3), *to walk in honesty* (Ps. 15:2), *in righteousness* (Isa. 33:15), *in peace* (Mal. 2:6), *in wisdom* (Prov. 28:36), *in integrity* (Ps. 26:1), or, on the contrary, *in lies* (Jer. 23:14). The N.T. will speak likewise of *walking in love* (Eph. 5:2), *in the light* (1 Jn. 1:7), and, on the other hand, *in darkness* (Jn. 12:35), *in sins* (Eph. 2:2), *in lasciviousness* (1 Pet. 4:3). It is obvious that these terms should not be interpreted in isolation, in the sense of an independent morality, but theologically, in the setting of the service of God.

Thus, as the latter citations above show, the N.T. also makes use of the hebraism *to walk in*. It is especially in the Pauline Epistles and the Johannine writings that it is found. The apostle Paul even introduces it when it is no more a question of conforming one's life to certain notions, but of abandoning oneself to certain powers, such as the *flesh* and the *Spirit* (Rom. 8:4; Gal. 5:16), human nature (1 Cor. 3:3), and the new life which radiates from the risen Christ (Rom. 6:4). But then he prefers to say: *to walk by*, or he has recourse to a construction with the dative which cannot be translated literally. In Col. 2:6, indeed, he has the audacious figure of speech: *walk in him* (= in Christ Jesus). The meaning is: Let your conduct be that of persons who live in the fellowship of Christ. In other words: Live as Christians!

J. BURNIER

WAR

O.T.

Though it may be true that after war peace always comes (Eccl. 3:8), yet the latter is too often fleeting; and this state of affairs wrenches from the inspired writer the heart-cry, "And there was *again* war" (1 Chr. 20:5). The people of God engaged in war quite as much as the nations that surrounded them, and the O.T. is full of stories of battle. We shall examine three kinds of war: the holy war, fratricidal war, and war in eschatology. Of these three the first is undeniably the best documented.

1. *The holy war*. The Sixth Commandment (Exod. 20:13; Deut. 5:17; cf. Jer. 7:9) cannot be construed as a condemnation of the holy war. Its meaning is that the act of killing should never be premeditated, and examination of other passages in which the same verb is found compels us to translate it rather: "Thou shalt not assassinate!" Moreover, although the text just mentioned may be ambiguous, the mass of biblical evidence to prove the existence of the holy war is quite decisive. The chosen people, in order to achieve the grand design of Yahweh in a world of arms and battle, must themselves also take up arms and fight. Their real captain is Yahweh, for Yahweh is a fighter, a valiant warrior (Exod. 15:3; Ps. 24:8), present in the midst of His people in the sacred Ark (Num. 10:35f.; 1 Sam. 4:3–8); He makes war both in the soldiers' stead and by means of them (Exod. 14:25; Josh. 10:14,42; 1 Sam. 25:28; Neh. 4:14), and therefore receives the name Yahweh, "God of the armies of Israel" (1 Sam. 17:45). Hence the soldier is "consecrated" by Yahweh (Isa. 13:3) and the camp itself is a holy place (Deut. 23:14). Whether the wars conducted by the people of God are aggressive or defensive, they are the wars of Yahweh (1 Sam. 18:17; 25:28) and the memory of the wars of old time was preserved in a book (which has not come down to us) entitled *The book of the battles of Yahweh* (Num. 21:14).

Should the chosen people, the instrument

of God's plan, fall into sin, then Yahweh takes command of hostile armies to punish His own (Isa. 5:25–30; Jer. 5:15; Amos 5:27; 6:14), but these same hostile armies will in their turn be annihilated by Him (Isa. 10:5–19; 14:24–27; Jer. 51:59–64).

A war, then, is a holy war, when the chosen people are obeying their God in order to achieve His plan of salvation. Such wars mark the escape from Egypt, the long journey in the wilderness, the moment of entering the country which it has been promised to their forefathers they shall possess, and its conquest, and finally the campaigns of the kings to liberate their territory and to secure the national independence. But when Yahweh is punishing His people by war, it is a crime for them to reply with war, even though it is in self-defence, for that is to obstruct the achievement of the salvation that God wills for His children (Jer. 21:1–10; cf. Jer. 27:6).

2. *Fratricidal war.* When the chosen people fight for Yahweh's cause, it is always with a single heart. In the time of the Judges, even when the tribes go to war only in coalitions of one or two, it is for the purpose of attacking foreigners: Canaanites, Midianites or Philistines. But after the split in the nation, tribes or groups of tribes make war against each other: we are dealing simply with the fratricidal war branded in the words of the prophet: "They snatch on the right, but are still hungry, and they devour on the left, but are not satisfied; each devours his neighbour's flesh, Manasseh Ephraim, and Ephraim Manasseh, and together they are against Judah" (Isa. 9:20f.; cf. further, 1 Kings 12:21–24).

3. *War in eschatology.* The end of the ages will be marked by Yahweh's victory (Ps. 110:5–7; Joel 3) over the nations leagued against Him and against His Messiah (Ps. 2:1f.). This particular aspect of war is developed especially in the apocryphal and pseudepigraphical literature.

4. *Weapons.* Weapons are called "things of war" (Judg. 18:11; Jer. 21:4). They show great diversity both in form and in the materials of which they are made, such as flint, bronze and iron. They may be divided into defensive and offensive weapons. Among defensive weapons may be cited:

(*a*) the *shield* or *buckler*: including the small shield, probably round, and the large shield, which was oblong and definitely of wood covered with leather (Jer. 46:3); the golden shields mentioned in the 1st book of Kings (10:16) were for decoration.

(*b*) the *helmet*: uncommon in the reign of Saul (1 Sam. 17:38) but worn more frequently from the time of Uzziah onward (2 Chr. 26:14).

(*c*) *full armour:* always rare, and restricted to the equipment of commanders (1 Sam. 17:5,38; 1 Kings 22:34).

Offensive weapons were as follows:

(*a*) the *sling*: (1 Sam. 17:40).

(*b*) the *spear*: the short spear, very manoeuvrable (1 Sam. 18:10), and the great spear, heavier and able to transfix two men at a blow (Num. 25:7f.).

(*c*) the *dagger* and the *short sword* (Judg. 3:21); there is only one word for both in the original, so that it is difficult to distinguish them.

(*d*) the *bow and arrows*: (2 Kings 9:24); some were designed to carry burning material for setting fire to enemy installations, and are referred to as "fiery shafts" (Ps. 7:13).

(*e*) the *torch*: used at close quarters for the same purpose as the lighted arrow at a distance.

Finally, and much less common,

(*f*) the *war club*: (Prov. 25:18; Jer. 51:20).

War chariots, drawn by horses and manned by a crew of three, did not appear in the armies of Israel until the time of Solomon (2 Chr. 9:25). *Siege engines*, such as the catapults mentioned in 2 Chronicles (26:15), are also to be classed as offensive rather than defensive.

5. *Warriors.* Because of the very different qualities of penetration and handling possessed by the various kinds of weapon,

warriors very soon acquire specialized duties. Some soldiers carry the long spear and oblong shield (2 Chr. 26:14) and form shock battalions, comparatively mobile but solid, later supported by chariots. Others become archers, equipped with the bow, the quiver loaded with arrows, the short sword and the small protective shield (1 Chr. 5:18; 2 Chr. 26:14). Together with the slingers, the archers provide the fire power. It is possible that, after a certain date, armour was worn not only by the commanders but also by a particular class of soldier (2 Chr. 26:14).

Each great captain had his armour-bearer; specially equipped with a shield, his duty was to protect his master during the battle and sometimes to do him the service of putting him to death, so that he might not survive the disgrace of defeat (1 Sam. 31:4).

Once chariots had made their appearance in the army of Israel, specialization became still more noticeable; one soldier drove the chariot, and an archer did the shooting, covered by a third soldier, who carried the small shield and commanded the manoeuvres of the unit (cf. 1 Kings 9:22).

6. *The army.* All men of twenty years of age and upward were eligible for military service (Num. 1:3; 2 Chr. 25:5). At the period of the wilderness wanderings, the effective force was reckoned in thousands by tribes (Num. 31). By the time of Joshua the number of soldiers has increased to somewhere in the region of 40,000 (Josh. 4:13). Later still, the numbers become staggering (1 Chr. 27:1–5; 2 Chr. 14:8; 17:14–18). Because Yahweh wishes men to rely on His support alone and not on the number of their soldiers, He requires His people to practise a process of selection: in this way Gideon reduces his fighting men from 32,000 to 300 (Judg. 7).

In the wilderness period the army is recruited by a levy from each tribe (Num. 31). It is interesting to read the grounds for exemption from service envisaged by the law in the book of Deuteronomy (20:1–9). In the period of the monarchy, the incessant wars with neighbouring countries led to a special organization of the army: in the reign of David, for example, there were a picked corps ready for the king's immediate service (2 Sam. 10:7; 1 Chr. 19:8), a permanent body of mercenaries standing by at all times to resist unexpected attack (2 Sam. 8:18), and finally the troops levied in time of war, a form of conscription (2 Sam. 20:4,23).

The army was divided into groups of a thousand, a hundred, and fifty men, each commanded by officers called respectively captains of thousands, of hundreds and of fifties (Num. 31:14,48; 1 Chr. 26:26; 2 Chr. 25:5; 2 Kings 1:9). In the wilderness, the supreme command was undertaken by Moses or by a priest (Num. 31:6); in the monarchical period there was a commander-in-chief (2 Sam. 8:16; 1 Kings 4:4), almost as powerful as the king himself (2 Kings 4:13). During the reign of David, there was a general for the standing army and another for the conscripts (2 Sam. 8:16–18), but the real supreme commander, not forgetting the king, was always Yahweh (Exod. 7:4; 1 Sam. 17:45).

7. *Battle.* Sometimes this is nothing more than the razzia of nomads, seeking to enrich themselves without bloodshed (Gen. 34:27ff.). More frequently, it is battle in the ordinarily accepted sense, hand-to-hand fighting in battle array. For a long time fighting was on foot, preferably in mountain country (1 Sam. 14:4,13f.; 1 Kings 20:23). But the need to match the enemy compelled the adoption of the horse, despite the serious warnings of the law and the prophets against its use (Deut. 17:16; Isa. 30:16; cf. Ps. 20-8; 33:17f.). Archers were organized into mounted corps and chariots came into use. Strategy was also perfected, reaching its highest point at the time of the Maccabees, a fact attested by the work, discovered among the scrolls of Qumran, near the Dead Sea, entitled *The War of the sons of Light against the sons of Darkness.*

The best time of year for campaigning is the spring (2 Sam. 11:1). War is proclaimed by the sounding of the trumpet (Judg. 3:27;

2 Sam. 20:1; Jer. 42:14). Because battle acquires a sacral character, it is never joined without the offering of sacrifices to Yahweh (1 Sam. 7:9; 13:9–12), or the making of a vow (Judg. 11); hence is derived the phrase "to consecrate a battle", meaning "to prepare for battle" (Jer. 6:4; Joel 3:9; Mic. 3:5). The soldier was in a state of ritual purity throughout the whole of a campaign. That is why Uriah, on his return to Jerusalem while the war is still going on at a distance, refuses to touch his wife and sleeps outside his own house (2 Sam. 11:11–13). During the battle Yahweh was addressed with war-cries, intended to induce Him to act (1 Chr. 5:20), for frequently the tactics employed derived all their effectiveness from the divine intervention. Thus, in the time of Deborah, Yahweh causes the torrent to burst its banks, immobilizing the enemy chariots in the mud and so delivering their crews into the hands of the Hebrew soldiers (Judg. 5:20f.). The classic tactics were those of taking the enemy in the rear (2 Sam. 5:22–25) and of the pincer movement: thus Joab found himself one day attacked on two sides at once by the Arameans and the Ammonites (2 Sam. 10:9–14).

8. *The siege of fortified towns.* The towns of strategic importance in the land of Canaan were girdled with thick and lofty walls, sometimes even with double walls. Nothing had been gained by a battle, so long as armed centres of resistance remained unconquered; it was therefore necessary to reduce such fortified towns by siege. In the days before they had built their own protective walls (cf. 2 Chr. 11:5–12), the Hebrews had to take possession of the Canaanite fortresses, some of which, such as Jebus-Jerusalem (2 Sam. 5:6f.), were reputed to be impregnable. These latter could hold out for considerable periods, thanks to well stocked granaries, underground tunnels leading to springs out of the enemy's reach (2 Chr. 32:2ff.) and, as a last resort, the citadel, a sort of keep in which the defence could be concentrated (Judg. 9:51). The invested city would fall either as the result of a miraculous intervention by Yahweh (e.g., Jericho, Josh. 6), or of a stratagem (e.g., Ai, Josh. 8), or of treachery (Judg. 1:24); or it might fall to a full-dress assault (2 Sam. 12:26–29), after a breach had been made in the ramparts, or the gate had been fired, or an assault ramp had been built against the outer wall (2 Sam. 20:15). If the town surrendered without resistance, the inhabitants were let off with forced labour and tribute (Deut. 20:10f.); if not, then during the siege the surrounding crops would be destroyed or more probably used to supply the besieging forces (1 Sam. 23:1). Fruit trees, however, were rarely cut down (Deut. 20:19f.; but cf. also 2 Kings 3:25).

When the battle was over, the dead would be buried (1 Kings 11:15) and the booty either given to the ban, that is to say, dedicated to Yahweh (Josh. 6:18f.,21,24), or divided among the warriors (Num. 31:25–30; Josh. 22:8; Judg. 5:30). The conquerors were welcomed to the sound of musical instruments and rhythmic odes (Judg. 11:34; 1 Sam. 18:6f.); certain psalms were also used to celebrate victories (e.g., Ps. 68,76). To release the combatants from their dedication to the holy war and to enable them to take up normal life again, purificatory rites were necessary (Num. 31:24).

9. *War and the language of the O.T.* The imagery and terminology of battle have strongly influenced the language of the O.T. Of this anyone can be convinced simply by reading through the books of the old covenant; hence it would be a useless labour to quote all the relevant passages. Let us confine ourselves, therefore, to certain characteristic expressions. The protection of Yahweh is compared to that of a shield: ". . . thou dost bless the righteous, O LORD; thou dost cover him with favour as with a shield" (Ps. 5:12); but His help against the wicked is expressed by the offensive power of the sword: "Happy are you, O Israel! Who is like you, a people saved by the LORD, the shield of your help, and the sword of your triumph!" (Deut. 33:29). The power of Yahweh reacts to the onslaught of His enemies: "for lo, the wicked bend the

bow, they have fitted their arrow to the string" (Ps. 11:2). Finally, the quiver filled with arrows has provided a happy metaphor to express the wealth it means for a family to be blessed with sons: "Lo, sons are a heritage from the LORD . . . Like arrows in the hand of a warrior are the sons of one's youth. Happy is the man who has his quiver full of them!" (Ps. 127:3–5).

10. *Is war the last word of the O.T.?* Although the language of the O.T. reverberates with the noise of battle, the eschatological conflict will be followed by a time of peace, an age of prosperity, which is the final hope of the messengers of God. The prophet Isaiah describes it thus:
"It shall come to pass in the latter days . . . (that) they shall beat their swords into ploughshares, and their spears into pruning hooks; nation shall not lift up sword against nation, neither shall they learn war any more!" (Isa. 2:2,4; cf. also Ps. 46:10; Isa. 9:4; Hos. 2:18; Zech. 9:10).

The new age, envisaged by the men of God in the midst of the harshest trials of war, is the Age of the Messiah.

H. MICHAUD

N.T.

1. For the N.T., Jesus Christ alone is our *peace (Eph. 2:14), but this is in a world which refuses to recognize the fact (Jn. 1:11). It is a *world, indeed, in which no one should be surprised that there are wars and rumours of war (Matt. 24:6 and parallels), for it has turned away from God.

This, as it were, natural incidence of wars in a sinful world has two primary consequences for the witness of the N.T.:

(*a*) The need for armies, occupation forces and police is never disputed; and the manner in which soldiers perform their duties is noted with an objectivity free from any kind of passion (Acts 5:26; Matt. 27:27; Acts 12:4,6,18; 27:31ff. etc.). They are the agents of that *authority which does not bear the sword in vain (Rom. 13:4). Though their way of carrying out their orders may be cruel or troublesome to those in their

charge (Lk. 23:36; Jn. 19:2,23f.,32ff.; Acts 16:20ff.), yet they are also able, by maintaining order, to protect the Church and its representatives (Acts 21:32,35; 23:10,23,31; 27:42f.).

(*b*) Similes from the world of war are among the most common in the N.T., and not only in the book of Revelation, where the whole of history between the ascension and the return of Christ is described as the continuation of the battles of a war that is physical as well as metaphysical (Rev. 2:16; 9:16ff.; 11:7; 12:7; 16:14; 17:14, etc.). Jesus uses such language quite naturally (Matt. 22:7; Lk. 11:17ff.; 14:31; cf. 1 Cor. 9:7; 14:8) and St. Paul does the same: he fights the good fight (1 Tim. 1:18), he exhorts Timothy to become a good soldier of Jesus Christ (2 Tim. 2:3), because the Christian life is a military enterprise, demanding, just as does the service of the ordinary soldier, an unconditional commitment (2 Tim. 2:4). But the battle is not with flesh and blood (Eph. 6:12); hence, to avoid defeat, we must receive from God Himself—Him whose word is a two-edged sword (Heb. 4:12)—the offensive and defensive weapons that will give us the victory (Eph. 6:13–17; cf. 2 Cor. 10:4ff.; 1 Thess. 5:8).

2. When, on occasion, a soldier is singled out for individual notice, it is normally to emphasize that his situation does not exclude him from salvation. Some come to John to be baptized, and are not told to desert but to be content with their pay (Lk. 3:14); the centurion of Capernaum not only has his request granted by Jesus but is held up as an example of deep faith (Matt. 8:5–10 and parallels); the first heathen to confess the divinity of Jesus is an officer (Matt. 27:54) and another officer, the centurion Cornelius, is the first heathen to enter the Church (Acts 10:1,22; this captain had under him, among others, a "devout soldier", 10:7). These examples show that, for the N.T. writers, there is not necessarily an absolute incompatibility between the calling of arms and the Christian faith: soldiers are one of the indispensable instruments of the State.

3. In "this world" of war and rumours of war—where Jesus Himself is a cause of strife and division, because He compels men to face a more peremptory demand for choice than any that confronts them in the world alone (Matt. 10:34; cf. Lk. 12:51ff.)—there is, nevertheless, one place where war no longer has any business; and woe to anyone who attempts to bring it there! (Jas. 4:1–10; 1 Pet. 2:11; 2 Cor. 12:20). That place is the Church, whose mission is to be, as it were, an enclave in this world of the world where "death shall be no more, neither shall there be mourning nor crying nor pain" (Rev. 21:4). For the Church is the place where *peace is proclaimed and lived (Eph. 2:11–22; cf. Mk. 9:50f.; 1 Thess. 5:13), because there Jesus Christ, the prince of peace (Isa. 9:5), is preached and men live in Him. This peace is the fruit of the reconciliation effected on the *cross; it is thus rooted essentially in Jesus Christ and perishes as soon as He ceases to be its guarantee. Two things follow from this:

(a) First, salvation is more important than any external war or peace (Mk. 13:7); but this must mean also that such human events are quite definitely not of sufficient weight (Mk. 13:20) to rob the believers of their true peace (Rom. 8:35).

(b) Secondly, it is on the basis of the Gospel and of the Kingdom already to be seen in the Church, and not on the basis of humanist utopianism or of political programmes, that Christians must become "peacemakers" (Matt. 5:9): their struggle against war and the terrible disasters it brings in its train (cf. the descriptions of apocalyptic) are comparable to their struggle against disease (Jas. 5:13ff.) or sin (Matt. 19:15–20). It may be said, without hesitation, that the best way for Christians to do away with war is to show by their unity and love for one another (Jn. 13:34f.) that it has no future (Matt. 26:52; Rev. 13:10).

4. One passage raises problems. It is that in which Jesus, after recommending His disciples to sell their clothing to buy weapons, tells them that the two swords they already have will be enough (Lk. 22:36,38). It was certainly with one of these that St. Peter tried to defend Jesus in Gethsemane (Jn. 18:10; cf. Matt. 26:51 and parallels). But Jesus refuses to be defended by force of arms, just as He renounces any appeal to the assistance of twelve legions of angels (Matt. 26:53). None of the commentators I have consulted seems to offer a satisfactory explanation and possibly none is to be found. (At any rate, that of Boniface VIII, who in the Bull "Unam Sanctam" based on this text the Roman claims to both civil and religious power, is out of the question!) It is likely, however, that Jesus wishes to convey (cf. also Jn. 15:18–23) that henceforward (v. 36) the calling of an apostle will mean the constant danger of death (cf. e.g., 2 Cor. 11:23–28) and that they will have to defend their lives against ambushes that are not worth the trouble taken over them (cf. e.g., Acts 9:23–25!); then (v. 38), with a certain irony, He changes the subject.

J.-J. VON ALLMEN

WASHING

1. From the time of the patriarchs up till that of Jesus washing played an important part in Jewish customs, without possessing a religious significance. In these dusty lands, where people walk about in sandals, it was a sign of hospitality to wash the feet of a person whom one received into one's tent or into one's house (Gen. 18:4; 19:2; 24:32, etc.). Jesus reproached Simon for not having accorded Him this dignity (Lk. 7:44); it was usually the task of a servant, and Jesus humbled Himself to this rank before His disciples (Jn. 13:1–20). This custom was followed in the primitive Church, since for a woman to be inscribed on the roll of widows it was necessary that she should have "washed the feet of the saints" (1 Tim. 5:10). Pharisees, and Jews in general, used to wash their hands carefully before meals (Mk. 7:3). This tradition, which had become a ritual, was ignored by the disciples of Jesus (Matt. 15:2), who were attacked by those who adhered to the

tradition. The Bible also mentions the current usage of *water, with which wounds were washed (Acts 16:33) and also the bodies of dead persons (Acts 9:37) and various other objects (Lk. 5:2); Jesus sent the man who had been born blind to wash in the pool of Siloam (Jn. 9:7,11,15), whence he came back healed.

Not to wash oneself could be an indication of sadness, penitence, or grief: "Mephibosheth the son of Saul . . . had not washed his feet, nor trimmed his beard, nor cleaned his clothes from the day the king departed until the day he came back in safety" (2 Sam. 19:24); contrariwise, he who washed himself, or washed his face, by this action expressed his satisfaction or his joy: for example, David after the death of his son (2 Sam. 12:20) or the Christian who intends to fast (Matt. 6:17).

2. In the old covenant washings with a view to purification played a considerable part: they were even a sign of the covenant of God with His people. Even before Yahweh established it, on the occasion of the solemn meeting on Sinai, Moses commanded the people to purify and wash their clothes (Exod. 19:10).

Washings constituted a part of the unwritten law to which men and women were expected to submit in various circumstances: these are enumerated in Leviticus (ch. 15; cf. also Num. 19:7–10; 31:24). Whatever they were, "he who is to be cleansed shall wash his clothes" (Lev. 14:8); "on the seventh day . . . he shall wash his clothes, and bathe his body in water, and he shall be *clean" (Lev. 14:9).

With all the more reason these ablutions were prescribed for the priests. Aaron and his sons were washed with water at the entrance to the tent of meeting: it is the primary mark of their ordination to the priesthood which will belong to them in accordance with a perpetual law (Exod. 29:4,9; cf. Lev. 8:6). The Levites will be purified by the sprinkling "of water which cleanses from sin"; "they shall wash their clothes": it is in this way that Aaron will consecrate them and separate them from the children of Israel for the service of Yahweh (Num. 8:5–14). For the service of the sanctuary a laver of brass was placed between the tent and the altar: "When they go into the tent of meeting, or when they come near the altar to minister, to burn an offering by fire to the Lord, they shall wash with water, lest they die; they shall wash their hands and their feet, lest they die: it shall be a statute for ever to them" (Exod. 30:20). This rite was evidently demanded by the holiness of the presence of Yahweh. Similarly, the entrails and the legs of the victim for the burnt offering were washed (Lev. 1:9).

These requirements were particularly significant at the time of the great annual sacrifice of atonement for the sins of the people (Lev. 16). After having placed the sins of Israel on the scapegoat, Aaron shall enter into the tent of meeting, shall take off his garments, "and shall bathe his body in water in a holy place, and put on his garments" (v. 24). Likewise, he who shall have been in contact with the goat is to wash his clothes (vv. 26, 28). Occasionally also, when a crime has been committed, the neck of a heifer shall be broken in token of expiation, "and all the elders of that city . . . shall wash their hands over the heifer" (Deut. 21:1–9).

3. The law is only the "shadow of the good things to come" (Heb. 10:1); it foretells, however, the sacrifice which Jesus Christ has made, once for all, of His own body (Heb. 10:10), His power of purification and redemption. The men of the old covenant foresaw this, and the numerous expressions in which they use the verb to wash bear witness to this. Isaiah reproves the sin of the people: "Your hands are full of blood. Wash yourselves; make yourselves clean!" (1:15–16), and he foretells the salvation of Jerusalem: "When the Lord shall have washed away the filth of the daughters of Zion, and cleansed the bloodstains of Jerusalem from its midst by a spirit of judgment . . ." (4:4; cf. also Ezek. 16:4). The Psalmist yearns for pardon when he prays: "Wash me thoroughly from my

iniquity, and cleanse me from my sin" (Ps. 51:2). And how is the expression, also found in the Psalms (26:6; 73:13), "to wash one's hands in innocence", to be understood, except in a Christological sense? Jesus Christ will accomplish what nitre and potash cannot do (Jer. 2:22), namely, expunge the mark of sin before the Lord. As Jacob prophesied (Gen. 49:11), Shiloh "will wash his garments in wine and his vesture in the blood of grapes"; he it is who will be both Saviour and Judge (Rev. 19:15).

When the N.T. uses the verb to wash in connection with the sacrifice of Christ it evokes at once the purificatory virtue of this sacrifice and the Church's sacramental act which renders it efficacious in the life of the believer, namely, *baptism (Eph. 5:26; 1 Jn. 1:7; 5:6,8). Thus Paul reports to the Jews the words which Ananias spoke to him: "Rise and be baptized, and wash away your sins, calling on his name" (Acts 22:16). It may be assumed that baptism is implied in the words of Jesus to Peter: "He who has bathed does not need to wash. . . ." (Jn. 13:10), in those of Paul to the Corinthians: "But you were washed, you were sanctified . . ." (1 Cor. 6:11), or those addressed to the Hebrews: "Let us draw near with a true heart in full assurance of faith, with our hearts sprinkled clean from an evil conscience, and our bodies washed with pure water" (Heb. 10:22). And the book of Revelation (as also 1 Jn.) makes use of a bold synthesis in order to evoke this mystery of cleansing: Jesus is He who has "washed us from our sins by his blood" (Rev. 1:6); it is in the blood of the Lamb that the elect have washed their robes (7:14; 22:14).

ED. DISERENS

WATCH, see HOPE

WATER

When the angel of judgment says: "Worship him who made heaven and earth, the sea and the fountains of water" (Rev. 14:7), he is voicing a truth proclaimed by the whole Bible: God, who created the earth and "drew it forth from the water" (cf. Gen. 1:9; 2 Pet. 3:5), makes constant use of this water for the purpose of showing forth His wrath or His mercy, His favour or His judgment; He employs it—in a way that seems to us contradictory—to bless the earth, giving life by means of it to animals and plants, but also to curse it by causing them to perish. In addition water has a purifying quality, both in the literal and figurative sense.

1. *Water as a sign of blessing.* Water plays an immense part in the life of the Near East. Lack of it (either in the form of rain or of springs) leads to drought and barrenness of the soil, resulting in thirst and famine for animals and men: hence the *desert. In the desert, nomads with their flocks halt by wells and cisterns and it is in the same neighbourhood that permanent settlements arise.

"For land which has drunk the rain that often falls upon it, and brings forth vegetation useful to those for whose sake it is cultivated, receives a blessing from God. But if it bears thorns and thistles, it is worthless and near to being cursed . . ." (Heb. 6:7–8).

God is He who gives His blessing by sending "the early rain and the later rain" (Deut. 11:14); He sends His punishment on the idolatrous people and their king by withholding the rain, as is seen in the story of Elijah (1 Kings 17,18). Water, which also quenches a man's thirst, is a gift so freely bestowed by God that the need to purchase it is a sign of punishment at His hand (Deut. 2:6; Lam. 5:4). In the book of Jonah, the royal proclamation calling for repentance in response to the prophet's preaching of judgment, says: "let them not feed, or drink water" (3:7). In the N.T. the apostle lists thirst among the trials he has endured (2 Cor. 11:27; 1 Cor. 4:11), and on the cross Jesus said "(to fulfil the scripture), 'I thirst'." (Jn. 19:28). Further, water is a mark of hospitality in Palestinian custom (Lk. 7:44); should anyone give a drink of water to his neighbour, he gives evidence of the love of Christ (Mk. 9:41), and should that neighbour be an enemy, God will judge him so much the more severely (Rom. 12:20).

The most typical account of the divine dealings is that of the journeying of the people of God in the wilderness; it demonstrates how God used water to show forth at one time His goodness, at another His severity. Though He made His people wander for forty years (Num. 32:13) yet He led them to the Promised Land; and when they rebelled (Num. 20:5) Yahweh commanded Moses to strike the rock that water might come out of it and the people quench their thirst (Exod. 17:6; Num. 20:8ff; Ps. 78:15–16). It is understandable that the Promised Land should always be presented as a country "which drinks water by the rain from heaven" (Deut 11:11); nothing else could have kept alive the hopes of Israel.

To describe the miraculous renewal of the *Kingdom of God at the end of the ages the prophets use the imagery of the effect of rain or running water on parched ground; the idea of water and its beneficial action forms an integral part of their Messianic hope. It signifies the gift of the Spirit of God, the fullness of blessing that flows from it and the prosperity which is its most striking manifestation (Isa. 35:7; 44:3–4 etc.). And the language of the seer in the book of Revelation, when he is describing the holy city, strangely recalls that of the prophets. He says of the elect: "The Lamb in the midst of the throne will be their shepherd, and he will guide them to springs of living water": "To the thirsty I will give water without price from the fountain of the water of life" (Rev. 7:17; 21:6; 22:17; cf. Isa. 49:10; 55:1; 58:11). And just as Zechariah (14:8) saw living waters proceeding out of Jerusalem, "half of them to the eastern sea and half of them to the western sea", so the angel showed John "the river of the water of life, bright as crystal, flowing from the throne of God and of the Lamb" (22:1). By contrast, the rich man in the parable suffers horribly from thirst in Hades (Lk. 16:24).

If water is the image of the *Spirit of God, the source of (eternal) life, in the Kingdom at the end of the ages, it is clear that it represents the same reality in the earthly life of the believer and of the Church. To the pious Jew God is "the fountain of living waters" (Jer. 2:13); and the righteous man is compared to a tree planted by running water (Ps. 1:3; Jer. 17:8). John develops this comparison (the meaning of which seems beyond the comprehension of those who talk with Jesus) at some length in the story of the Samaritan woman and in passing in that of Nicodemus: he insists on the present effectiveness of the Spirit, which renews the life of the believer. Further, to express the superabundance of grace in Christian experience, Jesus said: "He who believes in me, as the scripture has said, 'Out of his heart shall flow rivers of living water' " (Jn. 7:38); while the apostle compares false teachers to "waterless springs" (2 Pet. 2:17). The Johannine usage is connected with the dual sacramental meaning that the N.T. gives to water, for both purification and regeneration are signified by it in Christian baptism.

2. *Water as a sign of cursing*. While water which quenches thirst and irrigates the land is a sign of blessing, water in the mass, the *sea, the "great waters", the "deep waters", are a means by which God can show His anger. In the literal sense the sea unleashed is fearful, terrifying (Ps. 107:23–32; Jn. 1; Matt. 8:23–27); but the hand of God can calm it and protect the sailors. By way of imagery, the "great waters" represent the perils which threaten to overwhelm the believer and from which God delivers him (2 Sam. 22:17; Ps. 32:6; 144:7; Isa. 43:2). They are a power working for evil, in such a way that Jude (v. 13) can say of false teachers that they are "wild waves of the sea, casting up the foam of their own shame". The sea is the fitting repository for those who cause offences (Matt. 18:6 and parallel passages) and for the swine in which the demons expelled from the two Gadarenes took refuge (Matt. 8:32). The prophets predict the destruction of the kingdoms of

Syria and Israel by the "waters of the River" (i.e., the Euphrates) (Isa. 8:7), the fall and extinction of Babylon (Jer. 51:55) and of Tyre (Ezek. 26:19) by the "waves that destroy" and the "waters of the deep". The voice of the great Judge at the end of the ages thunders "like the sound of many waters" (Rev. 1:15; 14:2; 19:6). Prophesying these events Jesus declared that "there will be . . . upon the earth distress of nations in perplexity at the roaring of the sea and the waves" (Lk. 21:25). And John describes the judgment of the "great harlot, who is seated upon many waters" (Rev. 17:1). But in the Kingdom where all things are made new the sea is no more (Rev. 21:1).

The two most significant narratives are those of the Flood (Gen. 6–8) and of the crossing of the Red Sea (Exod. 14). Not only are they among the most striking in the history of the Old Covenant, but in addition they are singled out by the fact that the N.T. gives us an interpretation of them.

The story of the Flood is that of the curse which God caused to come upon the whole earth because of Man and the corruption of all creatures. God determines on the death of every being which He has created: ". . . In that day all the fountains of the great deep burst forth, and the windows of the heavens were opened" (Gen. 7:11). Only Noah "found favour in the eyes of the Lord" (Gen. 6:8) who "remembered him" and the creatures who owed their salvation to the ark. Isaiah interprets the covenant which God afterwards made with Noah as a sign of His everlasting mercy (Isa. 54:9); for the Epistle to the Hebrews (11:7) the faith of Noah is a condemnation of the world, and the Second Epistle of Peter (3:5–6) recalls this judgment in its prophecy of the Last Things.

In the whole history of Israel the account of the crossing of the Red Sea has remained the supreme story of miraculous deliverance. Yahweh manifested His glory by throwing the Egyptians "into the midst of the sea". "The waters returned and covered the chariots and the horsemen and all the host of Pharaoh that had followed them into the sea" (Exod. 14:28). "They sank as lead in the mighty waters" (Exod. 15:10; Neh. 9:11). The Epistle to the Hebrews says that "by faith the people crossed the Red Sea" (11:29).

Without entering on an examination of the problems posed by their exegesis, attention must be drawn to two passages in the N.T., 1 Pet. 3:20–21 and 1 Cor. 10:1–2, which respectively interpret these two events as a "sign of baptism". This sacrament embodies in fact the meaning which the Bible gives to water: a sign of judgment and of favour, of death and of life.

ED. DISERENS

WAY

Like the word path, which is its O.T· parallel, "way" can have a concrete or a figurative sense.

In the first case, it is used to denote the *roads, ways, tracks* and *paths* which furrow Palestine (Acts 8:26) and the world (Matt. 10:5) (local sense). It can also mean a *walk* or a *journey* (Gen. 42:25; Matt. 10:10) (active sense), and even express a distance: a *sabbath day's journey* (Acts 1:12) = 2,000 cubits (= 1,000 yards) to which the doctors of the law, starting from Exod. 16:29, limited permitted travelling on the sabbath day.

In the figurative sense, the words way and path apply, either in the singular (Jer. 10:23), or in the plural (Dan. 5:23), first to human life in general. Thus the expression *to go the way of all the earth* means *to die* (see *Death). They apply especially to life in so far as man assumes responsibility for it and they show *bearing, manner of living, conduct* (1 Kings 15:26; Jas. 1:8; Jude 11).

From this derives a very important theological use in the expression: the *ways of God*. These are first of all the ways in which God walks Himself; there is His activity, present (Deut. 32:4; Acts 13:10) or future (Isa. 40:3; cf. Matt. 3:3 and parallel passages), His manner of acting (Isa. 55:8), His plans, His designs (Isa. 58:2; Rom. 11:33). But they are also the ways in which He commands men to walk (Jer. 7:23; Ps.

25:4), particularly the commandments of the law (Deut. 8:6); it will also be the moral teaching of Jesus (Matt. 22:16). The way of the Lord is sometimes qualified by a simple adjective, such as good (1 Kings 8:36), right (1 Sam. 12:23), perfect (Ps. 101:6) or by a noun phrase: the way of righteousness (Prov. 8:20; Matt. 21:32), of truth (Ps. 119:30). These expressions are not to be interpreted without reference to God: the way will only be good because God, who is good, will order it.

It is not surprising to discover the term *way* frequently in the preaching of the prophets, who are called to bring the people back from their evil ways (2 Kings 17:13). They invite men to turn aside from them (Zech. 1:4; Jon. 3:8,10), to amend them (Jer. 7:3,5; 26:13), but God Himself will give to His people the way He wishes them to take (Jer. 32:39).

An echo of these appeals is often found in a much reiterated theme in the Wisdom books of the O.T.: the contrast of the two ways, the good and the bad (Ps. 1:6; Prov. 4:18–19; 12:28; cf. Jer. 21:8). Jesus Himself will turn to this theme in order to warn those whom He calls to follow Him not to be held back by the difficulties which make this way narrow (Matt. 7:13–14).

The apostles' preaching, like Christ's, requires people to take up a new and characteristic life. This explains the presence of the word *way* in the Epistles to express the general bearing of Christians (2 Pet. 2:2) or to denote a particular attitude which is recommended to them (1 Cor. 12:31). When the apostle Paul writes (1 Cor. 4:17) that Timothy will remind the Corinthians of "his ways in Christ Jesus as he teaches them everywhere in the Churches", we must certainly understand the spiritual and moral directives which he gives to the Churches in the communion of Christ.

In a few contexts, the Acts of the Apostles uses the term *way* without any qualification (9:2; 19:9,23; 24:14,22; cf. also 22:4). Its meaning remains vague. Witness the numerous renderings offered by the ordinary versions: way (of the Lord), (new) doctrine, gospel, sect, religion. This particular use seems to be derived from the expression *the way of the Lord*. In a very general manner it must denote Christianity as a movement into which God draws men.

We must examine separately two important passages in the N.T. where *way* is used in an image perceptibly different from the figurative sense so far considered: Heb. 10:20 (cf. also 9:8) and Jn. 14:6.

The first of these texts is difficult. The writer speaks here of Christ's work in relation to the Israelite worship in the Tabernacle. By the blood of Jesus, he says, we have free access into the holiest place, that is into the presence of God in heaven. Jesus has indeed opened for us a new and living way through the veil which shut off the entrance to the Holy of Holies. In fact, it is not by tearing this veil, which here is only an image, but in His own flesh that Jesus has opened this way for us, thanks to which we can approach God freely (10:22; cf. 4:16). The *new and living way* is then the entrance to communion with God, thanks to the expiation of Jesus and His present intercession (7:25).

In Jn. 14:6, Jesus calls Himself the *way*. The context, notably vv. 1–5, of which v. 6 is the logical conclusion, forces us to recognize a particular sense here as well. There is no question here of a certain manner of living, but of the way by which access to the Father is obtained. Now the only way which can lead the disciples there is Jesus Himself who, through His death, goes to prepare a place for them and who will then come back to seek them, doubtless at the time of His return. Thus they will be in the way which leads to the Father if they remain attached to their Lord through faith (14:1).

J. BURNIER

WICKED

O.T.

In order to describe the wicked the O.T. has recourse to a very great diversity of terms. Originally each of these terms without doubt expressed a characteristic of a particular wicked man, or was a value-judgment passed on him by the community.

Subsequently, these words changed and a word which was perhaps more recent, and in any case more precise, served to characterize them all. It is the word which is translated in the English Bible as "wicked" and which would be more suitably translated as *impious* or *disobedient*, notions which are more dynamic and more Hebraic. It is in relation to something and to someone that men are wicked.

Wickedness shows itself on three levels: Yahweh, the people, and the law, which we would render in modern categories as the theological, social, and moral levels, but which for the Israelite represented the one level of the *covenant.

The wicked man is originally either he who does not acknowledge the covenant of Yahweh (but such persons are then the enemies from without) or much more often he who, while acknowledging its necessity, doubts its sufficiency: "Yahweh is too far away, he sees nothing, he can do nothing, it is as though he does not exist" (Ps. 10:4 and 13; 14:1; 53:2). In no sense is this atheism. The wicked man then seeks for other covenants with other gods (and the same is the reaction of the entire people when they seek for covenants with other peoples, which was, in effect, to enter into covenant with their gods). The first duty of the prophets is to denounce these covenants which in the view of the wicked man in no way exclude the service of Yahweh. If the prophets protest, it is in the first place because no man can serve two masters (Josh. 24:15; 1 Kings 18:21); and, secondly, it is because a covenant is not something neutral; it causes one to partake of the "life" and the power of God; contamination is therefore forbidden (the wicked man himself is contagious: Ps. 1). Besides, the wicked man will quickly come to the point of rejecting the covenant of Yahweh, he becomes more and more "sick" and, in relation to the covenant of Yahweh, is only a nonentity, which does not, however, cease to constitute a danger to the other members of the covenant (this is paradoxical only to our modern mentality which views the nonentity as neutral, but for the Israelite the nonentity is injurious, he disrupts).

1. This is why we believe, supported by a careful study of the Psalms, that *the original historic form* of the wicked man was the magician or sorcerer (Ps. 31; 57; 59). The O.T., moreover, has much to say about them and evinces no tenderness for them (Deut. 18:9–14): an expression translated as "workers of iniquity" may perhaps signify workers of charms, or at least workers of vanity or malefactors; another term translated as "enemy" could be associated with the necromancer. Magic is the earliest form of natural theology, and the magicians transgressed against Yahweh by declaring Him to be insufficient and by wishing to make use of powers which Yahweh did not wish to grant to men, or by wishing to seize them in a manner other than that which He wished. They trespassed against the state, whose foundations were shaken by them, against the law which placed a ban upon them, and against the Israelites whom they caused to be ill or impious.

2. *The second form* (closely related to the foregoing) is that of the idolater (see *Idol), who also enters into other covenants and recognizes other laws, inasmuch as he proceeds to reject the law; he then becomes one who is without law and, by a thorough determination to lie, steal, kill, and be the enemy of him who is "in the law" (as distinct from "under the law"), the wicked man does injury to the holiness of Yahweh, to the integrity of Israel, and to the law: he must therefore be destroyed.

There are, it is true, many other wicked men: transgressors, blasphemers, murderers, but with a certain theological precision they have been assigned to the second category: to do injury to one of the commandments or to despise righteousness was to attack Israel, to break the covenant, to array oneself against Yahweh, it was above all to be an idolater, even though in our eyes this idolatry is not primitive. It is important to understand that for the Israelite mentality one was "for or against", and so one could not infringe an order of Yahweh except on the order of an enemy. All evil done to a pious Israelite was necessarily the fruit of a deep-seated idolatry.

This is the explanation of the imprecations against the wicked (Ps. 109; 139) which are wrongly rejected or adopted *en bloc*. They are nothing other than:

(*a*) on the religious plane, sentences of excommunication. The wicked are cut off from the covenant and from communion by the power of God. In these instances the verdict which they have pronounced upon themselves is confirmed and Yahweh is asked to make it effective; to-day it would be excommunication.

(*b*) On the civil plane, they are means of action. The Judge (and for Israel Yahweh is the Judge) is asked, as in all civil society, to punish them according to their deserts; to-day this would mean asking God for more justice in our governments, and acting accordingly.

N.T.

The same term can designate the wicked man (Matt. 5:39), the evil one (Matt. 5:37), and evil, not in itself, but as wicked action (Matt. 5:11); or it can describe a person (Matt. 18:32), his works (Col. 1:21), the present age (Gal. 1:4; cf. Eph. 5:16), the present generation (Matt. 12:45), the whole world (1 Jn. 5:19). Where man is concerned, his conscience can be evil (though this should not be understood in the modern sense of a tortured conscience: Heb. 10:22) as well as his words and his works. This arises from a ground which is not objectively but voluntarily evil (Matt. 15:10–20 and Mk. 7:14–23, where heart has the Israelite sense of will), for the *world is not evil in itself (Jn. 17:15). There are also evil spirits (Matt. 12:45; see *Demons). The impression is received of an entire world that is organized as a hierarchy and is the enemy of the other world; between the two there exists no neutrality, nor any synthesis (cf. O.T. and Matt. 6:24). But that is not the whole picture. To begin with, this evil world receives its light and thus its life from

God who is good (Matt. 6:45), and this world was brought into existence by Him (Jn. 1:1ff.). There is no question at all of a dualism. Above all, this evil is not immanent in the world in such a way that whoever is *in* the world is infected by it. It is rather a propensity, a distortion which is received there; one then becomes *of* the world, or *of* the evil one (1 Jn. 3:12). This propensity is terrible, it is animosity against God, and it extends to every thing, every thing yearns for deliverance (Rom. 8:18ff.). He who is infected with it cannot rid himself of it by his own efforts; the bad tree cannot bring forth good fruit (cf. Matt. 7:18), and the evil generation that wishes to free itself of it by cleansing its house finds itself seven times more evil than previously (Matt. 12:43f.). A purification that involves complete separation is necessary (Heb. 10:22; see *Baptism).

"Wicked" can also have a significance that is purely profane (cf. Acts 17:5) or specifically moral; it designates him who breaks the law. This term can also have a specifically Christian significance: it then designates him who does not forgive (Matt. 18:32) or who is against the Church and its apostles (3 Jn. 10; 2 Thess. 3:2), or again the heretic (2 Jn. 11).

With regard to the wicked man, if he does not belong to the Church, it is necessary to pray for him (cf. Matt. 5:44); if he is a Christian, it is necessary to admonish him that he is endangering his salvation (cf. Matt. 18:15ff.) and it may be necessary to excommunicate him in order to drive him to repentance (cf. Matt. 18:15ff. and 2 Cor. 2:5ff.).

A. MAILLOT

WILDERNESS, *see* DESERT (NAMES, GEOGRAPHICAL)

WINE

O.T.

The O.T. uses chiefly two terms which may be translated respectively by wine and must (there are other terms too but these simply define the species of wine or its alcoholic content).

1. The etymology is vague, but in neo-Sumerian the word for wine includes the connotation "life-giving" and in the Sumerian-Accadian pantheon one and the same goddess will be called "wine of heaven", "wine", and "mother of wine" and will represent both wine and the vine. Similarly there is a goddess of must, whose Sumerian name is Siris, which may be equated with the Hebrew word, and Siris is a personification of the life of the gods.

2. *Wine and *joy.* For the O.T., wine is one of the most significant gifts which God has made to man (Gen. 49:11ff.; 27:28; Ps. 104:15). It may even be interpreted as the symbol of all God's gifts to man. But above all it suggests the end of God's goodness: to bring joy to man (Ps. 104:15; Eccl. 9:7; cf. Ecclus. 3:25–31, especially v. 27). It is intended to console man for the curse which vexes the earth and the work of the soil. At least this is the conclusion which seems to emerge from the two texts Gen. 5:29 and 9:20–27. In 5:29, the name Noah comes doubtless from a root meaning to rest. The LXX interprets it as coming from a root meaning to console: Noah will console man, or refresh man, we are told, from the burden of the curse which weighs on the ground—an allusion to the fact that he will be the first to plant the vine and to taste its fruit: Gen. 9:20–27 (moreover his Babylonian counterpart Uta-Naphishtim knows the plant which prolongs life).

Wine rejoices God Himself (Judg. 9:13). The joy which it procures is therefore a participation of divine joy and also, as we shall see further, of divine life (let us say at once however that this is why Daniel and his friends will not partake of the wine of Nebuchadnezzar: they refuse to share the joy of Nebo, they want only the joy of Yahweh).

It is also a sign of *covenants and of the joy which they are meant to bring; both covenants between men (see *Eating and Drinking, and cf. Gen. 14:18–20) and covenants made by God with men; hence we find wine as an element in the perpetual daily sacrifice (Exod. 29:38ff.; Num. 15:5) and it plays a great part in feasts (Lev. 23:13).

3. *Wine and installation in the Messianic kingdom.* To drink one's own wine is a great source of blessing, and inversely not to take advantage of the fruit of one's vineyards is considered nothing short of catastrophic (Zeph. 1:13).

In the former case, the fact is that a man is able to profit by all that God gives. To drink wine and especially one's own wine becomes a sign of *rest, of installation; man shows thereby that he is already in the Messianic land. That is why the ascetic, declaring that the time is not yet, abstains from wine. The Rechabites, loyal to the nomadic state which for them and for a prophet such as Hosea was the Messianic time, abstain from wine; their point of view is that even in Canaan the Israelites are pilgrims and travellers (Jer. 35). For the same reason also the Nazirites, during their novitiate, will not drink wine. And again that is why John the Baptist may not drink wine (here too as in the case of the Rechabites and Hosea there is the notion of the significance of desert life).

4. *Wine and life.* But wine is also closely bound up with *life. (Doubtless the primitive symbol from which all the other associations of the vine flow is at the back of this idea, but it is not easy to elucidate the connection.) Let us recall the Sumerian term. Dhorme claims, no doubt rightly, that the tree of life was a *vine. If *bread sustains the present life, wine procures to man for a brief moment the transport of intoxication (which must be distinguished from the vice of drunkenness for which the Bible has no indulgence) and thus the sense of release into another life; it opens up for man the gates which the angel with the flaming sword guards. But in this matter there is an ambiguity brought about by two opposed trains of thought. Inasmuch as it recalls that wider life, the drunken transport

has been considered almost with sympathy (Prov. 31:6; Zech. 9:15; 10:7; Ecclus. 31:27). But inasmuch as it proceeds from a demoniacal determination to seize that other life, it has been treated severely; for it is ephemeral and fallacious and the angel keeps good guard (Amos 2:8; Isa. 5:11; 28:1; Hab. 2:15; cf. also Lev. 10:9–10 where wine is forbidden the family of Aaron before their entry into the tent of meeting; finally cf. Eph. 5:18 where to be filled with wine is contrasted with being filled with the Spirit). Let us confine ourselves to noting this eschatological character of wine: it is the element in life which symbolizes the Promised Land, all future joy and blessedness. Hence abstinence from wine, while legitimate, is only so if practised from hope in the future coming of the Kingdom and not from a criticism of wine in itself.

5. *Wine and *blood.* In Babylon and no doubt in Canaan too it was considered that the vine clusters (like grains of corn) in order to produce wine were crushed in suffering and from this painful death there arose the wine of life. Hence there easily came about the assimilation of wine and blood—an assimilation favoured by the colour (Deut. 32:14) and especially by the fact that both wine and blood are directly bound up with life. Here we have a triad. Wine, the blood of the vine, (Deut. 32:14) will be substituted for the blood of the victim (Deut. 32:38). At Babylon, libations of wine and bloody sacrifices could be regarded as the same and wine could be mixed with blood (against Ps. 16:4).

6. *Various.* Wine is also the "fruit" of the people (see *Vine). It can be closely connected with anger (Jer. 25:15) whether by antithesis or by allusion to judgment: wine is good but the sin of those who drink it makes it a wine of anger.

N.T.

Here too we find the same associations with joy, the covenant blood, life and the future Kingdom. The new wine of Matt. 9:17 is the new covenant which shatters the framework of the old. The two wines of Jn. 2 may symbolize the two dispensations (the Jews who have become drunk with the old covenant, now however exhausted, can no more enjoy the new covenant which is far better). The cup of the *Lord's Supper is the cup of the new covenant.

Similarly the cup of the Last Supper is closely connected with joy, blood, the Kingdom, especially in Lk. 22:14–20, which by distinguishing the two cups allows us better to disentangle all these elements.

Finally, it has often been thought that the only reason which made Christ refuse wine on the cross was that He did not wish His sufferings to be alleviated; Mark in fact tells us that this wine was mixed with myrrh (Matthew, who perhaps did not properly understand the episode or wanted to bring it into closer conformity with the O.T.— Ps. 69:22—says it was mixed with gall). But would not the reason for the refusal of Christ be also that He had declared He would no more drink of the fruit of the vine until He drank it new in the Kingdom? In any case it is curious to note that Jesus Christ offers man wine as a symbol of His suffering and that man offers wine to Christ in order that those sufferings might be alleviated. These two wines must needs be mutually exclusive for Him who in shedding His blood has reopened the gates which lead to the tree of life, because He Himself is the true vine, the real tree of life.

A. MAILLOT

WISDOM

O.T.

1. Although the O.T. often speaks of wisdom in somewhat secular contexts, it affirms equally clearly that wisdom flows from God who alone possesses it fully (Isa. 31:2; Jer. 8:9; 2 Sam. 14:20; Prov. 21:30; Dan. 2:20–23). This wisdom of God is the wholeness and the perfection of His knowledge which nothing can escape (Job 10:4; 26:6; 31:4; Prov. 5:21; 15:3; 24:12). In God this completeness of knowledge con-

sists in the power of discrimination between good and evil, but the same faculty exists in man, since the recompense of the righteous and the punishment of the sinner is an essential tenet in the teaching of the sages not only in Israel but also throughout the ancient East. The theme recurs constantly in the collection of sayings which constitutes chapters 10–22 of Proverbs and forms the point of departure of the books of Job and Ecclesiastes as well as of the so-called Wisdom Psalms (Pss. 1; 37; 49; 73; 111). Yet, unlike for example the theology of Deuteronomy with which the wisdom literature offers an undeniable kinship, the retributive providence of God is not related to the covenant but to His activity in creation.

The wisdom of God is manifested above all in the *creation of the world; such is the teaching of the whole of sapiential literature both canonical and apocryphal, Israelite and Egyptian. Sometimes the emphasis is placed on the creation of the universe (Prov. 3:19ff.; 8:22–31) sometimes and more often on the creation of man (Prov. 14:31; 17:5; 22:2; Job 4:17; 10:8ff.; 12:7–10; Eccl. 3:14; 7:13; 11:5; Ps. 94:9; 104:24; Isa. 40:13; Jer. 10:12; 51:15; Tob. 3:11; Baruch 3:32–35, etc.). Some of these texts lie behind a current of speculations concerning the pre-existing or hypostatic character of wisdom: according to Prov. 8:22ff. it seems that wisdom existed prior to the creation of the world and as a power of order and design was associated with God, the power of creation itself; but as this text is isolated in the O.T. it is doubtless better to see in those texts which personify wisdom the use of a literary device in speaking of one of the most important of the divine attributes. History too is the theatre in which the wisdom of God is manifested, although it is especially extra-canonical texts such as Ecclesiasticus (cf. the famous eulogy of the ancestors of Israel, chap. 44ff.) and the Wisdom of Solomon which bring out this aspect of divine wisdom.

2. The knowledge and still more the action which characterize divine wisdom are reflected in what the O.T. says about human wisdom. For man also may and must be wise, provided he will only allow himself to be instructed in the ways of wisdom. It is true that some texts imply that wisdom is the exclusive privilege of God and that man's attempt to acquire wisdom is impious and delusive; the book of Job seems to allude to a tradition according to which the sin of the first man consisted in ravishing the wisdom reserved to God (15:7ff.) while the command forbidding man to take of the tree of the knowledge of good and evil, i.e., total knowledge, points in the same direction (Gen. 2:17). Other texts insist on the insurmountable gulf between the wisdom of God and the ignorance of man (Job 11:6–9; Isa. 40:14,28; Ps. 92:6; 139:12; Prov. 8:22) and Ecclesiastes bases all his pessimism on the incommensurability between the plane of divine wisdom and the weakness and limitations of human knowledge. The solution of the problem is given us in the book of Job, which, after showing us in a fine passage (chap. 28) that God alone is the master of mysterious and unfathomable wisdom, concludes however that a type of wisdom is possible for man, i.e., wisdom of a practical kind consisting solely in submission to God and abhorrence of evil (28:28).

The thought typical of more orthodox Wisdom literature is still more affirmative (Proverbs, Ecclesiasticus).

Ecclesiasticus declares that God has shed His wisdom on all His works and on all flesh and that every man possesses the portion which divine wisdom has imparted to him (1:10). This wisdom, which is accessible to every man, is in the first place the privilege of those whom the O.T. calls the wise and of whom King Solomon is the most perfect specimen (1 Kings 3:12). The wise constituted a class alongside of the priest and prophet (Jer. 18:18). Their function was to teach wisdom, with the grace of which they had themselves been liberally endowed whether by *revelation or tradition. Their duty then was to give counsel. They offered a real body of teaching, the encyclopaedic character of which was remarkable for the period since it included the most diverse spheres of life and nature (cf. 1 Kings 4:32ff.), but the element of knowledge is always secondary to that of action. To be wise is not so much to be able to fathom the ultimate secrets of life as the ability to order one's life well: the wise man is a man who succeeds.

3. Three means are open to the man who will take the trouble to listen to the voice of wisdom:

(a) Wisdom is prudence: the search for balance, moderation, and the avoidance of extremes is expressed in many sayings of the book of Proverbs as in many wisdom texts of the Egyptians. To be wise is to give proof of discrimination in the choice of acquaintances—a matter where reserve is fitting even in the married state. To be wise is also to be able to control one's tongue and silence is the object of much praise (Prov. 10:19; 11:13; 17:27).

(b) Success in life is not to be attained, by any means whatsoever. The moral requirements of the law and the prophets shape the teaching on wisdom and give to Israelite wisdom a different emphasis from that of neighbouring peoples. This means that no wisdom is possible apart from respect for the person and goods of others (Prov. 1:13ff.; Job 24:2): the false balance is abhorrent to Yahweh (Prov. 11:1) and adultery is condemned not because of its disagreeable nature but because it involves breaking a bond established by the Creator; and we should also recall the fact that he who does not care for the poor insults the God who created all men (Prov. 14:31).

(c) The moral aspect of wisdom is itself the result of the religious basis of the latter: "The fear of the Lord is the beginning of wisdom" (Prov. 1:7; 9:10; 15:33; Ps. 111:10; Job 28:28) which means that religion is not only the point of departure but the culmination and crown of all the sapiential teaching, for it is the fear of God which permits one to refrain from evil (Prov. 3:7; 8:13). The centre of gravity of religion as inspired by the

wisdom teaching does not lie in the cultus, and ritual demands are of little importance for it (Prov. 3:9ff.); on the other hand prayer is frequently urged (Prov. 15:8,29) although it is admitted that prayer itself can become a matter of vain repetitions (cf. Ecclesiastes). Before Ecclesiasticus (130 B.C.) wisdom religion is not to be identified with submission to the written law (Ecclus. 19:20). The fear of God is, above everything, faith in the just working of divine retribution and a submissive and humble attitude in the recollection of the divine presence. The purely religious demand moulds the wisdom teaching to such an extent that the two things are sometimes identified: the wise man is essentially the pious man (Job 37:24; 42:8). The piety of Job and the impiety of his friends are equated with the wisdom of the one and the folly of the others. The religion of Israel with its dynamic power was able to control and inspire the cult of wisdom, which in itself was far from being the exclusive possession of the elect people, and to imprint upon it the specific mark of the holiness of the one God who is unwilling to leave any human concern outside the domain of His sovereignty.

ED. JACOB

N.T.

1. In modern times the word wisdom has taken on a very special meaning: it implies an insight which links knowledge to life and action. It denotes essentially a manner of life which is based on knowledge and a sure grasp of truth. But in the N.T. wisdom has in the first place a meaning in the realm of knowledge itself. It suggests an expansion of knowledge flowing from faith. That is why wisdom is sometimes confirmed by knowledge (1 Cor. 12:8; Col. 2:3) or understanding (Rev. 17:9).

Yet two distinct realities are covered by the same term, and for that reason St. Paul is at pains to stress the ambiguity of the word. Firstly, wisdom may mean wisdom after the flesh (1 Cor. 1:26), i.e., the wisdom which is sought after by the Greeks and generally speaking by philosophers as a whole (1 Cor. 1:21) and by the *world in so far as the latter asserts its independence over against its Creator. Such wisdom is the sum of knowledge which men can acquire through the use of their natural faculties; it is for example the wisdom which Moses gained among the Egyptians (Acts 7:22). It is characteristic of the adult, it is the knowledge of which men boast (cf. Matt. 11:25, which contrasts the wise and the understanding with little children). Although worldly, it is not without power. Paul implicitly admits that, like the language which reflects it, it has a certain superiority (1 Cor. 2:1) and it derives this superiority from its persuasive power ("the plausible words of wisdom", 1 Cor. 2:4). To the extent in which this wisdom is not swollen by pride and does not claim to exceed the sphere which is proper to it, it is by no means criticized or depreciated in the N.T. But as soon as this wisdom desires to measure itself against the wisdom of the spirit which flows from God, it is confounded: then it becomes nothing more than pride and vanity, and we see that God is resolved to confound the wisdom of the wise (1 Cor. 1:19). In fact, it reveals its inadequacy as soon as it aspires to the knowledge of God: "In the wisdom of God, the world did not know God through wisdom" (1 Cor. 1:21). Furthermore, when this wisdom of man is confronted by the wisdom of God (1 Cor. 1:24) a sort of inversion occurs. The former loses its true qualities; it becomes the opposite of itself, madness (1 Cor. 3:19) although by a tragic blunder it takes the wisdom of God for madness (1 Cor. 1:21).

2. But although not recognized by human wisdom (which proves indeed that there is not affinity between these two types of wisdom and that the second is not the expansion of the first) the wisdom of God is in truth an authentic wisdom and even an ultimately triumphant wisdom, though it is a wisdom which is not that of this age or of the rulers of this age who are "doomed to pass away" (1 Cor. 2:6). The characteristic feature of the wisdom of God is that it is "mysterious and hidden" (1 Cor. 2:7). Hence it is not based on rational evidence, unlike the former type of wisdom which, as the apostle well sees, is rationally demonstrable in such a way as to carry conviction and exert its sway over the mind (1 Cor. 2:1 and 2:4). Thus the wisdom of God does not consist in non-temporal and universally valid truth immediately intelligible, but rather in the beneficent providential design of God underlying history and working out the fulfilment of history. It is just because the wisdom of God concerns the divine plan underlying history that it is not totally intelligible to us at once. When St. Paul speaks of the mystery of the strange hardening of the heart of Israel—a process through which God is pursuing the fulfilment of His redemptive plan—he exclaims: "O the depth of the riches and wisdom and knowledge of God!" (Rom. 11:33).

The folly of human wisdom lies just in its incapacity to understand and recognize the deep plan of God which is being realized in the history of salvation and especially in the event of the *cross (1 Cor. 1:20) or again in its failure to understand the message of prophets and apostles who are revealers of the divine plan (Lk. 11:49–50). When Jesus praises His Father for hiding the secret from the wise and understanding and for revealing it to babes who have no pretension to wisdom (Matt. 11:25) He is referring to the secret relation between the Father and the Son in virtue of which the Son alone can reveal the Father (11:27): hence He is here calling attention to the very heart of the history of salvation. That is why the word wisdom can in the last resort be applied preeminently to Christ Himself, the centre of this history, who by the will of God was made unto us wisdom, righteousness, sanctification, and redemption (1 Cor. 1:30). Hence it becomes possible to speak of Christ as of a wisdom which is the object of knowledge—a knowledge which supersedes all other knowledge, and thus Paul can say: "I decided to know nothing among you except Jesus Christ and Him crucified" (1 Cor. 2:2).

3. If Christ is thus the wisdom of God, in His function as consummator of the divine plan in history, it becomes possible to identify Him also with what the O.T., and especially the Wisdom literature, called the wisdom of God, a kind of divine hypostasis described also as the spirit of God by the Wisdom of Solomon (1:6,7; 7:22; 8:1). The N.T. preserves only a few vague literary traces of this hypostasis: e.g., Lk. 11:49 and perhaps also the enigmatic conclusion of the teaching of Jesus on the Baptist (Matt. 11:7–19): "Wisdom is justified by her deeds" (Joh. Weiss thinks that we should see in this wisdom Christ Himself). But if such a hypostasis no longer plays any important part in the thought of the N.T., Christ inherits its attributes: He too is identified with the Spirit of God (1 Cor. 15:45; 2 Cor. 3:17). But His relation with God is quite different from that of the hypostasis: He is the Son equal in dignity with the Father. The wisdom of God is henceforth united to God by a precise and concrete bond, that of filiality. And God, the Father of Jesus Christ who became wisdom for our sakes, may be called "the only wise" (Rom. 16:27).

4. If wisdom is thus linked to the trinitarian mystery of the being of God and to His redemptive activity in a stream of saving history, then for man too wisdom assumes another meaning: it ceases to be the accumulation of the knowledge which he can acquire by his own unaided faculties and enlightenment. It becomes a charismatic gift. Because God is wise and manifests this wisdom in the person of Jesus Christ, and because in Jesus Christ we have the fullness of the Godhead (Col. 2:10) it follows that in giving to us Jesus Christ He gives us also His wisdom. A charismatic gift, wisdom is dependent on the word of Christ which fills it with its content and power: "Let the word of Christ dwell in you richly . . . in all wisdom" (Col. 3:16). It is by the *word that wisdom is inspired and nourished in us exactly like faith. Hence we see that the gift of wisdom figures in the catalogues of gifts drawn up by St. Paul (1 Cor. 12:8). Eph. 1:17 connects in an unmistakable manner the gift of wisdom with the revelation of God in Jesus Christ— a gift by means of which we shall know perfectly, within the limits of faith, God Himself.

The wisdom of the believer will consist in recognizing the wisdom of God which is manifested in the history of salvation. The true function of charismatic wisdom is to confess the mystery of God, "of Christ, in whom are hid all the treasures of wisdom and knowledge" (Col. 2:2–3). Both wisdom and knowledge are associated in the plan of God: wisdom and knowledge will therefore be equally given to man (1 Cor. 12:8). As it is difficult for us to distinguish clearly between wisdom and knowledge in God, so it is difficult for us to analyse the distinctive marks of wisdom and knowledge as charismatic gifts in man. In any case, wisdom is not a type of gnosis, for it must respect the hiddenness and mystery of the Godhead. Rev. 13:18 and 17:9 show clearly that wisdom is and remains the understanding of mysterious things. Hence it is not given to all men, it is never to be equated with a universal faculty of man: "This calls for wisdom: let him who has understanding reckon the number of the beast . . ." (13:18).

5. But this wisdom has not merely a cognitive aspect; it has inevitably also a practical and moral aspect. It is remarkable that the latter is not emphasized by James alone, but that it appears already in Paul, e.g., Col. 4:5, "Conduct yourselves wisely toward outsiders." We have here an injunction to spiritual prudence, a prudence which consists in seizing the favourable moment for witnessing to Christ. Only in fact the perfect can apprehend at once the wisdom of God and recognize it for what it is in reality (1 Cor. 2:6). It is to be noted also in regard to this practical wisdom that it is a question of respecting, for the purposes of teaching and evangelization, the mystery of *revelation. And when Paul declares (Eph. 5:15): "Look carefully then how you walk, not as unwise men, but as wise", it is again a question of behaving in a way which suggests not pagan moderation,

but rebirth into the new life of the Spirit, accession to the dignity of children of light, hence of beings who are aware of the mysterious and hidden wisdom of God. In the Epistle of James, the practical significance of the word is simply more emphasized: wisdom implies the patience by which we bear trials (1:5; 3:17) or meekness (3:13,15), i.e., all the qualities which are so many signs of the regeneration of man when the grace and wisdom of God seize upon him. The supernatural origin of this practical wisdom is not in doubt, for it is contrasted with wisdom that is "earthly, sensual, devilish", and the hymn to wisdom in James 3:13–18 bears a curious resemblance to the hymn to charity of 1 Cor. 13.

If there is thus throughout the N.T. a radical opposition between human wisdom, the origin of which, in fact, is not philosophically elucidated by the authors of the N.T., and on the other hand the mysterious wisdom of God, it does not follow that the wise according to this world are perpetually excluded from the understanding of revelation. Doubtless, among those that are called there are few wise according to the flesh (1 Cor. 1:26), and as soon as one boasts of one's wisdom one becomes mad (Rom. 1:22). Nevertheless the good news of salvation must be proclaimed to the wise also as St. Paul did at Athens (Acts 17:16–34). On that occasion the wise were not converted to the faith, which does not prevent the apostle from affirming: "I am under obligation both to Greeks and to barbarians, both to the wise and to the foolish" (Rom. 1:14). But of course it is necessary for the wise according to the flesh to be converted and to renounce his wisdom—at least in so far as he wishes to use it arrogantly, and to become foolish and mad in the eyes of the world in order to become wise in the sight of God (1 Cor. 3:18).

R. MEHL

WITNESS

The words witness and to witness have in the first place a strictly juridical connotation.

The witness is he who has a direct knowledge of certain facts and declares before a court of justice what he has seen or heard. He bears witness to what he knows.

These terms have taken on a much wider meaning in current usage. To witness no longer bears solely on tangible facts but on opinions and convictions which have impressed themselves as true and convincing on him who proclaims them. In witnessing of this kind there enters an element of faith which eludes purely empirical verification.

The Bible uses these words both in their literal and wider meanings. In this connection let us note that the Bible makes a very large use of technical juridical language. Its revelation is essentially concerned with relationships involving God with man and man with his *neighbour. The use of the language of law expresses the seriousness of these relationships.

1. *Witness in its literal juridical sense.* To bear witness in a court of law is a serious matter. The law of Moses requires the deposition of several witnesses in the case of a charge involving the possibility of the death penalty. It employs terrible sanctions against false witnessing (Deut. 17:2–13; 19:15–19; Num. 35:30). The Sanhedrin maintains an appearance of legality by bringing forward several false witnesses against Jesus (Matt. 26:60; cf. Acts 6:13; 7:58).

The apostolic Church also insists on a plurality of witnesses as an essential guarantee in all cases of judgment given by ecclesiastical authority (1 Tim. 5:19; 2 Cor. 13:1; cf. Matt. 18:16).

2. *Witness in the language of revelation.* (a) Witnessing in the specifically biblical sense is also concerned with facts; but these facts are deeds and words of God; they have an ultimate meaning which faith alone can discern. In this sphere the fact and its interpretation are indissolubly bound up together. The "cloud of witnesses" evoked in chapters 11 and 12 of the Epistle to the Hebrews consists of men who have believed

the promises of God, who have recognized His hand in the deliverances or the judgments of which they have been the object, and who have waited for the future deliverance of which these initial events were a precursory sign. The people of God are the witnesses to God among the heathen; they proclaim and confess the living and true God (Isa. 43:10–12).

In the language of the N.T., witnesses are in the first place those who knew the historical Jesus, were associated with His ministry and were the eyewitnesses of His passion and resurrection. Their witness is therefore concerned with *facts*. But their witness does not stop there: who is Jesus? He alone can be a witness to Him who recognizes by faith that Jesus is the One whom God has sent, as the Scriptures foretold, and who confesses Him as Lord and Saviour. Hence we are here face to face with revealed and proclaimed truth and this revelation is the work of the Holy Spirit (Lk. 24:48; Acts 1:8,21–22; 2:32; 5:32; 10:37–43; 13:30–31; 26:16). Later the term witness is extended to include those who without having known Jesus according to the flesh have known and confessed Him as the living One and the Lord; such is the case of St. Paul (Acts 22:15; 26:16; cf. 1 Cor. 15:1–11) and of all those who following the apostles confess publicly their faith in the crucified and risen Lord, the Christ.

Witnessing consists in oral confession and preaching of the Gospel. But to be authentic it presupposes the commitment of the whole person and life of the witness. Already in late Judaism many believers had sealed with their blood the confession of their faith and the word witness had become synonymous with martyr. The apostolic Church recognizes this inescapable character of the sufferings and trials which accompany the confession of the true faith. It is significant that the Greek word witness has passed into our modern languages as meaning "martyr" (cf. Rev. 6:9; 17:6).

(*b*) The witness of God the Father, the Son and the Holy Spirit.

1. God is often invoked as witness by the believer against his adversaries. Thus Samuel invokes God and His anointed as witnesses of his conduct (1 Sam. 12:5). St. Paul calls upon God as witness to his conduct, his feelings, and the motives which have actuated him (2 Cor. 1:23; Rom. 1:9; Phil. 1:8; 1 Thess. 2:5,10). On the other hand, God, assembling His people to the great assize of judgment, takes as His witness the heavens and the earth (Isa. 1:2).

2. Jesus Christ is described as the faithful and true witness (Rev. 1:5; 3:14). The terms to witness and witness play an exceptionally important part in the vocabulary of St. John's Gospel. Jesus is the witness come from heaven to whom God Himself, His works, the Scriptures, and John the Baptist bear witness. He attests what He has seen and heard (Jn. 3:11–13; 3:31–33; 5:31–47; 8:13–18). It is interesting to observe to what an extent John keeps strictly to the juridical principle of a plurality of witnesses; the witness of John the Baptist (cf. Jn. 1:7–8,31), of Moses, of God, and of the works. In the great trial of humanity the Son of Man is the witness whose mere presence brings about the separation of light and darkness, so that men judge themselves by the attitude they take up with regard to Him. He has come into the world "to bear witness to the truth" (Jn. 18:38). After the resurrection the chief witness will be the *Holy Spirit. It is He who seals the word of God in the hearts of believers. He "does not speak on His own authority" but speaks whatever He hears (Jn. 16:7–15). The first Epistle of John mentions three witnesses: the Spirit, the water of baptism, and the blood of the crucified (1 Jn. 5:6–9), three witnesses which agree.

The book of Revelation frequently uses the phrase "the testimony of Jesus" to describe the proclamation of the Gospel message (Rev. 1:2,9; 12:17; 20:4). Finally it mentions the witness of angels (22:16).

3. In regard to contracts, objects may be used as "witnesses" or evidence of the deed; thus the stone, the pillar erected by Jacob

and Laban (Gen. 31:45–48; Galeed means witness). Similarly Joshua erects a pillar as witness at Shechem: "Behold this stone shall be a witness against us: for it has heard all the words of the Lord which He spoke to us" (Josh. 24:27).

The tables of the law contained in the ark are called the tables of testimony, for the commandments of God are inscribed on them; by extension the *ark is sometimes called the testimony (Exod. 25:16,21,22; 26:34; 31:18; 32:15; Num. 17:4). The Song of Moses and the book of the law testify against the disobedient people. Scripture as a whole is the testimony to the work of God.

S. DE DIÉTRICH

WOE ! *see* BLESSED

WOMAN

O.T.

In a certain number of passages the O.T. reflects the ideas prevalent in the oriental world on the subject of woman: she is considered much more like a thing than a person; she occupies an entirely subordinate place in society. She is a being in permanent tutelage: before marriage her father is her owner (e.g., 1 Sam. 18:17); afterwards it is her husband, while at her husband's death she falls under the tutelage of the eldest son. She enjoys a certain consideration only as mother of the sons whom she has presented to the family.

This tendency was, in the end, predominant in late Judaism. There was however another and more favourable estimate of woman in the O.T. Women sharing in certain public demonstrations may be seen, notably at popular religious festivals (Deut. 12:12; 2 Sam. 6:19), at sacred dances (Judg. 21:21), at a sacrificial meal (1 Sam. 1:4). They possess the right to undertake certain responsibilities in the sanctuary (Exod. 38:8). In law, daughters have a right to succeed to a father's property in the absence of a son (Num. 27:8).

The O.T. points out the important rôle played by certain women of influence—judges or prophetesses—and makes mention of some others more modestly as examples, put forward as models for our faith (Miriam, sister of Moses, Exod. 15:20; Deborah, Judg. 4 and 5; Huldah, 2 Chr. 34:22ff.; Rahab, Josh. 2:9 (cf. Heb. 11:31); Ruth, 1–4; the widow of Zarephath, 1 Kings 17:12; the Shunammite, 2 Kings 4:8ff., etc.).

Finally, and above all, the O.T. in the first two chapters of Genesis asserts the unity of the married couple according to the will of the Creator. *Man and woman together are created in the image of God and together they receive the vocation to rule over creation (Gen. 1:25–28). Woman has been created at the side of man to be a help-meet for him (Gen. 2:18). She is therefore not an inferior being, but man's partner, his opposite member whose specific function is to complete him and bring his solitude to an end (Gen. 2:23). In order to join himself to her, a man will leave those who are the dearest and nearest to him in the world, his father and mother (Gen. 2:24).

N.T.

1. Bearing in mind how far late Judaism had degenerated from the teaching of Gen. 1 and 2, the attitude shown by Jesus towards women is, first, seen to be revolutionary.

To be sure, in so far as the love of Jesus is specially manifest towards little ones and the poor and the humble, it is natural that it should be also shown to women. But there is more than that. Jesus, from the outset, put woman on an equality with man: equal in face of the calling of grace, equal in face of the help which Jesus brings (e.g., Jn. 4:7ff.; Mk. 5:23ff.; 7:24ff.; Lk. 10:38–42). Though women were not sent like the disciples with the power of working miracles, yet they had in the larger circle of the disciples a special mission to give service, assistance and hospitality (Lk. 8:2; Mk. 15:40f.). Lastly, among them were some of the first witnesses of the resurrection (Mk. 16:1; Jn. 20:1,17).

As a sign of the importance which Jesus attached to women, we may note, in conclusion, the numerous feminine characters who are brought into the parables.

2. Both the Acts and the Epistles mention a number of women engaged in one way or another in the service of the Gospel (Acts 1:14; 12:12; 16:13ff.; 17:4,12; Rom. 16:1,3,12,15; 1 Cor. 1:11; Col. 4:15; 2 Tim. 1:5; Phil. 4:2–3). These texts do not permit us to define exactly the rôle which they played in the life of the Church. Some of them indeed were the moving spirits of a particular family or of a Christian cell which met under their hospitable roofs. Others were accustomed to exercise a more exactly defined and more regular ministry, such as Phoebe, deaconess of the Church at Cenchreae (Rom. 16:1), Priscilla, who was apparently responsible for instructing Apollos (Acts 18:24–26); so also perhaps the feminine "presbyters" that Tit. 2:3–5 speaks of. One might also mention the rôle of the widows, some of whom seem to have had a real ministry of intercession (1 Tim. 5:5). Finally, it would appear established that the primitive Church had its prophetesses (cf. Acts 21:9).

In any case the apostle Paul explicitly recognized that women might be called to prophesy; hence to speak in the Church, as well as men (1 Cor. 11:5).

In a general way Paul asserts clearly the equality of man and woman "in Christ"; and this implies reciprocity sexually (1 Cor. 7:4) and absolute equality before the grace and calling of the Holy Spirit (Gal. 3:28; 1 Cor. 11:11,12).

But while this fundamental truth was maintained, Paul was nevertheless not a mere revolutionary. It seems that in a certain degree primitive Christianity had rather to hold in restraint a spirit of emancipation derived from Hellenistic culture. This would explain how on the social level Paul never ceased to defend a hierarchy of the sexes, which led to a special attitude demanded of women—women to be silent and veiled in the assemblies: 1 Cor. 11:5–6 and 14:34; though he is there concerned not so much with fundamental principles as with rules of propriety, the apostle's exhortation being given essentially for the sake of order and witness among the heathen (cf. 1 Pet. 2:12). The same need to put a brake on a false emancipation of women is to be observed in the later Epistles (1 Tim. 2:11ff.; 3:14; 5:13).

3. While the N.T. affirms the absolute equality of man and woman before grace, the indissoluble unity of the couple whose most perfect expression is in the union of Christ with His Church (Eph. 5:21–33), it does not therefore recognize any the less that woman has her own specific qualities. The exhortations addressed to women are different from those addressed to men. There exists a kind of being and of appearing which is proper to woman. But this mode of behaviour has, like everything else, been perverted by sin. Relations between men and women have been vexed and distorted; the husband's authority has turned to a passion to dominate, an abuse of power; woman's submission has become voluntary capitulation, slavery. Sin produces in the one a kind of aggravated masculinity, or femininity in the other.

The teaching of the N.T. reverses this situation by means of a profound inward restoration. It gives back to each its true worth by bestowing on them their true measure, that which is given in Christ, and which alone can lead to the fullness of human life. In this new perspective man learns that in Christ there is no authority without love and without solicitude for his partner and taking care of her (Eph. 5:28–29). Woman recovers the true meaning of submission, which is not a matter of resignation or abdication, but what should be a sign of the submission of Christ, who submitted even as far as death to His Father and to men, His brethren (cf. Phil. 2:5–9). This submission after Christ (Col. 3:18; Eph. 5:21) is the submission of a being who is free and responsible, who does not use her liberty as a prey to be grasped, but in order to act as a "servant". So it belongs to woman, in her capacity as a woman, to bear witness more particularly to what is the stuff of the whole Christian ethic.

H. MEHL-KOEHNLEIN

WONDERS, see MIRACLE

WORD

1. *The importance of the Word.* The place occupied by the Word in the relationships between God and the world, between God and man, and between men themselves is so important that it covers the whole field of revelation. The word does not concern only this or that aspect of the work of God, it does not express only those elements which are intellectually or perceptibly communicable, but it is the essential mode whereby God intervenes in the world: it is by His Word that He creates the heavens and the earth (Gen. 1); it is through His Word that He reveals Himself to men (Jn. 1); it is, finally, by the proclamation of His Word that the history of the Church develops and is fulfilled (Acts 4:29,31). Apart from the Word, another mode of *revelation, more intuitive, for example, or more immediately sensible, must not be expected. The Holy Spirit Himself creates nothing new. All He does is to illuminate the Word, and to make possible its audition and its proclamation (Jn. 14:26).

Likewise an essential distinction should not be made between what, in O.T. and N.T., are "words", that is, articulated statements, and what are "deeds", that is, historical acts, miracles, signs, sacraments, manifestations of the Kingdom, all things which, although they are silent, are none the less eloquent. The whole history of salvation, of which Scripture is the witness, is the Word which God addresses to the world.

2. *The biblical notion of the Word.* From what has just been said it follows that the biblical notion of the "word" must not, on the one hand, be intellectualized, nor, on the other, limited to a simple verbal expression.

There is, in fact, a great temptation to trace the biblical notion of "word" back to a philosophical concept, to a rational expression of eternal verity, and thus—since the term is the same: *logos*—to confuse the biblical perspectives with those of Greek thought. It is true that foreign terms have been introduced into the biblical language, but it was so that they might at once be informed with a new and fundamentally original significance. Whereas, for the Alexandrian philosophers, the term *logos* evoked a rationality, a timeless order disclosing itself in the eternal sequence of things, the Bible associated the Word with a unique historical phenomenon. The Word became a direct and personal challenge of God to man, a mediating figure, and no longer a means of exchange in the rational order. In this respect it is significant that, for the Bible, the Word is something which can be announced, which is made the object of *preaching (Acts 8:4; 2 Tim. 4:2, etc.). The Word does not point to a reality of which it is only the intellectual expression. It is that reality itself. It is an event. It is not rationality, but a deed.

That is why the reality of the Word is in no way exhausted by its verbal expression. It is the merit of Reformed theology that it rediscovered the incontestably central importance of the "Word of God". But the risk of this theology is that it should become the victim of a confusion of terms, and should too readily assimilate what is ordinarily understood by "word" to the much vaster biblical notion of Word. The preaching of the Word is not confined to utterance, however appropriate it may be for the faithful transmission of biblical "thought". Revelation is above all a *deed*, and it is this deed as a whole which is the Word. The Word of God is more than an utterance of God. It is an act of God. For God acts by His Word and He speaks by His action.

3. *The Word of God.* It is not the word in itself, the speech or the deed detached from its living and intimate relation with Him who is its author, that is important to the believer, but what God says to man. It is only because it is the Word *of God* that the Word possesses interest and life.

The analysis of the notion of the Word of God, in the O.T. as also in the N.T., discloses the presence of two elements, sometimes distinct from each other, sometimes intermingled. On the one hand, the Word of God conveys an element of knowledge; on the other, it is charged with a dynamic element.

(a) *The Word of God, element of knowledge.* By His Word God transmits to man a truth, He conveys to Him understanding and wisdom. The Word of God possesses a power of information. It is addressed to man as a person who is responsible, that is to say, capable of giving—or of refusing—a response (Isa. 50:2). It is directed to the intelligence, it instructs in knowledge (Deut. 4:36; 2 Tim. 3:16). With regard to this didactic aspect of the Word, it must be emphasized again that, as we explained above, it was not a philosophical concept, the mode of expression of a truth which is impersonal and outside of time, an object of speculation. It is never a dimension in itself, but it points back always to Him from whom it proceeds. And, finally, it is in the relationship which it holds with God, and not in terms and formulas, that its truth resides. It instructs, in fact, to the degree that it brings man face to face with the living God and causes man to become aware of his position of responsibility before Him who speaks, challenged in the presence of his challenger. The Word, it must be stressed, has to do with the field of knowledge, not as a vehicle of an impersonal and general wisdom, but in that it is the Word *of God*. It is through the Word that man knows God and knows himself, and that he discovers the creation, the nature and history, the order—and the disorder—of the universe, and the place which the Creator assigns to all things.

(b) *The Word of God, dynamic element.* While the word (the *logos*) is for Greek wisdom an impersonal element of an eternal truth, in the biblical revelation it becomes a temporal event. It enters into history, charged with explosive power. It represents a potential of energy, it has a force of life. Since it is itself living, it has the power of giving life. It represents the irruption of a creative force into the world.

Its intervention cannot leave the things and the beings which it touches indifferent. It has a power of fecundity: it does not return to God fruitless (Isa. 55:10f.). But, here again, it can be a dynamic element only in the measure that it is the Word *of God*, proceeding from the very source of life.

For the Bible, therefore, the Word, which is both an element of knowledge and an element of power, creates on the one hand a relationship of truth and on the other a current of energy between God and the world, between Him who gives and him who receives, between Him who speaks and him who hears. This double aspect of the Word of God is found throughout the biblical revelation.

4. *The creative Word.* God speaks and the thing comes into being. By His Word He *creates the world, He causes beings and things to arise from nothing. Not only does He bring to life by His sovereign Word, but He also reduces chaos to order (Gen. 1). The creative Word is also always a word of order, assigning to each thing its place, or re-establishing each thing in its original order, destroyed by sin. The creative and regulative Word is also a redemptive Word. The Word which is able to create worlds and to organize them, to stir up the elements (Ps. 147:15–18) and to control them (Matt. 8:24–27), which is able to say to a paralytic: "Rise and walk", is also able to forgive sins (Matt. 9:1–8) and to create the elements and conditions of a life of a new order, redeemed from sin and condemnation.

5. *The prophetic Word.* The expression "the word of the Lord came..." is extremely frequent in the O.T. (1 Kings 6:11; 13:20; Jer. 1:4,11; 2:1; 13:8; 16:1; 24:4; 28:12; 29:30; Ezek. 3:16; 6:1; 7:1; 12:1; Hos. 1:1; Mic. 1:1; Zeph. 1:1; Mal. 1:1, etc.). In the history of prophecy this "word" is displayed more and more in the form of divine declarations or oracles, whereby the Lord addresses His called ones by means of words and makes them witnesses of the things *heard*. It should be noted, however,

that the Word of the Lord has not always had this auditive character and that it was also often expressed by means of *figures*. "The word of the Lord came to me, saying, Jeremiah, what do you *see?*" (Jer. 1:11,13). It is true that a figure is never given without words which accompany it and explain it (cf. the vision of Isaiah, chapter 6). But the figure conveys a revelation, a word of the Lord (Amos 7:1f.; 8:1f.; 9:1f.). Thus the prophet is sometimes called to "see" the Word, to apprehend the revelation not merely by hearing, but also by vision. A figure can also speak. It is not only the words of the prophets which are prophetic, nor only their visions, but the whole history of Israel. For the Word of God is creative not only of words, but also of forms, of signs, of deeds. It is creative of history. And it is through this history, illumined and indicated by the spoken word, that it is granted to receive the Word, to "see" it and not just to hear it. And the day was to come when the Word would be no longer communicated through prophetic signs, but manifested in the flesh in such a way that it would be possible to *behold* its glory (Jn. 1:14).

6. *The Word made flesh.* The Word of God is the expression of His love, even when it is judgment. The worst that could happen is not that this Word should be severe, for if it condemns it is to raise again, to call to repentance and to salvation, but that it should become rare or silent (1 Sam. 3:1). God, however, did not wish to deprive the world of His Word. In a sovereign act of love He sent Him "to set up his tent among us" (Jn. 1:14). Jesus is not a master of wisdom, although He taught and spoke; He is not in the first place a preacher of the Word, although He did preach; His words have authority and surpass those of the scribes and doctors only because He Himself is the Word. The words of Jesus demand faith in Him who pronounces them. They do not refer to a general truth, but to His person. They will not pass away, not because they proceed from an eternal wisdom, but because they are *His* words (Mk. 13:31).

The words and actions of Jesus are inseparable. His word is active in His *miracles (Matt. 8:16; Lk. 7:14; Mk. 1:25; 4:39, etc.). To abide in His Word is the same as to *abide in Him (Jn. 8:31). Thus the Word is not given as something distinct from Jesus, but it is manifested in His person, in the historic reality of His coming: He is the Word. In Him the fundamental unity of word and action is realized. In Him the Word has all its dynamic force and the action all its power of eloquence. The first chapter of St. John's Gospel is an echo of the first chapter of Genesis and provides a living key to the creation of the world by the Word. For, in fact, it is in Christ that all things were created; everything was created by Him and for Him, and in Him all things hold together (cf. Col. 1:16f.).

7. *The apostolic Word and the Word preached.* The ministry of the Word has been entrusted to the Church, to whom grace was given to receive the Word, to bear it, and to give it to the world. Announced by the prophets, and having come amongst us in the person of Jesus of Nazareth, the Word has been passed on by those who were, by seeing as well as by hearing (Lk. 1:2), its witnesses. And it is on this witness of the prophets and apostles that the Church is being built (Eph. 2:20).

The preaching of the Church consists not so much in recalling and declaring the words of Jesus as in proclaiming Jesus Himself. To preach the Word is to preach Jesus Christ.

Jesus Christ, moreover, is not proclaimed only by words, for faithful preaching does not depend on persuasive utterances of wisdom, but it must be accompanied by a demonstration of the Spirit and of power (1 Cor. 2:4). Miracles, brotherly love, the law of the Kingdom accepted and practised, in a word, the life of the Church, one, holy, apostolic, and universal, is also a preaching of the Word, preaching to which our time would be well advised to give attention still more than to utterances.

8. *The written Word.* The Bible is not a

collection of sentences. It is, from beginning to end, a testimony rendered to the Word, that is to say, to the creative, regulative, and redemptive work of God in Jesus Christ. It is for this reason that *Scripture testifies in the first place not to words, but to a history, a history in which words are inserted into the deeds from which they cannot be dissociated. It is in the performance of these deeds, and chiefly of the deed which is the incarnation of the Word in Jesus, that the words reported in the Bible must be received and understood. To claim to disengage them from their carnal setting, to liberate them from their history in order to make of them general principles, is to rob them of their truth and of their power as the Word of God for the sake of turning them into nothing more than precepts of philosophy and ethics.

It remains none the less true, of course, that it is essentially by means of words that we arrive at the testimony rendered to the Word and set down in O.T. and N.T. But these words, which are thoroughly human, are nothing in themselves, and by themselves have no authority. In order that they may become a source of knowledge and acquire the potency of an event, it is necessary that the Holy Spirit should illumine them and "read" them in such a way that the Word of God resounds through the human word and it is no longer words that are seen, but, as though under the action of a photographic bath, the figure of the Saviour, prophet, sacrificer, and king, in whom the whole history of salvation is located. Then the written word becomes in its turn the Word of God.

J.-PH. RAMSEYER

WORK

1. *The work of God.* It is the active energy of God Himself which constitutes the prototype of all work. In fact the biblical texts vigorously declare that God works. He works from the origin of things: He is the Creator, the Preserver, and the Saviour of the world (Gen. 1:31–2:3; Ps. 19:2; 65; Prov. 8:22–31; Isa.

40:21–31; 45:9–13; 64:8; Jn. 1:1–3,10; 5:17; Rev. 15:2–3).

2. *Work, the normal condition of man.* It is clear from the biblical texts that work reflects the divinely established order of things. The works of man are the counterpart of the works of God (the same word is used of both). The first man was placed in the garden of Eden to dress it and to keep it (Gen. 2:15). Work is the normal lot prescribed for man by his Creator. It is through work that God associates man with His own creative action (cf. 1 Cor. 3:9). Work is the sign by which God symbolizes the fact that man is His collaborator.

Thus the necessity of work flows from the ordinances of divine wisdom (Ps. 104:19–24; Isa. 28:23–29). The whole creation works (Prov. 6:6–11). Idleness is condemned. Work is God's specific command to man (Exod. 20:9; 1 Thess. 4:11; 2 Thess. 3:10).

The work of man is therefore good in so far as it is the response to this divine order and forms an integral part of the pattern of the divine purpose and activity.

3. *The deterioration of work as a result of the Fall.* But the order of creation willed by God has been wrecked by the Fall; the work of man which was to be a means of grace and a joy is now caught in the toils of *sin. In Gen. 3:16–19 we see that the work wrought by sinful man becomes toilsome and painful. The effect of sin is that human work is now accomplished in *suffering; a curse weighs on it. This is not to say that all work, since the Fall, is bad in itself; but the sinful state of man robs his work of its value. Instead of serving to praise God, it becomes a means of glorifying and exalting the creature. It is now an end in itself and thus an idolatry (cf. Eccl. 2:4–11,20–23; Lk. 12:16–22). It is a means of exploiting and oppressing man's neighbour (cf. Exod. 1:11–14; 2:23; Jas. 5:4).

Nevertheless, because in spite of everything divine grace continues to act in this unfortunate situation of humanity, work can still be in certain cases a source of blessing (e.g., the work of Noah). Moreover the divine instruction, ceaselessly operative at the heart of this disturbance caused by the Fall, continues to remind man of the true significance of work. This aim is fulfilled in particular by the institution of the *sabbath. In fact the sabbath foreshadows the great *rest reserved to the people of God. By the very fact that it implies the limitation of work it reminds man that the true end of his life is not work in itself but the glory and service of God (Exod. 20:8–11; 31:12–17; Isa. 58:13–14).

Again when the Israelites are bidden to sacrifice to God the first-fruits of their cattle and their crops, the work of mankind is replaced in its true perspective: the earth belongs to God, and man who by his work causes it to bear fruit is only the administrator of the property of God! Thus the ministry of divine grace throughout the ages points to the way by which work may be sanctified.

4. *Work in the order of redemption.* But it is in the new order of life inaugurated by Jesus Christ that human work finds its true meaning and place.

Christ Himself like the apostles has set an example of work. Jesus worked with His hands; He was a carpenter (Mk. 6:3). St. Paul was a tent-maker (Acts 18:3). Thus the Bible honours all manual labour. But it does not make any real distinction between the forms of work. What matters is the spirit in which work is done.

Thus the work of Christ is presented to us in two aspects. On the one hand He considered it to be a charge which had been entrusted to Him by His Father (Jn. 9:4) and on the other, He thought of it as a service towards men (Matt. 20:28).

In the light of this the work of man takes on a new quality. Of course it does not altogether cease to be toilsome. In the N.T. one at any rate of the terms used to denote work still contains the idea of hardship and fatigue. The pejorative connotation of work still persists. It is further true that even for believers there is the danger of performing vain works (cf. Jn. 6:27; 1 Cor. 15:58). Nevertheless in Jesus Christ every man is called upon to impart to his work a new quality, namely, the significance and the dignity of a labour carried through by divine grace and for the divine glory. It will be a work done "in" and "for" the Lord (Rom. 14:7–8; Eph. 6:5–9; Col. 3:23–24).

In this new perspective the man who works is seen to be an administrator of the riches of God (1 Cor. 4:1–2; cf. Matt. 25:14–30), and a servant of his neighbour (Matt. 25:40; Gal. 5:13; 1 Pet. 4:10). Work of this kind will not be in vain. It has without doubt a value even if this value is other than what it appears in the sight of men. Hence it will receive its recompense. In fact it should be observed that the Bible is not unaware of the idea of a just *reward (cf. Lev. 19:13; 2 Chr. 15:7; Jer. 22:13; Lk. 19:11–27; 1 Cor. 9:7–10). But it extends this idea beyond the limits of human justice and human deserving (cf. Matt. 20:1–6).

On the judgment day the true worth of each man's work will be disclosed. But the ultimate acceptance of the labourer will be an act of divine grace as much as of divine justice (cf. 1 Cor. 3:8–15). What matters most of all, in the new vision of things which Christ unfolds, is that human work should be a participation in the creative and re-creative work of God. In the measure in which that is true of them, the *works of believers will have eternal value, for they are integrated in the great work of God (cf. Rev. 14:13).

H. MEHL-KOEHNLEIN

WORKS

The Greek noun which our N.T. translations render by "work" signifies not only *the result of an activity*, but also *the activity itself*. Further, in those places where, in the O.T., our translations have the noun work, or the corresponding verbs, the original Hebrew presents a diversity of terms, which sometimes bear the passive sense (work completed), sometimes, and more often, the active sense (activity, actions), and sometimes both senses at one and the same time.

1. *God and His works.* (*a*) In the O.T. the works of God are in the first place exalted deeds by which God raised up Israel, delivered them from the Egyptian captivity, led them through the wilderness, and caused them to enter into the Promised Land (Exod. 34:10; Deut. 3:24; 11:3,7; 32:4; Josh. 24:31; Judg. 2:7,10; Ps. 66:3–6; 77:12,17–21, etc.). Such is the basis of the primitive Israelite notion of the divine *work: the sovereign intervention of the Lord in the history of His people.

The prophets declare that this intervention is not only a fact of the past, but that *God still intervenes in the present* (Isa. 5:12,19; 22:11; Jer. 10, etc.). To remain insensible of this intervention is to renounce the *covenant and to expose oneself to divine judgment.

With the prophetic message the original notion undergoes a double extension. On the one hand, and more and more, *God intervenes, by His works, in the life of the nations* (*Gentiles*), without, however, impairing the central rôle of Israel (Isa. 19:25; Jer. 50:25; 51:10; Hab. 1:5). The Gentiles also are reached by the judgment and the grace of the God of Israel. On the other hand, the consciousness develops that, by His exalted deeds in history, God reveals Himself as the *creator who takes care of His creation. Passages such as Isa. 45:11–13; 60:21; 64:8 indicate typically the enlargement of the notion of the covenant in that of creation. In the light of the covenant Israel discovers that its Lord is not only the master of the nations, but the creator of the whole world, which is His work (Gen. 2:2–3. These verses, like the whole passage Gen. 1:1–2:4, form part of the so-called priestly document, which is posterior to the Exile). At the heart of this work two elements are brought into particular prominence: the heavens (Ps. 8:4; 19:2; 102:6) and man (Ps. 138:8; 145:10; Job 10:3; 14:15). The most recent books of the O.T. and later Jewish literature develop this triple aspect—universalistic, cosmic, and anthropological—of the work of God.

(*b*) According to the N.T. these exalted deeds of God are manifested in the saving works of Christ (Matt. 11:2,19), in whom both the word and the action are united (Lk. 24:19). John, however, is the only one of the evangelists to make regular use of the notion of "the work(s) of God" who Himself plans *the whole of the salvation realized in Christ Jesus*. This is only natural since he also is the only one to view Christ in a systematic manner, whereas the three first evangelists content themselves with bringing together, without elaborating (at least consciously), the elements of the primitive Gospel tradition. The works which Jesus performs testify to Him and to the salvation which He brings (Jn. 5:36; 10:25; 14:11; 15:24); they demonstrate that Jesus performs the one and unique work of God Himself (Jn. 4:34; 5:17; 9:3; 17:4). The object of these works is that men may participate in them by faith (Jn. 6:29). Just as God has performed His works in Christ, so also He will perform them, through the glorified Christ, in believers (Jn. 14:12).

An analogous conception, but more explicit and still more vast, is found in Paul and in the Acts. The work of God, as Habakkuk conceived it (Hab. 1:5 cited Acts 13:41), is revealed as in fact being, in the perspective of the new covenant, the establishment of the new community, the building up of the *Church (cf. Rom. 14:20; 1 Cor. 15:58; Eph. 4:12; Phil. 1:6).

2. *The inclusion of man in the work of God.* Defined in this way, the work of God brings a judgment upon the works of men. It reveals that some are good and others bad. In the O.T. all the works of man performed in conformity with the saving will of God are good, and all those which are contrary to His will or independent of it are bad (cf. Ps. 28:4–5; 90:17; 2 Kings 22:17; Isa. 57:12, etc.). The N.T. defines— in opposition to the deviations of later Judaism—the relationship between man and God from which the goodness of the works of man proceeds. This relationship is *faith, the committal by man of himself to God. Apart from faith the works of man, however well intentioned they may be,

can only be bad (Jn. 6:28–29; Col. 1:21–23). It would, however, be wrong to put faith in solid opposition to works: faith is only opposed to the works *of the *law* (Rom. 3:20; Gal. 2:16). Of itself it gives rise to its own proper works, the "works of faith" (Gal. 5:6; 1 Thess. 1:3; 2 Thess. 1:11) without which no one will be saved (Rom. 2:6–7; cf. Matt. 3:8; Acts 26:20; see *Reward).

Thus a human work is valid before God only when it is the consequence of faith. But as such it is fully valid and necessary (Matt. 5:16; Eph. 2:10; Jas. 2:17–26). As was the case with Christ, the word and the action are united in the believer (Rom. 15:18; 2 Cor. 10:11). In faith the entire life of man, including its most "secular" aspects, is a good work. It is especially so with respect to his occupation (1 Thess. 4:11; 2 Thess. 3:10–12; Eph. 4:28). Much more, man is called, with the help of the Holy Spirit who operates in him, *to labour in the work of God itself*, that is to say, the building up of the Church (1 Cor. 3:9; 9:1; 16:10; Phil. 2:30; Acts 13:2; 14:26; 15:38). Man's most intimate life is thus bound to the work of God. Paul testifies to this with rejoicing (Col. 1:24; 2 Cor. 4:7–15; 12:7–10, and perhaps 2 Thess. 2:6–7, if it is right that, as many not unreasonably think, St. Paul himself was to be the "obstacle" which delays the manifestation of the mystery of iniquity). In a word, good work is the work of God, with which God, through Christ, has condescended to associate the believer by giving him a *ministry (Eph. 4:12).

J.-L. LEUBA

WORLD

O.T.

We do not find in the O.T. any theoretical and scientific exposition of the conception of the world held by the ancient Israelites. The subject is treated somewhat theoretically when the story of the creation of the world is told (cf. Gen. 1); but it is most frequently the case that these conceptions must be sought in the comparison of a number of very varied narratives (Gen.

28:10–15; the ladder of Jacob's dream shows us well enough the very relative dimensions of this world). The general picture is very consistent and it is very close to that which we encounter among the neighbouring peoples in whose general civilization Israel shared. In the great mythological texts of Ras Shamra, as in the material which the Greek writers have preserved for us of the Phoenician mythology, we see pretty clearly what was the mythology of the ancient Canaanites, which was similar to, though not identical with, that of the peoples of Mesopotamia—an extremely abstruse mythology in which there are only allusions to the origins of the world and to the constitution of this world. These accounts are quite parallel to what we find in several poetic passages of the O.T. It is in these conceptions, becoming simplified and refined in the course of the centuries, that we see the point of departure of the theological work of Israel.

In the priestly narrative of Gen. 1 we have a product of theological thought and not a point of departure. Yet it is from here that we must start, for it is the most "scientific" account that we have. We find here beneath the surface the ideas of the Canaanites and Mesopotamians, but they have been fully reconsidered, organized, and in particular purified of every mythological illusion which might then have been regarded as an affront to the majesty of Yahweh, the only God, and consequently the only *creator. We find here, clearly and consistently stated, the conception of the world which appears only fragmentarily in numerous other texts.

At first there existed only a watery chaos. One of God's first acts was to place in the middle of this chaos the flat land, surmounted by a solid firmament. Underneath this canopy the mountains could be seen when the waters which were still under this sort of vault had been gathered together into the seas. The waters which are above the canopy of the heavens can fall on the earth in the form of rain through suitable apertures; they can also come in tumultuous waves when, in the days of the Flood, God

opens all the windows of heaven. The
*waters which are below the earth can gush
forth and give rise to the springs which are
so precious in Palestine, where they are not
so abundant as might be wished. Inside
the firmament the sun, the moon, and the
stars revolve in the courses which God has
appointed them. Despite certain figures of
speech (Ps. 19:6), these are merely luminaries, but for a long time they were
envisaged as independent divine beings:
from force of habit the priestly account of
the creation speaks of "the host" of the
heavens (Gen. 2:1). Besides this very
deliberately monotheistic text we find
numerous allusions to more ancient
mythological conceptions. Sometimes these
are recollections, but more frequently they
are simple figures of speech which have
remained in the language. God has divided
the sea into two, as in Babylonian myth the
god Marduk divided the goddess Tiamat,
who was the personification of the primitive
abyss (Job 26:12, transl. Dhorme). God
fixes a limit for the seas which they must not
pass (Prov. 8:29). Men can reach the vault
of the heavens by building a very high
tower (Gen. 11:4).

The affirmation that God is the Creator
is encountered very early; but it is from
second Isaiah onwards that it plays a
theological rôle. Sometimes it is just
affirmed simply and sometimes details are
given which serve to emphasize the power
or the sovereign goodness of God (Isa.
40:12ff., 21ff., etc.). Later it is spoken of in
the same spirit. But in the poetic texts we
find numerous mythological allusions which
show us that the Israelites had had ideas
very close to those of the Canaanites and
Mesopotamians: Isa. 51:9, the conflict
against the primaeval monster (cf. Isa.
27:1); Ps. 74:13; Job 38:4, an imposing
picture of creation which we find also in
Prov. 8:22ff., but carefully purged of anything that was then regarded as an allusion
to other gods (cf. also Job 26:7-14). At a
period which is not very ancient the
Israelites set the dwelling-place of God and
His throne above the vault of the heavens
(cf. Ezek. 1:22,26; 10:1; Ps. 11:4; Isa. 66:1).

According to Gen. 28:10-15 communica-
tions are possible between heaven and
earth, while in Job 1:7 material means for
realizing this are no longer spoken of.

With regard to the general conception of
the world it is necessary to understand that,
for the Israelites, the earth is not the centre
of an organized universe: it alone is truly
organized and the stars exist only as
adjuncts to its functioning. It is only much
later that, under the influence of the Greek
thinkers and natural philosophers, the
conception was formed of a truly organized
universe of which the earth remained the
centre, not only geographically, but really.
The theological endeavour of the Israelites
aimed above all to remove all trace of the
mythological elements of the ancient conceptions, for any other divine power would
have been a rivalry to Yahweh, an offence
to His glory and power. The general idea
which had been formed of the world was
not changed, however, but it was affirmed
all the more resolutely that God alone is the
Creator and Organizer of everything that
exists on the earth, in the seas, and beneath
the heavens.

The notion that the Israelites had of a
very limited and confined world, stretching
from the Mediterranean Sea to the Iranian
plateau, and from the Caucasus mountains
to the Arabian desert, certainly encouraged
the view that they formed little by little of
a *God who is the governor of all, the
conception even of a God who is unique
and who alone has a real existence. When
in course of time this view of the world was
enlarged, the idea of God was also enlarged
and continued to embrace a universe which
was constantly expanding.

G. NAGEL

N.T. (I)

For the biblical authors, as for the
majority of the ancients, the world is composed of three parts: the terrestrial world,
the world above, and the world beneath the
earth. Cf. Phil. 2:10, where reference is
made to "things in heaven, things on earth,
and things under the earth".

1. *The terrestrial world.* According to Ezek. 5:5 the city of *Jerusalem is placed at the centre of the earth and is destined, according to Jewish beliefs, to become also the centre of the new world. The Promised Land, Palestine, is also called "the earth" without qualification, as in Matt. 5:5 (where the term has a supernatural sense).

Beyond Palestine and the neighbouring lands, such as the land of the Philistines, Phoenicia, Syria, and Egypt, there are many more distant lands of which the O.T. already has knowledge. It is sufficient for us to recall that the geographical consciousness of the Israelites extended to the north as far as the Caucasus, to the south as far as Ethiopia, to the west as far as Tarshish (which may possibly signify Spain, but more probably Carthage), and to the east as far as India, perhaps even as far as China (cf. Isa. 49:12, where the land of "Sinim" is mentioned). The horizon of the N.T. includes Illyria, Italy, and Spain as well, that is to say, nearly the whole inhabited earth according to the traditional Greek ideas.

The earth was created by God as a place of habitation for plants, animals, and men. But many N.T. authors, and notably the apostle Paul, assume, following Gen. 3:17, that the earth was cursed because of the transgression of man. According to certain Jewish conceptions, preserved in the apocryphal books, the animals suffer severely from the consequence of the Fall of man (cf. in particular the *Book of Adam and Eve*). This is precisely the way in which the apostle Paul sees things (cf. Rom. 8:19f.). Jesus Himself shared the conviction that in its present state creation was no longer what it ought to be (see *Devil), while at the same time, by an extraordinary act of faith, discovering the earth of God behind the dark veil woven by the Fall (Matt. 6:28–29). Unless these ideas are taken into account, Christian eschatology and its promises of a new world will be improperly understood.

We should notice also that the terrestrial world is often called "the world" without qualification (Jn. 11:27; Matt. 4:8; cf. Lk. 4:5). We also find the expression "to come into the world" for "to become incarnate on earth" (Jn. 1:9; 16:21, etc.). Finally, "the world" can also designate men: thus the Gospel must be proclaimed to "the whole world" (Mk. 14:9).

2. *The world above*; see *Heaven.

3. *The world beneath the earth.* It is called Sheol by the Hebrews and Hades by the Greeks. The world beneath the earth should not necessarily be represented as being a place of torment, that is, "hell" in popular Christian theology. It is simply the place where the dead are gathered together. For the wicked, however, it can become a place of torment, as for the bad rich man of Lk. 16:23ff. On the other hand, after their *death the righteous can enjoy a certain felicity, especially those who have been gathered into "Abraham's bosom". But there is no indication that Abraham is in "heaven", for he is not out of sight of the wicked.

Conversely, certain Jewish apocryphal books, such as the book of II Enoch, locate in the heavenly region the place of imprisonment of certain fallen angels. On the contrary, however, the Epistle of Jude (13) and the second Epistle of Peter (2:4) appear to make "tartarus" the place of their imprisonment.

But the prophets and psalmists had already introduced revelations which give the righteous dead the hope of a more glorious destiny at the end of time. The book of Daniel even promises the resurrection, which will bring in lasting and just happiness (Dan. 12:2; cf. 2 Macc. 7:14; 4 Esdr. 7:32ff.). In harmony with these hopes, the Wisdom literature sometimes teaches the Greek ideal of the immortality of the soul, especially the book of Wisdom (2; 3; 5; 15). This is the first of the two conceptions which prevailed in the N.T. (*redemption, *resurrection). For the apostle Paul, Hades is already vanquished in principle by the resurrection of Christ. At the end of time death itself will be destroyed (1 Cor. 15:26), which scarcely leaves any further place for a "hell". The book of

Revelation, however, retains a place of eternal suffering for the *Devil and his followers.

4. *The world viewed as a whole.* The universe is commonly designated in the O.T. by the expression "heaven and earth", or, more exactly, "the heavens and the earth." This expression is found again in the N.T., cf. 2 Pet. 3:13, which foretells the creation of new heavens and a new earth (cf. Rev. 21:1). Sometimes also, when giving the sense of *terra firma* to the word "earth", "heaven and earth and sea" are spoken of (Acts 4:24; 14:15; Rev. 10:6). But the N.T. is also familiar with the use of the word *kosmos* (world) for the universe (Acts 17:24; 1 Cor. 3:22, where the "world" includes also the angels, cf. 1 Cor. 4:9,13; 6:2–3). Again, the expression "all" is frequently employed (as in German *das All*, cf. Eph. 1:10; 3:9; 4:6; 1 Cor. 8:6; 2 Cor. 5:18). 1 Cor. 15:28 expresses the supreme hope in these words: "that God may be present in a total manner in the universe" (the usual translation, "that God may be all in all", is incorrect and awkward).

That the world in its entirety has been *created by God is something which all the biblical authors teach or assume. For Christianity, the creative Word is incarnate in Christ (Jn. 1:1–4; Col. 1:16–18). As for creation *ex nihilo*, it is quite plainly taught by John (1:1–3) and by Paul (1 Cor. 8:6; Rom. 11:36).

5. *The world from the eschatological point of view.* Our world is not regarded by the Bible as infinite in space. Is it infinite in time? Certainly not in essence. What God has created He can also destroy. Basically, according to the conception of the N.T., which is already found in certain parts of the prophetic books, our world has long since been ripe for annihilation. But God postpones the fateful moment in order to allow time for sinners to be converted. The end is near, however, and the second Epistle of Peter even establishes a parallel between the destruction of the ancient world by water (at the time of Noah) and the destruction of the present world by fire (3:5 ff.), which will prepare the way for a new world. Strictly speaking, therefore, this Epistle recognizes three successive worlds. But for the thought of the N.T. taken as a whole the two first worlds (that of Noah and our own) are reckoned as only one. They constitute the "present age" as opposed to the world to come (see *Time). What distinguishes the situation of the Christian is that, thanks to the gift of the *Holy Spirit and to his membership in the *Church, he can even now, by anticipation and in a hidden manner, participate in the world to come.

Regarding this coming age, it goes without saying that we cannot *represent* it otherwise than by images borrowed from our world which are consequently very inadequate (cf. Rev. 21 and 22). But thinking which is controlled by the biblical revelation can, at least partially, mark out, like geometrical positions, lines that are able to assist in its delineation. It will be a world which, like our own, will include a visible part, but in which sin and corruption in all their forms will be abolished, where the grievous barrier separating the "living" from the "dead" will have disappeared, and where God will reign in undisputed sway.

J. HÉRING

N.T. (II)

The "world". In the N.T. alone *world* is a term that is properly theological (the word is lacking, however, in O.T. Hebrew and our versions translate as world a word which means the inhabited earth, e.g., Ps. 90:2; Isa. 14:17), but the uses of the word in the account and the doctrine of salvation are governed by the conception formed in the O.T. of the relation between God and the creature, although the term itself has its origin elsewhere, in the theological reflection of the surrounding peoples.

1. At first the world is simply, without any suggestion of depreciation, *the whole of created reality*, in the sense when the O.T. speaks of "all things" or "heaven and

earth": the world was made by the Word (Jn. 1:10; cf. Heb. 1:2; 11:3); the world and all that is in it (Acts 17:24); all things are yours . . . whether the world, or life, or death . . . (1 Cor. 3:22); there is no idol in the world (1 Cor. 8:4), idols are not realities; what will it profit a man to gain the whole world if he loses his own soul, that is to say, his life? (Matt. 16:26). Given that man is the creature *par excellence*, in whom in particular the intention of God the Creator is manifested, and who is in some sense the mouthpiece of creation before God, then world becomes quite naturally the designation for *human reality*, the world of peoples, the historic world fashioned by the activity of man, and that too, often, without any pejorative implication. Light has come into the world (Jn. 1:9), has appeared in history; God so loved the world (Jn. 3:16); Jesus came into the world (Jn. 11:27; 1 Tim. 1:15); the casting away of the Jews was the reconciliation of the world (Rom. 11:15), that is to say, of all peoples.

2. Because the world is essentially that of man, who is the creature in rebellion against God, the term (by a transformation similar to that of the word *flesh) is loaded with a pejorative significance: world very frequently designates *humanity in rebellion against God*, the whole of human reality in so far as it is distinguished by this rebellion and destined for judgment.

The world is *this world*, because man shuts himself off from the wisdom of God in order that he may follow his own, and refuses to know God and to receive life from Him (Jn. 1:10; 1 Cor. 1:20). This refusal can take the form of philosophical reasoning or of ideology, but it is also displayed in religion properly so called. Both pagans and Jews contribute equally to the wisdom of the world, the former by imagining a world that is governed by their reason, in which they are masters of the problems of existence and where God is superfluous, and the latter by demanding of God that He will reveal His power and save them in accordance with their own ideas; it is plain that in the attitude of both

alike the same rebellion against God is displayed (1 Cor. 1:22). The world is what it is because of the sin of the first man (Rom. 5:12), who wished to be as God, that is to say, because of pride, or because of covetousness (1 Jn. 2:17; Tit. 2:12), which is the desire to possess life without receiving it from God. Here we should notice that amusements such as dancing, sport, cinema, etc., should not be called worldly in themselves: they are evil only to the degree that they become substitutes for grace and are used as such; nor should it be forgotten that the Pharisee who was satisfied that he was not "as other men" was only a worldling of another kind.

The world is often presented as a *personal power* which possesses man. Just as there is a Spirit of God, there is a *spirit of the world* which blinds the understanding (1 Cor. 2:12); the *elements of the world* (Gal. 4:3,8f.; Col. 2:20f.) are "powers" which hold man in servitude; the devil is the *prince of this world* (Jn. 12:31; 16:11; 1 Jn. 5:19) or, which is an equivalent expression, the *god of this age* (2 Cor. 4:4). The world which man fashions and constitutes by fleeing from God becomes a power from which he cannot escape, which blinds him and leads him to death (cf. Jn. 8:34).

3. When Jesus is called the *Saviour of the world* (Jn. 4:42; 1 Jn. 4:14) the meaning is that He delivers those who have fallen under this domination and this servitude. He was sent into the world in order to perform there the works of the Father (Jn. 10:36ff.) and to destroy there the works of the Devil (1 Jn. 3:8); by revealing God and by calling man who is prisoner of the world He breaks the world's dominion and creates a situation of decision, in which man will give a response which either will bring him forth into liberty or will confirm his servitude. His aim is that the world may know that He loves the Father and that He does what the Father commands Him (Jn. 14:31), that is to say, may acknowledge Him as the commissary of God and His revelation, and for this cause He goes even

to death, which is the manifestation of the cleavage between God and man and the supreme opportunity offered to man by God (cf. 2 Cor. 5:19–21).

Jesus came into the world (Jn. 16:28), but He is not of the world (Jn. 8:23; 17:16); His Kingdom is not of this world (Jn. 18:36). He entered into history fashioned by sin as a stranger, as the presence of God destroying the calm of the world by the offer of true and lasting peace (Jn. 14:27). Thus He draws upon Himself the *hatred of the world* (Jn. 7:7; 15:18) which wishes to remain as it is; but it is precisely in this way that He is the Saviour, the true bread, who gives life to the world (Jn. 6:32f.).

4. The situation of Christ is reflected in that of the Church and of each believer. We have been rescued from this present evil age (Gal. 1:4) and from the powers of darkness: no longer can the world claim us as its property, because redemption has transported us into the Kingdom of the Son of God's love (Col. 1:13f.). By the cross of Jesus Christ the world is crucified to the believer and the believer to the world (Gal. 6:14); in the curse borne by Christ is seen the judgment which God pronounces on the world and the falsity of the latter's promises, and by God's graciously accomplished salvation the believer is delivered from the desperate and wicked desire to obtain life by his own effort—provided that he grasps by faith the gift of God: the victory which overcomes the world is our faith (1 Jn. 5:4). Like Christ, those who believe in Him are *not of the world*; the Church, which owes her existence to Christ on whom she is founded, is with Him the unassimilable stranger *in the world* (Jn. 17:11,16), an object of the hatred of the world which she disturbs and threatens (Jn. 15:8; 1 Jn. 3:13). But it is precisely in this that she has her *raison d'être*; she is sent into the world as Jesus was sent to it, with a view to the confrontation of God and man, to testify to the judgment and the grace revealed in Jesus Christ (Jn. 17:18f.). Thus Jesus does not ask the Father to ensure to the Church a life of tranquillity

by withdrawing her from the world, but to preserve her from the Evil One, so that she may suffer neither assimilation nor elimination, but may faithfully be the sign of the contradiction and of the promise (Jn. 17:15).

CHR. SENFT

WORSHIP

1. It is generally admitted that the purpose of worship is to establish and, by means of its symbols and rites, to give expression to, a relationship between man and the Godhead. Whether by magic, sacrifice, prayer or any other means, worship, it is believed, must create between the world of the gods and that of men an intercourse which benefits both sides, a kind of circuit of vital and mystic forces which meets the needs of the gods as it does those of men. Worship, the occasion of an encounter between the faithful and those more or less impersonal realities which they reverence, becomes a source of renewal, a guarantee of happiness for heaven as well as for earth; it is rarely disinterested, since it presupposes a contract between humanity and divinity: "I give to you that you may give to me."

Religious practices, stimulated by this desire to enter into contact with the world of spirits and gods, possess, despite their very great multiplicity, a striking similarity. It is easy to discern in cultures widely separated by time and distance a whole series of identical rites and myths. Man, whether he be Babylonian, Greek, Chinese, Kanaka or Hottentot, finds himself face to face with the same mysteries, is puzzled by the same phenomena; he cannot but be struck by the various crises in human existence, such as birth, puberty, and death, by the unbroken succession of days and nights, by the regular cycle of the seasons and by the mysterious orbit of the stars. Almost everywhere similar rites of initiation and purification are practised, agrarian cults are celebrated according to the same patterns and, at the time of the solemn festivals, the faithful dramatize the same struggle between the powers of light and life and the forces of chaos.

2. This same general law is operative in the realm of the Bible. In the cult, as it is described in Scripture, are to be found features which bear a strange resemblance to pagan ceremonies. Just like the surrounding nations, Israel has its sacred seasons such as the *Sabbath and the Passover, its sacred places such as the oak of Mamre, its consecrated persons such as the priests and the Nazirites (*ministry). Israel shares with neighbouring peoples the practice of *circumcision, lawful and unlawful days, *clean and unclean animals (*sacrifices), and the great ceremonies of the harvest and grape-gathering seasons.

It cannot be denied that there are connections between the religious customs of the people of God and those of the pagans, near or distant, but the evident similarities must not be allowed to hide the special character of biblical worship. The actions and the words may at certain points be the same, but the spirit which animates them is of a completely different order.

3. According to Holy Scripture, the cult is a service which the chosen people owes to its God, but this service is not limited to certain religious ceremonies, to certain ritual acts. It extends to every domain of life. God must be served on all the planes of human existence, as biblical legislation testifies (*Justice). It is significant that Hebrew has one word to denote work, service and worship; in biblical thought there is no watertight division between daily work and the adoration of God; in the very first pages of Scripture manual activity and the service of the Creator are inseparably linked. The cult, in the narrow sense in which we understand it to-day, forms part of a vast service which God expects of His people, or, better still, everything which the believers do can and ought to be an act of worship, carried out for the honour of God.

4. To serve God signifies for Israel, as for the Church, having personal dealings with Someone. The *God of the Bible is not in any sense an emanation of nature, some cosmic force, a rational or moral idea, but the living God who intervenes in human history and creates for Himself a people in order that He may save the world. *Israel, as later the *Church, delivered from slavery, owes its existence only to divine favour, it has been chosen to serve God; it has no meaning except by virtue of this service which it has to perform for its Master and which consists in standing quite simply before the world as the witness of the living God. A *covenant, sealed at a particular moment and in a specific place, determines for all time the relationship between the chosen people and their God; the two partners, closely linked together, are not, however, on an equal footing: one commands, the other must obey; one has taken the initiative in everything and intends to keep it to the end, the other is just a subject invited to walk humbly with his God. It belongs, then, to God and to God alone to fix and to modify the conditions of the service which He demands of believers. He is and remains free to choose the seasons, the places and the methods of this service. God always reserves the right to accept or reject the offerings, the *prayers and the good *works of His people. Man cannot lay hands on Him, as he can on the *idols which he fashions for himself and whose existence depends only on his good pleasure. The service of God means in the first instance the recognition of His authority at every time and over all domains.

5. The drama reaches a crisis between Israel or the Church and God just because, sooner or later, the faithful imagine that they can contain God within His own revelation, tie Him down to certain objects or to certain persons, making themselves master of Him and finally, under the pretext of serving Him, serving themselves. The people of God, whether Israel or the Christian community, tend to want to make use of their God, and it happens all too often that in their splendid religious festivals, their manifold offerings, their abundant prayers they are seeking only their own satisfaction and adoring them-

selves under the cover of a religion which appears outwardly edifying.

It is then that there comes about an intervention on the part of the prophets whose mission it is to set the chosen people once more face to face with the demands, as well as with the promises, of the true God. The believers must first be reminded that their God is a jealous God who brooks no rival. The service of God is an exclusive service. It is impossible for the faithful to follow at the same time the Baalim and Yahweh, to put their trust simultaneously in Mammon and in God. Every time that the people of God look for their bread, their happiness and their salvation elsewhere than in the God who has bound Himself to them, every time that they conclude with the powers of the world a delusive alliance, they are lost and fall into a slavery at once political and religious. Believers have no other choice: they must either be servants of God or become slaves to idols.

The prophets remind them, too, that God does not allow Himself to be bought. He is dazzled neither by the multitude of the sacrifices nor by the splendour of the cultic ceremonies. The Lord rejects a worship belied by the everyday life of the worshippers. He spurns with horror the homage offered to Him by hypocritical lips and by hands stained with the blood of the poor. Piety which serves as a mask for a shameful life is hateful to Him. A long and violent indictment puts these things in their right perspective: God demands *righteousness and *truth, He condemns a worship which is sacrilegious because it is false, He requires above all not prayers and burnt offerings, but lives which are wholly consecrated to Him, in which respect for justice and mercy can be discerned. The prophets do not condemn, *ipso facto*, every religious practice, but they clearly indicate that God absolutely refuses all compromise with evil; He rejects the bargain that His unworthy people think they can make with Him; He has no need of those paltry and blasphemous ceremonies in which men place so much faith, since He is not one of those

idols whose very existence depends on the number of sacrifices and on the prosperity of his devotees. God would rather let the holy places be desecrated, and hand the chosen people over to pagan powers than make common cause with the infidel and the rebel.

6. However, the prophets in particular and Scripture as a whole do not envisage the substitution of a code of ethical rules for a system of religious practices; that would be risking a rapid fall into moralism and legalism. Believers can, behind the outward semblance, direct their worship to themselves and reject God just as easily by means of meritorious works as by religious practices. In biblical thought, worship, in the strict sense, retains all its significance. Its aim is to bring successive generations of worshippers face to face with the mighty works of God; it reminds them of the absolutely unmerited election to which they owe their very existence; it fits them into the framework of the redemptive plan of the Creator and directs their attention towards the realization of the divine purpose (*Prophecy O.T.).

Worship serves as a link uniting the present with the past so rich in the high deeds of the Lord of Israel and the Church, and with the future so rich in the promises of the heavenly Kingdom. It lets believers know whence they come and whither history is leading them; it sets before them at one and the same time the wonderful kindness and the holy demands of God. Worship actualizes the Word which binds the chosen people to their God, bringing it nearer to them and giving it new life for those who have gathered together in answer to its summons; thus it opens to the chosen people a way of service by strengthening their faith, by rousing their hopes, by awakening in them the love of God. Worship is the acceptable meeting-place for the faithful with their God while they await the coming of His Kingdom.

7. To serve God, then, means to encounter One who demands a complete

obedience, who exacts an absolute sub-mission, who wills to be the sole Lord of a man's whole life and of all life. To serve God is to measure one's unworthiness for such a vocation, to face an impossible yet obligatory task, to despair of one's own powers and to discover on the way Him whom the Scripture calls the *Servant of the Lord; it is to learn that He takes upon Him our wretchedness and insufficiency and that He inspires in us the passion for service.

R. MARTIN-ACHARD

ZION, *see* NAMES (GEOGRAPHICAL)

AUTHORS

General Editor: JEAN-JACQUES VON ALLMEN

S. AMSLER, Cup, Face, Nations O.T., Piety, Seek, Suffering

F. BAUDRAZ, Covet, Fulfil, Gehenna, Generation, Grace, Light, New, Parable, Shadow

M. BERNOULLI, Adoption, Disciple, Laying on of Hands

CH. BIBER, Confess, Freedom, Multitude, Name N.T., Persecution, Revelation N.T., Right Hand, Stumbling-block

S. BICKEL, Nations N.T.

P. BONNARD, Ascension, Build, Covenant N.T., Elect N.T., Holy, Jesus, Love, Resurrection, Righteous, Salvation N.T., Scripture, Transfiguration

M. BOUTTIER, Angel N.T., Blessed, Descend, Joy, Mystery, Priesthood N.T., Reconciliation, Seal, See

J. BURNIER, Judgment N.T., Life N.T., Prophecy N.T., Ransom, Walk, Way

M. CARREZ, Clean N.T., Dove, Earnest, Glory N.T., Language, Miracle N.T., Sacrifices N.T., Send, Slave

O. CULLMANN, Authorities

S. DE DIÉTRICH, Neighbour, Witness

ED. DISERENS, Call, Fear N.T., Washing, Water

A. GOY, Promise N.T.

J. HÉRING, Demons, Devil, Heaven, Jews, Sin N.T., Temple N.T., World N.T.

ED. JACOB, God O.T., Man O.T., Revelation O.T., Wisdom O.T.

A. LELIÈVRE, Angel O.T., Ark, Blood, Eating and Drinking, Oath, Obey, Remnant

J.-L. LEUBA, Apostle, Know, Law N.T., Names (Personal) O.T., One, Reward, Teaching, Works

D. LYS, Anointing, Clean O.T., Fear O.T.

A. MAILLOT, Bread, Falsehood, Hymn, Prayer, Vine, Wicked, Wine

J.-CL. MARGOT, Inheritance

R. MARTIN-ACHARD, Amen, Glory O.T., Justice, Miracle O.T., Prophecy O.T., Worship

CH. MASSON, Cross, Israel N.T.

R. MEHL, God N.T., Good, Money, Wisdom N.T.

H. MEHL-KOEHNLEIN, Follow, Forgiveness, Man N.T., Woman, Work

PH.-H. MENOUD, Church, Endure, Faith, Holy Spirit, Ministry N.T., People N.T., Tradition

F. MICHAELI, Circumcision, Elect O.T., Israel O.T., Law O.T., Life O.T., Promise O.T., Salvation O.T., Servant

H. MICHAUD, Anger, Dream, Name O.T., People O.T., War O.T.

G. NAGEL, Feasts O.T., Idol O.T., Image O.T., Sacrifices O.T., World O.T.

A. PÉRY, Poor

G. PIDOUX, Covenant O.T., Creation, Judgment O.T., Ministry O.T., Priesthood O.T., Sin O.T., Temple O.T.

J.-PH. RAMSEYER, Growth, Harvest, Hope, Lord's Supper, Repentance, Word

J.-D. ROBERT, Fasting

H. ROUX, Advent

CHR. SENFT, Blasphemy, Blessing, City, Curse, Gospel, Idol N.T., Image N.T., Preaching, Truth, World N.T.

E. TROCMÉ, Time

P. VALLOTTON, Temptation

J.-J. VON ALLMEN, Baptism, Death, Family, Feasts N.T., Garment, Marriage, Names (Geographical), Names (Personal) N.T., Numbers, Rest, Shepherd, War N.T.

INDEX